Lecture Notes in Computer Science 5815

Commenced Publication in 1973
Founding and Former Series Editors:
Gerhard Goos, Juris Hartmanis, and Jan van Leeuwen

Mario Fritz   Bernt Schiele
Justus H. Piater (Eds.)

Computer
Vision Systems

7th International Conference, ICVS 2009
Liège, Belgium, October 13-15, 2009
Proceedings

 Springer

Volume Editors

Mario Fritz
ICSI & UC Berkeley
1947 Center Street, Suite 600
Berkeley, CA 94704, USA
E-mail: mfritz@eecs.berkeley.edu

Bernt Schiele
TU Darmstadt
Department of Computer Science
Hochschulstrasse 10
64289 Darmstadt, Germany
E-mail: schiele@informatik.tu-darmstadt.de

Justus H. Piater
University of Liège
Department of Electrical Engineering and Computer Science
GrandeTraverse 10
4000 Liège - Sart Tilman, Belgium
E-mail: Justus.Piater@ulg.ac.be

Library of Congress Control Number: 2009934939

CR Subject Classification (1998): I.5, I.4, I.3, I.2, I.2.10, I.5.4, C.3

LNCS Sublibrary: SL 1 – Theoretical Computer Science and General Issues

ISSN   0302-9743
ISBN-10   3-642-04666-5 Springer Berlin Heidelberg New York
ISBN-13   978-3-642-04666-7 Springer Berlin Heidelberg New York

springer.com

© Springer-Verlag Berlin Heidelberg 2009
Printed in Germany

Typesetting: Camera-ready by author, data conversion by Scientific Publishing Services, Chennai, India
Printed on acid-free paper   SPIN: 12767250   06/3180   5 4 3 2 1 0

Preface

Computer vision research has taken great strides over the past decade. To deploy research results in large-scale, real-world applications, progress on scientific frontiers must be complemented by corresponding research and development concerning issues such as systems integration, scalable architectures and representations, automated configuration, adaptation and recovery, closing perception-action-loops, real-time and embedded implementations, benchmarking, etc. The International Conference on Computer Vision Systems (ICVS) is a regular forum with this perspective on systems. It brings together researchers and developers from academia and industry, fostering research and technology transfer relevant to real-world, deployed computer vision systems.

This volume contains the papers presented at ICVS 2009 in Liège, Belgium, continuing the established series of conferences held so far in Europe and North America.

A total of 96 submissions were received. Each of them was reviewed by at least 3 program committee members in a double-blind procedure. Overall, 45 contributed papers were accepted, 21 for oral presentation and 24 as posters. The contributions cover a broad spectrum of aspects related to computer vision systems such as learning, recognition, HCI, robotic applications, real-time constraints, cognitive systems, and architectures, to name just a few.

In addition, ICVS 2009 featured two invited speakers who presented complementary issues of high importance to computer vision systems. James M. DiCarlo from the Massachusetts Institute of Technology is a leading researcher in computational models of brain mechanisms that underlie biological vision, the ultimate example of deployed vision systems and an important source of inspiration for artificial systems. Jay Yagnik is the Head of Computer Vision and Audio Understanding Research at Google Inc., overseeing research and development in computer vision aimed at extremely large-scale application.

We wish to thank the program committee for providing their reviews as well as feedback to the authors. We would also like to thank the local organizers for the local arrangements.

August 2009

Mario Fritz
Bernt Schiele
Justus H. Piater

Conference Committee

General Chair

Justus H. Piater   University of Liège, Belgium

Program Co-chairs

Mario Fritz   ICSI & UC Berkeley, USA
Bernt Schiele   TU Darmstadt, Germany

Program Committee

Balasundram P. Amavasai	Sheffield Hallam University, UK
Antonios Argyros	Foundation for Research and Technology, Greece
Nick Barnes	National ICT, Australia
Christian Bauckhage	Fraunhofer-Institut IAIS, Germany
Carlos Beltran	University of Genoa, Italy
Alexandre Bernardino	Instituto Superior Técnico, Portugal
Horst Bischof	Graz University of Technology, Austria
Alain Boucher	IFI Hanoi, Vietnam
François Brémond	INRIA Sophia Antipolis, France
Jorge Cabrera	University of Las Palmas de Gran Canaria, Spain
Régis Clouard	GREYC Laboratory, France
Patrick Courtney	Perkin Elmer Life Science, UK
James Crowley	INRIA LIG, France
Bruce Draper	Colorado State University, USA
Mark Everingham	University of Leeds, UK
Bob Fisher	University of Edinburgh, UK
Gian Luca Foresti	University of Udine, Italy
Jannik Fritsch	Honda Research Institute Europe GmbH, Germany
Antonios Gasteratos	Democritus University of Thrace, Greece
Vassilios Gatos	National Center for Scientific Research Demokritos, Greece
Riad Hammoud	Delphi Corporation, USA
Václav Hlaváč	Czech Technical University in Prague, Czech Republic

Jesse Hoey	University of Dundee, UK
David Hogg	University of Leeds, UK
Edgar Körner	Honda Research Institute Europe GmbH, Germany
Yiannis Kompatsiaris	CERTH - ITI, Greece
Costas Kotropoulos	Aristotle University of Thessaloniki, Greece
Aleš Leonardis	University of Ljubljana, Slovenia
Dimitrios Makris	Kingston University, UK
Bärbel Mertsching	University of Paderborn, Germany
Giorgio Metta	Italian Institute of Technology, Italy
Bernd Neumann	Hamburg University, Germany
Lucas Paletta	Joanneum Research, Austria
Nikolaos Papamarkos	Democritus University of Thrace, Greece
Claudio Pinhanez	IBM T.J. Watson Research Center, USA
Axel Pinz	Graz University of Technology, Austria
Fiora Pirri	University of Rome La Sapienza, Italy
Ioannis Pratikakis	National Center for Scientific Research Demokritos, Greece
Paolo Remagnino	Kingston University, UK
Gerhard Sagerer	Bielefeld University, Germany
Gerald Schaefer	Aston University, Germany
Konrad Schindler	TU Darmstadt, Germany
Anastasios Tefas	Aristotle University of Thessaloniki, Greece
Panagiotis Trahanias	CVRL ICS FORTH, Greece
Marc Van Droogenbroeck	University of Liège, Belgium
Sergio Velastin	Kingston University, UK
Sven Wachsmuth	Bielefeld University, Germany
Sebastian Wrede	Bielefeld University, Germany

Additional Reviewers

Panagiota Antonakaki
Chiara Bartolozzi
Niklas Beuter
Manuel Boissenin
Anastasia Bolovinou
Alexia Briassouli
Andrea Carbone
Carlo Ciliberto
Andrew Dankers
Julian Eggert
Raphael Golombek
Stephan Hasler
Patrick Holthaus
Serena Ivaldi

Lorenzo Jamone
Marco Kortkamp
Manuel Lopes
Ingo Lütkebohle
Letizia Marchegiani
Ruben Martinez-Cantin
Stuart Meikle
Hans Meine
Plinio Moreno
Jean-Christophe Nebel
Georgios Papadopoulos
Ugo Pattacini
Matia Pizzoli
Francesco Rea

Jonas Ruesch
Denis Schulze
Konstantinos Sfikas
Frederic Siepmann

Agnes Swadzba
Matteo Taiana
Marko Tscherepanow
Heiko Wersing

Local Organization and Arrangements

Benoît Macq
Michèle Delville
Céline Dizier

Table of Contents

I Human-Machine Interaction

Recognizing Gestures for Virtual and Real World Interaction 1
  David Demirdjian and Chenna Varri

Multimodal Speaker Recognition in a Conversation Scenario 11
  Maria Letizia Marchegiani, Fiora Pirri, and Matia Pizzoli

FaceL: Facile Face Labeling 21
  David S. Bolme, J. Ross Beveridge, and Bruce A. Draper

Automatic Assessment of Eye Blinking Patterns through Statistical
Shape Models 33
  *Federico M. Sukno, Sri-Kaushik Pavani, Constantine Butakoff, and
  Alejandro F. Frangi*

Open-Set Face Recognition-Based Visitor Interface System 43
  Hazım Kemal Ekenel, Lorant Szasz-Toth, and Rainer Stiefelhagen

Cascade Classifier Using Divided CoHOG Features for Rapid Pedestrian
Detection 53
  Masayuki Hiromoto and Ryusuke Miyamoto

II Sensors, Features and Representations

Boosting with a Joint Feature Pool from Different Sensors 63
  Dominik Alexander Klein, Dirk Schulz, and Simone Frintrop

A Multi-modal Attention System for Smart Environments 73
  B. Schauerte, T. Plötz, and G.A. Fink

Individual Identification Using Gait Sequences under Different
Covariate Factors 84
  Yogarajah Pratheepan, Joan V. Condell, and Girijesh Prasad

Using Local Symmetry for Landmark Selection 94
  Gert Kootstra, Sjoerd de Jong, and Lambert R.B. Schomaker

Combining Color, Depth, and Motion for Video Segmentation 104
  *Jérôme Leens, Sébastien Piérard, Olivier Barnich,
  Marc Van Droogenbroeck, and Jean-Marc Wagner*

Stable Structural Deformations 114
    Karin Engel and Klaus Toennies

Demand-Driven Visual Information Acquisition 124
    Sven Rebhan, Andreas Richter, and Julian Eggert

III   Stereo, 3D and Optical Flow

A Real-Time Low-Power Stereo Vision Engine Using Semi-Global
Matching 134
    Stefan K. Gehrig, Felix Eberli, and Thomas Meyer

Feature-Based Stereo Vision Using Smart Cameras for Traffic
Surveillance 144
    *Quentin Houben, Jacek Czyz, Juan Carlos Tocino Diaz,
    Olivier Debeir, and Nadine Warzee*

Development and Long-Term Verification of Stereo Vision Sensor
System for Controlling Safety at Railroad Crossing 154
    Daisuke Hosotani, Ikushi Yoda, and Katsuhiko Sakaue

Generation of 3D City Models Using Domain-Specific Information
Fusion 164
    Jens Behley and Volker Steinhage

Bio-inspired Stereo Vision System with Silicon Retina Imagers 174
    Jürgen Kogler, Christoph Sulzbachner, and Wilfried Kubinger

A Fast Joint Bioinspired Algorithm for Optic Flow and
Two-Dimensional Disparity Estimation 184
    Manuela Chessa, Silvio P. Sabatini, and Fabio Solari

IV   Calibration and Registration

GPU-Accelerated Nearest Neighbor Search for 3D Registration 194
    Deyuan Qiu, Stefan May, and Andreas Nüchter

Visual Registration Method for a Low Cost Robot 204
    *David Aldavert, Arnau Ramisa, Ricardo Toledo, and
    Ramon López de Mántaras*

Automatic Classification of Image Registration Problems.............. 215
    Steve Oldridge, Gregor Miller, and Sidney Fels

Practical Pan-Tilt-Zoom-Focus Camera Calibration for Augmented
Reality 225
    Juhyun Oh, Seungjin Nam, and Kwanghoon Sohn

V   Mobile and Autonomous Systems

Learning Objects and Grasp Affordances through Autonomous
Exploration 235
  Dirk Kraft, Renaud Detry, Nicolas Pugeault, Emre Başeski,
  Justus Piater, and Norbert Krüger

Integration of Visual Cues for Robotic Grasping 245
  Niklas Bergström, Jeannette Bohg, and Danica Kragic

A Hierarchical System Integration Approach with Application to Visual
Scene Exploration for Driver Assistance............................ 255
  Benjamin Dittes, Martin Heracles, Thomas Michalke,
  Robert Kastner, Alexander Gepperth, Jannik Fritsch, and
  Christian Goerick

Real-Time Traversable Surface Detection by Colour Space Fusion and
Temporal Analysis 265
  Ioannis Katramados, Steve Crumpler, and Toby P. Breckon

Saliency-Based Obstacle Detection and Ground-Plane Estimation for
Off-Road Vehicles 275
  Pedro Santana, Magno Guedes, Luís Correia, and José Barata

Performance Evaluation of Stereo Algorithms for Automotive
Applications.. 285
  Pascal Steingrube, Stefan K. Gehrig, and Uwe Franke

VI   Evaluation, Studies and Applications

White-Box Evaluation of Computer Vision Algorithms through Explicit
Decision-Making 295
  Richard Zanibbi, Dorothea Blostein, and James R. Cordy

Evaluating the Suitability of Feature Detectors for Automatic Image
Orientation Systems... 305
  Timo Dickscheid and Wolfgang Förstner

Interest Point Stability Prediction................................. 315
  H. Thomson Comer and Bruce A. Draper

Relevance of Interest Points for Eye Position Prediction on Videos 325
  Alain Simac-Lejeune, Sophie Marat, Denis Pellerin,
  Patrick Lambert, Michèle Rombaut, and Nathalie Guyader

A Computer Vision System for Visual Grape Grading in Wine
Cellars 335
    Esteban Vazquez-Fernandez, Angel Dacal-Nieto, Fernando Martin,
    Arno Formella, Soledad Torres-Guijarro, and Higinio Gonzalez-Jorge

Inspection of Stamped Sheet Metal Car Parts Using a Multiresolution
Image Fusion Technique 345
    Eusebio de la Fuente López and Félix Miguel Trespaderne

Who's Counting? Real-Time Blackjack Monitoring for Card Counting
Detection 354
    Krists Zutis and Jesse Hoey

VII   Learning, Recognition and Adaptation

Increasing the Robustness of 2D Active Appearance Models for
Real-World Applications 364
    Ronny Stricker, Christian Martin, and Horst-Michael Gross

Learning Query-Dependent Distance Metrics for Interactive Image
Retrieval 374
    Junwei Han, Stephen J. McKenna, and Ruixuan Wang

Consistent Interpretation of Image Sequences to Improve Object
Models on the Fly 384
    Johann Prankl, Martin Antenreiter, Peter Auer, and Markus Vincze

Nonideal Iris Recognition Using Level Set Approach and Coalitional
Game Theory 394
    Kaushik Roy and Prabir Bhattacharya

Incremental Video Event Learning 403
    Marcos Zúñiga, François Brémond, and Monique Thonnat

A System for Probabilistic Joint 3D Head Tracking and Pose Estimation
in Low-Resolution, Multi-view Environments 415
    Michael Voit and Rainer Stiefelhagen

Robust Tracking by Means of Template Adaptation with Drift
Correction 425
    Chen Zhang, Julian Eggert, and Nils Einecke

A Multiple Hypothesis Approach for a Ball Tracking System 435
    Oliver Birbach and Udo Frese

Fast Vision-Based Object Recognition Using Combined Integral Map ... 445
    Tam Phuong Cao, Guang Deng, and Darrell Elton

Author Index 455

Recognizing Gestures for Virtual and Real World Interaction

David Demirdjian[1,2] and Chenna Varri[2]

[1] MIT CSAIL, Cambridge MA 02142, USA
[2] Toyota Research Institute, Cambridge MA 02142, USA

Abstract. In this paper, we present a vision-based system that estimates the pose of users as well as the gestures they perform in real time. This system allow users to interact naturally with an application (virtual reality, gaming) or a robot.

The main components of our system are a 3D upper-body tracker, which estimates human body pose in real-time from a stereo sensor and a gesture recognizer, which classifies output from temporal tracker into gesture classes. The main novelty of our system is the bag-of-features representation for temporal sequences. This representation, though simple, proves to be surprisingly powerful and able to implicitly learn sequence dynamics. Based on this representation, a multi-class classifier, treating the bag of features as the feature vector is applied to estimate the corresponding gesture class.

We show with experiments performed on a HCI gesture dataset that our method performs better than state-of-the-art algorithms and has some nice generalization properties. Finally, we describe virtual and real world applications, in which our system was integrated for multimodal interaction.

1 Introduction

Traditional interaction devices such as keyboards and mice are progressively being replaced by more intuitive interaction modalities. The success of touch-screen devices (e.g. iPhone) and motion sensors (e.g. Wii console) illustrates the need for average users to interact with modern devices in a more natural fashion. Recent years have seen the emergence of many systems using speech and gestures, where users interact with an application or a machine by talking to it, pointing or looking at icons and performing gestures. Such systems are still under research but their application for virtual reality, gaming and human-robot interaction for instance is obvious.

To be useful, vision-based gesture recognition systems should be able to recognize user's state (e.g. pointing) and gestures. To be usable, they must be accurate, robust and fast. With this in mind, we designed a system for the real-time estimation of user's body pose and gestures. Our system uses 3D sensing (stereo) to achieve accuracy and robustness to change of illumination. High gesture recognition rates are achieved by employing a novel algorithm based on bag-of-features representations.

In the following sections, we present the architecture of our system. In Section 2 we review previous work on human pose estimation and gesture recognition systems. Section 3 introduces our vision-based body pose estimation technique. A framework

M. Fritz, B. Schiele, and J.H. Piater (Eds.): ICVS 2009, LNCS 5815, pp. 1–10, 2009.

for gesture recognition based on the concept of temporal bag-of-features is then described in Section 4 and evaluated in Section 5 using an extensive experimental evaluation. Finally, in Section 6 we demonstrate the use of our system as a Human-Machine Interaction (HMI) device for recognizing typical gestures in virtual and real world environments.

2 Previous Work

Approaches for human body pose can be roughly divided into model-free and model-based categories. In model-free approaches [2,11], specialized appearance models or detectors are trained on individual body parts and combined with geometric constraints. This requires expensive manual labeling of the body parts and, modeling appearance under different view-points might be difficult. In addition, these techniques only provide 2D information. Model-based approaches [18,5,7] minimize the reprojection of a parametric 3D model to the image. Probabilistic techniques such as [18] employ particle filtering to recursively estimate the posterior pose distribution. Such framework is attractive but requires thousands of samples to provide accurate results, which makes them too slow to use in practice. Deterministic techniques [5,7] estimate pose using local optimization algorithms. These techniques are fast but rely on good initialization and are prone to tracking failure.

In this paper, we present a hybrid approach that combines multiple hypotheses (as in particle filtering) and local optimization (as in deterministic techniques) to achieve robustness, accuracy and speed.

Recent techniques [13] estimate gestures by detection of temporal events directly from video streams, i.e. without intermediate pose representation. Although these techniques provide high recognition rates, they do not provide human pose information. For HMI applications such as the ones described in this paper, obtaining human pose is important because it provides information about arm pointing direction used for deictic reference estimation. Gesture recognition is usually approached as learning temporal sequence models. [14] proposes a two phase approach for recognizing multi-scale gestures by first using Dynamic Time Warping (DTW) to eliminate significantly different gesture models, and then apply Mutual Information (MI) to match the remaining models. In this work, accurate learning of complex trajectories or long sequences can be computationally difficult. Graphical models have been the most successful in modeling temporal sequences. Directed graphical models, like Hidden Markov Models (HMM) [16], and many extensions have been used successfully to recognize gestures [3] and activities [15]. Undirected graphical models have also been used. Sminchisescu *et al.* [19] applied Conditional Random Fields (CRFs) [12] to classify human motion activities (i.e. walking, jumping, etc). Although these graphical models have been successful in recognizing temporal sequences, they are sensitive to training parameters and require large amounts of training data to learn good generalized models.

In this paper we present an approach that relies on temporal bag-of-features representation [13] and show that it outperforms previous methods and has nice generalization properties. The vision system (see Figure 1) consists of a commercial stereo camera connected to a standard 3-GHz PC. Pose is estimated by the articulated pose algorithm

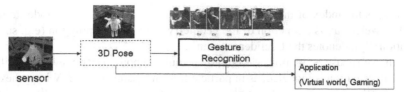

Fig. 1. System overview

(Section 3). Sequences of body poses are then used in the gesture-recognition system to identify gestures (Section 4).

3 Human Pose Estimation

We define a 3D articulated model (see Figure 2) by a set of limbs connected to each other by rotational joints that can be 1-dof (hinge), 2-dof (saddle) or 3-dof (spherical). In our system, only the upper body parts are modeled (head, torso, arms, forearms and hands). We parameterize pose as $\theta = (C, \phi_1, ...\phi_M)$, where C is the 3D torso location and $\phi_1, ..., \phi_M$ is the set of articulated angles. The dimension of θ is 20.

Fig. 2. (Left) Example of depth image. (Right) Corresponding pose.

Limbs are modeled using 3D meshes consisting of N_f polygons overall. Let P_k and u_k be the respective location and orientation of the kth polygon center of the model. P_k and u_k are functions of θ and expressed using exponential maps [4].

Modeling the space of poses θ reachable by the human body is important because it improves estimation robustness by reducing the search directions. In our work we model this space by setting limits μ_k and λ_k for each joint ϕ_k and constraints as:

$$\mu_k \leq \phi_k \leq \lambda_k \tag{1}$$

3.1 Pose Estimation Algorithm

In our system input data consists of 3D points M_i provided by a stereo camera. Similar to [5,7], we estimate articulated pose by minimizing a fitting error function $E(\theta)$ based on the distance between 3D model and 3D points:

$$E(\theta) = \sum_{i=1}^{i=N_f} w_i ||M_i - P_{k(i)}(\theta)||^2 \tag{2}$$

where $k(i)$ is the index of the closest polygon center $P_{k(i)}$ on the 3D model to scene point M_i. Weight w_i is a function of the geometry of the model polygon (e.g. surface, orientation). $||.||$ denotes the Euclidean distance.

To achieve robust estimation, we employ a multi-hypotheses framework similar to [8]. Pose distribution is modeled, as in particle filtering, using a set of N hypotheses or particles $(\alpha_t^{(i)}, \theta_t^{(i)})$ where $\alpha_t^{(i)}$ and $\theta_t^{(i)}$ are the weight and pose of the ith hypothesis at time t. In our system, a number of $N = 4$ hypotheses is usually enough to provide robust tracking. At time t, the multi-hypotheses set is updated as follows:

1. Novel hypotheses are added to the previously estimated set $(\theta_{t-1}^{(i)})$. These novel hypotheses are application-dependent and chosen as poses with high occurrence priors (e.g. user standing and pointing straight ahead, or with both arms down)
2. Local optimization is performed on all hypotheses using the articulated ICP algorithm described in Section 3.2
3. Weights $\alpha_t^{(i)}$ are recomputed from fitting error (2) and dynamic Gaussian priors as described in [8]
4. Hypotheses corresponding to the N highest weights $\alpha_t^{(i)}$ are selected for the next iteration. Estimated pose θ is set as the hypothesis with the highest weight.

3.2   Articulated ICP

Equation (2) in step 2 of the previously described multi-hypotheses framework is minimized using a variant of the Iterative Closest Point (ICP) algorithm to register articulated objects [7]. An iteration of the ICP algorithm can be summarized as follows:

1. **Rendering**: Estimate location and visibility of model points $P_k(\theta_{t-1})$ at pose θ_{t-1}
2. **Matching**: For each 3D point M_i in the scene, find the index $k(i)$ closest to the visible model point $P_k(\theta_{t-1})$.
3. **Optimization**: Estimate pose θ, which minimizes fitting error function $E(\theta)$ in equation (2) while preserving joint constraints (1)
4. **Stop criteria**: If $E(\theta)$ is smaller than a threshold or there has been more than n iterations stop, otherwise go to step 1.

Rendering. The 'Matching' part of our algorithm relies on visible points in the current frame. Our application uses OpenGL routines for obtaining visible model points. The whole model is first rendered at pose θ_t in color C_0. Then each point $P_k(\theta_t)$ is rendered in a unique color C_k. Once all points are rendered the frame is scanned for colors where color C_i indicates a corresponding visible point $P_i(\theta_t)$.

Matching. The matching step consists of finding for each scene point M, its corresponding model point P. It is the most time consuming step. We have implemented different algorithms including kd-trees (for fast nearest neighbor search) and exhaustive search. The overhead due to the construction of kd-trees makes them too slow in practice. Best speed performance were obtained with a GPU-implementation of exhaustive search.

4 Gesture Recognition Framework

In temporal sequences, we wish to learn a mapping of observations x to class labels $y \in \Omega$, where x is a sequence of local observations, $x = \{x_1, x_2, \ldots x_t\}$. Here, $x_k \in \mathbb{R}^d$ and t, the sequence size can vary between observations. x_k corresponds to pose θ_k estimated using the algorithm described in Section 3.

We re-formulate the bag of features technique introduced for visual categorization [9,1] into a general approach for temporal sequences. Here we introduce temporal descriptors and a codebook that contains codewords commonly shared between classes.

4.1 Temporal Descriptors

A temporal descriptor provides a compact (i.e. low dimensional) and useful description of the temporal texture at a given time. The descriptor is estimated over a window, whose size depends on the time scale s (see Figure 3). The time scale s corresponds to the granularity of the description.

We define our descriptors by convolving a Gaussian with the signal and its first temporal derivative over the window of interest centered at a given time t. We define the descriptor $D_{t,s}$ associated with the raw feature x at time t and scale s as: $D_{t,s}(x) = (G_s * x, G_s * \frac{\partial x}{\partial t})$ where G_s* denotes Gaussian convolution over a window of size $\sigma = 2s$. So for every time t, and every scale s, we have a descriptor $D_{t,s}$ of size $2d$, where d is the dimension of the input data x_k.

4.2 Codebook Construction

The codebook corresponds to a discrete quantization of the descriptor space into representative classes (codewords) that suffice to describe the input signal. In our case, codewords represent generic structures contained in temporal sequences. Codewords

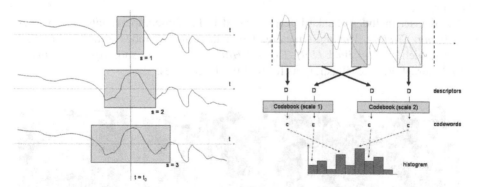

Fig. 3. (Left) Descriptors evaluated in a sequence for the point $t = t_0$ for three different scales. (Right) Encoding process. First, the descriptors are evaluated in the query sequence at every frame and time scale. Then the descriptors are converted to codewords using the dictionary. Finally, a histogram vote of codewords in the sequence is constructed and used as a representation for the sequence.

evaluated over small time scales represent micro-structure of the signal, while code-words evaluated over larger time scales represent semantically more meaningful struc-tures. This is analogous to phonemes in speech, where the codebook is an attempt at finding unit bases that describe the temporal sequences completely.

Following previous work, we construct the codebook by clustering the descriptors corresponding to a set of training sequences using a standard algorithm such as k-means [10]. A codebook is generated per time scale s.

4.3   Encoding and Classification of Temporal Sequences

Once the codebook is constructed, temporal sequences are encoded by accumulating histograms of quantized vectors corresponding to the codebook. As illustrated in Fig-ure 3, given a temporal sequence, the descriptors are first evaluated in the sequence at every location (position t in the sequence) and scale s. Each descriptor $D_{t,s}$ is then assigned to a codeword from the codebook corresponding to scale s. A histogram is then built by estimating the frequency of each codeword in the sequence.

This discrete quantization of the descriptor space and the histogram representation of the codebook reduces the complexity of the signal, and allows a simple classifier to learn the sequence classes easily.

Histograms are then trained using a multi-class SVM classifier. At testing, histograms are constructed as in training (using a temporal window of interest) and passed to the trained classifier, which returns the predicted class of gesture.

5   Database Collection and Experimental Evaluation

We conducted experiments comparing our bag-of-features technique with state-of-the-art sequence models such as HMMs and CRFs. We collected a dataset containing 10 types of arm gestures performed several times by 13 subjects. An average of 90 ges-ture sequences per class were collected (each sequence is comprised of one gesture instance).

The dataset includes standard gestures used in human-computer interaction, such as *Pointing, Circling, Waving, Greeting*. The dataset also includes some less intuitive gestures, such as *Flip Back (FB), Expand Horizontally (EH)* and *Expand Vertically (EV)*. Figure 4 provides illustrations for 6 of the 10 gestures.

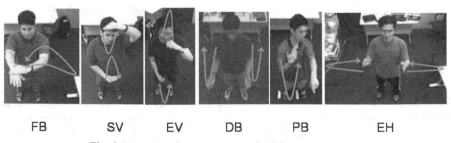

FB   SV   EV   DB   PB   EH

Fig. 4. Example of gestures recognized by our system

Table 1. (Left) Recognition performance (percentage accuracy) for different fractions μ of the initial training set. (Right) Effect of the number of time scales ($\#TS$) in the codebook on the recognition performance (percentage average accuracy and standard deviation).

Methods	μ=0.2	μ=0.5	μ=1.0
BOF	**0.85**	**0.93**	**0.95**
CRF	0.71	0.85	0.89
HMM	0.68	0.72	0.78

#TS	1	3	5
accuracy	0.71 (0.07)	0.83 (0.06)	0.95 (0.03)

The dataset was collected using a stereo camera. The algorithm described in section 3 was then applied to recover the pose θ of the subjects in each frame. The joint angles corresponding to the subject's upper body were retained as observations for our experiments. The models compared in this experiment are:

– BOF: our algorithm as described in Section 4 using temporal bag-of-features representations in a multi-class SVM classifier. For our bag-of-features representation, we used 5 time scales and a codebook of size 40 per scale.
– HMM: Using the pose features as observations, we trained an HMM model per class. During evaluation, test sequences were passed through each of these models, and the model with the highest likelihood was selected as the recognized gesture.
– CRF: We train a standard CRF chain where every class label has a corresponding state. The CRF predicts a label per frame. During evaluation, we found the Viterbi path under the CRF model, and assigned the sequence label based on the most frequently occurring gesture label per frame. We ran additional experiments that incorporated different long range dependencies.

When using HMM, we used some preliminary dimensionality reduction using Principal Component Analysis (PCA) and Linear Discriminant Analysis (LDA) for better performance. In addition, the number of Gaussian mixtures and states were set by minimizing the error on training data. When using CRF, multiple regularizer values and dependency window sizes were explored: we only show here the results with the highest accuracy.

To test the efficiency of our approach we divided the available data into two equal sized training and testing sets. The evaluation metric used for all the experiments was the percentage of sequences for which the correct gesture label was predicted.

We performed a set experiments to compare the different algorithms with respect to the size of the training dataset. To do so, we trained the algorithms using only a fraction μ of the training set. Table 1 (left) shows the recognition performance as μ varies from 0.2 to 1.0. The BOF shows exceptional performance (95% for $\mu = 1.0$), surpassing the other algorithms. The best results for the CRF were obtained using a regularizer value of 100 and a dependency window of size 2. As μ decreases, the performance of BOF degrades significantly less than the other algorithms. These results suggest that our bag-of-features representation is less sensitive to the amount of training data (even with only 20% of training data, BOF still performs better than the best results for HMMs).

Table 1 (right) shows the average and standard deviation of the accuracy of BOF as a function of the number of time scales in the codebook. The recognition rate significantly degrades with decreasing number of time scales, which clearly demonstrates the need to employ descriptors at multiple time scales.

6   Applications

Our system was implemented in Visual Studio C++ on a standard PC computer
(3-GHz PC). The overall speed –including stereo processing, pose estimation and
gesture recognition– is about 14-17Hz. To achieve high speed, the application was
multi-threaded and some components were implemented using GPU programming (e.g.
matching step of the ICP algorithm). Below we present two applications, in which the
visual system was utilized. Corresponding videos can be found at [6].

6.1   Virtual World Manipulation

In this application (Figure 5), a user can create and manipulate geometric objects in a 3D
world using multimodal interaction (speech and gestures). The user manipulates objects
by either speaking commands (e.g. "Create a blue cube here") or by making gestures
(e.g. user making a 'resize' gesture to resize the object created last). The setup consists
of a large display, on which the virtual scene is rendered. A stereo camera is placed on
top of the display and provides input to our system to estimate 3D arm locations and
gesture recognition. In our multimodal system, speech is processed using GALAXY
[17], an architecture for integrating speech technologies to create conversational spoken
language systems.

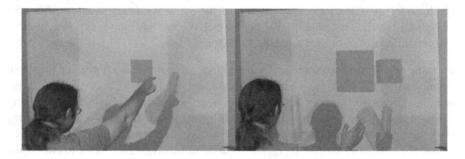

Fig. 5. Application for Virtual World Manipulation. (Left) user speaking "'create a red cube
here'" while pointing at the screen. (Right) user resizing an object.

6.2   Smart Room

In this application, a user can manipulate both real and virtual objects in a smart environment. The user can turn on/off devices (e.g. lamps, projectors, screens) and manipulate desktop objects (e.g. create and move windows, start applications, browse slides)
using speech and gestures. In addition to providing gesture recognition, our system is
also used to estimate the user's location in the room. Users's location is passed to a
microphone array to enhance audio signals from the user. The location of physical objects is manually given prior to using the system. Deictic references, i.e. objects the
user is referring to, are estimated using a 3D map containing both user and objects (see
Figure 6).

Fig. 6. Application for interaction with a smart room. (Left) user resizing a desktop window using gestures. (Middle) user turning on a lamp by pointing at it and saying "'turn this on'". (Right) 3D world map containing both user and object models.

Fig. 7. Examples of pose estimation results

7   Conclusion

In this paper, we have a presented a vision-based system that provides user pose estimation and recognizes gestures in real-time. Robustness and accuracy of pose estimation is achieved by using 3D input (stereo) and a multi-hypotheses model fitting framework. We also demonstrated with experiments the high recognition rate of our gesture recognizer based on temporal bag-of-features representation. We also described two HCI applications for virtual and real world interaction, in which our system was deployed.

Acknowledgment

We gratefully thank Sybor Wang for his help with collecting the data, which was used to evaluate the gesture recognition approach presented in this paper.

References

1. Agarwal, S., Awan, A.: Learning to detect objects in images via a sparse, part-based representation. IEEE Trans. Pattern Anal. Mach. Intell. 26(11), 1475–1490 (2004)
2. Andriluka, M., Roth, S., Schiele, B.: People-tracking-by-detection and people-detection-by-tracking. In: IEEE Conference on Computer Vision and Pattern Recognition, 2008 (2008)

3. Brand, M., Oliver, N., Pentland, A.: Coupled hidden markov models for complex action recognition. In: CVPR (1996)
4. Bregler, C., Malik, J.: Tracking people with twists and exponential maps. In: CVPR 1998 (1998)
5. Delamarre, Q., Faugeras, O.D.: 3D articulated models and multi-view tracking with silhouettes. In: Proceedings of ICCV 1999, pp. 716–721 (1999)
6. Demirdjian, D.:
   http://people.csail.mit.edu/demirdji/projects/iwall2.htm
7. Demirdjian, D., Darrell, T.: 3D articulated pose tracking for untethered deictic reference. In: Proceedings of ICMI 2002, Pittsburgh, PA, USA (2002)
8. Demirdjian, D., Taycher, L., Shakhnarovich, G., Grauman, K., Darrell, T.: Avoiding the streetlight effect: Tracking by exploring likelihood modes. In: IEEE International Conference on Computer Vision, pp. 357–364 (2005)
9. Dorko, Gy., Schmid, C.: Selection of scale-invariant parts for object class recognition. In: ICCV, vol. 01, p. 634 (2003)
10. Duda, R., Hart, P., Stork, D.: Pattern Classification, 2nd edn. Ch.4. John Wiley, Chichester (2001)
11. Felzenszwalb, P., Huttenlocher, D.: Pictorial structures for object recognition. International Journal of Computer Vision 61 (June 2005)
12. Lafferty, J., McCallum, A., Pereira, F.: Conditional random fields: probabilistic models for segmenting and labelling sequence data. In: ICML (2001)
13. Laptev, I., Marszalek, M., Schmid, C., Rozenfeld, B.: Learning realistic human actions from movies. In: IEEE Conference on Computer Vision and Pattern Recognition, 2008. CVPR 2008. pp. 1–8 (2008)
14. Li, H., Greenspan, M.A.: Multi-scale gesture recognition from time-varying contours. In: ICCV, pp. 236–243 (2005)
15. Oliver, N., Horvitz, E., Garg, A.: Layered representations for human activity recognition. In: Fourth IEEE Int. Conf. on Multimodal Interfaces, pp. 3–8 (2002)
16. Rabiner, L.R.: A tutorial on hidden markov models and selected applications in speech recognition. Proc. of the IEEE 77, 257–286 (1989)
17. Seneff, S., Hurley, E., Lau, R., Pao, C., Schmid, P., Zue, V.: Galaxy-ii: A reference architecture for conversational system development. In: ICSLP, vol. 3, pp. 931–934 (1998)
18. Sminchiesescu, C., Triggs, B.: Kinematic jump processes for monocular 3d human tracking. In: CVPR (2003)
19. Sminchisescu, C., Kanaujia, A., Li, Z., Metaxas, D.: Conditional models for contextual human motion recognition. In: Int'l Conf. on Computer Vision (2005)

Multimodal Speaker Recognition in a Conversation Scenario

Maria Letizia Marchegiani, Fiora Pirri, and Matia Pizzoli

Sapienza Università di Roma
Dipartimento di Informatica e Sistemistica (DIS), via Ariosto 25
00185, Rome, Italy

Abstract. As a step toward the design of a robot that can take part to a conversation we propose a robotic system that, taking advantage of multiple perceptual capabilities, actively follows a conversation among several human subjects. The essential idea of our proposal is that the robot system can dynamically change the focus of its attention according to visual or audio stimuli to track the actual speaker throughout the conversation and infer her identity.

1 Introduction

We propose a framework for real-time, multi-modal speaker recognition combining acoustic and visual features to identify and track people taking part to a conversation. The robot is provided with acoustic and visual perception: a colour camera and a pair of microphones oriented by a pan tilt unit. The robot follows a conversation among a number of people turning its head and focusing its attention on the current speaker, according to visual and audio stimuli. It tracks the participants exploiting a learning phase to settle both visual-audio descriptors and integration parameters. People are identified against a set of individuals forming the knowledge base. Multi-people, multi-modal detection and tracking scenarios have been modelled in the context of *smart rooms*[1], e-learning, meeting and teleconferencing support (see [2] for a review), but also in robot-person interface. Recently, multi-modal features have been used in domestic environments in order to annotate people activities for event retrieval [3], perform face and speech recognition, people tracking, gesture classification and event analysis (e.g. [4]). A conversation scenario has been addressed in [5]; here a robot interacts with several people performing changes in focus and showing different emotions.

The mentioned works do no directly address the problem of multi-modal identity estimation. To fill the gap we introduce a completely new model of a conversation scenario. In particular, four audio and visual descriptors of features are defined for both real time tracking and identification. Visual and audio identification is obtained by combining the outcome of these descriptors analysis with a generalised partial linear model (GPLM)[6,7]. Finally, the process undergoes a dynamic update.

In Section 2 we introduce the data acquisition modalities with the representation of their different descriptors, both audio and video, and the general behaviour of the entire system. In Section 3 and 4 the acoustic and visual scene modelling is defined in details. In Section 5 the GPLM and the complete identification process are described.

M. Fritz, B. Schiele, and J.H. Piater (Eds.): ICVS 2009, LNCS 5815, pp. 11–20, 2009.

In Section 6, due to lack of space, we only hint the update problem and the dynamic clustering steps. Experiments are discussed in section 7.

2 Data Acquisition

The knowledge base is a complex data structure that includes both the voice and visual features of $R = 30$ subjects, male and female. Each speaker's voice is modelled as a Gaussian mixture density (GMM). The models are trained with the first 18 Mel Frequency Cepstral Coefficients (MFCC) of a particular set of part of speech, made up of very short word utterances of the English phonemes (a single word contains a single phoneme, such as: put, pet, do, etc.). These particular utterances allow to collect only a small set of vocal samples per speaker (two or three examples for phoneme), rather than a whole conversation. Furthermore experiments prove better performance on short words, in particular when the system works in real-time and the active speaker has to be recognised by a short observation sequence. The j-th phoneme pronounced by the i-th speaker is described by a mono-dimensional vector of the audio signal, and its relative MFCC by a 18-dimensional matrix S_j^i for each utterance. Given the number of phonemes N_f (in this case 44) and the number R of voice sampled, $\mathbf{S}^i = [S_1^i S_2^i ... S_j^i ... S_{N_f}^i]$, with $i = 1, ..., R$ and $j = 1, ..., N_f$, indicates the complete features matrix of the speaker i.

Face appearance features are coded in 2 coefficient matrices. Columns of both matrices encode the observations, namely the people features. In the first matrix, rows encode the Karhunen-Loève coefficient vectors of the *eigenfaces* [8]. In the second matrix, rows encode the values of the non-parametric 2D face colour density, taken at each bin.

The acquisition process continuously performs the following tasks:

1. tracking people in the field of view over the frame stream, shifting the focus to include the current speaker into the field of view according to the angle θ determined by voice analysis;
2. extracting appearance based features, given the number of people in the current field of view and an hypothesis on the current speaker, returned by the voice analysis;
3. collecting the visual and voice descriptors to feed the multi-people identification process.

Fig. 1. Our robot is endowed with visual and audio capabilities in order to track the current speaker. Pan angle is set according to the voice source estimated direction θ. Besides the speaker (bold in the figure), other subjects are detected in the camera FOV, spanned by 2α.

By "field of view"(FOV) we mean the width and the height of the scene that can be observed with the camera lens. Given our audio set-up allowing only for horizontal speaker localisation, being f the camera focal length, w the image width and θ the currently estimated voice source, we refer the term FOV to the interval $FOV = [\theta - \alpha, \theta + \alpha]$ with $\alpha = \tan^{-1}(w/2f)$ (see Figure 1).

3 Acoustic Scene Modelling

In this section we present our approach to locate the active speaker and estimate the likelihood of the speaker features recorded during the conversation, with respect to the models created, as described in Section 2. The result is an ordered sequence of voice likelihoods that is suitably combined with the visual features, described in the next section, to produce the dataset further used to identify the speaker in the scene. We adopt the real-time algorithm proposed by [9], based on the time delay of arrival and the cross-correlation measure to compute, every 200 ms, the angle θ between the sound source and the robot on the horizon plane.

Each speaker's voice i is modelled as a GMM λ_i. Since each voice feature set i corresponds to a mixture, we also indicate the speakers with their corresponding voice model λ_i. The GMM are often selected for this kind of tasks, being able to describe a large class of sample distributions for acoustic classes relative to phonetic events, such as vowels, nasals or fricatives [10]. In order to obtain the models, we extract MFCC up to the 18th order, as a trade off between complexity and robustness after 25 experiments. The parameters initialisation of the EM algorithm and the number of Gaussian components are provided by the the mean shift clustering technique ([11]); we get a varying number of components χ, with $7 \leq \chi \leq 15$. For each utterance x_t acquired during a conversation and the associated MFCC matrix $\mathcal{A}_t$, composed of N_A 18-dimensional coefficients, we obtain, through the complete features matrix and the GMM, a probability $p(x_t^j|S^i)$ for all coefficient components x_t^j, $j = 1, \ldots, N_A$. Thus, the expectation is

$$E(\lambda_i|\mathcal{A}_t, S^i) = \sum_{k=1}^{N_{A_t}} p(\lambda_i|x_t^k, S^i)\, p(x_t^k|S^i) \tag{1}$$

The identification process, on the other hand, also involves clustering of speakers voices labels (see Section 6). To prevent the robot from turning its head to follow noises or random sounds in the environment, we trained a linear classifier based on support vector machine (SVM), able to distinguish between speech and no-speech frames. We consider the short term energy and the zero crossing rate of the signal received ([12], [13], [14]) as discriminant features for SVM classification. The short term energy is the sum of the squares of the amplitude of the fast Fourier transform of the samples in a frame and the zero crossing rate is the number of times the signal changes its sign within the same frame. The set that we use to train the classifier is composed of 10 different speech frames for each speaker in the knowledge base and the same amount of frames including silence or background noise (see Figure 3).

Acquisition and processing of voice features is performed in real time: both the voice detection and the localisation procedure work with frames of length $\Delta = 200ms$, the

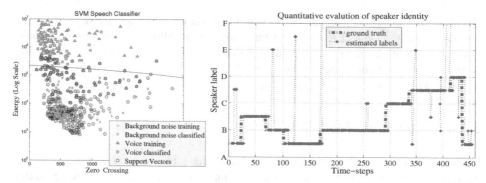

Fig. 2. On the left: SVM classification of voice against background noise. On the right, quantitative evaluation of a speaker identity estimation performance over 450 time-steps.

identification process with frames of length $5\varDelta = 1s$. Specifically, given the signal $u(t)$, acquired by the microphones at time t, and the frame $u_\varDelta(t)$, containing the values of $u(t)$ in the time interval $(t - \varDelta, t)$, the SVM classification implements a filter that provides a signal $\hat{u}_\varDelta(t)$, defined as follows:

$$\hat{u}_\varDelta(t) = \begin{cases} u_\varDelta(t - \varDelta) & \text{if } u_\varDelta(t) \text{ does not include a human voice} \\ u_\varDelta(t) & \text{otherwise} \end{cases} \tag{2}$$

This filtered frame is used for speaker localisation and identification. The angle between the robot and its interlocutor is computed for each part of signal $\hat{u}_\varDelta(t)$. The segment of conversation which we link to an identity, among the sampled voices, is represented by the utterance x_t corresponding to 5 consecutive frames $\hat{u}_\varDelta(t)$. On this premises, the acoustic scene modelling provides the list of the M most likely speakers. The first part $\hat{S}$ of the list includes the labels associated with the models λ_i, maximising $E(\lambda_i | \mathcal{A}_t, \mathbf{S}^i)$, given the utterance at time t and its MFCC matrix $\mathcal{A}_t$. The other values, modulo expectation, concern people indicated by the visual analysis, if not already in $\hat{S}$.

4   Visual Face Descriptors

Visual scene analysis starts with a multi scale face detector. The core of visual feature extraction is the integration of the detection and tracking facilities, by a finite state machine with detection and tracking states. Once a face is detected, the face area is divided in regions of interest on which different detectors are scanned to locate the eyes and the mouth. If these detections succeed over a number of different frames the computational process enters the tracking state in which the eye and mouth detectors are scanned across a predicted face region that is computed from the previous frame by a face tracker, based on mean shift.

Pre-processing involves equalisation, aligning and segmentation of face images. For the alignment, we rely on the position of eyes and mouth: assuming all faces are frontally detected, the images are rotated and scaled to compensate the angle γ formed by the eyes. Being d the computed distance between eyes, $\sigma = \bar{d}/d$ is the scale factor needed to obtain the desired distance $\bar{d}$, (x_c, y_c) is the centroid of the eyes and mouth,

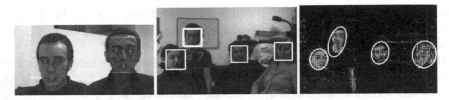

Fig. 3. Detection and tracking of facial features

$a = \sigma \cos \gamma$ and $b = \sigma \sin \gamma$. The transformation H that maps the original to the transformed image is expressed by the 2×3 matrix

$$H = \begin{pmatrix} a & b & (1-a)x_c - by_c \\ -b & a & bx_c + (1-a)y_c \end{pmatrix} \tag{3}$$

A fixed size region of interest is centred on (x_c, y_c) to extract, from the transformed image, an aligned face image. Three kind of visual descriptors are defined for each detected face in the scene: a probability that the subject is currently speaking based on mouth movements; a compressed representation of the intensity image; a non-parametric colour distribution.

This descriptor sizes the significant mouth movements, in so contributing to the cross-relation between audio and visual features for the recognition of the speaker in the scene. Indeed, the problem is to evaluate the amount of pixel changes needed to tell that the mouth is articulating a phrase. To face this problem we define a binary mask M_B by thresholding differences of frames from subsequent time steps. Each pixel is treated as an i.i.d. observation of a binary random variable x representing the detected change. Assuming a Binomial distribution for the binary variables within the mask, we estimate the parameter μ using a Beta prior distribution characterised by the hyperparameters α and β. While the μ parameter accounts for the influence of the number of pixels that have changed over the all pixel set, the two binomial proportions α and β enforce or weaken the amount of changes according to the effective number of samples that seem to vary. The best values for our implementation are $\alpha > 0.7$ and $\beta < 0.2$. Let N_B be the size of the observations, with ρ the number of pixels set to 1 by the mask (those changing). The likelihood that the observations come from a windows in which the mouth has significantly moved, as for articulating speech utterances (of course also for smiling or yawning) is thus defined as

$$\sum_{x \in M_b} p(x|\mu_B, N_B - \rho + \beta, \rho + \alpha)\mu \tag{4}$$

Note here that μ is re-estimated from each detected M_B, and thus μ underlines the model which most likely is induced by mouth activity. In any case the M_Bs are chosen, among those having best expectation, also according to the chosen voice models.

Karhunen-Loève(KL) coefficients provide efficient compression and are suitable to encode frontal faces that have been previously aligned. Compression is achieved by projecting D-dimensional face data into a D'-dimensional subspace spanned by the D' principal directions. Being c_i the D'-dimensional KL coefficient column vector representing the visual features of the i-th subject, we measure the similarity between

i and j in face intensity images by computing the coefficient Mahalanobis distance $d_{\mathcal{M}}(\mathbf{c}_i, \mathbf{c}_j) = (\mathbf{c}_i^\top \mathbf{\Lambda}^{-1} \mathbf{c}_j)^{1/2}$, where $\mathbf{\Lambda}$ is the diagonal matrix, with the eigenvalues corresponding to each KL coefficient.

The similarity in colour space is based on the Bhatthacharyya distance between non parametric densities of colour features. More precisely, given two histograms specified by the vectors of bin value $\mathbf{h}_j$ of the face colour features, $j = 1, \ldots, R$, the Bhatthacharyya distance is defined as $d_{\mathcal{B}}(\mathbf{h}_i, \mathbf{h}_j) = (1 - (\tilde{\mathbf{h}}_i^\top \mathbf{\Omega}^{-1} \tilde{\mathbf{h}}_j))^{1/2}$, here $\tilde{\mathbf{h}}$ is the vector obtained by computing the square root for every element of $\tilde{\mathbf{h}}$ and $\mathbf{\Omega}$ is the diagonal matrix mentioning the normalisation coefficients, such that $0 \le d_{\mathcal{B}} \le 1$. These colour descriptors, although are not robust against changes in face illumination conditions, compensate degradation of shape cues caused by poor resolution or changes in head orientation.

5   Discovering People Identities

In this section we discuss how to infer the current speaker identity based on the extracted multi-modal features. Data are collected during a time lapse $t : t + 1sec$ and descriptors are computed for each of these intervals. Each time lapse defines a trial; from each trial a data structure is formed which is peculiar since the descriptors have been generated from different sample spaces. The voice descriptor computes a probability with respect to MFCC codes, hence it returns the likelihood that A or B or C, etc. are speaking. It is clear that if the MFCC of two people with very similar voices are stored in the database, say A and Z, even if Z is not in the room, any time A will speak there will be a good chance that the voice estimator will return a high likelihood also for Z. The lips descriptor will tell who in the scene is moving the lips, so this feature needs to be combined with a voice and a face to be instantiated with a speaker. Indeed, people can articulate the mouth also, for example, for laughing and yawning. Finally, the two normalised distances tell who is plausibly in the camera FOV in the current trial, but cannot tell who is speaking.

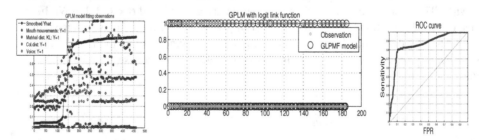

Fig. 4. On the left: the behaviour of each descriptor, at the value $\hat{Y}$, chosen for $Y = 1$. The central table illustrates 187 of the 498 matches obtained during testing with the GPLM. On the right the ROC curve. The false positive rate and true positive rates are defined as $FPR = FP/(FP + TN)$, $TPR = TP/(TP + FN)$. Sensitivity (TPR) is plotted in function of the false positive rate for different cut-off points. Each point on the ROC plot represents a sensitivity/specificity pair corresponding to a particular decision threshold for $\hat{Y}$: if the decision theroshold is chosen to be 0.5 then $FPR < 0.1$; if it is 0.9 then $FPR = 0.5$.

Trials will nominally include all the people enumerated in the knowledge base (see Section 2). The chosen labels are those in the union of the sets of descriptors with best classification. Note that if B is in the set since it has a good classification w.r.t the distance features on a region labelled Q_2, this does not imply it will yield a good classification with respect to voice or to another region Q_j, $j \neq 2$. That is why we take the union of the sets, instead of the intersection, that might be the empty set. Note also that distances are normalised over the whole dataset and not with respect to the chosen ones (see Section 4). We use regression in order to find the correct row given a trial . In particular we use a semi-parametric regression model. The model will estimate the parameters $\beta = (\beta_1, \beta_2)$ and a function g which, when applied to a trial, will return the row that most plausibly indicate the current speaker. To estimate these parameters, however, we had to resort to a training phase. Using the voices and the images in the knowledge base, and suitably adding errors for simulating environment influences, we have defined a set of 925 simulated trials, 427 of which have been used for training and the remaining for testing. We can now introduce the model. Given the descriptors $X_1, \ldots, X_4$ a semi-parametric regression model for inferring the row corresponding to the speaker is defined as:

$$E(Y|\mathbf{UT}) = P(Y = 1 \mid \mathbf{U}, \mathbf{T}) + \epsilon = f(X_2\beta_1 + X_3\beta_2 + g(X_1, X_4)) \tag{5}$$

Here f is the standard logistic distribution $f(z) = (exp(z)/(1 + exp(z)))$, $\mathbf{U} = (X_2, X_3)^\top$, $\mathbf{T} = (X_1, X_4)^\top$, and β and g are the parameters and function to be estimated. Note that we have grouped on one side the normalised distances $\mathbf{U} = (X_2, X_3)$, for which we want to estimate the parameters β_1 and β_2, and on the other side we have grouped the two probabilities $\mathbf{T} = (X_1, X_4)$. Differently from other regression models, the general non parametric regression model (5) is optimal for capturing the combination of linear and non-linear characters of the descriptors. Figure 4 illustrates the different behaviours of the features descriptors considering 427 trials. Here YHAT denotes the $\hat{Y}$ estimated by regression, that has been set to 1, with a decision threshold of 0.67. We estimate g and β according to the algorithm proposed by [6,7], here for the logit case. The iterative steps of the algorithm are reported in [15].

The goal of an empirical analysis of the data collected is to use the finite set of observations obtained for training, that is, $(\mathbf{X}_{ji}, Y_j), j = 1, \ldots, 427, i = 1, \ldots, 4$ to estimate β, g. These values, together with the canonical logit f are used to finally predict a speaker identity. Estimation amounts to the following steps:

1. Analysis of predictors performance to prove their impact on Y. Estimation of the β and of the unknown function g using the training set of the 427 trials, from the 925 obtained by simulation (using the data collected in the knowledge base). Validation of g and β with the remaining 498 trials, for all the plausible $Q_i, i = 1, \ldots, m$ in the camera FOV (in our case $m = 2, 3, 4, 5$).
2. Prediction, in real time, of the speaker identity given the current observations and the knowledge of the current trial dimension (that is, $m^2 \times 5$, with m the number of identified regions in the camera FOV, $Q_i, i = 1, \ldots, m$), considering the whole dataset.
3. Convergence of the identification process after a burning period. Expectation of the features of each identified speaker can be used to track the conversation

dynamically and refine the probability of the identity of each speaker using a dynamical model, not described here.

We consider each descriptor $X_1, \ldots, X_4$ as an explanation or predictor of the speaker identity. By looking at the performance of each explanation (see Figure 4) and also because we have two probabilities and two distances, we have chosen to group the two probabilities, that is, lips movements (X_1) and MFCC (X_4) with the non-parametric g. The iterative algorithm, with training data, starts with an initial approximation of $\hat{g} = f^{-1}((Y + 0.5)/2)$, with Y set to 1 on the correct regions labelled Q_i, and with initial values of $\hat{\beta}$ set to 0.

Now, to estimate μ a smoother matrix $\mathcal{M}$ is defined using kernel approximation. We have used the Epanechnikov kernel, defined with respect to the elements of $\mathbf{T}$

$$K_{\mathbf{h}}(X_j - X_i) = \prod_{w=1,2} (1/h_w)(3/4)(1 - ((X_{jw} - X_{iw})/h_k)^2) \cdot (\|(X_{jw} - X_{iw})/h\| \leq 0.75) \quad (6)$$

Here $h_w = 0.4$ and $w = 1, 2$ because $\mathbf{T}$ is $k \times 2$, with $K = 427$ in the training phase and $K = 498$ in the testing phase. Note that the kernel is evaluated with respect to the matrix $\mathbf{T}$, mentioning all the trials both in the training and testing phases. Then the smooth matrix $\mathcal{M}$, according to [6], can be formed by the following elements κ_{ij} of $\mathcal{M}$:

$$\frac{(\mathcal{L}''(Y, \mu_j))K_{\mathbf{H}}(X_j - X_i)}{(1/n)\sum_{j=1}^{n}(\mathcal{L}''(Y, \mu_j))K_{\mathbf{H}}(X_j - X_i)} \quad (7)$$

Convergence is achieved when difference of likelihood and the estimates of β is below a certain threshold τ. We used $\tau = 0.1E\text{-}004$ and for our set of trials 48 iterations were needed to converge on the data train set with $K = 427$. On data test the error is 0.4%. The error rate is, indeed, very low, as shown in the ROC curve displayed in Figure 4, reporting the behaviour of the estimator on data test.

6   Updating

One main problem for the online application of the system is the knowledge base dimension. If the knowledge base is large, then online acquisition for the voice descriptors and the visual descriptors, concerning the two distances, is a quite hard task. Indeed, it requires a huge set of comparisons, since nothing is known about the people in the scene. So the question is: is there a time t at which the system knows who is in the scene and can rely on that for online identification?

Experiments show that a time t at which all people have spoken is difficult to predict, and if no constraint is put on the scene, some people can leave and new people can join. Thus there is not a fixed set that can be devised after a specified time.

To solve this problem and induce a partial knowledge of the people in the scene, we assume that changes are smooth: not all current people suddenly disappear nor are substituted altogether with new ones. So in a time lapse at most one person joins the conversation and one leaves, and partial updates can be inferred for voice and face similarities acquired up to time T. More specifically, for the same effective speaker, the list $\hat{S}$ of the most probable relative labels, estimated via the acoustic analysis, tends to involve the same ones. After a specified time T (burning period), clusters of different cardinality, for each different list $\hat{S}$, are generated, with the associated frequency of occurrence. Thus, if at time $t > T$ there are δK new people, with $\delta K \geq 2$, in the list, only the most probable labels $\hat{S}_{mp}$ are maintained, while the others are replaced with the labels mentioned in the most likely cluster, of the same cardinality. This includes $\hat{S}_{mp}$, according to the likelihood computed after the burning period. These clustering on voices is integrated with an analogous clustering on visual distances and are thus used for setting a dynamic model in which known states and unknown new states are devised. The dynamic of this process, unfortunately, cannot be further described here.

7 Experiments and Conclusion

The described framework has been tested in real conversation scenarios, involving several people standing around the robot and producing audio and visual stimuli (see Figure 1). Experiments with up to 5 people, after a burning period of 2-3min, and with one people change, have a mean error rate of a person every 10 experiments. A P3-DX robotic platform has been extended by an alloy chassis supporting a laptop, which actually runs the software and presents a GUI. The head is made of a pan tilt unit orienting a pair of omnidirectional microphones, by Behringer, and a an AVT Marlin colour camera. Both the sensor types provide fast acquisition through the firewire bus. Computation is performed by a Pentium M based laptop computer, running the multi-modal data acquisition, segmentation, preprocessing and feature extraction C++ software, and a MATLAB engine for the regression and identification scripts. Audio signal is acquired and sampled at 44100 Hz, 16 bits/sample, using a Fireface 400 mixer interface, by RME Intelligent Audio Solution. Training was performed off-line using acquired sequences from a knowledge base including 30 subjects (see Section 2). 925 randomly generated trials with cardinality 2, 3, 4 and 5 are built from the stored sequences, with the constraint that every generated set must contain the real speaker. The heaviest computation is required by visual descriptors, mainly for the detection and tracking of the facial features. The system relies on a multiscale detector based on [16] and a mean shift tracker introduced in [17], that uses the backprojection of a 30×32 colour histogram encoding the H and S levels in the HSV colour space (see Figure 3). The same histogram representation is also used to estimate the 2D colour pdf of a specified Q region, as described in Section 4. The back-projected image is also conveniently used as a segmentation mask. On the other hand, the choice for the detector was mainly motivated by the performance level achieved by the face/eye/mouth cascades during the experiments. The overall performance of the vision process depends on the number of people in the scene. The described set-up allowed the acquisition / feature extraction loop to run at ≈ 12 Hz in the case of only two people in the camera field of view, which decreases to ≈ 5 Hz if the people in the FOV are 5. Online experiments proved that comparison of descriptors to the whole KB causes a sensible loss of performance, and brought the need to maintain a low number of known individuals in the KB. Evaluation was performed by setting up different conversation scenarios (Figure 1). We observed the robot shifting its attention towards the real speaker's direction and verified his/her identity through the robot's GUI. The system ignores audio/video data collected during the changes of pose, to produce a sort of saccade. A quantitative performance analysis has been carried out on audio/video sequences gathered by the robot in such scenarios. A total of about 1 hour of conversation, with 2, 3, 4, 5 people in the camera FOV has been collected and manually labelled: the real speaker's identity has been assigned to each time-step to form the ground truth; the time step used amounts to 1 second. This experiment involved 10 people among the 30 stored in the knowledge base. It is worth noting that, since the sequence is collected directly by the robot, the number of errors in speaker identification is affected by errors in the speaker localisation process too. Along the entire sequence, the total number of errors is averaged out over the number of time-steps and the resultant percentage of successful speaker identifications was about 85%.

References

1. Pentland, A.P.: Machine understanding of human action. M.I.T. Media Laboratory (1995)
2. Waibel, A., Schultz, T., Bett, M., Malkin, R., Rogina, I., Stiefelhagen, R., Yang, J.: Smart: the smart meeting room task at isl. In: Proc. of ICASSP, pp. 752–755 (2003)
3. Desilva, G.C., Yamasaki, T., Aizawa, K.: Interactive Experience Retrieval for a Ubiquitous Home. In: ACM CARPE (2006)
4. Reiter, S., Schreiber, S., Rigoll, G.: Multimodal meeting analysis by segmentation and classification of meeting events based on a higher level semantic approach. In: IEEE ICASSP, pp. 294–299 (2005)
5. Bennewitz, M., Faber, F., Joho, D., Schreiber, M., Behnke, S.: Multimodal conversation between a humanoid robot and multiple persons. In: Proc. of the Workshop on Modular Construction of Humanlike Intelligence (2005)
6. Müller, M.: Estimation and testing in generalized partial linear modelsa comparative study. Statistics and Computing 11, 299–309 (2001)
7. Severini, T., Staniswalis, J.: Quasi-likelihood estimation in semiparametric models. J. Amer. Stat. Assoc. 89, 501–511 (1994)
8. Turk, M.A., Pentland, A.P.: Face recognition using eigenfaces. In: Proc. of IEEE CVPR, pp. 586–591 (1991)
9. Murray, J.C., Erwin, H., Wermter, S.: Robotics sound-source localization and tracking using interaural time difference and cross-correlation. In: AI Workshop on NeuroBotics (2004)
10. Reynolds, D., Rose, R.: Robust text-independent speaker identification using gaussian mixture speaker models. IEEE TSAP 3(1) (1995)
11. Comaniciu, D., Meer, P.: Mean shift: A robust approach toward feature space analysis. In: IEEE TPAMI (2002)
12. Rabiner, L., Sambur, M.: An algorithm for determining the endpoints of isolated utterances. The Bell System Technical Journal 54, 297–315 (1975)
13. Atal, B., Rabiner, L.: A pattern recognition approach to voiced-unvoiced-silence classification with applications to speech recognition. IEEE TSP 24(3), 201–212 (1976)
14. Childers, D., Hand, M., Larar, J.: Silent and voiced/unvoied/ mixed excitation(four-way),classification of speech. IEEE TASSP 37(11), 1771–1774 (1989)
15. Marchegiani, M.L., Pirri, F., Pizzoli, M.: Multimodal speaker recognition in a conversation scenario. Technical Report 7, DIS, Sapienza Univerità di Roma (2009)
16. Viola, P., Jones, M.J.: Robust real-time face detection. IJCV 57(2), 137–154 (2004)
17. Bradski, G.R.: Real time face and object tracking as a component of a perceptual user interface. In: 4th IEEE WACV (1998)

FaceL: Facile Face Labeling

David S. Bolme, J. Ross Beveridge, and Bruce A. Draper

Colorado State University
Fort Collins, CO, USA
bolme@cs.colostate.edu

Abstract. FaceL is a simple and fun face recognition system that labels
faces in live video from an iSight camera or webcam. FaceL presents
a window with a few controls and annotations displayed over the live
video feed. The annotations indicate detected faces, positions of eyes,
and after training, the names of enrolled people. Enrollment is video
based, capturing many images per person. FaceL does a good job of
distinguishing between a small set of people in fairly uncontrolled settings
and incorporates a novel incremental training capability. The system
is very responsive, running at over 10 frames per second on modern
hardware. FaceL is open source and can be downloaded from http://
pyvision.sourceforge.net/facel.

1 Introduction

This paper presents Facile Face Labeler (FaceL), a simple open source tool meant
to illustrate the essence of face recognition in less than five minutes. When FaceL
is opened, it presents to the user a live video feed, face detection, and the ability
to teach the system the identities of a few people. When trained, FaceL displays
those identities back to the user over the video signal in real time. We call
this annotation of video *Face Labeling*. The FaceL user interface is shown in
Figure 1.

The primary motivation for FaceL is to provide real time demonstrations of
face recognition performance. Colorado State University has been distributing
an open source face identification evaluation system for over seven years[1]. This
system runs from the command line to batch process face imagery to perform
careful empirical evaluations of face recognition algorithm accuracy. This system
is still available and widely downloaded, but it does not provide the experience
of running a face recognition application with a camera and an observable result.
FaceL fills that void.

FaceL also represents a timely coming together of technology. In recent years,
webcams have become standard built-in features of most laptops and many desktop computers. OpenCV provides an implementation of the Viola and Jones
cascade face detector [2], which is accurate and fast enough to detect faces in
a live video feed. Robust real-time eye localization is provided by correlation
filters learned through a new technique developed by us[3]. A support vector

M. Fritz, B. Schiele, and J.H. Piater (Eds.): ICVS 2009, LNCS 5815, pp. 21–32, 2009.

Fig. 1. FaceL User Interface. (Left) Clicking in a face detection rectangle enrolls the face. (Right) After training Foreheads are labeled.

classifier is used to assign labels to faces [4]. Finally, `python` and the PyVision Computer Vision Toolkit[5] integrates the components into a cohesive user interface.

Most modern face recognition systems focus on the problem of identifying a novel (probe) face by finding the most similar image in a large database of face images. As such, most face recognition systems can be viewed as nearest-neighbor classifiers. In contrast, FaceL uses the Support Vector Classifier (SVC) to select the best of a small number of classes, typically one person per class. The support vector classifier appears to be very reliable for small numbers of people in uncontrolled environments [6]. In particular, it performs well under uncontrolled lighting with people moving their heads and adopting different expressions. However, one of the known issues with the SVC as it is used in FaceL is that performance degrades as the number of classes increases. In practice, we have not experimented with more than 8 people at a time.

Another distinct property of FaceL is that it can quickly enroll many images of a person from live video. In this way FaceL captures many different *views* of a person which include differences in expression and pose. Therefore, the system can produce an accurate model of faces under a variety of conditions, helping it to reliably label faces. A user can also add new images based upon observed performance, essentially helping FaceL to overcome mistakes.

Care has been taken to make FaceL easy to use and it is available both as a ready to run compiled application and as part of a larger open source library called PyVision (http://pyvision.sourceforge.net). The PyVision library is under a BSD license, which allows researchers and commercial vendors to integrate there own algorithms into the system.

2   Related Work

Face recognition has been an important and active field in computer vision research for many years. Multiple advancements in computer vision have come from the study of face recognition since Turk and Pentland first demonstrated the utility of eigenfaces [7] in the early nineties.

Modern commercial face recognition systems perform very well under controlled scenarios [6] and have demonstrated their utility for many applications including security and entertainment. For security, face recognition is now in use at banks, airports, government facilities, and border control. For entertainment, face recognition technology has found a home in personal photograph applications including Facebook, YouTube.com, Google Picasa, Google Images, and Apple iPhoto. All these systems now perform some sort of face detection and recognition, annotating images with identifying information such as names and supporting identity-based image retrieval. This development is transforming the public perception of face recognition from a science fiction technology to a tool that is used in every day life.

While the tools just cited are useful, they do not provide a live experience. To fill that niche, FaceL is designed to provide an interactive face recognition experience that is accessible to the general public. Users of photo cataloging software may wonder why some faces are not detected in photos or why some faces are mislabeled. By providing a video interface to a face recognition algorithms, FaceL provides a dynamic and entertaining way to explore face recognition technology.

Prior to FaceL, we spent a significant amount of time developing a similar system called Scarecrow (a strawman for face recognition) [8]. Scarecrow was intended to be an educational tool that could quickly demonstrate the fundamentals of face recognition. Scarecrow had a simple Bayesian-based face detector[9] and an Eigenfaces-based face recognition algorithm. The system was written in C++ using the QT library for the user interface. Unfortunately, because Scarecrow used a simple 15 year old face recognition algorithm it could not accurately identify people unless the images were taken under very controlled conditions.

Scarecrow often produced inaccurate or some times even embarrassing results, it was therefore never released publicly. Many lessons were learned from Scarecrow that have made FaceL a success. Scarecrow illustrated that better registration was needed through the use of better face detection and the addition of a robust eye locator. The most notable change is that FaceL has abandoned the notion of a standard nearest neighbor face recognition algorithm, like Eigenfaces, which are designed to identify thousands of people. Instead FaceL trains an SVC to classify a face as belonging to a small number of labels.

We conducted a brief survey of free webcam-based face recognition demonstration systems and discuss four of these systems here, and a more complete list can be found on the FaceL website. Of these, most of the open source demonstrations are limited to face detection and are based on sample code provided with OpenCV [10] (the same detector used in FaceL). OpenCV is the only system that we were able to run on MacOS X, Linux, and Windows[1]. However, installing and running OpenCV requires significant software development skills and is therefore beyond the reach of many users.

We know of one other open source system similar to FaceL called Malic [11]. Malic captures video from a webcam and uses OpenCV for face detection and a Gabor filter based algorithm from the CSU Face Recognition Evaluation System [1] for identification. This project appears to have been abandoned in 2006. We spent a few hours trying to install Malic and its dependencies but were never able to get the system to run. This is the only other open source system that we know of that attempts face recognition in addition to face detection.

Pittsburgh Pattern Recognition [12] recently released a free demonstration application for their face detection and tracking software. Stand alone executables are available for Windows and Mac and are easily installed and run. The user interface for the demonstration is extremely simple, providing a video window with overlaid detection information and one control which selects the minimum face size. Their detector performs better under poor lighting conditions than OpenCV and detects face profiles and faces rotated up to 45°. Frame rates are approximately the same as FaceL.

NeuroTechnology has a free demonstration application for their VeriLook SDK[13] that performs face verification on Windows[2] The user interface is more complex than FaceL and appears targeted towards software developers. The primary differences between Verilook and FaceL is that VeriLook has a more traditional face recognition algorithm that outputs a similarity score. Verification is performed on the video by pressing a button labeled "M" for "Match". The system then captures a user defined number of frames and outputs a similarity score for any enrolled face that pass a threshold. The VeriLook face identification algorithm is impressive and only made three or four mistakes for the approximately 50 times we pressed the "match" button with 8 people enrolled.

3   Face Processing

There are three main components to the FaceL face labeling system: face detection, eye localization, and face labeling. FaceL processes a live video stream which means that these components must be fast. Because the system needs to operate using a variety of cameras in a variety of settings, they need to be robust to changes in lighting and background. They also need to be accurate enough to distinguish between a small number of face classes.

---

[1] Most tests were run on a MacBook Pro running MacOS 10.5. Windows XP and Kubuntu Linux were tested on the same machine using Parallels and a Logitech QuickCam 5000 Pro USB webcam.

[2] Verilook did not run on Windows XP on Parallels, but did install and run without issues on a Windows Vista machine.

3.1   Face Detection: OpenCV Cascade Face Detector

Face detection is performed by the OpenCV cascade face detector, which is based on the Viola and Jones face detection algorithm[2], as extended by [14] (See Figure 2). OpenCV includes both the code and training files for the cascade classifier. The training files specify a decision tree which discriminates between face and non-face image subwindows. The classifier is easy to use and is nicely suited for video processing. The output of the classifier is a set of rectangles which indicate face detections. We have found that the face detector performs very well detecting frontal faces under a variety of conditions and is also fast enough to run in real time [15].

The face detector uses several optimizations to improve run-time. First, the Haar-based features used for classification are computed from an integral image. This integral image allows each feature to be computed in constant time regardless of the size of the feature. The second optimization is the use of a cascaded decision tree. This is a decision tree that is built in layers where the purpose of each layer is to reject non-face subwindows. The idea is that most of the non-face subwindows are rejected quickly in the first few layers of the decision tree, which saves processing time while still allowing for high accuracy.

To further improve run-time, images are down sampled to 320×240 pixels before passing them to the cascade classifier. The minimum detection size was also set to 60 pixels. The result is that the minimum face size detected by the system is approximately 120 pixels across in the original 640×480 image. This setting is ideal for FaceL which expects the faces to be approximately 3 to 4 feet from the camera. However it also means that the system has difficultly detecting faces that are more than 5 feet from the camera. The tuned face detection algorithm takes between 15ms and 22ms to process a frame.

Fig. 2. Face detection (blue rectangles) and eye localization (blue dots) are displayed in real time in the video window

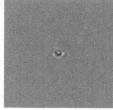

Fig. 3. Eye localization using ASEF Filters. From left to right: output from the face detector, the left eye ASEF filter, the correlation output from the left filter, and the image with the left and right correlation peaks marked in red. (The right eye filtering results are not shown.)

3.2   Eye Localization: Average of Synthetic Exact Filters

The second step in the system is to accurately register or align the faces. Faces are registered by locating the eyes and then rotating and scaling the faces such that the eyes are in fixed locations. We have found that accurate localization and subsequent registration of faces to a canonical size and position is critical for producing accurate labels.

Each eye is located by convolving the face with an Average of Synthetic Exact Filters (ASEF) filter (Figure 3) trained to detect eyes[3]. ASEF filters are simple correlation filters that are trained to produce sharp peaks corresponding to the eyes in the face image. The location of these peaks correspond to the location of the eyes.

ASEF filters are constructed from a set of training images and corresponding synthetic output. In this case the synthetic output is a bright peak at the location of the eye and zero every where else. An *exact filter* is constructed which exactly maps a training image to the desired output. This exact filter is usually very specific to the particular training image. By averaging a few thousand exact filters, the features of the filter that are idiosyncratic are averaged out while features appearing in many of the exact filters remain. The resulting filters have the appearance of an eye and perform very well at locating eyes in face images.

Originally FaceL used the same filters that were produced using the FERET dataset as seen in[3]. We found that these filters performed well for frontal images but had some difficulty when presented with poses that were to the left or right of frontal. We believe this is because the FERET images are taken under controlled lighting with the person looking directly at the camera.

To correct this deficiency, we retrained the filters on the PIE Illum dataset which includes frontal poses and four neighboring poses (27,5,29,9,7) to expose the filters to broader variations of pose and lighting. The resulting filters perform much better in the settings where we have tested FaceL. Eyes are correctly located for most faces detected by the cascade classifier.

One advantage of using correlation filters to detect eyes is that correlation is very fast. The subwindows produced by the face detector are rescaled to 128×128. Those images are then correlated with two filters (one for each eye), using the FFT to speed up the computation. A real valued discrete FFT and inverse FFT from OpenCV are used because they require approximately half the time and memory as a full complex FFT. Eye detection has been benchmarked at under 3ms per face.

Correlation filters are also much faster than other common techniques for locating eyes. Gabor jet based methods often correlate the image with up to 80 different gabor filters which takes far more time than convolving with the two specially tuned filters of ASEF. Further more, ASEF filters have been benchmarked at almost three times faster than cascade classifiers trained to detect eyes.[3]

3.3 Labeling: Support Vector Classifier

Before classification some common preprocessing is done to the image to improve the accuracy of the classifier and reduce the time needed to classify the image. The first step uses the eye coordinates to geometrically align the face. A 128×160 pixel image of the face is constructed by translating, rotating, and scaling the original frame to place the eye coordinates at (26,40) and (102,40).

A high pass filter is applied to the image to remove some of the effects of lighting. This is done by converting the image to gray scale and convolving the face image with a Gaussian of radius $\sigma = 8.0$. This produces a smoothed image emphasizing the low frequencies. To obtain the higher frequencies the smoothed image is subtracted from the original face image. These images are then normalized to have a mean pixel value of zero and a standard deviation of one.

Principal Components Analysis (PCA) is used to perform dimensionality reduction. PCA training is performed on the enrolled images. The eigenvectors corresponding to 95% of the energy in the distribution are retained and define a subspace into which both enrolled images and new images are projected. The PCA basis is also used to whiten the data before classification. This takes the original distribution of the face images, which is assumed to be an elongated hyper ellipsoid, and non uniformly rescales it using the Eigenvalues such that the point cloud has unit variance in every direction. This transformation has been shown to have a positive effect on the accuracy of the Eigenfaces algorithm [1].

Finally, the system uses a SVC from `libsvm`[4] to classify the faces as belonging to a small number of user definable classes. A typical SVC finds a decision boundary that optimally separates two classes by maximizing a linear margin between those two point distributions. The `libsvm` library has extended this to a multiclass classifier by constructing a SVC for each possible pair of classes. A voting strategy is then used to assign the final classification.

One consequence of extending a two-class SVC to a multiclass problem is that labeling will only work well for a small number of classes. This is different from many face recognition algorithms which distinguish between hundreds of people by basing decisions on similarity computations between pairs of face images. FaceL therefore performs well only when distinguishing a small number of names, poses, or expressions.

In order to produce an accurate label, parameters of SVC needs to be tuned to produce good decisions. The PyVision SVC automatically tunes the classifier based on the method suggested by the authors of libsvm[16]. The enrolled images are first randomly partitioned. Two thirds are used as a training set and one third is used as a validation set. Tuning uses a Radial Basis Function (RBF) kernel to produce a nonlinear decision boundary and performs a grid search to find optimal values of C which is a penalty parameter for the error and γ which controls the radius of the RBF kernel.

4   Using the Application

FaceL can be downloaded from the PyVision website at http://pyvision. sourceforge.net/facel. A binary distribution is currently only available for MacOS 10.5. All libraries and components used by FaceL are cross platform so running FaceL on other systems should be possible. FaceL has been tested and runs on Linux from the source code distribution. On windows OpenCV has difficulty retrieving images from a webcam so additional work is needed.

FaceL requires a webcam for a live video feed. Video capture is delegated to the OpenCV library and therefore FaceL should support any webcam available to OpenCV. On Mac OS, FaceL has been tested with firewire and build-in iSight cameras as well as a few USB webcams from Microsoft and Logitech with no problems.

After starting FaceL, a window is displayed that contains live video feed from the webcam. Face detection and eye localization is run on each video frame. A blue rectangle is rendered around each face detection and small blue circles are rendered for each eye.

To enroll a face, the user simply clicks within the blue detection rectangle. FaceL will add the next 64 images of that face to its training dataset. After those images are collected the system prompts the user for a label such as the person's name. This step is repeated for each person enrolled in the database.

Once at least two distinct labels have been enrolled, the user trains the SVC by clicking the "Train Labeler" button. For a small dataset (128 faces), training takes less than 10 seconds. Training time increases with more enrolled faces. Once the SVC is trained the video resumes and faces in the video will have green labels on their foreheads. Additional faces can be enrolled at any time by using the same enrollment process and retraining the labeler. As will be discussed below, this incremental learning proves to be very useful.

4.1   Accuracy and Improving Recognition

Poor lighting conditions have the largest effect on the accuracy of FaceL. If the person's face is dark and the background is bright, face detection often fails. Because the face detector is pre-trained the best way to correct this problem is to set up the camera facing away from bright backgrounds or light sources such as windows. In extreme cases it also helps to use a lamp or other light source to illuminate the face.

Fig. 4. Using live feedback at over 10fps users can quickly search out expressions or poses that confuse the labeler. Here the real "Douglas" is in the center of the image. In this case the users found that a smile in combination with some poses where associated with the label "Douglas".

Another cause of difficulty is uncooperative subjects. Users can attempt to confuse the labeler by finding a pose or expression that causes a face to be mislabeled. Because FaceL runs at over 10fps with immediate feedback to the user it is easy for users to quickly search for poses, expressions, lighting, etc. that cause a failure in labeling. Figure 4 shows one such example where the system learned to associate a smile with the label "Douglas" and hence all four people found ways to cause the system to label them "Douglas".

This amusing aspect of FaceL has two serious implications for fielded biometric systems. The first is that any system that allows a user to interact with an authentication system may be able to discover ways of gaming the system. In other words, they could experiment with changes until the system falsely associates them with another person's identity and unlocks whatever the system is endeavoring to protect. Hence, any system meant to provide security should probably avoid real-time feedback of the type illustrated by FaceL.

The second implication concerns the nature of enrollment. Traditional approaches to face biometrics have tended to take a rather narrow view of enrollment, often assuming only a single image is necessary. We have found that FaceL performs best when a variety of views are captured. Thus, users are encouraged to present as many views of their face as possible by rotating their head up, down, left, and right by up to 10° and also to assume different expressions. This goes a long way toward making FaceL more robust.

However, the "five Douglases" problem, where FaceL provides realtime feedback on the circumstances under which it becomes confused, opens the door for a staged and more intelligent approach to enrollment. So, if a user finds a view that causes difficulty, an additional video sequence of that view can be enrolled

Process	Time	Relative CPU Usage
Face Detect Time:	16.1ms	
Eye Locate Time:	2.8ms	
Face Label Time:	12.5ms	
Other Processing:	72.1ms	
Total Time:	104ms	Frames/Sec: 9.7fps

Fig. 5. Performance window measures the execution time of FaceL components for each frame processed

by clicking the face and entering the corrected label. When the system is re-trained it will use the additional frames for training and the resulting classifier will no longer make the same mistakes.

4.2   Real-Time Labeling

The video in FaceL is very responsive. Processing times can be seen in Figure 5. We have found that FaceL runs at about 10 to 20 fps for a frame with one face. Tuning the face detector had the largest effect on the speed of the system. By sacrificing the ability to detect small faces the speed of face detection can be greatly improved. Eye localization time and face labeling time are of course proportional to the number of faces detected. Acquiring an image from the camera seems to be the most time consuming task in the image processing pipeline and could possibly be improved by interfacing directly with Quicktime instead of using the OpenCV abstraction.

4.3   Tasks Other Than Identification

Many face recognition systems are focused only on accurately identifying a person in an image. FaceL, however, has no such bias, and therefore can be trained

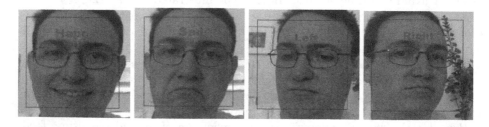

Fig. 6. FaceL can be trained to recognize expressions (left two images) or pose (right two images)

to perform other tasks (See Figure 6). For example, the system does very well at detecting which direction a persons head is looking: "Left", "Center", or "Right", or at distinguishing a small set of expressions: "Happy" or "Sad". These are also some simple ways to test the system with only one person.

5   Conclusions and Future Work

In our experience over the past few months we have found FaceL to be an interesting and fun way to demonstrate face recognition technology. FaceL has a responsive and intuitive user interface that makes using the application easy. Finally, the OpenCV face detector, ASEF eye locator, and SVC labeling algorithms perform well with a small number of cooperative people.

Almost every person with a background in computer vision to whom we have demonstrated FaceL has said something to the effect: "Couldn't you do _____ with this!" As it stands, FaceL is serves to demonstrate real-time face recognition projected over a live video feed. In the future we intend to introduce features that make FaceL more useful as a face recognition tool such as the ability to detect faces, locate eyes, and label whole directories of images. which make FaceL more useful and more educational. We would also like FaceL to be more educational by exposing more of the inner workings of the algorithms.

Another key contribution of FaceL from the standpoint of biometrics is the compelling manner in which it opens up the notion of incremental and intelligent enrollment. Enrolling a large number of different views and additional enrollments for problem views has proven very useful in producing a robust classifier. Similar procedures may prove very useful in any biometric system where video enrollment and fast face processing algorithms are available.

Acknowledgments

We thank Yui Man Lui, Patrick Flynn, and other FaceL Beta testers for volunteering their time and for providing useful feedback. We also thank Ward Fisher and Jilmil Saraf for their work on Scarecrow and for the knowledge and experience that we gained from that system.

References

1. Bolme, D.S., Beveridge, J.R., Teixeira, M.L., Draper, B.A.: The CSU face identification evaluation system: Its purpose, features, and structure. In: Crowley, J.L., Piater, J.H., Vincze, M., Paletta, L. (eds.) ICVS 2003. LNCS, vol. 2626, pp. 304–313. Springer, Heidelberg (2003)
2. Viola, P., Jones, M.J.: Robust real-time face detection. Int. J. Comput. Vision 57(2), 137–154 (2004)
3. Bolme, D.S., Draper, B.A., Beveridge, J.R.: Average of synthetic exact filters. In: CVPR (2009)
4. Chang, C.C., Lin, C.J.: LIBSVM: a Library for Support Vector Machines (2007)

5. Bolme, D.S.: Pyvision - computer vision toolbox. WWW Page (2008),
   http://pyvision.sourceforge.net
6. Phillips, P., Scruggs, W., O'Toole, A., Flynn, P., Bowyer, K., Schott, C., Sharpe, M.: FRVT 2006 and ICE 2006 large-scale results. National Institute of Standards and Technology, NISTIR (2007)
7. Turk, M.A., Pentland, A.P.: Face recognition using eigenfaces. In: CVPR (1991)
8. Fisher, W.: An introduction to and analysis of Scarecrow. Master's thesis, Colorado State Univ. (2008)
9. Saraf, J.: An assessment of alternative features for a semi-naive Bayesian face detector on single face images. Master's thesis, Colorado State University (2007)
10. Garage, W.: Opencv libarary (April 2009), http://opencv.willowgarage.com
11. Suga, A.: Malic - malib with csufaceideval and opencv (January 2006), http://malic.sourceforge.net
12. Pittsburgh Pattern Recognition: Webcam face tracker (April 2009), http://demo.pittpatt.com/
13. NeuroTechnology: Verilook demo (April 2009), http://www.neurotechnology.com/download.html
14. Lienhart, R., Maydt, J.: An extended set of haar-like features for rapid object detection. In: ICIP (2002)
15. Beveridge, J., Alvarez, A., Saraf, J., Fisher, W., Flynn, P., Gentile, J.: Face Detection Algorithm and Feature Performance on FRGC 2.0 Imagery. In: Biometrics: Theory, Applications, and Systems (2007)
16. Hsu, C.W., Chang, C.C., Lin, C.J.: A practical guide to support vector classification. LibSVM (2007)

Automatic Assessment of Eye Blinking Patterns through Statistical Shape Models

Federico M. Sukno[1,2], Sri-Kaushik Pavani[2,1], Constantine Butakoff[2,1], and Alejandro F. Frangi[2,1,3]

[1] Networking Research Center on Bioengineering, Biomaterials and Nanomedicine (CIBER-BBN), Spain
[2] Research Group for Computational Imaging & Simulation Technologies in Biomedicine; Department of Information and Communication Technologies, Universitat Pompeu Fabra, Barcelona, Spain
[3] Catalan Institution for Research and Advanced Studies (ICREA), Spain

Abstract. Several studies have related the alertness of an individual to their eye-blinking patterns. Accurate and automatic quantification of eye-blinks can be of much use in monitoring people at jobs that require high degree of alertness, such as that of a driver of a vehicle. This paper presents a non-intrusive system based on facial biometrics techniques, to accurately detect and quantify eye-blinks. Given a video sequence from a standard camera, the proposed procedure can output blink frequencies and durations, as well as the PERCLOS metric, which is the percentage of the time the eyes are at least 80% closed. The proposed algorithm was tested on 360 videos of the AV@CAR database, which amount to approximately 95,000 frames of 20 different people. Validation of the results against manual annotations yielded very high accuracy in the estimation of blink frequency with encouraging results in the estimation of PERCLOS (average error of 0.39%) and blink duration (average error within 2 frames).

1 Introduction

Spontaneous eye blink has been shown to provide substantial information regarding fatigue [12]. Even though the mechanism controlling eye blinking is not well understood yet, it seems conceivable (from a physiological point of view) "that modifications in the level of activity by mental, emotional and sleepiness-associated changes affect frequency and duration of spontaneous blinking" [2].

Several studies have experimentally demonstrated an increase in the blink frequency as a function of the time-on-task in diverse situations, like driving a car [15] and in aviation [7]. For example, The U.S. Department of Transportation reported distinctive patterns in the blinking frequency right before a person falls asleep (a sudden increase after a relative decrease in the blinking rate) [14] while Caffier *et al.* [2] found an increase in the duration of the blinks as a person gets more drowsy.

Among several measurements designed to monitor the ocular activity, the *PERcentage of eye CLOSure* (PERCLOS) was found to be the most reliable

M. Fritz, B. Schiele, and J.H. Piater (Eds.): ICVS 2009, LNCS 5815, pp. 33–42, 2009.

and valid determination of a driver's alertness level [4]. A PERCLOS drowsiness metric was established in a 1994 driving simulator study as the proportion of time in a minute that the eyes are at least 80% closed [17].

Systems to monitor eye blinking are usually built using infrared devices. For example, Caffier *et al.* [1] used an array of (infrared) light emitting diodes and sensors clipped to the ear piece of an empty spectacle frame. Apart from the fact that these methods need specialized and expensive equipment, the devices are not user-friendly as they provide substantial visual obstruction to the driver. D'Orazio *et al.* [5] and Smith *et al.* [13], simplified the setup using standard cameras in front of the drivers. In both cases, however, there was no attempt to validate the PERCLOS measurements against ground truth.

In this work, we present an alternative method based on state of the art facial biometric techniques to analyze the blinks of a user in a non-intrusive fashion. The proposed system is composed by a face detector [10] followed by a segmentation based on Active Shape Models with Invariant Optimal Features (IOF-ASM) [16] to extract the contours delineating the different facial features. A statistical analysis of the resulting shape sequence allows to accurately estimate a number of blinking parameters.

A brief description of the face detection and segmentation algorithms is presented in Section 2, followed by the techniques designed to extract the blinking measurements from the shape sequences in Section 3. The results of the automatic measurements and validation against manual annotation are presented in Section 4, on 360 video sequences of 20 people from the studio part of the AV@CAR database [8]. Section 5 concludes the paper.

2   Automatic Face Segmentation

2.1   Detection

The aim of the face detector is to determine if there are face(s) in the image or not. If there are face(s), the detector outputs the position and the size of each face. We used the detector proposed in [10], which uses Haar-like features [9] with optimally weighted rectangles. This detector, when tested on the MIT+CMU dataset, produced a false acceptance rate of 5×10^{-6} while correctly classifying 93% of the faces in the database at real-time speeds.

2.2   Segmentation

For the segmentation of the prominent facial features our system employs Active Shape Models with the Invariant Optimal Features (IOF-ASM)[16]. This algorithm combines local image search with global shape constraints based on a Point Distribution Model (PDM) [3] and can automatically locate the outlines of eyes, mouth, nose, brows and silhouette contour of the face with an average error of approximately 2% of the inter-eye distance. As a result, it is possible to extract facial features based on either shape (directly using the resulting

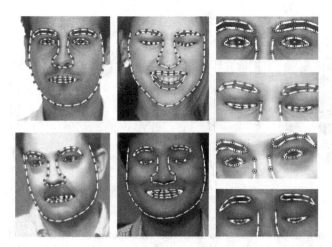

Fig. 1. Examples of the training images with the annotation template superimposed. There are clearly two separate lines delineating the eyes, even when fully closed.

parametrization in model space) or image intensities, taking into account region correspondences.

The system described in this paper was trained on 1078 images from the AR and Equinox databases [6] [11], with the same parameters specified in [16]. Fig. 1 shows some examples of the training images, with the 98-point annotation template superimposed. It can be seen that both databases contain images with open and closed eyes, hence constituting an appropriate training set for the models to handle blinking.

3   Estimation of Eye-Blink Parameters

Given a video stream (a sequence of images), the techniques described in the previous section allow to extract the corresponding sequence of shapes. Each shape is composed by 98 landmarks, among which there are 8 landmarks for each eye.

A simple way to quantify the *aperture* of the eyes is to measure the distances between *vertically* corresponding landmarks, as indicated in Fig. 2. There are six of such distances (three for each eye), which we average to obtain $a(t)$, an estimation of the eye aperture at time t.

Fig. 2 shows an example of $a(t)$ for a video sequence of AV@CAR. This example immediately brings up three observations:

- There are a number of minima easily identifiable that, as we shall see later, correspond to blinks.
- The signal is quite noisy, although the amplitude of this *noise* is smaller than the amplitude of the peaks indicating the minima.
- Even though they correspond to blinks, the values of $a(t)$ at the minima do not reach as close to zero as intuitively expected.

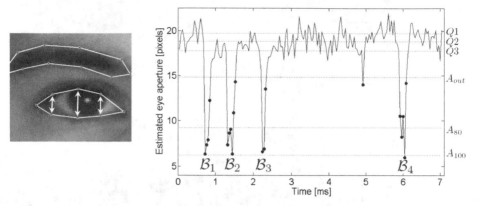

Fig. 2. Landmark distances used to estimate the *aperture* of the eyes (Left) and an example of the resulting signal over time with the decision thresholds indicated (Right). Outlier samples are highlighted by individual markers. Four out of the five outlier clusters are identified as blinks.

The first two points suggest the need for robust estimation techniques to soften the effect of the noise. The intuitive alternative of low-pass filtering does not seem appropriate here, as this would reduce our temporal resolution.

The fact that $a(t)$ does not reach zero during eye closure is because of the manner the training set was annotated. As it can be seen in Fig. 1, even when the eyes are fully closed there are two separate lines for the contours of the eyes, and $a(t) > 0$.

The values of $a(t)$ for fully closed and fully open eyes are likely to be person dependent. Therefore, there is a need to estimate them automatically (preferably without the need for ground truth labeling). For this purpose, we treat the values of $a(t)$ as the samples of a distribution. As eyes are open most of the time, blinks will be detected as outliers.

Our strategy starts off by setting the reference level for open-eyes, A_0, as the median of $a(t)$. Eye blinks are detected by splitting the set of outlier samples into disjoint subsets, each corresponding to a downward peak (or *valley*) of $a(t)$. All samples in a peak are neighbors and the peak is considered a blink only if its minimum is low enough (that is, if the eye got fully closed). Since there are typically several blinks, each having different amplitude, we take their average as the reference value, denoted by A_{100}. Now, since we are interested in measuring the time that the eyes are closed 80% or more (following the definition of PERCLOS [17]), the threshold for the minimum amplitude of a peak to be *low enough* is $A_{80} = A_0 - 0.8(A_0 - A_{100})$ (we are interested only on the downward outliers). Notice that the calculation of A_{80} is iterative, as it sets the threshold to validate when a valley is considered a blink, which in turn will be used to calculate A_{80}.

Fig. 2 shows an example with four blinks, $\mathcal{B}_k$, and the resulting thresholds, where $Q1$, $Q2$ and $Q3$ are the quartiles of $a(t)$. The estimated median is $A_0 = Q2$ and a sample is considered an outlier if its amplitude is below $A_{out} = Q3 - 1.5(Q1 - Q3)$. There are five groups of outlier samples which could potentially

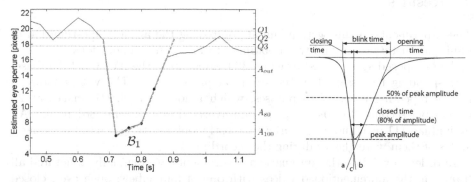

Fig. 3. On the left, an example of the aperture signal over time (continuous line) and the regression lines computed to estimate the duration of the blink (dashed lines). On the right, a schematic drawing of a blink signal, as measured with infrared devices: the blink duration is estimated from lines tangent to the signal at 50% amplitude [1].

become blinks. However, the minimum of the peak found at $t \approx 5$ seconds is much higher than the minima of the other four peaks. The first iteration yields $A_{100} = 7.83$, so we get $A_{80} = 10.0$. Then the peak at $t \approx 5$ is discarded and only four blinks remain. At the second iteration $A_{80} = 8.8$ and no more blinks are discarded, hence the process has converged.

3.1   Duration of the Blinks

Once the occurrences of blinks are determined, there is the need for estimating their duration. Two main durations are usually computed: a) the time of the whole blink, which starts and ends with the eyes fully open, and b) the time the eyes are fully closed, where "fully" actually means above a certain percentage (80% in our case).

Fig. 3 shows a portion of $a(t)$ together with a schematic drawing of a typical blink wave [1]. It is clear that the starting time of a blink is easier to detect than the ending time. Indeed, Caffier *et al.* proposed to measure the durations based on linear approximations of the ascending and descending flanks [1]. We proceeded in an analogous way, using linear regression to estimate each flank. Fig. 3 shows the estimated regression lines (dashed lines) plus a third line (*peak line*) interpolating the samples below A_{80} (the peak value was not important then we did not use regression here). The samples used to estimate the flanks were those from the blinks B_k augmented with neighboring samples. The gap between the flanks and the peak line were linearly interpolated. In the descending flank there seems to be a single line, the ascending line clearly shows two different slopes as the eye opening happens in a much smoother way. As it will be shown in the experiments, this fact seriously complicates the validation due to the relatively low frame rate of standard video cameras compared with the temporal resolution of infrared devices like the one used in [1].

4   Results

The experiments in this section aim at comparing the automatic estimation of blink parameters to ground truth obtained from manual annotations.

The proposed system was tested on 360 videos from the AV@CAR database, corresponding to session 1 of the studio acquisitions [8]. The videos show 20 people repeating a set of 18 phrases, which amount to $94,931$ images at 25 frames per second ($3m\,10s$ per person on average) and showing 861 blinks. All individuals (11 men and 9 women) were mostly looking straight into the camera, and 8 of them wore glasses during the recording.

In order to validate the automatic measurements, we manually annotated all frames in the aforementioned videos with one of four labels: open eyes, closed eyes, opening eyes and closing eyes. With the help of these labels we created a ground truth signal for the aperture $a(t)$. At frames labeled with fully open or fully closed eyes we set $a(t)$ to A_0 and A_{100}, respectively, and we performed linear interpolation during frames with opening and closing labels.

4.1   Estimation of the Reference Levels

As explained in Section 3, the estimation of A_0 and A_{100} must be done from long enough sequences. As the duration of the test videos ranged from 5.08 to 22.16 seconds, we concatenated all the videos from each user and used the resulting sequence to estimate the reference values. Fig. 4 shows the estimation error averaged over all users for different durations of the sequence (when the first t seconds were used). The error was computed as the difference with respect to the value obtained using all available frames. As expected, the estimation of A_{100} takes longer to stabilize, as it requires the occurrence of blinks. For the

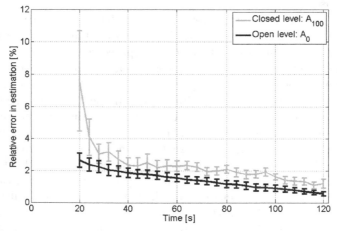

Fig. 4. Relative error in the estimation of the reference levels while varying the length of the sequence used for the estimation. The error bars correspond to the standard error.

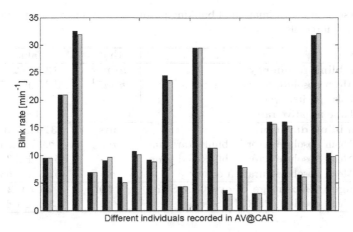

Fig. 5. Blink frequencies for all 20 users from session-1 of AV@CAR database. Black bars indicate the values computed from manual ground truth, and light-gray bars indicate the values estimated by the automatic system.

experiments reported in this paper we used the first minute of video to estimate the parameters. This delay in the measurements is perfectly acceptable for our needs, as PERCLOS is defined in [7] as the time eyes are closed averaged over a minute.

4.2 Estimation of Blink Parameters

Table 1 summarizes our results. We observed a very high accuracy in the detection of blinks, even in cases of successive blinks with very short time between them. This can be observed not only in the low estimation error for the frequencies, but also in the low number of false positives (detection of non-existing blinks) and false negative (non-detected blinks which actually occurred). To provide a relative error metric we divided these numbers by the total number of blinks and reported them as rates, although this is not strictly correct as the upper bound is much higher than 100%.

The occurrence of blinks was accurately detected for all users, in spite of the considerable dispersion in their blink frequencies. Fig. 5 shows these frequencies together with the estimated values.

The second set of measurements reported in the table corresponds to the blink duration. The overall error is about 1.5 frames and it is mostly influenced by the estimation of the end point. Indeed, as shown in Fig. 3, the end point of a blink is considerably smoother than its starting point. This makes it difficult to accurately estimate the end-point even manually for a human observer.

Regarding the PERCLOS, the estimation errors that were obtained are very low in absolute terms. However, in relative terms it represents approximately 20% of the measured values. We discuss this point in the next section.

Table 1. Results in the estimation of blinking parameters. Averages are provided with 95% confidence intervals.

Parameter	Units	Value
Mean blink frequency	min^{-1}	**13.5 ± 2.1**
Mean absolute frequency error	min^{-1}	0.37 ± 0.15
False positive rate	%	2.67
False negative rate	%	4.41
Mean blink duration	**ms**	**310 ± 7.3**
Mean absolute error in blink-start time	ms	19.9 ± 1.64
Mean absolute error in blink-end time	ms	51.2 ± 3.35
Mean absolute duration error	ms	62.3 ± 3.68
Average PERcentage of eye CLOSure	$\times 10^3$	**20 ± 6.2**
Mean absolute PERCLOS error	$\times 10^3$	3.9 ± 1.8

Table 2. Comparison of frame classification accuracy

Correct frame classification rate	Open-eye frames	Closed-eye frames	All frames (4 labels)
Smith et al. [13]	92.8%	87.6%	92.2%
This work	99.5%	80.5%	97.1%

5   Discussion and Conclusions

In this paper, we presented an automatic system for monitoring eye-blinking parameters based on statistical techniques for facial analysis. The system operates on video sequences provided by a standard video camera and it is composed by three blocks: detection, segmentation and parameter estimation. The detection and segmentation blocks are based on statistical models, which were trained on databases completely independent from the test set. The parameter estimation block, on the other hand, does not require training: it only introduces an adaptation delay at the beginning, which was set to 1 minute.

From the results in the previous section, it is clear that blink frequencies can be accurately estimated. Comparison to other works is unfortunately difficult since in most cases there were no ground truth annotations available. As an exception, Smith et al. report blink detection on approximately 1, 200 frames (18 blinks in total). They report the number of missclassified frames, which allowed as to address a comparison in Table 2. Ignoring the differences in the type and amount of the test data, our system showed a higher correct classification rate, although the one of Smith et al. showed lower false negative rate.

An important question is whether 25 FPS provide enough temporal resolution. At first glance, the errors in the estimation of blink duration shown in Table 1 suggest that this frame rate is not sufficient. However, the average blink duration was longer than 6 frames and above 70% of all blinks lasted more than 150 ms. This coincides with values reported in the literature: Caffier et al. [2] reported average blink durations ranging from 230 to 280 ms, with minimum durations around 75 *ms* occurring in very few cases (in our case there were only two blinks of 75 *ms* and 9 blinks of 100 *ms*).

Results on the PERCLOS measurements were also somehow contradictory. On the one hand, Wierwille *et al.* [17] classified users into three states of alertness based on the PERCLOS measurements: *Awake* (PERCLOS < 0.075), *Questionable* ($0.075 <$ PERCLOS < 0.15) and *Drowsy* (PERCLOS > 0.15). This classification can be successfully used with our method because the mean PERCLOS error we obtain is 0.0039. However, the average PERCLOS score observed in our datasets was approximately 0.02, which leads to a considerable estimation error, if analyzed in relative terms. This average is indeed considerably smaller than the values reported in the literature. The same effect, to a lesser extent, was observed in the blinking frequency and obeys to a limitation inherent to the test data. As mentioned before, there were 18 short videos for each person, which implies a non-continuous recording. We believe that overall blinking rates and durations of these people were higher than those shown in the video sequences.

Acknowledgements

This work was partially funded by grants TEC2006-03617/TCM and DEX-520100-2008-40 from the Spanish Ministry of Innovation & Science.

References

1. Caffier, P.P., Erdmann, U., Ullsperger, P.: Experimental evaluation of eye-blink parameters as a drowsiness measure. European Journal of Applied Physiology 89(3-4), 319–325 (2003)
2. Caffier, P.P., Erdmann, U., Ullsperger, P.: The spontaneous eye-blink as sleepiness indicator in patients with obstructive sleep apnoea syndrome - a pilot study. Sleep Medicine 6(2), 155–162 (2005)
3. Cootes, T.F., Taylor, C.J., Cooper, D.H., Graham, J.: Active shape models - their training and application. computer vision and image understanding 61(1), 38–59 (1995)
4. Dinges, D.: PERCLOS: A valid psychophysiological measure of alertness as assesed by psychomotor vigilance indianapolis. Technical report, Federal Highway Administration, Office of Motor Carriers, Tech. Rep. MCRT-98-006 (1998)
5. D'Orazio, T., Leo, M., Guaragnella, C., Distante, A.: A visual approach for driver inattention detection. Pattern Recognition 40(8), 2341–2355 (2007)
6. Martínez, A., Benavente, R.: The AR face database. Technical report, Computer Vision Center, Barcelona, Spain (1998)
7. Morris, T.L., Miller, J.C.: Electrooculographic and performance indices of fatigue during simulated. Biological psychology 42(3), 343–360 (1996)
8. Ortega, A., Sukno, F.M., Lleida, E., Frangi, A.F., Miguel, A., Buera, L., Zacur, E.: AV@CAR: A spanish multichannel multimodal corpus for in-vehicle automatic audio-visual speech recognition. In: Proc. 4th Int. Conf. on Language Resources and Evaluation, Lisbon, Portugal, vol. 3, pp. 763–767 (2004),
http://www.cilab.upf.edu/ac

9. Papageorgiou, C.P., Oren, M., Poggio, T.: A general framework for object detection. In: ICCV 1998: Proceedings of the International Conference on Computer Vision, Washington, DC, USA, pp. 555–562 (1998)
10. Pavani, S.-K., Delgado-Gomez, D., Frangi, A.F.: Haar-like features with optimally weighted rectangles for rapid object detection. Pattern Recognition (in press, 2009)
11. Selinger, A., Socolinsky, D.: Appearance-based facial recognition using visible and thermal imagery: a comparative study. Technical report, Equinox Corporation (2002), http://www.equinoxsensors.com
12. Sirevaag, E.J., Stern, J.A.: Ocular Measures of Fatigue and Cognitive Factors. In: Engineering Psychophysiology: Issues and Applications, L. Erlbaum Associates Press, Mahwah (1998)
13. Smith, P., Shah, M., da Vitoria Lobo, N.: Determining driver visual attention with one camera. IEEE Trans. Intell. Transport. Syst. 4(4), 205–218 (2003)
14. Stern, J.: Eye activity measures of fatigue, and napping as a countermeasure. Technical report, U.S. Department of Transportation. Technical Report FHWA-MC-99-028 (1999)
15. Stern, J.A., Beideman, L., Chen, S.C.: Effect of alcohol on visual search and motor performance during complex task performance. In: Adverse effects of environmental chemicals and psychotropic drugs: neurophysiological and behavioral tests, vol. 2, pp. 53–68. Elsevier, Amsterdam (1976)
16. Sukno, F.M., Ordas, S., Butakoff, C., Cruz, S., Frangi, A.F.: Active shape models with invariant optimal features: Application to facial analysis. IEEE Trans. Pattern Anal. Mach. Intell. 29(7), 1105–1117 (2007)
17. Wierwille, W.W., Ellsworth, L.A., Wreggit, S.S., Fairbanks, R.J., Kirn, C.L.: Research on vehicle based driver status/performance monitoring: development, validation, and refinement of algorithms for detection of driver drowsiness. Technical report, National Highway Traffic Safety Administration Final Report: DOT HS 808 247 (1994)

Open-Set Face Recognition-Based Visitor Interface System

Hazım K. Ekenel, Lorant Szasz-Toth, and Rainer Stiefelhagen

Computer Science Department, Universität Karlsruhe (TH)
Am Fasanengarten 5, Karlsruhe 76131, Germany
{ekenel,lszasz,stiefel}@ira.uka.de

Abstract. This work presents a real-world, real-time video-based open-set face recognition system. The system has been developed as a visitor interface, where a visitor looks at the monitor to read the displayed message before knocking on the door. While the visitor is reading the welcome message, using the images captured by the webcam located on the screen, the developed face recognition system identifies the person without requiring explicit cooperation. According to the identity of the person, customized information about the host is conveyed. To evaluate the system's performance in this application scenario, a face database has been collected in front of an office. The experimental results on the collected database show that the developed system can operate reliably under real-world conditions.

1   Introduction

Face recognition is one of the most addressed topics in computer vision and pattern recognition research communities. Closed-set face identification problem, assigning test images to a set of known subjects, and face verification, comparing test images with the ones from claimed identity to check whether the claim is correct or not, have been extensively studied. However, on open-set face recognition, determining whether the encountered person is known or not and if the person is known finding out who he is, there exists only a few studies [1,2]. In [1] a transduction-based approach is introduced. To reject a test sample, its k-nearest neighbors are used to derive a distribution of credibility values for false classifications. Subsequently, the credibility of the test sample is computed by iteratively assigning it to every class in the k-neighborhood. If the highest achieved credibility does not exceed a certain level, defined by the previously computed distribution, the face is rejected as unknown. Otherwise, it is classified accordingly. In [2] accumulated confidence scores are thresholded in order to perform video-based open-set face recognition. It has been stated that in open-set face recognition, determining whether the person is known or unknown is a more challenging problem than determining who the person is.

Open-set identification can be seen as the most generic form of face recognition problem. Several approaches can be considered to solve it. One of them is to perform verification and classification hierarchically, that is, to perform first verification to determine whether the encountered person is known or unknown and then, if the person is known, finding out who he is by doing classification (Fig. 1a). An alternative approach

M. Fritz, B. Schiele, and J.H. Piater (Eds.): ICVS 2009, LNCS 5815, pp. 43–52, 2009.

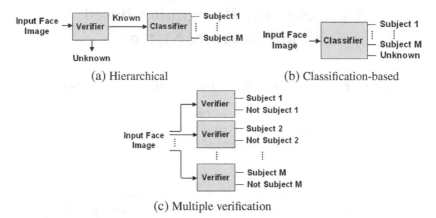

(a) Hierarchical   (b) Classification-based

(c) Multiple verification

Fig. 1. Possible approaches for open-set face recognition

can be training an unknown identity class and running just a classifier (Fig. 1b). A third option is running just verifiers. A test image is compared against each known subject to see whether it belongs to that subject or not (Fig. 1c). If all the verifiers reject, then the image is classified as belonging to an unknown person. If one or more verifiers accept, then the image is classified as belonging to a known person. Among these approaches, we opt for the last one, which we name as the multi-verification approach. The main reason for this choice is the better discrimination provided by the multi-verification approach. The first method requires a verifier to determine known/unknown persons. This requires training the system with face images of known and unknown persons. Since human faces are very similar, generating a single known/unknown verifier can not be highly discriminative. In the second method, training a separate unknown class would not be feasible, since the unknown class covers unlimited number of subjects that one cannot model. On the other hand, with the multi-verification approach, only the available subjects are modeled. The discrimination is enhanced using the available data from a set of unknown persons for support vector machine (SVM) based verifiers.

The system has been developed as a visitor interface, where a visitor looks at the monitor before knocking on the door. A welcome message is displayed on the screen.

Fig. 2. A snapshot of visitor interface in operation

While the visitor is looking at the welcome message, the system identifies the visitor unobtrusively without needing person's cooperation. According to the identity of the person, the system customizes the information that it conveys about the host. For example, if the visitor is unknown, the system displays only availability information about the host. On the other hand if the visitor is known, depending on the identity of the person more detailed information about the host's status is displayed. A snapshot of the system in operation can be seen in Fig. 2.

2   Open-Set Face Recognition System

This section briefly explains the processing steps of the developed open-set face recognition system.

2.1   Face Registration

In the system, faces are detected using Haar-like features based cascade of classifiers [3]. Region-of-interest based face tracking is utilized to compensate misses in the face detector. Eye detection is also based on cascade of classifiers [3]. Cascades were trained for left and right eyes. They are then applied to detected face regions to find the eye locations taking also anthropometric relationships into account. According to the eye center positions the face is aligned and scaled to 64×64 pixels resolution.

Sample augmentation. Imprecise registration reduces classification rate significantly. In order to mitigate the effects of improper registration, for every available training frame 25 additional samples are created by varying the detected eye positions for each eye independently in the four-neighborhood of the original detection. When these positions are modified, the resulting aligned faces are slightly different in scale, rotation and translation. Finally, the number of representatives are reduced to the original number of samples by k-means clustering [2].

2.2   Face Representation

Face representation is done using local appearance-based face representation. There are three main reasons to opt for this algorithm:

- Local appearance modeling, in which a change in a local region affects only the features that are extracted from the corresponding block, while the features that are extracted from the other blocks remain unaffected.
- Data independent bases, which eliminate the need of subspace computation. In the case of real-world conditions, the variation in facial appearance is very high, which causes difficulty to construct suitable data-dependent subspaces.
- Fast feature extraction using the discrete cosine transform (DCT), which enables real-time processing.

This method can be summarized as follows: A detected and aligned face image is divided into blocks of 8×8 pixels resolution. The DCT is applied on each block. Then, the obtained DCT coefficients are ordered using zig-zag scan pattern. From the ordered coefficients, M of them are selected and normalized according to a feature selection and feature normalization strategy resulting in an M-dimensional local feature vector [4]. In this study, we utilized $M = 5$ coefficients by leaving out the first coefficient and using the following five coefficients. This local feature vector is then normalized to unit norm. Finally, the feature vectors extracted from each block are concatenated to construct the global feature vector. For details of the algorithm please see [4].

2.3   Verification

Support vector machines based verifiers are employed in the study [5]. Support vector machines (SVMs) are maximum margin binary classifiers that solve a classification task using a linear separating hyperplane in a high-dimensional projection-space. This hyperplane is chosen to maximize the margin between positive and negative samples. A polynomial kernel with degree 2 is used in this study. Confidence values are derived directly from the sample's distance-to-hyperplane, given a kernel K and the hyperplane parameters w and b,

$$d(x_i) = K(w, x_i) + b. \tag{1}$$

2.4   Multiple Verification

As mentioned earlier, this work formulates the open-set face recognition problem as a multiple verification task. An identity verifier is trained for each known subject in the database. In testing, the test face image is presented to each verifier and N verifications are performed, where N denotes the number of known subjects. If all of the verifiers reject, the person is reported as unknown; if one accepts, the person is accepted as known and the verified identity is assigned to him; if more than a single verifier accepts, the person is accepted as known and the identity of the verifier with the highest confidence is assigned to him. Verifier confidences are inversely proportional to the distance-to-hyperplane. Given a new sample x, a set of verifiers for every known subject $\{v_1, \ldots, v_N\}$, and a distance function $d(v_i, x)$ of sample x from subject i training samples using classifier v_i, the accepted identities are

$$identities_x = \{i | i \in [1 \ldots n], d(v_i, x) < t\}. \tag{2}$$

The best score is $d_x = min\{d(v_j, x) | j \in identities_x\}$ and the established identity is $id = argmin_j\{d(v_j, x) | j \in identities_x\}$.

For video-based identification, n-best match lists, where $n \leq N$, are used. That is, at each frame, every verifier outputs a confidence score and among these confidence scores, only the first n of them having the highest confidence scores are accumulated. Before the accumulation, the scores are first min-max-normalized so that the new score value in the n-best list is

$$s_i' = 1 - \frac{s_i - s_{min}}{s_{max} - s_{min}} \qquad i = 1, 2, ..., n. \tag{3}$$

Then, the scores are re-normalized to yield a sum of one, $\sum_{i=1}^{n} s_i' = 1$, in order to ensure an equal contribution from each single video frame.

3 Evaluation

The data set consists of short video recordings of 54 subjects captured in front of an office over four months. There is no control on the recording conditions. The sequences consist of 150 consecutive frames where face and eyes are detected. Fig. 3 shows some captured frames. As can be seen, the recording conditions can change significantly due to lighting, motion blur, distance to camera and change of the view angle. For example, as the subject comes closer to the system, his face will be tilted more to see the interface. The subjects are assigned to two separate groups as known and unknown subjects. The term known refers to the subjects that are added to the database during training, whereas unknown refers to the subjects that are not added to the database. Unless otherwise stated, in the experiments, five subjects, who are the members of a research group, are classified as known people. 45 subjects who are mainly university students and some external guests, are classified as unknown people. The recordings of four additional subjects are reserved for the experiment, at which the effect of number of known subjects to the performance is analyzed. The set of recording sessions is then further divided into training and testing data. Known subjects' recordings are split into non-overlapping training and testing sessions. From the 45 recordings of unknown subjects, 25 are used for training and twenty of their recordings are used for testing. The organization of the used data can be seen in Table 1. As can be noticed, for each verifier training, there exists around 600 frames (4 sessions, 150 frames per session) from the known subject. On the other hand, the number of available frames from the unknown subjects is around 3750 frames (25 sessions, 150 frames per session). In order to limit the influence of data imbalance during verifier training, unknown recordings are undersampled to 30 images per used training session, making a total of 750 frames.

Table 1. Data organization for open-set face recognition experiments

Training data		
Known	5 subjects	4 sessions
Unknown	25 subjects	1 session
Testing data		
Known	5 subjects	3 – 7 sessions per person
Unknown	20 subjects	1 session per person

(a) Artificial light, far away   (b) Artificial light, motion blur   (c) Daylight, brighter   (d) Daylight, darker

Fig. 3. Sample images from the data set

Table 2. Frame-based verification results

CCR	FRR	FAR	CRR	FCR
90.9 %	8.6 %	8.5 %	91.5 %	0.5 %

Open-set face recognition systems can make three different types of errors. False classification rate (FCR) indicates the percentage of correctly accepted but misclassified known subjects, whereas false rejection rate (FRR) shows the percentage of falsely rejected known subjects and false acceptance rate (FAR) corresponds to the percentage of falsely accepted unknown subjects. These three error terms have to be traded off against each other in open-set face recognition by modifying a threshold and cannot be minimized simultaneously. In the case of SVM-based verifier it is obtained by moving the decision hyperplane. The equal error rate (EER) is defined as the point on the ROC curve where $FAR = FRR + FCR$.

3.1   Frame-Based Verification

Frame-based verification implies doing verification using a single frame instead of an image sequence. Each frame in the recordings is verified separately, that is, the decision is taken only using a single frame at a time. The results of this experiment, at the closest measurement point to the point of equal error, are reported in Table 2. In the table CCR denotes the correct recognition rate and CRR denotes the correct rejection rate. The threshold value used was $\Delta = -0.12$. The SVM classification is modified by shifting hyperplane in parallel towards either class, so that the hyperplane equation becomes $wx + b = \Delta$.

Obtained receiver operating characteristic (ROC) curve can be seen in Fig. 4. To analyze the effect of FRR and FCR on the performance, they are plotted separately in the figure. The dark gray colored region corresponds to the errors due to false known/ unknown separation and the light gray colored region corresponds to the errors due to misclassification. Similar to the finding in [2], it is observed that determining whether a person is known or unknown is a more difficult problem than finding out who the person is.

3.2   Video-Based Verification

As the data set consists of short video sequences, the additional information can be used to further improve classification results. We evaluated two different cases. In the case of progressive verification, the frames up to a certain instant, such as up to one second, two seconds etc., are used and the decision is taken at that specific instant. The performance is calculated by averaging the results obtained at each instant. In the case of video-based verification, the decision is taken after using the frames of the entire video.

Table 3 shows the improved results with the help of accumulated scores. In both cases the video-based score outperforms the progressive scores because the accumulation over the whole image sequence outweighs initial misclassifications that are present in the progressive-score rating.

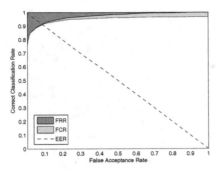

Fig. 4. ROC curve of frame-based verification

Table 3. Progressive score and video-based classification results

	CCR	FRR	FAR	CRR	FCR
Frame	90.9	8.6	8.5	91.5	0.5
Progressive	99.5	0.5	0.1	99.9	0
Video	100	0	0	100	0

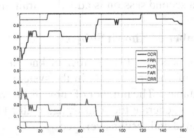

Fig. 5. Classification score development after n frames

Fig. 5 shows the development of the classification rates for a single subject over a sequence. The results usually stabilize after about 15 frames, which implies that only 15 frames can be used to make a decision. Using more data usually increases the performance further.

The following experiments were performed with basic frame-based classification using SVM-based classification and no further optimizations. The hyperplane decision threshold for SVM classification was not modified here and $\Delta = 0$ was used.

3.3 Influence of the Number of Training Sessions

The influence of the amount of training data on the verification performance is analyzed in this experiment. The more training sessions are used the more likely is a good coverage of different poses and lighting conditions. This results in a better client model with more correct acceptances and fewer false rejections. For this experiment, the available data is partitioned into training and testing sets as explained in Table 1. However, the amount of used training sessions has varied from one to four sessions. Consequently,

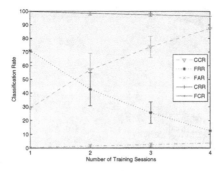

Fig. 6. Classification score by number of training sessions

multiple combinations of training sessions are possible if less than the maximum of four sessions are used for training. In these cases of all the combinations 30 randomly selected combinations are used due to the large number of possibilities and the obtained results are averaged. Fig. 6 shows the classification rates with respect to number of training sessions used. The standard deviation range is also given if multiple combinations exist. The classification results improve as more sessions are added. The highest increase is obtained when a second session is added for training.

3.4 Influence of the Number of Known Subjects

In order to evaluate the influence of the number of known subjects that the system can recognize, the number of known subjects in the system is varied. Four additional subjects are added to the database. The number of subjects known to the system is varied from one to nine. In order to generate the results, again all 511 possible combinations of known clients are generated and results averaged.

Due to limited available data only tests with up to nine known subjects were performed. Security applications on the other hand have to recognize hundreds of known people. Nevertheless, the objective of this work is to develop a smart interface where a small group of people is required to be identified. Moreover, it has been shown in the literature [2] and also in this paper that the main source of problem arises because of the difficulty in separating the known and unknown subjects. Fig. 7 illustrates the change of classification rates as the number of subjects known to the system is increased. It can be seen that the correct classification rate nearly remains the same as more subjects are added. The correct rejection rate decreases as more subjects are added overall by 8%. The false classification and false rejection rates remain nearly the same.

3.5 Sample Augmentation

In order to increase the system's overall robustness to misalignment, the training set is augmented with deliberately misaligned training images. A training input image is added multiple times with slight variations of the eye detection locations and thus varied registration. Table 4 presents the results of using sample augmentation and shows that sample augmentation indeed further improves the results and reduces the influence of incorrect registration.

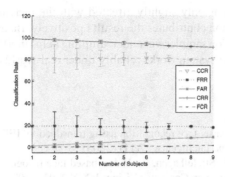

Fig. 7. Performance with respect to number of subjects

Table 4. Influence of sample augmentation

	CCR	FRR	FAR	CRR	FCR
Non-augmented	87.2 %	12.5 %	3.7 %	96.3 %	0.3 %
Augmented	92.9 %	6.3 %	12.6 %	87.4 %	0.8 %

Table 5. Effect of undersampling. Originally, 150 frames are available.

# frames	CCR	FRR	FAR	CRR	FCR
30	87.2 %	12.5 %	3.7 %	96.3 %	0.3 %
60	85.2 %	14.7 %	2.7 %	97.3 %	0.1 %
90	83.5 %	16.5 %	2.4 %	97.6 %	0.0 %
150	83.5 %	16.5 %	2.3 %	97.7 %	0.0 %

3.6   Undersampling the Unknown Class

As 25 subjects are used to model the unknown class each having one session of about 150 recorded frames, there is an imbalance of positive and negative samples for training: 3750 frames for the unknown class and only 600 for the known class. Akbani et al. [6] analyzed the impact of imbalanced data sets and proposed methods to overcome the problem. Undersampling, albeit being simple, is also shown to yield good improvements. Table 5 shows that undersampling improved the correct classification rate while slightly raising the false acceptance rate because less data was used to model the unknown class.

4   Conclusion

A multi-verification based open-set face recognition system is presented in this paper. The system operates fully automatically and runs in real-time (at frame rate 30 frame/s) on a laptop computer with a 1.6GHz Pentium M processor. It has been observed that using video information improves the results significantly compared to the frame-based results. The performance increases as the used amount of training data increases. The correct classification rate is only slightly affected with the increasing number of subjects. Sample augmentation contributes the results positively. Balancing the amount of known and unknown person samples via undersampling helps in SVM training. Overall, it has been shown that the system works reliably under real-world conditions.

References

1. Li, F., Wechsler, H.: Open set face recognition using transduction. IEEE Transactions on Pattern Analysis and Machine Intelligence 27(11) (2005)
2. Stallkamp, J., Ekenel, H., Stiefelhagen, R.: Video-based face recognition on real-world data. In: International Conference on Computer Vision, ICCV 2007 (2007)
3. Jones, M.J., Viola, P.: Fast multi-view face detection. Technical Report TR2003-96, Mitsubishi Electric Research Laboratories, Cambridge, MA, USA (2003)
4. Ekenel, H., Stiefelhagen, R.: Analysis of local appearance-based face recognition: Effects of feature selection and feature normalization. In: CVPR Biometrics Workshop, New York, USA (2006)
5. Schölkopf, B., Burges, C.J.C., Smola, A.J.: Advances in Kernel Methods -Support Vector Learning. MIT Press, Cambridge (1998)
6. Akbani, R., Kwek, S., Japkowicz, N.: Applying support vector machines to imbalanced datasets. In: Boulicaut, J.-F., Esposito, F., Giannotti, F., Pedreschi, D. (eds.) ECML 2004. LNCS (LNAI), vol. 3201, pp. 39–50. Springer, Heidelberg (2004)

Cascade Classifier Using Divided CoHOG Features for Rapid Pedestrian Detection

Masayuki Hiromoto[1] and Ryusuke Miyamoto[2]

[1] Kyoto University, Yoshida-hon-machi, Sakyo, Kyoto, 606-8501, Japan
hiromoto@easter.kuee.kyoto-u.ac.jp
[2] Nara Institute of Science and Technology,
8916-5, Takayama-cho, Ikoma, Nara, 630-0192, Japan
miya@is.naist.jp

Abstract. Co-occurrence histograms of oriented gradients (CoHOG) is a powerful feature descriptor for pedestrian detection, but its calculation cost is large because the feature vector is very high-dimensional. In this paper, in order to achieve rapid detection, we propose a novel method to divide the CoHOG feature into small features and construct a cascade-structured classifier by combining many weak classifiers. The proposed cascade classifier rejects non-pedestrian images at the early stage of the classification while positive and suspicious images are examined carefully by all weak classifiers. This accelerates the classification process without spoiling detection accuracy. The experimental results show that our method achieves about 2.6 times faster detection and the same detection accuracy in comparison to the previous work.

1 Introduction

Pedestrian detection from visual images is a recent challenging problem in the field of computer vision. Many variations of pedestrian appearance, such as their clothes, poses, and illumination, make it difficult to distinguish pedestrians from other objects.

For accurate pedestrian detection, selection and combination of feature descriptors and classification algorithm are important issues. As feature descriptors, many schemes have been proposed, e.g. Harr-like features [1], local self-similarities [2], contour-based methods [3], and gradient-based methods [4,5]. In combination with the above features extraction methods, classification algorithms, such as principal component analysis (PCA), support vector machine (SVM), and group learning like AdaBoost, are used for pedestrian detection.

Among those works, detection algorithms based-on histograms of oriented gradients (HOG) [4] are now popularly used for pedestrian detection. Many HOG-based detection algorithms are proposed because of its robustness for rotation, deformation and illumination change. Co-occurrence histograms of oriented gradients (CoHOG) [6] is one of the feature descriptors derived from the original HOG, and it is reported that CoHOG achieves excellent detecting performance and outperforms other feature descriptors.

M. Fritz, B. Schiele, and J.H. Piater (Eds.): ICVS 2009, LNCS 5815, pp. 53–62, 2009.

On the other hand, real-time processing of pedestrian detection is indispensable for practical applications such as driver assistance, video surveillance and robot navigation. Although pedestrian detection with CoHOG features achieves good recognition as mentioned above, its computational cost to calculate Co-HOG features and classify them is too large because dimension of the vector is very high (about 35,000 dimensions if the window size is 18×36).

In this paper, we focus on the pedestrian detection algorithm based on Co-HOG and propose a cascade-structured classifier to accelerate detection process. Since Watanabe et al. [6] classify CoHOG features using a linear SVM, the high-dimensional vector impacts the calculation costs. In our approach, however, the feature vector is divided into many small vectors and each small vector is evaluated by a weak classifier respectively. The weak classifiers are arranged in 'stronger'-order, serially chained, and constructed as a rejection tree, which we call a 'cascade'. By using the cascade structure, most negative images are rejected before evaluated by all weak classifiers, while positive ones are strictly evaluated by all of them. Since the candidate windows in a practical image are mostly negative, this cascade classifier improves the processing time without spoiling detection rate.

This paper is organized as follows. In Sect. 2, pedestrian detection using Co-HOG is described. In Sect. 3, our proposed cascade classifier is introduced and the arrangement order of weak classifiers is discussed. In Sect. 4, detection rate and processing time of the proposed method is evaluated to compare with the original method using SVM, and finally Sect. 5 gives our conclusions.

2 Co-occurrence Histogram of Oriented Gradients

CoHOG is a powerful feature descriptor, proposed by Watanabe et al. [6], which can express complex shapes of objects by using co-occurrence of gradient orientations with various positional offsets. In this section, CoHOG feature and its classification method using SVM is described.

2.1 CoHOG Feature

CoHOG is a high-dimensional feature that uses pairs of gradient orientations. From the pairs, a histogram called co-occurrence matrix is build as shown in Fig. 1. The co-occurrence matrix $C = (C_{i,j})$ is defined over an $n \times m$ image of gradient orientations I, as

$$C_{i,j} = \sum_{p=0}^{n-1} \sum_{q=0}^{m-1} \begin{cases} 1, & \text{if } I(p,q) = i \text{ and } I(p+x, q+y) = j, \\ 0, & \text{otherwise,} \end{cases} \tag{1}$$

where x and y represent an offset. An image of gradient orientations, I, is generated from an original visual image by computing gradient orientations as $\theta = \arctan(v/h)$, where v and h are vertical and horizontal gradient calculated by appropriate filters. Then θ is divided into eight orientations per 45 degrees

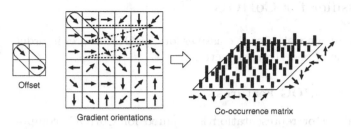

Fig. 1. A co-occurrence matrix of gradient orientations. For a given offset, a histogram of pairs of gradient orientations is calculated over an input image.

Fig. 2. Offsets for co-occurrence matrices. The center small white circle and the other 30 black circles are pairs for the offsets.

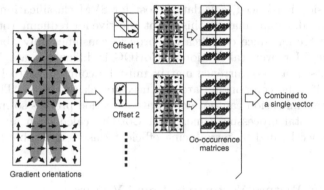

Fig. 3. CoHOG calculation. Co-occurrence matrices are computed for all offsets and small regions and combined into a single long vector.

and eight labels are used for representing an orientation for each pixel. Therefore, the size of the co-occurrence matrix C becomes 8×8. The offsets, (x, y), which define pairs of pixels, are shown in Fig. 2. Because of the symmetry, only a half of the offsets are used within the maximum distance. The number of valid offsets is 31 including a zero offset. The co-occurrence matrices are computed for all combinations of the offsets and small regions as shown in Fig. 3. By using index k for small regions, each co-occurrence matrix C with an offset (x, y) can be expressed as a 64-dimensional vector $\boldsymbol{f}_{k,x,y}$. The final CoHOG descriptor is generated by concatenating small vectors $\boldsymbol{f}_{k,x,y}$ into a long vector $\boldsymbol{F}$.

2.2 Classification of CoHOG

Since the CoHOG descriptor is informative enough, accurate pedestrian detection is achieved with a simple learning and classification algorithm, such as linear SVM [7] used by Watanabe et al. [6]. With linear SVM, CoHOG feature $\boldsymbol{F}$ is classified as $SVM(\boldsymbol{F}) = \text{sign}(\boldsymbol{w} \cdot \boldsymbol{F})$, where '·' means inner product and $\boldsymbol{w}$ is a vector learned by using many positive and negative training data.

3 Cascade Classifier for CoHOG

In this section, we propose a novel cascade classifier for CoHOG features in order to reduce processing time of pedestrian detection.

3.1 Computation of CoHOG Features

Since high-dimensional vector representation is required for CoHOG, computational cost for detection process is large. However, as pointed out in [6], many zero or small value components, which do not affect classification performance, are included in the feature vectors. This means that the feature vector is redundant and the dimension can be reduced by using PCA, etc. If the vector dimension is reduced, calculation cost for SVM classification is proportionately reduced. Unfortunately, this is not effective for reducing total processing time of detection since classification process consumes only about 20% of the total time. Moreover, calculation of CoHOG is difficult to accelerate since all components in a co-occurrence matrix must be counted up to build a histogram even if some components are not used for classification. Thus, simply reducing vector dimension can not accelerate detection process so much. In order to reduce total processing time, both CoHOG calculation and classification must be accelerated by introducing efficient classifier suitable for CoHOG features.

3.2 Dividing Feature Vector into Small Vectors

As discussed above, CoHOG calculation needs to be accelerated for rapid detection. CoHOG calculation is performed on each co-occurrence matrix and components in a single matrix can not be calculated separately because of the characteristic of histogram computation. Therefore, if we want to reduce calculation cost of CoHOG, the co-occurrence matrix is a minimum unit that can be omitted. In consideration of this issue, we propose dividing the feature vector into small vectors $\boldsymbol{f}_{k,x,y}$ and evaluating them by weak classifiers respectively as

$$eval(\boldsymbol{F}) = \sum_{k,x,y} h_{k,x,y}(\boldsymbol{f}_{k,x,y}), \qquad (2)$$

where $h_{k,x,y}$ is a weak classifier, instead of evaluating a high-dimensional single vector $\boldsymbol{F}$ with SVM, as $eval(\boldsymbol{F}) = SVM(\boldsymbol{F})$. Once the vector is divided into small vectors, CoHOG calculation and classification against each small vector can be executed independently. Therefore, if we use the smaller number of weak classifiers, the total processing time can be effectively decreased.

3.3 Cascade Classifier

With the divided vectors of CoHOG, a straightforward idea to accelerate detection process is to omit some weak classifiers whose response value $h_{k,x,y}(\boldsymbol{f}_{k,x,y})$

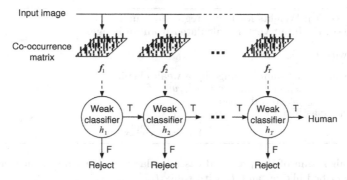

Fig. 4. Proposed cascade classifier that consists of serially chained weak classifiers h_t. small vectors $\boldsymbol{f}_t$ generated from input images are evaluated by weak classifiers h_t respectively. Only an image that passes all weak classifiers is finally classified as a pedestrian.

is relatively small. However, we found that omitting weak classifiers seriously affects detection performance through some preliminary experiments.

Therefore, instead of reducing the number of weak classifiers, we propose a cascade-structured classifier. As shown in Fig. 4, the proposed cascade classifier consists of serially chained weak classifiers that behave as a rejection tree. Every weak classifier evaluates a sample image, and if the sample is positive, the subsequent process is continued, but otherwise, the classification process is terminated immediately. This idea is inspired by detection algorithm by Viola and Jones [1] and other algorithms using group learning. By configuring weak classifiers to filter out only 'obviously negative' images, the detection performance can be kept high because positive or suspicious images are well examined by all weak classifiers.

With this structure, it is very important how to configure and arrange the weak classifiers. For the former issue, we simply adopt a linear regression model as a weak classifier,

$$h_{k,x,y}(\boldsymbol{f}_{k,x,y}) = \boldsymbol{w}_{k,x,y} \cdot \boldsymbol{f}_{k,x,y}. \tag{3}$$

Using this weak classifier, the cascade classifier behaves as shown in Fig. 5. If we make c_{cutoff} small, many negatives are rejected soon and processing time is reduced, but some positive images are also misclassified. The relation between processing speed and detection accuracy is a trade-off.

In order to achieve the same detection performance of [6] when using all weak classifiers, $\boldsymbol{w}_{k,x,y}$ is extracted from a SVM model learned by the same method in [6], as shown in the following equation:

$$\sum_{k,x,y} \boldsymbol{w}_{k,x,y} \cdot \boldsymbol{f}_{k,x,y} = SVM(\boldsymbol{F}). \tag{4}$$

The latter issue, arrangement of weak classifiers, is discussed in the next subsection.

$\boldsymbol{w}_t$ $(t = 1, \cdots, T)$: Weights for linear regression models.
$\boldsymbol{f}_t$ $(t = 1, \cdots, T)$: Input vectors calculated from an image.

- Start with $c = 0$.
- For $t = 1, \cdots, T$:
  - Evaluate the sample image by a weak classifier h_t
  - Add the response value: $c \leftarrow c + \boldsymbol{w}_t \cdot \boldsymbol{f}_t$
  - If $c < c_{\text{cutoff}}$, stop iteration.
- The final classifier is:

$$C = \begin{cases} 1 & c \geq c_{\text{thrd}} \\ 0 & \text{otherwise} \end{cases}$$

Fig. 5. The algorithm of the proposed cascade classifier. For convenience, $w_{k,x,y}$ and $f_{k,x,y}$ are described like w_t and f_t with suffix t.

3.4   Order of Arranged Weak Classifiers

In order to achieve high detection rate with rapid processing by the proposed cascade classifier, arrangement order of weak classifiers must be studied. If 'powerful' weak classifiers are located at the beginning of the cascade, most samples are classified correctly in early stage of classification process. This means that we can regard an non-pedestrian image as negative with a little computational time. Here, the 'powerful' weak classifier should be a classifier that produces little miss-classification. We evaluate performance of a weak classifier h_t using weights given for each positive or negative example as follows.

$$\varepsilon_t = \sum_i w_i |h_t(x_i) - y_i|. \tag{5}$$

The pairs of (x_i, y_i) are example images where $y_i = 0, 1$ for negative and positive examples respectively, and w_i is a weight for example x_i. By using error values ε_t, weak classifiers are sorted and arranged to construct a cascade classifier.

In this paper, weights for examples are defined by two methods. One is using a constant value as a weights, $w_i = \frac{1}{2m}, \frac{1}{2l}$ for $y_i = 0, 1$ respectively, where m and l are the number of negatives and positives respectively. The other is updating weights by each iteration of selecting a weak classifier with minimum error. This is similar to AdaBoost algorithm [8]. In this case, a procedure to arrange weak classifiers is shown in Fig. 6.

- Initialize weights for examples:
  $w_i = \frac{1}{2m}, \frac{1}{2l}$ for $y_i = 0, 1$
- For $t = 1, \cdots, T$:
  - Normalize the weights, $w_i \leftarrow \frac{w_i}{\sum w_i}$.
  - Using the weights, select the best weak classifier with the lowest error ε_t as h_t.
  - Update the weights: $w_{t+1,i} = w_{t,i} \beta_t^{1-e_i}$,
    where $e_i = 0$ if example x_i is classified correctly, $e_i = 1$ otherwise, and $\beta_t = \frac{\varepsilon_t}{1-\varepsilon_t}$.

Fig. 6. The algorithm of arranging weak classifiers by an iterative method

4   Experimental Results

This section describes experimental results of performance evaluation to compare the proposed cascade classifier with the original SVM classifier used in [6].

4.1   Data Set

As a date set, we use the DaimlerChrysler data set [9], which contains human images and non-human images cropped into 18×36 pixels. With this data set, we divided the example images into 3×6 small regions that are units for calculating co-occurrence matrices. Therefore the number of co-occurrence matrices for an example image is $(3 \times 6) \times 31 = 558$.

4.2   Experiments

We implement the training and detection algorithm as software. The programs are written in C++ and executed on the 3.2 GHz Intel Core i7 processor.

We perform two experiments: One is comparison of the arrangement method for weak classifiers described in Sect. 3.4 to examine how the detection rate changes when applying the proposed cascade classifier for processing acceleration. With this experiment, we select the best arrangement method for the proposed cascade classifier. The other experiment is comparison of the proposed classifier with the original SVM classifier by evaluating processing time and detection results using some test images.

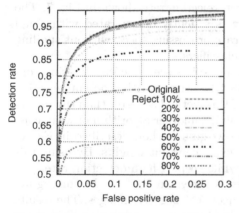

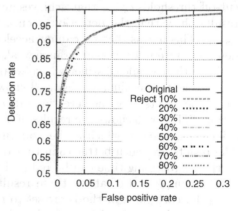

Fig. 7. Detection performance of the cascade classifier with not arranged weak classifiers. If the rejection rate increases, the detection performance is traded off for processing acceleration.

Fig. 8. Detection performance of the cascade classifier with arranged weak classifiers using constant weights. Processing acceleration can be achieved without large decrease of the detection rate.

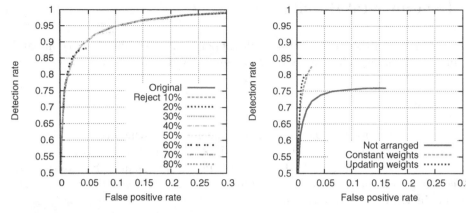

Fig. 9. Detection performance of the cascade classifier with arranged weak classifiers with the updating-weights method. Almost same detection performance to the original method is achieved with large acceleration of processing speed.

Fig. 10. Comparison of the detection performance with three arranging methods with rejection rate of 70%

Arrangement Methods for Weak Classifiers. First, the cascade classifier whose weak classifiers are not sorted but arranged in original order of SVM classifier in [6] is evaluated. Figure 7 shows Receiver Operating Characteristic (ROC) curves, which indicate relation between detection rate and false positive rate. Each ROC curve is drawn by changing the final threshold c_{thrd} in Fig. 5. The 'Original' curve means that the cascade structure is disabled and all the weak classifiers perform evaluation. The other curves are drawn with different cut-off thresholds c_{cutoff} that achieves given rejection rate shown in Fig. 7. The results show that the detection accuracy is saliently deteriorated with small c_{cutoff}. This means that we cannot accelerate processing speed without spoiling detection rate if we do not arrange weak classifiers.

Then the cascade classifier whose weak classifiers are sorted by ε_t using constant weights is evaluated. Figure 8 shows ROC curves with different rejection rate. The results show the detection rate of this method is better than the results in Fig. 7. Figure 9 shows the results of applying another algorithm of weak classifiers arrangement, which is the updating-weights method described in Fig. 6. The results are much better than that of using constant weights. By using this method, processing time can be reduced while keeping high detection rate.

The comparison of above three results is shown in Fig. 10. In this figure, c_{cutoff} for each three methods are set to reject 70% negative images. The results show that the proposed cascade classifier with arranging weak classifiers using the updating-weights method achieves higher detection rate than the other two methods. In practical use, for example, 0.8 detection rate with 0.02 false positive rate is achieved with this 70% rejection rate, which means that we can accelerate processing speed about three times faster than the method where all weak classifiers are used.

Fig. 11. Detection results of the original method (top) and of our proposed method (bottom). The proposed method achieves the same detection performance as the original method in spite of the fast processing.

Detection Examples. With the proposed cascade classifier, processing time for pedestrian detection is evaluated using some example images. For a dense scan of a 320 × 240 image with 3 pixel jumps vertically and horizontally under five different scales, the proposed cascade classifier takes about 0.3 seconds while the original SVM classifier in [6] takes 0.78 seconds. The rejection rate of the proposed method is set to 70%. Due to the cascade classifier, the processing speed becomes 2.6 times faster than the original method. Note that this depends on the characteristics of the used images. Processing time increases if an image is filled by pedestrians. However, in practical use like surveillance or driver assistance, there are several people in an image and so most of the evaluated windows are negative.

Results of pedestrian detection are shown in Fig. 11. There are some miss detections because of low resolution of DaimlerChrysler data set used for training. If we use high resolution data set such as INRIA data set [4], more accurate detection can be achieved. As shown in Fig. 11, in spite of processing acceleration, detection accuracy is not spoiled by introducing the proposed cascade classifier.

5   Conclusions

In this paper, we propose a novel cascade classifier for rapid pedestrian detection using CoHOG feature descriptors. With the proposed cascade classifier, many negative images are rejected at the early state of the classification process and this reduces the total processing time effectively. Since the arrangement order of the weak classifiers that constructs the cascade classifier is very important, we have studied two arranging algorithms to select the superior algorithm through experimental evaluations. The proposed cascade classifier is compared to the original SVM classifier, and the results show that our classifier achieves 2.6

times faster processing while keeping same detection rate of the original work. In addition, our cascade classifier is capable of much faster detection if we tolerate deterioration of detection accuracy. This flexibility is also a large advantage of the proposed classifier.

Acknowledgments

This work was partly supported by a Global Center of Excellence (G-COE) program of the Ministry of Education, Culture, Sports, Science and Technology of Japan and by Grant-in-Aid for Young Scientists (B) 20700048 and for JSPS Fellows 20·2451.

References

1. Viola, P., Jones, M.: Robust real-time object detection. Int'l J. Computer Vision 57(2), 137–154 (2004)
2. Shechtman, E., Irani, M.: Matching local self-similarities across images and videos. In: Proc. IEEE Conf. Computer Vision and Pattern Recognition (2007)
3. Leordeanu, M., Hebert, M., Sukthankar, R.: Beyond local appearance: Category recognition from pairwise interactions of simple features. In: Proc. IEEE Conf. Computer Vision and Pattern Recognition (2007)
4. Dalai, N., Triggs, B., Rhone-Alps, I., Montbonnot, F.: Histograms of oriented gradients for human detection. In: Proc. IEEE Conf. Computer Vision and Pattern Recognition, vol. 1, pp. 886–893 (2005)
5. Lowe, D.: Distinctive image features from scale-invariant keypoints. Int'l J. Computer Vision 60(2), 91–110 (2004)
6. Watanabe, T., Ito, S., Yokoi, K.: Co-occurrence histograms of oriented gradients for pedestrian detection. In: Proc. the 3rd IEEE Pacific-Rim Symposium Image and Video Technology, pp. 37–47 (January 2009)
7. Hsieh, C., Chang, K., Lin, C., Keerthi, S., Sundararajan, S.: A dual coordinate descent method for large-scale linear SVM. In: Proc. the 25th international conference on Machine learning, pp. 408–415 (2008)
8. Freund, Y., Schapire, R.: A decision-theoretic generalization of on-line learning and an application to Boosting. Journal of Computer and System Sciences 55(1), 119–139 (1997)
9. Munder, S., Gavrila, D.: An experimental study on pedestrian classification. IEEE Trans. Pattern Anal. Mach. Intell. 28(11), 1863–1868 (2006)

Boosting with a Joint Feature Pool
from Different Sensors

Dominik A. Klein[1], Dirk Schulz[2], and Simone Frintrop[1]

[1] Institute of Computer Science III,
Rheinische Friedrich-Wilhelms-Universität,
53117 Bonn, Germany
[2] Forschungsgesellschaft für Angewandte Naturwissenschaften e.V. (FGAN),
53343 Wachtberg, Germany

Abstract. This paper introduces a new way to apply boosting to a joint feature pool from different sensors, namely 3D range data and color vision. The combination of sensors strengthens the systems universality, since an object category could be partially consistent in shape, texture or both. Merging of different sensor data is performed by computing a spatial correlation on 2D layers. An AdaBoost classifier is learned by boosting features competitively in parallel from every sensor layer. Additionally, the system uses new corner-like features instead of rotated Haar-like features, in order to improve real-time classification capabilities. Object type dependent color information is integrated by applying a distance metric to hue values. The system was implemented on a mobile robot and trained to recognize four different object categories: people, cars, bicycle and power sockets. Experiments were conducted to compare system performances between different merged and single sensor based classifiers. We found that for all object categories the classification performance is considerably improved by the joint feature pool.

1 Introduction

Object classification in sensor data is an important task for many applications. Especially autonomous mobile robots that have to act in a complex world rely on knowledge about objects in their environment. Imagine for example an automatically controlled car driving in city traffic or a universal housekeeping robot cleaning up your room. Various machine learning and pattern recognition methods have been studied to meet these demands. One area of active research in the field of object classification are boosting techniques [1, 2, 3, 4, 5, 6, 7]. An exhaustive survey can be found in [8].

While most approaches for object classification use camera data [9, 5, 6, 10, 11, 12, 13], several groups also have investigated the use of other sensor data such as laser range finders [14, 15] or infrared cameras [16]. A reason for choosing different sensors is that each sensor has different strengths and drawbacks and some sensors capture information that others are not able to provide. Laser scanners for example provide accurate depth information and infrared cameras enable the detection of people or animals at night.

M. Fritz, B. Schiele, and J.H. Piater (Eds.): ICVS 2009, LNCS 5815, pp. 63–72, 2009.
© Springer-Verlag Berlin Heidelberg 2009

In this paper, we introduce an approach to automatically exploit the advantages of different sensors. We provide a feature pool that consists of a collection of feature candidates from different sensor layers. In a training phase, the boosting algorithm Gentle AdaBoost automatically selects the most distinctive feature at a time to obtain an optimal classification performance. Thus, it depends on the object type which features from which sensor layers are selected. To further improve the results, we introduce new corner-like features and a new measure to extract color information based on hue-distance.

We show the classification performance in various experiments for four different object classes: cars, people, bicycles and power sockets. Depending on the object type, different layers are chosen with different priorities. In all cases, the classification profited considerably from the fusion of data from different sensors; the classification performance was considerably higher than the classification rate of each sensor on its own.

The combination of data from different sensors has also been investigated by other groups. A straightforward solution is to train a classifier on the data from each sensor independently and in a second step combine the results. For example, Zivkovic and Kröse integrated a leg detector trained on 2D laser range data and a part-based person detector trained on omnidirectional camera images this way [17]. Frintrop et al. trained classifiers to detect chairs and robots on the range and the remission data of a laser scanner [18]. Nüchter et al. applied the same approach to people detection [19]. Here, the authors suggest two ways to join the two cascades: serial or interleaved. Both versions represent a logical "and" operator. In our approach instead, the boosting algorithm decides automatically which features to choose for an object type. It is thus a general approach to optimizing the sensor fusion for a certain object category. The result is a single, more concise classification cascade that achieves a faster classification with a better classification performance.

This paper comprehends results of the master's thesis[1] of Klein [20] and some further enhancements.

2   Adaptive Boosting with Haar-Like Features

The Adaptive Boosting algorithm, short AdaBoost, forms a strong classifier as a weighted sum of as many weak-classifiers as are needed to reach a given precision on the training data [2]. Therefore it iteratively picks the weak-classifier out of a huge amount of possible candidate classifiers that performs best on a weighted training set. Subsequently it reweights the training set according to the outcome of the chosen weak-classifier: a failure raises the weight of the example, a correct match lowers its weight.

There are different versions of AdaBoost that differ on how weights are updated and how classifier performance is measured. We use Gentle AdaBoost with squared error metric to decide which candidate classifier is considered next, because it has been shown to outperform standard Discrete AdaBoost in [4], and

---

[1] Available at www.iai.uni-bonn.de/~kleind/

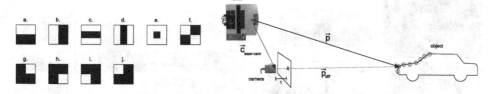

Fig. 1. Utilized Haar-like features. The sum of values in white regions is subtracted from those in black regions. a.-f.: standard features. g.-j.: new corner-like features.

Fig. 2. Projection of a 3D point cloud. For every point $|p_{diff}|$ is recorded at the intersection pixel between p_{diff} and the image plane of the camera.

we confirmed this result during our own experiments. In addition we arrange strong classifiers of increasing complexity in a cascade structure as proposed by Viola and Jones [5, 6] to speed up the system.

A common approach in computer vision to build weak classifiers is to use Haar-like features [9], which are inspired by Haar wavelet functions. In general, they consist of a positive and a negative area, whose values add to a common sum (cf. Fig. 1). For efficient computations, areas have upright rectangular borders, because it allows the use of integral images to compute this sum in a constant time. An integral image, also known as summed area table, is an intermediate step between per pixel values and sums of values in rectangular regions [5]. For every pixel position, the sum of all pixel values left and above this position is stored. This integral image can be computed in a single pass over the image by building the integral image in normal reading direction and just adding the current pixel value to sums computed before. With this integral image, the sum of any rectangular region can be computed with the four values at its corners.

Regions are combined to form simple templates that match to edge, line or center-surround features. To further enlarge the over-complete candidate pool and approximate diagonal features, we introduce new, corner-like features (cf. Fig. 1, g-j). In contrast to the diagonal features in [7] that are computed on rotated integral images, our features have the advantage that they can be computed as fast as the basic haar-like features of [9] with the standard upright integral image.

A feature is defined by its type, size and position with respect to a subwindow in an image. Variations in size do not only include scaling but also aspect ratio. This combinatorial multiplicity results in an over-complete set of some hundred thousands up to millions of different features. Every feature becomes a single weak-classifier by computing an optimal CART (classification and regression tree) for the training set. Because our training sets are rather small and generalization capability decreases by depth of the CARTs, we only use stubs. The coordinate system of the subwindow is also normalized to fit into the unit square (Fig. 4). This enables to handle differently stretched object instances in an elegant way.

Fig. 3. Conversion of the coordinate system of the sensor layers to unit square. Sensor layers are red, green, blue, hue-distance, intensity, distance and remission.

Fig. 4. Object coordinate systems normalized to unit square for handling different aspect ratios

3   A Joint Feature Pool from Different Sensors

3.1   Sensor Fusion

Our robot is equipped with a color vision camera and a rotating SICK LMS 291 laser scanner. The beams of the laser scanner uniformly meter the encircled sphere. By clocking their time of flight a laser scanner supplies accurate distance information, and by quantifying the amount of laser-emitted light that is reflected or scattered back by the surfaces in the scene it provides remission information. Thus our robot is able to perceive an RGB image and a 3D point cloud of its surrounding area. After a conversion from spherical into Cartesian coordinates the visible part of the point cloud is projected onto the image plane of the camera (cf. Fig. 2). Note that the centers of reception of the sensors should be as close together as possible to avoid wrong assignments in case that an object is exclusively seen by one of the sensors. Although we use a lower resolution for the image layer of the laser, the layer is not densely-packed and we need to interpolate the missing values. In our case, we have to additionally correct the barrel distortion of the camera, before we obtain correctly correlated sensor layers.

The coordinate system of a sensor layer l is normalized by its width w_l and height h_l to fit into the unit square,

$$|(x, y)|_l = \left(\frac{x}{w_l}, \frac{y}{h_l} \right).$$

Thus, the position of an object is specified by the same coordinates in every layer, even if they vary in physical resolution (Fig. 3).

Altogether, we use seven sensor layers: red, green, blue, intensity and hue-distance from the camera, and distance as well as remission values from the laser (cf. Fig. 8). The hue channel from HSV color space encodes pure color

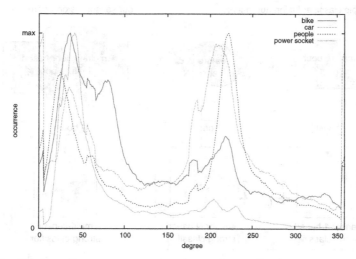

Fig. 5. Distribution of hue occurrence for object classes (10 degree smoothed average)

information without saturation and brightness as an angle in a color wheel. However, the computation of weak-classifiers from Haar-like features needs a totally ordered set which is naturaly given in case of continuous intensity values, but not in case of angles. Therefore we do not use angles directly. Instead, we use the distance between the hue angles and one specifically chosen hue angle. This particular value depends on the object type and is calculated from the positive training examples: we choose the most frequent hue by building a coarse additive histogram (Fig. 5). If the color distribution of an object type has only a few strong peaks, this choice tends to be more reliable than the use of a single predetermined hue value, because that constant reference hue could be located between two strong peaks and thus would not allow to discriminate between those peaks in the hue distance norm. Otherwise, if the color is uniformly distributed for an object type, there is no difference.

3.2 Integration of Different Sensors

A straightforward approach to exploit the information of different sensors is to train one classifier for each sensor and somehow join the outcome. For instance Frintrop et al. linked range and remission based classifiers by a logical "and" operator [18]. Instead of this, our approach is to learn only one classifier per object type that uses information of all sensors simultaneously (cf. Fig. 6). Because of our mapping to unit square coordinates, every feature is well defined on every sensor layer. Now it is a rather natural extension to enlarge the pool of candidate classifiers to all layers. It is up to AdaBoost to decide which weak-classifier from which sensor is best.

Thus, it only depends on the characteristics of the object type how much a certain sensor layer contributes to the final decision. The most distinctive features from every sensor are estimated and combined to supplement each

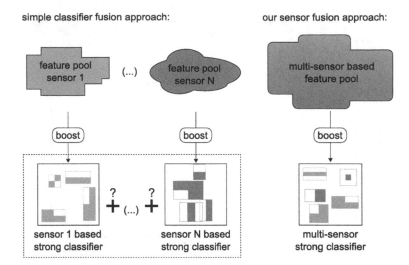

Fig. 6. Overview to our approach: utilizing AdaBoost to combine multiple sensors in a single strong classifier

other. Furthermore the computational effort for classification is much lower. On average, one can expect that a multiple sensor classifier cascade is much smaller than each single sensor cascade used in the decoupled approaches, because they achieve a lower average classification error of selected weak-classifiers. A heuristic for combining the cascades of different sensors is no longer needed in this approach, therefore, it is also more general.

4   Experiments

We conducted experiments to discover if and how much a classifier benefits from our training on merged sensor data and from the new corner-like features. For this purpose, we built a training and a test set[2] for four different object categories: people, cars, bicycles and power sockets. Table 1 shows their configuration. An example is a labeled rectangular region inside of an image. During learning negative examples are bootstrapped from those parts of training images that do not contain positive examples. We also add images that do not contain positive examples but only clutter to enlarge the choice for negative examples.

First, we trained one classifier with all Haar-like features (cf. Fig. 1) on all sensor layers (cf. Fig. 3) for each object type. Then we decomposed those cascades into weak-classifiers and summed up their weights by sensor layer to discover how much a certain layer contributes to the final decision of the cascades. Fig. 7 shows the results of these experiments. It can clearly be seen that the laser distance layer is favored over all others. Power sockets themselves are complanate at a

---

[2] Note that because of our special sensor fusion we cannot use common benchmark tests. More example pictures from training and test sets can be found in [20].

Table 1. Components of training and test sets (number of positive examples / images)

	car	people	bike	power socket
training	115 / 191	115 / 173	95 / 180	66 / 137
test	34 / 35	49 / 30	31 / 29	27 / 36

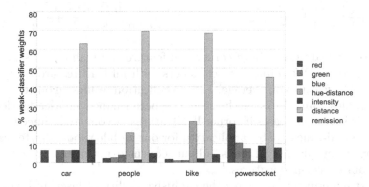

Fig. 7. Distribution of weak-classifier weights by sensor layers

Fig. 8. (a.) Person classified with a cascade trained with features from intensity (b.), hue-distance (c.), distance (d.) and remission (e.) data

wall and hardly visible in distance data, but the distance data is still useful for rejecting non-flat negative examples. In this case sensor fusion pays off most, weak-classifiers are shared equally between the sensor layers of laser and camera. Categories with a more protruding shape, namely car, people and bike, benefit still more from the distance layer. It can also be seen that hue-distance as a unified layer for color features is a worthwhile extension. While the utility of red, green and blue layers on their own seem to have strong correlation with each other and with intensity, hue-distance adds some unique information.

In further experiments, we restrict the pool of candidate features to certain types or sensor layers to compare performances. Some of the sensor layers with a classified person are shown in Fig. 8. We evaluate the performance with recall, precision, and the F-measure. Recall is a measure of completeness, whereas precision is a measure of exactness. Because they are interdependent opposite goals, the F-measure combines them into a single value by calculating the harmonic mean.

Table 2. Results of classifiers trained on all sensor layers. Length is number of combined weak-classifiers.

	car	people	bike	p.sock.
length	47	77	99	142
recall	1	0.98	0.97	0.85
precision	1	1	0.65	0.88
F-measure	1	0.99	0.78	0.87

Table 3. Results of classifiers trained on all sensor layers without the corner-like features

	car	people	bike	p.sock.
length	62	111	162	142
recall	0.94	0.98	0.94	0.89
precision	0.94	0.98	0.69	0.63
F-measure	0.94	0.98	0.79	0.73

First, we evaluate the gain of corner-like features by training classifiers with and without them. We found that classifiers with all features are composed of 31% corner-like features on average. The classification results on our test sets are shown in Tables 2 and 3. As can be seen, the performance of cascades decreases and/or their length increases if corner-like features are omitted. Since we are interested in a real-time capable application for our mobile robot, shorter cascades are an important advantage. Thus, all subsequent experiments are carried out including our corner-like features.

The next experiment compares the exclusive ability of laser and camera for object recognition. For each object type one cascade was trained with the distance and remission layers from the laser sensor and one with the intensity and hue-distance layers from vision. Tables 4 and 5 show the results. Two observations can be made. First, performances of classifiers from single sensors are worse than those from all sensors and cascades grow considerably in length (cf. Tab. 2). For example the sizes of car classifiers increased by 236% (laser only) respectively 853% (camera only) while the F-measures slightly decreased. Second, performance of a sensor depends on object categories. It shows that the power socket category performs better with data from the camera than with data from the laser while car, people and bike categories show better results and shorter cascades with laser data.

After this we evaluate our sensor fusion approach against the approach to first learn separated classifiers and then fuse the results (cf. Fig. 6). We learned cascades with merged hue-distance, intensity, distance and remission layers and compared them to classifiers generated by a logical "and" concatenation of the cascades from camera-only and laser-only data (Tab. 4 and 5) as proposed in [18]. Tables 6 and 7 comprise the results on our test sets. It is self-evident that linking classifiers by a logical "and" can only improve precision, but possibly degrades the recall. This also arises in our experiments: while results from power sockets and cars perform comparably well with both methods, our approach shows superior results on the people and bike categories. It is able to exploit the pros of every sensor, thus can improve precision and recall. Furthermore, in theory a strong-classifier trained on the same examples but with a super-set of candidate weak-classifiers has at most the same size as one trained with less weak-classifiers. Therefore, the execution time of n concatenated single sensor classifiers is on average at least n times longer than the time spent by one classifier trained with a joint feature pool. In practice, the sensor fusion approach proposed here is more than twice as fast as the "and" concatenation of classifiers.

Table 4. Results of classifiers trained only on laser data (distance and remission layers)

	car	people	bike	p.sock.
length	111	123	135	418
recall	1	0.96	0.97	0.85
precision	0.89	1	0.6	0.29
F-measure	0.94	0.98	0.74	0.43

Table 5. Results of classifiers trained only on camera data (intensity and hue-distance layers)

	car	people	bike	p.sock.
length	401	1008	373	172
recall	0.94	0.67	0.52	0.89
precision	0.89	0.97	0.59	0.86
F-measure	0.91	0.8	0.55	0.87

Table 6. Results of classifiers trained on distance, remission, intensity, and hue-distance layers

	car	people	bike	p.sock.
length	58	128	108	87
recall	1	0.98	0.94	1
precision	1	1	0.78	0.75
F-measure	1	0.99	0.85	0.86

Table 7. Results of classifiers from Tab. 4 linked by logical "and" operator with classifiers from Tab. 5

	car	people	bike	p.sock.
length	512	1131	508	590
recall	0.94	0.65	0.55	0.74
precision	1	1	0.74	1
F-measure	0.97	0.79	0.63	0.85

5 Conclusions and Future Work

In this paper, we have introduced a new approach to combine the significant parts of information from different sensors for object classification. Gentle AdaBoost selects the best weak-classifiers built from a joint feature pool from different sensors. In several experiments, we have shown that the presented approach outperforms results from separate sensor classifications as well as from a simple fusion of separately trained cascades. The proposed approach is generic and can be applied to other object types as well.

Moreover we have shown that corner-like features are a reasonable extension of the standard feature set. In our experiments, classifiers trained with corner-like features outperform those trained without. Already the fact that they have been selected by Gentle AdaBoost proofs their advantage. The same holds for our new feature channel based on hue-distances.

While the test and training sets in our experiments are comparably small (a fact that is explained by the time-consuming acquisition of sensor data with our mobile robot), our results imply that these sets are big enough to define the characteristics of object types and to classify objects reliably. In future work we will investigate if larger training sets can even improve the performance. We also plan to use classifiers trained with this approach as initializer for object tracking to go one step further towards autonomous behavior of mobile robots.

We meet another challenge with improving the sensors. Acquisition time for the laser is much to long ($\approx$ 4 seconds per frame) to record data of fast moving objects or while driving with the robot. We will examine the applicability of TOF camera *ZCAM* or its successor *Natal* to tackle this drawback.

References

1. Schapire, R.E.: The strength of weak learnability. Machine Learning 5 (1990)
2. Freund, Y., Schapire, R.E.: A decision-theoretic generalization of on-line learning and an application to boosting. Technical report, AT&T Bell Laboratories (1995)
3. Freund, Y., Schapire, R.E.: A short introduction to boosting. Journal of Japanese Society for Artificial Intelligence 14(5), 771–780 (1999)
4. Friedman, J., Hastie, T., Tibshirani, R.: Additive logistic regression: a statistical view of boosting. Annals of Statistics 28 (2000) (2000)
5. Viola, P., Jones, M.: Rapid object detection using a boosted cascade of simple features. In: Proc. of CVPR (2001)
6. Viola, P., Jones, M.: Fast and robust classification using asymmetric adaboost and a detector cascade. In: NIPS (2002)
7. Lienhart, R., Maydt, J.: An extended set of haar-like features for rapid object detection. In: Proc. International Conference on Image Processing, pp. 900–903 (2002)
8. Meir, R., Rätsch, G.: An introduction to boosting and leveraging. In: Mendelson, S., Smola, A.J. (eds.) Advanced Lectures on Machine Learning. LNCS, vol. 2600, pp. 118–183. Springer, Heidelberg (2003)
9. Papageorgiou, C.P., Oren, M., Poggio, T.: A general framework for object detection. In: Proc. of Int'l Conf. on Computer Vision. IEEE Computer Society Press, Los Alamitos (1998)
10. Huang, C., Al, H., Wu, B., Lao, S.: Boosting nested cascade detector for multi-view face detection. In: Proc. of the Int'l Conf. on Pattern Recognition (2004)
11. Mitri, S., Frintrop, S., Pervölz, K., Surmann, H., Nüchter, A.: Robust Object Detection at Regions of Interest with an Application in Ball Recognition. In: IEEE 2005 International Conference Robotics and Automation, ICRA 2005 (2005)
12. Barreto, J., Menezes, P., Dias, J.: Human-robot interaction based on haar-like features and eigenfaces. In: Proc. Int. Conf. on Robotic and Automation (2004)
13. Laptev, I.: Improvements of object detection using boosted histograms. In: Proc. British Machine Vision Conf. BMVC 2006 (2006)
14. Arras, K.O., Mozos, O.M., Burgard, W.: Using boosted features for the detection of people in 2D range data. In: Proc. of ICRA (2007)
15. Premebida, C., Monteiro, G., Nunes, U., Peixoto, P.: A lidar and vision-based approach for pedestrian and vehicle detection and tracking. In: Proc. ITSC (2007)
16. Zhang, L., Wu, B., Nevatia, R.: Pedestrian detection in infrared images based on local shape features. In: OTCBVS Workshop, CVPR (2007)
17. Zivkovic, Z., Kröse, B.: Part based people detection using 2D range data and images. In: Proc. of IROS (2007)
18. Frintrop, S., Nüchter, A., Surmann, H., Hertzberg, J.: Saliency-based object recognition in 3D data. In: Proc. of Int'l Conf. on Intelligent Robots and Systems (2004)
19. Nüchter, A., Lingemann, K., Hertzberg, J., Surmann, H.: Accurate object localization in 3D laser range scans. In: Int'l Conf. on Advanced Robotics (2005)
20. Klein, D.A.: Objektklassifizierung in fusionierten 3D-Laserscans und Kameradaten mittels AdaBoost. Master's thesis, University of Bonn (December 2008)

A Multi-modal Attention System
for Smart Environments

B. Schauerte[1], T. Plötz[1], and G.A. Fink[2]

[1] Dept. Intelligent Systems, Robotics Research Institute, TU Dortmund, Germany
[2] Dept. Pattern Recognition in Embedded Systems, Faculty of Computer Science,
TU Dortmund, Germany

Abstract. Focusing their attention to the most relevant information is a
fundamental biological concept, which allows humans to (re-)act rapidly
and safely in complex and unfamiliar environments. This principle has
successfully been adopted for technical systems where sensory stimuli
need to be processed in an efficient and robust way. In this paper a
multi-modal attention system for smart environments is described that
explicitly respects efficiency and robustness aspects already by its architecture. The system facilitates unconstrained human-machine interaction
by integrating multiple sensory information of different modalities.

1 Introduction

The selective choice of salient, i.e. potentially relevant and thus interesting, sensory information and focusing the processing resources on it is a fundamental
problem of any artificial and biological system that requires fast reactions on
sensory stimuli despite limited processing resources. Therefore, during the last
decades substantial research effort has been devoted to the investigation of attention (e.g. [1,2,3]) and its applications (e.g. [4,5]). In recent years human-machine
interaction (HMI) within smart environments has become very popular. Such
environments typically contain medium- to large- size multi-modal sensor networks, most prominently cameras and microphones. Consequently, HMI in smart
environments requires efficient and robust processing of huge amounts of sensory
information. Thus focusing the attention is a crucial task.

In this paper we present a multi-modal attention system that has been designed to support real-life applications for intuitive HMI within smart environments. Complementing the formal presentation in our previous work (cf. [6]), in
this contribution we focus on the aspect of system design and practical implementation aspects. In addition to an overview of the core components (saliency
and attention) we explicitly consider system integration. The latter is of major
importance for practical applications. Intuitive HMI should not impose any behavioral constraints for humans. They should be allowed to act as natural as
possible and to interact with the smart environment using their natural means.
This implies the practical consequence that the full information required for exhaustive scene analysis is typically not accessible when restricting to the use of
single sensors or even of single modalities only. In order to deal with this, our

M. Fritz, B. Schiele, and J.H. Piater (Eds.): ICVS 2009, LNCS 5815, pp. 73–83, 2009.
© Springer-Verlag Berlin Heidelberg 2009

system follows a rigorous multi-modal multi-sensor integration approach. Reasoned by the very dynamic application domain an attention system for smart environments needs to fulfill certain constraints w.r.t. extensibility, flexibility and robustness aspects, and efficiency issues for real-time reactiveness. Our attention system respects these aspects already at the level of system architecture.

2   System Design

2.1   Architecture

The general architecture of the proposed system that is partitioned into conceptual sub-systems, i.e. connected groups of functional modules, is shown in Fig. 1. It contains two major parts: the *Saliency Sub-System*, responsible for the calculation of the multi-modal saliency, and the *Attention Sub-System*, which implements the methods to guide the attention. Within the first part of the system *Sensor-Specific Saliency Computation* extracts salient signals of a sensor and then transfers them into a common spatial saliency representation (Sec. 2.2). The latter serves as input for the subsequent *Hierarchical Saliency Computation*, which is based on a hierarchical combination scheme. Whereas in its first stage (sensor-type dependent) uni-modal combinations are derived, multi-modal combination forms the second phase of saliency calculation. A major advantage of this two-stage combination approach is the principal possibility for parallelization of the computations. Eventually, the spatial saliency world model is calculated in the post-processing module, where spatial and time filtering is applied. Based on the spatial saliency world model, *Attention Selection* identifies those regions inside the smart room, which attract the focus of attention. The selected regions are then used to realize the concrete *Attention Mechanism*.

Due to well specified interfaces, modules or even sub-systems can easily be exchanged. In order to fulfill the reactiveness constraint of smart environment applications the described system is designed to exploit the inherent parallsism of the serial stages of sensor data processing. The organization in modules allows for a flexible distribution of tasks within the network and thus guarantees scalability. Modules are grouped in processes and parallel calculations inside the processes are performed in threads. Also on this level, distribution of tasks (here processes) within the network is possible by design. Inter-process communication is enabled by serialization. Sub-systems organized in such processes can

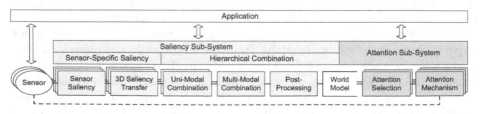

Fig. 1. Architecture concept

be selectively added/removed during runtime, e.g. to add additional sensors or attention mechanisms.

The advantage of our modular system architecture becomes especially manifest when addressing the development and evaluation of particular sub-systems. Special modules can be used to replay and/or simulate input data as well as to visualize the output and the states of specific sub-systems. The configuration of each module is stored in XML format and parameters of all modules can be modified at runtime by a unified network interface, e.g. to modulate the attention/saliency at runtime.

2.2   Spatial Saliency Representation

The choice of the representation for the saliency distribution is an important – if not the most important – design decision. We use a voxel representation, i.e. a regular tesselation of the environment's volume in sub-volume boxes (voxel). Spatial distributions in the modeled environment are approximated as functions over the voxel set. Using the unit interval as codomain, this representation is able to model probabilities and fuzzy sets. We utilize a fuzzy interpretation and therefore a fuzzy set represents salient voxels (saliency space). Additional crisp sets are used to represent opaque voxels, i.e. those sub-volume boxes that are occupied by known objects, and sensor-dependent binarized versions of visual saliency spaces. The binarized saliency space can optionally be used by the combination. It indicates whether a sensor perceives a voxel as salient and enables the integration of the characteristics and the history of sensory data.

3   Saliency Sub-System

3.1   Sensor-Specific Saliency Computation

Visual Saliency. The definition of visual saliency determines, which parts of the image are salient and should attract the visual attention. In our system the choice of the saliency model is not restricted to a particular one. However, for practical reasons we prefer to use object-based models (cf. e.g. [7,8]) instead of space-based models (cf. [8, p. 3f.]), The latter tend to suppress salient objects with homogeneous texture (cf. [7]). In order to determine salient objects we use a combination of a modulatable model [9] and the color-spatial distribution [7]. Adaptations had to be made to achieve real-time computations, which is a usual challenge of computational saliency models (cf. e.g. [4,10] and [8, p. 4]).

A simple ray casting algorithm is used to backproject the saliency map into the voxel-based spatial saliency representation. Each ray originates from the projection center through the pixel center and is associated with the pixel's saliency. The algorithm stops tracing, if the ray intersects a voxel that is occupied by a known opaque object.

The saliency of each voxel is calculated by aggregating the saliencies of the intersecting rays. We use *max* as aggregation function, because it can be calculated iteratively by applying the binary *max* function. Hence we avoid to store the intersecting rays of each voxel. Moreover, the binary *max* function is commutative, associative and idempotent, which are important properties for the backprojection algorithm. Since 0 is the neutral element of *max*, casting rays with a saliency of 0 can be omitted without introducing an error. By casting only rays with a saliency larger than ϵ we introduce an error bounded by ϵ. Depending on post-processing and selection of the focus of attention this heuristics has usually no negative influence on attention mechanisms. Since most pixels of a saliency map have very low intensity values, substantially increased performance is obtained due to the application of this pruning technique.

Additionally, the pixel- and voxel- resolutions are optimized. If the voxel resolution is too high, some voxels in the field of view of a camera may not be intersected by rays. In contrast, if the pixel resolution is too high, more rays than necessary are casted, resulting in low performance. Therefore we choose a pixel resolution and calculate the highest voxel resolution, which guarantees that no voxel is missed, or vice versa (e.g. Sec. 5.1).

Auditory Saliency. While there exist numerous models of visual saliency (e.g. [2,7]), only very few auditory saliency models have been developed (cf. [5,11]). In the considered application area of smart environments, sound sources that emit high energy signals should attract the attention, e.g. speaking persons. Therefore we define the auditory saliency based on the emitted energy.

Since salient acoustic signals recorded by a single microphone correspond to points in time and/or specific frequencies, there is no reasonable method to transfer and combine this information into the spatial saliency representation. Therefore we merge the uni-modal combination with the transfer into the spatial representation, exploiting the flexible modular architecture.

First we localize salient sound sources with the SRP-PHAT method [12, Ch. 8]. Then we transfer valid localization hypotheses into the spatial saliency representation. Since audio signals do not provide reliable information about the emitting objects' spatial dimensions, assumptions about the emitting object are required. Persons are the most likely salient sound source and, therefore, we use a cylindrical shape as model of a persons upper body.

3.2   Hierarchical Saliency Combination

The Visual Combination. has two tasks, namely to fuse the visual saliency information and to localize salient objects. For the latter the principle of volumetric intersection is applied because no additional information about the objects is available that allows for localization by a single view. Therefore, salient objects have to be perceived as salient in at least two views, which need to be combined into a unified representation. View combination has to consider certain severe challenges like varying scene coverage, potential sensor failure, view-dependent saliencies, occlusions and reconstruction failures. The latter corresponds to differences between the real and the reconstructed object shape (cf. [13]).

We use pairwise intersection followed by a union as combination scheme. This combination incorporates the principle of volumetric intersection that is capable of dealing with most of the aforementioned challenges. A potential negative side-effect of this procedure is that it unites the pairwise reconstruction error, if an object is recognized as salient by more than two cameras. However, depending on the camera arrangement in most practical applications this effect is of minor importance. We address this problem by integrating the perception functions and by determining those voxels that are perceived as salient by the local maximum number of cameras. All other voxels of the combination result are set to 0. By applying this *core extraction* afterwards, we can use powerful combination schemes that originally were not designed to localize objects, e.g. normalized convex combinations. In addition, we minimize the global reconstruction error by optimizing the camera positions offline (Sec. 5.1) and by optimizing the camera orientations online (Sec. 4.2).

Audio-Visual Combination. In general, all fuzzy aggregations are supported to aggregate the audio and visual saliency space. Basically, variants of three plausible audio-visual combination schemes for overt attention [3] can be expressed as fuzzy aggregations, namely early interaction, linear integration and late combination. Although the authors of [3] identified the linear combination scheme as the scheme that is most likely used by humans, we do not restrict the audio-visual combination to this particular one. Instead, we allow to (dynamically) choose the combination scheme that is most appropriate for the attention mechanism. The behaviors of the combination schemes differ depending on whether objects are salient in one or more modalities.

Post-Processing creates the world model by aggregation of the stream of multi-modal combination results, i.e. filtering in the time domain. We use a convex combination with an exponential weight decay as aggregation, because it can be efficiently implemented with a binary weighted addition of the current multi-modal combination result with the previous world model. Other convex combinations are supported, but the weight functions have to be positive and monotonically decreasing over the time domain to model the influence of a short term memory. In addition, spatial filtering can be used to suppress noise.

4   Attention Sub-System

4.1   Focus of Attention Selection

The selection of the focus of attention (FoA) determines, which salient regions inside a smart environment attract the attention. Salient regions consist of neighboring voxels with a high saliency in the current world model. Thresholding is used to determine these voxels and connected components labeling is used to group them into initial hypotheses of salient regions, which are then filtered to obtain the final regions that form the FoA.

The ordered execution of filters is a flexible method to implement certain tasks. We use filters to incorporate prior knowledge and to respect other aspects of attention, e.g. the serial shift of attention and inhibition of return (IoR). IoR prevents attention from returning to already-attended objects. It can also be implemented by attenuating the world model before determining the salient voxels (cf. e.g. [14] for a 2D variant of the IoR method). Attenuation is also used to implement habituation, i.e. the decreasing response to continuing stimuli.

4.2 Attention Mechanisms

Covert Attention is the act of focusing on one of several possible sensory stimuli. The common way of using saliency is to serially concentrate complex algorithms on those regions of an image that are particularly most relevant for some task, e.g. for object recognition (cf. [15]). We consider an additional (serial) selection and processing of the best views as a natural transfer of the covert attention to a multi-camera environment.

The definition of the "best" view depends on application-dependent selection criteria (e.g. [16]). We distinguish between two types: Firstly, low-level criteria express relations between cameras and regions, e.g. the number of visible objects in a view. Secondly, application-dependent high-level criteria like, e.g., the visibility of human faces are evaluated. Since these criteria can be conflicting, we model the ranking of the views as a multi-objective optimization problem.

Naturally, the objective functions of the criteria have different measures and react differently on changes in the environment. Therefore, values of different objective functions should not to be compared directly. This is avoided by using weighted majority voting as single aggregate function to rank the views.

Overt Attention directs the sense organs towards salient stimuli to optimize the perception of the stimulus sources. Thus active control of cameras (cf. [17]) appears to be a natural realization of the visual overt attention.

We use the minimization of the accumulated estimated reconstruction error over the salient objects as primary objective to optimize the camera orientations. We reduce the complexity of the estimation problem by considering the horizontal plane only, resulting in a reconstruction polygon and an error area. Furthermore, we assume a circular object shape, because it is of maximum symmetry and thus the object orientation is irrelevant. Depending on the saliency definition the salient regions allow for the estimation of the object's radius. However, we apply a constant radius for all regions because the estimated radius prioritizes bigger objects, which is, usually, an unwanted effect.

The search space of possible camera orientations is continuous and allows for infinitesimal variations with equal error. Hence, we use the centering of salient regions in the views as a secondary criterion to obtain a finite search space. It is sampled via sliding windows to determine the global optimum. The error function can be calculated efficiently, in particular with pre-calculations for stationary cameras. This is important since the number of sliding windows is in the order of the number of salient regions to the power of the number of active cameras.

In addition to the obvious optimization of the visual saliency model, the overt attention improves the perception of salient objects in two ways that are especially important for recognition tasks: It increases the number of cameras that see salient regions and favors multifarious views.

The camera orientations are adjusted in saccades, i.e. fast simultaneous movements of the cameras. During the saccades the processing of camera images is suppressed, realizing a simplified visual saccadic suppression. The saccadic suppression is necessary, because heavy motion blur and erroneous pan/tilt readouts during servo motion would degrade the spatial saliency model.

5   Experimental Results

As it is important to react sufficiently fast on changes in the environment to support natural HMI, the practical applicability of the presented system depends on its latency. The proposed attention system is intended to save computational resources. However, it requires additional resources to create the spatial saliency model and to determine the focus of attention. Hence, it is necessary to know the break-even point at which the use of the attention system begins to be benefical. Therefore, we evaluate the run-time of components that are necessary to determine the focus of attention, because the latency is measured by the required run-time, which also serves as an indicator for computational requirements.

Since it is impossible to consider all scenarios and configurations in a smart environment, we evaluated the run-time of a meaningful configuration in a smart meeting room. For the sake of representativeness, we exclude results that depend mainly on the chosen saliency definition. The latter results in substantially varying, thus hardly generalizable, run-times for saliency computations – ranging from several milliseconds to seconds (cf. [10]). Furthermore, we evaluate the run-time of the visual backprojection independently of the saliency by using randomized saliency maps with a specified percentage of salient pixels. Therefore the evaluation is largely independent of a specific scene and thus representative. Also, we exclude the network latency, because it is not substantial and depends on other network traffic. Since reactivity is critical to support the visual perception of all camera-based applications through the overt attention mechanism (Sec. 4.2), we evaluate the run-time of the camera orientation optimization.

5.1   Experimental Setup

Fig. 3 shows a representative example of the data flow in the presented system as well as the organization of the described modules in processes. The results of the processing steps are visualized and each (parallel) processing stage is annotated with the average run-time. The system is not executed on a single host because of load balancing aspects and unapt scheduling behavior due to the large number of dependent threads/processes. The chosen organization minimizes the network traffic because the voxel representation is encapsulated within a single process.

An office room with a pentagonal shape of $6,625 \times 3,760$ mm and a height of $2,550$ mm is used for evaluation. The evaluation is performed on *Intel Core 2 Duo 6320* 1.86 GHz dual core processors running LINUX, which are interconnected by Gigabit Ethernet. The camera images are taken by 4 *Sony EVI-D70P* pan-tilt-zoom cameras with an effective resolution of 752×582 pixels. The cameras are positioned roughly in the corners in order to minimize the expected

COMPONENT	∅RT	SD
Audio Transfer	< 0.2	0.00
Visual Combination	2.9	0.13
Core Extraction	3.5	0.89
A/V Combination	0.6	0.03
Post-Processing	0.3	0.06
Attention Selection	1.2	0.08
Total	8.4	0.91

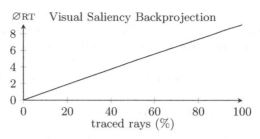

Fig. 2. Average run-times ∅RT (ms) with standard deviation SD

reconstruction error for a single region and the best camera pair (cf. Sec. 4.2). 16 microphones grouped in 2 circular arrays are used to record acoustic signals.

The resolution of the saliency maps was chosen to be 64×48, thus the voxel resolution is $67 \times 39 \times 27$ (see Sec. 3.1). This results in sub-volume boxes with approx. 10 cm side length, which is sufficiently accurate for most applications. Saliency maps and spaces are represented by floating point arrays, therefore vectorization is used to achieve real-time performance.

The table and cabinets in the room as well as the irregularities of the room are modeled as opaque objects. Note that modeling known opaque objects improves the model quality as well as the speed of the backprojection.

5.2   Results

The average run-times ∅RT and the standard deviation SD of the main components are listed in Fig. 2. It can be seen that the computational requirements as well as the overall latency are low, even on off-the-shelf hardware. However, the quality of the spatial saliency model could be improved at the cost of additional resources by increasing the voxel resolution.

The average time to backproject the visual saliency depends on the amount of traced rays (cf. Fig. 2) that is determined by the pixel saliency and the ray casting threshold. No zoom was used and the cameras were directed towards the far corners, thus a large sub-volume of the room was covered. The pairwise combination scheme for the 4 visual saliency spaces requires an average time of 2.9 ms. Transfering the hypotheses of salient sound sources into the spatial model requires below 0.2 ms for realistic numbers of sound sources (< 8). The optional *core extraction* requires 3.5 ms, depending on the number and values of the local maxima (caused by the iterative nature of the algorithm). Maximum was used as audio-visual combination and required 0.6 ms, which is representative for audio-visual combination schemes. Post-processing consisted of temporal integration with exponential weight decay and required 0.3 ms.

Selecting the focus of attention, i.e. thresholding, grouping and filtering, required 1.2 ms. Static thresholding and connected components labeling took 1.2 ms on average. The computation time for filters depends on their complexity in combination with the – usually low – number of initial region hypotheses. Three simple filters were used in the evaluation to suppress disturbances. Executing these filters

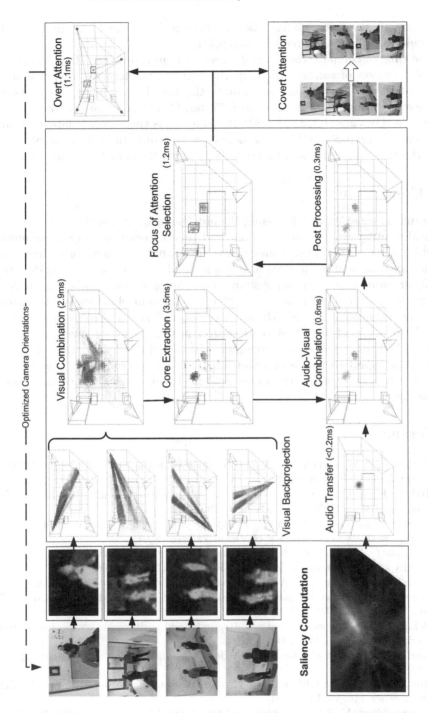

Fig. 3. Exemplary data flow of the described attention system. Each processing step is visualized by its result. The parallel execution stages are marked with their average run-times.

and extracting additional information for each region, e.g. which sensor perceive the region as salient, required less than 0.1 ms.

The time to compute the optimal camera orientations (Sec. 4.2) depends on the distribution of salient regions in the room. Therefore we used a uniform distribution of $6 - 8$ regions to evaluate the run-time (w/o pre-calculations). The average time is 1.1 ms and the $(.75, .95, .99, .999, 1)$-quantiles of the measured run-times are $(1.3, 2.8, 4.7, 8.2, 16.8)$ ms. Thus the expected latency is low, especially if compared to the time necessary to adjust the camera orientations (e.g. the max. angular velocities are $0.08°/\text{ms}$ for pan and $0.05°/\text{ms}$ for tilt).

6   Conclusion

Filtering information and focussing its processing by reasonable selection is a natural strategy when aiming for fast and reliable reactions on enivronmental stimuli. In recent years this concept was successfully adopted for technical attention systems that are applied for complex and dynamic application domains.

We developed an attention system that follows a multi-modal multi-sensor integration approach for robust and efficient human-machine interaction within smart environments. It explicitly focusses on efficiency and robustness aspects already at the level of system architecture. In this paper we gave an overview of the novel attention system together with a detailled discussion of system integration aspects, which is of major importance for practical applications. We demonstrated the effectiveness of the system by evaluating the computational requirements in a smart room.

References

1. Treisman, A.M., Gelade, G.: A feature-integration theory of attention. Cognitive Psychology 12, 97–136 (1980)
2. Itti, L., Koch, C., Niebur, E.: A model of saliency-based visual attention for rapid scene analysis. TPAMI 20, 1254–1259 (1998)
3. Onat, S., Libertus, K., König, P.: Integrating audiovisual information for the control of overt attention. Journal of Vision 7, 1–16 (2007)
4. Longhurst, P., Debattista, K., Chalmers, A.: A GPU based saliency map for high-fidelity selective rendering. In: AFRIGRAPH, pp. 21–29 (2006)
5. Kalinli, O., Narayanan, S.: A saliency-based auditory attention model with applications to unsupervised prominent syllable detection in speech. In: INTERSPEECH, pp. 1941–1944 (2007)
6. Schauerte, B., Richarz, J.: et al.: Multi-modal and multi-camera attention in smart environments. In: ICMI (2009)
7. Liu, T., Sun, J.: et al.: Learning to detect a salient object. In: CVPR, pp. 1–8 (2007)
8. Sun, Y., Fisher, R.: Object-based visual attention for computer vision. Artificial Intelligence 146, 77–123 (2003)
9. Navalpakkam, V., Itti, L.: Search goal tunes visual features optimally. Neuron 53, 605–617 (2007)

10. Frintrop, S., Klodt, M., Rome, E.: A real-time visual attention system using integral images. In: ICVS (2007)
11. Kayser, C., Petkov, C.I., et al.: Mechanisms for allocating auditory attention: an auditory saliency map. Current Biology 15, 1943–1947 (2005)
12. Brandstein, M.S., Ward, D. (eds.): Microphone Arrays: Signal Processing Techniques and Applications. Springer, Heidelberg (2001)
13. Dyer, C.R.: Volumetric scene reconstruction from multiple views. In: Davis, L.S. (ed.) Foundations of Image Understanding, pp. 469–489. Kluwer, Dordrecht (2001)
14. Ruesch, J., Lopes, M.: et al.: Multimodal saliency-based bottom-up attention: A framework for the humanoid robot icub. In: ICRA, pp. 962–967 (2008)
15. Walther, D., Koch, C.: Modeling attention to salient proto-objects. Neural Networks 19, 1395–1407 (2006)
16. Doubek, P., Geys, I., van Gool, L.: Cinematographic rules applied to a camera network. In: OMNIVIS, pp. 17–30 (2004)
17. Bakhtari, A., Naish, M., Eskandari, M., et al.: Active-vision-based multisensor surveillance: An implementation. TSMC 36, 668–680 (2006)

Individual Identification Using Gait Sequences under Different Covariate Factors

Yogarajah Pratheepan, Joan V. Condell, and Girijesh Prasad

School of Computing and Intelligent Systems, University of Ulster, UK

Abstract. Recently, gait recognition for individual identification has received increased attention from biometrics researchers as gait can be captured at a distance using low-resolution capturing device. Human gait properties can be affected by different clothing and carrying objects (i.e. covariate factors). Most of the literature shows that these covariate factors give difficulties for individual identification based on gait. In this paper, we propose a novel method that generates dynamic and static feature templates of the sequences of silhouette images (Dynamic Static Silhouette Templates (DSSTs)) to overcome this issue. Here the DSST is calculated from Motion History Images (MHIs). The experimental results show that our method overcomes issues arising from differing clothing and the carrying of objects.

1 Introduction

Early medical studies showed that individual gaits are unique, varying from person to person and are difficult to disguise [1]. In addition, it has been shown that gaits are so characteristic that we recognize friends by their gait [2]. Humans have distinctive features that distinguish one person from another. The way an individual normally walks (i.e. gait) is one of those distinctive features that may be used for individual identification. Gait can be obtained from images taken at a distance which by itself form a strong advantage when compared to other biometrics such as iris or face recognition.

The identification based on gait analysis typically proceeds by extracting the silhouette of the walking person. The gait features used for identification can be broadly classified into two categories, namely static and dynamic features. The static features reflect the geometry based measurements of the anatomical structure of the human body such as the person's height, length or width of the different body segments. The dynamic features are the features which describe the kinematics of the locomotive process, such as the angular motion of the lower limbs. Recent research on gait using static features for individual identification proved that a promising recognition rate can be achieved [3]. On the other hand Cutting et al. [4] argued that dynamic features contribute significantly more in individual recognition than static features. Moreover, Stevenage et el. [5] supported the argument that gait-related features are more important than body-related features for the purpose of human identification. Some researchers have preferred to fuse both static and dynamic cues with a belief that fusion would yield the optimal gait recognition rate [6].

M. Fritz, B. Schiele, and J.H. Piater (Eds.): ICVS 2009, LNCS 5815, pp. 84–93, 2009.

Despite the fact that static and dynamic features were proved by recent experiments to achieve promising gait recognition rates, their use in the development of an individual identification system is impractical. This is mainly because the body-related parameters are not robust as they are dependent on covariate factors [7,8] which would certainly affect the recognition performance. For example, if we have already seen some individuals and their walking sequences with normal conditions (i.e. without covariate factors) then the question is, how can we identify an individual (i.e. an already known person) in a new walking sequence with a different appearance (i.e. someone who appears with covariate factors)? A solution may be proposed for this problem as, **"Have I seen this person before?"**. Bouchrika et al. [9] developed a model-based approach and only considered dynamic features to solve this problem. But the computational cost of model-based methods is relatively high [10]. Also, recent experiments proved that the static features helped achieve a good gait recognition rate (e.g. [3]). Therefore this paper shows the implementation of a novel hybrid model-free method combined with static and dynamic information of the gait as a single template that makes the development of a biometric system practical. Our static features do not include clothing or the carrying of objects information (i.e. covariate factors) for individual identification. The primary concept of this method is the removal of covariate factors for upper body part. Our combined static and dynamic feature gives better results for individual identification and makes the development of biometric system practical.

In Section 2, details of feature extraction are described. Section 3 provides details of the proposed recognition algorithm while Section 4 presents the experimental results. Finally Section 5 gives the conclusion to the work.

2 Feature Extraction

2.1 Motivation

The main motivation of our proposed template is to construct similar features for the same person even if that person appears with different clothing or carrying objects. Here the feature refers to the combined static and dynamic gait information. There are different approaches available for gait recognition such as holistic (e.g. [6,12]), and model-based (e.g. [8,9]) approaches. Holistic approach means using motion information directly without the need for a model reconstruction. Model-free approaches usually use sequences of binary silhouettes (e.g. [11,12]), extracting the silhouettes of moving objects from a video using segmentation techniques such as background subtraction. Unlike these methods, in this paper, a method is proposed which simply extracts a feature template, Dynamic Static Silhouette Template (DSST), from a sequence of silhouettes of images for recognition.

The DSST is generated using dynamic and static feature templates called Dynamic Silhouette Templates (DSTs) and Static Silhouette Templates (SSTs). The DST considers the motion characteristic of the gait as part of the body in motion during walking, such as the leg. This motion characteristic is generated

Fig. 1. (a) Sample of individual walking sequences used for training and (b) Sample of individuals with different clothing and carrying objects used for testing

from the lower part of the Motion History Image (MHI). The static characteristic of the gait is the torso which remains steady during walking. This static characteristic is generated using the upper part of the MHI.

Two different walking sequences are considered, i.e. individuals with normal conditions for training and individuals with different clothing and carrying objects for testing, see Figure 1. First, the silhouettes are extracted from Gait sequences, normalized to a fixed size and centralised. Then the gait period is estimated from the silhouette sequence. The silhouette sequence is further divided into several cycles according to the estimated gait period. The MHI is computed for each cycle. In each MHI a DST, SST and DSST are computed. But in the testing sequence, the calculated SST is going to give unwanted information as it contains clothing and carrying objects as well. In this case it is necessary to remove the unwanted information that is available in the calculated test sequence SST. Here the human body symmetry property is used to remove the covariate factors as the human body is typically close to symmetric when people are walking naturally [13,14].

2.2   Pre-processing

In our proposed algorithm, silhouettes are the basis of gait-based individual identification. The silhouettes are extracted using a Gaussian model-based background estimation method [15]. The bounding box of the silhouette image in each frame is computed. The silhouette image is extracted according to the size of the bounding box and the extracted image is resized to a fixed size (128*100 pixels) to eliminate the scaling effect. The resized silhouette is then aligned centrally with respect to its horizontal centroid. After this preprocessing the gait period is estimated in an individual's walking sequence.

2.3   Gait Period Estimation

Human walking repeats its motion in a stable frequency. Since our proposed gait feature templates depend on the gait period, we must estimate the number of frames in each walking cycle. A single walking cycle can be regarded as that period in which a person moves from the midstance position (both legs are closest together) to a double support position (both legs are farthest apart), then the midstance position, followed by the double support position, and finally back to the midstance position. The gait period can be estimated by calculating the number of foreground pixels in the silhouette image [16]. Because sharp changes in the gait cycle are most obvious in the lower part of the body, gait period estimation makes use only of the lower half of the silhouette image, with the gait period being the median of the distance between two consecutive minima of the distribution of foreground pixels. Here the gait period is calculated as the number of frames between two consecutive minima of the distribution of foreground pixels. The number of frames are now used to generate MHI images.

2.4   Motion History Image (MHI)

A motion history image (MHI) is a temporal template. Let $I(u, v, k)$ be the kth frame of pixels intensities of an image sequence and let $D(u, v, k)$ be the binary image that results from pixel intensity change detection. That is by thresholding $|I(u, v, k) - I(u, v, k-1) > th|$, where th is the minimal intensity difference between two images for change detection. An MHI, say H_θ, contains the temporal history of motion at that point represented by θ which is the period of time to be considered. The implementation of the MHI is then as follows [17]:

$$H_\theta(u, v, k) = \begin{cases} \theta & if \ \ D(u, v, k) = 1 \\ max[0, H_\theta(u, v, k-1)] \ otherwise \end{cases} \quad (1)$$

Moreover, in Bobick's problem definition [17], it is not known when the movement of interest begins or ends. Therefore they needed to vary the observed period θ. Because we assume that the beginning and the end of a gait are known, we do not need to vary θ. Therefore we modify the MHI operator into:

$$H(u, v, k) = \begin{cases} k & if \ \ D(u, v, k) = 1 \\ H(u, v, k-1) \ otherwise \end{cases} \quad (2)$$

where $H(u, v, k) = 0$ for $k = 0$ and $0 \le k \le K$, where k is the sequence of frames during which the motion is stored. Examples of MHIs are shown in Figure 2. Based on this MHI we generate the DST and the SST.

Static Silhouette Template (SST). The SST can be generated using the following algorithm:

$$SST_i(x, y) = \begin{cases} MHI_i(x, y) \ if \ \ MHI_i(x, y) = K \ and \ (x < \tfrac{2}{3} * H) \\ 0 \ \ \ \ otherwise \end{cases} \quad (3)$$

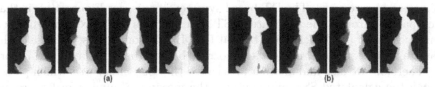
(a)   (b)

Fig. 2. (a) MHIs for four differet individuals with normal conditions (b) MHIs for four different individuals carrying objects

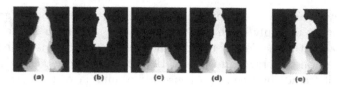

Fig. 3. (a), (b), (c) and (d) represent MHI, SST, DST and DSST features respectively. (e) DSST with covariate factor.

where H is the height of the MHI in pixels and $2/3$ is taken into account because of the assumption that useful gait information lies on the lower part of the body (e.g. legs), i is the gait-cycle number in the gait sequence, SST_i is the i-th static silhouette template and K is the maximum intensity value of $MHI_i(x, y)$.

Dynamic Silhouette Template (DST). The DST can be generated using the following algorithm:

$$DST_i(x, y) = \begin{cases} 0 & if \quad x < (\frac{2}{3} * H) \\ MHI_i(x, y) & otherwise \end{cases} \tag{4}$$

where i is the gait-cycle number in the gait sequence, DST_i is the i-th dynamic silhouette template.

Dynamic Static Silhouette Template (DSST). The DSST is defined as:

$$DSST_i(x, y) = DST_i(x, y) + SST_i(x, y) \tag{5}$$

If we consider the training sequences, the individuals gait image sequence is first converted to an MHI then the SST, DST and DSST are calculated (see Figure 3(a)-(d)). But if we consider the SST that is generated from the test sequence then we need to remove the covariate factors (see Figure 3(e)). Therefore for the calculated SSTs from the test sequences, the human body symmetry property is applied to remove the covariate factors. Finding the symmetric axis is not an easy task when covariate factors exist. Here we applied the Distance Transform (DT) [20] and the *body major axis* technique to overcome the covariate factor issue and find the human body symmetry axis. Here only vertical lines are taken into consideration because the main goal is to find the vertical axis that corresponds to the symmetric axis.

A distance transform of a binary image specifies the distance from each pixel to the nearest zero pixel. The DT based symmetric axis, see Figure 4(c), is that which passes through the calculated SST and contains the maximum summed intensity value of pixels belonging to that line. But in some cases, because of the covariate factor we could not get the correct body symmetric axis, see Figure 4(c). Therefore we also find another axis called the *body major axis* which passes through the calculated SST and contains the maximum number of foreground pixels. In some instances (i.e because of human body shape or some other factors), this technique also does not give good results, see Figure 4(d). Therefore

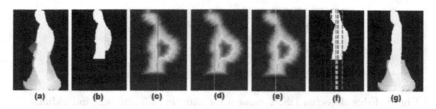

Fig. 4. (a) and (b) represent MHI and SST respectively. (c) Corresponding DT matrix based on Euclidean distance. Red, Green and Yellow lines are shown in (c), (d) and (e) represent the DT symmetric axis, *body major axis* and the mean of DT symmetric axis and *major body axis*. Pink and blue lines are shown in (f) represent right and left bound of the human body. (g) represents final DSST image without covariate factor.

the final human body symmetric axis is calculated by taking the mean value of the DT axis and the *major body axis*, see Figure 4(e). This final *human body symmetric axis* gives a good body symmetry value. Also left and right most body vertical lines are calulated for each individuals. The mean value of the left most vertical lines and body symmetry value give the left width of human body. Similarly the right body width is calculated. The Human body width parameters are important to remove the covariate factors. Any foreground pixels which belong outside of these widths are considered as covariate factors, see Figure 4(f). The final DSST template image is shown in Figure 4(g).

3   Recognition

Here, we use two different sets of walking sequences - one set of sequences for training and another set of sequences for testing. We applied two different approaches (i.e. Hausdorff distance and Support Vector Machine) to identify individuals in gait sequences. In this section, the two approaches are explained.

3.1   Approach-1

Canny edge detection [18] is applied to the DSST images, see Figure 5. The feature set obtained during training is stored in the system database as a template (say shape $\mathbf{A}$). During identification, the feature extracted from the test sequence (say $\mathbf{B}$) is compared to the template by the matcher, which determines the degree of similarity between the two features. Here, the problem of individual recognition is how to decide if a "Shape" $\mathbf{B}$ is an instance of a particular "Shape" $\mathbf{A}$. Here we used the modified version of the Hausdorff distance method based on Felzenszwalb's work [19] for comparing shapes. Felzenszwalb compared the shapes $\mathbf{A}$ and $\mathbf{B}$ using a **dot** product function:$\mathbf{A}.\mathbf{B}^d$, where the dilation [20] of $\mathbf{B}$ by d is denoted $\mathbf{B}^d$ and it consists of the set of points that are at a distance at most d from some point in $\mathbf{B}$.

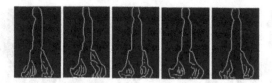

Fig. 5. Edge detected DSST images for sample of 5 different individuals

3.2 Approach-2

Support Vector Machine - SVM. The problem of learning a binary classifier can be expressed as that of learning the function $f : R^n \rightarrow \pm 1$ that maps patterns x onto their correct classification y as $y = f(x)$. In the case of an SVM, the function f takes the form,

$$f_{svm}(x) = \sum_{i=1}^{N} y_i \alpha_i k(x, x_i) + b \tag{6}$$

where N is the number of training patterns, (x_i, y_i) is training pattern i with its classification, α_i and b are learned weights, and $k(.,.)$ is a kernel function. Here, we use a linear function as the kernel for which $\alpha_i > 0$ are denoted *support vectors*.

The surface $f(x) = 0$ defines a hyperplane through the feature space as defined by the kernel $k(.,.)$. The weights α_i and b are selected so that the number of incorrect classifications in the training set is minimized, while the distances from this hyperplane to the support vectors are maximized. This is achieved by solving the optimization problem [21]:

Minimize:

$$\alpha^* = arg \min_{\alpha} \frac{1}{2} \sum_{i=1}^{N} \sum_{j=1}^{N} \alpha_i \alpha_j y_i y_j k(x_i, x_j) - \sum_{k=1}^{N} \alpha_i$$

with constraints, $0 \leq \alpha_i \leq C$ and $\sum_{i=1}^{N} y_i \alpha_i = 0$. The constant C affects the tolerance to incorrect classifications. Using optimal parameters α_i, equation (6) with any support vector (x_i, y_i) as in data can be used to find b.

In each binary SVM, only one class is labelled as "1" and the other is labelled as "-1". The one-versus-all method uses a winner-takes-all strategy. Multi-class SVMs are usually implemented by combining several two-class SVMs. If there are M classes, SVM will construct M binary classifiers by learning. In our experiment we use multi-class SVMs.

4   Results

We used the well-known SOTON dataset to evaluate the proposed algorithm. The SOTON gait sequence dataset was developed by the University of Southampton [22]. The walking sequences were filmed in a controlled laboratory environment and captured with a digital video camera at 25 frames per second. We

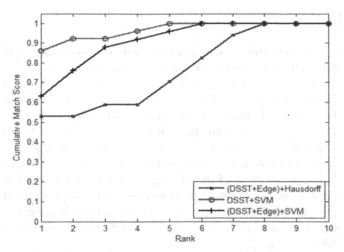

Fig. 6. Individual identification performance in terms of rank order statistics

Table 1. Performance on SOTON Hid (small) dataset

	Rank 1(%)	Rank 2(%)	Rank 3(%)
Edge(DSST) + Hausdorff	52.9	52.9	58.8
Edge(DSST) + SVM	63.0	76.0	88.0
DSST + SVM	86.0	92.3	92.3

used normal walking sequences for training and different clothing (i.e. jacket) and carrying object (i.e. back bag and shoulder bag) walking sequences for testing. There are 10 subjects (i.e. 10 different individuals) with 180 sequences (i.e. 90 sequences for training and 90 sequences for testing) used for this experiment. First, the gait period is estimated. Using that gait period the MHI is calculated. Then the DST, SST and DSST are generated. The proposed algorithm was tested to determine its ability to identify individuals by using Edge(DSST) + Hausdorff, Edge(DSST) + SVM and DSST + SVM (see Fig 6).

The Cumulative Match Score (CMS) evaluation method which was introduced by Phillips et. el in the FERET protocol [23] is used for our individual identification approach. We correctly classified 86.0% of the walking sequences at *Rank* = 1 using our proposed DSST + SVM method while the Edge(DSST) + Hausdorff and Edge(DSST) + SVM approaches achieved a reduced performance (see Table 1). A recognition rate of 73.4% is achieved at *Rank* = 1 by Bouchrika et al. [9] for all the covariate factors including footwear, clothing, load carriage and walking speed. But they have not showed the experimental results for shoulder bag and back bag. We can conclude that our derived features have a potential discriminative capability to identify individuals with artifacts which include a shoulder bag and a back bag.

5 Conclusion

In this paper, a gait recognition algorithm has been proposed for individual identification using a Dynamic Static Silhouette Template (DSST) under covariate
factors. The performance of the proposed algorithm is evaluated experimentally
using the SOTON data set [22]. The experimental results showed that the performance of the proposed algorithm is promising for covariate factor sequences.
Therefore this proposed algorithm provides a better solution to the identification of individuals even when they appear with different clothing or carrying objects. The proposed method has therefore enhanced applicability for the
surveillance-based application of identifying individuals. The method however
produced inferior results on some walking sequences. Examples were when some
of the scenarios such as the individuals fully covering their body with a different
clothing style or individuals carrying objects that fully covered the individuals'
legs motion information.

Removing covariate factors from test sequences is important in our method.
Our *symmetric axis* based covariate factors removal worked very well. If we
apply more robust methods to remove the covariate factors then we could get a
higher recognition rate. One of the future directions of this research would be to
consider different methods to remove the covariate factors.

References

1. Murray, M.P., Drought, A.B., Kory, R.C.: Walking patterns of normal men. J.
   Bone Joint Surg. 46 A(2), 335–360 (1964)
2. Cutting, J., Kozlowski, L.: Recognizing friends by their walk: gait perception without familiarity cues, Bull. Psychon. Soc. 9(5), 353–356 (1977)
3. Wang, L., Ning, H., Tan, T., Hu, W.: Fusion of static and Dynamic body biometrics for Gait Recognition. IEEE Transcations on Circuits and Systems for Video
   Technology 14(2), 149–158 (2004)
4. Cutting, J.E., Proffitt, D.: Gait Perception as an Example of How we may Perceive
   Events. Intersensory per. and sensory integration, 249–273 (1981)
5. Stevenage, S.V., Nixon, M.S., Vince, K.: Visual Analysis of Gait as a Cue to Identity. Applied Cognitive Psychology 13(6), 513–526 (1999)
6. Lam, T., Lee, R., Zhang, D.: Human gait recognition by the fusion of motion and
   static spatio-temporal templates. Pattern Recognition 40(9), 2563–2573 (2007)
7. Veres, G.V., Nixon, M.S., Carter, J.N.: Modelling the Time-Variant Covariates for
   Gait Recognition. In: Proc. of 5th Intl. Conf. on Audio-and Video-Based Biometric
   Person Authentication, pp. 597–606 (2005)
8. Wagg, D.K., Nixon, M.S.: On Automated Model-Based Extraction and Analysis
   of Gait. In: Proc. of Conf. Automatic Face and Gesture Recognition, pp. 11–16
   (2004)
9. Bouchrika, I., Nixon, M.: Exploratory Factor Analysis of Gait Recognition. In: 8th
   IEEE International Conference on Automatic Face and Gesture Recognition, pp.
   1–6 (2008)
10. Wang, L., Tan, T.N., Hu, W.M., Ning, H.Z.: Automatic Gait Recognition Based
    on Statistical Shape Analysis. IEEE Trans. on Image Processing 12(9), 1120–1131
    (2003)

11. Foster, J.P., Nixon, M.S., Prügel-Bennett, A.: Automatic gait recognition using area-based metrics. Pattern Recognition Lett. 24, 2489–2497 (2003)
12. Wang, L., Tan, T.: Silhouette analysis-based gait recognition for human identification. IEEE Trans. PAMI 25(12), 1505–1518 (2003)
13. Haritaoglu, I., Cutler, R., Harwood, D., Davis, L.S.: Backpack: detection of people carrying objects using silhouettes. In: Proc. of Seventh IEEE International Conference on Computer Vision, vol. 1, pp. 102–107 (1999)
14. Weiming, H., Min, H., Xue, Z., Tieniu, T., Jianguang, L., Maybank, S.: Principal axis-based correspondence between multiple cameras for people tracking. In: IEEE Transactions Pattern Analysis and Machine Intelligence, pp. 663–671 (2006)
15. Stauffer, C., Grimson, W.E.L.: Adaptive background mixture models for real-time tracking. In: Proc. IEEE Computer Society Conference on Computer Vision and Pattern Recognition (CVPR 1999), vol. 2, pp. 246–252 (1999)
16. Sarkar, S., Phillips, P.J., Liu, Z., Vega, I.R., Grother, P., Bowyer, K.W.: The humanID gait challenge problem: data sets, performance, and analysis. IEEE Trans. PAMI 27(2), 162–177 (2005)
17. Bobick, A., Davis, J.: The recognition of human movement using temporal templates. IEEE Transaction on Pattern Analysis and Machine Intelligence 23(3), 257–267 (2001)
18. Canny, J.: A computational approach to edge detection. IEEE Trans. PAMI 8(6), 679–698 (1986)
19. Felzenszwalb, P.F.: Learning Models for Object Recognition. In: IEEE Conference on Computer Vision and Pattern Recognition, pp. 1056–1062 (2001)
20. Gonzalez, R.C., Woods, R.E.: Digital Image Processing, 2nd edn. Pearson Education, London (2003)
21. Gunn, S.R.: Support Vector Machines for Classification and Regression. Technical Report, Image Speech and Intelligent Systems Research Group, University of Southampton, pp. 1–66 (May 1998)
22. Shutler, J.D., Grant, M.G., Nixon, M.S., Carter, J.N.: On a large sequence-Based Human Gait Database. In: Proc. 4th International Conference on Recent Advances in Soft Computing, Nottingham (UK), pp. 66–71 (2002)
23. Phillips, P.J., Moon, H., Rizvi, S.A., Rauss, P.J.: The FERET Evaluation Methodology for Face Recognition Algorithms. IEEE Transactions on Pattern Analysis and Machine Intelligence 22(10), 1090–1104 (2000)

Using Local Symmetry for Landmark Selection

Gert Kootstra, Sjoerd de Jong, and Lambert R.B. Schomaker

University of Groningen, Postbus 407, 9700 AK Groningen, The Netherlands
G.Kootstra@ai.rug.nl
http://www.ai.rug.nl/~gert

Abstract. Most visual Simultaneous Localization And Mapping (SLAM) methods use interest points as landmarks in their maps of the environment. Often the interest points are detected using contrast features, for instance those of the Scale Invariant Feature Transform (SIFT). The SIFT interest points, however, have problems with stability, and noise robustness. Taking our inspiration from human vision, we therefore propose the use of local symmetry to select interest points. Our method, the MUlti-scale Symmetry Transform (MUST), was tested on a robot-generated database including ground-truth information to quantify SLAM performance. We show that interest points selected using symmetry are more robust to noise and contrast manipulations, have a slightly better repeatability, and above all, result in better overall SLAM performance.

1 Introduction

One of the fundamental tasks of an autonomous robot is to build a map of the environment and use it for self localization. The problem of Simultaneous Localization and Mapping (SLAM) has therefore received much attention in the last decade [1]. Nowadays, approaches using laser range finders are very successful. SLAM using vision, however, remains a challenging research topic, e.g., [2,3].

Using a camera has the advantage over a laser-range finder that it is a passive sensor that is low cost, low power, and lightweight. A camera furthermore provides a rich source of information, which enables the use of sophisticated detection and recognition methods. The difficulty, however, is to extract relevant information from the high-dimensional visual data in real time. In this paper, we propose the use of local symmetry.

Most visual SLAM systems use visual landmarks to create a map of the robot's environment. It is important to select robust, stable landmarks that will be recognizable in future encounters. Furthermore, the number of selected landmarks should be limited, since the computational complexity of the SLAM algorithms strongly depends on the number of landmarks.

Usually, interest-point detectors are used for landmark selection. Most approaches use contrast features to detect interest points. Examples are the Scale-Invariant Feature Transform (SIFT) [4,5], Speeded Up Robust Features (SURF) [6,7], and Harris corners [8]. We propose the use of local symmetry to detect interest points. We compare our method with SIFT, since it is among the best performing interest point detectors in SLAM [9], as well as in object recognition [10].

Although systems using SIFT have successfully been applied to SLAM, there are three important drawbacks. The interest points are very susceptible to noise, not all selected landmarks are recognized when the robot returns to a previously visited location,

M. Fritz, B. Schiele, and J.H. Piater (Eds.): ICVS 2009, LNCS 5815, pp. 94–103, 2009.

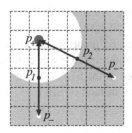

Fig. 1. The Fast Radial Symmetry Transform [21]. Each pixel in the image votes for symmetry at a given radius r. In this example, two pixels p_1 and p_2 are shown. Using the orientation of a pixel's gradient, a vote is made for bright symmetrical forms on a dark background at p_-, and the reverse, p_+. Doing this for all pixels in the image gives the symmetry transform of the image, $\psi_r(o, s)$, at octave o and scale s.

and too many interest points are found in an image, but only few points are so stable that they can be tracked over a number of successive frames. Thus SIFT has problems with robustness, repeatability, and stability.

We propose a landmark selection mechanism using local symmetries instead of local contrast, and show that it performs better regarding the above mentioned problems. Our choice for symmetry is motivated by human behavior. Symmetry is detected very rapidly, especially when patterns have multiple axes of symmetry [11]. Moreover, humans pay attention to locally symmetric parts of images [12,13]. Furthermore, humans use symmetry to segregate a figure from its background [14]. These findings suggest that symmetry is used in pre-attentive vision, and can therefore be used for context-free object segmentation and landmark selection.

Using symmetry to select landmarks exploits the fact that most man-made indoor environments contain many symmetrical objects and forms. Since symmetry is a strong non-accidental property, we believe that its use will result in the selection of valuable landmarks for the visual SLAM system.

Although contrast features have received most attention in computer vision research (e.g., [4,15]), symmetry is successfully used in a number of studies. In earlier work, for instance, Marola [16] used symmetry for detection and localization of objects in planar images. Symmetry has furthermore been used to control the gaze of artificial vision systems [17,18] Heidemann [19] showed that interest points detected with color symmetry are robust to noise and 3D object rotation. Moreover, he showed that symmetry detection results in points that are more robust to changing light conditions than Harris corners and that these points are more unique compared to other locations in the image.

To detect local symmetry in an image, a number of symmetry operators exist. Reisfeld et al. [20], for instance, developed a mirror-symmetry operator by comparing the gradients of neighboring pixels. Heidemann [19] extended this work to the color domain. Reisfeld et al. also proposed a radial-symmetry operator that promotes patterns that are symmetric in multiple symmetry axes. A faster operator to detect radial symmetry, the Fast Radial Symmetry Transform (FRST), is proposed in [21].

In this paper, we use FRST as a basis of our model to determine local symmetry. We develop the model to a novel scale- and rotation-invariant interest-point detector, which we call the MUlti-scale Symmetry Transform (MUST). We discuss the use of MUST for selecting landmarks for visual SLAM.

We show that landmarks selected using local symmetry are more robust to noise and have a higher repeatability, and require fewer computations. Most importantly, we show that the overall performance of the SLAM system increases when interest points are selected using local symmetry instead of SIFT.

2   Methods

In this section we first explain the selection of interest points using local symmetry. We then discuss the visual buffer to select stable interest points as landmarks. We end with a description of the Kalman Filter implementation for visual SLAM.

2.1   Interest Points Based on Local Symmetry

As a basis of our interest point detector, we use the Fast Radial Symmetry Transform [21], and extended it to a multi-scale and rotational-invariant detector, MUST. The basis of the FRST is given in Fig. 1, and MUST is depicted in Fig. 2.

To obtain a multi-scale interest-point detector, we use a pyramid approach similar to that used in [4]. The symmetry response is calculated at five spatial octaves, $\mathcal{O} = \{-1, 0, 1, 2, 3\}$. In the first octave, -1, the gray-scaled input image, I_{-1}, has twice the resolution of the original image, similar to [4]. For each next octave, the input image of the previous octave is smoothed with a Gaussian kernel and down-sampled by a factor of two. Within each octave, there are three scales, $s \in \{0, 1, 2\}$, with progressive smoothing. This gives a pyramid of gray-scaled images, $I_{o,s}$, for a given octave o and scale s.

The symmetry transform, $\Psi(o, s)$, for octave o and scale s, is calculated by investigating the local radial symmetry at a set of different radii. The size of the radii depends on the scale s. The set of radii used to calculate the symmetry response is defined as $\mathcal{R}_s = (1 + s/(s_{max} - 1)) \cdot \mathcal{R}$, where $s_{max} = 3$ and $\mathcal{R} = \{1, 3, 5\}$. The symmetry transform is then:

$$\Psi(o, s) = \frac{1}{|\mathcal{R}_s|} \sum_{r \in \mathcal{R}_s} \psi_r(o, s) \tag{1}$$

where $\psi_r(o, s)$ is the symmetry response at octave o and scale s for radius r.

$\psi_r(o, s)$ is determined by first calculating the gradients of the input image $I_{o,s}$ with horizontally and vertically aligned Sobel filters, resulting in a magnitude map, $G_{o,s}$, and an orientation map, $\Theta_{o,s}$. Then, each pixel p votes for the existence of symmetry based on its gradient, $\Theta_{o,s}(p)$, its magnitude, $G_{o,s}(p)$ and the given radius r. This is related to the Hough transform. A pixel votes for the existence of both a bright symmetrical form on a dark background, and a dark symmetrical form on a bright background at respectively location p_+ and p_-:

$$p_+ = p + r \cdot (\cos \Theta_{o,s}(p), \sin \Theta_{o,s}(p)) \tag{2}$$

$$p_- = p - r \cdot (\cos \Theta_{o,s}(p), \sin \Theta_{o,s}(p)) \tag{3}$$

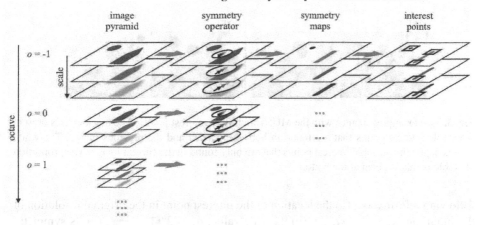

Fig. 2. MUST, the MUlti-scale Symmetry Transform. Symmetry is calculated at multiple octaves and scales. At the first octave, $o = -1$, the image is double its original size. For every next octave, the image is down-scaled by a factor two. Within an octave there are three scales with progressive Gaussian blurring. For every image in the image pyramid, the symmetry response, $\psi_r(o, s)$, is calculated at three different radii by applying the symmetry operator. The average of these responses results in the symmetry map, $\Psi(o, s)$. In the last step, the interest points are obtained by finding points that have a local maximal or minimal symmetry value. The local neighborhood of such an interest point is described by the SIFT descriptor.

where p_+ and p_- are rounded to the nearest pixel. Subsequently, an orientation projection map, O_r, and a magnitude projection map, M_r, are built. Initially, all values in these maps are set to zero. Then, for every pixel p, the maps are updated according to:

$$O_r(p_+) = O_r(p_+) + 1 \, , \, O_r(p_-) = O_r(p_-) - 1 \tag{4}$$

$$M_r(p_+) = M_r(p_+) + G_{o,s}(p) \, , \, M_r(p_-) = M_r(p_-) - G_{o,s}(p) \tag{5}$$

Finally, the symmetry map for radius r at octave o and scale s is determined by:

$$\psi_r(o, s) = F_r * A_r \tag{6}$$

and

$$F_r(p) = M_r(p) \cdot O_r(p)/k_r \tag{7}$$

where $O_r(p)$ has a upper value of k_r, and a lower value of $-k_r$. k_r has been experimentally established in [21] at $k_r = 8$ for $r = 1$, and $k_r = 9.9$ otherwise. A_r is a Gaussian kernel of size $r \times r$ with a standard deviation of $0.25r$.

This gives us the symmetry response $\psi_r(o, s)$ for the radius r at octave o and scale s. By averaging the symmetry responses over all radii in $\mathcal{R}_s$, according to equation (1), we obtain the full symmetry response at octave o and scale s, $\Psi(o, s)$.

Next, the interest points in every octave and scale are determined by finding the points in $\Psi(o, s)$ that are either a maximum or a minimum in the neighborhood of 11×11 pixels. Each interest point i found in the symmetry maps is stored. We store the

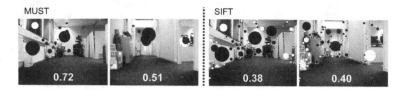

Fig. 3. Two examples images with the MUST and SIFT interest points. The black circles present the stable interest points that are found in both the current and the previous image. The white circles depict the unstable interest points that are only found in the current image. The proportion of stable points is given at the bottom.

following information: (a) the location of the interest point in the original resolution of the input image, $\mathbf{x}_i = (x_i, y_i)$, (b) its scale value, $\sigma_i = 2^{o_i + s_i/s_{max}}$, (c) its symmetry strength, $v_i = \Psi(o_i, s_i, \mathbf{x}_i)$, (d) its orientation, γ_i, and (e) the descriptor of the interest point, $\mathbf{d}_i$. The later two are described in the next paragraph.

To calculate the orientation and the descriptor of the interest points, we use the corresponding methods of the SIFT algorithm [4]. The orientation of the interest point is determined by finding the dominant gradient in the local neighborhood of the interest point. This orientation is used to obtain a rotationally invariant descriptor of the local neighborhood patch. The neighborhood is described by histograms of gradients. The size of the neighborhood depends on the scale value of the interest point. This makes that the descriptor is also scale invariant. To calculate the histograms of gradients. the patch is divided in 4 by 4 squares. A histogram of gradients is then calculated for each square. Since there are 16 squares, and each histogram contains 8 bins, this gives us a feature vector with 128 values. The magnitude of the feature vector is normalized to 512. For more detailed information about the method to calculate the descriptor, we refer to [4].

Figure 3 shows the interest points found by MUST on two of the images used in our experiments as compared to the SIFT interest points. Note that SIFT results in a large number of interest points, of which many are unstable. MUST, on the other hand, results in less, but more stable points.

2.2 The Visual Buffer

Both MUST and SIFT result in a large number of interest points when applied to the camera images taken by the robot. In our experiments, MUST detects on average 40 interest points per image, and SIFT 124. To be practically usable, the state matrix of the Extended Kalman Filter should contain a few hundred landmarks in total. Furthermore, most interest points are unstable, and therefore useless for SLAM. We propose a visual buffer test the stability of the interest points, similar to [2,5].

The buffer contains the last N camera images. The interest points in the current image are compared to those in the $N-1$ previous images. An interest point i passes the buffer if it meets two criteria: 1) The point matches in at least M of the previous images. Two points, i and j, match when the descriptors, $\mathbf{d}_i$ and $\mathbf{d}_j$, are sufficiently similar. This is true when the Euclidean distance is below the threshold τ_1: $\|\mathbf{d}_i - \mathbf{d}_j\| < \tau_1$, and when the *best-to-next-best ratio* is smaller than the threshold δ_1: $\|\mathbf{d}_i - \mathbf{d}_j\|/\|\mathbf{d}_i - \mathbf{d}_l\| < \delta_1$, where $\mathbf{d}_l$ is the descriptor of the second most-similar region in the previous image. This ratio ensures uniqueness. Additionally, to avoid spurious interest points, the symmetry strength of the interest point should be $v_i \geq \lambda \cdot v_{max}$, where v_{max} is the strength of the most symmetrical point that is successfully matched in the current image, 2) The estimates of the position of the landmark in the environment are congruent. The landmark's position is estimated by triangulation using the bearings of the interest point in the current image and the previous images, and the displacement of the robot. This results in a set of estimates of the range and bearing, $P = \{\mathbf{p}_k | \mathbf{p}_k = \langle r_k, \theta_k \rangle \wedge 1 \leq k \leq K\}$. The landmark is accepted if $\mathrm{var}(R) < \rho$, where var is the variance, and $R = r_k$.

2.3 Visual SLAM

We use a standard implementation of the Extended Kalman Filter (EKF) as basis of the SLAM system [22]. Our method and results, however, are also valid for other SLAM approaches. We will not discuss the full EKF method, rather only the incorporation of the landmark observations.

A landmark i with descriptor $\mathbf{d}_i$ that results from the buffer is classified as either a new landmark, or a previously observed landmark that is already in the map. It concerns a previously observed landmark if the landmark in the database with the most similar descriptor, $\mathbf{d}_j$, fulfills three criteria: 1) Similarity in descriptors: $\|\mathbf{d}_i - \mathbf{d}_j\| < \tau_2$, 2) A small best-to-next-best ratio to only match unique landmarks δ_2: $\|\mathbf{d}_i - \mathbf{d}_j\|/\|\mathbf{d}_i - \mathbf{d}_l\| < \delta_2$, where $\mathbf{d}_l$ is the second most similar descriptor in the database, 3) A small distance in the EKF map, measured by the Mahalanobis distance: $\sqrt{(\mathbf{x}_i - \mathbf{x}_j)^T \mathbf{S}_j^{-1} (\mathbf{x}_i - \mathbf{x}_j)} < \eta$, where $\mathbf{S}_j$ is the uncertainty covariance matrix, discussed in the next paragraph.

The landmark is classified as new only if none of the three criteria is fulfilled. For a new landmark, the state matrix and covariance matrix are augmented using the observation, $\mathbf{z}_i$, and the uncertainty covariance matrix, $\mathbf{S}_i$, where $\mathbf{z}_i$ is set to mean(P), and $\mathbf{S}_i$ is determined using the uncertainty of the observation, cov(P), and the uncertainty of the robot's position in the EKF. When a landmark is matched with an existing landmark in the database, $\mathbf{z}_i$ and $\mathbf{S}_i$ are used to update the EKF.

3 Experiments

We performed a number of experiments with a Pioneer II DX robot equipped with a Sony D31 camera to test the use of local symmetry for visual SLAM and to compare it to using standard SIFT. To be able to repeat the experiments, we created a SLAM database. This database contains camera images and odometry information, along with the ground truth position of the robot. The data was recorded in ten different runs, in which the robot drove four laps of approximately 35 meters through an office environment and hallway with an average speed of 0.3 m/s. Camera images of 320 x 240 pixels were stored at 5 Hz. At intervals of one meter, the true location of the robot was logged by hand. This enabled us to quantify the performance of the SLAM estimation.

SIFT and MUST result in different types of interest points, which might have an influence on the best settings for the other parameters in the SLAM system. We therefore optimized the parameters for the visual buffer (N, M, τ_1, δ_1, and ρ) and for the SLAM system (τ_2 and δ_2) for both MUST and SIFT separately. Any differences in performance can therefore be subscribed to the interest-point detectors.

3.1   Robustness

To test the performance of our model for landmark selection in indoor environments, we took images from one of the runs in our database with intervals of 3 meters to represent the complete environment. To test the noise robustness of MUST, we smoothed the image with a Gaussian kernel, and added Gaussian noise to the pixels. In addition, we manipulated the contrast and brightness of the images to test the robustness to changing light conditions[1]. The reason to not use the dataset in [23] is that it contains images of outdoor scenes, which contain fewer symmetrical objects than indoor environments.

The robustness is measured by the proportion of matching interest points between the original and the manipulated images. Two interest points match when criterion 1 of the visual buffer (see Sect. 2.2) is met, where $\tau_1 = 0.6$ and $\delta_1 = 0.75$. Additionally, the distance between the two points in the image should be less than 3 pixels.

3.2   Repeatability

For good SLAM performance, it is crucial that landmarks added to the map are observable on future encounters. We therefore test the repeatability of the interest points. For every experimental run, we selected three parts of the robot's trajectory, and aligned the sequences of images of the four consecutive laps that are approximately at the same position. The interest points in the images in the first lap are then compared to the images taken at approximately the same position in the later laps.

The average proportion of interest points that are matched in lap 2, 3, and 4 is the measure of repeatability. An interest point matches when criterion 1 of the visual buffer is met (see section 2.2), where where $\tau_1 = 0.6$ and $\delta_1 = 0.75$. Unlike the evaluation of the robustness, we do not put a constraint on the spatial distance between the two observed interest points, since there is variation in the exact position and orientation of the robot. This may cause relatively large displacements of the interest points.

3.3   Visual SLAM Performance

Because we logged the ground-truth position of the robot at intervals of 1 meter, we can quantify the performance of the complete visual SLAM system. For that, we compare the estimated position of the robot made by the EKF with the ground-truth position. The SLAM performance is the average Euclidean distance between the estimated and ground-truth positions in the last of the four laps.

---

[1] The functions used for the manipulations are: (1) *Gaussian pixel noise*: $I'(x,y) = I(x,y) + X(\alpha_g)$, where $I(x,y) \in [0,1]$ is the intensity of pixel (x,y), and $X(\alpha_g)$ is a random sample from the normal distribution $N(0, \alpha_g^2)$. (2) *Gaussian smoothing*: $I' = I * G_s$, where G_s is a Gaussian mask of size $s \times s$, with a standard deviation of $\sigma = s/6$. (3) *Contrast manipulation*: $I'(x,y) = I(x,y) + \alpha_c \left(I(x,y) - \bar{I}_{x,y} \right)$, where $\bar{I}_{x,y}$ is the local average in a neighborhood of 21×21 pixels around pixel (x,y). The contrast for $\alpha_c > 0$, and decreases otherwise. (4) *Brightness manipulation*: $'(x,y) = I(x,y)^{\log \alpha_b / \log 0.5}$. For $\alpha > 0.5$, the pixels are brightened, for $\alpha < 0.5$, the pixels are darkened.

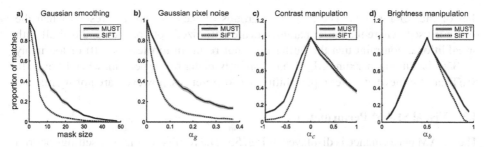

Fig. 4. Robustness to noise and changing light condition. The lines show the mean proportion of matching interest points between the distorted and the original images over 57 runs. The gray areas around the lines display the 98% confidence intervals. Note that these intervals are small, and therefore not very visible.

4 Results

4.1 Robustness

Figure 4 shows the robustness results. The proportion of matching interest points between the original and the manipulated images are displayed on the y-axis. In Fig. 4a and 4b, the results for the addition of noise are given. MUST is significantly less affected by the noise than SIFT. The performance of MUST is more than twice that of SIFT, making it much more robust to noise. Figure 4c shows the performance with respect to contrast manipulation. Although the performance of both methods is similar for the contrast enhancement, MUST shows a significantly better performance when the contrast is reduced. Also with enhanced brightness the use of MUST results in considerably better performance (see Fig. 4d). There is no difference with reduced brightness.

4.2 Repeatability

The repeatability results can be appreciated in Fig. 5a. The first two bars show the repeatability results for all detected interest points, in other words when the visual buffer is not used. The repeatability of the MUST interest points is significantly higher then

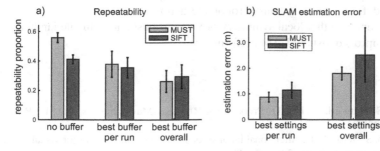

Fig. 5. a) The mean repeatability proportion over the ten runs. The error bars give the 95% confidence intervals. b) The mean estimation error over the ten runs. The 95% confidence intervals are represented by the error bars.

that of the SIFT points. The two other groups of bars display the results when the buffer is used, where the buffer parameters are optimized both per run and overall with an additional contraint that the buffer does not result in too few (< 50) or too many (> 350) landmarks per run. MUST has a slightly better result per run, whereas overall, SIFT has a somewhat better repeatability. The differences, however, are not significant.

4.3   Visual SLAM Performance

The SLAM performance is displayed in Fig. 5b. The results for the best settings per run show that MUST results in a significantly lower estimation error. Also when the overall best settings are used, MUST performs significantly better than SIFT. This suggests that MUST selects better quality landmarks.

Not only does MUST result in better performance, it also reduces the amount of selected landmarks. MUST selects on average 40 interest points per image, and SIFT 124. This greatly reduces the number of computations in the matching process, which is quadratic in the number if interest points. Since both models are similarly fast in detecting interest points in the images, the full SLAM system is faster using MUST.

5   Discussion

In this paper, we proposed a new interest point detector, MUST, for landmark selection based on local symmetry. The model exploits the presence of symmetrical forms in indoor environments. The interest points selected by our model are less sensitive to noise and changing light conditions and more stable than points selected on the basis of contrast by the SIFT model [4]. The repeatability of all selected interest points is higher for our model than for SIFT. Most importantly, the use of symmetry results in better visual SLAM performance. This shows that exploiting symmetry results in valuable and robust landmarks for the representation of the environment. Moreover, MUST results in less interest points, which improves the processing time of the SLAM system.

Although the visual buffer successfully reduces the number of landmarks in the map, its effectiveness can be further enhanced, judging from the fact that the repeatability drops when the visual buffer is used.

Symmetry detection can results in the selection of complete objects. This could result in semantically more meaningful landmarks and maps of the environment, which could be exploited, for instance, in human-robot interaction.

We can conclude that local symmetry provides robust and valuable landmarks, that results in improved visual SLAM performance.

References

1. Thrun, S., Burgard, W., Fox, D.: Probabilistic Robotics, Massachusetts. The MIT Press, Cambridge (2005)
2. Frintrop, S., Jensfelt, P.: Attentional landmarks and active gaze control for visual slam. IEEE Transactions on Robotics 24(5) (2008)
3. Davison, A.J., Reid, I.D., Molton, N.D., Stasse, O.: Monoslam: Real-time single camera slam. IEEE Transactions on Pattern Analysis and Machine Intelligence 29(6), 1–16 (2007)

4. Lowe, D.G.: Distinctive image features from scale-invariant keypoints. International Journal of Computer Vision 60(2), 91–110 (2004)
5. Se, S., Lowe, D.G., Little, J.: Mobile robot localization and mapping with uncertainty using scale-invariant visual landmarks. International Journal of Robotics Research 21(8), 735–758 (2002)
6. Bay, H., Tuytelaars, T., Van Gool, L.: SURF: Speeded up robust features. In: Leonardis, A., Bischof, H., Pinz, A. (eds.) ECCV 2006. LNCS, vol. 3951, pp. 404–417. Springer, Heidelberg (2006)
7. Murillo, A.C., Guerrero, J.J., Sagues, C.: Surf features for efficient robot localization with omnidirectional images. In: IEEE International Conference on Robotics and Automation (ICRA), Rome, Italy, pp. 3901–3907 (2007)
8. Davison, A.J., Murray, D.: Simultaneous localization and map-building using active vision. IEEE Transactions on Pattern Analysis and Machine Intelligence 24(7), 865–880 (2002)
9. Mozos, Ó.M., Gil, A., Ballesta, M., Reinoso, O.: Interest point detectors for visual SLAM. In: Borrajo, D., Castillo, L., Corchado, J.M. (eds.) CAEPIA 2007. LNCS (LNAI), vol. 4788, pp. 170–179. Springer, Heidelberg (2008)
10. Moreels, P., Perona, P.: Evaluation of features detectors and descriptors based on 3d objects. International Journal of Computer Vision 73(3), 263–284 (2007)
11. Palmer, S.E., Hemenway, K.: Orientation and symmetry: Effects of multiple, rotational, and near symmetries. Journal of Experimental Psychology: Human Perception and Performance 4(4), 691–702 (1978)
12. Kootstra, G., Nederveen, A., de Boer, B.: Paying attention to symmetry. In: Everingham, M., Needham, C., Fraile, R. (eds.) British Machine Vision Conference (BMVC 2008), Leeds, UK, pp. 1115–1125 (2008)
13. Kootstra, G., Schomaker, L.R.: Prediction of human eye fixations using symmetry. In: Cognitive Science Conference (CogSci), Amsterdam, NL (2009)
14. Driver, J., Baylis, G.C., Rafal, R.D.: Preserved figure-ground segregation and symmetry perception in visual neglect. Nature 360, 73–75 (1992)
15. Itti, L., Koch, C., Niebur, E.: A model of saliency-based visual attention for rapid scene analysis. IEEE Transactions on Pattern Analysis and Machine Intelligence 20(11), 1254–1259 (1998)
16. Marola, G.: Using symmetry for detecting and locating objects in a picture. Computer Vision, Graphics, and Image Processing 46, 179–195 (1989)
17. Backer, G., Mertsching, B., Bollmann, M.: Data- and model-driven gaze control for an active-vision system. IEEE Transactions on Pattern Analysis and Machine Intelligence 23(12), 1415–1429 (2001)
18. Sela, G., Levine, M.D.: Real-time attention for robotic vision. Real-Time Imaging 3, 173–194 (1997)
19. Heidemann, G.: Focus-of-attention from local color symmetries. IEEE Transactions on Pattern Analysis and Machine Intelligence 26(7), 817–830 (2004)
20. Reisfeld, D., Wolfson, H., Yeshurun, Y.: Context free attentional operators: The generalized symmetry transform. International Journal of Computer Vision 14, 119–130 (1995)
21. Loy, G., Zelinsky, A.: Fast radial symmetry for detecting points of interest. IEEE Transactions on Pattern Analysis and Machine Intelligence 25(8), 959–973 (2003)
22. Durrant-Whyte, H., Bailey, T.: Simultaneous localization and mapping: Part I. Simultaneous localization and mapping: Part I. 13(2), 99–108 (2006)
23. Mikolajczyk, K., Tuytelaars, T., Schmid, C., Zisserman, A., Matas, J., Schaffalitzky, F., Kadir, T., Van Gool, L.: A comparison of affine region detectors. International Journal of Computer Vision 65(1/2), 43–72 (2005)

Combining Color, Depth, and Motion for Video Segmentation

Jérôme Leens[2], Sébastien Piérard[1], Olivier Barnich[1],
Marc Van Droogenbroeck[1], and Jean-Marc Wagner[2]

[1] INTELIG Laboratory, Montefiore Institute, University of Liège, Belgium
[2] Haute École de la Province de Liège, Département Ingénieur Industriel, Belgium

Abstract. This paper presents an innovative method to interpret the content of a video scene using a depth camera. Cameras that provide distance instead of color information are part of a promising young technology but they come with many difficulties: noisy signals, small resolution, and ambiguities, to cite a few.

By taking advantage of the robustness to noise of a recent background subtraction algorithm, our method is able to extract useful information from the depth signals. We further enhance the robustness of the algorithm by combining this information with that of an RGB camera. In our experiments, we demonstrate this increased robustness and conclude by showing a practical example of an immersive application taking advantage of our algorithm.

1 Introduction

One of the main tasks in computer vision is the interpretation of video sequences. Traditionally, methods rely on grayscale or color data to infer semantic information.

In the past few years, new methods based on *Time-of-Flight* cameras have emerged. These cameras, hereinafter referred to as *ToF* (or *range*) cameras, produce low-resolution *range* images (also called *depth maps*), whose values indicate the distance between a pixel of the camera sensor and an object. Although distances measured by ToF cameras are relevant from a physical point of view, the technology has its own limitations: (1) since the size of a pixel on the sensor plane is larger than with a CCD camera, the resolution is relatively small, (2) distances are not measured precisely, (3) the calibration procedure is difficult, and (4) surface properties influence the reflections on objects, and consequently affect the measured distances.

To our knowledge, there is no theoretical model that embraces all the issues related to the acquisition of range data, but this hasn't stopped some companies to deliver products based on ToF cameras. Figure 1 shows a 3D model extracted from a range sensor; that model is used for an interactive game. For such an application, a complete 3D model of the scene cannot be deduced from the sole range image of a ToF camera. For example, there is no way to estimate the thickness of an object from a frontal depth map. Consequently, an elaborated

M. Fritz, B. Schiele, and J.H. Piater (Eds.): ICVS 2009, LNCS 5815, pp. 104–113, 2009.
© Springer-Verlag Berlin Heidelberg 2009

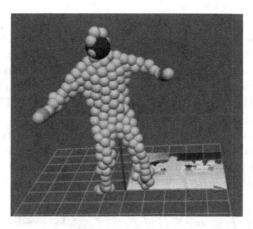

Fig. 1. A 3D model reconstructed from a range image (image reproduced with the permission of SOFTKINETIC http://www.softkinetic.net)

model is required for an application that handles 3D objects in conjunction with ToF cameras.

In this paper, we detail a different approach that deals with pixels instead of objects. Such a pixel-based method allows to limit the number of assumptions about the scene and ignores the notion of any 3D model. More precisely, we aim to analyze the dynamic content of a scene by applying a background subtraction technique on a depth map. Our method is complementary to 3D model-based approaches as it can be used as a pre-processing step to locate objects in the foreground.

Background subtraction consists in separating pixels belonging to the background, where no motion is detected, from pixels of moving objects contained in the foreground. Silvestre [1] has briefly compared several background subtraction techniques on range maps for the purpose of video-surveillance. However, if one aims at an interactive application, it might not be sufficient to accurately segment the users, especially when they are located close to background objects. This is a similar problem to the confusion between background and foreground color occurring with color cameras: if a person's colors match those of the background, the person cannot be correctly detected.

In this paper, we propose to counter the aforementioned problems by combining depth and color information to enhance the robustness of a background subtraction algorithm.

We discuss the principles and limitations of Time-of-Flight cameras in Sec. 2 and 3. In Sec. 4, we explain how to combine motion detections coming from different modalities. Experimental results are given in Sec. 5. Section 6 concludes the paper.

2   Principles of Time-of-Flight Cameras

Time-of-Flight (ToF) cameras have already been described in several technical publications [1,2,3,4] and, therefore, we limit our discussions to the basic principles of PMD (Photonic Mixer Device) ToF cameras.

PMD-cameras illuminate the whole scene with an infrared light ($\lambda = 870$ nm) whose envelope is modulated in amplitude: $s(t) = a + b \, \cos(\omega t)^1$ (where $a > b > 0$, t is the time, and ω relates to a modulation frequency of 20 MHz). Each pixel of the sensor receives the sum of a time-delayed and attenuated signal reflected by the scene plus some additional ambient light in a small solid angle. It is assumed that the receiver is only sensitive to infrared. The received signal is thus $r(t) = k_a + k_b \, s(t - \Delta t) = a' + b' \, \cos(\omega(t - \Delta t))$.

In a PMD-camera, the device continuously multiplies the received signal $r(t)$ with 4 internal signals, given by $f_\theta(t) = a + b \, \cos(\omega t + \theta\frac{\pi}{2})$ with $\theta \in \{0, 1, 2, 3\}$, and computes their intercorrelations cor_θ. If the period of integration (shutter time) T is a multiple of $2\pi/\omega = 50$ ns, then

$$\mathrm{cor}_\theta = \frac{1}{T} \int_{<T>} f_\theta(t) r(t) \, dt = aa' + \frac{bb'}{2} \, \cos(\omega \Delta t + \theta \frac{\pi}{2}) \ . \tag{1}$$

The distance d between the camera and the target is estimated by $c \, \Delta t/2$, where $c \simeq 3 \, 10^8$ m/s is the speed of light. It is computed using the four intercorrelation values. Note that there is a distance ambiguity after $\pi c/\omega \simeq 7.5$ m, due to the Δt-periodicity of cor_θ. If j represents the complex number, we have the following estimation for the distance

$$d = c \, \frac{\arg\left(\mathrm{cor}_0 - j \, \mathrm{cor}_1 - \mathrm{cor}_2 + j \, \mathrm{cor}_3\right)}{2 \, \omega} \ . \tag{2}$$

The amplitude b' of the received signal is also provided. It is related to the peak-to-peak amplitude A of the intercorrelations:

$$A = bb' = \sqrt{\left(\mathrm{cor}_0 - \mathrm{cor}_2\right)^2 + \left(\mathrm{cor}_1 - \mathrm{cor}_3\right)^2} \ . \tag{3}$$

It measures the strength of the incoming signal. The amplitude obviously decreases as the distance between the sensor and the object increases. This has led some authors [5] to establish a relationship between A and a grayscale (luminance) image. But this relationship is incorrect in some cases like, for example, clouds seen through a window, where the amplitude A will be equal to 0 to the contrary of the luminance.

The continuous component a' of the received signal is the third information a PMD-camera can provide. It is expressed by the intensity I, and estimated as

$$I = aa' = \frac{\mathrm{cor}_0 + \mathrm{cor}_2}{2} = \frac{\mathrm{cor}_1 + \mathrm{cor}_3}{2} \ . \tag{4}$$

In conclusion, as shown in Fig. 2, a PMD camera provides three values per pixel: d, A and I. These values can be interpreted as follows:

 - d is the estimated distance between the illuminated object and the sensor,
 - A estimates the quality of the signal used for the determination of d, and
 - I is related to the temporal average amount of received infrared light.

---

[1] Several papers wrongly assume that $a = 0$ and establish incorrect equations. This paper gives the correct expressions.

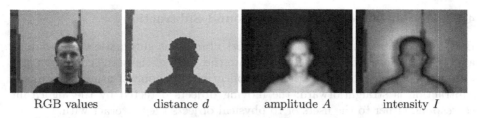

RGB values   distance d amplitude A intensity I

Fig. 2. A color image and the 3 channels provided by a PMD-camera

One must note that the aforementioned interpretations must be handled with care: the intuitive interpretation of the three channels provided by a range camera is, at best, delicate. In the next section, we detail the various limitations that must be taken into account when using a PMD range camera.

3   Limitations of Time-of-Flight Cameras

The signals given by a PMD-camera (d, A and I) are imperfect. Differences exist between the theoretical principle and its implementation: some delays are introduced by the electronics and the wave envelope isn't a perfect sinusoid [3]. Furthermore, a static error, called *wiggling effect*, has been observed on d. It is an oscillating and periodic function of the true distance [2,3]. As noted in [6], a temporal analysis of d shows that its standard deviation is proportional to its mean. Thus, the variance of the noise on d is depth-dependent. [7] showed that both d and A depend on the shutter time T. As of today, there is no available theoretical model explaining all these effects.

Other imperfections come from the scene itself [2]. Because of the low resolution of the sensor, each pixel corresponds to a wide solid angle, leading to errors. Furthermore, the estimated distance depends on the reflectivity and the orientation of the observed object [2]. Moreover, as Fig. 2 shows, artefacts appear in the A and I channels near distance discontinuities. Finally, our experiments showed a dependence of A and I over multi-paths.

Some authors tried to reduce the error on the estimated distances using the information contained in the A or I channels [2,5]. But due to error dependencies, A, I and T should be used simultaneously to correct d. Even then, getting a perfect measure is impossible if the content of the scene is unknown.

4   Combining Depth with Other Modalities

The three channels provided by the PMD-camera are not suited for precise distance measurements, but it is possible to simplify the problem. We model all the defects on the channels as an additive noise and try to recover useful information from these noisy signals using a widely used video segmentation technique: background subtraction, which is described below.

4.1   Motion Detection and Background Subtraction

Background subtraction is one of the most ubiquitous automatic video content analysis technique. Its purpose is to isolate the parts of the scene corresponding to moving objects. For an interactive application, the point of using background subtraction is straightforward: the moving objects detected by the algorithm correspond either to the users or to physical objects they interact with.

Numerous methods for background subtraction have been proposed over the past years (see [8,9] for surveys). From a review of the literature on the subject, it appears that recent *sample-based* techniques [10,11,12] are particularly well-suited for our needs: they are fast, versatile, and resilient to important amounts of noise. Furthermore, these techniques are pixel-based: they analyze the temporal evolution of each pixel independently. As a result, they do not make any assumption about the content of the images they process.

We use the ViBe algorithm presented in [10]. Our main motivation is the robustness to noise exhibited by ViBe as shown in the experiments of [10]. ViBe has other advantages: it is fast, simple to implement and shows a great accuracy on the contours of the silhouettes. Hereinafter we explain our motivations to apply ViBe on conventional color or grayscale images, and on range images separately. Then in Sec. 4.2, we combine both techniques.

Application to a Color or Grayscale Image. For most interactive applications, a background subtraction technique is a useful tool. The sole binary silhouettes of the users can provide sufficient amount of information in simple applications who often take advantage of the high precision of the silhouettes obtained with conventional cameras.

However, the use of RGB or grayscale images has a few intrinsic limitations. Due to the lack of 3D information, the system cannot recognize simple actions such as pointing a finger to an area of the screen. Furthermore, background subtraction itself imposes major restrictions on operating conditions: the illumination of the scene must be controlled and the colors of the users may not match those of the background.

Application to a Range Image. If applied on a range image, background subtraction does not suffer from the two limitations mentioned in the above paragraph. Indeed, the range camera uses its own light source and is only slightly affected by the ambient lighting. It can even be used in complete darkness. Furthermore, since it does not use color information, it is not sensitive to users' colors. Unfortunately, a problem occurs when the users are physically too close to the background of the scene. In such a worst-case situation, it is impossible to discriminate between the objects and the background because of the noisy nature of depth maps. Furthermore, due to the low resolution of the PMD sensor, the use of ViBe on the sole depth map cannot produce precise segmentation.

From the above discussions, it appears that an optimal solution to get robust silhouettes consists in combining the benefits of several motion segmentations obtained from various modalities. In the next section, we present a method to combine both segmentation maps and describe the technical issues raised by such a combination.

4.2 Combining Color, Depth, and Motion

Our experimental setup is made of an RGB-camera and a PMD-camera fixed on a common support, one on top of the other. Both cameras are equipped with similar objectives, but their field of view are different. The first major issue in using a couple of cameras is that of image registration.

Image Registration. With a precise distance channel, we could theoretically link the two focal planes. First, a projective model must be chosen for each camera and internal and external parameters must be computed. The distance estimation then helps to locate which 3D point is projected on the PMD-pixel. This point can be reprojected with the model of the RGB-camera to get the corresponding RGB-pixel. This process is valid as long as no other object stands between the 3D point and the RGB-camera. This correspondence has to be computed for each PMD-pixel.

The two cameras can follow the pin-hole model [13]. Their sensor geometries are similar and their optical systems are identical. The determination of the internal and external parameters of the RGB-camera is a classical problem [14,15]. The calibration of a PMD-camera is more difficult. First, its low resolution (160×120 pixels) makes it difficult to associate a pixel with a 3D point. Unfortunately, there is no way to determine the external parameters without using these correspondences. Second, it is hard to build an appropriate calibration object. A plate with holes is inadequate because there are significant artefacts near the edges. Moreover, many paints don't absorb infrared light (black paintings are not necessarily the best ones). This complicates the determination of the internal parameters.

An alternative to the calibration of both cameras is to establish a static mapping between PMD- and RGB-pixels. Unfortunately, the linearity and the continuity of this mapping are only guaranteed if the observed world is flat or if both cameras share the same optical center.

In our application, a very precise matching is not required and we deliberately want to avoid both an uncertain calibration and any assumptions about to the scene content. This led us to use a static affine mapping between the RGB image and the depth map. From our experiments, it has proven to be sufficient, as the optical centers of both cameras are close to each other and the targets are far from the camera.

Motion Segmentations Combination. We consider the behavior of the background extraction algorithm on the grayscale channel of a color camera and on the different channels of a range camera. An extended case study of the usability of the 4 channels is given in Table 1.

We detect motion on the grayscale image and on each channel of the range camera. Combining the motion maps allows us to deal with most of the practical scenarios. Three practical examples of successful combination follow:

Table 1. Usability of motion detection on the grayscale channel of the color camera and on each channel of the range camera

Operating conditions	grayscale	distance	amplitude	intensity
low target/background contrast	no	yes	yes/no[1]	yes/no[1]
small target to background distance	yes	no	yes/no[2]	yes/no[2]
distance to background larger than 7.5 m	yes	no	yes	yes
low scene illumination	no	yes	yes	yes
fluctuations in scene illumination	no	yes	yes	yes

[1]When the difference in reflectance between the target and the background is small, amplitude and intensity cannot be used if the distance between them is short.
[2]Amplitude and intensity can be used if the difference in reflectance between the target and the background is large.

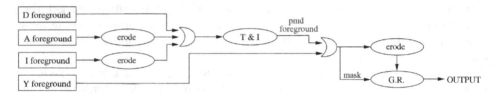

Fig. 3. Complete description of our method. *"G.R."* stands for *"Geodesic Reconstruction"* and *"T&I"* stands for *"Transformation and Interpolation"*.

1. If the target is physically close the background and the scene illumination is low, distance and grayscale information are useless for motion segmentation. However, amplitude and intensity channels are still usable if the reflectance properties of the background and the target differ.
2. Under low illumination conditions or when the targets and the background looks similar, depth is a meaningful channel for motion detection.
3. Background subtraction on the luminance channel is impossible in presence of large fluctuations of the scene illumination, but the channels of a PMD-camera are not perturbed by this phenomenon.

The complete segmentation process is drawn in Fig. 3. To refine the segmentation maps near the edges, the motion masks of I and A are eroded. An affine transform is used to map the images generated from the two cameras. A logical (non-exclusive) "or" is used to combine the different foregrounds and noise is removed by morphological filtering.

5 Results and Application

This section presents some segmentation results. We also illustrate our method by projecting the segmented depth map and RGB texture in a 3D engine.

5.1   Motion Segmentation Results

As shown on Fig. 4, users too close to the background cannot be correctly segmented given the sole depth map. As a matter of fact, the minimal distance at which the detection becomes possible is conditioned by the amount of noise present in the depth channel. However, by taking advantage of the grayscale image, our algorithm manages to successfully segment those users.

Figure 5 illustrates a case with poor motion detections for all the modalities. Since most of the locations of the segmentation errors differ for each modality, the proposed method showed to be able to produce accurate results, even in such a pathological situation.

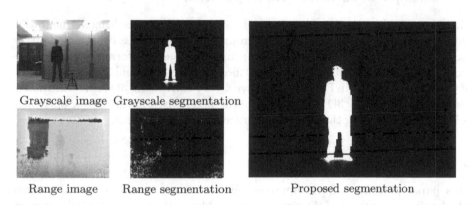

Fig. 4. This figure shows that the failure of the background subtraction algorithm in one of the used modalities (*range* in this case) does not harm the motion detection resulting from the proposed fusion method

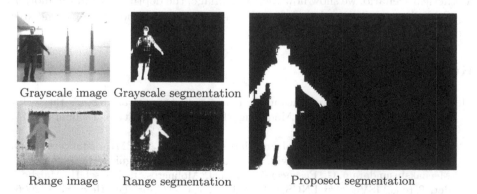

Fig. 5. Even when none of the used modalities produces a satisfactory motion detection, the proposed fusion method is still able to successfully segment the video stream

Fig. 6. Application of the proposed algorithm in an immersive application. The depth signal serves to construct a mesh and an RGB texture is mapped on that mesh.

5.2   Example of an Immersive Application

Finally we combine in real time the depth signal with the resulting segmentation map to project users in a virtual 3D environment. A 3D mesh is constructed on the basis of the segmented depth signal. By using the affine transform described previously to map the RGB image onto the 3D mesh, we create a valid 3D representation of the scene. As show in Fig. 6, we achieve a very convincing 3D representation of the scene without any 3D model, despite the pixel-based nature of our approach. It is worth mentioning that the whole process runs in real time.

6   Conclusions

This paper presents a novel approach for the interpretation of a video scene which takes advantages of the signals provided by a PMD Time-of-Flight camera. By combining these signals with those of a RGB camera and processing them with a background subtraction algorithm, we are able to extract meaningful information from the depth signals, despite their noisy nature. As a showcase for a practical scenario, we show how the RGB image, the depth map and the motion segmentation can be combined for an interactive application or an immersive human-machine interface.

References

1. Silvestre, D.: Video surveillance using a time-of-flight camera. Master's thesis, Informatics and Mathematical Modelling, Technical University of Denmark, DTU (2007)
2. Lindner, M., Kolb, A.: Lateral and depth calibration of PMD-distance sensors. In: Bebis, G., Boyle, R., Parvin, B., Koracin, D., Remagnino, P., Nefian, A., Meenakshisundaram, G., Pascucci, V., Zara, J., Molineros, J., Theisel, H., Malzbender, T. (eds.) ISVC 2006. LNCS, vol. 4292, pp. 524–533. Springer, Heidelberg (2006)
3. Lindner, M., Kolb, A.: Calibration of the intensity-related distance error of the PMD TOF-camera. In: SPIE: Intelligent Robots and Computer Vision XXV, vol. 6764, pp. 6764–35 (2007)
4. Blais, F.: Review of 20 years of range sensor development. Journal of Electronic Imaging 13(1), 231–243 (2004)

5. Oprisescu, S., Falie, D., Ciuc, M., Buzuloiu, V.: Measurements with ToF cameras and their necessary corrections. In: International Symposium on Signals, Circuits and Systems (ISSCS), pp. 1–4 (July 2007)
6. Falie, D., Buzuloiu, V.: Noise characteristics of 3D time-of-flight cameras. In: International Symposium on Signals, Circuits and Systems (ISSCS), July 2007 vol. 1, pp. 1–4 (2007)
7. Radmer, J., Fusté, P., Schmidt, H., Krüger, J.: Incident light related distance error study and calibration of the PMD-range imaging camera. In: Society, I.C. (ed.) Conference on Computer Vision and Pattern Recognition, Piscataway, NJ, pp. 23–28 (2008)
8. Piccardi, M.: Background subtraction techniques: a review. In: Proceedings of the IEEE International Conference on Systems, Man and Cybernetics, vol. 4, pp. 3099–3104 (2004)
9. Radke, R., Andra, S., Al-Kofahi, O., Roysam, B.: Image change detection algorithms: A systematic survey. IEEE transactions on Image Processing 14(3), 294–307 (2005)
10. Barnich, O., Van Droogenbroeck, M.: ViBe: a powerful random technique to estimate the background in video sequences. In: International Conference on Acoustics, Speech, and Signal Processing (ICASSP 2009), April 2009, pp. 945–948 (2009)
11. Elgammal, A., Harwood, D., Davis, L.: Non-parametric model for background subtraction. In: Vernon, D. (ed.) ECCV 2000. LNCS, vol. 1843, pp. 751–767. Springer, Heidelberg (2000)
12. Wang, H., Suter, D.: A consensus-based method for tracking: Modelling background scenario and foreground appearance. Pattern Recognition 40(3), 1091–1105 (2007)
13. Fuchs, S., May, S.: Calibration and registration for precise surface reconstruction with ToF cameras. In: DAGM Dyn3D Workshop (September 2007)
14. Hartley, R., Zisserman, A.: Multiple View Geometry in Computer Vision, 2nd edn. Cambridge University Press, Cambridge (2004)
15. Zhang, Z.: A flexible new technique for camera calibration. IEEE Transactions on Pattern Analysis and Machine Intelligence 22(11), 1330–1334 (2000)

Stable Structural Deformations

Karin Engel and Klaus Toennies

Otto-von-Guericke University Magdeburg, Germany

Abstract. Recently, we introduced a hierarchical finite element model in the context of structural image segmentation. Such model deforms from its equilibrium shape into similar shapes under the influence of both, image–based forces and structural forces, which serve the propagation of deformations across the hierarchy levels. Such forces are very likely to result in large (rotational) deformations, which yield under the linear elasticity model artefacts and thus poor segmentation results. In this paper, we provide results indicating that different implementations of the stiffness warping method can be successfully combined to simulate dependent rotational deformations correctly, and in an efficient manner.

1 Introduction

In many applications, such as object recognition, tracking and medical image segmentation, specific shapes of arbitrary complexity have to be detected in images. The shape decomposition approach allows representing objects of similar types (shape classes) using a combination of a set of basis functions, where the basis can be either pre–defined in an a priori manner [1] or obtained via training [2]. If, however, the object deforms in a non–linear manner, invalid shapes may result when the model parameters are chosen independently. Shape models that include a structural decomposition of the object into parts and a description of parts and relations between them are especially suitable for representing valid non–linear variation in a shape class as indicated by [3,4,5,6,7,8,9,10,11], among others. In [12], we introduced a hierarchical decomposition approach, which extends the ability of finite element models (FEM) of shape in the sense that it enables structural variability in terms of elastic co–variations between specific deformable shapes. The resulting shape description allows to separately analyse the deformation behavior of shapes and their structural relations, while the different levels of the shape hierarchy can influence each other during the segmentation process. A significant result of using finite element vibration modes in the shape–structure hierarchy is that it combines noise robustness from deformable shape models and validation of structure from structural models without the need for training as with probabilistic structural models, e.g. [5,6,7,9].

An energy–minimising prototypical shape model can deform from its equilibrium shape into similar shapes under the influence of forces [14, 1]. Since the structural interpretation of images is an ill–posed problem, whose solution does not continuously depend of the data and which has many possible solutions, our approach for regularised partial matching employs a shape hierarchy. In our

M. Fritz, B. Schiele, and J.H. Piater (Eds.): ICVS 2009, LNCS 5815, pp. 114–123, 2009.

case, the parametrisation of shape parts is determined by a set of constraints corresponding to finite element vibration modes given by a shape model from a preceding hierarchy level. As a result, complex deformations can be described by a superposition of hierarchically dependent displacement fields defined over linear sub–shape regions. The linear elasticity model that is commonly used in real–time animations of deformable objects is, however, not invariant to rigid body transformations, i.e. not stable. In order to avoid artefacts due to large rotational deformations (such as an increase in volume), the stiffness warping method can be applied to factor out the effect of local rotations [15, 1, 16]. In this paper, we introduce the stiffness warping in the context of structural image analysis, and adapt its principles to hierarchical FEM. We will show that our implementation allows for improving the shape–structure interactions in an efficient simulation of non–linear deformations.

This paper is structured as follows. In section 2.1 we briefly introduce our shape model for use in part–based recognition, and describe how such model can be build in section 2.2. Section 2.3 describes the hierarchical shape matching and the proposed hierarchical stiffness warping is introduced in section 2.4. Finally, we present case studies for applying our model to recognition and classification tasks and analyse the improvements over [12] in section 3. A conclusion is drawn in section 4 along with suggestions for further research.

2   Method

Our method builds on the assumption that valid instances of the desired compound object can be reconstructed from a set of a-priori constrained model parameters. We therefore employ the hierarchical finite element decomposition of shape. The quality of such a model instance projected into the image domain and deformed according to (image–based) external forces can be evaluated in a straightforward manner and provides contextual shape information for eliminating false interpretations of the data in a top–down manner.

For simulating rotational deformations correctly, the stiffness warping method effectively re-references each finite element to its initial pose at each time step of the deformable simulation. Here this principle is adapted such that stable deformations due to linear elastic forces can be efficiently computed by exploiting the hierarchical shape constraints.

2.1   Hierarchical Decomposition–Based Shape Modelling

A parametric deformable template $\mathcal{T}(\mathbf{p})$ represents the objects undeformed shape (rest shape or equilibrium shape) and a set of parameters $\mathbf{p}$ that define how it deforms under applied forces. In our case, the rest shape of a n–dimensional object is modelled as a continuous domain $\Omega \subset \mathbb{R}^n$. Its deformation is described by a boundary value partial differential equation, which is solved for the unknown displacement field $u(\mathbf{x})$, $\mathbf{x} \in \Omega$ using the finite element method [14]. It yields an algebraic function that relates the deformed positions $\mathbf{x}(t) = \mathbf{x}(0) + \mathbf{u}(t)$

of all finite element nodes to the forces acting on the deformable template. The dynamic equilibrium equation has the form

$$\frac{\partial^2 \mathbf{u}}{\partial t^2}\Big|_{t>0} = \mathbf{M}^{-1}\Big(-\mathbf{C}\frac{\partial \mathbf{u}}{\partial t}\Big|_{t>0} - \mathbf{K}\mathbf{u}(t) + \mathbf{f}(t)\Big), \tag{1}$$

where $\mathbf{K}$ encapsulates the stiffness properties as well as the type of mesh and discretisation used, $\mathbf{u}(t) = u(\mathbf{x}, t)$ and $\mathbf{f}(t)$ is a vector of nodal loads. To simplify analysis $\mathbf{C}$ may approximate a velocity–dependent damping force, and $\mathbf{M}$ may represent a constant function of material density. For simulating the deformation of the template, the finite element equations (1) are integrated over time until an equilibrium is reached [14]. The deformed shape $\mathcal{T}(\mathbf{p}^t) = \mathbf{x}(t)$ can be expressed in terms of a linear mixture of $m = m_2 - m_1$ displacement fields,

$$\mathbf{x}(t) = \mathbf{x}(0) + \sum_{k=m_1}^{m_2} \phi_k \mathbf{q}_k(t), \tag{2}$$

where $m_1 \geq 1, m_2 \leq s$, for s degrees of freedom (DOF) of the system. The modal vectors ϕ_k are solutions to the eigenproblem [1],

$$(\mathbf{K} - \omega_k^2 \mathbf{M})\phi_k = 0, \tag{3}$$

and span the *shape space* $\mathcal{S}(\mathcal{T})$ [17], which allows comparing shape instances based on their modal coordinates $\mathbf{q}_k(t)$. Assuming the center of mass at the origin of the local frame of reference, the affine transformation $\theta(\xi), \xi = \{\mathbf{c}, \psi, \mathbf{s}\}$, defines the position $\mathbf{c}$, orientation ψ and scaling $\mathbf{s}$ of a model instance in the image coordinate frame. A model instance can thus be characterised by the vector of affine and non–rigid shape parameters $\mathbf{p}^t = (\xi, \mathbf{q}(t))$.

The preference of a template to deform into specific shapes is in our case imposed by additional constraints in terms of (typically) non–linear transformations of the weight vector $\mathbf{q}$. We employ a *hierarchical mixing* process to model elastic co–variations in shape, such that a hierarchical shape model

$$\mathcal{T}(\mathbf{p}) = \bigcup_{v=1}^{\mathcal{V}} \mathcal{T}_v^{(l)}(\mathbf{p}_v), \tag{4}$$

represents the decomposition of a complex shape into $\mathcal{V}$ discrete shapes, which contribute to different hierarchy levels l. The shape parts at each level $l - 1$ are coupled to form a higher level l of the hierarchical shape model, while any $\mathcal{T}_v^{(l-1)}$ may represent a compound shape on its own. As a result, each compound deformable shape is characterised by a mixture of dependent parameter vectors $\mathbf{p}_v^t$, whose union defines a valid shape region in $\mathcal{S}(\mathcal{T})$.

The desired structural constraints on the dependent displacements at the lower levels are introduced by across–level spring forces subject to specific link nodes that define the boundaries of the top–level finite elements (figure 1). In contrast to [18], this yields a hierarchy of FEM, whose nodes are subject to external model forces, which are derived from the image in a bottom–up fashion, and by employing the deformable model paradigm. More specifically, the structural dependencies are propagated to neighbouring nodes of level l as well as to nodes at consecutive levels (cf. sect. 2.3), such that sub–shape displacements invoke deformations of the top–level shape, and vice versa.

2.2 Model Generation

A prototypical hierarchical model can be specified from domain knowledge by deciding on the decomposition of a shape exemplar into simpler components, e.g. functional shape units such as body parts, and formalising assumptions about the allowed deviation from their equilibrium shape and configuration. Depending on the number and location of the link nodes different structural attributes of a compound shape can be represented by the top–level model, including high–order relations, such as parallelism (figure 1). We employ the following rules for building such hierarchical model based on an example segmentation: First, the sample is decomposed by outlining the shape parts, which are subdivided into geometrically simpler finite elements. Next, the shape parts are mapped to nodes of the top–level model, i.e. compact shapes are mapped to a single top–level node (using a single internal link node), while more elongated shapes whose orientation does not vary arbitrarily might be constrained by at least two top–level nodes (using at least two link nodes). Finally, the top–level model is also triangulated. The decomposition may continue through additional levels yielding a hierarchy of deformable shapes, structures, super–structures, et cetera.

2.3 Hierarchical Shape Matching

A hierarchical shape model deforms from an initial estimate $\mathcal{T}(\mathbf{p}^0)$ into an object instance $\mathcal{T}(\mathbf{p}^t)$ supported by features derived from the image I. In our case, solving equation 1 yields a balance of internal and external forces. The set of parameter values $\mathbf{p}^t$ maximises the quality of fit of model and data, i.e. the deformed model instance represents a locally optimum segmentation result.

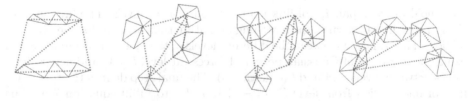

Fig. 1. Examples of hierarchical FEM of two levels. Different structural attributes, e.g. the spatial configuration of the sub–shapes (solid lines), are explicitly defined by the top–level model (dotted lines). In comparison to tree–structured models, such as [7], and coupled shapes, e.g. [18], parallelism (left figure), distant relations and curved shapes (right figure) can be represented.

The external model forces $\mathbf{f}(t)$ are created by a sensor–based sparse sampling of a scalar potential field $\mathcal{P}$, whose local minima coincide with features of interest,

$$\mathbf{f}(t) = -\nabla \mathcal{P}(\mathbf{x}(t)), \tag{5}$$

i.e. Gaussian potential forces [19] can be used for the shapes at the lowest level $l = 1$. The input for the higher level nodes $\mathbf{x}_{w,j}^{(l)}, l > 1$, depends on the behaviour of the underlying morphological FEM at level $l - 1$. Therefore, the deformation energy and the correspondence with the expected image features is measured for the associated shape instance using a combined objective function $\mathcal{Q} \in [0, 1]$ that evaluates the quality of fit. The gradient $\Delta \mathcal{Q}_v \approx \frac{\partial \mathcal{Q}(\mathbf{p}_v, l)}{\partial t}\big|_{t>0}$ is used to set up the across–level spring forces,

$$\mathbf{f}_{w,j}^{(l)}(t) \propto \Delta \mathcal{Q}_v(\mathbf{x}_{v,i}^{(l-1)}(t) - \mathbf{x}_{w,j}^{(l)}(t-1)), \tag{6}$$

where $\mathbf{x}_{v,i}^{(l-1)}(t)$ denotes the current position of the link node i of the associated sub–shape $\mathcal{T}_v^{(l-1)}$.

The hierarchical shape constraints facilitate the initialisation and deformable shape fit as follows: Each global shape model ($l > 1$) restricts the parametrisation of the associated morphological FEM $\mathcal{T}_v^{(l-1)}$ according to the displacements of the top–level nodes. I.e. after initialising an instance of the global model, the instances of the local models are aligned to it by propagating the displacements of the link nodes $\mathbf{x}_{w,j}^{(l)}$ in the global model to the linked low–level nodes $\mathbf{x}_{v,i}^{(l-1)}$. In this case, the displacement of each top–level link node directly affects the DOF associated with a specific low–level link node, and is imposed as a displacement boundary condition (BC) on the particular finite element equations (1). For initialisation (i.e. at time $t = 0$), these equations are solved for the static case, i.e. neglecting inertia and damping forces, such that a single iteration of the hierarchical fit results in a transform $\theta_{vw}(\mathbf{x})$ that maps a point $\mathbf{x}$ defined in the v–th local coordinate frame, to a point in the global coordinate frame defined by top–level shape $\mathcal{T}_w^{(l)}$. In our case, equation

$$\mathbf{x}_{v,i}^{(l-1)}(t) = \theta_{vw}^{-1}(\mathbf{x}_{w,j}^{(l)}(t)), \tag{7}$$

must hold for each pair i, j of link nodes at consecutive levels. The first steps of the iterative hierarchical shape matching algorithm then account for the bottom–up flow of information between the different levels of the model. It is implemented using the hierarchy of Gaussian potential forces (at level $l = 1$) and across–level forces between levels $l-1$ and l (equation 6). The final step defines the top–down flow of information from level l to $l - 1$. In order to fulfill equation 7 at time $t > 0$, this is – similar to the initialisation step – realised through displacement BC on the system of linear discrete equilibrium equations (1).

Thereby, the model naturally considers the relationships between the different shape parts, and we only need to estimate the optimum affine transformation parameters for the top–level model, as well as for all lower level shapes, whose parametrisation is only partially constrained by it. In case of a single link between two shapes, equation 7 constrains only the relative position of the two coordinate frames. Additional initial constraints between pairs of shapes v and w,

$$\mathbf{s}_{w \to v} = \mathbf{s}_w^{-1} \mathbf{s}_v, \quad \psi_{w \to v} = \psi_w - \psi_v, \tag{8}$$

may likewise be implemented in terms of a parametric transform θ_{vw}. This concept allows to improve the specificity (i.e. the ability to exclude invalid shapes) and precision of the model (i.e. the ability to include all valid shapes) without altering its compact representation in terms of a small set of parameters. It also allows for abstract prior models, since alternatively constraints on the relative orientation and scale of shape parts would require the definition of additional link nodes, yielding more complex – and possibly less precise – structural models.

2.4   Hierarchical Stiffness Warping

The linear elasticity model that is commonly used in real–time animations of deformable objects employs the linear Cauchy strain, $\epsilon(u) = \frac{1}{2}(\nabla u + \nabla u^T)$, and provides only a first order approximation at the undeformed state. Large rotational deformations included in a transformation from $\mathbf{x}(0)$ to the deformed nodal positions $\mathbf{x}(t)$ may thus yield artefacts (figure 2), which can be avoided using stiffness warping [15, 1, 16].

This method modifies the stiffness matrix $\mathbf{K}$ at each time step of the simulation in order to factor out the effect of local rotations. The elastic net forces are computed by employing a tensor field that describes the nodal rotations $\mathbf{R}_i$, such that

$$\mathbf{K}_{ij} \mathbf{u}_i(t) = \mathbf{R}_i \sum_{j \in \mathbf{N}_i} \mathbf{K}_{ij} (\mathbf{R}_i^{-1} \mathbf{x}_j(t) - \mathbf{x}_j(0)). \tag{9}$$

The nonzero elements in sub–matrix $\mathbf{K}_{ij} \in \mathbf{K}$ are those for which there is an element boundary, and $\mathbf{N}_i = \{j\}$ denotes the set of nodes adjacent to i.

As an alternative to using for each node the single rotation matrix from an underlying rigid body reference frame [15], the nodal rotations $\mathbf{R}_i$ can be estimated by applying a matrix decomposition on A_i, which is found by solving [20],

$$\sum_{j \in \mathbf{N}_i} \|\mathbf{d}_{ij}(t) - R_i \mathbf{d}_{ij}(0)\|^2 = \min! \leftrightarrow R_i = A_i B_i, \tag{10}$$

where $\mathbf{d}_{ij}(t) = \mathbf{x}_j(t) - \mathbf{x}_i(t), t \geq 0$,

$$A_i = \sum_{j \in \mathbf{N}_i} \mathbf{d}_{ij}(t) \mathbf{d}_{ij}^T(0) \quad \text{and} \quad B_i = \Big(\sum_{j \in \mathbf{N}_i} \mathbf{d}_{ij}(0) \mathbf{d}_{ij}^T(0) \Big)^{-1}.$$

Here both approaches are adopted to efficiently simulate *dependent rotational deformations* correctly. For each shape v of level l, the desired rotation field is estimated using equation 10 based on the relative rotation $\mathbf{R}_v^{(l)}$ w.r.t. the rest directions $\mathbf{d}_{v,ij}^{(l)}(t) = \mathbf{x}_{v,j}^{(l)}(t) - \mathbf{x}_{v,i}^{(l)}(t)$ at $t = 0$. Since, however, the rotational part of the deformation at a node may depend on structural deformations, our

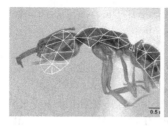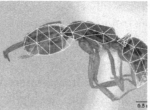

Fig. 2. Large rotational deformations due to structural deformations from the initial estimate (left figure) may in the linear case yield artefacts (middle). These can be avoided using the stiffness warping method (right).

method aims at more efficiently computing the mesh rotation for shapes v whose variation in size and orientation is restricted by the top–level model.

If the global model $\mathcal{T}_w^{(l+1)}$ shares with the local shape $\mathcal{T}_v^{(l)}$ at least two links, which introduce structural constraints in terms of dependent rotation, the rotational part of the sub–shape deformation can be approximated based on the global rigid–body frame of level $l + 1$. More specifically, we use the relative rotation $\mathbf{R}_{w,mn}^{(l+1)}$ based on the rest directions of the particular link nodes m, n of $\mathcal{T}_w^{(l+1)}$, and let

$$\mathbf{K}_{v,ij}^{(l)}\mathbf{u}_{v,i}^{(l)}(t) = \mathbf{R}_{w,mn}^{(l+1)} \sum_{j\in\mathbf{N}_i} \mathbf{K}_{v,ij}^{(l)}\big((\mathbf{R}_{w,mn}^{(l+1)})^{-1}\mathbf{x}_{v,j}^{(l)}(t) - \mathbf{x}_{v,j}^{(l)}(0)\big). \qquad (11)$$

Using the field of nodal rotations w.r.t. the initial orientation of the local and global reference frames, resp., assembled into $\mathbf{R}_v^{(l)}$, the elastic forces can be computed in the non–rotated reference frame based on the pre–computed system matrix for each shape v. Therefore, the stiffness matrix $\mathbf{K}_v^{(l)}$ in equation 1 is replaced at every time step by a warped version, $(\mathbf{R}_v^{(l)})^T\mathbf{K}_v^{(l)}\mathbf{R}_v^{(l)}$.

3   Experimental Evaluation

In our case, the simulation of specific, structurally deformable object instances in images incorporates a small set of link nodes (typically 1–2), which connect the local shapes to the top–level model, is subject across–level forces (equation 6), which serve the propagation of deformations from the top to the lower hierarchy levels. Such structural forces may result in large rotational deformations, which yield artefacts under the linear elasticity model. Evaluating the local rotation for each node is the most expensive operation in the stiffness warping method, because it involves solving equation 10 and computing a polar decomposition. If the rotational part of the local deformation can be estimated from the associated top–level model nodal rotations, we can employ the proposed hierarchical stiffness warping according to equation 11 for linearising the particular restoring forces, and obtaining stable deformations.

To demonstrate the advantages of this approach, we compared it to both, the linear (i.e. non–warped) and the (node–wise) warped stiffness case according to equation 9. In the linear case, the stiffness matrices of all shape models $T_v^{(l)} \subset T$ were evaluated once and used throughout the simulation to compute the internal elastic forces. In the warped stiffness case, we used constant stiffness matrices $\mathbf{K}_v$ and dynamically warped them along the particular rotation fields. In the example applications, we used class–specific hierarchical FEM to represent (A) the lateral views of different ant genera in 2D–colour images[1], and (B) the frontal views of human faces in 2D–colour and grey–scale images[2], respectively.

Sub–shapes, which are constrained in size and orientation by a global model, were modelled in both examples. In case study A, the orientation of the sub–shapes that represent thorax and back of the ants was constrained by the structural model at level $l = 2$. In B for example the orientation of sub–shapes that represent the upper and lower lips were constrained by a top–level model of the mouth ($l = 2$). All experiments have been done setting the elastic moduli to $E = 2, \nu = 0.4$ and the material density to $\rho = 1$, i.e. the volume of the material should not change substantially during the model–based segmentation.

If rotational deformations were not factored out, the resulting segmentations were in many cases insufficient w.r.t. the shape prior. For example, in some cases the volume of the deformed ant shape templates increased by more than 15% w.r.t. the initial references. This resulted in an invalid overlap of sub–shapes and thus over–segmentations of the desired objects (figure 2). Such artefacts were avoided using stiffness warping. In the node–wise warped stiffness case the artefacts w.r.t. volume preservation were at the order of 6%. Similar results were obtained using the hierarchical stiffness warping (figure 3). The difference in the segmentations obtained using equivalent initial estimates was at the order of 1% for the ant segmentations (A), and 3% for the face segmentations (B). We can conclude from these results that the hierarchical method avoids deformation artefacts with similar accuracy.

The stiffness warping yielded an increase in the significance of the criterion Q, which penalises non–affine deformations based on the strain energy associated with the model, and is used in equation 6 to effect the model–based segmentation [12]. As a result, we observed a less divergent behaviour of the shape parts during the hierarchical matching using both the hierarchical and node–wise warping.

However, by applying the hierarchical stiffness warping the convergence of the deformable segmentation was achieved much faster. We computed savings in the number of iterations of the simulations at the order of 40%. The hierarchical method further accelerated the numerical simulation from $67ms$ per step to $30ms$ in case study A, and from $84ms$ per step to $39ms$ in B[3]. We found evidence that the computationally more expensive solution, which requires extracting the

---

[1] Our particular database of 120 images has been obtained from MCZ database by Harvard University and AntWeb by the Californian Academy of Sciences.

[2] To consider variations in pose, illumination and facial expression, 200 example images were collected from The Yale Face Database, BioID Face Database, Calltech Face Database and MIT–CBCL Face Recognition Database.

[3] 3.2 GHz P4, unoptimised Matlab/C–code.

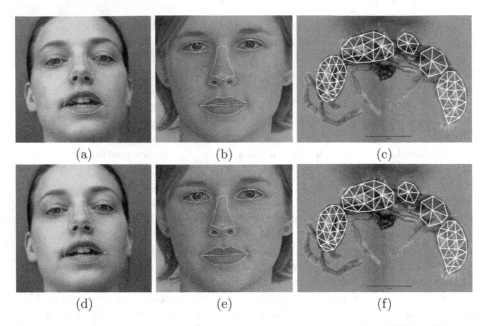

Fig. 3. Typical segmentation results using class–specific hierarchical FEM of human faces and ant genera. The top row provides results in the node–wise warped stiffness case. The results in the bottom row were obtained from the same initial estimates using the hierarchical stiffness warping. Corresponding results in (c) and (f) differ by less than 0.5% in volume.

relative rotation of each node at each hierarchy level, would neither improve the simulated deformations nor the criterion function Q ($p > 0.1$, one–sided t–tests).

4   Conclusion and Outlook

A hierarchical FEM provides a framework for the multi–scale decomposition of complex (and typically non–linear) variation in a specific shape class into dependent displacement fields defined over linear sub–shape regions. In order to obtain stable structural deformations, i.e. a physically plausible dynamic behaviour of a hierarchy of linear FEM, our method employs a strategy for factoring out the effect of rotational deformations. Our results showed that different implementations of the stiffness warping method can be successfully combined to simulate dependent rotational deformations correctly, and in an efficient manner.

For now the applicability of our model to the structural interpretation of images may be restricted to cases where general assumptions on the structural decomposition of the object anatomy can be exploited for identification and combination of the shape parts. Future work will focus on the evaluation of possible decompositions of a particular shape, which may differ within and across hierarchy levels. We believe that the proposed approach for obtaining stable structural deformations will support the evaluation of structural prior models.

References

1. Sclaroff, S., Pentland, A.: Modal matching for correspondence and recognition. IEEE Trans. Patt. Anal. Mach. Intell. 17(6), 545–561 (1995)
2. Cootes, T., et al.: The use of active shape models for locating objects in medical images. Imag. Vis. Comp. 12(16), 355–366 (1994)
3. Pentland, A.: Recognition by parts. In: Proc. IEEE ICCV, pp. 612–620 (1987)
4. Ullman, S., Basri, R.: Recognition by linear combinations of models. IEEE Trans. Patt. Anal. Mach. Intell. 13(10), 992–1005 (1991)
5. Heap, A., Hogg, D.: Improving Specificity in PDMs using a Hierarchical Approach. In: Proc. BMVC, pp. 80–89 (1997)
6. Al-Zubi, S., Toennies, K.D.: Extending active shape models to incorporate a-priori knowledge about structural variability. In: Van Gool, L. (ed.) DAGM 2002. LNCS, vol. 2449, p. 338. Springer, Heidelberg (2002)
7. Felzenszwalb, P., Huttenlocher, D.: Pictorial structures for object recognition. Int. J. Comp. Vis. 61(1), 55–79 (2003)
8. Ren, X., et al.: Recovering human body configurations using pairwise constraints between parts. In: Proc. IEEE ICCV, pp. 824–831 (2005)
9. Zhe, L., et al.: Hierarchical part–template matching for human detection and segmentation. In: Proc. IEEE ICCV, pp. 1–8 (2007)
10. Wang, Y., Mori, G.: Multiple tree models for occlusion and spatial constraints in human pose estimation. In: Proc. ECCV, pp. 710–724 (2008)
11. Felzenszwalb, P., et al.: A discriminatively trained, multiscale, deformable part model. In: Proc. IEEE CVPR, pp. 1–8 (2008)
12. Engel, K., et al.: A two–level dynamic model for the representation and recognition of cortical folding patterns. In: Proc. IEEE ICIP, pp. 297–300 (2005)
13. Zhu, L., Yuille, A.: A hierarchical compositional system for rapid object detection. In: Proc. NIPS (2005)
14. Pentland, A., Sclaroff, S.: Closed–form solutions to physically based shape modeling and recognition. IEEE Trans. Patt. Anal. Mach. Intell. 13(7), 715–729 (1991)
15. Terzopoulos, D., et al.: Elastically deformable models. In: Proc. ACM SIGGRAPH, pp. 205–214 (1987)
16. Müller, M., et al.: Stable real–time deformations. In: Proc. ACM SIGGRAPH, pp. 49–54 (2002)
17. Kendall, D.: A survey of the statistical theory of shape. Stat. Sci. 4, 87–120 (1989)
18. Tao, H., Huang, T.: Connected vibrations: a modal analysis approach to non-rigid motion tracking. In: Proc. IEEE CVPR, pp. 1424–1426 (1998)
19. Xu, C., Prince, J.: Snakes, shapes, and gradient vector flow. IEEE Trans. Imag. Proc. 7(3), 359–369 (1998)
20. Huang, J., et al.: Geometrically based potential energy for simulating deformable objects. Vis. Comput. 22(9), 740–748 (2006)

Demand-Driven Visual Information Acquisition

Sven Rebhan, Andreas Richter, and Julian Eggert

Honda Research Institute Europe GmbH,
Carl-Legien-Strasse 30,
63073 Offenbach am Main, Germany

Abstract. Fast, reliable and demand-driven acquisition of visual information is the key to represent visual scenes efficiently. To achieve this efficiency, a cognitive vision system must plan the utilization of its processing resources to acquire only information relevant for the task. Here, the incorporation of long-term knowledge plays a major role on deciding which information to gather. In this paper, we present a first approach to make use of the knowledge about the world and its structure to plan visual actions. We propose a method to schedule those visual actions to allow for a fast discrimination between objects that are relevant or irrelevant for the task. By doing so, we are able to reduce the system's computational demand. A first evaluation of our ideas is given using a proof-of-concept implementation.

Keywords: scene representation, scheduling, attention, memory.

1 Introduction

Cognitive systems are surrounded by a vast amount of (visual) information. To acquire the currently relevant information is a challenge for both biological and technical systems. But how do we decide what is relevant? How many details of the current scene do we process? Which locations in the scene contain information we need? And what information do we need to store about these locations?

Already the work of Yarbus [1] showed that the task one currently performs has an outstanding role in determining what is relevant. In his work, Yarbus showed that the scanpaths of a human observer on a photo vary dramatically, dependent on the task. But how does the task influence our perception of the scene? To get an insight into this question many experiments were performed. The so called "change blindness" experiments revealed that, even though our subjective perception tells otherwise, only parts of the scene are perceived (e.g. [2]). *Where* we look is determined by the task and the knowledge about both the current scene and the world [3,4]. However, a very important question remains: Which details are stored about a visited location? In [5] an experiment was conducted, suggesting that only those object properties relevant for solving the current task are stored in memory. The subjects were blind to changes of other properties of the object. This experimental evidence was confirmed by later experiments [6]. The psychophysical experiments show that we perceive

M. Fritz, B. Schiele, and J.H. Piater (Eds.): ICVS 2009, LNCS 5815, pp. 124–133, 2009.

the visual vicinity only partially. *What* details we perceive is also determined by the current task and our knowledge. Here, attention is a crucial aspect [7] and guiding this attention is assumed to be an active process [8].

First models for guiding attention were proposed under the names *active perception* [9], *active and purposive vision* [10] and *animate vision* [11]. Although the idea behind these approaches is more general, these models mainly focus on the modulation of sensor parameters in order to guide attention. However, the results show that using an active system it is possible to solve some problems that are ill-posed for a passive observer. In newer approaches on scene representation, more elaborated attention control mechanisms were implemented [12]. In these models the long- and short-term memory (LTM & STM) of the system is used along with the gist of a scene to accumulate task-relevant locations in a map. The memorized properties of the objects are used to bias the low-level processing in order to speedup the visual search.

However, all models mentioned focus solely on the spatial aspect of attention. That is, they use the world and scene knowledge to determine *where* to look. Once they have focused on a certain location, the complete feature vector is stored in the STM. This contradicts the experiments showing that only the task-relevant properties are stored for an object. It is our goal to build a cognitive vision system that also accounts for this aspect of vision. Thus, it must be able to selectively acquire information in both the spatial *and* feature domain to acquire only the information relevant for solving the current task. For example: If the task requires to know the color of an object, we only want to measure and store the color of the object. If the task requires to identify the object, we only want to acquire the minimal set of information that identifies the object and so on. Here, the static processing pathways of all state-of-the-art models do not hold anymore. Rather, a more flexible solution is required that allows to dynamically "construct" a processing pathway. However, this flexibility raises a new fundamental question [13] not tackled in current approaches: In which order should the system execute visual routines to acquire information?

In this paper, we concentrate on exactly this question and give a first idea on how a scheduling algorithm for visual routines could look like. We propose a method that incorporates knowledge about the task, the world and the current scene to determine which information is relevant. To decide in which sequence visual routines should be executed, the attention guidance process itself needs to carefully plan the utilization of the system resources, taking the cost and gain of each operation into account. In this work, we concentrate on simple search tasks, as they are often a basic atomic operation for other, more complex, tasks.

In section 2, we briefly present our system architecture. Afterwards we propose a memory architecture (section 3) that accounts for both the special needs of our scheduling process and the generic representation of knowledge. In section 4, we describe our scheduling algorithm used to control attention in the spatial and feature domain. We show first results using a proof-of-concept implementation and close with a discussion and an outlook in section 6.

2   System Architecture

In order to investigate the execution sequence of visual routines, we need a flexible system architecture as mentioned before. Such a flexible architecture was first proposed in [14], where different elementary visual routines are called on demand. Our system architecture as shown in Fig. 1 is based on this work and comprises four major parts: a relational short- and long-term memory, the attention control, a tunable saliency map and visual routines for extracting different object properties. The relational memory stores the knowledge about the world (LTM) and the current scene (STM). We will give a more detailed view on the memory in section 3. The focus of this paper is the attention control, as it determines which locations and features are attended (for details see section 4). Furthermore, a saliency map is used to find the objects in the current scene. By doing so, it can use top-down information to speedup the visual search task similar to [15]. Finally, the system comprises a bank of visual routines, each of them specialized to determine a certain property of a focused object [16]. The execution of a visual routine is selectively triggered by the attention control mechanism. Currently, our system comprises three elementary visual routines for measuring the color, the disparity-based distance z from the camera (calibrated stereo setting) and a pixel mask of an object. Along with the object mask we store its rectangular bounding box, having a width of w and a height of h where we define $w \geq h, \forall(w, h)$. Based on these properties, more complex ones like the position in the three-dimensional space x, the physical size s and a coarse shape r can be calculated. Here, the physical size is defined as $s \propto w/<z>$, and the coarse shape is defined as the aspect ratio r of the bounding box $r = h/w$. Note that $<z>$ is the averaged distance z using the object mask.

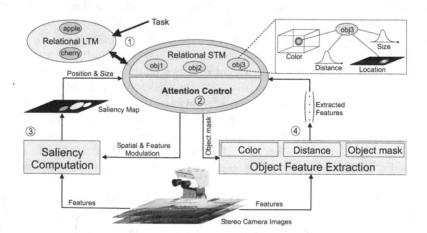

Fig. 1. The overall system architecture mainly consists of four parts: a relational memory(1), the attention control(2), a tunable saliency(3) and several feature extraction components(4)

3 Memory Architecture

In our approach, the system's memory does not just serve as a "data store" for the world knowledge. More importantly, it provides a suitable representation for deciding which properties are characteristic for the different objects. A flexible and general memory architecture, fulfilling our requirements, was proposed in [17], which we use as a basis for our implementation as shown in Fig. 2. This memory architecture allows for freely definable link patterns, inheritance of information and hypothetical nodes in both short- and long-term memory. It is important to note that property nodes are "anchored" by storing direct links to the sensory representation (see Fig. 2). Figure 2 shows that all nodes are equivalent. The role of the node is entirely defined by its incoming and outgoing links. These properties of the memory architecture distinguish the chosen memory architecture from standard AI models. In the following illustrations, we merge the labels attached to the nodes into the node names for better readability.

Additionally to storing knowledge about the world and the current scene, in our case the LTM also stores knowledge about the process of acquiring information (see [18] for details). For example, if we want to measure the color of an object, we first need to know where the object is and which dimensions it has. This dependency on other properties is consistently represented as links between those property nodes in the LTM. As both STM and LTM share the same object structure, transferring information is straightforward. When searching for a certain object in the current scene, a hypothetical object is instantiated in the STM (see *obj1* in Fig. 2). The object instance inherits (dashed line) all object properties from the long-term memory and thus can access these properties as predictions (see *shape1*). Using the visual routines, the predictions can be confirmed on demand (see *size1*). The scheduling of visual routines to confirm property predictions is the task of the attention control.

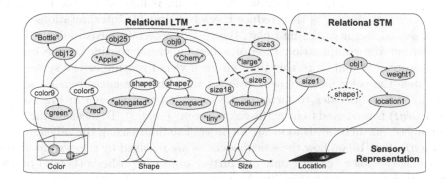

Fig. 2. The memory architecture allows a relational representation of knowledge with an identical structure for both STM and LTM. Nodes representing visual properties are "anchored" by storing direct links to sensory representations. Nodes can inherit information from other nodes (dashed line) and represent hypotheses (see *shape1*).

4 Attention Control and Scheduling

We now want to focus on the key element of this paper, the attention control mechanism. So what is the role of attention? As mentioned earlier, we understand attention as a selection process, deciding where to look and which details to store about that location. So the problem is twofold. First, there is a spatial aspect of attention, namely to locate object candidates in the current scene. A lot of work has been done in this direction, the probably most prominent one is [15]. The authors state that modulating low-level features using knowledge about an object can speedup visual search. Once focusing on a location the system needs to assure that the attended object has all properties requested by the task. This leads to the second, not well researched aspect of attention: attention in the feature domain. The system needs to acquire the information *relevant* for solving the current task. But how does it know what is relevant? For tasks already containing a hint on which property is relevant, the system can simply trigger the respective visual routine. If the task is to "find a small object", the system immediately knows that it needs to analyze the size of an object candidate.

However, for finding a specific object the procedure is more complex. In order to keep the computational and storage demand low, the goal is to find the minimal set of measurements ensuring that the attended object is the searched one. This way, the amount of information that needs to be stored in the STM and the computation time are minimized. In our approach the system uses its LTM knowledge to determine characteristic properties of the searched object. Please note that the discriminative power of a certain property strongly depends on concurrently active object hypotheses. In Fig. 3, the system has to search an apple and knows that an apple is "green", "small" and "compact". Now the system must decide on which property it wants to focus. If it measures the color "green", there are two valid hypotheses (bottle and apple), for the size "small" also two hypotheses remain (lemon and apple) and for the shape "compact" four hypotheses remain (see Fig. 3a). So the gain is highest for the color and the size measurements, as they reduce the set of possible interpretations most. Now a second factor comes into play, the cost of a certain measurement. Here, we interpret the computation time of a certain visual routine as the cost of the measurement and store this time for each visual routine in the system. In our system the color measurement is faster than the size measurement, so the attention control decides to measure the color. As you can see in Fig. 3a, an object (*obj1*) is predicted to have the color "green" (*color1*). To measure the color of an object, one first needs to locate an object candidate using the saliency map (*location1*). See [18] on how these dependencies are resolved by the system. After confirming the color "green", only one further object hypothesis (bottle) beside apple remains as shown in Fig. 3b. As a consequence of the color measurement, most hypotheses were rejected and the discriminative power of both the size and shape increased. Now, either measuring the size "small" or the shape "compact" would uniquely confirm the object candidate to be an apple. Again, the speed of the visual routines biases the selection. For our system the measurement of the size is faster, so the prediction that the focused object is small is added to

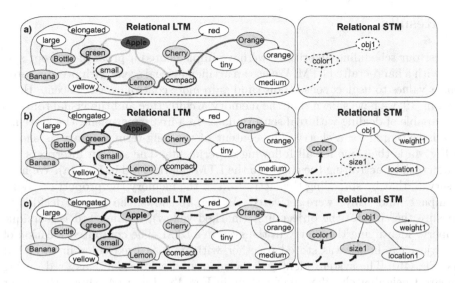

Fig. 3. a) To search the apple it is activated in the LTM (red). By propagating the activation, attached sensory representations are activated in the LTM (yellow). Propagating the activation further triggers competing object hypotheses (blue). b) After measuring the color of the object candidate, two hypotheses (bottle and apple) remain. c) By measuring the size the object candidate is confirmed to be the apple.

the STM (*size1*). After confirming the size, only the apple remains as a valid object hypothesis and is thus linked to the object candidate (see Fig. 3c). If a measurement contradicts the searched object, another object candidate will be located. To formalize our approach, we use the following notation: The LTM graph $G = (V, E)$ consists of the object nodes O, property nodes P where $V = O \cup P$ and edges E. In summary, the scheduling works as follows:

1. Locate an object candidate o_c using the saliency map and set $O_r = O$.
2. Activate the searched object $o_s \in O$ and collect its attached properties $P_s = \{p \in P | (o_s, p) \in E\}$.
3. Find all remaining competing object hypotheses O_h sharing properties with the searched object $O_h = \{o \in O_r | \exists p \in P_s : (o, p) \in E\}$.
4. Calculate the discriminative power $d_i = |D_i|^{-1}$ against the remaining hypotheses where $D_i = \{o \in O_h | \exists (o, p_i) \in E\}, \forall p_i \in P_s$.
5. Trigger the visual routine on the object candidate o_c for the most discriminative property $p_i : d_i \leq d_j \forall j$. If multiple properties minimize the set, select the fastest one. Remove the selected property from the set $P_s = P_s \setminus p_i$.
6. Find the property node $p_m \in P$ that matches the measurement best and determine the attached objects $O_m = \{o \in O | \exists (o, p_m) \in E\}$. Calculate the remaining objects $O_r = O_h \cap O_m$. If the search object is rejected $o_s \notin O_r$, go to step 1. Otherwise, if $|O_r| > 1$, continue with step 3. For $O_r = \{o_s\}$ we have found the object.

5   Results

To test our scheduling algorithm, we have implemented a proof-of-concept system with a hand-crafted LTM. We use an artificial visual scene with precomputed sensor values to neglect sensor noise and gain more control over the scene. However, in [19] we have shown that the memory architecture and the visual routines are capable of dealing with real sensory data. In a first experiment, the system's task is to search for a cherry. The content of the long-term memory as shown in Fig. 4a is the same for all following experiments. The system interprets the search task by activating the cherry in the LTM (marked red in Fig. 4a). We have observed, that by spreading this activation in the memory the properties "red", "compact" and "tiny" were activated. As Fig. 4b shows, the system decided to measure the color of the object first (marked yellow), because red is a unique property identifying the cherry in the system's LTM. The computed location of an object candidate was stored together with its measured color in the STM (see Fig. 4b). The system identified the measured color *color_1* as "red" using a nearest neighbor classifier (dashed line in Fig. 4b). Figure 4c shows that after this measurement the system classified the object candidate (*obj_1*) as a cherry (dashed line). Starting from this point, the system could predict further properties of that object like its size or shape. The system only stored one property for this object in its STM, where other systems would have stored the property vector containing three elements.

In a second experiment, the system's task was to search for an apple (see Fig. 5a). For better visualization, we reset the STM. In Fig. 5b we observed that

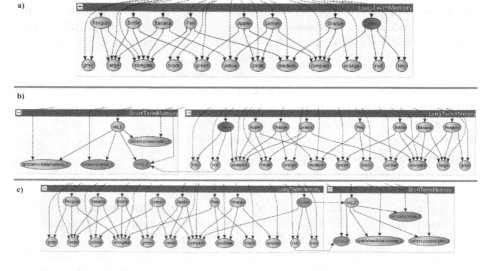

Fig. 4. a) Search for a cherry. Based on the long-term memory, the system knows cherries are red. b) The saliency map selects an object candidate and its color is measured. c) Because object *obj_1* is red, it is identified as a cherry. See the text for the color code.

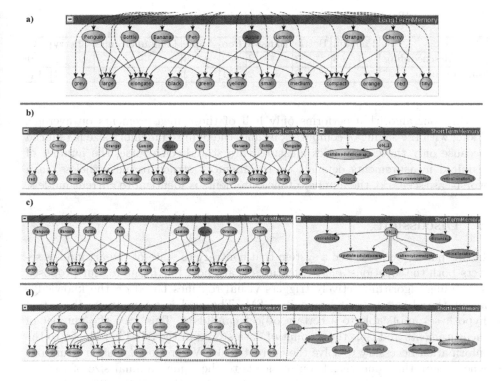

Fig. 5. a) Search for an apple. b) First, the color of the object candidate is measured to minimize the set of remaining hypotheses. c) Then, the need to distinguish between the bottle and the apple triggers the measurement of the size. d) Finally, the object *obj_1* is identified to be an apple.

the system decided to measure the color first. It did so, even though two possibilities were given because both the color "green" and the size "small" would trigger two hypotheses. This decision was due to the fact that the predefined computation time (cost) was smaller for the visual routine measuring the color. Figure 5b shows that a green object was found in the scene (dashed line). Furthermore, a second hypothesis (bottle) beside the apple remained (see Fig. 5b). The system started another refinement step as shown in Fig. 5c. Here, the system decided to measure the size "small" to distinguish between the remaining hypotheses. Again the system chose the faster visual routine although a shape measurement would have identified the object. Figure 5c shows that the object candidate was indeed small, which only left the apple as a valid hypothesis. The system identified object *obj_1* as an instance of the apple (see dashed line in Figure 5d). Again the system only stored the minimal number of properties required to identify the object.

To emphasize the memory and computation savings of our algorithm, we measured the number of computed and stored properties for all objects in the LTM (see Table 1). As current state-of-the-art models (e.g. [15]) always store the complete property vector, they always perform three measurements. Compared

Table 1. Comparison of properties measured per object

Object	Penguin	Bottle	Banana	Pen	Apple	Lemon	Orange	Cherry	Ø
without scheduling	3	3	3	3	3	3	3	3	3.0
our approach	1	2	2	1	2	2	1	1	1.5

to this, our algorithm performs only half of those measurements on average. Along with the saving of computation time, the required memory size is reduced because only those properties measured are stored. Of course, the number of required measurements depends on the memory structure, nevertheless, in a worst-case scenario, the number of measurements is identical to current models.

6 Discussion

In this paper, we presented a system that contrary to state-of-the-art models selects both the locations *and* the features it attends. Furthermore, our proposed scheduling algorithm actively triggers visual routines based on the knowledge about the object to search and its LTM. The goal is to minimize the set of hypotheses applicable to a certain object candidate. This way, the number of measurements and thus the amount of data stored in the STM is reduced to the information necessary to solve the current task. We proposed that in situations where more than one visual routine leads to the same minimal size of the hypotheses set, the costs (in our case the computation time) of the different visual routines are taken into account. In this paper, the cost parameters where chosen by hand, representing the approximated computation time of the different visual routines.

In future work, the performance of our system needs to be tested on real-world scenes. One possible problem in such a setup could be the influence of noise of real sensor data on the scheduling algorithms. Here, a more sophisticated and probabilistic activation spreading algorithm might be required. The reason is that the activation for the property nodes and thus also for the object nodes is more ambiguous for noisy measurements. Another interesting aspect for further investigations is the triggering of an object hypothesis using a fast feed-forward pathway for prominent features as proposed for neocortical structures in [20]. This would confine the initial set of hypotheses and speedup the identification. In such a regime, the proposed algorithm would act as a refinement process. Furthermore, we want to investigate the relation between our scheduling algorithm and decision and game theory problems, where a gain (the number of excluded hypotheses) is often weighted against a risk (an ambiguous measurement).

References

1. Yarbus, A.L.: Eye Movements and Vision. Plenum Press, New York (1967)
2. Pashler, H.: Familiarity and visual change detection. Perception and Psychophysics 44(4), 369–378 (1988)

3. Just, M.A., Carpenter, P.A.: Eye fixations and cognitive processes. Cognitive Psychology 8(4), 441–480 (1976)
4. Henderson, J.M., Weeks, P.A., Hollingworth, A.: The effects of semantic consistency on eye movements during complex scene viewing. Experimental Psychology: Human Perception and Performance 25(1), 210–228 (1999)
5. Ballard, D.H., Hayhoe, M.M., Pelz, J.B.: Memory representations in natural tasks. Cognitive Neuroscience (1995)
6. Triesch, J., Ballard, D.H., Hayhoe, M.M., Sullivan, B.T.: What you see is what you need. Journal of Vision 3(1), 86–94 (2003)
7. Intraub, H.: The representation of visual scenes. Trends in Cognitive Sciences 1(6), 217–221 (1997)
8. Tsotsos, J.K.: On the relative complexity of active vs. passive visual search. International Journal of Computer Vision 7(2), 127–141 (1992)
9. Bajcsy, R.: Active perception vs. passive perception. In: Proceedings of the IEEE Workshop on Computer Vision: Representation and Control, pp. 55–62 (1985)
10. Aloimonos, Y.: Introduction. In: Active Vision Revisited, pp. 1–18. Lawrence Erlbaum Associates, Hillsdale (1993)
11. Ballard, D.H.: Animate vision. Artificial Intelligence 48(1), 57–86 (1991)
12. Navalpakkam, V., Itti, L.: Modeling the influence of task on attention. Vision Research 45(2), 205–231 (2005)
13. Hayhoe, M.: Vision using routines: A functional account of vision. Visual Cognition (7), 43–64 (2000)
14. Eggert, J., Rebhan, S., Körner, E.: First steps towards an intentional vision system. In: Proc. International Conference on Computer Vision Systems (2007)
15. Navalpakkam, V., Itti, L.: Search goal tunes visual features optimally. Neuron 53(4), 605–617 (2007)
16. Ullman, S.: Visual routines. Cognition 18 (1984)
17. Röhrbein, F., Eggert, J., Körner, E.: A cortex-inspired neural-symbolic network for knowledge representation. In: Proceedings of the 3rd International Workshop on Neural-Symbolic Learning and Reasoning (2007)
18. Rebhan, S., Einecke, N., Eggert, J.: Consistent modeling of functional dependencies along with world knowledge. In: Proceedings of World Academy of Science, Engineering and Technology: International Conference on Cognitive Information Systems Engineering, vol. 54, pp. 341–348 (2009)
19. Rebhan, S., Röhrbein, F., Eggert, J.P., Körner, E.: Attention modulation using short- and long-term knowledge. In: Gasteratos, A., Vincze, M., Tsotsos, J.K. (eds.) ICVS 2008. LNCS, vol. 5008, pp. 151–160. Springer, Heidelberg (2008)
20. Körner, E., Gewaltig, M.O., Körner, U., Richter, A., Rodemann, T.: A model of computation in neocortical architecture. Neural Networks 12(7–8), 989–1006 (1999)

A Real-Time Low-Power Stereo Vision Engine Using Semi-Global Matching

Stefan K. Gehrig[1], Felix Eberli[2], and Thomas Meyer[2]

[1] Daimler AG Group Research, 71059 Sindelfingen, Germany
[2] Supercomputing Systems AG Technoparkstr. 11, Zuerich,
8005 Zuerich, Switzerland

Abstract. Many real-time stereo vision systems are available on low-power platforms. They all either use a local correlation-like stereo engine or perform dynamic programming variants on a scan-line. However, when looking at high-performance global stereo methods as listed in the upper third of the Middlebury database, the low-power real-time implementations for these methods are still missing. We propose a real-time implementation of the semi-global matching algorithm with algorithmic extensions for automotive applications on a reconfigurable hardware platform resulting in a low power consumption of under 3W. The algorithm runs at 25Hz processing image pairs of size 750x480 pixels and computing stereo on a 680x400 image part with up to a maximum of 128 disparities.

1 Introduction

3D perception is a crucial task both for automotive and for robotics applications. Besides time-of-flight systems such as RADAR or LIDAR, stereo cameras are a very popular and inexpensive choice to perform this task.

Stereo vision has been an active area of research for decades. A few years ago, a benchmark to compare stereo algorithms with respect to (w.r.t.) accuracy was established [1]. This benchmark database ranks the current published stereo algorithms. Among the top-performing algorithms in this database, we found semi-global matching (SGM) [2] to be the most efficient. We will focus on this algorithm for the remainder of this paper.

Roughly speaking, SGM performs an energy minimization in a dynamic-programming fashion on multiple 1D paths crossing each pixel and thus approximating the 2D image. The energy consists of three parts: a data term for photo-consistency, a small smoothness energy term for slanted surfaces that change the disparity slightly (parameter P_1), and a smoothness energy term for depth discontinuities (parameter P_2). Based on this algorithm, we introduce the first real-time global stereo implementation besides dynamic programming that runs at 25 Hz with less than 3W power consumption.

This paper is organized in the following way: Prior work of the field is presented in Section 2. Section 3 explains our system design. The next section describes implementation details to obtain real-time performance. Results of the hardware setup can be found in the Section 5. Conclusions and future work comprise the final section.

M. Fritz, B. Schiele, and J.H. Piater (Eds.): ICVS 2009, LNCS 5815, pp. 134–143, 2009.

2   Related Work

Today, several real-time stereo vision systems are available on low-power platforms. One of the first stereo hardware engines is described in [3]. Recently, the census-based stereo system by the company Tyzx became popular [4]. Phase-based correlation has also been implemented on a field-programmable gate-array (FPGA) [5]. In this work, also a nice overview of existing reconfigurable stereo engines is provided. Dynamic Programming as a global method on a single scan line has also been implemented on an FPGA [6] .

In the automotive field, the car manufacturer Toyota delivers a stereo object detection system for the Lexus LS460 [7] produced by Denso. Autoliv cooperates with Sarnoff in the field and offers an ASIC solution for correlation stereo called Acadia [8]. The company MobilEye offers a stereo engine in its latest automotive ASIC EyeQ2 [9]. All these available stereo engines operate with local correlation-variants.

For some of the top-performing stereo algorithms near real-time implementations on the graphics card (GPU) exist. Semi-global matching runs at 13Hz for QVGA size images [10]. Belief propagation was shown to be real-time capable on the GPU for small images [11]. The power consumption of these GPUs is well above 100W.

Despite the enormous amount of work on real-time stereo vision, there is still a need for a high-performance, low-power implementation of a global stereo method. We close this gap with our contribution.

3   System Design

3.1   Design Considerations

SGM has to traverse many paths along the image for all pixels and disparities. The paths all start at the image margin so running the algorithm in one scan is not possible. The main limitation is the number of memory accesses for the accumulated costs for every pixel, disparity, and path. In order to fit modern FPGA resources we decided to run the algorithm on 8 paths, computing 4 paths simultaneously (see Figure 4) keeping the memory bandwidth on a manageable level. The intermediate results are stored into an external memory during the first scan, and then read back during the second scan for accumulation. This memory bandwidth reduction and the choice of the FPGA as computing device yield the desired low-power engine.

The core of the SGM algorithm is the cost calculation along the 8 paths. Here, parallelization is limited since it is necessary to have the result of the previous pixel in the path available. However, the costs for all disparities at the current pixel only depend on results from the previous pixel along the path (see Figure 5). We instantiate this part 16 times in parallel on the FPGA.

We consider two 750x480px input greyscale images with 12 bits per grey-value as input. Due to mounting tolerances and missing stereo overlap, the actual region of computation is limited to 680x400px. In automotive and robotics applications with these image sizes, a disparity range of 0 through 127 suffices. For larger disparities, similarity is often hard to establish due to the significant different view angles. Ideally, SGM would be computed everywhere at full resolution. We decided to reduce the image size by a factor of 2 in width and height for the full image and to run a second SGM at full resolution for a smaller region of interest (ROI) where the full resolution is needed. This subsampling step is mandatory to keep the necessary data for path accumulation in internal memory on automotive FPGAs. The ROI can be changed on a frame-by-frame basis.

For the outdoor scenario with uncontrollable lighting conditions, a different metric to the ones proposed in [2] has to be used. We have to cope with different brightness in the left and right image and with vignetting effects due to inexpensive lenses. The proposed similarity criterion mutual information is sensitive to vignetting artifacts [12]. We slightly deviated from a pixel-wise matching cost using a small 3x3 correlation window to minimize the effect of foreground fattening. The mean-free sum-of-absolute differences (ZSAD) turns out to be very efficient and robust for the task at hand.

The experimental system explained below is a PC-based system used to validate the design and to test different SGM variants. The target system is derived from the experimental system, has limited parametrization options and runs in an embedded system. The SGM building blocks were implemented in VHDL on the FPGA from scratch.

3.2   Experimental System

The experimental system is built on a general purpose personal computer (PC) with x86 CPU. The stereo image data is received over a frame grabber from the cameras. The necessary pre-processing step to properly align the cameras, rectification, is done in software and only the SGM algorithm is executed on the PCIe-FPGA card (see Figure 1).

Figure 2 shows the overview of the blocks running on the FPGA. The optional Gauss filter alleviates negative effects of a slight stereo decalibration [13]. The

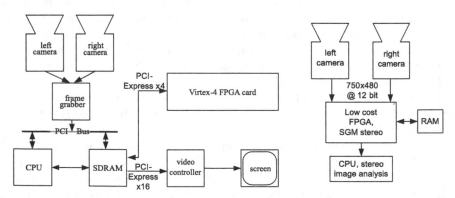

Fig. 1. Hardware blocks of the experimental system (left) and the target system (right)

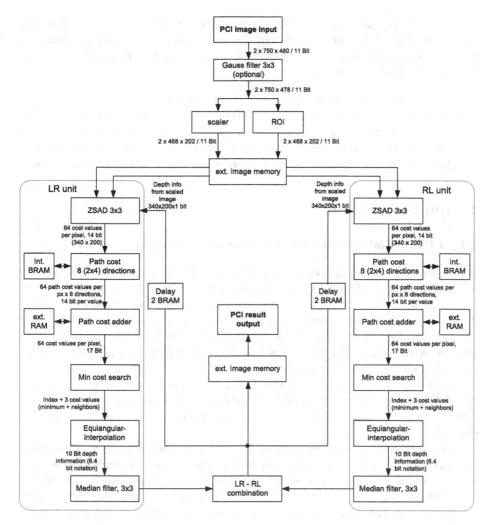

Fig. 2. System Overview. The critical blocks w.r.t. latency and resources are ZSAD correlation, path calculation, and memory communication.

critical blocks w.r.t. latency and resources are the correlation block, the SGM path calculator and adder with the associated external RAM access controller. The pre-processing (Gauss, scaler) and post-processing (median, sub-pixel interpolation, LR-RL-combination to detect occlusions) blocks are standard operations and are only performed once per pixel. Thus, they are not time-critical blocks.

3.3   Target System

In the target system, the SGM algorithm works in an embedded system with the stereo cameras directly connected to the low-cost FPGA. The FPGA executes the complete pre-processing of the input images, SGM stereo calculation and post-processing. The input images and the stereo result are then forwarded to a CPU for further analysis of the raw result images (see Figure 1). Differences to the experimental system are:

- The rectification is done by the FPGA, not in software
- The experimental system has two SGM engines in the high-end FPGA for a full right-left check, i.e. computing SGM a second time with the right image as the reference image. The target system only contains one of these, therefore the result uses a simplified right-left-check to detect occlusions.

4   Implementation

4.1   FPGA Platform for the Experimental System

The experimental system uses a Xilinx Virtex-4 FPGA on a 64-Bit PMC-Module from Alpha Data (ADM-XRC-4FX module with a Virtex-4 FX140 FPGA). The card contains a PCI/PCI-X to localbus bridge including four DMA-units. Apart from the localbus connection, the FPGA has four independent 32-bit DDR2 blocks with 256 MB each available. Virtex-4 FPGAs have an almost identical logic structure compared to the low-end Spartan-3 FPGAs which are used on the target system (Spartan-3a 3400DSP).

The image data is transferred with DMA from and to the PC main memory. The FPGA uses three external 32-bit DDR2 memories, one for image and result storage and one for each of the two stereo processing engines as temporary storage.

The image data is transferred from the PC and filtered to form the internal image format on which the algorithm works. These are two stereo image pairs, a scaled and a ROI image pair which are stored in external memory. In the first step, the core algorithm starts to read a image pair top down, line by line from left to right. In this order, the ZSAD correlation is calculated and forwarded to the SGM core.

4.2   Main SGM Blocks

The ZSAD core is fully pipelined and produces one cost value per clock cycle. To match the throughput of the SGM core, four such ZSAD units work in parallel. The line buffers for the input images, specifically the line buffers for the search image had to be designed to deliver the required bandwidth for four correlation units. As a first step in ZSAD, the means of both the reference and the search 3x3 pixel areas are calculated (see Figure 3). The 3x3 pixels of the two areas are subtracted from each other, the means are subtracted and then the absolute values are summed to form a cost value. To reduce the number of bits for the cost value, the result is divided by 8, i.e. 3 bits are truncated. This is done to match the 14 bit cost width of the implemented SGM core.

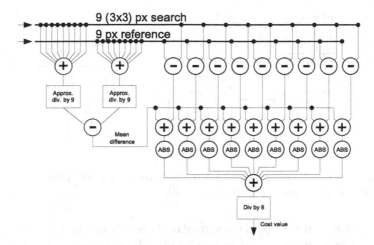

Fig. 3. ZSAD calculation core. The ZSAD cost is calculated for every pixel and disparity.

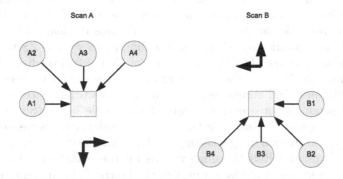

Fig. 4. Processing the 8 path accumulations in two scans

The SGM core calculates four SGM directions: one horizontal to the left and three vertical down, including two diagonal down paths (see Figure 4).

The basic SGM operation is shown in Figure 5, where the smoothness constraint via P_1 and P_2 is incorporated ($L(p - r, d)$ is the accumulated cost from the previously visited pixel p at disparity d, $C(p, d)$ is the ZSAD value). The history of the SGM path costs is kept inside the FPGA in fast local memory. Only the accumulated costs of these first four paths are stored in external memory which consists of an array of 64 values with 16 bits each for every pixel in the image (340x200). This external 16 bit restriction is also responsible for the 14 bit restriction for each single SGM-path and the 17 bit restriction for the final accumulated costs over eight paths

The second step does the same operation backwards, reading the image pair from bottom to top, again calculating the same correlation costs, but in reverse order. This allows us to calculate the missing four SGM paths in the inverse

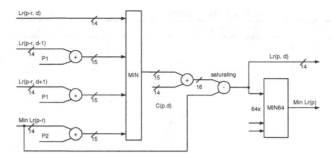

Fig. 5. The core processing unit calculating the lowest cost path. This path calculation is performed for every pixel, disparity, and path.

directions. During this step, the accumulated costs from the first step are read back from external memory and accumulated with the currently calculated paths to form the final costs over eight paths.

For each pixel, the minimum cost of 64 values is then calculated which yields a 6 bit index value. To further enhance the depth precision, an additional interpolation is done which expands the result to a total of 10 bits. We use the equiangular interpolation as suggested by [14] since it yields better sub-pixel precision for cost metrics based on absolute differences such as ZSAD compared to the standard parabola fit. After the interpolation, a 3x3 median filter is performed similar to [2] before the data is verified in the right-left check.

During the first and second scan, the algorithm works on the down-scaled image and produces an overview result of the whole input. Since the image is scaled by a factor of two, the 64 disparities calculated correspond to 128 disparities in the original image. During the third and fourth scan, the algorithm works on an unscaled ROI the same way as for the scaled overview to further enhance the precision of a selected part of the image. False matches in the ROI caused by the limited disparity range are avoided in the following way: We set the correlation costs for disparity 63 to 0 whenever 63 (31.5 for the scaled image) or a larger disparity has been established in the overview image. This drives the ROI SGM result towards the overview SGM result for large disparities. The combination of both results is straightforward.

In our experimental system, two SGM engines are instantiated, one with the left image as reference, one with the right image (full RL-Check). The disparity is invalidated if the resulting disparities differ by more than 1. On the target system, we use a fast Right-To-Left consistency check traversing the accumulated costs at a 45° angle, looking again for the minimum cost and invalidating the disparity if the values differ (fast RL-Check) [2]. Thus, we only need one SGM engine.

5   Results

Computational Speed: Our stereo engine runs with clock speeds of up to 200MHz on the Virtex4 FPGA. For the low-cost FPGA clock speed of 133 MHz,

Fig. 6. Resulting Disparity Maps for the Van Scene (top left). SGM with ZSAD (top right) works well, SGM with BT (bottom left) has more invalid pixels while SGM with HMI works comparably to ZSAD (bottom right). Small disparities are mapped to black, invalid pixels are marked dark green.

we obtain a maximum frame rate of 27Hz. On the Virtex 4, a full RL-Check, i.e. computing SGM twice per disparity map, is used and two disparity images of size 340x200 per image pair are calculated. The same speed is achieved on the low-cost FPGA using the fast RL-Check. The high end FPGA has twice the performance at the same clock speed because it contains the SGM engine twice to calculate the left- and right-image referenced results at the same time.

Resources: The FPGA resources for the Virtex-4 experimental system, including DDR2 controllers, are about 60000 LUT4 logic elements for two SGM engines and 150 Block-RAMs (300kB) of internal memory. For the target system, the resources are halved using the fast RL-Check, i.e. only one SGM engine.

Power Consumption: Based on our implementation on the low-cost FPGA, the FPGA has a power consumption of less than 2W. Up to one extra Watt can be generated due to bit toggles when transferring data to the external memory.

Algorithmic Performance: We computed results on the Middlebury test data with our ZSAD similarity criterion. We obtained 5.86% wrong pixels (disparity deviates by more than one pixel to ground truth based on all pixels) for Tsukuba, 3.85% for Venus, 13.28% for Teddy and 9.54% for the Cones image pair based on all pixels with ground truth. Invalid pixels were interpolated via propagation of the last valid disparity value. These results are slightly worse than the SGM results with mutual information [2] which is not surprising since the similarity criterion has been selected for robust performance under difficult imaging conditions which are not present in the Middlebury database.

Fig. 7. Resulting Disparity Maps for the Construction Site Scene (top left). SGM with ZSAD (top right) works well while SGM with BT (bottom left) and SGM with HMI (bottom right) fail. The image pair has a strong vignetting effect and different brightness. Small disparities are mapped to black, invalid pixels are marked dark green.

Real-World Results: We show a few results from our experimental system. In the van scene (Figure 6) with rather favorable lighting conditions and excellent lenses, our ZSAD SGM variant and the literature SGM (Birchfield-Tomasi(BT) and Hierarchical Mutual Information(HMI) [2]) versions perform comparably well with more invalid pixels for the literature variants. For the construction site scene (Figure 7), the situation is very different. Here, the lenses have a strong vignetting artifact that cannot be compensated with global statistics such as mutual information. Hence the HMI-SGM performs poorly. The BT metric fails, especially on the road, because the image pair has different brightness in addition. The ZSAD-SGM yields a dense disparity map with correct occlusion detection and no noticeable outliers. A more detailed and stringent evaluation of the algorithm and a comparison to other real-time stereo algorithms can be found in [15].

6   Conclusions and Future Work

We have introduced a real-time low-power global stereo engine. The results using SGM are very encouraging. The key design choices to obtain real-time performance are subsampling and result reuse for full resolution computation, parallelization of the most time-consuming block (path calculator), and minimizing the external memory bandwidth by combining 4 paths in one scan. We expect this engine to be the basis for many future camera-based driver assistance and robotic systems. Ongoing work is the further reduction of the FPGA resources and the incorporation of issues such as calibration sensitivity [13] and additional robustness in difficult weather conditions such as rain and backlight.

References

1. Scharstein, D., Szeliski, R.: Middlebury stereo vision and evaluation page, http://vision.middlebury.edu/stereo
2. Hirschmueller, H.: Accurate and efficient stereo processing by semi-global matching and mutual information. In: Proceedings of Int. Conference on Computer Vision and Pattern Recognition 2005, San Diego, CA, vol. 2, pp. 807–814 (June 2005)
3. Konolige, K.: Small vision systems. In: Proceedings of the International Symposium on Robotics Research, Hayama, Japan (1997)
4. Woodfill, J.I., et al.: The tyzx deepsea g2 vision system, a taskable, embedded stereo camera. In: Embedded Computer Vision Workshop, pp. 126–132 (2006)
5. Masrani, D.K., MacLean, W.J.: A real-time large disparity range stereo-system using fpgas. In: Narayanan, P.J., Nayar, S.K., Shum, H.-Y. (eds.) ACCV 2006. LNCS, vol. 3852, pp. 42–51. Springer, Heidelberg (2006)
6. Sabihuddin, S., MacLean, W.J.: Maximum-likelihood stereo correspondence using field programmable gate arrays. In: Int. Conference on Computer Vision Systems (ICVS), Bielefeld, Germany (March 2007)
7. Tech-News: Toyota' lexus ls 460 employs stereo camera (viewed 2009/04/15), http://techon.nikkeibp.co.jp/english/NEWS_EN/20060301/113832/
8. Sarnoff-Inc.: The acadia video processors - acadia pci (viewed 2009/07/15), http://www.sarnoff.com/products/acadia-video-processors/acadia-pci
9. MobilEye: Eye q2 system - vision system on a chip (viewed 2009/07/15), http://www.mobileye.com/manufacturer-products/brochures
10. Ernst, I., Hirschmüller, H.: Mutual information based semi-global stereo matching on the gpu. In: Bebis, G., Boyle, R., Parvin, B., Koracin, D., Remagnino, P., Porikli, F., Peters, J., Klosowski, J., Arns, L., Chun, Y.K., Rhyne, T.-M., Monroe, L. (eds.) ISVC 2008, Part I. LNCS, vol. 5358, pp. 228–239. Springer, Heidelberg (2008)
11. Yang, Q.: Real-time global stereo matching using hierarchical belief propagation. In: British Machine Vision Conference (BMVC), pp. 989–998 (September 2006)
12. Hirschmueller, H., Scharstein, D.: Evaluation of cost functions for stereo matching. In: Proceedings of Int. Conference on Computer Vision and Pattern Recognition 2007, Minneapolis, Minnesota (June 2007)
13. Hirschmueller, H., Gehrig, S.: Stereo matching in the presence of sub-pixel calibration errors. In: Proceedings of Int. Conference on Computer Vision and Pattern Recognition 2009, Miami, FL (June 2009)
14. Shimizu, M., Okutomi, M.: An analysis of subpixel estimation error on area-based image matching. In: DSP 2002, pp. 1239–1242 (2002)
15. Steingrube, P., Gehrig, S.: Performance evaluation of stereo algorithms for automotive applications. In: ICVS 2009 (October 2009)

Feature-Based Stereo Vision Using Smart Cameras for Traffic Surveillance

Q. Houben[1], J. Czyz[2], J.C. Tocino Diaz[1], O. Debeir[1], and N. Warzee[1]

[1] LISA, Université Libre de Bruxelles, CP165/57, Belgium
[2] Macq Electronique S.A., 1140 Brussels, Belgium

Abstract. This paper presents a stereo-based system for measuring traffic on motorways. To achieve real-time performance, the system exploits a decentralized architecture composed of a pair of smart cameras fixed over the road and connected via network to an embedded industrial PC on the side of the road. Different features (Harris corners and edges) are detected on the two images and matched together with local matching algorithm. The resulting 3D points cloud is processed by maximum spanning tree clustering algorithm to group the points into vehicle objects. Bounding boxes are defined for each detected object, giving an approximation of the vehicles 3D sizes. The system presented here has been validated manually and gives over 90% of good detection accuracy at 20-25 frames/s.

1 Introduction

This work presents an application of stereo vision to vehicle detection and classification on motorway. Traffic analysis is an active research domain. The behavior of the road users and the type of vehicle they use becomes a main issue for motorway administrators. We propose here a stereo camera pair and a distributed computing architecture to tackle the problem of real-time vehicle recognition and to determine its main characteristics (dimensions, class and velocity of the vehicle). Traffic video analysis is attractive since hardware becomes more and more inexpensive and powerful, allowing real-time results. The installation of cameras is relatively cheap and the maintenance cost is low. Most of the existing solutions are based on a monocular system. Foreground/Background methods are massively used since they demand small computer effort and are simple to implement [1]. Other methods use tracked features that are compared to models [2], [3] or clustered into vehicles [4]. Some approached are based on object detection techniques [5], [6]. All these methods give limited information about the dimensions of the vehicle (length, width, height) and perform poorly in vehicle class recognition. In the approach discussed in this work, two smart cameras are positioned over the road (on a bridge for example) with a distance of approximately 2 m between them. The stereo allows to obtain 3D information of the scene and to determine the dimensions of the vehicle. This accurate 3D information leads to more precise vehicle classification compared to monocular systems. With the height information a distinction can be made, for example, between a

M. Fritz, B. Schiele, and J.H. Piater (Eds.): ICVS 2009, LNCS 5815, pp. 144–153, 2009.
© Springer-Verlag Berlin Heidelberg 2009

minivan and an estate car. In addition to well known Harris corners [7], we use also edge-based features which are very well adapted to vehicles. Indeed, some vehicles have large flat regions which do not contain any corners, and thus there is no 3D information for these regions. This complicates subsequent processing. In this case the edge-based features have proved to be useful for providing meaningful point of interest.

As we are interested in a real-time system and because vehicles can move quite fast on a motorway, the computational requirements for processing the stereo image flow is large. We have therefore opted for a distributed architecture based on smart cameras carrying out features extraction and a central node that collects and process the pre-computed features. Using this approach the system can process 752x480 gray-scale image at 20-25 frames/s. This distributed approach has another advantage: the data transmitted is limited to features as opposed to complete frame data in a classical single PC-based architecture.

2   Algorithm Description

In this section, we first present an overview of the stereo system. Then we describe in more detail the algorithms chosen for solving the problem.

2.1   System Overview

The purpose of the presented system is to provide a realistic solution for high accuracy counting, classification and speed measurement of vehicles on motorways. Stereo vision is well adapted to this task as it provides real 3D measurements of the scene that can be used to determine vehicles sizes, and hence vehicle classes and velocities. Since the system must be real-time, a trade-off has to be found between algorithmic complexity and hardware requirements. A solution based entirely on some powerful standard PC hardware is less attractive because the PCs cannot be easily mounted above a motorway, hence the high volume video data must be transferred on several meters, or even dozens of meters, to the side of the road. For this reasons, it is relevant to process locally the image data, extract important features and send only the features to a central processing unit over the network. This reduces drastically the bandwidth requirements between cameras and the central processing unit.

The proposed system is therefore composed of two smart cameras mounted above the motorway connected to an industrial PC via a standard 100Mbit Ethernet network. The smart cameras utilize a CMOS sensor, an FPGA (Field Programmable Gate Array) and a 32-bit RISC processor for capturing images, extracting the features and sending the results to the PC. The industrial PC is a fan-less machine that collects the features coming from the smart cameras, performs the feature matching and 3D back-projection, and grouping resulting 3D points into vehicles that can be tracked.

In the following we describe in more detail the algorithms developed for counting and classifying the vehicles.

2.2 Feature-Based Stereo Reconstruction

In stereo vision two major issues have to be considered: the cameras system calibration and the identification of matching points between the two images. We will focus here on the second point, assuming that the calibration has been already obtained using standard methods [8], [9].

Given the camera calibration data, both acquired images are first rectified. Using rectified images reduces significantly the complexity of the matching, since two corresponding points in the left and right image will have equal vertical coordinates. Different features are identified separately on each image. The first characteristic points used in our implementation are the classical Harris corner points [7]. Each point of the left image is compared to the points lying on the same horizontal line in the right image. A maximum disparity is set to reduce the search space and accelerate the process. Several similarity measurement systems between surrounding pixels area have been studied in the literature. Our method uses normalized cross-correlation C of the pixel values in a square window W_1 and W_2 around the two points, defined by

$$C = \frac{\sum (p_1(i,j) - \bar{p}_1)(p_2(i,j) - \bar{p}_2)}{\|(p_1(i,j) - \bar{p}_1)(p_2(i,j) - \bar{p}_2)\|} \tag{1}$$

where the sum is taken over (i,j), index of points in the square windows W_1 and W_2, $p_1(i,j)$ and $p_2(i,j)$ are the intensities at the pixel (i,j) in the image 1 and image 2 respectively, and p_1, p_2, their mean over the square windows $W1$ and $W2$.

A list of scores in the right image is obtained for each point of the left image and in a similar way for each point of the right image. A "winner-take-all" strategy is then used to match the different points: a match is considered as valid if the correlation is maximum among all the correlations computed on the same horizontal line in the left image and in the right image. Furthermore we check symmetrically that the determined match gives a maximum correlation in the left image. This method is relatively fast and presents few outliers. However, the number of 3D points determined in this way is insufficient to obtain dense 3D point cloud in all kinds of lighting conditions and for all kinds of vehicles. In particular truck trailers often present texture-less surfaces (i.e. with few Harris features) which produce insufficient number of 3D points for further clustering.

For this reason we introduce a second type of features points based on Canny edges [10]. Edges are firstly detected in both images using a Canny edge detector. We slightly modify the algorithm so that horizontal edges are not detected. The rectified stereo image pair are then scanned horizontally line by line. To save computation time these lines are distant of five pixels each. Each intersection between these horizontal lines and the detected edges defines a new point of interest. See Figure 1. In order to characterize these points we introduce an 8-dimensional vector that is build using: (i) the strength of the edge r (Canny filter response), (ii) a five pixel long intensity profile along the edge e, (iii) and the average intensity taken on the 3 pixels to the left and the right side of the intersection point m^l and m^r.

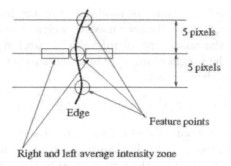

Fig. 1. Circles show the edge-based feature points taken as the intersection of an image scan line with an edge. In addition to edge intensity profile the average intensity taken on 3 pixels to the left and the right (depicted by rectangles in the figure) of the point is used to characterize the feature.

For each hypothetical match, a score S is computed between feature vectors i and j using the following equation

$$S = \alpha C(e_i, e_j) + \frac{\beta}{1 + |m_i^r - m_j^r + m_i^l - m_j^l|} + \frac{\gamma}{1 + |r_1 - r_2|} \tag{2}$$

where $C(e_i, e_j)$ is the normalized correlation between two edge intensity profiles, r_i, r_j are the Canny responses, m_i, m_j are the average intensities and α, β and γ are design parameters that are set empirically. The score S is built is such a way that it will be large when the two features come from the same physical object and small otherwise. The final matching is then done in the same way as for the Harris features: we consider that a match is valid if the score S is maximum among all the scores on the same epipolar line in the left image and in the right image.

These two types of features together cover well all objects of interest (trucks, cars, motorbikes).

2.3   3D Point Back-Projection, Clustering and Tracking

Once the matching is obtained, the image projections can be back-projected to give 3D points in the world coordinates. The coordinates are obtained using Least Mean Square, minimizing algebraic distance [11]. The plane equation of the road and its principal axis are supposed to be known. The 3D points lying above the road level are considered as belonging to a vehicle. The aggregation of the 3D points into vehicle groups is achieved by the minimum spanning tree clustering algorithm: all the 3D points form an undirected graph whose vertices are the 3D points. For each edge of the graph, we define a weight given by the distance between the 3D points. The minimum spanning tree is built in such way to that every point is connected to the tree and the sum of the edge weights is minimum. The weights used here are based on Euclidean distance. The edges that have a weight greater than a threshold are cut, forming distinct clusters.

This threshold is defined by a constant modulated by the points density around the two considered points. The distance used to weight the edges is anisotropic due to the nature of the tackled problem: vehicles are longer in the direction parallel to the road. The weight of an edge between two vertices (x_1, y_1, z_1) and (x_2, y_2, z_2), is therefore defined as :

$$d^2 = A_x(x_1 - x_2)^2 + A_y(y_1 - y_2)^2 + A_z(z_1 - z_2)^2 \qquad (3)$$

where A_x , A_y and A_z are parameters adjusted to give more importance to the direction parallel to the road, x is the horizontal axis perpendicular to the road, y, the axis parallel to the road and z, the axis normal to the road. After clustering, matching errors resulting in aberrant 3D points are extracted by examining the distribution of the height coordinates of points inside each group. Isolated points of the distribution are considered as outliers and are eliminated. Bounding boxes of the groups are then defined around the point clouds. These boxes give a good approximation of the dimensions of the vehicle (length, width, and height) and are easy to track.

For tracking the vehicles we adopt the Kalman filter framework. At each time step, the tracker keeps an internal list of active targets (vehicles) and updates the state-vector of the vehicle using a system model and the measurements provided by the detected bounding box. Each bounding box resulting from the clustering operation is considered as a possible vehicle detection. The bounding box that is closest to an active target is used as measurement vector for the Kalman filter. When no active targets are in the vicinity of a detected box, a new target is created. Likewise, when an active target does not have a corresponding bounding box it will be erased after a number of time steps. Trajectories with insufficient length are eliminated.

3   Implementation on a Distributed Architecture

In this section we describe how the algorithms presented in the previous section are implemented on a distributed architecture in order to achieve real-time. The system is composed of a pair of smart cameras and an industrial fan-less PC, currently the AEC-6920 Embedded PC from Aaeon Technology. This PC is equipped with a Core 2 Duo CPU running at 2.0 GHz and 1 GByte of RAM. The smart cameras and the central processing node are connected via a classical Ethernet 100BaseTX network. In the following we describe the hardware of the smart cameras, and the distribution of the different processing tasks in the system.

3.1   Smart Camera Hardware Description

The electronic board, that is at the heart of the smart camera, has been developed by the company Macq Electronique. This board has been designed specifically for computer vision tasks. The smart camera is composed of three main units: a CMOS video sensor, an FPGA and a general purpose low power PowerPC processor. The high level architecture of the board is depicted in Figure 2.

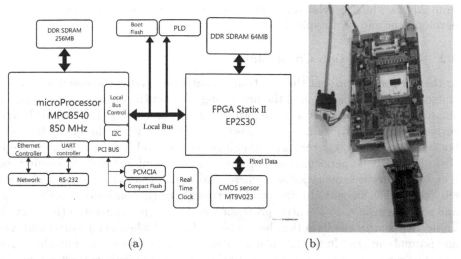

Fig. 2. (a) Block diagram architecture of the smart camera. (b) A prototype of the smart camera.

An FPGA can be seen as a reconfigurable electronic chip that can be configured to perform dedicated computing tasks.

The choice of the combination of an FPGA with a PowerPC over a DSP is motivated by the fact that vision algorithms usually require high processing power for very repetitive low-level tasks like filtering, feature extraction, image manipulation. An FPGA is clearly well adapted to this kind of processing. In particular feature extraction is usually a local operation, in the sense that it gets access to one neighborhood of pixels at the same time to obtain a result. Feature extraction can therefore be easily implemented on an FPGA. At the same time, for some higher level tasks it is convenient to have a processor that can run C/C++ programs independently of its specific architecture which is not the case for DSP's. It allows us to use standard code and libraries without any modifications. Also many DPS's do not support floating point operations, algorithms must then be adapted. Furthermore, a CMOS sensor can be directly interfaced with the FPGA with very little additional hardware. This reduces the costs and simplifies the dataflow since an external camera is no more necessary. Power consumption constraints limit the processing power of the device. The Freescale MPC8540 based on a PowerPC e500 core has been chosen because of its low thermal dissipation and relatively high computational power (32bit processor running at 850 MHz). From an electronic design point of view the design of the board is somehow simplified because the MPC8540 contains already a memory controller, an Ethernet controller and other standard interfaces.

We have opted for the CMOS sensor MT9V023 from Aptina because much less circuitry is required to operate CMOS sensors compared to CCD sensors. Also the MT9V023 sensor is physically robust yet it is sensitive to light and has a wide dynamic range. The FPGA mounted on the board is a Stratix II EP2S30 from Altera which is relatively large to be able to contain many processing for development and prototyping.

3.2 Implementation Constraints

In this section, we present the constraints that have guided the design of the architecture and the partition of the processing tasks in the distributed system. To summarize the main steps of the algorithm are: (i) image rectification, (ii) Harris corner detection, (iii) Canny edge detection, (iv) feature matching, (v) 3D point back-projection, (vi) clustering of 3D points in boxes and (vii) box tracking. Steps (i) to (iii) must be performed on both images thus doubling the processing time if executed on the same processor, whereas steps (iv) to (vii) are to be performed only once. This suggests to decentralize steps (i) to (iii) on local smart cameras and send the results to a central processing node that performs step (iv) to (vii). Table 1 compares the data that has to be exchanged when using smart cameras and normal cameras. In the case of normal cameras, the image data must be transferred to the central processing node. In the second case, only extracted features coordinates and a small surrounding neighborhood have to be sent over the network. For Harris corners, the coordinates can be coded as two 16bit numbers, and the neighborhood is 5 by 5 pixels (25 bytes) giving in total 29 bytes per feature. In the case of edge-based features, the 8-dimensional feature vector is composed of 6 integers, each coded on one byte, and two floating numbers coded on 4 bytes, thus a total 14 bytes per features. On average, there are approximately 400 strong Harris corners and 600 edge-based features on a frame.

From the table, the amount of data to be transferred over the network is almost 20 times less when using smart cameras rather than normal cameras. Furthermore the computation of Harris corners and edge-based feature is quite intensive as it takes about 27ms and 22ms respectively on a standard PC with Intel dualCore CPU running at 2.0GHz for the chosen frame size. Thus, it is interesting to decentralize the feature extraction computation in order to alleviate the computational burden of the central node.

Task partition in the system. In the current system, the image rectification and feature extraction are executed in the smart cameras. The remaining tasks are done in the central processing node. In the smart cameras, the Harris corners and Canny edge detection are performed by the FPGA directly on the frame data flow coming out the video sensor. Results and the frame data are then sent with a time stamp to the smart camera CPU via the Local Bus (see Figure 2). The extracted Harris corners are then prepared to be sent over the network to

Table 1. Exchange data sizes for normal and smart cameras

	Normal cameras	Smart cameras
image data (bytes)	$2 \times 752 \times 480$	-
Harris corners (bytes)	-	$2 \times 400 \times (4 + 25)$
Edge-based features (bytes)	-	$2 \times 600 \times 14$
Total per frame (bytes)	721920	40000

the central node. Edge-features are constructed following the method described in Section 2.2. Due to development difficulties on the FPGA, the image rectification is currently done on the smart camera CPU. Since features are already extracted, rectification is applied only to features as opposed to the entire frame as described in Section 2.2. However, the global accuracy of the method is not affected by this permutation of tasks.

Execution times in the FPGA. The computation of Harris corners can be done in one pass directly on pixels coming from the video sensor. The corresponding processing block in the FPGA runs at 40 MHz and can fully process one pixel per clock cycle. The computation of Harris corners takes then a little more than 9ms. Although it is possible to implement a Canny edge detector in one pass [12], for simplicity we use a two-pass approach: in the first pass, the gradients and gradient orientations are computed, non-maxima suppression is applied. In the second pass the hysteresis thresholding is applied. The execution time for the edge detector is about 19ms.

The role of the central node is to collect and organize data coming from the smart cameras, carry out the feature matching, 3D back-projection, clustering and tracking. Traffic analysis results can be stored locally or sent further to a server. On average, the matching of Harris features takes 24ms, and the matching of edge-based features takes 8ms. 3ms are spent for computing the backprojection of 3D points and more 3ms are spent for clustering the points into vehicles. Tracking is almost negligible (less than a ms). In summary the central node can process a stereo frame in about 40ms. However a small latency is introduced to collect corresponding data from the two cameras. At the end the system runs between 20 and 25 frame/s (40-50ms/frame).

4   Experimental Results

To validate the vehicles detection method, a test was conducted on 3 sequences extracted from a long video of a 4 lanes motorway. Since the final system contains a video sensor, it is not possible to replay the test sequences. Hence the system is simulated in software in order to be able to process recorded sequences. The three test sequences contain a realistic set of vehicle types. See Figure 3. A total of 214 vehicles went through the zone covered by the two cameras. A human operator identified the detection errors. These can be classified into 3 categories: the vehicle is not detected, the object detected is not a vehicle and the vehicle is detected several times The causes for the miss-detection case are either a bad contrast between a dark car and the shadowed road (see Figure 3(f)) or a missed image in the camera flow. The first cause could be avoided by using more advanced feature extraction.The second category does not appear on the analyzed sequence but could be a problem if a mark on the road is permanently miss-matched. The third category is due either to tracking problem or to over-segmentation of the 3D points, which induces double detections of the same vehicle. This could be avoided using the tractory analysis, which is not yet used here. The results of the 3 sequences (s1, s2, s3) are presented in Table 2.

Fig. 3. (a) (b) (c) Three consecutive frames on a motorway: vehicles are pre-detected (blue boxes), detected when their trajectory is long enough (green boxes), and tracked. (d) (e) Two frames showing a detected truck. Note the car partially occluded behind the truck which is however pre-detected and then detected. (f) Images with a missed vehicle (on the left)

Table 2. Error types for the three sequences

	s1	s2	s3
Number of vehicles	107	44	63
Number of detected vehicles	110	44	63
Total not detected / Total not detected in %	6 / 5.6%	5 / 11.4%	7 / 11.1%
Total false detections / Total false detections in %	9 / 9.4%	5 / 11.4%	7 / 11.1%
Over-segmentation / Tracking error	7 / 2	3 / 2	2 / 5

The dimensions of the vehicle are consistent with the vehicle actual characteristics. A test was conducted on 20 vehicles. This test compares the dimensions given by the algorithm of some well identified vehicles (sedans, estate cars, SUV, minivans...) to dimensions furnished by the constructor. The height measurement presents a precision of 92.1%, the length 76.58% and the width 83.35%. Speed measurement has not been validated yet, but current speeds obtained with this methods seem plausible.

5   Conclusion

In this work a realistic application of multi-camera system for real-time traffic monitoring has been presented. Based on a multi-feature matching and a 3D tracking, the system detects vehicles with detection rates about 90% and determines their dimensions with accuracy above 75%. Also the method gives good results even with fast change of lighting condition. The system is based on smart cameras that perform part of the processings and communicate results to a central processing node.

References

1. Kastrinaki, V., Zervakis, M., Kalaitzakis, K.: A survey of video processing techniques for traffic applications. In: Image and Vision Computing, vol. 21, pp. 359–381. Elsevier, Amsterdam (2003)
2. Dickinson, K.W., Wan, C.L.: Road traffic monitoring using the trip ii system. In: IEE Second International Conference on Road Traffic Monitoring, pp. 56–60 (1989)
3. Hogg, D.C., Sullivan, G.D., Baker, K.D., Mott, D.H.: Recognition of vehicles in traffic scenes using geometric models. In: Proceedings of the International Conference on Road Traffic Data Collection, London. IEE (1984)
4. Beymer, D., McLauchlan, P., Coifman, B., Malik, J.: A real-time computer vision system for measuring traffic parameters. In: Proceedings of the IEEE Computer Vision and Pattern Recognition, pp. 495–501. IEEE, Los Alamitos (1997)
5. Arth, C., Leistner, C., Bischof, H.: Tricam: An embedded platform for remote traffic surveillance. In: Proceedings of the IEEE CVPR embedded CV workshop, p. 125. IEEE, Los Alamitos (2006)
6. Alefs, B., Schreiber, D.: Accurate speed measurement from vehicle trajectories using adaboost detection and robust template tracking. In: International IEEE Conference on Intelligent Transportation Systems, pp. 405–412. IEEE, Los Alamitos (2007)
7. Harris, C., Stephens, M.: A combined corner and edge detector. In: Proceedings of the 4th Alvey Vision Conference, pp. 147–151 (1988)
8. Zhang, Z.: Determining the epipolar geometry and its uncertainty: A review. IJCV 27(2), 161–195 (1998)
9. Zhang, Z.: Determining the epipolar geometry and its uncertainty. IEEE TPAMI 22, 1330–1334 (2000)
10. Canny, J.: A computational approach to edge detection. IEEE Trans. on Pattern Analysis and Machine Intelligence 8, 679–714 (1986)
11. Hartley, R.I., Zisserman, A.: Multiple view geometry in computer vision, 2nd edn. Cambridge University Press, Cambridge (2004)
12. Neoh, H.S., Hazanchuk, A.: Adaptive edge detection for real-time video processing using fpgas. In: GSPx 2004 - Global Signal Processing Expo and Conference (2004)

Development and Long-Term Verification of Stereo Vision Sensor System for Controlling Safety at Railroad Crossing

Daisuke Hosotani[1,3], Ikushi Yoda[2,3], and Katsuhiko Sakaue[2,3]

[1] Research Institute, Koito Industries, Ltd,
100 Maeda-cho, Totsuka-ku, Yokohama, Kanagawa, 244-8567, Japan
[2] Information Technology Research Institute,
National Institute of Advanced Industrial Science and Technology,
AIST Tsukuba Central 2 Tsukuba, Ibaraki, 305-8568, Japan
[3] System and Information Engineering, University of Tsukuba,
Tennodai, Tsukuba, Ibaraki, 305-8577, Japan

Abstract. Many people are involved in accidents every year at railroad crossings, but there is no suitable sensor for detecting pedestrians. We are therefore developing a stereo vision based system for ensuring safety at railroad crossings. In this system, stereo cameras are installed at the corners and are pointed toward the center of the railroad crossing to monitor the passage of people. The system determines automatically and in real-time whether anyone or anything is inside the railroad crossing, and whether anyone remains in the crossing. The system can be configured to automatically switch over to a surveillance monitor or automatically connect to an emergency brake system in the event of trouble. We have developed an original stereovision device and installed the remote controlled experimental system applied human detection algorithm in the commercial railroad crossing. Then we store and analyze image data and tracking data throughout two years for standardization of system requirement specification.

1 Introduction

The recent diversification of people's lifestyles has led to increasing demands for automated technologies for safety and security services. However, conventional sensors can monitor spaces only in terms of points (contact sensors), lines (infrared sensors), and planes (ultrasonic sensors), and their resolution is very low. They can therefore be used only for turning warning systems on and off and other limited purposes. To overcome those limitations, we have been developing a system that uses multiple stereo cameras for precise detection of people in a 3-D monitoring space [1]. One application for this technology is automatic monitoring of railway crossings.

Ohta et al. investigated the use of two stereo cameras to detect obstacles [2]. In that study, however, the test site is an empty street and they couldn't obtain

M. Fritz, B. Schiele, and J.H. Piater (Eds.): ICVS 2009, LNCS 5815, pp. 154–163, 2009.
© Springer-Verlag Berlin Heidelberg 2009

enough data for verification. There is currently no other research on monitoring pedestrian traffic with a stereo camera all day in a real environment.

Poseidon is a real application system designed to help lifeguards [3] and is used only in pools. There has also been research on using single-lens cameras to track people [4, 5], but those systems were evaluated only with static datasets or with data obtained in a static laboratory environment. A few studies have used stereo cameras for detecting pedestrians [6, 7]. Fascioli used a stereo camera to detect objects on pedestrian crossings [6], but the stereo camera needs to be installed at directly above a monitoring area. A pedestrian recognition method for a driving assistance system has been proposed [7], but that proposal focuses on a learning method based on segmented images.

Other existing sensing technologies for managing safety at crossings include:

1. Electromagnetic sensors consisting of loop coils that are installed under the road surface at crossings and detect metal objects passing over by changes in inductance, and
2. Photoelectric sensors that detect objects that block light when passing between an emitter and receiver.

Those sensors cannot detect objects below a certain size, and are not effective in detecting people. The also have low resolution, so even if they can detect an object, they are not suited to monitoring changes in the object's situation. Because about 35% of the cause of accidents at crossings are pedestrians [4], we developed a stereo vision sensing technology that can detect all people at a crossing and allow action to be taken flexibly according to the situation.

Specifically, stereo cameras are placed so as to cover the center of the crossing and monitor people passing through for dangerous behavior or the presence of people just before a train is to pass through (Fig. 1). The use of stereo cameras allows extraction of distance information to use as a key for excluding shadows of persons, changes in daylight and other factors that are problematic for frame-differencing video methods. Furthermore, using color data along with the distance information makes it possible to differentiate birds, scraps of paper blowing around, and other objects that might cause false readings at railroad crossings.

We have already conducted basic short-term experiments using commercially-available stereo cameras combined with a personal computer, and devised a basic method for estimating the position of people from the acquired distance data [10]. In this paper, we describe an original stereo vision device that implements that method. We also describe the features of an experimental safety control system for actual railroad crossings and present evaluation results for long-term operation of the system.

Section 2 of this paper describes the ubiquitous stereo vision (USV) [11], and section 3 describes the method of using USV distance information to distinguish people from other objects. Section 4 explains the specifications of a system installed at a crossing. Image and pedestrian tracking data recorded at an actual railroad crossing is used to validate and analyze system operation in Section 5. Section 6 summarizes the study and highlights issues for future research.

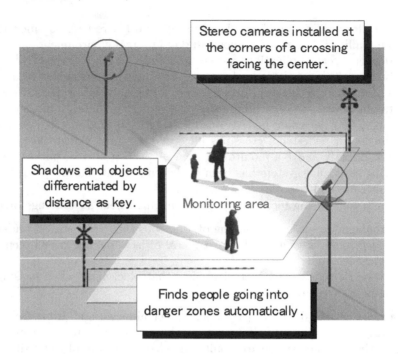

Stereo cameras installed at the corners of a crossing facing the center.

Shadows and objects differentiated by distance as key.

Monitoring area

Finds people going into danger zones automatically.

Fig. 1. Concept of a USV-based railroad crossing safety management system

2   Ubiquitous Stereo Vision (USV)

2.1   Overview of USV

The conditions in outdoor environments such as railroad crossings, where there are extreme variations in lighting conditions throughout the day and in crowded shopping areas on holidays, make it very difficult to differentiate people using motion-difference-based image processing. We attempted to solve this problem using USV. USV is essentially a system capable of detecting the presence of multiple people and differentiating individuals based on range information and color image data obtained from stereo cameras installed at multiple points. In this work, we implement a safety management system for railroad crossings by exploiting the main feature of USV systems, which real-time acquisition of range data in actual environments. The range information we deal with here is a 3-D reconstruction obtained by suitable transformation of range data acquired by cameras. Object recognition based on this range information is can adapt practically to severe changes in outdoor conditions, such as weather and shadows.

2.2   USV Device

While the stereo vision system has the advantage of robustness against environmental changes, execution of the stereo matching algorithm requires high-speed computation.

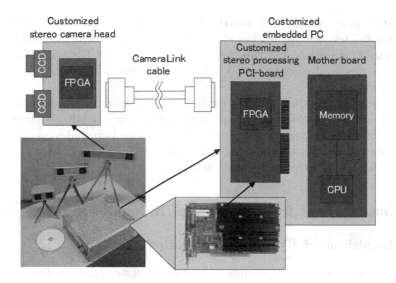

Fig. 2. Outline of USV Device

Table 1. Specification of Original USV Device

Customized Stereo Camera Head	
Imager	1/3-inch CCD image sensors
Resolution	VGA (640x480) or QVGA (320x240)
Frame Rate	30fps
Baseline	50mm, 120mm, and 180mm
Camera Calibration	Calibrated at the factory
Image Format	Grayscale or color (bayer)
Output Interface	CameraLink
Customized Stereo Processing PCI-board	
Resolution	VGA (640x480) or QVGA (320x240)
Disparity Frame Rate	15 fps (VGA mode) or 30 fps (QVGA mode)
Stereo Algorithm	Sum of Absolute Differences (SAD) with 7x7 - 15x15 block matching.
Host Interface	Standard PCI 66
Post Processing interface	
Drivers	Linux and Windows drivers provide access to the depth image and camera through images.
Control API	Includes programming interfaces for parameter control.

We therefore developed a hardware implementation (FPGA) of the algorithm as a stereo vision device (USV devices).

This USV device has the three components described below (Fig. 2, Table. 1).

- **Stereo camera**: Acquires two synchronized raw images and outputs them through the CameraLink interface.

- **Stereo processing PCI board**: Receives two raw images via the CameraLink interface, applies the stereo matching algorithm, and outputs the disparity image and the two raw images over the PCI bus interface. This board runs on drivers for the Windows and Linux personal computer operating systems.
- **Embedded personal computer**: Receives the two raw images and the disparity image and computes range information from the disparity image. It then executes the person detection algorithm. This personal computer is specially equipped for improved power supply capacity and greater robustness against high temperature environments.

3   Measurement from 3D Range Information

3.1   Acquisition of 3D Range Information

Multiple stereo cameras are mounted on utility poles or other facilities near the crossing so as to face the monitored area and acquire range information.

3.2   Human Detection

Finding the heads of people from the acquired range information is mathematically equivalent to a multi-point search problem. However, considering the accuracy of acquired range images and the requirement for real-time operation, we treat it here as an image processing problem.

First, we use the extraction method to obtain multi-level range information projections and then apply the person detection algorithm to detect the position of the person passing below the camera in each frame [11].

3.3   Neighborhood Connection

The head positions obtained for the frames are connected as a time series and used as person movement data to count the number of persons remaining in the area. When there are l movement lines in the preceding frame, $f - 1$, the head position of the mth movement line is taken to be $t_m^{f-1} = (x_m^{f-1}, y_m^{f-1})$. In that case, the heads of c persons appear in the most recent frame, f. The coordinates of this n^{th} person's head is in the same way expressed as $p_n^f = (x_n^f, y_n^f)$. Let D denote the distance between the coordinates of the beginning of the line of motion and the coordinates of the head. We then apply the following tracking algorithm that connects nearest neighbor points to form the line of motion for that person.

```
for m = 0; m < l; m = m + 1 do
  for n = 0; n < c; n = n + 1 do
```

$$D(m, n) = \sqrt{(x_m^{f-1} - x_m^f)^2 + (y_m^{f-1} - y_m^f)^2}$$

```
  end
end
for k = 0; k < l; k = k + 1 do
  D (a, b) = minimum (D)
```

$$t_a^f = p_b^f$$

```
  for i = 0; i < c; i = i + 1 do
    delete (D (a, i) )
  end
  for j = 0; j < l; j = j + 1 do
    delete (D (j, b) )
  end
end
```

4 Development of Remote Experiment System for Safety at Commercial Railroad Crossings

4.1 Experimental Railroad Crossing Site

In February 2007, we installed an experimental safety control system for commercial railroad crossings at an actual crossing near the Tokyu Jiyugaoka Station. The system has been in continuous operation since then. The station is located in a popular shopping area on the outskirts of central Tokyo and is used by more than 120,000 passengers every day. We used this installation to test the durability of the hardware and verify the accuracy of person detection.

4.2 Remotely Controlled Experimental System

Two stereo cameras were mounted on utility poles at the site of the experiment (Fig. 3 & 4). One personal computer is connected to each camera via an optical cable and repeaters. The computer creates the range information and the person tracking information within the monitoring area. This system receives various signals that indicate the status of the crossing from the crossing equipment (Table 2). In addition, the crossing is connected to our laboratory by an ordinary commercial optical line in a virtual private network, allowing remote control of the system as well as data transfer and storage.

4.3 Acquired Data

This system tracks all of the persons passing through the monitoring area at about 10 fps, and the data for those lines of motion are recorded over the entire time period from first train departure to last train arrival. During the time the crossing closing signal is being issued, raw images are saved an two-second intervals.

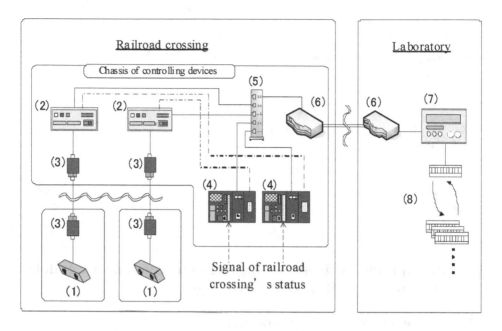

Fig. 3. Outline of experimental system, (1) Stereo camera heads, (2) Customized embedded personal computers, (3) CameraLink cable - Optical fiber cable repeater, (4) Programmable Logic controller, (5) Switching hub, (6) Router, (7) Client computer, (8) Removable hard disks

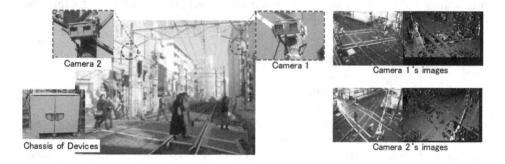

Fig. 4. Overview of Crossing and obtained images

Table 2. Signals of railroad crossing's status

Device	Signal level	
	High level	Low level
Crossing gate	Gate closing	Gate opening
Track circuit	Train within 20 m	Nothing
Infrared car sensor	Car on crossing	Nothing

Table 3. Specification of verification data

Term	For 2 years from February, 2007
Time	6 a. m. to 1 a. m.; the time period from the first train of the day to the last.
Weather	Alternately clear, overcast, rain and snow.
Camera deployment	2 stereo cameras mounted on poles facing to the center of the railroad crossing.
System frame rate	10 frames/second.
Camera images	Single color, 640 × 480 pixels.
3D reconstructions	Calculations based on 640 × 480 points.

5 Analysis of Recognition Results

5.1 Experimental Railroad Crossing Site

Concerning the accuracy of the system, we verified the effects of long-term changes in the environment such as seasonal changes and the effects of short-term environmental changes such as weather. To do so, we used the accumulated intermittent raw image data and line of motion data to analyze the error in detecting people in the crossing during the times the crossing was closed.

For this purpose, we used the data obtained from one of the two cameras set up at the crossing as described in section 4. The data for when the crossing was closed was obtained over a total of 36 days in the months of February, May, August and September of 2008. From each month, we selected three days of clear weather, three days of cloudy weather and three days of rainy weather. For each day, one set of crossing closed scene data was sampled for every hour at equal intervals from 6:00 a.m until 1:00 a.m., giving a total of 20 sets of data. The data for each scene included about 400 frames over the time from when the crossing closed signal began to when the track circuit signal was raised (from when the crossing barrier began to lower until the train approached to within 20 m of the crossing). The overall total of 288,000 frames of data acquired were examined visually. The 6-m-wide and 10-m-long railroad crossing area was divided into an up-bound side half and a down-bound side half, with the half closest to the camera taken as the monitoring area.

Success for intrusion detection was defined as the case in which a line of motion of an arbitrarily specified length h or greater appears in the time from when a given pedestrian enters the monitoring area until that person leaves the area. The verification procedure involved first examining the intermittent raw images to distinguish persons passing through the crossing. If there exists line of motion whose length is at least h frames for that person, then the detection is judged to be successful. If the length of the motion line is less than h frames, then the detection is judged to have failed. In the case that there is a line of motion that is at least h frames long but does not correspond to a pedestrian, it as counted as an extraneous detection. For this evaluation, we set h to three.

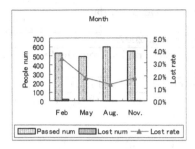 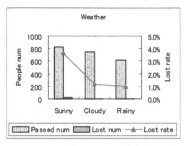

Fig. 5. Error rate trend (Month & Weather conditions)

The verifications results showed that there were no extraneous detections for any of the data. Because among causes of extraneous detections, low objects like equipments of crossings or shadows were rejected by the person detection algorithm. In addition, if extra detections occurred from fake range data in one frame, these didn't become a long tracking line. Because fake range data were generated by faults of stereo matching and these were less apt to appear at a same point in a series of video frames.

On the other hand, a number of failures to detect occurred among the 1650 people passing by.

The detection failure rate by month and weather condition are presented in Fig 5.

5.2   Considerations

The results presented in Fig 5 show that the detection failure rate was higher for February than other months, and for clear days than for cloudy or rainy days. The reason for that is sunlight reflected from structures on sunny days entering the camera lens directly and interfering with the stereo image processing in some of the scenes. That problem can be dealt with by remounting the camera at a more suitable height and angle or by increasing the dynamic range of the camera. We surmise that another factor is that many people use umbrellas on rainy days, which increases the range points that form a body and facilitates detection.

6   Conclusions and Future Work

Applying USV technology for which basic testing has already been completed, we developed a stereo vision device using hardware circuitry. Long-term operation experiments are continuing with a permanently installed system for railway crossing safety management mounted at a commercial railroad crossing. We used data collected by that system to verify the effects of environmental changes on the accuracy of the intrusion detection system.

In future work, we will continue to collect data in the field and use artificial weather facilities and other means to acquire data under snow and fog conditions, which is difficult to do at the present site. We will then use that data to verify detection accuracy under more diverse conditions and identify the factors that affect system accuracy. On the basis of those results, we will define the system requirements, and continue to improve the person detection algorithm.

References

1. Yoda, I., Sakaue, K.: Concept of Ubiquitous Stereo Vision and Applications for Human Sensing. In: Proc. 2003 IEEE International Symposium on Computational Intelligence in Robotics and Automation (CIRA2003), Kobe, Japan, pp. 1251–1257 (July 2003)
2. Ohta, M., Shibayama, N., Hanawa, K.: Obstacle Detection System for Level Crossing Using Stereo Cameras. In: Proc. World Congress on Railway Research 2003 (WCRR 2003), Edinburgh, England, (September-October 2003)
3. HP of poseidon system from Vision-IQ works, http://www.vision-iq.com/
4. Zhao, T., Nevatia, R.: Tracking multiple humans in complex situation. IEEE Transaction on PAMI 26(9), 1208–1221 (2004)
5. Mittal, A., Davis, L.S.: M2Traker: A multi-view approach to segment and tracking people in a cluttered scene. Int. Journal of Computer Vision 51(3), 189–203 (2003)
6. Fascioli, A., Fedriga, R.I., Ghidoni, S.: Vision-based monitoring of pedestrian crossings. In: Proc. 14th International Conference on Image Analysis and Processing (ICIAP 2007), Modena, Italy, pp. 566–574 (September 2007)
7. Zhao, L.: Stereo- and Neural Network-based Pedestrian Detection. IEEE Transaction on ITS 1(3), 148–154 (2000)
8. East Japan Railway Company: Corporate catalogue, (2008) (in Japanese), http://www.jreast.co.jp/youran/pdf/all.pdf
9. Cabinet office, Government of Japan: Traffic safety white paper 2008 (in Japanese) (2008)
10. Yoda, I., Sakaue, K., Hosotani, D.: Multi-point Stereo Camera System for Controlling Safety at Railroad Crossings. In: Proc. International Conference on Computer Vision Systems (ICVS 2006), New York, USA, p. 51 (January 2006)
11. Yoda, I., Sakaue, K., Yamamoto, Y., Hosotani, D.: Human Body Sensing Using Multi-Point Stereo Cameras. In: Proc. 17th International Conference on Pattern Recognition (ICPR 2004), Cambridge, UK, vol. 4, pp. 1010–1015 (August 2004)

Generation of 3D City Models Using Domain-Specific Information Fusion

Jens Behley and Volker Steinhage

Institute of Computer Science III,
Rheinische Friedrich-Wilhelms-Universität,
53117 Bonn, Germany

Abstract. In this contribution we present a building reconstruction strategy using spatial models of building parts and information fusion of aerial image, digital surface model and ground plans. The fusion of sensor data aims to derive reliably local building features and is therefore controlled in a domain specific way: ground plans indicate the approximate location of outer roof corners and the intersection of planes from the digital surface model yields the inner roof corners. Parameterized building parts are selected using these corners and afterwards combined to form complete three-dimensional building models. We focus here on the domain specific information fusion and present results on a sub-urban dataset.

1 Introduction

In the recent years three-dimensional city models became increasingly important in many applications. For instance, many manufacturers of navigation systems integrate the ability to visualize urban environments in a three-dimensional ego view. In this view, prominent buildings or landmarks are visualized to enable a more intuitive navigation. Besides this, Goggle Earth and other programs enable the user to view their environment from above and at many places even three-dimensionally. Three-dimensional city models are also commonly used in the field of town-planning, pollution simulation and virtual tourism. The increasing demand for either simple or complex building models can't be accommodated by solely manual reconstruction. Therefore automated reconstruction is an on-going research topic in the computer vision community.

In this paper we propose a reconstruction process that employs the information fusion of aerial images with ground plans and aerial images with airborne laser scanning data to extract reliable local building features, i.e. roof corners, and a domain-specific building modelling [1].

The paper is organized as follows. First, we discuss related work in section 2. We briefly introduce the used sensor data and modelling by parameterized building parts in section 3. Then, we describe in section 4 our approach to reconstruct buildings using these parameterized building parts. Section 5 presents some implementation details. Section 6 presents our current results and finally section 7 concludes and suggests some improvements to further increase the automation.

M. Fritz, B. Schiele, and J.H. Piater (Eds.): ICVS 2009, LNCS 5815, pp. 164–173, 2009.
© Springer-Verlag Berlin Heidelberg 2009

2   Related Work

Building reconstruction from images and other inputs is a classical application in computer vision. In the last decade several approaches have been presented to solve this problem by using aerial images [1, 2, 3, 4, 5]. Digital surface maps (DSM) were also used to reconstruct buildings [6, 7]. A more general overview on building reconstruction is given in [8, 9].

Using more than one source of information is advantageous, since inadequacies in one data source can be accommodated by another data source. Thus many research groups investigate the fusion of different data sources for reconstruction. To model buildings, several standard representations from computer graphics have been utilized, e.g. boundary representation or CSG. Also domain-specific representations have been developed. In the remainder of this section, we summarize the most relevant related work concerning information fusion and domain-specific modelling.

Haala and Brenner [10] use ground plans and DSM to reconstruct buildings. Their approach uses the ground plans to extract rectangular regions to position CSG models. In the next step the parameters of the models are optimized to minimize the error in respect to the DSM. In contrast to [10] we use aerial image additionally, since the ground plans don't resemble the observable roof outline neither topologically nor geometrically. Furthermore, we use the different sensor sources in a interwoven fashion. This means that information from one sensor source guides the feature extraction of another sensor source and vice versa.

Fischer et al.[1] use parameterized building parts and multiple aerial images to reconstruct buildings. A tight coupling of two-dimensional and three-dimensional features and aggregates enables a robust reconstruction. Starting with corners and edges, two dimensional corner observations are derived and via stereo reconstruction enriched to three-dimensional corner observations. These corner observations are used to select building parts, which are combined to complete three-dimensional building models. The major part of this process is adopted in this paper and the main points will be summarized in the next sections. In contrast to [1] we integrate different sensor sources to further improve the automated reconstruction.

Lafarge et al. [7] also use parameterized building parts and a DSM to reconstruct buildings. First, a subdivision in two-dimensional support regions is performed. The support regions are used to position three-dimensional parameterized building parts. A Markov Chain Monte Carlo approach is used to determine the parameter settings of the building parts. However, the extraction of the precise roof outline is difficult due to the density of airborne laser scanning and can only be approximated. We tackle this problem by using a aerial image where the resolution is naturally much higher. Furthermore, our building modelling enforces geometrically correct reconstructions, which is not mandatory in the approach by Lafarge et al. How this geometrical correctness could be assured, will be one topic of the next section.

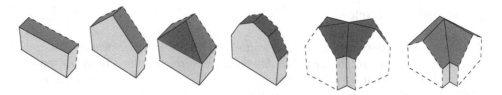

Fig. 1. Some building parts: flat, gable, mansard and hip roof terminal; gable roof X-connector, gable roof L-connector. Plug faces are drawn dashed. Note, that we distinguish between different types of plug faces, i.e. the mansard roof plug face is only connectable to the mansard roof terminal in this collection of building parts. However, the gable and hip roof are connectable, since they have the same type of plug face.

3 Sensor Data and Modelling Approach

We use aerial imagery with a resolution of about 10 cm, while the digital surface model (DSM) generated from airborne laser scanning, shows a not regularized resolution of about 50 cm, i.e. the data points are not interpolated to a grid. The aerial images are so called orthophotos, which implies that a slight perspective distortion is visible and ground plan and DSM are slightly translated in respect to the observeable roofs in the aerial image. The building ground plans describe the building outline measured in the height of 1 m above the ground. All these data are referenced in the common Gauss-Krüger coordinate system and was kindly provided by the land register and surveying office of the city of Bonn.

The modelling is based on typed and parameterized building parts (cf. [1]). The types correspond to different roof types and shapes of ground plans. Building parts must be connected("plugged") via typed *plug faces* and hence a topological and geometrical correctness can be assured. Some of the building parts, which we use, are shown in figure 1. Based on the number of plug faces (dashed lines in figure 1) building parts with one plug face will be called *terminals*, while building parts with more than one plug face will be called *connectors*.

Building parts are encoded hierarchically by a boundary representation (cf. [11]). All faces and corners (vertices) are labeled with domain specific attributes; e.g. wall faces, roof faces, ridge corners, etc. Furthermore, edges are labeled with their orientation in respect to the ground plane, i.e. 'horizontal', 'vertical' and 'sloped'. We also classify normals of adjoining faces to the left and right side of an edge. The combination of corner, edge and face labels enables a robust so called indexing of building parts by matching of these labels [1]. We use symbolic parameters in the coordinates of the vertices to parameterize the building parts. When connecting two building parts the same parameters are unified, if they appear in the plug face, and renamed otherwise. This ensures consistent parameterization even in the connected building parts and in the final building hypothesis accordingly. The selection and combination of building parts into complete three-dimensional building models is described in the next section.

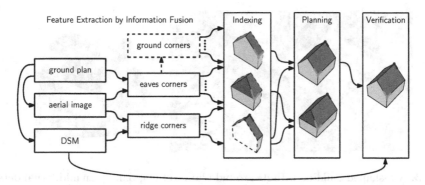

Fig. 2. Our reconstruction strategy and the data flow depicted by arrows. First, information fusion of aerial image, ground plan and DSM is used to derive eaves (green) and ridge corners (blue). These corner observations are used to index building parts. Next, the building parts are combined to complete building hypotheses by a planning procedure. Finally, the hypothesis that minimizes the error in respect to the DSM is selected as reconstruction result.

4   Reconstruction Strategy

The following strategy is motivated by the underlying building model and the provided data. We can identify three classes of corners in the building model, namely eaves (outer roof corners), ridge (inner roof corners) and ground corners. These classes are extracted from the data in different ways. We therefore call our feature extraction domain-specific. Figure 2 highlights the main stages in our reconstruction process – feature extraction, indexing, planning and verification. First, we use the ground plan to extract the region of interest from the aerial image and DSM. Furthermore, we use the ground plan to infer the location of the eaves corners in the aerial image. However, wall corners in the ground plan have generally not the same location as the corresponding roof corners, due to overhanging roofs. But these roof corners are located in the proximity of the ground corners. Furthermore, not all wall corners correspond to roof corners at all because of convex and concave recesses by terraces, balconies etc (cf. figure 3). We account this fact by a shape generalization of the ground plan, which removes small sized border lines caused by terraces, balconies etc. The orientation of the remaining ground plan walls determine the orientation of eaves in the aerial image. Roof planes can be derived from the DSM using a plane segmentation. Intersecting these planes results in the inner three-dimensional roof edges. We determine the position of ridge corners using the intersections of this inner roof edges. Moreover, the intersections of horizontally inner roof edges with the ground plan induce another type of ridge corners, the ridge points of gable roofs, and their approximate (due to roof overhangs) location (cf. section 5). Ground corners can not be observed directly neither in the aerial image nor the DSM. In the current version of our approach we predict the location of ground corners by using the location of eaves corners.

Fig. 3. A L-shaped building with its ground plan. In the ground plan additional details occur, which are not observable in the roof outline. Also a displacement due to roof overhangs is visible. The middle picture shows results of the eaves corners (green) and ridge corners (blue) extracted by our feature extraction (see section 5). The picture on the right shows our reconstruction result.

In summary, the corner and edge features extracted from the ground plan as well as the three-dimensional planes, edge, and corner features derived from DSM determine their approximate locations in the aerial image. The detection of these features in the aerial images by image processing procedures is therefore guided by the derived knowledge from the ground plan and the DSM. Furthermore, the two-dimensional features extracted in the aerial image will verify the features derived from the ground plan and the DSM.

Next, the locations of the eaves and ridge corners in the aerial image are combined with the plane information derived by the plane segmentation algorithm. This yields three-dimensional *corner observations* with three-dimensional position, adjacent edges and adjoining faces, and qualitative labels for the corner itself ('eaves', 'ridge' and 'ground'), every edge ('horizontal', 'vertical' and 'sloped') and every face ('horizontal', 'vertical' and 'sloped'). Details on the implementation of the feature extraction are given in the next section.

We adopt the concepts of Fischer et al. [1] to index and combine building parts, and estimate their parameters. In the following only a short summary is given and improvements are explained more detailed.

The aforementioned labeling is crucial for the selection of the buildings parts. Building parts are selected by matching of the reconstructed corner labels with the labels of the building parts. This process is called *indexing*. In contrast to the approach of Fischer et al. we use additional labels to narrow down the amount of indexed building parts. First, we exploit the different ways of corner extraction to derive corner labels, as mentioned before. Next we use the planes from the DSM to derive normals with corresponding labels 'horizontal', 'vertical' and 'sloped'. In our building parts every edge has two adjoining faces and so has every edge of a corner observation. For all faces that can not be observed an additional label 'unknown' is introduced, and this label can be matched with every normal orientation.

Next, the building parts are combined to building hypotheses. A planning algorithm generates a plan to combine the terminals and connectors in complete building hypotheses (cf. [1]). Every indexed building part is associated with the indexing corner observation. A complete building hypothesis is composed of one building part for every corner observation and after combining the building parts no plug faces are left. As mentioned before, a building part must be connected via connectable plug faces. A plug face P_A of a building part A is connectable to a plug face P_B, if the type of P_A equals the type of P_B (cf. figure 1) and the normals n_A and n_B of P_A and P_B satisfiy $n_A \cdot -n_B > 1 - \epsilon \in \mathbb{R}$, i.e. the normals are nearly parallel and opposed oriented.

We end up with one or more complete building hypotheses. Now, the parameter estimation is performed using the Levenberg-Marquardt approach. Parameter estimation is done by minimizing the error of the building part corners to the corresponding corner observations. Our approach results in the hypothesis that minimizes the error of the roof planes to the DSM.

5   Domain-Specific Information Fusion

As mentioned in the previous section, we use a domain-specific information fusion to robustly extract features. This means we employ different ways of feature extraction for different domain-specific entities – eaves, ridge and ground corners. In the following section we describe more precisely our methods and implementation details.

5.1   Eaves Corners

Outer roof corners, so called eaves corners, are detected using ground plan information and the aerial image. For this purpose, corners c_I in the aerial image I are detected using the Harris detector [12] and image edges e_I are detected using a non-maximum suppression on the gradient followed by a Hough transformation [13]. The hough transformation is used to determine the direction of edges. To eliminate noise and unnecessary details in the aerial image an edge preserving non-linear diffusion [14] is applied before edges and corners are detected. Corners c_G and edges e_G, which correspond to eaves corners and eaves edges, exists in the generalized ground plan G. This fact is used to determine corners c_I in the aerial image which correspond to these ground plan corners c_G. For each c_G and all corners c_I in the aerial image, a rating r is computed by the euclidean distance $d(c_I, c_G)$ to c_G and the local gradient count $g(e_I, e_G)$ of the edges e_I in the local neighborhood of c_I:

$$r = \frac{1}{2} \sum_{e_I} (g(e_I, e_G) - t_1) + \frac{1}{2}(t_2 - d(c_G, c_I)) \tag{1}$$

In this term $g(e_I, e_G)$ describes the gradient count of such image edges e_I which are nearly parallel to the corresponding ground plan edge e_G and pass through c_I. The gradient count is only locally evaluated near every corner c_I, since the complete edges can be occluded. The corner c_I with the highest positive rating

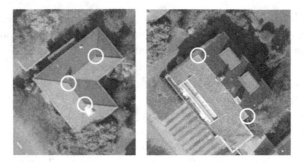

Fig. 4. The different types of ridge corners. The left figure shows the ridge corners, which results from intersection of inner roof edges. The second type of ridge corners is shown in the right figure.

r is regarded as match. Thus, the values t_1 and t_2 are thresholds to suppress candidates with low gradient count of adjoining edges and great distance to the ground plan corner. The parameters are determined empirically and a size of the local window around every corner of 30 pixels and $t_1 = 15$ and $t_2 = 50$ yield good results. Figure 3 shows extracted eaves corners with corresponding ground plan corners. The associated height parameter of such a corner observation is derived using the plane segmentation, which is described in the succeeding section. Every corner extracted by this procedure is labeled as eaves corner.

5.2   Ridge Corners

To determine the location of inner roof corners, so called ridge corners, we derive inner roof edges from the DSM. Since a house must have a certain height, we truncate all points below 2 meters above the ground. Then, a plane segmentation is obtained by region merging on the Delaunay triangulation $T = \{\tau_i\}_{i \in \mathbb{N}}$ of the DSM points [15]. In this region merging algorithm adjoining regions $R_i = \{\tau_k\}_{k=1,\ldots,|R_i|}$, $R_j = \{\tau_l\}_{l=1,\ldots,|R_j|}$, $R_i \cap R_j = \emptyset$ are merged to one region $R = R_i \cup R_j$, if the region normals μ_i, μ_j are similar oriented, i.e.

$$\mu_i \cdot \mu_j > cos(\theta), \quad 0 < \theta < \frac{\pi}{2} \quad \text{and} \quad \mu_i = |R_i|^{-1} \cdot \sum_{\tau_j \in R_i} n_j. \tag{2}$$

The algorithm is initialized with one region for every triangle, merges every two regions R_i, R_j which maximize the dot product $\mu_i \cdot \mu_j$ and is iterated as long as adjoining regions satisfy equation 2. A threshold of $\theta = 25$ degrees produces in most cases good results. After the merging, all regions R_i with $|R_i| < 0.1 \cdot |T|$ are removed, since these regions are assumed to be caused by vegetation, etc.

Merging of co-planar regions is the next step. This is achieved by a interpolation of planes with singular value decomposition from the DSM points of the region triangles. Now, adjoining regions are merged, if the corresponding planes are co-planar. Dormers are currently not modelled and hence regions are eliminated, which are mostly enclosed by another region, i.e. such a region is neighbored to the surrounding region with more than 75% of its boundary. This local inspection is the main advantage over global plane estimators like RANSAC [16] or Hough transformation. Experiments showed that global estimators tend to subsume co-planar dormers to a single plane. Now, we can extract the inner roof edges by intersecting the remaining planes. Intersection of these edges yields the ridge corners. Every ridge corner is located and verified in the aerial image as before the eaves corners.

Gable roofs reveal a second type of ridge corner, which is formed by horizontally roof edges and adjoining walls (cf. figure 4) and these ridge corners thus can not be derived by intersection of inner roof edges. The second type of ridge corner is derived by projecting every horizontally oriented ridge edge onto the ground plan. The intersection of projected edge and ground plan edge yields the missing ridge corners. Then, this T-shaped corner hypothesis is verified – as in the case of the eaves corners – in the aerial image. Using the height information of the plane intersection and the involved planes, a spatial corner observation is created which is labeled as ridge corner. Furthermore the height of every eaves corner is determined by using the derived planes.

5.3   Ground Corners

In our building model, ground corners have the same location as the eaves corners – currently the models don't support roof overhangs. Thus, the ground corners are approximated by the projection of the eaves corners onto the ground. The height is interpolated by the mean of the ground DSM.

6   Evaluation

Our domain-specific information fusion and the aforementioned improvements were integrated into the reconstruction system from Fischer et al. [1]. The automatic reconstruction extracts features as described in section 5 and uses the corner observations to index building parts. In most cases, only some roof corners are needed to reconstruct a building, because missing corners are added by the building parts. But due to occlusion, weak contrasts in the aerial image, etc. some of the buildings are not automatically reconstructible, since too few corner observations could be infered. Therefore, our system offers the user a semi-automated reconstruction which enables him to initialize our approach by selecting the eaves corners in the aerial image. This semi-automatic approach allows the reconstruction of buildings even in difficult cases. In very bad cases, the user can lastly initiate the reconstruction by manually indexing, i.e. choosing and adjusting the needed building parts and selecting the corresponding points to eaves and ridge corners in the aerial image. The selection of up to three points for every building part in the aerial image is sufficient to reconstruct a building by manual indexing. The rest of the reconstruction process, generation and verification of building hypothesizes, is performed as before.

The reconstruction processes has been applied to a suburban region with 105 buildings located in the district "Gronau" of Bonn, where detached houses are

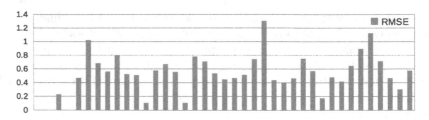

Fig. 5. The root mean squared error (RMSE) of the automated reconstruction. The error is calculated in respect to a reconstruction by manual indexing.

predominant. In total 40 (37.7%) buildings were fully automated reconstructed, 27 (25.4%) were semi-automated reconstructed and the remaining 38 (35.8%) buildings were reconstructed with manual indexing. In average 7.9 seconds were needed to reconstruct automatically a building using a building part database consisting of flat, gable and hip roof terminal and flat roof L-connector, gable roof L-connector. Figure 5 shows the root mean squared error (RSME) from the reconstructed buildings in respect to a reconstruction by manual indexing. The parameters of the manual indexing were adjusted to resemble the DSM when necessary. The RMSE is calculated by evaluating the height in the automated reconstruction and the manual reconstruction at every DSM point inside the roof boundary. A quantitative comparison with other approaches is difficult due to different data sets and accuracy of the used sensors. In contrast to [5, 7] we reconstruct buildings of level of detail 2 [17], i.e. the roof type is modelled and details like dormers are missing. But as mentioned before, these type of building models are advantageous in domains, where only a small bandwidth can be guaranteed or storage space is limited.

7   Conclusion

We proposed an approach to reconstruct buildings using a domain-specific building modelling and information fusion. We presented a fully automated procedure as well as a semi-automated procedure for robust reconstruction of buildings. To assure complete reconstruction results, we also provide a third way by initial manual model indexing. The benefit of information fusion is that complex and erroneous computations can be avoided by using only relevant information from the appropriate data source. We call this domain-specific information fusion. E.g., the localization of buildings in the aerial images and DSM is achieved by using the ground plans. Furthermore, ground plans determine the rough position of the eaves corners in the aerial image and the direction of adjoining edges. The usage of a DSM allows a canonical derivation of heights. Our building model based on typed models of building parts assures a generic modelling approach on the one hand and valid reconstruction results on the other hand. Future improvements on the automation of the reconstruction should be achieved by exploiting more subtle information in the fusion of sensor data, like the relative positions of roof boundary and ground plan boundary and symmetries in ground plans. We are currently developing an active contour approach, which localy modifies the ground plan boundary to follow the gradient in the aerial image. Concurrently, unnecessary or additional corners are removed in the ground plan. We also want to extend the building model by dormers and roof overhangs to increase the geometrical details of the buildings.

References

[1] Fischer, A., Kolbe, T., Lang, F., Cremers, A.B., Förstner, W., Plümer, L., Steinhage, V.: Extracting buildings from aerial images using hierarchical aggregation in 2d und 3d. Comp. Vision and Image Underst. 72(2), 195–203 (1998)

[2] Mohan, R., Nevatia, R.: Using perceptual organization to extract 3-d structures. Trans. on Pattern Anal. and Machine Intell. 11(11), 1121–1139 (1989)

[3] Henricsson, O., Gruen, A.: Automated 3-d reconstruction of buildings and visualization of city models. In: Proc. of the Workshop on 3D City Models (1996)

[4] Jaynes, C., Riseman, E., Hanson, A.: Recognition and reconstruction of buildings from multiple aerial images. Comp. Vision and Image Underst. 90, 68–98 (2003)

[5] Zebedin, L., Bauer, J., Karner, K., Bischof, H.: Fusion of feature- and area-based information for urban buildings modeling from aerial imagery, pp. 677–690 (2008)

[6] Vosselman, G.: Building reconstruction using planar faces in very high density height data. Int. Arch. of Photogr. and Rem. Sens. 32(3/2W5), 87–92 (1999)

[7] Lafarge, F., Descombes, X., Zerubia, J., Pierrot-Deseilligny, M.: Building reconstruction from a single dem. In: Proc. of the CVPR (2008)

[8] Brenner, C.: Building reconstruction from laser scanning and images. In: ITC Workshop on Data Qual. in Earth Observ. Techn. (2003)

[9] Mayer, H.: Automatic object extraction from aerial imagery - a survey focusing on buildings. Comp. Vision and Image Underst. 74(2), 138–149 (1999)

[10] Haala, N., Brenner, C.: Virtual city models from laser altimeter and 2d map data. Photogr. Engineering and Rem. Sens. 65(7), 787–795 (1999)

[11] Foley, J.D., Van Dam, A., Feiner, S.K., Hughes, J.F.: Computer Graphics: Principles and Practice. Addison-Wesley, Reading (1995)

[12] Harris, C., Stephens, M.: A combined corner and edge detection. In: Proc. of The 4th Alvey Vision Conf, pp. 147–151 (1988)

[13] Duda, R., Hart, P.: Use of the hough transformation to detect lines and curves in pictures. Comm. of the ACM 15(1), 11–15 (1972)

[14] Perona, P., Malik, J.: Scale-space and edge detection using anisotropic diffusion. Trans. on Pattern Anal. and Machine Intell. 12(7), 629–639 (1990)

[15] Gorte, B.: Segmentation of tin-structured surface models. In: Joint Conf. on Geospatial theory, Processing and Applications (July 2002)

[16] Fischler, M.A., Bolles, R.C.: Random sample consensus: A paradigm for model fitting with applications to image analysis and automated cartography. Comm. of the ACM 24, 381–395 (1981)

[17] Kolbe, T., Gröger, G.: Towards unified 3D city models. In: Proc. of ISPRS Comm. IV Workshop Challenges in Geospatial Analysis, Integration and Visualization II (2003)

Bio-inspired Stereo Vision System with Silicon Retina Imagers

Jürgen Kogler, Christoph Sulzbachner, and Wilfried Kubinger

AIT Austrian Institute of Technology GmbH
A-1220 Vienna, Austria
{juergen.kogler,christoph.sulzbachner,wilfried.kubinger}@ait.ac.at

Abstract. This paper presents a silicon retina-based stereo vision system, which is used for a pre-crash warning application for side impacts. We use silicon retina imagers for this task, because the advantages of the camera, derived from the human vision system, are high temporal resolution up to $1ms$ and the handling of various lighting conditions with a dynamic range of $\sim120dB$. A silicon retina delivers asynchronous data which are called *address events* (AE). Different stereo matching algorithms are available, but these algorithms normally work with full frame images. In this paper we evaluate how the AE data from the silicon retina sensors must be adapted to work with full-frame area-based and feature-based stereo matching algorithms.

1 Introduction

Advanced Driver Assistance Systems (ADAS) currently available on the market perform a specific function like lane departure warning (LDW), collision warning, or high beam assist. ADAS are entering only slowly into the market because cost-effective solutions are still missing, which would allow extensive market penetration and an increase in number of sensors and supported safety functions.

For example BMW offers for the latest series 5 and 6 a LDW system as optional equipment which costs $\sim950\$$. This price is for vehicles in the higher price segment acceptable, but not for low price and economy vehicles. Recent studies (2005 [12]) have been made to evaluate customer desirability and willingness to pay for active and passive safety systems in passenger cars. The result is that an acceptable price is below the current market prediction, so manufactures need to find cheaper solutions to increase the customer acceptance.

In the EU-funded project ADOSE[1] we use a *Silicon Retina Sensor* for reducing the costs. That kind of sensor overcomes limitations of classical vision systems with high temporal resolution, allowing to react to fast motion in the visual field, on-sensor pre-processing to significantly reduce both memory requirements and processing power, and high dynamic range for dealing with difficult lighting situations encountered in real-world traffic situations. Efficient pre-processing of visual information on the focal plane of the silicon retina vision chip allows cost

---

[1] www.adose-eu.org

M. Fritz, B. Schiele, and J.H. Piater (Eds.): ICVS 2009, LNCS 5815, pp. 174–183, 2009.

effective computation of scene depth using a single low-cost, low-power *Digital Signal Processor* (DSP).

The silicon retina is specifically tailored to serve as a pre-crash sensor for side impacts (e.g., for the pre-ignition and preparation of a side airbag). In this paper we describe the principle of this sensor technology and how we use the specific silicon retina data in stereo matching algorithms.

2   Bio-inspired Silicon Retina Imagers

The silicon retina imager is derived from the human vision system and is represented by an analog chip which delivers intensity changes as output. Fukushima etal [2] describe in their work an early implementation of an artificial retina. The first retina imager on silicon basis is described in the work of Mead and Mahowald [7], which have also established the term *Silicon Retina*. The work from Litzenberger etal [5] describes a vehicle counting system using the same silicon retina sensor described in the work from Lichtsteiner etal [6], which is developed at the AIT[2]/ETH[3] and also used for the described stereo vision system in this paper.

The silicon retina delivers, for each pixel that has exceeded a defined intensity change threshold, the coordinates of the pixel, a timestamp and the polarity which signals a rising intensity (ON-event) or a falling intensity (OFF-event). The description of the exact data structure from the silicon retina is described in section 2.1. For the setting of the threshold, which defines when an intensity change should trigger an AE, 12 different bias voltages are available in the silicon retina sensor. Each pixel of the silicon retina is connected via an analog circuit to its neighbors which are necessary for the intensity measurements. Based on these additional circuits on the sensor area, the density of the pixels is not as high as on conventional monochrome/color sensors, which results for our sensor in a resolution of 128×128 pixels with a pixel pitch of $40\mu m$.

Due to the low resolution and the asynchronous transmission of AEs from pixels where an intensity change has been occurred, a temporal resolution up to $1ms$ is reached. In figure 1 on the right side the speed of a silicon retina imager compared to a monochrome camera (Basler A601f) is shown. The top image pair on the right shows a running LED pattern with a frequency of $45Hz$. Both camera types recognize the LED movement. The frequency of the LED pattern in the bottom right image pair is $450Hz$. The silicon retina can capture the LED hopping sequence, but the monochrome camera can not capture the fast moving pattern and therefore, more than one LED is visible in a single image. A further benefit of the silicon retina is the high dynamic range up to $120dB$ for various lighting conditions, which is demonstrated in figure 1 on the left side. The top left image pair shows a moving hand in an average illuminated room with an illumination of $\sim 1000\frac{lm}{m^2}$. In both images the hand is clearly visible. In the bottom left image pair a moving hand is captured from both camera types

---

[2] Austrian Institute of Technology GmbH.
[3] Eidgenössische Technische Hochschule Zürich.

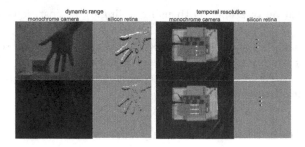

Fig. 1. *Left*: The top pair shows a hand moved under office illumination conditions ($\sim 1000 \frac{lm}{m^2}$) and the lower pair on the left side shows the same scene with an illumination of $\sim 5 \frac{lm}{m^2}$. *Right*: The LED running speed in the top image pair is $45Hz$ and in the lower image pair on the right $450Hz$.

too, but in a room with an illumination of $\sim 5 \frac{lm}{m^2}$. Here, only the silicon retina sensor recognizes the hand.

2.1 Address-Event Data Format

The silicon retina is free running and sends only data if the intensity changes generate AEs. These AEs can happen anytime and therefore the silicon retina sensor adds a timestamp, represented by a 32 bit value, to the AEs (location and polarity) and forwards the AEs to the processing unit. The location of the event is addressed by its coordinates (x,y). Both values (x,y) are mapped to a 7 bit representation in the data format. The polarization p of an event is described by one bit. A high bit denotes an OFF-event and low bit an ON-event.

Table 1 shows a comparison between a monochrome sensor and a silicon retina imager with the same resolution for a typical application. Both imagers have different types of data representation and therefore the calculation of the transfer rate is carried out, which makes a direct comparison of both sensors possible. For future purpose the AE data structure will be improved so that the bits/AE decreases and the transfer performance will increase. The data amount of a silicon retina imager with an average address event rate of 50000 AE/s is at the moment ~ 2.3 times lower than a monochrome sensor with $60 fps$.

2.2 Address-Event Converter

Before the AE data can be used with full frame image processing algorithms, the data structure is changed into a frame format. For this reason an address event to frame converter has been implemented.

The silicon retina sensor delivers permanently ON- and OFF-events, which are marked with a timestamp t_{ev}. The frame converter collects the address events over a defined time period $\Delta t = [t_{start} : t_{end}]$ and inserts these events into a frame. After the time period a frame is closed and the generation of the next frame starts. The definition of an event frame is

Table 1. Data rate of a monochrome sensor and a silicon retina imager

	128 × 128 monochrome sensor	128 × 128 silicon retina
Transfered Data	983.040[a] pix/s	50.000[b] AE/s
Data Size	8[c] bit/pix	64[d] bit/AE
Transfer rate	7.5 MBit/s	~3.2 MBit/s

[a] at 60 fps.
[b] average address events (AE) per second (measured with fast movements in front of the camera $\Longrightarrow$ distance $\sim 1m$).
[c] 256 grayscale values.
[d] 32 bit timestamp, 15 bit data and 17 bit reserved.

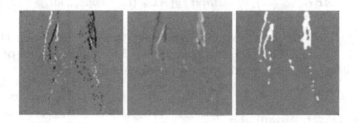

Fig. 2. Different results of AE to frame converter

$$AE_{frame} = \int_{t_{start}}^{t_{end}} AE_{xy}(t_{ev})dt_{ev} \qquad (1)$$

Different algorithm approaches need a different frame format. The silicon retina stereo camera system in this paper is evaluated with two algorithms derived from two different categories. The first algorithm is an area-based approach, which works with the comparison of frame windows. The second algorithm is a feature-based variant which matches identified features. Both categories need differently constructed frames from the converter. Due to this reason, the converter offers configurations to fulfil these requirements. Figure 2 shows on the left side the output frame of the converter with the collected ON- and OFF-events. The resolution of the timestamp mechanism of the silicon retina is $1ms$, but for the algorithm used in this paper a Δt of the $10ms$ and $20ms$ is used. The Δt is changed for different conditions which produce a different number of events.

The image in the middle of figure 2 shows a frame built for an area-based matching algorithm. For this reason each event received in the defined time period is interpreted as a gray value, with

$$AE_{frame} = \int_{t_{start}}^{t_{end}} graystep(AE_{xy}(t_{ev}))dt_{ev}. \qquad (2)$$

The background of the frame is initialized with 128 (based on a 8 bit grayscale model) and each ON-event adds a gray value and an OFF-event subtracts one.

In 3 the function for generating a gray value frame is shown. The 8 bit grayscale model limits the additions and subtractions of the $\Delta_{grayvalue}$ and saturates if an overflow occurs.

$$graystep(AE_{xy}(t_{ev})) = \begin{cases} AE_{frame_{xy}} + \Delta_{grayvalue} & AE_{xy}(t_{ev}) = ON_{event} \\ AE_{frame_{xy}} - \Delta_{grayvalue} & AE_{xy}(t_{ev}) = OFF_{event} \end{cases}$$
(3)

The right image in figure 2 shows a frame built for a feature-based image processing algorithm. Multiple received events within the defined time period are overwritten in this case of frame building. Equation 4 shows the frame building and the used simplify function is illustrated in (5).

$$AE_{frame} = \int_{t_{start}}^{t_{end}} simplify(AE_{xy}(t_{ev}), conv_{on})dt_{ev}$$
(4)

The simplify function gets a second parameter ($conv_{on}$) to decide the event variant (only ON or OFF). This frame is prepared for different kind of feature-based algorithms and also for algorithms based on segmentation.

$$simplify(AE_{xy}(t_{ev}), conv_{on}) = \begin{cases} ON_{ev} & AE_{xy}(t_{ev}) = ON_{ev} \wedge conv_{on} = 1 \\ ON_{ev} & AE_{xy}(t_{ev}) = ON_{ev} \wedge conv_{on} = 0 \\ ON_{ev} & AE_{xy}(t_{ev}) = OFF_{ev} \wedge conv_{on} = 1 \\ 0 & AE_{xy}(t_{ev}) = OFF_{ev} \wedge conv_{on} = 0 \end{cases}$$
(5)

Both specialized generated frames (middle and right in figure 2) can optionally filtered with a median filter to reduce noise and small objects. With this settings every Δt a new frame from the left and right address event stream is generated. These frames are now handled as images for the stereo matching algorithms described in the next section.

3   Stereo Matching

The main task of this stereo vision sensor is the extraction of depth information from the viewed scenery for the application mentioned in section 1. It is a challenging task to handle the asynchronous incoming AEs for the stereo matching process. Hess [4] used a global disparity filter in his work to find a main disparity of the received events. In a second approach he worked with a general disparity which considers each incoming event separately, but this is a time consuming task and needs a new kind of a stereo matching implementation. In our work we evaluate the opportunity to use standard stereo vision algorithms for AE data from silicon retina imagers. In section 3.1 the suitability of an area-based algorithm is analyzed and a feature-based approach is described in section 3.2.

3.1   Area-Based Approach for AE Stereo Matching

For the evaluation of the area-based stereo matching of AE images a simple correlation method is used. In the work from Scharstein and Szeliski [8] many different area-based approaches are compared and evaluated, and for the silicon retina stereo matching a *Sum of Absolute Differences* (SAD) algorithm is used. Before the silicon retina output is processed by the SAD algorithm the data stream is converted into a grayvalue frame (Figure 2 in the middle). A block matching, only with ON- and OFF- events, would produce a lot of similar costs and a lot of mismatches may appear. The grayscale images have more than two values and therefore, the statistical significance of the block is larger.

Derived from the application scenario the distance of a closer coming object must be estimated. Therefore, the distance measurement does not have to be exact and the search space is restricted to one horizontal scanline without a prior rectification step. For each pixel the disparity is calculated and after that the average disparity is calculated which represents the main disparity of the whole object. Results of the algorithm are shown in section 4.2.

3.2 Feature-Based Approach for AE Stereo Matching

For feature-based stereo matching, features must be extracted from the image. Shi and Tomasi [10] give more detail about features in their work. For the evaluation of the feature-based stereo matching with silicon retina cameras, a segment center matching approach is chosen. Tang etal [11] describe in their work an approach for matching feature points. An assumption, derived from the application scenario is, that an object comes closer to the sensor and the distance of the object must be estimated. That means no occlusions with other objects and exact distance measurements of each pixel respectively the closer coming object.

Additional processing is required for the extraction of the segment centers, but usually the stereo matching process is less costly. For the segment extraction a morphological *erosion* followed by a *dilation* is applied [3]. After that the *flood fill* labeling [1] function is used, which labels connected areas (segments). A pixel-by-pixel matching is not possible and therefore, it must be defined how the whole segment shall be matched. In a first step the features are ordered downwards according to their area pixel count. This method is only useful, if the found segments in the left and right image are nearly the same. As representative point of the segment the center is chosen. The center of the corresponding segment in the left and right frame can differ. Due to this reason the confidence of the found centers are checked. This mechanism checks the differences of center points, if they are too large, the center points are ignored for the matching. If the center points lie within the predefined tolerances, the disparity is calculated which stands for the disparity of the whole object. Results of the algorithm are shown in section 4.3.

4   Experimental Results and Discussion

This section presents results of the stereo matching on AE frames. In a first step the sensor setup and configuration used for the tests are described.

4.1 Stereo Sensor Setup

The stereo system consists of two silicon retina imagers and are mounted on a $0.45m$ baseline. Both cameras are connected to an Ethernet switch, which joins both address event data streams packaged in UDP packets and sends it to the further processing unit. The left and the right camera must have the same knowledge of time, therefore we have realized a master-slave synchronization concept where the master camera sends the timestamp to the slave. In a first step for the offline processing and algorithm evaluation a PC-based system is used.

The silicon retina cameras of the stereo vision system are also equipped with lenses which must be focussed before they can be used. Due to the fact that an output is only delivered if intensity changes are recognized in front of the sensor, a stimuli is necessary which generates an continuous sensor output and can used for the adjustment of the camera lenses. Therefore, we are using blinking lights to get focused camera (depth of field is infinity). The input AE frames for the algorithms are shown in figure 3.

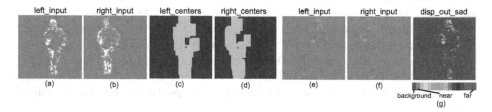

Fig. 3. (a,b): Input pair for the feature-based algorithm. (c,d): Segment centers as disparity representatives. (e,f): Input pair for the area-based algorithm. (g): Disparity output of the SAD.

4.2 Results of the Area-Based Approach

The algorithm parameter of the SAD is the correlation window size. We tested the algorithm with an object at three different distances ($2m$, $4m$, $6m$) and different settings of the address event converter.

In figure 4 the results of the SAD algorithm processing AE frames are given. On the x-axis the different converter settings at three different distances are shown. The first number represents the object distance in meters, the second value describes the time period for collecting address events and the last value represents the graystep for the accumulation function described in section 2.2. For each distance all four converter settings with four different SAD correlation window sizes are tested. The output on the y-axis is the average relative error of the distance estimation based on 500 image pairs.

The results in figure 4 show that the average relative disparity error increases with the distance of the object. In near distances the results are influenced by the correlation window size, especially there is a significant difference between

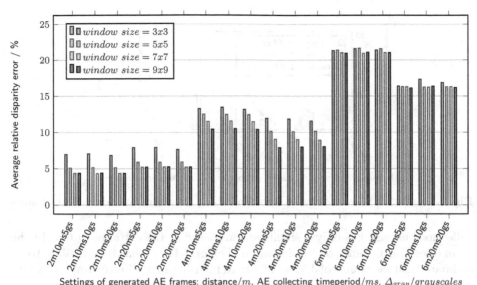

Fig. 4. Results of the area-based stereo matching algorithm on address event frames

the usage of a 3×3 window and a 9×9 window. In the distance of $4m$ and $6m$ the results with a timestamp collection time Δt of $20ms$ are better. The third parameter of the generated input AE frame is the grayscale step size which has no influence at any distance. Generally we reach with the SAD stereo matching approach used for AE frames in the main operating distance of $4m$ an minimal error of 8%. That is equivalent to an estimated distance range of $3.68m$-$4.32m$. In figure 3 (e,f,g) an example of an input stereo pair for the area-based algorithm and the SAD disparity output are shown.

4.3 Results of the Feature-Based Approach

This section shows results of the feature-based stereo matching on AE frames. The algorithm parameter of the feature center matching is the morphological erosion and dilation function at the beginning of the algorithm.

In figure 5 the results of the feature-based algorithm processing AE frames are given. For the center matching only the collecting time period Δt of the address events is varied, which is shown with the second value from the descriptors on the x-axis. All converter settings with three different morphological erosion and dilation settings are tested. The structuring element is always a square. The results on the y-axis shows the average relative disparity error of the feature center matching at three different distance with two different address converter settings and with three different morphological function combinations. The results are based on 500 image pair samples.

The results in figure 5 show that the average relative disparity error depends on the sizes of the structuring elements. At all distances the morphological combination *erosion=3* and *dilation=5* produces the best results. The timestamp

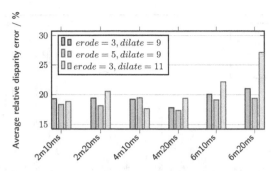

Fig. 5. Results of the feature-based stereo matching algorithm on address event frames

collection time Δt has only a significant influence at the distance of $6m$. In the main operating distance of $4m$ the minimal error is 17%. That is equivalent to an estimated distance range of $3.32m$-$4.68m$. In figure 3 (a,b,c,d) an example of an input stereo pair for the feature-based algorithm and the segment centers are shown.

5   Future Work

As presented in this paper, several algorithms which are suited for monochrome or color stereo matching can be used for silicon retina image processing, too. The algorithms have to be adapted and the address event representation of the information has to be converted to conventional data structures representing images (AE frames). This conversion is a time-consuming process and therefore, the advantage of the asynchronous data delivery and high temporal resolution of the silicon retina sensor is not used very efficiently. Additionally, the results showed us, that the feature-based approach produces errors, which are too high for the estimation of the distance. The area-based approach is better and the estimated distances are precise enough for the usage in the distance estimation of approaching objects.

In the next step we will analyze how we can process the delivered data from the silicon retina camera in a more efficient way. For this reason we want to design an algorithm which can handle the asynchronous data and processes each incoming event without any frame generation strategies. Additionally we would like to implement a suitable calibration and rectification step for the silicon retina stereo vision system, which makes a more exact distance estimation possible. The next version of the algorithm shall run on an embedded platform based on a TMS320C64x+ DSP core from *Texas Instruments* for the evaluation of real time capabilities.

Acknowledgments

The research leading to these results has received funding from the European Community's Seventh Framework Program (FP7/2007-2013) under grant agreement $n°$ ICT-216049 (ADOSE).

References

1. Burger, W., Burge, M.J.: Digital Image Processing An Algorithmic Introduction using JAVA, 1st edn. Springer-Science/Business Media LLC (2008)
2. Fukushima, K., Yamaguchi, Y., Yasuda, M., Nagata, S.: An Electronic Model of the Retina. Proceedings of the IEEE 58(12), 1950–1951 (1970)
3. Gonzalez, R.C., Woods, R.E.: Digital Image Processing, 2nd edn. Prentice Hall/Pearson Education International (2002)
4. Hess, P.: Low-Level Stereo Matching using Event-based Silicon Retinas. In: Semesterarbeit am Institut für Neuroinformatik, ETH Zürich (2006)
5. Litzenberger, M., Kohn, B., Gritsch, G., Donath, N., Poscha, C., Belbachir, N.A., Garn, H.: Vehicle Counting with an Embedded Traffic Data System using an Optical Transient Sensor. In: Proceedings of the IEEE Intelligent Transportation Systems Conference (ITSC 2007), Seattle, USA (2007)
6. Lichtsteiner, P., Posch, C., Delbruck, T.: A 128128 120dB 30mW Asynchronous Vision Sensor that Responds to Relative Intensity Change. In: IEEE International Solid-State Circuits Conference (ISSCC 2006), San Francisco, USA (2006)
7. Mead, C., Mahowald, M.: A silicon model of early visual processing. Neural Networks Journal 1(1), 91–97 (1988)
8. Scharstein, D., Szeliski, R.: A Taxonomy and Evaluation of Dense Two-Frame Stereo Correspondence Algorithms. International Journal of Computer Vision 47(1-3), 7–42 (2002)
9. Schreer, O.: Stereoanalyse und Bildanalyse. Springer, Heidelberg (2005)
10. Shi, J., Tomasi, C.: Good Features to Track. In: Proceedings of the IEEE Computer Vision and Pattern Recognition Conference (CVPR 1994), Seattle, USA (1994)
11. Tang, B., AitBoudaoud, D., Matuszewski, B.J., Shark, L.K.: An Efficient Feature Based Matching Algorithm for Stereo Images. In: Proceedings of the IEEE Geometric Modeling and Imaging Conference (GMAI 2006), London, UK (2006)
12. Frost, Sullivan: European Markets for Advanced Driver Assistance Systems, B844-18 (2006)

A Fast Joint Bioinspired Algorithm for Optic Flow and Two-Dimensional Disparity Estimation

Manuela Chessa, Silvio P. Sabatini, and Fabio Solari

Department of Biophysical and Electronic Engineering, University of Genoa
Via all'Opera Pia 11a - 16145 Genova - Italy
{manuela.chessa,silvio.sabatini,fabio.solari}@unige.it

Abstract. The faithful detection of the motion and of the distance of the objects in the visual scene is a desirable feature of any artificial vision system designed to operate in unknown environments characterized by conditions variable in time in an often unpredictable way. Here, we propose a distributed neuromorphic architecture, that, by sharing the computational resources to solve the stereo and the motion problems, produces fast and reliable estimates of optic flow and 2D disparity. The specific joint design approach allows us to obtain high performance at an affordable computational cost. The approach is validated with respect to the state-of-the-art algorithms and in real-world situations.

1 Introduction

The extraction of stereo and motion information, which can be directly used by a robot to interact with the environment, requires the processing of the visual information in a fast and reliable way. In the literature, several algorithms for the computation either of the optic flow [1] or the binocular disparity [2] have been proposed, which are characterized by high performances either in term of accuracy of the estimates or in term of the execution time [3]. Though, real-time system solutions for both motion and depth, which partially share the computational resources are very seldom. On the contrary, in the visual system of mammals the analysis of the dynamics and of the 3D spatial relationships occur jointly in the *dorsal* cortical pathway, which projects visual information from the primary visual cortex (V1) to the occipital areas V3 and MT (V5), up to the parietal lobe, by specializing as an "action stream" for guiding in real-time the actions that we direct at objects in the world [4]. Bioinspired computer vision techniques, although conceptually valuable, have always been characterized by a high computational cost, as the price to pay for their higher flexibility. Usually, these bioinspired solutions were indeed developed as models of how the visual cortex works, and their functionality were demonstrated on simple synthetic images, but were not designed to form a systematic alternative to computer vision, working on raw images and real video sequences [5] [6] [7] [8], but see [9]. It is also worth mentioning, that several neuromorphic solutions, at an affordable cost, have been proposed [10][11][12] with the aim of providing efficient sensor modules for machine vision. Yet, even though such solutions have the merit of

M. Fritz, B. Schiele, and J.H. Piater (Eds.): ICVS 2009, LNCS 5815, pp. 184–193, 2009.

solving excellently the specific sensorial problem, they do not have the necessary generality to guarantee a rich and flexible perceptual representation of the visual signal to be used for a more advanced visual analysis.

In this paper, we propose a joint neural architecture for the computation of both 2D (horizontal and vertical) disparity and optic flow, whose performances are comparable to the state-of-the-art algorithms (also not bioinspired) in terms of accuracy (see Section 4) and execution time. Specific emphasis is given to the sharing of the resources for the computation of both the features and to a proper combination of the information extracted by a set of spatial orientation channels, that allows us to tackle the aperture problem that arises in both optic flow and 2D disparity estimation.

2   Neuromorphic Computational Paradigms for Visual Processing

Disparity and optic flow features can be extracted from a sequence of stereo image pairs, using a distributed bioinspired architecture that resorts to a population of tuned cells. In the literature, many authors analyze different approaches to design those populations of neurons, and to properly combine their responses in order to obtain reliable information from the visual signal [13]. In distributed representations, or population codes, the information is encoded by the activity pattern of a network of *simple* and *complex* neurons, that are selective for elemental vision attributes: oriented edges, direction of motion, color, texture, and binocular disparity [14]. In particular, we consider neurons tuned to specific values of disparity and velocity, whose receptive fields (RFs) overlap with the ones of the other neurons of the population. To decode information at a specific image location the whole activity of the population within a neighborhood of this location is considered.

2.1   Population Coding

Considering that the image motion is described as an orientation in the space-time domain [15], numerous models for the detection of velocity are based on spatio-temporal filtering of the image sequence with 3D Gabor filters (e.g., [5][6]). Similarly, the tuning to binocular disparity is obtained from physiological and modeling studies [16][8], that demonstrated that a difference in the phase of the left and right spatial receptive field profiles of a binocular simple cell of area V1 can encode the disparity information (*phase-shift-model*)[1][8][7]. Given the distributed character of the representation, proper decoding mechanisms have to be considered to estimate the value of a given feature from the whole activity of the population. Common and simple approaches for decoding the population codes are the Winner Takes All (WTA) method and the weighted sum [13].

---

[1] Yet, models based on a difference in the position of the left and right RFs (*position-shift-model*) or hybrid approaches have been proposed.

2.2   Multichannel Representation and Cooperation

To come up with more complex visual descriptors and to solve the problem of visual motion and depth perception, the outputs from area V1 have to be combined in higher cortical levels, through feed-forward convergence, recursive interactions and selection processes. The combination of the information extracted by single cells with respect to different orientation channels represents a widely used computational paradigm in the visual cortex. The different orientation channels could be used to remove the inherent ambiguities of local motion and stereo estimates, consequence of the well known aperture problem. In optic flow computation, motion along an edge cannot be discriminated when the edge is larger than the population RFs, used to estimate *image velocity* **v**, since only the component of the feature orthogonal to an edge can be computed. A similar problem arises for a stereo active vision system with convergent axes [17], where 2D (horizontal and vertical) disparities are present and it is possible to define the *vector disparity* **δ** as the vector difference in positions of identified corresponding points in the left and right eyes, each measured with respect to the point of fixation as origin [18]. From this perspective, a multidimensional representation of the visual signal over several spatial orientation channels is instrumental to provide a structural reference with respect to which to evaluate motion and stereo information.

3   Neural Architecture

The proposed population approaches for the computation of horizontal and vertical disparities and optic flow share a common algorithmic structure (see Fig. 1): (i) the distributed coding of the features across different orientation channels, through a filtering stage (that resembles the filtering process of area V1), (ii) the decoding stage for each channel, (iii) the estimation of the features through channel interactions, and (iv) the coarse-to-fine refinement.

3.1   Feature Coding Strategy

A population of spatio-temporal units, characterized by a spatial orientation θ and tuned to different velocities v_i^θ and to different disparities δ_i^θ, is used to represent the feature values. Each unit (a quadrature pair of simple cells) is described by a 3D Gabor filter, in order to maintain the sensitivity to the 3D orientation in the spatio-temporal domain.

A set of Gabor filters [19], with the form $h(\mathbf{x}, t) = g(\mathbf{x})f(t)$, that uniformly cover the orientation space and optimally sample the spatio-temporal domain, is chosen. The spatial component of the filters, $g(\mathbf{x})$, is built by exploiting its separability, to keep low the computational cost [20]. A Gabor filter rotated by an angle θ with respect to the horizontal axis is defined by:

$$g(x, y; \psi, \theta) = e^{\left(-\frac{x_\theta^2}{2\sigma_x^2} - \frac{y_\theta^2}{2\sigma_y^2}\right)} e^{j(\omega_0 x_\theta + \psi)} \tag{1}$$

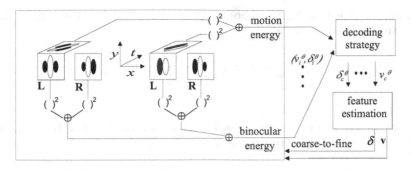

Fig. 1. The joint architecture for the computation of 2D disparity and optic flow. The box on the left represents a complex unit of the distributed population. Each unit, characterized by a spatial orientation θ, codes for its preferred velocity v_i^θ and for its preferred disparity δ_i^θ. The motion energy and the binocular energy responses, obtained by the $N \times M \times K$ cells, are decoded (upper-right box), thus obtaining an estimate of the component velocity v_c^θ and disparity δ_c^θ for each spatial orientation. These estimates are then combined to obtain the full velocity $\mathbf{v}$ and the full disparity δ (lower-right box). The obtained features are used to perform a coarse-to-fine refinement.

where ω_0 is the spatial radial peak frequency, σ_x and σ_y determine the spatial supports of the filter, ψ is the phase of the sinusoidal modulation and (x_θ, y_θ) are the rotated spatial coordinates. In the spatial domain, the orientation space is uniformly sampled using N filters oriented from 0 to 2π and having the same radial peak frequency. It is worthy to note that, to avoid the introduction of a loss of balance between the convolutions with the even and odd Gabor filters, the contribution of the DC component is removed. In the following, we describe how the specific tuning to velocity and disparity values is obtained.

Optic flow. The temporal component of the 3D filter is defined by:

$$f(t; \omega_t) = e^{\left(-\frac{t^2}{2\sigma_t^2}\right)} e^{j\omega_t t} 1(t) \tag{2}$$

where σ_t determines the filter support in time domain, ω_t is the temporal peak frequency and $1(t)$ denotes the unit step function. Each cell is tuned to the velocity with magnitude v^θ and direction orthogonal to the preferred spatial orientation θ of the filter. The spatial frequency ω_0 is kept constant while the temporal peak frequency is varied by the rule $\omega_t = v^\theta \omega_0$. For each spatial orientation, a set of M tuning velocities are chosen (accordingly to the limit imposed by the temporal support of the filter and by the Nyquist theorem).

The described quadrature pair of spatio-temporal receptive fields $h(\mathbf{x}, t)$ are applied to the sequence of images in input $I(\mathbf{x}, t)$, thus obtaining a complex response:

$$Q(\mathbf{x_0}, t; v^\theta) = \int_{-\infty}^{\infty} \int_{-\infty}^{\infty} h(\mathbf{x_0} - \mathbf{x}, t - \tau) I(\mathbf{x}, \tau) d\mathbf{x} d\tau \tag{3}$$

Following [15] it is possible to compute the *motion energy*, as the squared modulus of the complex response:

$$E(\mathbf{x_0}, t; v^\theta) = |Q(\mathbf{x_0}, t; v^\theta)|^2 = \left| e^{j\psi(t)} \int_0^t Q(\mathbf{x_0}, \tau; v^\theta) e^{-j\omega_t \tau} d\tau \right|^2 \qquad (4)$$

where $\psi(t) = \psi + \omega_t t = \psi + \omega_0 v^\theta t$.

The response of the motion energy unit has its maximum when the tuning velocity is equal to the velocity present in the stimulus.

Disparity. Following the *phase-shift model*, to obtain the tuning to a specific disparity the left and right RFs, $g^L(\mathbf{x})$ and $g^R(\mathbf{x})$ respectively, are centered at the same position in the left and in the right images, but have a proper binocular phase difference $\Delta\psi = \psi^L - \psi^R$. For each spatial orientation, a set of K binocular phase differences, uniformly distributed between $-\pi$ and π, are chosen to obtain the tuning to different disparities $\delta^\theta = \Delta\psi/\omega_o$, oriented along the direction orthogonal to the orientation of the RF. Then, the left and right RFs are applied to the binocular image pair in input $I^L(\mathbf{x})$ and $I^R(\mathbf{x})$, thus obtaining a complex response:

$$Q(\mathbf{x_0}; \delta^\theta) = \int_{-\infty}^\infty g^L(\mathbf{x_0} - \mathbf{x}) I^L(\mathbf{x}) d\mathbf{x} + \int_{-\infty}^\infty g^R(\mathbf{x_0} - \mathbf{x}) I^R(\mathbf{x}) d\mathbf{x} \qquad (5)$$

The *binocular energy* [16][8] is obtained as the squared responses of a quadrature pair of binocular units:

$$E(\mathbf{x_0}; \delta^\theta) = |Q(\mathbf{x_0}; \delta^\theta)|^2 = |Q^L(\mathbf{x_0}; \delta^\theta) + e^{-j\Delta\psi} Q^R(\mathbf{x_0}; \delta^\theta)|^2 \qquad (6)$$

and it has its maximum when the product of the stimulus disparity and the spatial peak frequency equals the binocular phase difference.

3.2   Feature Decoding and Estimation

Once the features along each spatial orientation have been coded by the population activity, it is necessary to read out this information, to obtain a reliable estimate. The decoding strategy, the number of the cells in the population and their distribution are jointly related. To decode the population by a WTA strategy a large number of cells along each spatial orientation would be necessary, thus increasing the computational cost and the memory occupancy of the approach. To obtain precise feature estimation, while keeping the number of cells as low as possible, thus an affordable computational cost, a *weighted sum* (i.e. a center of gravity) of the responses for each orientation is calculated. The *component velocity* v_c^θ is obtained by:

$$v_c^\theta(\mathbf{x_0}, t) = \frac{\sum_{i=1}^M v_i^\theta E(\mathbf{x_0}, t; v_i^\theta)}{\sum_{i=1}^M E(\mathbf{x_0}, t; v_i^\theta)} \qquad (7)$$

where v_i^θ are the M tuning velocities and $E(\mathbf{x_0}, t; v_i^\theta)$ are the motion energies for each spatial orientation. Similarly, we decode the *component disparity* δ_c^θ. Other decoding methods [13], such as the *maximum likelihood* estimator, have been considered, but the center of gravity of the population activity is the best compromise between simplicity, low computational cost and reliability of the estimates.

As we have described in Section 2.2, a single oriented filter cannot estimate the feature, but only the component orthogonal to the filter orientation i.e. the velocity v_c^θ or the disparity δ_c^θ. Following [21][22] the aperture problem is tackled by combining the estimates of v_c^θ and δ_c^θ for each spatial orientation, in order to obtain a robust estimate of the full velocity $\mathbf{v}$ and of the full disparity $\boldsymbol{\delta}$.

3.3 Multiscale Processing and Coarse-to-Fine Refinement

In the frequency domain, the Gabor filters, used in the architecture, act as band pass filters centered in a single spatial radial peak frequency. However, experimental studies have shown the presence of different spatial frequency channels, and, since information in natural images is spread over a wide range of frequencies, it is necessary to use a technique that allows us to get information from the whole range. Here, we have adopted a pyramidal decomposition, in order to keep as low as possible the computational cost. Moreover, by exploiting the pyramidal decomposition, a coarse-to-fine refinement is implemented. The features, obtained at a coarser level of the pyramid, are expanded and used to warp the sequence of the spatially convolved images, then the residual optic flow and disparity are computed. In this way, the "distance" between corresponding points is reduced, thus yielding to a more precise estimate, since the remaining feature values lie in the filters' range.

4 Comparisons and Results

The proposed algorithm analyzes the visual information by using a biologically plausible strategy. However, in order to use effectively this model in a robotic system, it is important to compare the obtained results with the ones of the well-established algorithms from the literature. It is worth noting that both the accuracy and the computational requirements (e.g. execution time) should be taken into account for the extraction of features, especially when aiming to embed the algorithm in a robotic system. For what concerns the accuracy, the quantitative evaluation of optical flow and disparity algorithm is performed by comparing the results for selected test sequences, for which the ground truth data are available [1][2] (Fig. 2(a-h)). It is worth noting that these test beds contain horizontal disparities, only. Thus, to benchmark the validity of our approach in active vision systems, and thus with images that contain 2D disparities, we have used the dataset described in [23] (Fig. 2(i-n)). The presented results have been obtained by using $N = 16$ oriented filters, each tuned to $M = 3$

Table 1. Comparison between the proposed distributed population code and some state-of-the-art algorithms for optic flow estimation. The reliability has been computed by using the average angular error (AAE) proposed by Barron [24]. (*)Results from http://vision.middlebury.edu/flow/.

Algorithm	Yosemite	Rubberwhale	Hydrangea
2D-CLG [Bruhn & Weickert, IJCV 61(3), 2005]	1.76	16.75	
SPSA-learn [Li & Huttenlocher, ECCV 2008]	2.56	5.22	2.43
Black-Anandan 2 modified by Simon Baker (*)	2.61	8.14	
Black-Anandan modified by Deqing Sun (*)	3.1		
Distributed population code	**3.19**	**8.01**	**5.79**
Dynamic MRF [Glocker et al., CVPR 2008]	3.63		
Fusion [Lempitsky et al., CVPR 2008]	4.55	3.68	
Pyramidal LK modified by Bouguet (*)	6.41	18.69	15.86
CBF [Trobin et al., ECCV 2008]	6.57		
Group Flow [Ren, CVPR 2008]		5.32	
FMT [Ho & Goecke, CVPR 2008]		10.07	
Proesman [Ho & Goecke, CVPR 2008]		17.43	

Table 2. Comparison between the proposed distributed population code and some state-of-the-art algorithms for disparity estimation. The reliability has been computed in terms of percentage of bad pixels for non-occluded regions (see http://vision.middlebury.edu/stereo/).

Algorithm	Venus	Teddy	Cones
Reliability DP [Gong & Yang, CVPR 2005]	2.35	9.82	12.9
Go-Light [Su & Khoshgoftaar, ICIP 2007]	2.47	14.5	9.78
SSD + MF [Scharstein & Szeliski, IJCV 47, 2002]	3.74	16.5	10.6
Infection [Olague et al., Artificial Life 2006]	4.41	17.7	14.3
Distributed population code	**4.5**	**11.7**	**6.4**
Adaptive weight[Yoon & Kweon, PAMI 28, 2006]	4.61	12.70	5.50
Phase-based [El-Etriby et al., ISIE 2007]	6.71	14.5	10.8
Phase-diff [El-Etriby et al., ICCVG 2006]	8.34	20.0	19.8
SO [Scharstein & Szeliski, IJCV 47, 2002]	9.44	19.9	13.0
DP [Scharstein & Szeliski, IJCV 47, 2002]	10.1	14.0	10.5

different velocities and to $K = 9$ binocular phase differences. The used Gabor filters have a spatio-temporal support of $(11 \times 11) \times 7$ pixels $\times$ frames and are characterized by a bandwidth of 0.833 octave and spatial frequency $\omega_0 = 0.5\pi$. Tables 1 and 2 show the comparison with some state-of-the art algorithms. Even if there are some algorithms that perform better than the proposed approach, the feature maps we obtain are reliable and accurate. The approach is also applied to real-world scenes, acquired by two stereo cameras, moving in a non-static environment. Figure 3 shows some of the obtained optic flow fields and disparity maps.

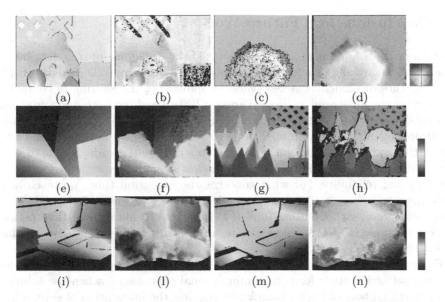

Fig. 2. The ground truth (a)(c) and the estimated (b)(d) optic flows for the Rubberwhale and the Hydrangea sequences. The different colors represent velocity direction. The ground truth (e)(g) and the estimated (f)(h) disparities for the Venus and the Cones image pairs. Disparity values are coded from red (near objects) to blue (far objects). The ground truth (i)(m) and the estimated (l)(n) horizontal and vertical disparities for a stereo pair acquired by two virtual cameras with convergent axes.

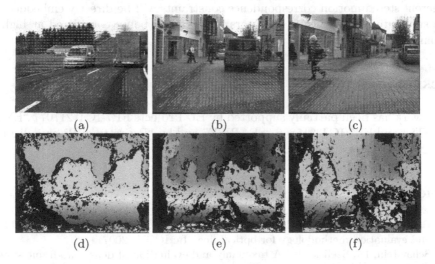

Fig. 3. Optic flow (a-c) and disparity maps (d-f) computed in different real-world situations. The images are acquired by moving stereo cameras, thus both ego-motion and independent motion of other objects in the scene are present. Disparity values are coded from red (near objects) to blue (far objects).

5   Conclusions and Future Work

The major contributions of this paper are: (1) the development of a distributed neuromorphic architecture for the estimation of motion and 2D disparity fields in a sequence of binocular stereo pairs, by mimicking the sharing of computational resources evidenced in cortical areas; (2) the handling both horizontal and vertical disparities; (3) the application of such bioinspired approach in real-world situations; (4) a good compromise between reliability of the estimates and execution time. The proposed solution, based on a distributed code, is able to keep the computational cost of the algorithm as low as possible, without loosing in accuracy and reliability. For what concerns the execution time, we reach near real-time performances (7 frames/second for images of 256×256 pixels on a QuadCore processor), by using Intel IPP libraries. To obtain real-time performances on standard VGA image we are implementing the proposed algorithm on architectures based on GPU.

From a broader perspective, we observe that the design approach followed for the cortical architecture leads to computational advantages, when the solution of a perceptual task of higher complexity requires the integration of several features, such as orientation, binocular disparity, and motion. By example, in typical real-world situations, as it occurs during stereo camera movements, stereopsis extends to time-varying images, thus requiring the integration of static (binocular) and temporal correspondence [25]. In these situations, by generalizing the local visual operators to binocular motion energy units [26], the architecture will be able to provide an early rich description of 3D motion events. In this way, coherent stereo-motion correspondence constraints will be directly embedded in the structure of such visual operators, rather than being considered at higher semantic level of data fusion.

Acknowledgements

This work has been partially supported by EU Projects FP7-ICT 217077 "EYE-SHOTS" and FP7-ICT 215866 "SEARISE" and by "Progetto di Ricerca di Ateneo 2007" (University of Genoa).

References

1. Baker, S., Scharstein, D., Lewis, J., Roth, S., Black, M., Szeliski, R.: A database and evaluation methodology for optical flow. In: ICCV (2007)
2. Scharstein, D., Szeliski, R.: A taxonomy and evaluation of dense two-frame stereo correspondence algorithms. Int. J. of Computer Vision 47, 7–42 (2002)
3. Tombari, F., Mattoccia, S., Di Stefano, L., Addimanda, E.: Classification and evaluation of cost aggregation methods for stereo correspondence. In: CVPR (2008)
4. Milner, A.D., Goodale, M.: The visual brain in action. Oxford Univ. Press, Oxford (1995)
5. Heeger, D.: Model for the extraction of image flow. JOSA 4(8), 1455–1471 (1987)

6. Grzywacz, N., Yuille, A.: A model for the estimate of local image velocity by cells in the visual cortex. Proc. R. Soc. Lond. B 239, 129–161 (1990)
7. Chen, Y., Qian, N.: A coarse-to-fine disparity energy model with both phase-shift and position-shift receptive field mechanisms. Neural Computation 16, 1545–1577 (2004)
8. Fleet, D., Wagner, H., Heeger, D.: Neural encoding of binocular disparity: Energy models, position shifts and phase shifts. Vision Res. 36(12), 1839–1857 (1996)
9. Bayerl, P., Neumann, H.: A fast biologically inspired algorithm for recurrent motion estimation. IEEE Trans. Pattern Anal. Mach. Intell. 29(2), 246–260 (2007)
10. Shimonomura, K., Kushima, T., Yagi, T.: Binocular robot vision emulating disparity computation in the primary visual cortex. Neural Networks 21(2-3), 331–340 (2008)
11. Higgins, C., Shams, S.: A neuromorphic vision processor for spatial integration of optical flow. In: ICCNS 2001 (2001)
12. Dale, J., Johnston, A.: A real-time implementation of a neuromorphic optic-flow algorithm. Perception 31, 136 (2002)
13. Pouget, A., Dayan, P., Zemel, R.S.: Inference and computation with population codes. Ann. Rev Neurosci 26, 381–410 (2003)
14. Adelson, E., Bergen, J.: The plenoptic and the elements of early vision. In: Landy, M., Movshon, J. (eds.) Computational Models of Visual Processing, pp. 3–20. MIT Press, Cambridge (1991)
15. Adelson, E., Bergen, J.: Spatiotemporal energy models for the perception of motion. JOSA 2, 284–321 (1985)
16. Ohzawa, I., De Angelis, G., Freeman, R.: Stereoscopic depth discrimination in the visual cortex: neurons ideally suited as disparity detectors. Science 249, 1037–1041 (1990)
17. Morgan, M.J., Castet, E.: The aperture problem in stereopsis. Vision Res. 37(19), 2737–2744 (1997)
18. Serrano-Pedraza, I., Read, J.C.A.: Stereo vision requires an explicit encoding of vertical disparity. J.Vision 9(4), 1–12 (2009)
19. Daugman, J.: Uncertainty relation for resolution in space, spatial frequency, and orientation optimized by two-dimensional visual cortical filters. JOSA A/2, 1160–1169 (1985)
20. Nestares, O., Navarro, R., Portilla, J., Tabernero, A.: Efficient spatial-domain implementation of a multiscale image representation based on Gabor functions. J. of Electronic Imaging 7(1), 166–173 (1998)
21. Pauwels, K., Hulle, M.V.: Optic flow from unstable sequences containing unconstrained scenes through local velocity constancy maximization. BMVC 1, 397–406 (2006)
22. Theimer, W., Mallot, H.: Phase-based binocular vergence control and depth reconstruction using active vision. CVGIP: Image Understanding 60(3), 343–358 (1994)
23. Chessa, M., Solari, F., Sabatini, S.: A virtual reality simulator for active stereo vision systems. In: VISAPP (2009)
24. Barron, J., Fleet, D., Beauchemin, S.: Performance of optical flow techniques. Int. J. of Computer Vision 12, 43–77 (1994)
25. Jenkin, M., Tsotsos, J.: Applying temporal constraints to the dynamic stereo problem. In: CVGIP, vol. 33, pp. 16–32 (1986)
26. Sabatini, S., Solari, F., Cavalleri, P., Bisio, G.: Phase-based binocular perception of motion in depth: Cortical-like operators and analog VLSI architectures. EURASIP Journal on Applied Signal Processing 7, 690–702 (2003)

GPU-Accelerated Nearest Neighbor Search for 3D Registration

Deyuan Qiu[1,*], Stefan May[2], and Andreas Nüchter[3]

[1] University of Applied Sciences Bonn-Rhein-Sieg,
Sankt Augustin, Germany
dqiu2s@smail.inf.h-brs.de
[2] INRIA, Sophia-Antipolis, France
stefan_may@arcor.de
[3] Jacobs University Bremen, Germany
andreas@nuechti.de

Abstract. Nearest Neighbor Search (NNS) is employed by many computer vision algorithms. The computational complexity is large and constitutes a challenge for real-time capability. The basic problem is in rapidly processing a huge amount of data, which is often addressed by means of highly sophisticated search methods and parallelism. We show that NNS based vision algorithms like the Iterative Closest Points algorithm (ICP) can achieve real-time capability while preserving compact size and moderate energy consumption as it is needed in robotics and many other domains. The approach exploits the concept of general purpose computation on graphics processing units (GPGPU) and is compared to parallel processing on CPU. We apply this approach to the 3D scan registration problem, for which a speed-up factor of 88 compared to a sequential CPU implementation is reported.

Keywords: NNS, GPGPU, ICP, 3D registration, SIMD, MIMD.

1 Introduction

Nearest Neighbor Search (NNS) algorithms aim to optimize the process of finding closest points in two datasets with respect to a distance measure. It is a commonly employed geometrical algorithm in computer vision. In the context of 3D vision, NNS is used frequently in 3D point cloud registration. The registration of large data sets, such as acquired by means of modern 3D sensors, is computationally expensive.

In recent years, growing interest has been attracted by GPUs (Graphics Processing Units) on account of their immense computational power assembled in compact design. Increasing programmability enables general purpose computation and yields a powerful massively parallel processing alternative to conventional multi-computer or multi-processor systems. Moreover, costs of commodity graphic cards are lower when measured in cost per FLOPS.

---

[*] This work was supported by B-IT foundation, Applied Sciences Institute, a cooperation between Fraunhofer IAIS and University of Applied Sciences Bonn-Rhein-Sieg.

M. Fritz, B. Schiele, and J.H. Piater (Eds.): ICVS 2009, LNCS 5815, pp. 194–203, 2009.

Being of a recursive nature, traditional NNS is difficult to be implemented on GPUs. We take advantage of Arya's priority search algorithm [1], to fit NNS in the SIMD (Single Instruction Multiple Data) model, so that it is possible to be accelerated by use of a GPU. *GPU-NNS*, the proposed algorithm, is implemented using *CUDA*, nVidia's parallel computing architecture [11]. Additional approaches are also applied to accelerate the NNS process, such as single-element priority queue and array-based k-d tree (see 3.1). GPU-NNS is used to implement a 3D registration algorithm: *GPU-ICP* (see 3.2). As a standard scan matching algorithm, ICP is widely used for 3D data processing [6]. The analysis on the standard sequential CPU-based ICP algorithm shows that the most time-consuming part of ICP is NNS. In the proposed GPU-ICP implementation, not only NNS, but also the remaining stages are accelerated by GPU. The experiment shows that GPU-ICP performs 88 times faster than a k-d tree based sequential CPU ICP algorithm, which runs on a Intel Core 2 Duo E6600 CPU.

The following sections are structured as follows: Section 2 outlines work related to GPU-based NNS. Section 3 explains our GPU-NNS and GPU-ICP implementation. Section 4 analyzes the results of two experiments: registering two 3D scans and indoor 3D mapping. Section 5 concludes with an outlook on future work.

2   Related Work

NNS is typically implemented using brute force methods on GPUs, which are by nature highly parallelizable. This property makes brute force based NNS methods easily adaptable for a GPU implementation and there have been a couple of implementations available. Purcell et al. used cells to represent photon locations [12]. By calculating the distances between the photons in the cells that are intersected with a search radius, and a query point, k nearest neighbors are located to estimate the radiance. Purcell et al. stressed that k-d tree and priority queue methods are efficient but difficult to be implemented on GPU [12]. Bustos et al. stored indices and distance information as quaternions in RGBA channels of a texture buffer. They used three fragment programs to calculate Manhattan distances and to minimize them by reduction [2]. Rozen et al. adopted a bucket sort primitive to search nearest neighbors [13]. Van Kooten et al. introduced a projection based nearest neighbor search method for the particle repulsion problem [15], which chooses a viewport encompassing every particle (or as many as possible), and projects particles onto a projection plane. The approach takes advantage of the hardware accelerated functionalities of GPUs, such as projection and 2D layout of the texture buffer for grid calculation. Garcia et al. implemented a brute force NNS approach using CUDA, showing that it is multiple times faster than CPU k-d tree approach in high dimensional situations [4].

Other than brute force implementations, GPU-based NNS with advanced search structures are also available in the field of global illustration. In the context of ray tracing, the NNS procedure builds trees with a different manner from a triangle soup, and takes also triangles but not points as the objects of interest. These algorithms cannot be used as general point-based NNS algorithms. On the other hand, the NNS algorithm for photon mapping shares a similar model with a general point-based NNS problem. Foley built a k-d tree on CPU and used the GPU to accelerate the search procedure [3]. Horn et al. extended Foley's work by restarting the search at half of the tree but not from the root [5]. Singh presented an SIMD photon mapping framework, using stack based k-d tree traverse to search k nearest neighbors [14]. Lieberman et al. used quad-tree for the similarity joint algorithm [8]. Zhou et al. implemented k-d tree based NNS on GPU for both ray tracing and photon mapping, using the CPU as a coordinator [16]. He applied a heuristic function to construct k-d trees. In the k-d tree traverse stage, range searching is used to find the k nearest neighbors.

In recent GPU-accelerated NNS implementations, most NNS kernels are based on brute force methods. They are easy to implement but possess the natural drawback of low efficiency compared with advanced data structures. On the other hand, brute force methods mostly need reduction kernels in order to find the minimum in distance. A reduction kernel is slow due to its non-parallel nature, even implemented by highly optimized blocks. Tree-based NNS algorithms have shown a performance leap in global illumination. Hints and inspirations can be gained from these algorithms. Therefore the purpose for which they were designed makes them not easily adoptable for non-graphics purposes.

3   Massively Parallel Nearest Neighbor Search

The NNS problem can be stated as follows: Given a point set S and a query point q in metric space M, the problem is to optimize the process of finding the point $p \in S$, which has the smallest Euclidean distance to q. Our massively parallel nearest neighbor search algorithm, GPU-NNS, is implemented on the CUDA architecture. Instead of using the brute force and linear search method, we use a space partitioning structure, k-d tree, to improve the search process. In the following, the terms *host* and *device* refer CPU and GPU respectively.

3.1   GPU-NNS

Next we describe our GPU-NNS procedure which features three steps.

Array-based k-d Tree. Before the search procedure, a piece of page-locked memory is allocated on the host side. A left-balanced k-d tree is built for S by splitting the space always on the median of the longest axis. Being left-balanced, the k-d tree can be serialized into a flat array, and thus stored in the page-locked memory [7]. Since the device memory cannot be dynamically allocated, the array-based k-d tree is downloaded to the device before NNS stage. It is worth mentioning that in order to satisfy the coalescing of CUDA global memory, a Structure of Array (SoA) is used.

Priority Search Method. Because recursion is not possible with CUDA, the traditional k-d tree search method cannot be used. However, the priority search method provides a way to put NNS on the GPU [1]. Priority queues are maintained by the registers in the GPU. The priority search algorithm iteratively executes the follow three steps: (1) Extract the element with the minimal distance to the query point from the queue. (2) Expand the extracted node, insert the higher node in the queue and then expand the lower node. The step is repeated till the leaf node. (3) Update the nearest neighbor so far. The complete GPU-NNS algorithm is shown in Algorithm 1.

Algorithm 1. GPU-NNS Algorithm

Require: download the k-d tree, model point cloud and scene point cloud to GPU global memory.
1: assign n threads, where n = number of query points.
2: assign arrays pair[n] and distance[n] in GPU memory for results.
3: **for** every query point **in parallel, do**
4:     assign the query point to a thread
5:     allocate a dynamic list for the thread
6:     construct dynamic queue q
7:     Initialize q with the root node
8:     do **priority search**, find: *pair* with shortest distance d
9:     **if** $d <$ distance threshold **then**
10:         pair[threadID] = *pair*
11:         distance[threadID] = d
12:     **else**
13:         pair[threadID] = non-pair flag
14:         distance[threadID] = 0
15:     **end if**
16: **end for**

Single-element Priority Queue. Registers are scarce resources in GPU hardware, i.e., the more threads are launched at a time, the less registers can be assigned to each. If the space is unevenly partitioned (e.g., in a point cloud of real scene), a k-d tree based NNS routine performs frequently backtracking to find the real nearest neighbor. In this case, a long queue has to be maintained for each search thread. Such long queues are either not affordable by GPU registers or not desirable in terms of a long search time. In our approach, early termination is achieved by fixing the length of the queues. The insertion of nodes is ignored when the queues are filled. It is observed from experiments that single-element queues also result in valid search. With single-element queues, the process needs fewer steps, especially extractions to find the minimum. A 3D registration experiment in section 4 shows that a GPU-NNS with a single-element queue performs valid matching while consuming less time. In [10] a series of evaluations is presented stating that approximation does not significantly deteriorate the quality of 3D registration using approximate nearest neighbors in an ICP framework.

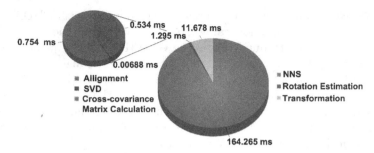

Fig. 1. The pie chart depicts the timing of different stages of one ICP iteration with two point clouds of 68229 points. In the standard sequential CPU implementation, the tree is constructed using the sliding midpoint splitting rule of ANN library, with a bucket size of 1. The tree is searched by an approximate nearest neighbor search method, with maximal visited points of 50. Matrix calculation, i.e., the singular value decomposition (SVD) for the closed form minimization of the ICP error function is implemented by NewMat library.

3.2   GPU-Based 3D Registration

The ICP algorithm is a standard algorithm of 3D registration [6]. The algorithm iterates over three steps: (1) Find point correspondences by the nearest neighbor criteria. (2) Estimate the transformation using a mean square error function. (3) Transform the points. Terminate if an error criterion is fulfilled, otherwise go back to (1). Fig. 1 shows the runtime of different stages of a standard sequential CPU-based ICP algorithm in which NNS consumes the majority of the time. The proposed approach accelerates not only the NNS stage but also the remaining parts of the ICP algorithm, namely the transformation, alignment and covariance matrix calculation. Fig. 2 illustrates the coordination between the host and the device of the GPU-ICP algorithm.

In our implementation, a stepwise reduction of the search radius is applied to refine the iterations. The model point cloud is stored in the texture buffer, not global memory, since they are cached in multiprocessors. Matrix operations are performed by employing the CUBLAS library (CUDA implementation of basic linear algebra methods). Counting the number of valid pairs is implemented with the compact method of CUDPP (CUDA Data Parallel Primitives Library). The block size is configured to be 192 or 256 to get the optimal compromise of enough active threads and enough registers per multi-processor.

4   Experiments and Results

We analyze the results of the GPU-ICP algorithm and compare its performance with that of the OpenMP-based ICP algorithm run on an Intel® Core^{TM}2 Duo 6600 CPU [9]. The GPU-ICP algorithm is performed on a nVidia GeForce GTX280® GPU.

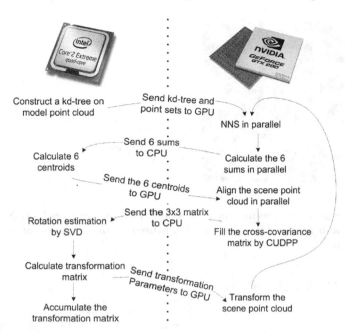

Fig. 2. The coordination between CPU and GPU in the GPU-ICP algorithm. Notice that other than constructing the k-d tree, CPU does only negligible work. The data transfer over the PCIe is minimized. Pictures of the chips are taken from manufacturer websites.

Experiment 1 – Registering two 3D Scans. The 3D scan registration experiment is based on two partially overlapping 3D point clouds captured by a SICK laser scanner in an office-like indoor environment as shown in Fig. 3. Both of the scans have 68229 points. Other than the OPENMP-based ICP algorithm, the performance of GPU-ICP is also compared with a sequential CPU-based ICP (the same implementation as the one of Fig. 1), which uses a single CPU and sets the maximal visited points to 50 as an early termination condition.

The convergence test on GPU-ICP with different queue lengths is presented in Fig. 4 (a). The convergence, which represents the matching quality, is measured by variation. Variation is defined by root mean squared error of the distances between nearest neighbors. The root operation is eliminated in implementation. It is observed that although the executions with different queue lengths perform at different convergence speeds at the beginning, they all converge to a similar variation limit, so as the one with a single-element queue. Figure 4(b) shows the time consumed by different queue length configurations, as well as the two CPU implementations. When registering 68229 points, GPU-ICP with single-element queues performs more than 88 times faster than the standard sequential CPU implementation. Fig. 5 compares the matching results between GPU-ICP and CPU based ICP. Notice that the purple is the blend of the red and the blue when point clouds are aligned. GPU-ICP with single-element priority queues performs similar matching results in shorter time. Fig. 6 compares the speed of the three

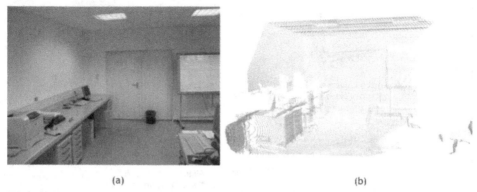

(a)   (b)

Fig. 3. The experimental scene, where the point clouds are captured. (a) An office-like indoor environment. (b) The point cloud captured in the environment, displayed in fake depth color.

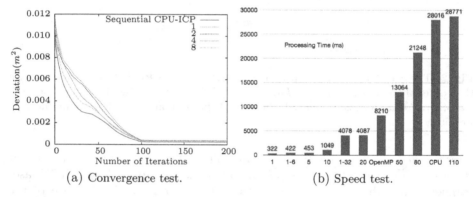

(a) Convergence test.   (b) Speed test.

Fig. 4. The result of the 3D registration experiment of 68229 points. 1-6 means the queue length is increased gradually in iterations as follows: 1, 2, 3, 4, 5, 6, and 1-32 as: 1, 2, 4, 8, 16, 32. It is observed from the speed test that GPU-ICP is 88 times faster than the sequential CPU-based ICP.

implementations: standard CPU-based ICP, OPENMP-based ICP and GPU-ICP. When registering 68229 points, OPENMP multi-threading on a dual core machine achieves a speedup of around 3 compared to the sequential execution, while a speedup of 88 is achieved by GPU implementation. It is observed that with more points, the speedup ratio of GPU-ICP to CPU implementations is improved. Data (68229×2 points which amount to around 7 MB) are transfered to the GPU only once in an ICP process, which take less than 3 milliseconds if the GPU is connected by PCIe 2.0.

The same experiment is also tested on a contemporary system, which has an Intel® Core^{TM} i7-965 Extreme Edition CPU and a GeForce GTX 295 GPU. All experimental settings are the same as above. The results are in Table 1.

Experiment 2 – Indoor 3D Mapping. The proposed GPU-ICP algorithm is applied to an indoor mapping task. 180 frames are captured by an SR3000 Swiss

Fig. 5. Top view of the matched point clouds. Model point cloud is in red, scene in green, and transformed scene in blue. (a) Matching result of standard sequential CPU-ICP. (b) Matching result of GPU-ICP with single-element priority queue.

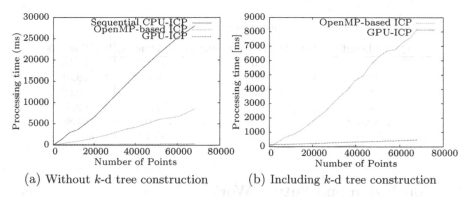

(a) Without k-d tree construction   (b) Including k-d tree construction

Fig. 6. The runtime comparison among sequential CPU implementation, OPENMP-based implementation and GPU-ICP

Table 1. Testing results of three ICP methods on a contemporary system

Sequential CPU-ICP	OPENMP-based ICP	GPU-ICP
13140 ms	2800 ms	260 ms

Ranger Camera®, with resolution of 25344 points[1]. The mapping environment and the result of GPU-ICP are shown in Fig. 7 and the mapping performance is listed in Table 2. Total time includes file operation, data transfer and matching process. 1-2-3-4-5-6 means the queue length increases during the iterations from 1 to 6. Since the number of points in every frame is less than that of *Experiment 1*, the speedup ratio of GPU-ICP is somewhat less (see Fig. 6b).

---

[1] The data are taken from http://www.robotic.de/242/

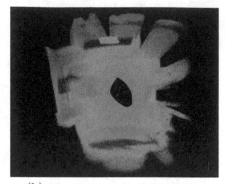

(a) Experimental environment.   (b) Mapping result of GPU-ICP.

Fig. 7. The mapping result is attained with increasing queue length from 1 to 6 and 130 iterations. Notice that the result is produced by the pure ICP process, without any preprocessing or refinement.

Table 2. The runtime of the mapping experiments

Queue Length	Number of Iterations	Total Time (s)	ICP Time (s)
1	20	55.57	11.58
1	30	78.95	19.51
1	60	99.08	40.86
1	130	107.79	50.55
1-2-3-4-5-6	130	123.05	65.80
OPENMP-based ICP	130	463.78	454.30

5   Conclusion and Future Work

We developed a GPU-accelerated NNS approach that uses the k-d tree based priority search method. The performance is enhanced significantly by the massive parallelism of the GPU SIMD architecture. The GPU-NNS is applied in a 3D registration algorithm, GPU-ICP. When registering 68229 points, results show that a performance increase of up to 88 times can be obtained using a modern commercial video card. The resulting approach is meanwhile around 26 times faster than the MIMD-based ICP algorithm running on a dual-core CPU. The acceleration ratio of GPU-ICP to CPU implementations is greater when registering larger point clouds.

With the rapid development of GPU technology, the k-d tree construction stage can be migrated to GPU, possibly using a breadth first, dynamic list based approach. In addition Nüchter et al. show that a larger bucket size improves NNS performance [10]. GPU-NNS could also increase the points in every leaf node. As for the GPU-ICP algorithm, more extensions can be implemented to make it a fully-fledged 3D registration algorithm, such as global relaxation, frustum culling and point reduction.

References

1. Arya, S., Mount, D.M.: Algorithms for Fast Vector Quantization. In: Proc. Data Compression Conference, pp. 381–390. IEEE Computer Society Press, Los Alamitos (1993)
2. Bustos, B., Deussen, O., Hiller, S., Keim, D.: A Graphics Hardware Accelerated Algorithm for Nearest Neighbor Search. In: Proc. of the 6th Int. Conf. on Computational Science, pp. 196–199 (May 2006)
3. Foley, T., Sugerman, J.: KD-Tree Acceleration Structures for a GPU Raytracer. In: Graphics Hardware, pp. 15–22 (July 2005)
4. Garcia, V., Debreuve, E., Barlaud, M.: Fast k Nearest Neighbor Search using GPU. In: Proc. Comp. Vision and Pattern Recognition Workshops (CVPRW), pp. 1–6 (June 2008)
5. Horn, D.R., Sugerman, J., Houston, M., Hanrahan, P.: Interactive k-D Tree GPU Raytracing. In: Proc. Symp. on Interactive 3D graphics and games, pp. 167–174 (April 2007)
6. Besl, P.J., McKay, N.D.: A Method for Registration of 3-D Shapes. IEEE Transactions on Pattern Analysis and Machine Intelligence 14(2), 239–256 (1992)
7. Jensen, H.W.: Realistic Image Synthesis Using Photon Mapping. AK Peters (July 2001)
8. Lieberman, M.D., Sankaranarayanan, J., Samet, H.: A Fast Similarity Join Algorithm Using Graphics Processing Units. In: Proc. of the 24th IEEE International Conference on Data Engineering, pp. 1111–1120 (May 2008)
9. Nüchter, A.: Parallelization of Scan Matching for Robotic 3D Mapping. In: Proceedings of the 3rd European Conference on Mobile Robots (September 2007)
10. Nüchter, A., Lingemann, K., Hertzberg, J., Surmann, H.: 6D SLAM with Approximate Data Association. In: Proc. of the 12th IEEE International Conference on Advanced Robotics (ICAR), pp. 242–249 (July 2005)
11. nVidia. NVIDIA CUDA Compute Unified Device Architecture Programming Guide. nVidia, version 2.0 edn. (June 2008)
12. Purcell, T.J., Donner, C., Cammarano, M., Jensen, H.W., Hanrahan, P.: Photon Mapping on Programmable Graphics Hardware. In: Doggett, M., Heidrich, W., Mark, W., Schillin, A. (eds.) Proc. of the ACM SIGGRAPH/EUROGRAPHICS Conf. on Graphics Hardware (2003)
13. Rozen, T., Boryczko, K., Alda, W.: GPU bucket sort algorithm with applications to nearest-neighbour search. In: Journal of the 16th Int. Conf. in Central Europe on Computer Graphics, Visualization and Computer Vision (February 2008)
14. Singh, S., Faloutsos, P.: SIMD Packet Techniques for Photon Mapping. In: Proc. of the IEEE/EG Symposium on Interactive Ray Tracing, pp. 87–94 (September 2007)
15. van Kooten, K., van den bergen, G., Telea, A.: GPU Gems 3, ch. 7, pp. 123–148. Addison Wesley Professional, Reading (2007)
16. Zhou, K., Hou, Q., Wang, R., Guo, B.: Real-Time KD-Tree Construction on Graphics Hardware. In: SIGGRAPH Asia 2008, p. 10 (April 2008)

Visual Registration Method for a Low Cost Robot

David Aldavert[1], Arnau Ramisa[2], Ricardo Toledo[1],
and Ramon López de Mántaras[2]

[1] Computer Vision Center (CVC)
Dept. Ciències de la Computació
Universitat Autònoma de Barcelona (UAB), 08193, Bellaterra, Spain
{aldavert,ricard}@cvc.uab.cat
[2] Artificial Intelligence Research Institute (IIIA-CSIC)
Campus de la UAB, 08193, Bellaterra, Spain
{aramisa,mantaras}@iiia.csic.es

Abstract. An autonomous mobile robot must face the correspondence
or data association problem in order to carry out tasks like place recognition or unknown environment mapping. In order to put into correspondence two maps, most methods estimate the transformation relating the
maps from matches established between low level feature extracted from
sensor data. However, finding explicit matches between features is a challenging and computationally expensive task. In this paper, we propose a
new method to align obstacle maps without searching explicit matches
between features. The maps are obtained from a stereo pair. Then, we use
a vocabulary tree approach to identify putative corresponding maps followed by the Newton minimization algorithm to find the transformation
that relates both maps. The proposed method is evaluated in a typical
office environment showing good performance.

Keywords: Registration, bag of features, robot localization.

1 Introduction

An autonomous mobile robot that navigates through an unknown environment
often has to carry out tasks such as detecting loop-closings, estimate motion from
robot sensors or build a map using a SLAM algorithm. To solve such problems
we must face the correspondence (or data association) problem, i.e. the problem
of determining if sensor measurements taken at different locations or at different
times correspond to the same physical object in the world.

This problem is usually approached extracting primitives from sensor measurements and searching for correspondences between them. From such correspondences an estimation of the robot motion and its uncertainty is obtained.
An algorithm typically used to align robot sensor measurements is the Iterative
Closest Point (ICP) algorithm [1]. The ICP algorithm searches at each iteration
explicit correspondences between features using the distance between feature

M. Fritz, B. Schiele, and J.H. Piater (Eds.): ICVS 2009, LNCS 5815, pp. 204–214, 2009.

descriptors as a likelihood measure. However, the search for explicit correspondences is the most expensive step since for each primitive of a set, a test against all the primitives from the other set must be done. Therefore, other methods like the Normal Distribution Transform (NDT) presented by Biber and Straßer [2], tried to avoid this step aligning sensor measurements without finding direct correspondences between primitives. The NDT transforms the laser scan to a 2D grid where each cell locally models the probability of measuring an obstacle using a normal distribution. The result of the transform is a piecewise continuous and differentiable probability density, that can be used to match another scan using Newton's algorithm. The previous methods use range information which is not discriminative enough to directly find correct correspondences between primitives, so that, such methods iteratively search the matching primitive. Therefore, some authors use robust invariant features [3][4][5] because they can provide primitives that are distinctive enough to find matches directly without using an iterative approach. However, there are situations where image local invariant features cannot be used to describe the world. For example, in poorly textured environments, the number of putative matches usually is not enough to ensure that the estimated robot motion is correct. In environments with repetitive textures, the amount of false correspondences rises rapidly and the transformation that relates both scans cannot be estimated reliably. These two problems are common in indoor or urban environments.

In this paper, we present a method to align local maps using stereo image data: First, local obstacle maps are obtained by scanning the environment with a stereo head. Then, using a *Vocabulary Tree*[6], signatures of obstacle maps are built with robust invariant features extracted from stereo images. Such map signatures are used as a fast reranking method to prioritize the maps that are more likely to be related. Finally, the Newton minimization algorithm is used to determine the robot motion. Our minimization algorithm searches explicit correspondences between primitives, which is a computationally expensive step. However, as our obstacle space is discrete and obstacles are restricted into the ground plane, the matching step can be notably speeded up. Moreover, colour image information is added to the probabilistic map in order to increase the convergence ratio and the robustness of the alignment estimation.

The paper is structured as follows: In section 2, methods used to build local obstacle maps and to obtain map signatures are presented. In section 3, the method used to align different obstacle maps is described. The experiments setup and results are shown in section 4. Finally in section 5, there is a discussion of the results and an overview of future work.

2   Local Stereo Maps

The local stereo maps are 2D occupancy grids where each cell models the probability of an obstacle occurrence. Those occupancy grids are constructed from image pairs acquired while rotating a stereo head mounted on a pan-tilt unit. The occupancy grid also stores colour information of the detected objects.

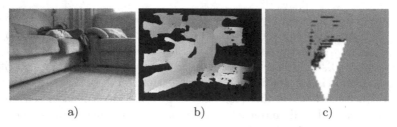

a)   b)   c)

Fig. 1. a) Original right stereo pair image. b) Dense disparity map. c) Occupancy grid obtained from dense reconstruction.

Additionally, a global signature of the local map is obtained using a *bag of visual words* approach.

2.1   Obstacle Maps

Obstacle maps are represented by a 2D occupancy grid in the X-Z world plane where each cell represents the probability that an obstacle is present. Obstacles are detected using a correlation based stereo algorithm that uses the SAD (Sum of Absolute Differences) function as similarity measure which, for a relatively small resolution, can obtain a dense stereo map in real time [7]. Once the dense stereo map is obtained, pixels are reprojected to 3D space by simply using a noise free triangulation operation. Let $m_l = [x_l, y_l]$ and $m_r = [x_r, y_r]$ be a corresponding pair of points in image plane coordinates. The 3D coordinates can be computed as follows:

$$X = \frac{bx_l}{x_l - x_r} \qquad\qquad Y = \frac{by_l}{x_l - x_r} \qquad\qquad Z = \frac{bf}{x_l - x_r} \ . \qquad (1)$$

where b is the baseline and f is the focal length of the camera. The resulting 3D world points that are within a height range, say $[Y_1, Y_2]$, are reprojected to a 2D occupancy grid in the X-Z world plane. To increase the field of view of the robot's cameras, the pan-tilt unit is used to take a stereo pair of images every 10° degrees covering an arc of 120° degrees, obtaining an overall field of view of 160° degrees. Figure 1 shows how a local map is built: First, a dense disparity map (Fig. 1.b) is obtained from stereo image pairs (Fig. 1.a). Then, obtained points are reprojected into the 2D occupancy grid (Fig. 1.c). Although the disparity maps have gaps in poorly textured regions, obstacles are found in the occupancy grid.

2.2   Maps Signature

Easily, a robot mapping a fairly large environment can store up to thousands of scans, making too computationally expensive to find correspondences for a new scan in the database using only the alignment method. Therefore, a visual appearance based signature is extracted for each newly acquired scan and used to select the most similar instances from the database. The signature used is based on the bag of words document retrieval methods that represent the subject

a)   b)

Fig. 2. (*Best viewed in colour*) Original image (a) is segmented obtaining (b)

of a document by the frequency in which certain words appear in the text. Recently these approaches have been adapted to visual object recognition by different authors [8][9] using local visual descriptors computed on image features as *visual words*: First a clustering algorithm is used to sample the descriptor space to obtain a set of *visual words*. Then, the frequency of the *visual words* in the image is used to create a histogram which is used as the signature of the local map. Finally, the Euclidean distance between histograms is used as a likelihood measure that two maps are related. In this work we use the *vocabulary tree* proposed by Nistér and Stewénius [6] to cluster the feature space.

In our experiments we have evaluated the performance of the vocabulary tree using two types of descriptors: Shape Context and SIFT [10], computed on regions detected by five state-of-the-art region detectors: Harris Affine, Hessian Affine, Harris Laplace, Hessian Laplace [11], MSER [12] and SURF [13], combinations of different detectors with complementary properties have been also evaluated.

2.3   Colour Obstacle Maps

In order to improve alignment results, instead of using only depth information to build local environment maps, we add colour information to each cell of the 2D occupancy grid. Essentially, each image pixel is assigned a red, green, blue or non-colour label and those labels are accumulated in the 2D occupancy grid. In order to achieve a certain degree of invariance to illumination changes, we have trained a *Support Vector Machine* (SVM) [14] for colour image segmentation. The input vector of the SVM is built as follows: the image is transformed to the Hue-Saturation-Lightness (HSL) colour space and a colour descriptor is computed from a region around each pixel. The descriptor is a histogram of six bins. Each pixel of the region votes in a bin determined by its *hue* and weighted by its *saturation*. The output of the SVM determines which label is assigned to the pixels of the image region. In Fig. 2 a segmentation example is shown.

3   Map Alignment

In this section we present the method used to align different local maps: First, the visual appearance signature is used to prioritize the most similar maps from the database as candidates to be aligned. Then, for the selected maps the Newton based iterative algorithm is used to find the registration parameters.

3.1   Signature Comparison

When a new scan is acquired by the robot, its appearance signature described in section 2.2 is computed and compared to the ones stored in the memory of the robot. Next, the k most similar scans of the database are selected and registered using the alignment method described in the next subsection. In our experiments we have used the Euclidean distance as a similarity measure between the signature histograms given that it is widely used in the literature [9][8][6].

3.2   Iterative Map Alignment

In order to align a new map with a map in the database, we need to find the transformation that relates both maps. Since our robot navigates in an indoor environment, we suppose that the ground is planar. Therefore, to align a query map against a database map we need to estimate a 2D rigid transformation:

$$M = \begin{bmatrix} cos\beta & -sin\beta & t_x \\ sin\beta & cos\beta & t_z \end{bmatrix} . \tag{2}$$

where β is the rotation between the two maps in the Y axis, while t_x and t_z are the translation between the two maps in the X and Z axis respectively. To find the parameters $p = [\beta, t_x, t_z]^\top$ of equation 2, an iterative method which at each step reduces the distance between the obstacles of the maps query map and the database map is used. This algorithm tries to find the parameters p that minimize the following function:

$$sc(p) = \sum_{c=1}^{4} \sum_{j=1}^{M_c} \sum_{i=1}^{N_c} e^{-\mathbf{x}_i^{c\top} C_i^{c-1} \mathbf{y}_j^c} . \tag{3}$$

where M_c is the number of obstacles of the query map with colour label c, $\mathbf{y}_j^c$ are the 2D coordinates of those obstacles, N_c is the number of obstacles in the database map with colour label c, $\mathbf{x}_i^c$ are the 2D coordinates of those obstacles and C_i^c is the covariance matrix modelling location uncertainty of $\mathbf{x}_i^c$.

Then, to align two obstacle maps, the following method is proposed:

1. Initialise the motion parameters to zero or by an estimation obtained from the robot odometry.
2. Apply the parameters of the transformation to the set of points S corresponding to the location of the obstacles in the query map.
3. From eq. 3 a score value is obtained.
4. Estimate new parameters values by optimizing the score using the Newton minimization algorithm.
5. While the convergence criterion is not meet, go to 2.

Given that eq. 3 is non-linear, to find the parameters p that maximize eq. 3 the Newton's algorithm is used. This method is similar to other computer vision methods used for registration of image information obtained from different sensors or aligning images related by an affine or projective transformation.

The Newton's algorithm iteratively finds the parameters p that maximize eq. 3 solving the following eq.:

$$\triangle p = -H^{-1}g \tag{4}$$

where g is the gradient of eq. 3 with elements:

$$g_i = \frac{\partial sc(p)}{\partial p_i} \tag{5}$$

and H is the Hessian of eq. 3 with elements:

$$H_{ij} = \frac{\partial sc(p)}{\partial p_i \partial p_j} \tag{6}$$

Then, the parameters are updated using the following:

$$p = p + \triangle p \; . \tag{7}$$

Equations 4 and 7 are iterated until the estimate of p converges. For each obstacle $\mathbf{y}$ of the query obstacle map, the elements of the gradient are, by the chain rule:

$$g_i = \frac{\partial sc(p)}{\partial p_i} = \frac{\partial sc(p)}{\partial \mathbf{y}} \frac{\partial \mathbf{y}}{\partial p_i} \tag{8}$$

where the partial derivate of $sc(p)$ respect $\mathbf{y}$ is the gradient of the eq. 3 and the partial derivate of $\mathbf{y}$ respect p_i is given by the Jacobian of equation 2:

$$\frac{\partial W}{\partial p} = \begin{bmatrix} -x_i sin\alpha - y_i cos\alpha & 1 & 0 \\ x_i cos\alpha - y_i sin\alpha & 0 & 1 \end{bmatrix} \; . \tag{9}$$

The Hessian matrix H is given by:

$$H = \sum_j \left[\frac{\partial sc(p)}{\partial \mathbf{y}} \frac{\partial W}{\partial p} \right]^{\top} \left[\frac{\partial sc(p)}{\partial \mathbf{y}} \frac{\partial W}{\partial p} \right] \tag{10}$$

Finally, the algorithm is iterated until a maximum number of iterations is reached or the update of the parameters fulfils the condition $\| \triangle p < \varepsilon \|$. Robot motion estimation is obtained from parameter vector p and the uncertainty of such estimation, i.e. the covariance matrix, is obtained from the inverse of the Hessian matrix.

3.3   Optimizing the Minimization Process

As seen in section 2, obstacles are detected using a 2D occupancy grid, so that, the location of the detected obstacles is discrete over the $X - Z$ plane. Therefore, for each location $\mathbf{y} = (i, j)$ of a 2D occupancy grid, we can calculate a priori its score:

$$SM(\mathbf{y}, c) = \sum_i e^{-\mathbf{x}_i^c C_i^{c-1} \mathbf{y}} \; . \tag{11}$$

Where y is the coordinates vector of the j obstacle with colour label c of the query map. Then, eq. 3 can be reduced to:

$$sc(p) = \sum_{c=1}^{4} \sum_{j=1}^{M} SM(y_j, c) \qquad (12)$$

Therefore, at each step of the minimization process we have to look up the value of eq. 11 and avoid calculating the exponentials of eq. 3. Although this calculation is computationally expensive, it only has to be done once and it greatly speeds up the matching algorithm.

4   Experimental Results

In this section, we analyse the results obtained with our alignment algorithm. To perform the experiments, a database of 50 panoramas has been acquired in a three room apartment with the mean distance between panoramas of approximately 0.5 meters. A testing environment with poor salient visual features was chosen in order to test the reliability of our method. We manually annotated the relations and the alignment parameters between the panoramas to create the ground truth. Data has been acquired using a mobile robot platform built at our department: It is based on a Lynxmotion 4WD3 robot kit and it has been designed to be as cheap as possible. All the experiments are executed on the robot's on-board computer, which is a VIA Mini-ITX EPIX PE computer with a VIA C3 1 GHz CPU, and stereo images are obtained from two Philips SPC900NC webcams with a resolution of 320×240 pixels. Stereo measurements are stored in a 2D occupancy grid that has 160 cells width per 120 cells height. Each cell represents a square with a side length of 0.05 meters, so that, the local map has a width of 8 meters and a depth of 6 meters.

4.1   Map Identification

As explained in Section 2.2, for a query map, the k most similar database maps are selected using a fast visual appearance method. This way the more computationally expensive alignment step does not have to be applied to every database map. To find the best parameters for our vocabulary tree, we have evaluated several trees with different depths and branch factors. Taking into account both, performance and computational cost, we have selected a branch factor of 5 and a depth of 6, so that the resulting tree has 15.625 leaves. As the performance of a bag of visual words approaches is typically improved with more detected features, it is interesting to combine complementary feature detectors. However, the computational cost of combining all possible feature detectors is prohibitive in our approach. Instead we have evaluated all the possible combination in order to find the one that maximizes performance while minimizing the number

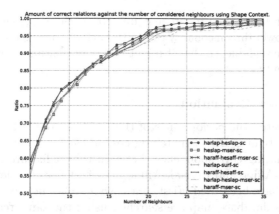

Fig. 3. Average ratio of correct relations according to ground truth among the k most similar appearance signatures using the Shape Context descriptor

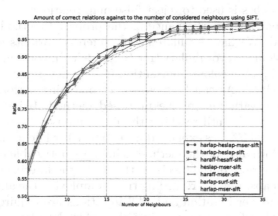

Fig. 4. Average ratio of correct relations according to ground truth among the k most similar appearance signatures using the SIFT descriptor

of applied detectors. With a similar idea in mind, we have compared two region descriptors with significantly different dimensionality. With a similar performance, it is favourable to chose the descriptor with lowest dimensionality. Figure 3 shows the average ratio of correct map relations (vertical axis) that are included between the k most similar appearance signatures (abscissa axis) using the shape context descriptor. Figure 4 shows the same results but using the SIFT descriptor. We require that 90% of k local maps selected by the vocabulary tree are truly related to the query local map. This ratio is achieved by the combination of the Hessian-Affine and the Harris-Affine detectors using the SIFT descriptor at k equal to 14. Another interesting option would be the combination of Harris-Laplace and Hessian-Laplace detectors with Shape Context descriptor that achieves 90% with k equal to 15. Even though an extra map alignment has to be done, the computational cost of the Laplace version of the detectors is much lower than its affine counterpart. Besides, the Shape Context has a markedly lower dimensionality than SIFT, thus it needs less computational effort and is more scalable, so that it might be an interesting option for mapping larger environments.

4.2   Performance Evaluation

Finally, we evaluated the performance of the whole system and we compared it against direct matching. Direct matching computes the alignment between the panoramas estimating correspondences between robust features. In this experiment, the Harris-Affine and Hessian-Affine covariant features detectors and the SIFT descriptor have been used. First, putative matches between features of the query map and a database map are searched using the same technique as [15]. Then, features are projected to the X-Z plane using stereo information and the RANSAC algorithm is used to reject possible false matches and find the 2D rigid transformation between the two maps. The ratio between correct matches and total putative matches is used to reject false map relations.

Figure 5 compares the performance of the proposed method and the direct matching method. We have evaluated four different variants of the proposed method: using colour and vocabulary tree (CIter + VT), vocabulary tree without colour (Iter + VT), only colour information (CIter) and the iterative alignment algorithm alone (Iter). As can be seen, direct matching performs significantly worse than all the variations of the proposed method. Using the vocabulary tree increases the recall until reaching the limit imposed by the number of selected neighbours (90.0%), as explained in section 4.1, while using colour slightly increases the performance of the method. The most noticeable effects of the vocabulary tree is the raise of the precision thanks to the filtering of most false relations between maps. Finally, regarding time complexity, the alignment method requires about 5ms per iteration and 14.7 iterations are required in average to align two maps. Therefore, the mean time elapsed in the alignment step is about

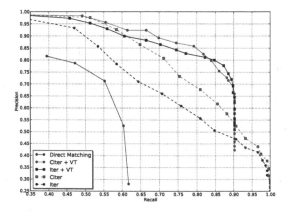

Fig. 5. Precision vs. Recall for each evaluated method

73ms. Classifying a map on the vocabulary tree takes on average 40ms, and given that 15 database maps are selected by the vocabulary tree, 1.1 seconds are required to find the possible relations between a query map and the database maps.

5   Conclusion

Although invariant visual feature matching has shown good performance in robot motion estimation, in environments with few visual salient features, that estimation tends to be unreliable. However, we have obtained better results modelling the distribution of the obstacles with a 2D occupancy grid and aligning them with the Newton minimization algorithm. Besides, when a visual appearance similarity measure is added to the occupancy grid, the recall increases up to 87.3% while keeping a good precision. Future work includes testing our method in larger data sets including different types of environments.

Acknowledgements

This work was supported by TIN 2006-15308-C02-02 project grant of the Ministry of Education of Spain, the CSD2007-00018 and the MIPRCV Consolider Ingenio 2010, the FI grant from the Generalitat de Catalunya, the European Social Fund, and the MID-CBR project grant TIN2006-15140-C03-01, and FEDER funds and the grant 2009-SGR-1434.

References

1. Besl, P.J., McKay, N.D.: A method for registration of 3-D shapes. IEEE Trans. Pattern Anal. Mach. Intell. 14(2), 239–256 (1992)
2. Biber, P., Straßer, W.: The normal distributions transform: A new approach to laser scan matching. In: Proc. of Int. Conf. on Intel. Robots and Systems (2003)
3. Newman, P., Ho, K.: SLAM - Loop Closing with Visually Salient Features. In: Proc. of the Int. Conf. on Robotics and Automation (ICRA), April 18-22 (2005)
4. Se, S., Lowe, D., Little, J.: Vision-based mobile robot localization and mapping using scale-invariant features. In: Proc. of Int. Conf. on Rob. and Aut. (2001)
5. Davison, A., et al.: MonoSLAM: Real-time single camera SLAM. IEEE Trans. Pattern Anal. Mach. Intell. 26(6), 1052–1067 (2007)
6. Nister, D., Stewenius, H.: Scalable recognition with a vocabulary tree. In: Proc. of the Conf. on Computer Vision and Pattern Recognition (CVPR), pp. 2161–2168 (2006)
7. Mühlmann, K., et al.: Calculating dense disparity maps from color stereo images, an efficient implementation. Int. J. Comput. Vision 47(1-3), 79–88 (2002)
8. Sivic, J., Zisserman, A.: A text retrieval approach to object matching in videos. In: Proc. of the Int. Conf. on Computer Vision, ICCV (October 2003)
9. Csurka, G.: Visual categorization with bags of keypoints. In: Workshop on Statistical Learning in Computer Vision, ECCV, p. 22 (2004)

10. Mikolajczyk, K., Schmid, C.: A performance evaluation of local descriptors. IEEE Trans. Pattern Anal. Mach. Intell. 27(10), 1615–1630 (2005)
11. Mikolajczyk, K., et al.: A comparison of affine region detectors. Int. J. Comput. Vision 65(1-2), 43–72 (2005)
12. Matas, J., et al.: Robust wide-baseline stereo from maximally stable extremal regions. Image and Vision Computing 22(10), 761–767 (2004)
13. Bay, H., et al.: Speeded-up robust features (SURF). Comput. Vis. Image Underst. 110(3), 346–359 (2008)
14. Nello, C., John, S.: An introduction to support vector machines and other kernel-based learning methods. Cambridge University Press, Cambridge (2000)
15. Lowe, D.G.: Distinctive image features from scale-invariant keypoints. Int. J. Comput. Vision 60(2), 91–110 (2004)

Automatic Classification of Image Registration Problems

Steve Oldridge, Gregor Miller, and Sidney Fels*

University of British Columbia, Electrical and Computer Engineering
{steveo,gregor,ssfels}@ece.ubc.ca
http://www.ece.ubc.ca/~hct

Abstract. This paper introduces a system that automatically classifies registration problems based on the type of registration required. Rather than rely on a single "best" algorithm, the proposed system is made up of a suite of image registration techniques. Image pairs are analyzed according to the types of variation that occur between them, and appropriate algorithms are selected to solve for the alignment. In the case where multiple forms of variation are detected all potentially appropriate algorithms are run, and a normalized cross correlation (NCC) of the results in their respective error spaces is performed to select which alignment is best. In 87% of the test cases the system selected the transform of the expected corresponding algorithm, either through elimination or through NCC, while in the final 13% a better transform (as calculated by NCC) was proposed by one of the other methods. By classifying the type of registration problem and choosing an appropriate method the system significantly improves the flexibility and accuracy of automatic registration techniques.

Keywords: Image Registration, Computational Photography, Panorama Stitching, Focal Stacking, High-Dynamic Range Imaging, Super-Resolution.

1   Introduction

Image registration is the process of calculating spatial transforms which align a set of images to a common observational frame of reference, often one of the images in the set. Registration is a crucial step in any image analysis or understanding task where multiple sources of data are combined. It is commonly used in computational photography [1], remote sensing [2,3], medical image processing [4,5], and other computer vision tasks.

Image registration methods vary significantly depending on the type of registration being performed. This paper introduces a system that attempts to automatically classify registration problems based on the variation between image pairs. Rather than rely on a single "best" algorithm to solve all types of registration,

---

* Support for this project was provided by Bell Research and the National Science and Engineering Research Council.

M. Fritz, B. Schiele, and J.H. Piater (Eds.): ICVS 2009, LNCS 5815, pp. 215–224, 2009.

the proposed system is made up of a suite of techniques. Image pairs are analyzed according to the types of variation that occur between them, and an algorithm designed to handle that variation solves for the misalignment. In instances where multiple types of variation are detected all potentially appropriate algorithms are run, and a normalized cross correlation of the results in their respective error spaces is performed to select which alignment is best.

This approach has significant advantages over single algorithmic approaches which perform poorly outside their respective domains. Conversely, when compared to simply running all available registration algorithms on the pair, the system is both more efficient and also easier to interpret. No single metric exists to compare the quality of a registration, particularly when error spaces are tuned to particular types of registration, so determining which solution is best from amongst several candidates is difficult. Using normalized cross correlation is possible, however it is less effective at comparing across all algorithms because the normalized combination of all error spaces often doesn't represent the best alignment if one or more of the error spaces is inappropriate.

Our system significantly improves the flexibility and accuracy of automatic registration, approaching what Zitová and Flusser [6] term 'the ultimate registration method,' which is 'able to recognize the type of given task and to decide by itself about the most appropriate solution.'

Section 2 looks at traditional taxonomies of registration and how these can be used to guide in the classification of registration problems. Section 3 examines the basis by which image pairs are classified by the system. Section 4 outlines the system created to automatically register images with different types of variation. The results of the classification of a large set of registration problems by our prototype system is shared in Section 5. Finally Section 6 concludes.

2   Related Work

Systems for automatic image registration exist, however they are most often limited to a single application such as stitching panoramas [7], super-resolution [8,9], high dynamic range (HDR) imaging [10,11], or focal stacking [1]. These techniques can be used on a limited subset of problems from other domains, however no single algorithm exists that will solve all types of registration. Yang et. al [12] extend the flexibility of their algorithm within other problem domains by analyzing the input image pairs and setting parameters accordingly, however the single underlying algorithm still fails in a number of their test cases.

Drozd et. al [13] propose the creation of an expert system based tool for autonomous registration of remote sensing data, and outline a plan to use information derived from image metadata and user tags to select from amongst correlation based, mutual information based, feature based, and wavelet based methods. Unfortunately their description is more of a preliminary proposal and doesn't provide results of the performance of their expert system or of how appropriate the registration techniques selected were at solving the problems they were chosen for. To our knowledge no other attempts at classifying registration have been made, either by rule based systems or by learning methods.

Image registration survey papers provide a methodological taxonomy for understanding the different algorithms used to solve the registration problem. Brown [14] divides registration into four components: feature space, search space, search strategy, and similarity metric. Within Brown's framework, knowledge of the types of variation that occur in image sets is used to guide selection of the most suitable components for a specific problem. Variations are divided into three classes; variations due to differences in acquisition that cause the images to be misaligned, variations due to differences in acquisition that cannot be easily modeled such as lighting or camera extrinsics, and finally variations due to movement of objects within the scene. These are labeled by Brown 'corrected distortions', 'uncorrected distortions', and 'variations of interest' respectively. This paper outlines a system that attempts to automatically detect these variations and use them as a basis for classification of the type of registration problem to be solved, which in turn guides in the selection of suitable algorithms. We focus on Brown's 'corrected distortions,' which are easier to detect and provide significant guidance in the selection process.

More recently, Zitová and Flusser [6] have differentiated the field of registration into area and feature based methods. The four basic steps of image registration under their model are: feature detection, feature matching, mapping function design, and image transformation and resampling. While they do not provide a model of variation equivalent to Brown's, they discuss in detail the advantages and drawbacks of each method, allowing a similar mapping of methodology from situation. In the conclusion of their survey of registration techniques they propose the creation of '*the ultimate registration method*,' which is 'able to recognize the type of given task and to decide by itself about the most appropriate solution.' This paper is an attempt at just that.

Examining these surveys reveals a number of common forms of variation: purely spatial variation, significant variations in intensity, significant variations in focus, variations in sensor type, and finally variations in structure. We have implemented three representative algorithms as a part of our system: a feature based method [7] for purely spatially varying problems, a median thresholding method [10] for intensity varying problems, and finally an area based method [15] for focus varying problems. We do not classify or solve for sensor or structure variations, however these are logical additions to the system.

3   Problem Classification

Image registration methods vary significantly depending on the type of registration being performed. Within our system image pairs are organized into the categories: spatially varying, intensity varying, focus varying, and unrelated, based on their primary form of variation. Examining the types of variations that occur in a pair or sequence of images allows photographers to select an appropriate application, or programmers to select an appropriate algorithm, in order to find the best alignment.

Similarly in our system each image pair is analyzed to determine the differences in their intensity histograms and hue/saturation histograms, the normalized

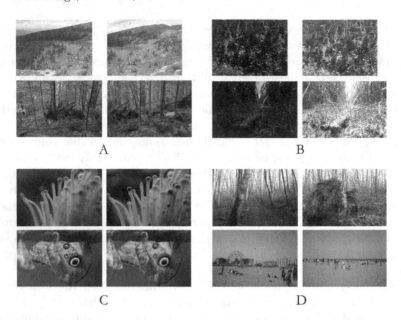

Fig. 1. Image pairs representative of the different types of variation that occur in registration problems. A: Spatially Varying B: Intensity Varying C: Focus Varying D: Unrelated.

power of each image, the number of matching features between the images, and the centroid of those matches. Differences between histograms are measured by their intersection. Figure 1 shows two representative image pairs of each type of registration, and Table 1 presents their corresponding values. These values are used by the system to classify what type of variations occur through the application of simple heuristic rules that utilize these operators. Our system is capable of running many algorithms and comparing the results to find the best solution, therefore it is much more important to make true positive classifications than it is to prevent false positives. The basis for these rules within each application domain is examined in detail below.

3.1   Purely Spatial Variations

Image pairs that differ purely spatially, as shown in Figure 1A, are the most common type of image registration problem. Applications that require registration of images that vary spatially include panorama stitching, super resolution, and remote sensing. Although area-based methods derivative of Lucas and Kanade [15] are capable of solving these types of registration problems, feature based methods like Autostitch [7] and Autopano are the most common technique applied and are generally considered much more accurate unless the image pairs contain little high-frequency information from which to find and match features.

Without first aligning the images, calculating the amount of *overlapping* high frequency content in the image pairs is difficult, so instead we calculate the

Table 1. Values used in the classification of image pairs corresponding to images from Figure 1. For each pair the number of features (N Feat), feature centroid (Centroid), overlap of intensity histogram (I), overlap of hue saturation histogram (HS), and power of each image (Power) is calculated.

Image Pair	N Feat	Centroid	I	HS	Power
A1 (Spatial)	967	(0.76,0.51)(0.22,0.61)	0.765	0.787	3.30%, 3.10%
A2 (Spatial)	605	(0.71,0.65)(0.30,0.65)	0.923	0.878	3.30%, 3.05%
B1 (Intensity)	944	(0.53,0.62)(0.53,0.62)	0.161	0.303	3.79%, 1.80%
B2 (Intensity)	1483	(0.53,0.60)(0.43,0.50)	0.425	0.651	3.60%, 3.24%
C1 (Focus)	139	(0.52,0.53)(0.52,0.53)	0.834	0.812	1.40%, 0.96%
C2 (Focus)	50	(0.52,0.36)(0.58,0.32)	0.862	0.834	0.16%, 0.43%
D1 (Unrelated)	24	(0.49,0.25)(0.44,0.28)	0.898	0.819	3.18%, 2.76%
D2 (Unrelated)	10	(0.47,0.6)(0.58,0.73)	0.746	0.704	1.88%, 1.73%

number of matched features [16] directly. Image pairs with on average more than one matched feature per 75x75 pixel patch are classified as 'purely spatial' because methods unconcerned with other forms of variation (i.e. feature based methods) are likely to be capable of solving for their alignment. Stitching problems with low overlap are likely to contain a low number of matching features, so we also calculate the centroid of the features detected, allowing us to distinguish these cases. Pairs with feature centroids greater than 30% translation from the origin are considered purely spatial require 1/5 as many matches. Section 5 shows how the results of the combination of these two rules allows us to positively classify purely spatially varying image pairs within our test set.

3.2 Intensity Variations

Significant intensity variations are common amongst high dynamic range image registration problems, and can also appear in panorama image pairs where there is a powerful light source in one of the frames. HDR techniques are predominantly area based; interest points required by feature based methods are most often detected at edges or corners, and are not consistent across large differences in intensity. For those image pairs where image intensity varies significantly, such as those shown in Figure 1B, median thresholding [10] can be used to find a more accurate registration.

Intensity varying image pairs can be easily detected by examining the differences in intensity histograms, providing a simple basis for their classification. Pairs with histograms that differ by more than 30% are classified as intensity varying. Section 5 demonstrates the effectiveness of this rule at finding intensity varying image pairs within our test set.

3.3 Focus Variations

Focus variations are found in image pairs used for focus stacking, and in pairs with motion or gaussian blur, shown above in Figure 1C,. Techniques are predominantly area based for the same reason as HDR techniques; the same edges and corners are not detected across images with different focal planes. Instead intensity based area methods like those derivative of Lucas and Kanade [15] must be used to find the correct alignment.

Focus stacking is used to combine images with limited depth of field, so images are likely to have a low amount of high frequency information. Image pairs are detected by examining the normalized power of each of the images, a measure proportional to the number of in focus pixels in the image. In a number of problems, particularly those relating to registering blurred images, only one of the images is lacking in focus. Image pairs where either image has a normalized power less the 2.5% are classified as focus varying. As we will see in Section 5 this rule is useful for positively classifying focus varying pairs, however it also classifies a number of other pairs which are not considered as primarily focus varying in our ground truth.

4   System

Using the rules described in Section 3 our system is able to identify the types of variation occurring between the image pair. If only a single type of variation is identified then the corresponding algorithm is run to solve for the transform that aligns the pair. As mentioned in Section 2, we have implemented three representative algorithms as a part of our system: a feature based method [7] for purely spatially varying problems, a median thresholding method [10] for intensity varying problems, and finally an area based method [15] for focus varying problems.

When multiple forms of variation are classified for an image pair the system uses all appropriate algorithms, solving for each transform. Normalized cross correlation of the proposed transforms is then performed, calculating the error of each transform across all appropriate error spaces to pick the best. For both our area based and median thresholding methods this value can be calculated directly using the same error function that they use to align the images. Unfortunately this is not directly possible in our feature based method, which uses the number of unmatched features as its metric for finding a transform. Instead an error space based on joint intensity of image patches is used.

5   Evaluation

Image registration methods vary significantly depending on the type of registration being performed. Knowing the types of variations that occur in a pair or sequence of images allows photographers to select an appropriate application or programmers to select an appropriate algorithm in order to find the best alignment. To test our algorithm we created a set of 64 image pairs from the categories: spatially varying, intensity varying, focus varying, and unrelated, based on their primary form of variation. These images were then classified in a user study by six independent photographers. For each pair we considered the classification to be valid if five of the six photographers classified the image pairs exactly the same, a process which eliminated four pairs. This set of uniformly classified pairs was then used as a ground truth for evaluating the system. For the remaining 60 images the photographers were on average 96% successful at correctly classifying the main form of variation. This allows us to compare how well our system is able to classify registration problems.

Using our two rules outlined in 3.1 we can positively identify 100% of the purely spatial varying problems within the data set. 38% of pairs classified as primarily spatially varying were also proposed as being intensity or focus varying. Once normalized cross correlation has been applied 76% of the purely spatial (according to our ground truth) pairs find the best alignment using the correspond spatial method. Examination of the remaining 24% of spatial pairs shows that in 60% of cases all error spaces agreed the solution chosen was the best, while 40% produced conflicting recommendations.

As expected, intensity varying image pairs can be easily detected by examining the differences in intensity histograms as proposed in 3.2. Using this rule we are able to find 100% of the intensity varying image pairs within the data set. 91% of ground truth intensity varying pairs were also indicated by either the spatial and/or focus varying rules. After NCC however 81% of the selected solutions were from the intensity varying method. The remaining 19% were selected from the spatially varying method.

Similarly, using the rule proposed in 3.3 we are able to classify 94% of the focus varying problems in our test set. 16% of ground truth pairs were also classified as spatially varying, however after NCC all of the solutions were selected from the focus varying method.

Fig. 2. Image pairs that were aligned using a method other than that suggested by their main form of variation

Table 2. Summary of the system's classification rate

Ground Truth Classification	Identified W	No Alt	After NCC
Spatial	100%	62%	76%
Intensity	100%	9%	81%
Focus	94%	78%	94%
Unrelated	38%	38%	38%
Total Related	98%	56%	87%

Unclassified image pairs are considered to be unrelated by the system. 38% of the unrelated image pairs were correctly identified by the system. A single focus varying problem was also indicated as being unrelated. This poor rate of classification of unrelated image pairs derives from nature of our rules, which were chosen to identify differences in intensity and focus between images, a common occurrence in unrelated images.

Overall the system is able to positively classify 90% of the problems correctly. Removing unrelated image pairs from the set increases the correct classification rate to 98%. 55% of the problems were correctly classified with no alternative variation suggested and were solved using their appropriate method. A further 32% selected the solution by the corresponding method for their classification through normalized cross correlation. Finally, for the remaining 13% of image pairs, 71% of the solutions selected by the system were lowest in all error spaces being considered, suggesting that they represent a better alignment than that proposed by the 'correct' method. Figure 2 shows this set of images. Table 2 summarizes the results of our system's performance classifying the test set.

Further verification of the resulting transforms created by the system is unfortunately a difficult prospect. The unbiased evaluation of registration techniques is a significant problem within the field, particularly when error surfaces or representations used by different methods don't agree upon a decisive 'best' solution. Zitová and Flusser [6] identify three measures of registration accuracy in their survey: localization error, matching error, and alignment error. Localization error represents mistakes in the location of feature based methods' interest regions. Matching error is measured as the number of false matches between features. Finally, alignment error measures the difference between the proposed alignment and the actual between-image geometric distortion. Localization and matching error are specific to feature based methods and measures of common problems with the steps of those methods, and are difficult to apply to area based approaches. Alignment error is a much more desirable measure, however this requires a ground truth.

Azzari et al. recently propose the use of a set of synthetic data with a known ground truth which they have made available online [17]. Their error measure consists of a combination of sum of square difference of image intensity and distance metrics that measure the displacement of known points within the image. Unfortunately their image sets are low resolution (320x240), limited to translation and rotation, and contain no variation in intensity or focus, sensor, limiting their usefulness. A much more robust and high resolution set is necessary for evaluation of modern registrations, and would be a critical contribution to the field of registration. Proof that the 13% of ground truth pairs that were aligned with the other methods selected by normalized cross correlation remains impossible to provide without such a data set. A visual inspection seems to suggest that in most cases they are, however this type of evaluation is empirical at best.

6 Conclusions and Future Work

We have introduced a novel automatic registration system that attempts to automatically classify registration problems based on the variation between image pairs. The system was validated using a test set of 60 pre-classified image pairs verified by an independent user study of photographers. The system was able to identify 98% of the related ground truth pairs' main form of variation. 55% of pairs were correctly identified by a single form of variation allowing immediate selection of an algorithm. A further 32% of pairs proposed transforms were correctly selected using normalized cross correlation on the solution space of the proposed algorithms. Visual inspection of the final 13% of pairs suggests that the alignments proposed are superior to the solution found by the 'correct' algorithm, however verification of this is hypothetical at best. Empirical evaluation of registration is impossible without knowledge of the ground truth alignments.

Although our system focused on spatial, intensity, and focus variations, extension into automatic registration for sensor and structure variations would greatly benefit researchers, particularly those within the medical imaging community. Such a system would require a greater degree of differentiation between problem types and would likely rely more heavily on image metadata to distinguish the variations between image pairs. Additionally learning based methods such as support vector machines, PCA analysis or Bayesian networks represent an avenue of improvement upon our simple heuristic rule based system. Our initial test set of 60 images is sufficient to prove the concept of the system and provide a frame of reference for establishing a set of rules that work for the given images, however a more robust approach would require a substantially larger set of classified images, particularly if using learning based methods. Ideally this set would also contain ground truth translations as proposed in [17], allowing for direct evaluation of performance post-classification.

The correspondence of a set of images using a system that selects which pairs to align would increase the flexibility of our system further. Autostitch [7] provides an excellent example of how this can be done for spatially varying problems.

Finally, our system deals with registration only. The inclusion of image resampling and transformation techniques appropriate to the type of variation detected, such as tone mapping or focal stacking, would greatly enhance the usefulness of this system as a tool for photographers and researchers alike.

References

1. Agarwala, A., Dontcheva, M., Agrawala, M., Drucker, S., Colburn, A., Curless, B., Salesin, D., Cohen, M.: Interactive digital photomontage. In: SIGGRAPH 2004: ACM SIGGRAPH 2004 Papers, pp. 294–302. ACM Press, New York (2004)
2. Lillesand, T.M., Kiefer, R.W.: Remote Sensing and Image Interpretation, 6th edn. Wiley, Chichester (2007)
3. Campbell, J.B.: Introduction to remote sensing, 4th edn. Guildford Press (2008)
4. Maintz, J., Viergever, M.: A survey of medical image registration. Medical Image Analysis 2(1), 1–36 (1998)
5. Pluim, J., Maintz, J., Viergever, M.: Mutual-information-based registration of medical images: a survey. IEEE Transactions on Medical Imaging 22(8), 986–1004 (2003)
6. Zitová, B., Flusser, J.: Image registration methods: a survey. Image and Vision Computing 21, 977–1000 (2003)
7. Brown, M., Lowe, D.G.: Recognising panoramas. In: Proceedings of Ninth IEEE International Conference on Computer Vision, October 16, vol. 2, pp. 1218–1225 (2003)
8. Flusser, J., Zitová, B., Suk, T.: Invariant-based registration of rotated and blurred images. In: Proceedings of IEEE 1999 International Geoscience and Remote Sensing Symposium, pp. 1262–1264. IEEE Computer Society Press, Los Alamitos (1999)
9. Zitová, B., Kautsky, J., Peters, G., Flusser, J.: Robust detection of significant points in multiframe images. Pattern Recogn. Lett. 20(2), 199–206 (1999)
10. Ward, G.: Robust image registration for compositing high dynamic range photographs from handheld exposures. Journal of Graphics Tools 8, 17–30 (2003)
11. Schechner, Y.Y., Nayar, S.K.: Generalized mosaicing: High dynamic range in a wide field of view. Int. J. Comput. Vision 53(3), 245–267 (2003)
12. Yang, G., Stewart, C., Sofka, M., Tsai, C.L.: Registration of challenging image pairs: Initialization, estimation, and decision. IEEE Transactions on Pattern Analysis and Machine Intelligence 29(11), 1973–1989 (2007)
13. Drozd, A.L., Blackburn, A.C., Kasperovich, I.P., Varshney, P.K., Xu, M., Kumar, B.: A preprocessing and automated algorithm selection system for image registration. SPIE, Vol. 6242, 62420T (2006)
14. Brown, L.G.: A survey of image registration techniques. ACM Computing Surveys 24, 325–376 (1992)
15. Lucas, B.D., Kanade, T.: An iterative image registration technique with an application to stereo vision (darpa). In: Proceedings of the 1981 DARPA Image Understanding Workshop, April 1981 pp. 121–130 (1981)
16. Lowe, D.G.: Distinctive image features from scale-invariant keypoints. International Journal of Computer Vision 60, 91–110 (2004)
17. Azzari, P., Di Stefano, L., Mattoccia, S.: An evaluation methodology for image mosaicing algorithms. In: Blanc-Talon, J., Bourennane, S., Philips, W., Popescu, D., Scheunders, P. (eds.) ACIVS 2008. LNCS, vol. 5259, pp. 89–100. Springer, Heidelberg (2008)

Practical Pan-Tilt-Zoom-Focus Camera Calibration for Augmented Reality

Juhyun Oh[1,2], Seungjin Nam[1], and Kwanghoon Sohn[2]

[1] Broadcast Technical Research Institute, Korean Broadcasting System, Seoul, Korea
{jhoh,sjnam}@kbs.co.kr
[2] School of Electrical and Electronic Engineering, Yonsei University, Seoul, Korea
khsohn@yonsei.ac.kr

Abstract. While high-definition cameras with automated zoom lenses are wide-ly used in broadcasting and film productions, there have been no practical cali-bration methods working without special hardware devices. We propose a prac-tical method to calibrate pan-tilt-zoom-focus cameras, which takes advantages from both pattern-based and rotation-based calibration approaches. It uses pat-terns whose positions are only roughly known *a priori*, with several image samples taken at different rotations. The proposed method can find the camera view's translation along the optical axis caused by zoom and focus operations, which has been neglected in most rotation-based algorithms. We also propose a practical focus calibration technique that is applicable even when the image is too defocused for the patterns to be detected. The proposed method is composed of two separate procedures – zoom calibration and focus calibration. Once the calibration is done for all zoom settings with a fixed focus setting, the remain-ing focus calibration is fully automatic. We show the accuracy of the proposed method by comparing it to the algorithm most widely used in computer vision. The proposed algorithm works also well for real cameras with translation off-sets.

Keywords: camera calibration, automated zoom lens.

1 Introduction

Automated zoom lenses have been widely used in augmented reality content produc-tion such as virtual studios. The zoom lens must be precisely calibrated with the at-tached sensor system for seamless insertion of graphic objects in a real scene. If the calibration is not accurately achieved, the graphic objects would not seem 'tied' to the scene and slide along with camera movements. Automatic calibration of a zoom lens is very difficult because of the zoom lens characteristics – variable field of view, variable and small) depth of field, and variable radial distortion. Calibration has been performed manually in most production sites in the absence of practical automatic calibration methods, taking too much time to get a satisfactory result.

A variety of camera calibration methods have been developed because of its impor-tance as a fundamental process in computer vision. Camera calibration is the process

M. Fritz, B. Schiele, and J.H. Piater (Eds.): ICVS 2009, LNCS 5815, pp. 225–234, 2009.

of determining camera parameters such as focal length, pixel skew, principal point, and radial distortion coefficients. For an automated zoom lens, these parameters should be determined with respect to the zoom and focus settings of the camera. Basically there are two categories in traditional camera calibration approaches. The first is to use *a priori* known calibration objects, to determine the camera parameters from the relationship between the known object points and the corresponding image points [1-3]. The second is to use only image points from multiple camera views and called self-calibration [4-9]. Most of the self-calibration methods are based on the assumption that the camera's movement is pure rotation. In pure-rotation condition the relationship of each image pairs is represented with a homography which yields eight constraints, and the camera parameters are extracted by finding the homography and decomposing it to camera intrinsic and rotation parameters. Unfortunately this pure-rotation assumption is not true in the real case, especially for a camera mounted on a pan-tilt head. The error caused by the inaccurate assumption is approximately 5% according to the error analysis in [10], assuming the translation offset of 0.5m and the scene depth of 5m. Qiang et al. [9] developed a self-calibration method that can handle translation offset, but their algorithm requires an active pan-tilt head.

While high-definition (HD) cameras with automated zoom lens which has wide focal length range are used in most broadcast and film productions, not many studies on the calibration of such cameras are found in the literature. Modeling and calibration of automated zoom lens was dealt with in [11]. Chen et al. [3] developed a practical zoom lens calibration method with high accuracy, but their method is to interpolate between the monofocal settings calibrated using Weng's method [2], which requires special hardware to move the pattern precisely for multiple image measurements.

The proposed algorithm is rotation-based, and does not require any specialized hardware but a few patterns attached on walls or desks. Multiple image measurements are obtained by rotating the camera, as in most rotation-based methods. Translation offset caused by the nodal point movement is considered in our method. Focus calibration based on 2-D point correspondences is followed by zoom calibration. While we could not find a similar approach in existing methods, our focus calibration is similar to the zoom calibration procedure in [7].

2   The Camera System

The camera to be calibrated is for virtual studio environments and different from typical surveillance cameras in a few aspects such as high resolution, varying translation offset, wide range of focal length change, and varying depth of field. The camera system is composed of an HD camera, a zoom lens, a tripod fixed on the floor, a pan/tilt head, and sensors attached to the pan/tilt head and the lens, as shown in Fig. 1. A control PC receives data from the sensor box. Zoom and focus values are normalized to 0.0~1.0. Rotation data from the camera head is of high resolution and can be used without calibration. It is also possible to control the lens to move to a particular zoom and focus setting via serial communication interface.

Fig. 1. The camera system, lens sensor, and sensor box

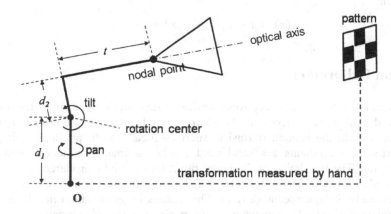

Fig. 2. The camera model

The camera is modeled as Fig. 2. d_1 is the height of the tilt axis from the world origin on the ground, and d_2 the offset from the tilt axis to the optical axis. t is the translation due to the nodal point movement of the lens. Then a model point in the pattern $\mathbf{M} = [X, Y, Z, 1]^T$ is projected to $\mathbf{m} = [x, y, w]^T$ on the image plane:

$$\mathbf{m} = \mathbf{K}[\mathbf{R}|\mathbf{t}](\mathbf{M} + \mathbf{t}_1) , \tag{1}$$

where $\mathbf{R}$ is the rotation matrix obtained from the pan and tilt angles. We assume that rotations take place at a single point where the pan and tilt axes intersect. The upper triangular matrix $\mathbf{K}$ contains the intrinsic parameters of the camera:

$$\mathbf{K} = \begin{bmatrix} f & s & x_c \\ 0 & af & y_c \\ 0 & 0 & 1 \end{bmatrix} . \tag{2}$$

The translation vectors $\mathbf{t}$ and $\mathbf{t}_1$ are given as:

$$\mathbf{t} = [0, -d_2-, t]^T , $$
$$\mathbf{t}_1 = [0, -d_1, 0]^T . \tag{3}$$

The linearly projected point (x, y) suffers radial distortion. We assume the centre of radial distortion is same to the principal point (c_x, c_y). The distorted point (x_d, y_d) is given as:

$$\begin{pmatrix} x_d \\ y_d \end{pmatrix} = L(r) \begin{pmatrix} x \\ y \end{pmatrix},$$

$$r = \sqrt{(x - c_x)^2 + (y - c_y)^2},$$

(4)

where $L(r)$ is the radial distortion function [16]. Although radial distortion is compensated well with commercial broadcast-level zoom lenses, it still has highly nonlinear characteristics. We use the second and fourth order terms for accurate distortion estimation:

$$L(r) = 1 + \kappa_1 r^2 + \kappa_2 r^4.$$

(5)

3   Zoom Calibration

The camera is calibrated for every zoom setting at first, while the focus is fixed to the setting with which the patterns can be clearly found. Parameters considered in our algorithm include the camera intrinsics, such as focal length, principal point, and radial distortion coefficients. $s = 0$ and $a = 1$ can be assumed with modern broadcast-level cameras. The translation of the nodal point (t) must be considered. The pattern poses are also included in the optimization, because it is quite difficult to measure them accurately without special devices. This results in optimization in a large number of dimensions with the parameter vector $\mathbf{p}$ given in (6). If two patterns are used $(N=2)$, the parameter dimensions are 18 (5 for intrinsics, 1 for nodal point translation, 12 for pattern pose update).

$$\mathbf{p} = \begin{bmatrix} f, c_x, c_y, \kappa_1, \kappa_2, t, r_{x1}, r_{y1}, r_{z1}, t_{x1}, t_{y1}, t_{z1}, r_{x2}, r_{y2}, r_{z2}, t_{x2}, t_{y2}, t_{z2} \end{bmatrix}^T.$$

(6)

We minimize the sum of squared reprojection errors between the pattern points $\hat{\mathbf{m}}$ reprojected using the estimated camera parameters $\hat{\mathbf{p}}$ and the corresponding image points $\mathbf{m}$,

$$\mathbf{p} = \operatorname*{argmin} \sum_n^N \sum_m^{M_n} \|\hat{\mathbf{m}}_{nm} - \mathbf{m}_{nm}\| + (\tilde{r}_{xn} - r_{xn})^2 + (\tilde{r}_{yn} - r_{yn})^2 + \cdots,$$

(7)

where total of N patterns are used and M_n points exist in n-th pattern. $\tilde{r}$ and $\tilde{t}$ are the initial pattern poses measured by hand. The squared pattern pose update terms are added for stability, because they are the differences of true values from the measured ones and assumed to be small. Levenberg-Marquardt algorithm [12] is used for the minimization of (7). The initialization of parameters can be done from rotation-based self-calibration methods as in other two-stage calibration techniques, or with the approximate focal lengths provided by the lens manufacture. We use the focal lengths printed on the lens' zoom ring and corresponding zoom motor readings, to build a lookup table to get an approximate focal length from a zoom setting.

4 Focus Calibration

The method introduced in section 3 is not applicable for the focus calibration procedure, where the focus is set out of the depth of field. Fig. 3 shows the effect of defocusing. Note that the field of view changes with focus operation, although the variation is small compared to zoom operation. It is clearly seen in Fig. 3 that calibration of different focus settings using pattern-based techniques is impossible.

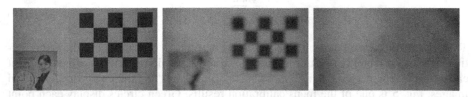

Fig. 3. The effect of defocusing: focused, set to infinite, and set to closest (0.6m) from the left. Zoom is fixed to 0.7.

We propose an automatic focus calibration method based on self-calibration. From each calibrated zoom-focus setting, the focus setting is modified a little and the optimal parameters that minimize the reprojection error are sought, as illustrated in Fig. 4 (a).

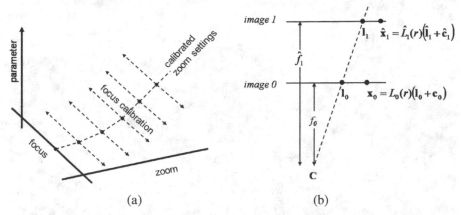

(a)   (b)

Fig. 4. The focus calibration. (a) the calibration order (b) calibration between adjacent focus settings.

In Fig. 4 (b), parameters for a new focus setting 1 are estimated from those of the adjacent focus setting 0. Let x_0 a point among the corner feature points extracted from *image 0* and the corresponding point x_1 is found in *image 1* using optical flow estimation. Then x_1 is compared to $\hat{x}_1$ obtained by reprojecting x_0 onto *image 1* using the parameter set $\hat{p}_{focus}$. From $l_1/\hat{f}_1 = l_0/f_0$, x_0 is reprojected to $\hat{x}_1$,

$$\hat{x}_1 = \hat{L}_1(r)\left(\frac{\hat{f}_1}{f_0}(L_0^{-1}(r)x_0 - c_0) + \hat{c}_1\right), \tag{8}$$

where $\mathbf{l}$ represents the points linearly projected with f only, ignoring the principal point and radial distortion. With focus calibration, only intrinsic parameters are assumed to vary. $\mathbf{p}_{focus} = [f, c_x, c_y, \kappa_1, \kappa_2]^T$ is updated to minimize the difference between $\mathbf{x}_1$ and $\hat{\mathbf{x}}_1$. A homography estimation between each focus step is performed to find outliers in point correspondences. The threshold to judge outliers must not be set too tight, because radial distortion is not considered in the homography estimation. Outliers from the homography estimation are excluded in cost function evaluations.

$$\mathbf{p}_{focus} = \text{argmin} \sum^{\#inliers} \|\hat{\mathbf{x}} - \mathbf{x}\|. \tag{9}$$

This focus calibration between adjacent focus settings is repeated until the focus setting reaches each end (closest or infinite). Feature extraction is not performed again at each focus step, because it is impossible to find good feature points in defocused images. Fig. 5 is one of the focus calibration results. Green circles display each point $\mathbf{x}_1$ found by optical flow estimation, which is shown in blue lines. Outliers are drawn in yellow. Red dots show each point reprojected by the estimated parameters $\mathbf{p}_{focus}$. Parameters are well estimated (red dots arrived in green circles) in spite of several outliers.

Fig. 5. An example of focus calibration

5   Experimental Results

We compared our experimental results with synthetic data with those of the standard calibration provided by OpenCV[13,14]. Although it is not a rotation-method that can be compared with a same dataset, we couldn't find a more similar method to ours that uses multiple measurements of *a priori* known patterns. We placed patterns about 10 units apart from the camera and rotated the pattern or the camera as much as possible, considering the field of view change by zoom variation. 11 zoom settings were used and each zoom setting has three image measurements with different rotations by a fixed rotation axis. Parameters were initialized to a single constant value for all zoom settings.

The experimental results with Gaussian noise of zero mean and standard deviation σ of up to five pixels added to the measurements are shown in Fig. 6. The proposed method shows superior results to those of OpenCV's. We suppose that a large part of the improvement is due to the use of known rotation information and multiple (two) patterns of different depths. Only three parameters are shown for comparison due to the limited space, but the results are almost the same for the remaining ones. The parameters converged from an initial position far away from the desired values in the parameter space. All parameters were measured in pixel units for the experiments with synthetic data, which were done for zoom calibration only.

For experiments with real images, we used Sony's professional HD camcorder PDW700 and Fujinon's HA18x7.6 standard zoom lens with focal length range of 7.6~137mm. Shotoku's TU-03VR pan-tilt head was used for rotation sensing. Pan and tilt resolutions of the camera head are 400,000/360° and 324,000/360° respectively. Shotoku's TY-03 lens encoder was attached to the lens to read zoom and focus motor settings. Focal length and other parameters were estimated in metric domain (in millimeter) for experiments with real images. The CCD sensor size of 9.59 ×5.39mm from the spec. sheet was used for conversion between image and metric domains.

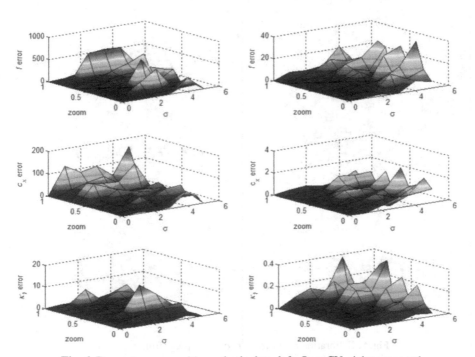

Fig. 6. Parameter errors with synthetic data, left: OpenCV, right: proposed

Fig. 7. Calibration result for a single zoom-focus setting. Reprojected pattern points are drawn in red, and reprojected reference object points are in green.

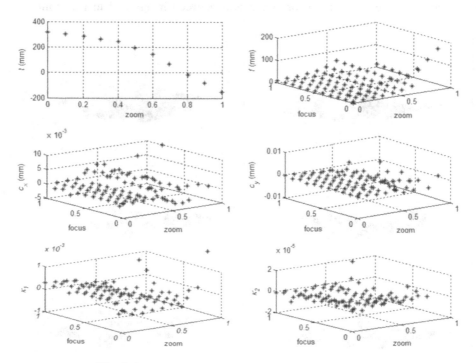

Fig. 8. Calibration result for $t, f, c_x, c_y, \kappa_1, \kappa_2$ (from top left)

Focal length was initialized with the lookup table built as explained in section 3. Five focal lengths and linear interpolation were used. Pattern poses were measured by hand, and all other parameters were set to zero.

Fig. 7 is the calibration result for a particular zoom-focus setting, using eight image samples with different rotations. The position of the reference wall object was measured by hand. Green dots exactly overlap the wall lines, showing that the parameters were accurately estimated including the radial distortion coefficients.

Fig. 8 shows the parameters estimated with real images. Translation offset was found to move backward from the front of the pan axis with the camera's zooming in. The focal length and other parameters converged only for in-focus images for high zoom settings above 0.6, because the blurring was too high and no information could be extracted from the images, as shown in Fig. 3. Reprojection errors were small (< 2 pixels), but not included in the results because it is meaningful only if the optical flow estimation for focus calibration is correct, which is not true for such regions. An alternative solution is to use more patterns located at different depths to cover the entire focus range. We expect the proposed focus calibration technique will reduce the number of patterns required for calibration in that case. Calibration in a brighter environment will also help, by narrowing the iris of the lens. Scattered data interpolation or other techniques to model the parameters as a function of focus and zoom [15] can be used for completion of the calibration results.

6 Conclusion

A practical calibration method for a pan-tilt-zoom-focus camera was presented. The proposed algorithm takes advantages from both pattern-based calibration and self-calibration approaches. It uses patterns whose positions are roughly known *a priori*, with several samples taken with different rotations. Pattern poses are updated as well as the camera parameters. We also proposed a practical focus calibration technique. Once the calibration is done for one focus setting, parameters for adjacent settings are estimated from the calibrated one. The focus calibration procedure is fully automatic. Once the user sets the camera to see a textured scene, the algorithm scans for the lens settings calibrated at the zoom calibration procedure, and perform focus calibration from the calibrated zoom settings. The camera lens is remotely controlled for this purpose. We compared the calibration results with those of a widely used calibration algorithm, to show the superiority of the proposed method in finding camera parameters including radial distortion coefficients. The proposed algorithm works also well for real cameras with translation offsets, but showed incorrect results at the high-zoom region. Our future work will attempt to reduce the calibration error and get stable results in the entire zoom region.

References

1. Zhang, Z.: A flexible new technique for camera calibration. IEEE Transactions on Pattern Analysis and Machine Intelligence 22(11), 1330–1334 (2000)
2. Weng, J., Cohen, P., Herniou, M.: Camera calibration with distortion models and accuracy evaluation. IEEE Transactions on Pattern Analysis and Machine Intelligence 14(10), 965–980 (1992)

234   J. Oh, S. Nam, and K. Sohn

3. Chen, Y., Shih, S., Hung, Y., Fuh, C.: Simple and efficient method of calibrating a motorized zoom lens. Image and Vision Computing 19(14), 1099–1110 (2001)
4. Hartley, R.: Self-calibration of stationary cameras. International Journal of Computer Vision 22(1), 5–23 (1997)
5. Seo, Y., Hong, K.: About the self-calibration of a rotating and zooming camera: Theory and practice. In: International Conference on Computer Vision (1999)
6. Agapito, L., Hayman, E., Reid, I.: Self-calibration of rotating and zooming cameras. International Journal of Computer Vision 45(2), 107–127 (2001)
7. Sinha, S., Pollefeys, M.: Pan-tilt-zoom camera calibration and high-resolution mosaic generation. Computer Vision and Image Understanding 103(3), 170–183 (2006)
8. Hemayed, E.: A survey of camera self-calibration. In: IEEE Conference on Advanced Video and Signal Based Surveillance (2003)
9. Ji, Q., Dai, S.: Self-calibration of a rotating camera with a translational offset. IEEE Transactions on Robotics and Automation 20(1), 1–14 (2004)
10. Hayman, E., Murray, D.: The effects of translational misalignment when self-calibrating rotating and zooming cameras. IEEE Transactions on Pattern Analysis and Machine Intelligence 25(8), 1015–1020 (2003)
11. Willson, R.: Modeling and calibration of automated zoom lenses. Department of Electrical and Computer Engineering, Carnegie Mellon University (1994)
12. Lourakis, M.: levmar: Levenberg-Marquardt nonlinear least squares algorithms in C/C++ (2004), http://www.ics.forth.gr/~lourakis/levmar
13. Bradski, G.: Open source computer vision library. Intel Corporation (2001)
14. Bouguet, J.: Complete camera calibration toolbox for matlab: tech. rep (2004), http://www.vision.caltech.edu/bouguetj/calib_doc/index.html
15. Sarkis, M., Senft, C., Diepold, K.: Modeling the variation of the intrinsic parameters of an automatic zoom camera system using moving least-squares (2007)
16. Hartley, R., Zisserman, A.: Multiple view geometry in computer vision. Cambridge Univ. Pr., Cambridge (2003)

Learning Objects and Grasp Affordances through Autonomous Exploration

Dirk Kraft[1], Renaud Detry[2], Nicolas Pugeault[1], Emre Başeski[1], Justus Piater[2],
and Norbert Krüger[1]

[1] University of Southern Denmark, Denmark
{kraft,nicolas,emre,norbert}@mmmi.sdu.dk
[2] University of Liège, Belgium
{Renaud.Detry,Justus.Piater}@ULg.ac.be

Abstract. We describe a system for autonomous learning of visual object representations and their grasp affordances on a robot-vision system. It segments objects by grasping and moving 3D scene features, and creates probabilistic visual representations for object detection, recognition and pose estimation, which are then augmented by continuous characterizations of grasp affordances generated through biased, random exploration. Thus, based on a careful balance of generic prior knowledge encoded in (1) the embodiment of the system, (2) a vision system extracting structurally rich information from stereo image sequences as well as (3) a number of built-in behavioral modules on the one hand, and autonomous exploration on the other hand, the system is able to generate object and grasping knowledge through interaction with its environment.

1 Introduction

We describe a robot vision system that is able to autonomously learn visual object representations and their grasp affordances. Learning takes place without external supervision; rather, the combination of a number of behaviors implements a bootstrapping process that results in the generation of object and grasping knowledge.

Learning of objects and affordances has to address a number of sub-aspects related to the object aspect of the problem (**O1–O3**) and to the action aspect (**A1, A2**):

O1 What is an object, i.e., what is "objectness"?
O2 How to compute relevant attributes (shape and appearance) to be memorized?
O3 How can the object be recognized and how can its pose determined?
A1 What is the (preferably complete) set of actions it affords?
A2 What action is triggered in a concrete situation?

A satisfactory answer to **O1** is given by Gibson [1] as temporal permanence, manipulability and constrained size in comparison to the agent. Note that manipulability can only be tested by acting on the potential object, and hence requires an agent with at least minimal abilities to act upon objects. For **O2** there are requirements discussed in the vision literature. In many systems, in particular in the context of robotics, the object shape is given a priori by a CAD representation and is then used for object identification and pose estimation (see, e.g., Lowe [2]). However, CAD representations are not

M. Fritz, B. Schiele, and J.H. Piater (Eds.): ICVS 2009, LNCS 5815, pp. 235–244, 2009.

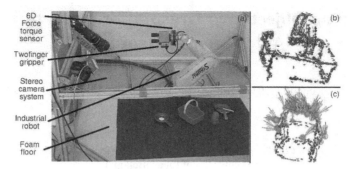

Fig. 1. (a) Hardware setup. (b, c) Outcome of the learning process in form of a geometric object model (b) and a grasp density (c).

available in a general context and hence for a cognitive system, it is important that it is able to learn object representations from experience. Important issues to be considered when coding objects are that the information memorized (1) is useful for the tasks to be performed with the representations (e.g., for matching or grasping), (2) is efficiently accessible internally, and (3) requires little storage space. **O3** has been addressed widely in the computer vision literature. In particular in the context of grasping, besides the actual recognition, the determination of the pose is of importance since it allows the system to associate learned grasps in object coordinates to an observes object instance.

In cognitive robotics, the automatic association of grasping actions to objects (**A1**, **A2**) is referred as learning *affordances* [3]. For maximum flexibility, it is desirable to represent the set of grasp affordances to the most complete extent possible **A1**. There are attempts to compute such a complete set by analytic means [4] which however in general require a pre-existing 3D surface model. In addition, analytic modeling of the interaction between a gripper and an object surface, besides being very time consuming, is very complex since it involves for example friction parameters that are difficult to estimate. Hence we decided to achieve such knowledge by letting the robot experiment in the real world. The decision on the grasp to be performed in a given situation **A2** involves additional considerations, in particular work-space constraints.

This paper describes a system that approaches the above problems in a way that does not require any explicit prior object or affordance knowledge. Instead, the system generates object and grasping knowledge by pure exploration (see Fig. 1). We present a robot-vision system driven by a number of basic behaviors that generate object and grasp-affordance knowledge within two learning cycles. In the first cycle, a multi-modal visual representation covering geometric as well as appearance information (see Fig. 2) is extracted by actively manipulating a potential object. In the second cycle, the robot "plays" with the object by trying out various grasping options. Successful grasp parameters are associated to the object model, leading to an increasingly complete description of the object's grasp affordance. This is done by largely autonomous exploration with only very little interaction between robot and humans. Only interaction that puts the system into a state from which learning can continue is permitted (e.g., putting the object back after playing has pushed it out of the workspace). No high level information such as object identities or demonstrations of ways to grasp it is given to the system.

However, this is not to imply that the system does not make use of any prior knowledge. Quite to the contrary, the system can only perform the complex learning tasks by utilizing a large degree of innate knowledge about the world with which it interacts. However, this knowledge is of rather generic structure. Specifically, the system

- has knowledge about its embodiment and the consequences of its movements in the three-dimensional world (kinematics and the ability to plan motions),
- has a sophisticated early cognitive vision (ECV) system [5, 6, 7] that provides semantically rich and structured 2D and 3D information about the world. This system contains prior knowledge about image features and their relations.
- has a set of procedural prior knowledge about how to: *a)* grasp unknown objects based on visual features, *b)* create visual object models based on object motion, *c)* evaluate a grasping attempt, *d)* estimate object pose based on a learned visual model and *e)* generalize from individual grasps to grasping densities.

This paper describes the various sub-modules and their interaction that lead to the autonomous learning of objects and associated grasp affordances. We show that, based on a careful balance of generic prior knowledge and exploratory learning, the system is able to generate object and grasping knowledge while exploring the world it acts upon. While the sub-modules have already been described [7, 8, 9, 10, 11, 12], the novel part of this work is the integration of these components into an autonomously learning system.

2 State of the Art

Concerning the aspects **O1–O3**, the work of Fitzpatrick and Metta [13] is closely related to our object learning approach since the overall goal as well as the hardware setup are similar: finding out about the relations of actions and objects by exploration using a stereo system combined with a grasping device. We see the main distinguishing feature of this work to our approach in the amount of prior structure we use. For example, we assume a much more sophisticated vision system. Also, the use of an industrial robot allows for a precise generation of scene changes exploited for the extraction of the 3D shape of the object. Similar to this work, we initially assume "reflex-like" actions that trigger exploration. However, since in our system the robot knows about its body and about the 3D geometry of the world and since the arm can be controlled more precisely, we can infer more information from having physical control over the object in terms of an exact association of visual entities based on proprioceptive information. Therefore, we can learn a complete 3D representation of the object (instead of 2D appearance models) that can then be linked to pose estimation. Modayil and Kuipers [14] addressed the problem of detection of objectness and the extraction of object shape in the context of a mobile robot using laser. Here also motion information (in terms of the odometry of the mobile robot) is used to formulate predictions. In this way, they can to extract a 2D cross section of the 3D environment, albeit only in terms of geometric information.

Object grasp affordances (**A1, A2**) can emerge in different ways. A popular approach is to compute grasping solutions from the geometric properties of an object, typically obtained from a 3D object model. The most popular 3D model for grasping is probably the 3D mesh [4], obtained e.g. from CAD or superquadric fitting [15]. However, grasping has also successfully been achieved using models consisting of 3D surface patches [16], 3D edge segments [8, 12], or 3D points [17]. When combined with pose estimation, such methods allow a robot to execute a grasp on a specific object. In our system, we start with edge-based triggering of grasping actions [8, 12] which is then verified by empirical exploration. This requires a system that is able to perform a large number of actions (of which many will likely fail) in a relatively unconstrained environment, this requires a representation of grasp affordances that translate the grasping attempts into a probabilistic statement about grasp success likelihoods.

Learning grasp affordances from experience was demonstrated by Stoytchev [18,19]. In this work, a robot discovers successful grasps through random exploratory actions on a given object. When subsequently confronted with the same object, the robot is able to generate a grasp that should present a high likelihood of success.

Means of representing continuous grasp affordances have been discussed by de Granville et al. [20]. In their work, affordances correspond to object-relative hand approach orientations, although an extension is underway where object-relative positions are also modeled [21].

3   The Robot-Vision System

Hardware setup: The hardware setup (see Fig. 1) used for this work consists of a six-degree-of-freedom industrial robot arm (Stäubli RX60) with a force/torque (FT) sensor (Schunk FTACL 50-80) and a two-finger-parallel gripper (Schunk PG 70) attached. The FT sensor is mounted between robot arm and gripper and is used to compute to detect collision. Together with the foam ground, this permits graceful reactions to collision situations which might occur because of limited knowledge about the objects in the scene. In addition, a calibrated stereo camera system is mounted in a fixed position in the scene. The system also makes use of a path-planning module which allows it to verify the feasibility of grasps with respect to workspace constraints and 3D structure discovered by the vision system.

Early cognitive vision system: In this work, we make use of the visual representation delivered by an early cognitive vision system [5, 7, 6]. Sparse 2D and 3D features, so-called *multi-modal primitives*, are created along image contours. 2D features represent a small image patch in terms of position, orientation, phase. These are matched across two stereo views, and pairs of corresponding 2D features permit the reconstruction of a 3D equivalent. 2D and 3D primitives are organized into perceptual groups in 2D and 3D (called 2D and 3D contours in the following). The procedure to create visual representations is illustrated in Fig. 2 on an example stereo image pair. Note that the resultant representation not only contains appearance (e.g., color and phase) but also geometrical information (i.e., 2D and 3D position and orientation).

The sparse and symbolic nature of the multi-modal primitives allows for the coding of relevant perceptual structures that express relevant spatial relations in 2D and 3D [22]. Similar relations are also defined for 2D and 3D contours to enable more global reasoning processes. In our context, the coplanarity and co-colority relations (i.e., sharing similar color structure) permit the association of grasps to pairs of contours. Figure 3(c) illustrates the association of grasp affordances to an unknown object

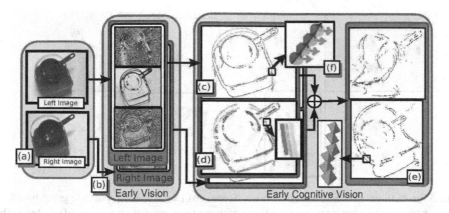

Fig. 2. An overview of the visual representation. (**a**) Stereo image pair, (**b**) Filter responses, (**c**) 2D primitives, (**d**) 2D contours, (**e**) 3D primitives, (**f**) close-up of (c).

by using appearance and geometrical properties of the visual entities. The formalization of the visual change of a primitive under a rigid-body motion allows for the accumulation of the primitives belonging to the object (see Sect. 4).

4   The First Learning Cycle: Birth of the Object

Within the first learning cycle, the "objectness" of visually-detected structure in the scene **O1** is first tested by trying to obtain physical control over such detected structure and then manipulating it. In case the structure changes according to the movement of the robot arm, a 3D object representation is extracted.

Initial grasping behavior: To gain physical control over unknown objects a heuristic grasp computation mechanism based on [8, 12] is used. Pairs of 3D contours that share a common plane and have similar colors suggest a possible grasp; see Fig. 3(a–c). The grasp location is defined by the position of one of the contours. Grasp orientation is calculated from the common plane defined by the two features and the orientation of the contour at the grasp location. Every contour pair fulfilling this criteria generates multiple possible grasps (see Fig. 3(b) for one such possible grasp definition).

Accumulation: Once the object has been successfully grasped, the system moves it to present it to the camera from a variety of perspectives to accumulate a full 3D symbolic model of the object [7]. This process is based on the combination of three components. First, all primitives are tracked over time and filtered using an Unscented Kalman Filter based on the combination of prediction, observation and update stages. The prediction stage uses the system's knowledge of the arm motion to calculate the poses of all accumulated primitives at the next time step. The observation stage matches the predicted primitives with their newly observed counterparts. The update stage corrects the accumulated primitives according to the associated observations. This allows the encoding and update of the feature vector. Second, the confidence in each tracked primitive is

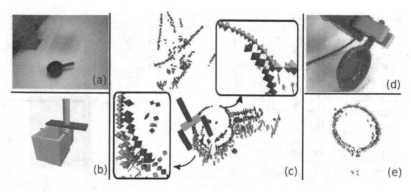

Fig. 3. (a–c) Initial grasping behavior: (a) A Scene, (b) Definition of a possible grasp based on two contours, (c) Representation of the scene with contours generating a grasp. (d) A step in the accumulation process where features from the previous scene get matched to the new scene. (e) Model extracted by the accumulation process.

updated at each time step according to how precisely the accumulated primitive was matched with a new observation. The third process takes care of preserving primitives once their confidences exceed a threshold, even if they later become occluded for a long period of time. It also ensures that primitives are discarded if their confidence falls below a threshold. New primitives that were not associated to any accumulated primitive are added to the accumulated representation, allowing the progressive construction of a full 3D model. Note that the sparse nature of primitives yields a condensed description.

The learning cycle: Figure 4 (top) shows how the two sub-modules described above interact to generate object models for previously unknown objects. The initial grasping behavior is used to gain physical control over an unknown object. In case no object has been grasped in the process (this is determined using haptic feedback i.e. the distance of the fingers after grasping) another grasping option is executed. After the object has been grasped, the accumulation process is used to generate an object model which is then stored in memory. This process can be repeated until all objects in the scene have been discovered (a naive approach here can be to assume that we have learned all objects if grasping fails for a certain amount of trials). Results of the first learning cycle can be seen in Figs. 1(b), 3(e) and [11].

5   The Second Learning Cycle: Learning Grasp Affordances

In the second learning cycle, the object representation extracted in the first learning cycle is used to determine the pose of the object in case it is present in the scene **O3**. A mechanism such as that triggering the grasps in the first learning cycle generates a large number of grasping options (see Fig. 4 bottom). A random sample of these are then tested individually. Successful grasps are then turned into a probability density function that represents a the grasp affordances associated to the object **A1** in the form of the success likelihood of grasp parameters. This grasp density can then be used to compute the optimal grasp in a specific situation **A2** [10]. The second learning cycle is invoked

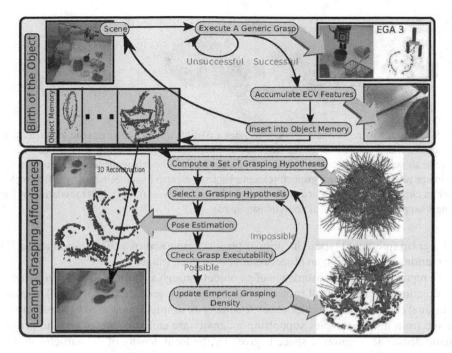

Fig. 4. The two learning cycles and the interaction between them. See text.

after the first learning cycle has successfully establish the presence and the shape of an object.

Pose estimation: In preparation for pose estimation, a structural object model is built on top of the set of ECV primitives that has been accumulated in the first learning cycle. An object is modeled with a hierarchy of increasingly expressive object parts [9]. Parts at the bottom of the hierarchy represent ECV primitives. Higher-level parts represent geometric configurations of more elementary parts. The single top part of a hierarchy represents the object. A hierarchy is implemented as a Markov tree, where parts correspond to hidden nodes, and relative spatial relationships between parts define compatibility potentials.

An object model can be autonomously built from a segmented ECV reconstruction [9] as produced by the first learning cycle (Sect. 4). Visual inference of the hierarchical model is performed using a belief propagation algorithm (BP; see, e.g., [23]). BP derives a posterior pose density for the top part of the hierarchy, thereby producing a probabilistic estimate of the object pose.

Grasp densities: When formalizing object grasp affordances, we mean to organize and memorize, independently of grasp information sources, the whole knowledge that an agent has about the grasping of an object. By *grasp affordance*, we refer to the different ways of placing a hand or a gripper near an object so that closing the gripper will produce a stable grip. The grasps we consider are parametrized by a 6D gripper pose

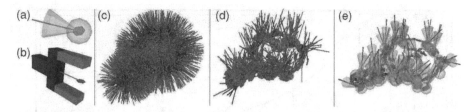

Fig. 5. Grasp density representation. (**a**) illustrates a particle from a nonparametric grasp density, and its associated kernel widths: the translucent sphere shows one position standard deviation, the cone shows the variance in orientation. (**b**) illustrates how the schematic rendering used in the top image relates to a physical gripper. (**c**) Samples from a grasp hypothesis density. (**d**) Samples from an empirical density learned from the hypothesis density in (c). (**e**) A 3D rendering of the kernels supporting the empirical grasp density in (d).

and a grasp (preshape) type. The gripper pose is composed of a 3D position and a 3D orientation, defined within an object-relative reference frame.

We represent the grasp affordance of an object through a continuous probability density function defined on the 6D object-relative gripper pose space $SE(3)$ [10]. The computational encoding is *nonparametric*: A density is simply represented by the samples we see from it. The samples supporting a density are called *particles* and the probabilistic density in a region of space is given by the local density of the particles in that region. The underlying continuous density is accessed by assigning a kernel function to each particle – a technique generally known as *kernel density estimation* [24]. The kernel functions capture Gaussian-like shapes on the 6D pose space $SE(3)$ (see Fig. 5).

A grasp affordance is attached to the hierarchical model as a new *grasp node* linked to the top node of the network. The potential between grasp node and top node is defined by the grasp density. When an object model is visually aligned to an object instance, the grasp affordance of the object *instance* is computed through the same BP process as used for visual inference. Intuitively, this corresponds to transforming the grasp density to align it to the current object pose, yet explicitly taking the uncertainty on object pose into account to produce a posterior grasp density that acknowledges visual noise.

The learning cycle: Affordances can initially be constructed from a grasp generation method that produces a minimum proportion of successful grasps (e.g., the initial grasping behavior in Sect. 4). In this work we used an approach where we initially use grasp hypotheses at random orientations at the position of the ECV primitives of the object model. We call affordance representations built with any of these weak priors *grasp hypothesis densities* [10]. These are attached to the object hierarchical model, which will allow a robotic agent to execute *random samples* from a grasp hypothesis density under arbitrary object poses, by using the visual model to estimate the 3D pose of the object.

Although grasp hypothesis densities already allow grasping, it is clear that physical experience with an object will add valuable information. We thus use samples from grasp hypothesis densities that lead to a successful grasp to learn *grasp empirical densities*, i.e. grasps that have been confirmed through experience [10]. In this way, we increase grasping performance for the blue pan from 46% to 81%. The process of computing hypothesis densities, pose estimation and execution of random samples from the grasp hypothesis density through which a empirical density is generated is shown in Fig. 4 (bottom).

6   Discussion and Conclusions

The descriptions of the presented sub-modules [7, 8, 9, 10, 11, 12] include an evaluation. We therefore only want to reiterate here a few important points that influence the performance and restrict the system. Because of the limitations of the robot system, the objects are limited by size (ca. 5–40 cm) and weight (up to 3 kg). Further restrictions are introduced by the vision system. The objects need to be describable by line-segment features and therefore can not be heavily textured. In addition the used stereopsis process can not reconstruct features on epipolar lines. This can lead to problems for the initial grasping behavior and the pose estimation process, but not the accumulation process.

Besides the blue pan object shown throughout this work we have successfully tested the full system on a toy knife and on a toy basket. The individual sub-components have been tested on more objects.

Autonomous systems benefit from an ability to acquire object and affordance knowledge without external supervision. We have brought together 3D stereo vision, heuristic grasping, structure from motion, and probabilistic representations combining visual features and gripper pose to autonomously segment objects from cluttered scenes and learn visual and affordance models through exploration. This enables an autonomous robot — initially equipped only with some generic knowledge about the world and about itself — to learn about objects and subsequently to detect, recognize and grasp them.

Acknowledgments

This work was supported by the Belgian National Fund for Scientific Research (FNRS) and the EU Cognitive Systems project PACO-PLUS (IST-FP6-IP-027657).

References

1. Gibson, J.: The Ecological Approach to Visual Perception. Houghton Mifflin (1979)
2. Lowe, D.G.: Fitting parametrized 3D-models to images. In: IEEE Transactions on Pattern Analysis and Machine Intelligence, vol. 13(5), pp. 441–450 (1991)
3. Sahin, E., Cakmak, M., Dogar, M., Ugur, E., Ucoluk, G.: To afford or not to afford: A new formalization of affordances toward affordance-based robot control. Adaptive Behavior 15(4), 447–472 (2007)
4. Bicchi, A., Kumar, V.: Robotic grasping and contact: A review. In: IEEE Int. Conf. on Robotics and Automation, pp. 348–353 (2000)
5. Krüger, N., Lappe, M., Wörgötter, F.: Biologically Motivated Multi-modal Processing of Visual Primitives. The Interdisciplinary Journal of Artificial Intelligence and the Simulation of Behaviour 1(5), 417–428 (2004)
6. Pugeault, N.: Early Cognitive Vision: Feedback Mechanisms for the Disambiguation of Early Visual Representation. PhD thesis, Informatics Institute, University of Göttingen (2008)

7. Pugeault, N., Wörgötter, F., Krüger, N.: Accumulated Visual Representation for Cognitive Vision. In: Proceedings of the British Machine Vision Conference, BMVC (2008)
8. Aarno, D., Sommerfeld, J., Kragic, D., Pugeault, N., Kalkan, S., Wörgötter, F., Kraft, D., Krüger, N.: Early reactive grasping with second order 3d feature relations. In: Recent Progress in Robotics: Viable Robotic Service to Human. Springer, Heidelberg (2008)
9. Detry, R., Pugeault, N., Piater, J.: A probabilistic framework for 3D visual object representation. IEEE Transactions on Pattern Analysis and Machine Intelligence (accepted, 2009)
10. Detry, R., Başeski, E., Krüger, N., Popović, M., Touati, Y., Kroemer, O., Peters, J., Piater, J.: Learning object-specific grasp affordance densities. In: International Conference on Development and Learning (to appear, 2009)
11. Kraft, D., Pugeault, N., Başeski, E., Popović, M., Kragic, D., Kalkan, S., Wörgötter, F., Krüger, N.: Birth of the Object: Detection of Objectness and Extraction of Object Shape through Object Action Complexes. Special Issue on "Cognitive Humanoid Robots" of the International Journal of Humanoid Robotics 5, 247–265 (2009)
12. Popović, M.: An early grasping reflex in a cognitive robot vision system. Master's thesis, The Maersk Mc-Kinney Moller Institute, University of Southern Denmark (2008)
13. Fitzpatrick, P., Metta, G.: Grounding Vision Through Experimental Manipulation. In: Philosophical Transactions of the Royal Society A: Mathematical, Physical and Engineering Sciences, vol. 361, pp. 2165–2185 (2003)
14. Modayil, J., Kuipers, B.: Bootstrap learning for object discovery. In: IEEE/RSJ International Conference on Intelligent Robots and Systems (IROS), vol. 1, pp. 742–747 (2004)
15. Biegelbauer, G., Vincze, M.: Efficient 3D object detection by fitting superquadrics to range image data for robot's object manipulation. In: IEEE International Conference on Robotics and Automation (2007)
16. Richtsfeld, M., Vincze, M.: Robotic grasping based on laser range and stereo data. In: International Conference on Robotics and Automation (2009)
17. Huebner, K., Ruthotto, S., Kragic, D.: Minimum volume bounding box decomposition for shape approximation in robot grasping. Technical report, KTH (2007)
18. Stoytchev, A.: Toward learning the binding affordances of objects: A behavior-grounded approach. In: Proceedings of AAAI Symposium on Developmental Robotics, pp. 17–22 (2005)
19. Stoytchev, A.: Learning the affordances of tools using a behavior-grounded approach. In: Rome, E., Hertzberg, J., Dorffner, G. (eds.) Towards Affordance-Based Robot Control. LNCS (LNAI), vol. 4760, pp. 140–158. Springer, Heidelberg (2008)
20. de Granville, C., Southerland, J., Fagg, A.H.: Learning grasp affordances through human demonstration. In: Proceedings of the International Conference on Development and Learning, ICDL 2006 (2006)
21. de Granville, C., Fagg, A.H.: Learning grasp affordances through human demonstration. Submitted to the Journal of Autonomous Robots (2009)
22. Baseski, E., Pugeault, N., Kalkan, S., Kraft, D., Wörgötter, F., Krüger, N.: A scene representation based on multi-modal 2D and 3D features. In: ICCV Workshop on 3D Representation for Recognition 3dRR 2007 (2007)
23. Pearl, J.: Probabilistic Reasoning in Intelligent Systems: Networks of Plausible Inference. Morgan Kaufmann, San Francisco (1988)
24. Silverman, B.W.: Density Estimation for Statistics and Data Analysis. Chapman and Hall, CRC, Boca Raton (1986)

Integration of Visual Cues for Robotic Grasping

Niklas Bergström, Jeannette Bohg, and Danica Kragic

Computer Vision and Active Vision Laboratory,
Centre for Autonomous System,
Royal Institute of Technology, Stockholm, Sweden
{nbergst,bohg,danik}@csc.kth.se

Abstract. In this paper, we propose a method that generates grasping actions for novel objects based on visual input from a stereo camera. We are integrating two methods that are advantageous either in predicting how to grasp an object or where to apply a grasp. The first one reconstructs a wire frame object model through curve matching. Elementary grasping actions can be associated to parts of this model. The second method predicts grasping points in a 2D contour image of an object. By integrating the information from the two approaches, we can generate a sparse set of full grasp configurations that are of a good quality. We demonstrate our approach integrated in a vision system for complex shaped objects as well as in cluttered scenes.

1 Introduction

Robotic grasping remains a challenging problem in the robotics community. Given an object, the embodiment of the robot and a specific task, the amount of potential grasps that can be applied to that object is huge. There exist numerous *analytical* methods based on the theory of contact-level grasping [1]. Even though these approaches work very well in simulation, they cannot simply be applied to object models reconstructed from typically sparse, incomplete and noisy sensor measurements.How to choose a feasible grasp from incomplete information about the object's geometry poses an additional challenge. This paper introduces a vision based grasping system that infers *where* and *how* to grasp an object under these circumstances. This involves a decision about where the hand is applied on the object and how it is orientated and configured.

Current state of the art methods usually approach this problem by concentrating on one of the two questions. The first group of systems, e.g. [2,3] typically infers grasps based on 3D features resulting in many hypotheses where to apply the grasp. For each hypothesis, a hand orientation is determined. Heuristics are then applied to prune the number of grasp hypotheses. A drawback of these approaches is the high dependency on the quality of the reconstructed data. The second group of approaches, e.g. [4,5] relies on 2D data and thus avoids the difficulty of 3D reconstruction. Grasp positions are inferred from a monocular image of an object. The difficulty here is the inference of a full grasp configuration from 2D data only. Additional 3D cues are required to infer the final grasp.

M. Fritz, B. Schiele, and J.H. Piater (Eds.): ICVS 2009, LNCS 5815, pp. 245–254, 2009.

In this paper, we propose a method that aims at integrating 2D and 3D based methods to determine both *where* and *how* to grasp a novel, previously unseen object. The first part of the system matches contour segments in a stereo image to reconstruct a 3D wire frame representation of the object. An edge image containing only successfully matched contour segments serves as the input to the second part of the system. Hypotheses about where a grasp can be applied on the 2D contours are generated. By augmenting the 3D model with this 2D based information, we can direct the search for planar object regions. Plane hypotheses that are supported by contour points with a high grasping point probability will carry a high weight. The normal of these planes then define the approach vectors of the associated grasps. In that way both methods complement one another to achieve a robust 3D object representation targeted at full grasp inference.

This paper is structured as follows. In the next chapter we review different grasp inference systems that are applied in real world scenarios. In Sec. 3 we give an overview of the whole system. Section 4 describes the contour matching approach and Sec. 5 the grasp point inference system. This is followed by Sec. 6 where the integration of these two models is described. An experimental evaluation is given in Sec. 7 and the paper is concluded in Sec. 8.

2   Related Work

The work by [2] is related to our system in several aspects. A stereo camera is used to extract a sparse 3D model consisting of local contour descriptors. *Elementary grasping actions* (EGAs) are associated to specific constellations of small groups of features. With the help of heuristics the huge number of resulting grasp hypotheses is reduced. In our system however, the number of hypotheses is kept small from the beginning by globally searching for planar regions of the object model. [3] decompose a point cloud derived from a stereo camera into a constellation of boxes. The simple geometry of a box and reachability constraints due to occlusions reduce the number of potential grasps. A prediction of the grasp quality of a specific grasp can be made with a neural network applied to every reachable box face. In contrast to that, we drive the search for a suitable grasp through information about 2D grasping cues. These have been shown to work remarkably for grasping point detection in [4,5].

In [4] an object is represented by a composition of prehensile parts. Grasping point hypotheses for a new object are inferred by matching local features of it against a codebook of learnt *affordance cues* that are stored along with relative object position and scale. How to orientate the robotic hand to grasp these parts is not solved. In [5] a system is proposed that infers a point at which to grasp an object directly as a function of its image. The authors apply machine learning techniques to train a grasping point model from labelled synthetic images of a number of different objects. Since no information about the approach vector can be inferred, the possible grasps are restricted to downward or outward grasps. In this paper, we solve the problem of inferring a full grasp configuration from 2D data by relating the 2D grasping cues to a 3D representation generated on-line.

There exist several other approaches that try to solve the problem of inferring a full grasp configuration for novel objects by cue integration. In [6], a stereo camera and a laser range scanner are applied in conjunction to obtain a dense point cloud of a scene with several non-textured and lightly textured objects. The authors extend their previous work to infer initial grasping point hypotheses by analysing the shape of the point cloud within a sphere centred around an hypothesis. This allows for the inference of approach vector and finger spread. In our approach however, we apply a stereo camera only and are not dependent on dense stereo matching. Due to the application of contour matching, we can obtain sparse 3D models of non-textured and lightly textured objects. [7] showed that their earlier 2D based approach is applicable when considering arbitrarily shaped 3D objects. For this purpose, several views of the object are analysed in terms of potential grasps. While the approach vector is fixed to be either from the top or from the side, the fingertip positions are dependent on the object shape and the kinematics of the manipulator. The best ranked grasp hypothesis is then executed. In our approach, we are not restricted to specific approach vectors whereas our grasp type is assumed to be one of the EGAs defined in [2]. Additionally determining the fingertip positions with the method proposed by [7] is regarded as future work. Finally, in [8] a framework is introduced in which grasp hypotheses coming from different sources e.g. from [2] are collected and modelled as *grasp hypothesis densities*. The grasp hypotheses are strongly dependent on the quality of the 3D object model. The density will therefore contain numerous potential grasps that may not be applicable at all. The authors propose to build a *grasp empirical density* by sampling from the hypotheses that are then grasped with the robot hand. In our case, we are also inferring potential grasps that may not be applicable in practice. However, we are not enumerating hypotheses from different sources but are integrating the information to infer fewer and better hypotheses that are ranked according to their support of 2D grasping cues.

3   System Overview

In our approach the process of grasp inference involves several steps: i) identification, ii) feature extraction, iii) cue integration and iv) grasping. A flow chart of the system is given in Fig. 1 and also shows the utilised hardware.

The first step involves figure-ground segmentation by means of fixation on salient points in the visible scene [9]. A combination of peripheral and foveal cameras is used that are mounted on a kinematic head. Figure 1 (b) and (c) show the left peripheral and foveal views of the head and (d) shows the segmented object.

In this paper, we focus on the feature extraction and cue integration. Full 3D reconstruction of objects with little or no texture from stereo vision is a difficult problem. However, it is debatable if a complete object model is always needed for grasping [7]. We propose a representation that is extractable from real world sensors and rich enough to infer how and where to grasp the considered

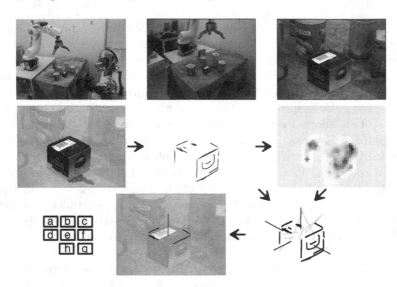

Fig. 1. (a): System setup with 6 DoF KUKA arm, a 7 DoF SCHUNK hand and the ARMAR 3 stereo head. (b,c): Left peripheral and foveal views. d-h: The steps of the grasping system.

object. A general observation that has driven our choice of representation is that many objects in a household scenario, including cups, plates, trays and boxes have planar regions. According to [2] these regions along with their coplanar relationships afford different EGAs. These grasps represent the simplest possible two fingered grasps humans commonly use.

The several steps to build such an object model composed of surfaces are shown in Fig. 1 (d-h). In the segmented foveal view (d) edges are detected and matched across the stereo images to form a 3D wire frame model (e). The projection of this wireframe in one of the images is used to predict where to grasp the object (f). The 3D model is then augmented with this information to detect planar regions that are supported by contour points with a high probability of being graspable (g). The four hypotheses with largest support are indicated with black lines, the others with dashed grey lines. The resulting surfaces provide hypotheses for how to grasp the object. The best hypothesis with respect to plane support and kinematic restrictions of the arm-hand configuration is finally shown in (h).

4   Partial 3D Reconstruction of Objects

Dynamic Time Warping (DTW) is a dynamic programming method for aligning two sequences. The method is described in detail in [10]. Below we give a brief overview of the key points of the algorithm, which is an extension to [11]. The different steps of the method are given in Fig. 2. The leftmost image shows the left foveal view of the object. Canny is used to produce an edge image from

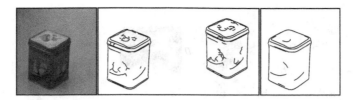

Fig. 2. Left: Left foveal view of object. **Middle**: Contours from left and right foveal views. **Right**: Successfully matched contours.

which connected edge segments (contours) are extracted. Spurious contours are filtered out by restricting their curvature energy and minimum length. The middle image pair shows the contour images from the left and right foveal views. Matching is performed between these two views. DTW is used both for solving the correspondence problem, i.e. which contour that belongs to which, and the matching problem, i.e. which point in the left contour corresponds to which point in the right contour. The latter is performed by calculating dissimilarities between the two contours based on the epipolar geometry, and finding the alignment that minimises the total dissimilarity. The former is performed by integrating the dissimilarity measure with gradient and curvature cues. This is one extension to [11], who could solve the correspondence problem more easily. Another difference is the extension of DTW to handle open and partial contours.

Many contours on the object surface correspond to texture. For 3D reconstruction, as well as 2D grasping point detection as described in Sec. 5, we are only interested in contours belonging to actual edges on the object. As seen in the middle image in Fig. 2, many contours stemming from texture do not have a corresponding contour in the other image and thus will be filtered in the DTW algorithm. Furthermore, shorter contours with higher curvature are less likely to be matched due to a too high total dissimilarity. The resulting matching is used to generate a sparse 3D model of the object.

5   Detecting Grasping Points in Monocular Images

Given the wireframe model reconstructed with the method introduced in the previous section, we search for planar regions that afford EGAs. As it will be shown later, fitting of planes to this raw model will result in many hypotheses stemming from noise and mismatches. In this section, we introduce a method that forms heuristics for searching and weighting of hypotheses according to their *graspability*. We introduce knowledge that comprises how graspable object parts appear in 2D and how these cues are embedded in the global shape of common household objects. Here, we are following a machine learning approach and classify image regions as graspable or not. We briefly describe how our feature vector is constructed and how the training of the model is done. A more detailed description can be found in [12].

Shape context (SC) [13] is a widely applied descriptor that encodes the property of *relative shape*, i.e. the relation of the global object shape to a local point

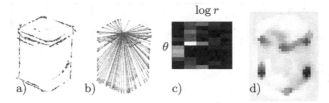

Fig. 3. Example of deriving the shape context descriptor for the matched contours shown in Fig. 2. (a) Sampled points of the contour with tangent direction. (b) All vectors from one point to all the other sample points. (c) Histogram with 12 angle bins and 5 log-radius bins. (d) Classification of the descriptors in each image patch.

on it. The descriptor is invariant to 2D rotation, scale and translation. Figure 3 shows an overview on the computation of SC. N samples are taken with a uniform distribution from the contour. For each point we consider the vectors that lead to the remaining $N-1$ sample points. We create a log polar histogram with K angle and radius bins to comprise this information. For the feature vector, we subdivide the image into 10×10 pixel patches. A patch descriptor is composed by accumulating the histograms of all those sample points that lie in the patch. We calculate the accumulated histograms at three different spatial scales centred at the current patch and concatenate them to form the final feature descriptor.

This feature vector is then classified by a grasping point model as either graspable or not. This model is an SVM that we trained off-line on the labeled database developed in [5]. An example of the classification results with an SVM trained on a pencil, a martini glass, a whiteboard eraser and two cups is shown in Fig. 3 d). Patches with a high graspability are characterised by rounded and parallel edges which indicate similarity to handles, rims or thin elongated structures. However, the approach direction is not easily inferred.

6   Cue Integration

To generate grasping hypotheses, we are interested in finding planar surfaces, i.e. finding contours that lie in the same plane. The set of plane hypotheses is defined as $\Pi = \{\pi_i\}$, $\pi_i = (\overline{n}_i, \mu_i)$, where $\overline{n}_i$ is the normal and μ_i the centre point on the plane. When searching for hypotheses, we start be selecting a point p_1 on one of the contours and a point p_2 nearby. We assume that these points are likely to lie in the same planar region(s) on the object. Then, there will be a third point p_3 on the remaining contours that defines such a region. By searching over the set of potential p_3, we try to find all these planes. Given p_1, p_2 and p_3, a plane hypothesis $\tilde{\pi}_i$ can be defined. Since the depth is quantised, the three selected points may produce a non optimal plane. Therefore we use RANSAC [14] over small contour regions defined by these points to optimise the plane. The hypothesis is accepted or rejected depending on the amount of contour points neighbouring p_1, p_2 and p_3 that are close enough to $\tilde{\pi}_i$. If accepted a more exact π_i is computed by performing regression on the full set of contour points not exceeding a certain distance to $\tilde{\pi}_i$. After the planes related to p_1 have been found, a new p_1 is selected and the procedure is repeated.

In order to restrict the search, whenever a contour point has been assigned to a plane it will be unavailable when choosing p_1. This will, apart from reducing the computational time, drastically reduce the number of hypotheses and remove most duplicates. This puts requirements on how the selection of p_1 is made. If chosen badly, it is possible to miss good hypotheses if for instance p_1 is not chosen from a contour corresponding to an actual edge. To solve this problem we use the information from the 2D grasping point detection. We start by extracting local maxima from the classification result. Because contour points in these regions are likely to be graspable, we choose p_1 from among these. As we will show in Sec. 7, this will result in a faster and more reliable search than randomly choosing p_1. The search for hypotheses continues until all points from regions with local maxima have been considered. We enforce that the normals are in the direction pointing away from the mean of all contour points.

As a final step planes are ranked according to graspability. For each plane

$$support(\pi_i) = \sum_{j \in \{all\ points\}} w(p_j) * P(p_j)/(\lambda_1 + \lambda_2) \tag{1}$$

where $w(p_j) = 1 - 2\frac{1}{1+e^{-d(p_j, \pi_i)}}$, $d(p_j, \pi_i)$ is the distance of p_j to the plane π_i, $P(p_j)$ is the probability that p_j is a grasping point, and $\lambda_{1,2}$ are the two largest eigenvalues from PCA over the inliers. This gives a support value that favours planes with dense contours whose points have a high graspability. Estimated planes may have a normal that does not correspond perfectly to the normal of the real plane. This plane will still get support from points that are close and are likely to stem from the real plane. Normalising with the sum of the eigenvalues ensures that planes without gaps are favoured over planes formed only from e.g. two sides. It also reduces the support for planes with points from falsely matched contours that will lie far from the actual object. Moreover, by calculating the eigenvalues we are able to filter out degenerate planes that have a small extension in one direction.

The normals of the final plane hypotheses are then defining the approach direction of the grasp and the smallest eigenvector of the related set of contour points the wrist orientation.

7   Experiments

The goal of the proposed method is to generate good grasping hypotheses for unknown objects in a robust and stable manner. Furthermore, as few false positives as possible should be generated. In this section, we will show that this is achieved for objects and scenes of varying geometrical and contextual complexity.

Figure 4 shows different objects used for the experiments. The corresponding matched contours are shown on the row below. The upper right of the figure contains the output of the grasping point detection. Finally, the last row shows the five planes with best support for each object. These four objects are selected to pose different challenges to our system: The hole puncher has a *complex geometric structure*, but with easily detectable edges. Due to many close parallel contours on the tape roll, we get some *false matches*. The tea canister object is *highly textured*, and its lid has many *parallel edges* which causes problems when finding the top plane. The magnifier box resides in a more complex scene in which Canny produces more *broken edges* that complicate the matching problem.

In all cases the two best hypotheses (red and green) shown in the bottom row are graspable, and correspond to how a human probably would have picked up the objects under the same conditions. For the puncher, the hypotheses give the choice of picking up from the object's front or top. This is an example of one of the benefits of our method: we do not need to constrain the approach direction. In the tape roll case there are several severe mismatches (marked in the figure). These correspond to a depth error of up to 50 cm, and are actually part of three plane hypotheses. Here the normalisation makes sure they get low support. Because of the parallel edges on the tea canister's lid, several hypotheses with good support are found on the top. The red hypothesis gets more support though, as it has more contour points close to the plane. In the case of the magnifier box, matching is harder, and we get much fewer and shorter edges. The longest contour is actually the one corresponding to the image of the magnifier. This affects the results from the support computations since the contours from the sides are not complete. The hypothesis from the right side clearly gets largest support. When finally choosing a grasp configuration kinematic constraints or other preferences will guide which of them to choose.

As mentioned in the previous section, the choice of the starting point is crucial to the performance of plane detection. We compared the method described in Sec. 6 to other approaches like random choice or a systematic search from the longest to the shortest contour. The assumption behind the latter method is that longer contours are more likely to originate from an actual edge of the object rather than from texture. We have performed an extensive evaluation of each method on the data in Fig. 4 to estimate their robustness, and will show how the proposed method outperforms the random and sequential method. Given the same input, all three methods will result in different plane hypotheses for each run due to the application of RANSAC in the plane estimation phase. The quality of a detected plane is measured by Eq. 1.

Figure 5 shows three representative examples for each of the three methods applied to the magnifier box. The two plane hypotheses that have the highest support are red and green. The best results for each method are shown in the leftmost column. Our method produced results similar to the top left example in Fig. 5 most times. The best result for the random selection only contains two hypotheses corresponding to real planes. The other two examples contain cases of missed planes (e.g. the top plane in the middle figure) and wrong planes being preferred over hypotheses corresponding to real planes. As with our method, the sequential selection produces more stable results. However, the problem of missed planes and ranking wrong planes higher than real ones persists.

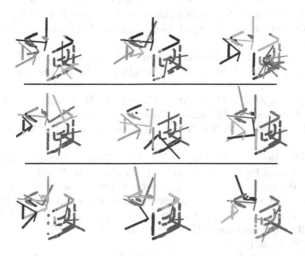

Fig. 4. Four objects, their matched contours, grasping point probabilities and finally the five best hypotheses for each object. The hypotheses are coloured, from best to worst, red, green, blue, cyan, magenta. False matches are circled in black. (Best viewed in colour).

Fig. 5. Top row: Proposed method. Middle row: Random selection. Bottom row: Sequential selection. Colours in the same order as in Fig. 4 (Best viewed in colour).

In cases of simple hardly textured objects in non-cluttered scenes, all three methods have a comparable performance. However, in real world applications we need to deal with objects of arbitrary geometry in complex scenes in which segmentation is hard due to sensory noise, clutter and overlaps.

8   Conclusion

We have presented a method for generating grasping actions for novel objects based on visual input from a stereo camera. Two methods have been integrated. One generates a wire frame object model through curve matching, and associates EGAs to it. The other predicts grasping points in a 2D contour image of the object. The first accurately predicts how to apply a grasp and the other where to apply it. The integration generates a sparse set of good grasp hypotheses. We have demonstrated the approach for complex objects and cluttered scenes.

Our future work will exploit the use of the method in an integrated learning framework. Hypotheses will be generated as proposed and used for picking up objects. The system will then be able to view the object from different directions in order to generate a more detailed model.

Acknowledgments. This project has been supported by the EU IST-FP7-IP GRASP (2008-2012) and the Swedish Foundation for Strategic Research through project CORS.

References

1. Nguyen, V.-D.: Constructing stable grasps. Int. J. on Robotics Research 8(1), 26–37 (1989)
2. Kraft, D., Pugeault, N., Baseski, E., Popovic, M., Kragic, D., Kalkan, S., Wörgötter, F., Krueger, N.: Birth of the Object: Detection of Objectness and Extraction of Object Shape through Object Action Complexes. Int. J. of Humanoid Robotics (2009)
3. Hübner, K., Kragic, D.: Selection of Robot Pre-Grasps using Box-Based Shape Approximation. In: IEEE Int. Conf. on Intelligent Robots and Systems, pp. 1765–1770 (2008)
4. Stark, M., Lies, P., Zillich, M., Wyatt, J.C., Schiele, B.: Functional Object Class Detection Based on Learned Affordance Cues. In: Gasteratos, A., Vincze, M., Tsotsos, J.K. (eds.) ICVS 2008. LNCS (LNAI), vol. 5008, pp. 435–444. Springer, Heidelberg (2008)
5. Saxena, A., Driemeyer, J., Kearns, J., Ng, A.Y.: Robotic Grasping of Novel Objects. Neural Information Processing Systems 19, 1209–1216 (2006)
6. Saxena, A., Wong, L., Ng, A.Y.: Learning Grasp Strategies with Partial Shape Information. In: AAAI Conf. on Artificial Intelligence, pp. 1491–1494 (2008)
7. Speth, J., Morales, A., Sanz, P.J.: Vision-Based Grasp Planning of 3D Objects by Extending 2D Contour Based Algorithms. In: IEEE/RSJ Int. Conf. on Intelligent Robots and Systems (2008)
8. Detry, R., Başeski, E., Krüger, N., Popović, M., Touati, Y., Kroemer, O., Peters, J., Piater, J.: Learning object-specific grasp affordance densities. In: Int. Conf. on Development and Learning (2009)
9. Björkman, M., Eklundh, J.O.: Attending, Foveating and Recognizing Objects in Real World Scenes. In: British Machine Vision Conference (2004)
10. Bergström, N., Kragic, D.: Partial 3D Reconstruction of Objects for Early Reactive Grasping. Technical report, CAS, KTH Stockholm (2009), http://www.csc.kth.se/~nbergst/files/techreport09.pdf
11. Romero, J., Kragic, D., Kyrki, V., Argyros, A.: Dynamic Time Warping for Binocular Hand Tracking and Reconstruction. In: IEEE Int. Conf. on Robotics and Automation, May 2008, pp. 2289–2294 (2008)
12. Bohg, J., Kragic, D.: Grasping Familiar Objects Using Shape Context. In: Int. Conf. on Advanced Robotics (June 2009)
13. Belongie, S., Malik, J., Puzicha, J.: Shape Matching and Object Recognition Using Shape Contexts. IEEE Trans. on Pattern Analysis and Machine Intelligence 24(4), 509–522 (2002)
14. Fischler, M.A., Bolles, R.C.: Random sample consensus: A paradigm for model fitting with applications to image analysis and automated cartography. Commun. ACM 24(6), 381–395 (1981)

A Hierarchical System Integration Approach with Application to Visual Scene Exploration for Driver Assistance

Benjamin Dittes[1], Martin Heracles[1,2], Thomas Michalke[1], Robert Kastner[3], Alexander Gepperth[1], Jannik Fritsch[1], and Christian Goerick[1]

[1] Honda Research Institute Europe GmbH, Carl-Legien-Str. 30, 67073 Offenbach,
firstname.lastname@honda-ri.de
[2] CoR-Lab Bielefeld, Bielefeld University, Universitätsstraße 25, 33615 Bielefeld
heracles@cor-lab.uni-bielefeld.de
[3] Darmstadt University of Technology, Landgraf-Georg-Straße 4, 64283 Darmstadt
robert.kastner@rtr.tu-darmstadt.de

Abstract. A scene exploration which is quick and complete according to current task is the foundation for most higher scene processing. Many specialized approaches exist in the driver assistance domain (e.g. car recognition or lane marking detection), but we aim at an integrated system, combining several such techniques to achieve sufficient performance. In this work we present a novel approach to this integration problem. Algorithms are contained in hierarchically arranged layers with the main principle that the ordering is induced by the requirement that each layer depends only on the layers below. Thus, higher layers can be added to a running system (incremental composition) and shutdown or failure of higher layers leaves the system in an operational state, albeit with reduced functionality (graceful degradation). Assumptions, challenges and benefits when applying this approach to practical systems are discussed. We demonstrate our approach on an integrated system performing visual scene exploration on real-world data from a prototype vehicle. System performance is evaluated on two scene exploration completeness measures and shown to gracefully degrade as several layers are removed and to fully recover as these layers are restarted while the system is running.

Keywords: Visual scene exploration, System integration, Hierarchical architecture, Driver assistance.

1 Introduction

In real-world scenarios, artificial intelligence systems face an overwhelming abundance of sensory data and high information density. One example is the domain of driver assistance, where camera images and range finder measurements are taken while driving on an inner-city road. Additionally, the amount of processing power available is limited. To handle this abundant data with limited resources,

M. Fritz, B. Schiele, and J.H. Piater (Eds.): ICVS 2009, LNCS 5815, pp. 255–264, 2009.

the system must select important positions in the input data space before launching a – usually computationally expensive – detailed analysis. Since our main focus is on driver assistance systems analyzing camera images we call this process visual scene exploration and the important positions 'visual targets'.

Several approaches for general visual scene exploration exist, presenting both algorithms (e.g. [1,2]) and integrated systems (e.g. [3,4]). However, the analysis of the integration process performed to arrive at such systems is very rarely done. It is much more common that specific systems are presented without a discussion about the benefits or drawbacks of the chosen integration approach. On the other hand, many existing vision systems are oriented strongly along the underlying software architecture, most notably blackboard[5], agent-based[6] or data-flow modeling[7].

Lömker et. al.[8] also see this problem of increasing system complexity and react with the introduction of a technical software environment on top a modern xml-based blackboard architecture[9]. Leibe et. al.[10] present a 3D scene analysis system with a strong decomposition and explicit top-down communication, but without formalizing it as a system integration approach.

In this work we will present a hierarchical system integration approach largely independent of the used software platform (necessary assumptions are discussed). It is based on the Systematica approach introduced in [11], a synthesis of the two major contributions to cognitive system architecture so far, the subsumption[12] and 3-tier[13] approaches. We go beyond this work by placing a strong restriction on the dependence of layers as the main decomposition principle. Furthermore, we go towards practical use with a generic mechanism to utilize top-down information while keeping independence at design- and run-time and a discussion of main design challenges when building practical systems.

We illustrate this approach on the problem of scene exploration in the driver assistance domain. As an integration problem, this is interesting because it does not simply require a sequence of processing steps producing a set of visual targets given the input data. Rather, there is a dualism between scene exploration (i.e. detecting important visual targets) and subsequent scene analysis (i.e. recognizing, tracking or storing these targets): based on a set of visual targets, the analysis of these targets may yield the necessity to tune parameters in the scene exploration sub-system. This may include setting parameters in other algorithms or directing the focus of the scene exploration to areas where important objects are expected to appear. This reflux of data from scene analysis to scene exploration is what we call top-down modulation and what makes system integration significantly more powerful, but also much more complex than sequential composition.

In Sec. 2 we will present our hierarchical system integration approach. We will then proceed to illustrate this integration process on the example of a concrete system instance performing visual scene exploration on a prototype vehicle in Sec. 3. An evaluation in Sec. 4 will show the behavior and positive qualities of this implemented system and discuss that this is a result of the integration approach. Discussion and outlook follow in Sec. 5.

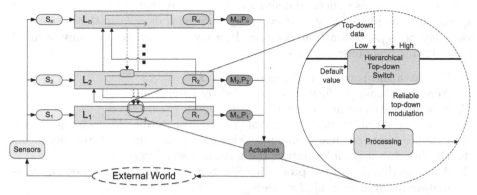

Fig. 1. The proposed hierarchical integration approach – **Left**: each layer L_i with internal processing runs in parallel and receives a sub-space S_i of the sensor data. It generates a representation R_i to be read by higher layers (solid lines), a motor command/priority pair M_i, P_i sent to actuators and top-down information sent to lower layers (dashed lines). Finally, it receives and integrates top-down information coming from higher layers (encircled box). **Right**: For each kind of top-down information received, the layer has to guarantee that it responds correctly *but does not depend* on the data. This is achieved by the 'top-down switch': a hierarchical switching module which chooses the valid top-down data from the highest layer and can fall back to a default if no top-down data is received.

2   The Incremental Architecture Approach

For the domain of large-scale artificial intelligence systems we see several requirements an integrated system has to fulfill:

- The high processing load requires sub-systems to be distributed to multiple processing units, thus they must be able to run asynchronously in parallel
- To allow collaboration of many researchers building the system, sub-systems must have clear interfaces and should continue to work without modifications when new sub-systems are added
- Operating in a real-world domain requires a high level of robustness to unexpected input and errors within the system, which is why sub-systems must be able to continue to work even if some of the other sub-systems are removed to save resources or fail.

We propose an approach decomposing the integration problem into hierarchically arranged layers $L_i, i = 1..n$. All layers run in parallel in an asynchronous manner and each layer can receive any subset S_i of available sensory data and produce motor commands M_i together with motor command priorities P_i to allow selecting among competing commands. Communication between layers is done through explicit channels: every layer L_i can access data and events produced in any lower layer $L_{j,j<i}$ through bottom-up channels and transmit data or events to any lower layer $L_{k,k<i}$ through top-down channels. Fig. 1(left) illustrates this schematically.

In addition to this structural definition, the main design principle defining our approach is the requirement that every layer L_i depends *only* on the presence of lower layers $L_{j,j<i}$ to function. As a result, a layer L_i may perform any or all of the following functions:

1. Receive a subspace S_i of all sensory data S
2. Access bottom-up information provided by lower layers
3. Synchronize to events emitted by lower layers
4. Provide a set of internal states, called a 'representation' R_i, to higher layers
5. Produce motor commands and priorities M_i, P_i and send to system actuators
6. Produce top-down information and send to lower layers
7. Allow modulation of the processing for items 4, 5 and 6 by top-down information received from higher layers.

As a result, a layer can depend on and synchronize to lower layers, as well as use all their representations for it's own processing. Every layer is added to the system as an *extension*: relying on all existing lower layers, but making no assumptions on anything that might be added later, except providing 'ports' where top-down modulation may be received. Since the arrival of this top-down information cannot be relied on by any layer, a layer *must not* depend on the presence or arrival of information from higher layers or wait for events from higher layers. In the following we will discuss the main challenges in composing systems in such a way:

Influence of Layer Ordering. The key to success or failure of a system integrated with this approach is the hierarchical composition of layers. The most obvious constraint imposed by the approach is the unidirectional dependence of layers, but sometimes this is not enough to arrive at a unique ordering. Communication between two layers can occasionally be formulated either as top-down modulation or as access to bottom-up representations, making the ordering seemingly arbitrary. However, there are additional guides: Firstly, the ordering defines the final behavior of each of the possible running sub-systems $L_{1..i,i=2..n}$ consisting of only a sub-set of layers. Thus, if one layer L_j is necessary for the first intended sub-system to function while another layer L_k would add additional functionality to the next-higher sub-system, L_j must be sorted under L_k. Secondly, it is often prudent to operate lower layers at higher frequencies than higher layers in order to avoid too fast top-down modulation leading to oscillation. Finally, the failure of one layer may cause the failure of all higher layers, therefore more reliable layers should be sorted lower.

On System Design Methodology In addition to finding a compromise between the constraints on the layer ordering every system design is the results of a more of less suited problem decomposition. For most problems, including the example chosen in Sec. 3, decomposition is a problem in itself as there is no "natural" way to achieve it. We believe no system integration approach can, by itself, solve this problem in an automated methodology and problem decomposition will remain an art that requires as much skill as theoretical background. Therefore, this contribution focuses on the formalization and implementation of integrated systems given a decomposition and cannot provide a complete methodology. However, experience has shown that a formalization helps both in the process of designing by suggesting crucial questions to be answered as well as in the communication about the design by providing a shared language.

Handling of Top-down Information. To provide the demanded independence of layers, the most important requirement is that layers must be able to react to top-down information *without* depending on it. More precisely, there are three cases to be considered: first, a layer must be able to function if the layer(s) sending the top-down information are not present yet; second, it must use the received top-down information immediately after higher layers appear; third, it must return to default operation if higher layers are removed or fail. This is non-trivial since processing is asynchronous and the number of layers sending top-down information may not even be known while designing the current layer. We propose to solve all three by the help of a 'top-down switch' (Fig. 1(right)), a component which receives all top-down data of one type, analyzes their temporal behavior and returns the valid top-down data from the highest layer, or a default if none is valid. Validity is computed by comparing the input's time t_{data} to the typical temporal behavior $\mu_{\Delta t}, \sigma_{\Delta t}$ of data coming from the sending layer. Given a scaling factor ν, data is considered valid if $t_{\text{now}} - t_{\text{data}} \leq \mu_{\Delta t} + \nu \sigma_{\Delta t}$. This is similar to the 'suppression' mechanism introduced in the subsumption architecture[12], but it i) allows a clear definition of the top-down interface, ii) accepts an arbitrary number of top-down inputs and iii) adds a temporal adaptation mechanism.

We see three beneficial system-properties resulting from this approach:

- *Incremental Composition.* Higher layers can be added at run-time, thus providing top-down modulation or additional motor commands and increasing system performance without restarting the whole system. The new top-down channels usually lead to the formation of new internal control loops; it is the responsibility of the added layers to prevent any negative effects, e.g. providing top-down modulation at a lower rate to avoid oscillation.
- *Graceful Degradation.* The removal of a layer only affects the layers on top of it, all lower layers will continue to function and still provide an acceptable, albeit lower level of performance.
- *Reduction of Design Space.* Extending an existing integrated system by adding a new layer does not require modification of existing layers: new layers passively consume existing sensor inputs and representations of lower layers and they provide top-down modulation to (existing) ports of the existing top-down switching modules.

3   The Visual Processing Hierarchy

To approach the problem of scene exploration we applied the above principles to an integrated system which employs several state-of-the-art methods. The system is designed with four layers (see Fig. 2): it combines saliency computation, drive path computation, visual target selection including inhibition of return and a parameterization with task-relevant modulatory data.

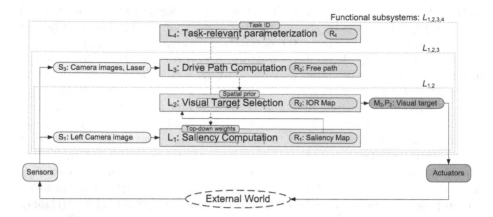

Fig. 2. Overview of the implemented hierarchical system – The figure shows the layers composing the implemented scene exploration system. It is composed of four layers performing saliency computation, visual target selection, drive path computation and task execution which communicate through the depicted bottom-up (solid) and top-down (dashed) channels. Top-down switching is done in three places: once for switching between top-down and default weights for the saliency, once for switching between top-down and default spatial prior for visual target selection and a third time for selecting the task id, although this switch is (currently) not receiving any top-down input. Since layer L_2 produces motor output, the first functional sub-system is $L_{1,2}$, followed by $L_{1,2,3}$ and $L_{1,2,3,4}$ (dotted boxes).

Saliency Computation. For the lowest layer L_1 we use an algorithm[14] which evaluates a multitude of image features (DoG, Gabor, RGBY, motion, . . .). It is tuned to real-world scenarios and allows setting weights to specify selectivity. The result is an image-sized, float-valued saliency map using either default weights, or the ones received by top-down modulation – therefore this is the first point in the system where top-down switching is needed.

Visual Target Selection. The core task of the scene exploration system is the selection of a visual target, performed in L_2. Here, we use the saliency map produced by L_1, multiply it with a top-down spatial prior and select the maximum as the current visual target. A top-down switching is needed to reliably integrate this top-down spatial prior under the constraint of loose coupling to the higher layers producing it. To get multiple visual targets per image, we apply an inhibition of return (IOR)[15] by subtracting a Gaussian at the last selected position from an IOR map. This map is provided to higher layers in case they need to focus processing on regions that have not been covered yet.

Drive Path Computation. In the car domain, one very helpful spatial prior can be extracted from the drive path in front of the car. The drive path itself is computed in L_3 by using segmentation on a number of sensors based on training regions in the camera images, combined with a temporal integration[4]. The result is a binary road map used to produce a spatial prior with a broad range of excitation around the edges of the drive path and very little on the path or in

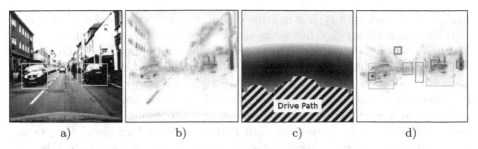

a)   b)   c)   d)

Fig. 3. Ground-truth information and internal processing results – The images show input and internal states of the system when processing one image with all layers running. a) Input left camera image with added ground truth information about target objects (turquoise boxes); b) saliency map computed in L_1 with top-down weights from L_4 *(for b,c,d: darker = higher activation)*; c) drive path spatial prior computed in L_3, with artificially highlighted drive path; d) integrated attention map with added resulting visual targets (red), computed in L_2, and ground-truth (green: hit, gray: not hit).

the sky. This spatial prior allows to focus on obstacles and the side of the road and is provided to L_2 as top-down modulation.

Task-relevant Parameterization. In addition to improving the spatial selectivity, a suitable set of top-down weights can greatly increase the performance of the saliency computation. Layer L_4 therefore receives a task identifier as a top-down input and gives a matching weight set (e.g. for cars) to L_1.

The described system has three points of top-down switching: one for receiving the top-down weights in L_1, one for receiving the spatial prior in L_2, one for settings the current task in L_4. All switches use the mechanism described in Sec. 2, without any specialization needed. All layers provide a default in case that no top-down information is received. In this manner, each layer is designed, implemented and started without caring about the subsequent higher layers.

4   Evaluation

The system described in Sec. 3 was implemented on a software infrastructure for data-flow oriented real-world capable processing systems[16]. The platform provides the main prerequisites for utilizing the benefits of the presented approach: Firstly, it allows sub-systems provided by researchers to be 'wrapped' into opaque larger modules with clear interfaces. Secondly, it allows these modules to be started or stopped in separate system processes, potentially on different machines, while providing robust data communication between these processes.

On this basis, each of the layers seen in Fig. 2 has been implemented as a module running in a separate process, communicating with the others through the software infrastructure. The final system is capable of running on-board a prototype vehicle but experiments for this work where done on a data stream (recorded on that vehicle) with additional hand-labeled ground-truth information. We chose a 30s data stream, recorded at 10Hz during a typical drive on an inner-city road, with typical lighting conditions and occasionally missing lane markings, on a cloudy day, but without rain (see Fig. 3 for samples).

When on-board the vehicle, the system is distributed on three 2-GHz dual-core computers, one performing sensor acquisition and preprocessing (disparity, pitch correction etc.), one with layers L_1, L_2 and L_4 and one with layer L_3. The most time-consuming layers are L_1 and L_3, both are currently running at 3Hz, which is enough to achieve interactive processing when driving with slow velocity. Layer L_2 is running with 12Hz to extract four visual targets per processed image[1], layer L_4 sends top-down information with a rate of 1Hz.

To evaluate system performance, we annotated the stream with ground-truth information, which can be seen in Fig. 3: for each image $I(t)$, all task-relevant objects $o_i(t) \subset I(t)$ where marked. The labeling is consecutive, i.e. the identifier i is used in all previous and following images for the same object. Thus, an object's appearance, movement through the stream and disappearance can be tracked. The scene exploration system produces a set of visual targets $v(t) = \{v_j(t), j = 1..n, v_j(t) \in I(t)\}$, in our experiments $n = 4$. We can define several related values: the first time an object i was marked $t_0^i = \arg\min_t o_i(t) \neq \{\}$, the first time an object i was hit $t_1^i = \arg\min_t \exists_j v_j(t) \in o_i(t)$, the number of marked objects $N^{\mathrm{obj}}(t) = |\{i, o_i(t) \neq \{\}\}|$ and the number of hit objects $N^{\mathrm{hit}}(t) = |\{i, \exists_j v_j(t) \in o_i(t)\}|$.

We now define two measures: the 'time-to-hit' indicates for each object o_i how much time passed between the appearance of the object and the first time it was hit: $q_1(o, v) = \langle t_1^i - t_0^i \rangle_i$. The 'local hitrate' indicates for each image how many of all objects in this image where hit by visual targets: $q_2(o, v) = \langle N^{\mathrm{hit}}(t)/N^{\mathrm{obj}}(t) \rangle_t$. Both together give a good impression of how early and how reliably the scene exploration is focusing on the important objects in the scene.

We evaluate both scene exploration performance measures once for the three functional sub-systems (see Fig. 2) and, most importantly, a fourth time for a full system run with induced shutdowns in layers L_3 and L_4 and subsequent restarts. The results of our experiments can be seen in Fig. 4 and caption.

5   Discussion and Outlook

In this work we introduced a novel, generic, hierarchical system integration approach for practical application in large-scale artificial intelligence systems. The system instance we used to show the benefits of the approach represents a functional, extendable effort towards visual scene exploration, incorporating several complex, state-of-the-art algorithms running asynchronously and communicating through explicit bottom-up and top-down channels. At the same time, it exhibits the described system properties: each layer implements one specific algorithm, depending only on lower layers; layers can fail or be deactivated at run-time without taking down the full system; layers can be started and restarted at run-time leading to a full recovery of system performance (see Fig. 4 and caption).

---

[1] Although L_2 is running faster than L_1 it cannot introduce oscillations because there are no top-down channels from L_2 to L_1.

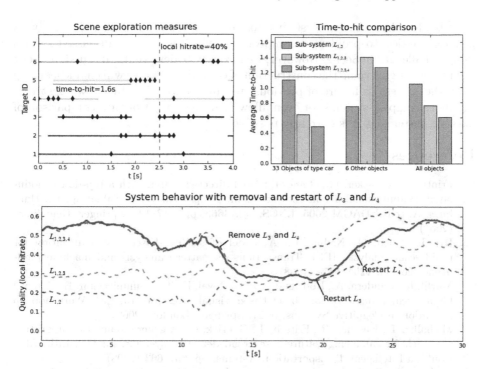

**Fig. 4. Performance during several system runs with varying active layers –
Top Left:** Each of the target objects is plotted over time (colored bars). Black diamonds indicate when an object was hit by a visual target, in this case with subsystem $L_{1,2}$. The first measure (time-to-hit) can be seen in this visualization as the difference between the appearance of an object and the first hit, the second measure (local hitrate) evaluates how many of the objects at one specific point in time where hit. **Top Right:** The figure compares the time-to-hit performance over the entire data stream for the three possible functional subsystems. **Bottom:** The figure shows the local hitrate recorded over four separate runs of the system. The first three (dashed lines) where done with stable (sub-)sets of the full system: lowest $L_{1,2}$, middle $L_{1,2,3}$, highest $L_{1,2,3,4}$. Since the local hitrate shows considerable jitter in raw data, measurements have been averaged over $7s$. The fourth run (solid red line) demonstrates the system's ability for graceful degradation and recovery. The system is started with all layers, after $12.5s$ L_3 and L_4 are removed and restarted after $19s$ and $23s$, respectively. As can be seen, the system performance drops to the performance of the remaining functional sub-system $L_{1,2}$ after the removal (asymptotically, due to the floating average) and recovers as higher layers are restarted.

In order to utilize this robustness, we plan to add a 'quality of service' controller which autonomously shuts down layers to save resources and restart failed layers.

The introduced performance measures are specific to the visual scene exploration domain, resulting from the absence of any measures allowing to compare system integration strategies in general. For the same reason we cannot quantify the reduction of design or integration time following this approach, a comparison of identical teams using different approaches seems unrealistic.

It is also clear that no system integration approach will be able to give a generic solution to problem decomposition, which is why we discussed several design challenges in Sec. 2. However, we strongly believe that a discussion about the principles governing the construction of cognitive systems will enable learning from the success or failure of previous systems. It will thereby allow constructing more complex systems, or even allow a more straightforward comparison of existing systems as it is currently possible.

References

1. Frintrop, S., Backer, G., Rome, E.: Goal-directed search with a top-down modulated computational attention system. In: Kropatsch, W.G., Sablatnig, R., Hanbury, A. (eds.) DAGM 2005. LNCS, vol. 3663, pp. 117–124. Springer, Heidelberg (2005)
2. Itti, L., Koch, C., Niebur, E.: A model of saliency-based visual attention for rapid scene analysis. IEEE Transactions on pattern analysis and machine intelligence 20(11), 1254–1259 (1998)
3. Marfil, R., Bandera, A., Rodriguez, J., Sandoval, F., Telecomunicacion, E.: A novel hierarchical framework for object-based visual attention. In: Intl. Workshop on Attention in Cognitive Systems, p. 27. Springer, London (2009)
4. Michalke, T., Kastner, R., Fritsch, J., Goerick, C.: A generic temporal integration approach for enhancing feature-based road-detection systems. In: 11th Intl. IEEE Conf. on Intelligent Transportation Systems, pp. 657–663 (2008)
5. Dodhiawala, R., Jagannathan, V., Baum, L.: Blackboard Architectures and Applications. Academic Press, Inc., London (1989)
6. Shoham, Y., et al.: Agent-oriented programming. Artificial intelligence 60 (1993)
7. Abram, G., Treinish, L.: An extended data-flow architecture for data analysis and visualization. In: 6th Conf. on Visualization (1995)
8. Lömker, F., Wrede, S., Hanheide, M., Fritsch, J.: Building modular vision systems with a graphical plugin environment. In: IEEE Intl. Conf. on Computer Vision Systems, pp. 2–2 (2006)
9. Wrede, S., Fritsch, J., Bauckhage, C., Sagerer, G.: An xml based framework for cognitive vision architectures. In: 17th Intl. Conf. on Pattern Recognition (2004)
10. Leibe, B., Cornelis, N., Cornelis, K., Van Gool, L.: Dynamic 3d scene analysis from a moving vehicle. In: Conf. on Computer Vision and Pattern Recognition (2007)
11. Goerick, C., Bolder, B., Janßen, H., Gienger, M., Sugiura, H., Dunn, M., Mikhailova, I., Rodemann, T., Wersing, H., Kirstein, S.: Towards incremental hierarchical behavior generation for humanoids. In: Intl. Conf. on Humanoids (2007)
12. Brooks, R.: A robust layered control system for a mobile robot. IEEE journal of robotics and automation 2(1), 14–23 (1986)
13. Gat, E., et al.: On three-layer architectures. Artificial Intelligence and Mobile Robots (1997)
14. Michalke, T., Fritsch, J., Goerick, C.: Enhancing robustness of a saliency-based attention system for driver assistance. In: Gasteratos, A., Vincze, M., Tsotsos, J.K. (eds.) ICVS 2008. LNCS, vol. 5008, pp. 43–55. Springer, Heidelberg (2008)
15. Klein, R.: Inhibition of return. Trends in Cognitive Sciences 4(4), 138–147 (2000)
16. Ceravola, A., Stein, M., Goerick, C.: Researching and developing a real-time infrastructure for intelligent systems - evolution of an integrated approach. Robotics and Autonomous Systems 56(1), 14–28 (2007)

Real-Time Traversable Surface Detection by Colour Space Fusion and Temporal Analysis

Ioannis Katramados[1], Steve Crumpler[2], and Toby P. Breckon[1]

[1] Cranfield University, School of Engineering, Cranfield, MK43 0AL, UK
{i.katramados,toby.breckon}@cranfield.ac.uk
[2] TRW Conekt, Stratford Road, Solihull, B90 4GW, UK
steve.crumpler@trw.com

Abstract. We present a real-time approach for traversable surface detection using a low-cost monocular camera mounted on an autonomous vehicle. The proposed methodology extracts colour and texture information from various channels of the HSL, YCbCr and LAB colourspaces by temporal analysis in order to create a "traversability map". On this map lighting and water artifacts are eliminated including shadows, reflections and water prints. Additionally, camera vibration is compensated by temporal filtering leading to robust path edge detection in blurry images. The performance of this approach is extensively evaluated over varying terrain and environmental conditions and the effect of colourspace fusion on the system's precision is analysed. The results show a mean accuracy of 97% over this comprehensive test set.

1 Introduction

This work addresses the problem of autonomous vehicle navigation in semi-structured or unstructured environments where geometrical road models are not applicable. Specifically, a real-time approach is presented which facilitates the detection of traversable surfaces via temporal analysis of multiple image properties. These properties are specifically selected to provide maximally descriptive image information with a minimal computational overhead per image frame. Initially, a multi-stage approach is proposed for feature extraction based on colour and texture analysis. This information is then stored in a temporal memory structure to improve algorithm robustness by means of noise filtering. The proposed methodology has been implemented on the SATURN unmanned ground vehicle as part of the MoD Grand Challenge competition (2008).

Engineering road and obstacle detection systems has long been at the centre of academic and industrial research, leading to a number of successful implementations, ranging from the early road-following systems [4,16] to the most recent fully automated vehicles in the DARPA Urban Challenge competition (2007) [1,5,14]. Additionally, significant research has been motivated by various vehicle platforms for Mars exploration missions [7,8]. However, the sensing and processing complexity of these systems has often led to costly solutions which whilst useful for exploiting the current limits of technology, do not address the

M. Fritz, B. Schiele, and J.H. Piater (Eds.): ICVS 2009, LNCS 5815, pp. 265–274, 2009.

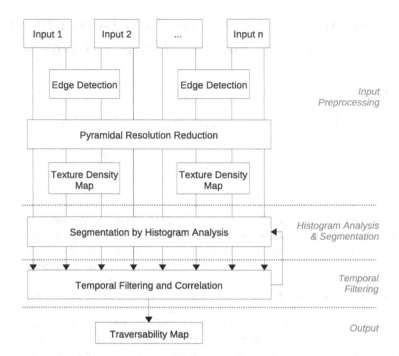

Fig. 1. Traversable area detection methodology

demand for low-cost autonomous platforms utilising widely available low-cost sensors. Creating such vision systems is not a new concept [3,11]. Embedded lane-departure warning systems [9,10], are increasingly becoming commonplace in commercial vehicles, motivated by the demand for improved driver safety. However, not every driving environment is as structured as a conventional roadway and an autonomous vehicle may also be required to traverse unstructured environments under varying conditions.

Several prior approaches focus on obstacle detection and avoidance by analysing basic image properties such as texture, colour, hue and saturation of the monocular image. Such approaches are often built on the assumption that the area directly in front of the vehicle is always traversable (initial state assumption) and use a "safe" window to derive the properties of that surface [13]. Obstacles and non-traversable areas are normally identified through a probabilistic model which is based on the similarity of each image pixel to the "safe window" [2,13,7]. This becomes the initial *a priori* model from which the system is driven as demonstrated by the Pebbles III robot [13]. The advantages of this approach include flexibility to changing conditions/terrains, limited training requirements and real-time performance. On the other hand, a major disadvantage is its inability to distinguish between surfaces with similar properties due to noise, illumination and environmental effects. To solve this problem Kröse *et al.* [12] proposed the use of optical flow-based techniques, however this is often sensitive to camera vibration and incurs additional computational cost. The work of [12] does however introduce the important aspect of temporal analysis (via frame-to-frame optical flow) as a driver to overcome the earlier limitations of [16,13]. By contrast, this paper proposes a real-time solution as inspired by the Navlab "Road Following" module [16] and Pebbles III robot [13], with some fundamental changes in the image feature selection from multiple colourspaces and the addition of a novel temporal memory model.

2 Feature Extraction for Traversable Area Detection

The following methodology aims to extract information from the video stream output of a vehicle-mounted camera in order to create a map of the traversable and non-traversable areas in real-time. The main challenge is the creation of an algorithm that is adaptable to variable environmental conditions while utilising the least possible computational resource that would facilitate execution on a low-cost processing unit. *Figure 2* provides some examples of such challenging conditions that were experienced during the MoD Grand Challenge competition. The proposed approach is divided into four incremental stages: a) *camera image pre-processing*, b) *multi-dimensional segmentation by histogram analysis*, c) *temporal information processing*, d) *traversable area mapping*. As illustrated in the overview diagram of *Figure 1*, the first stage deals with colour and texture extraction by using intensity-invariant channels of differing colourspaces. The resolution of each input channel is then pyramidically reduced in order to improve system performance and reduce noise (*Figure 1 centre*). Finally, the lower-resolution images are segmented and filtered using a temporal memory model that produces the "traversability" map (*Figure 1 lower*).

Fig. 2. Examples of challenging environmental conditions with shadows, reflections from standing water and wet prints

2.1 Camera Image Pre-processing

First we describe the noise-filtering approach that is applied prior to segmentation in order to eliminate shadows, reflections and water prints. This is achieved by combining individual channels from differing colourspaces to extract colour and texture information that is insensitive to illumination changes. Prior research [17,6,15,13] has shown that choosing the right colourspace is crucial for extracting accurate path and obstacle features. In fact this methodology combines the *HSL, YCbCr* and *LAB* colourspaces [15] to derive four illumination invariant features as listed below:

- **Saturation** (based on the S channel of the HSL colourspace)
  By converting the RGB colourspace to HSL, the saturation channel is extracted (as illustrated in *Figure 3*) and further resized to a coarse 64×48 saturation intensity map by Gaussian pyramid decomposition of the 320×240 input image.
- **Saturation-Based Texture**
  This can be derived by applying an edge detector on the S channel of the HSL colourspace (*Figure 3*). Then the texture is defined as the density of edges in different parts of the image. Practically, this is achieved by Gaussian pyramid decomposition of the output of the *Sobel* edge detector in order to generate a low-resolution 64×48 grid.
- **Mean Chroma** (based on combining the Cb and Cr components of the $YCbCr$ colourspace with the A component of the LAB colourspace)
  Chroma provides luminance-independent colour information in the $YCbCr$ colourspace. As with the S channel of the HSL colourspace, dark shadows and reflections alter the chroma level making their detection difficult. To solve this problem Wu et al. [17] propose the combination of the two chroma components (Cb and Cr) in order to detect features that are entirely light intensity invariant. However, the Cb and Cr components have a relatively small variation range when compared to the Y component. Based on this observation, the Cb and Cr values are scaled to fit the $0 - 255$ (8-bit) range and subsequently their mean value is derived. The A channel of the LAB colourspace also provides intensity invariant information, thus by combining it with the mean value of Cb and Cr, a map of colour distribution (*Figure 4a*) is created as described by *equation 1*.

$$chroma\ map = \frac{sCb + sCr + 2sA}{4} \tag{1}$$

where sCb is the Cb channel of the $YCbCr$ colourspace, sCr is the Cr channel of the $YCbCr$ colourspace and is the A channel of the LAB colourspace. These three parameters have been scaled to 8-bit ($0 - 255$ range).

An example of a *mean chroma* map is illustrated in *Figure 4a*, where most reflections have successfully been eliminated. This map is also pyramidically reduced to a coarse 64×48 grid.

- **Chroma-based texture** (based on the Cb and Cr components of the $YCbCr$ colourspace)
  This is derived by calculating the mean value of the Cb and Cr components to generate a new chroma map. The *Sobel* edge detector is subsequently applied to this map in order to calculate a chroma-based texture density using the process described in the saturation-based texture above (*Figure 3*).

At this point we have four 64×48 arrays (8-bit) representing a set of characteristic image properties. These arrays form the input of the segmentation algorithm as described in the following section.

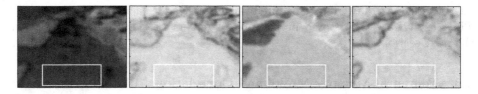

Fig. 3. Image analysis into four input channels: saturation, saturation-based texture, mean chroma and chroma-based texture

2.2 Segmentation by Histogram Analysis

Several prior path-following techniques have been developed around the assumption that the area immediately in front of the vehicle is initially traversable and thus they identify the pathway by comparison to "safe" window near the bottom of the image [13,2]. The current approach also adopts this idea since the "safe" window can always be validated by low-cost active short-range sensors such as ultrasonic or infrared. A histogram is calculated for each of the four input image arrays (from the pre-processing stage) within the safe area. The histogram resolution is then reduced by a factor of 8 in order to simplify its processing and improve performance. Thus four different histograms are derived, from which the dominant features of the traversable area are extracted by detecting the histogram peaks based on the assumption that each surface is characterised by a certain combination of saturation, chrominance and texture density levels. Each histogram peak is considered as a feature with five attached properties:

- **Left histogram peak edge**: The point where the left side of the peak meets the "mean level"[1] line
- **Right histogram peak edge**: The point where the right side of the peak meets the "mean level" line
- **Histogram peak value**: The peak value of the low-resolution histogram
- **Mean segment value**: The mean value of the left and right edges of the histogram peak
- **Age**: The time that the peak has remained consistent (in terms of persistence over multiple image frames). A peak is considered as a valid feature only if its age is above a certain threshold. In our tests, the age threshold was set to 10 frames (0.4 sec) with a maximum possible age of 30 frames (1.2 sec).

The left and right histogram peak edges form a histogram segment. Each image pixel is marked as traversable only if its value falls within one of the histogram segments. The remaining pixels are marked as non-traversable. In most cases, the histogram will have only one main segment thus the image will essentially be thresholded. However, more complex surfaces may result in two or more histogram peaks and thus two or more segments. This feature makes the current approach suitable for identifying simple as well as composite traversable surfaces.

---

[1] Defined as the mean of all the histogram values.

At this stage, we have four segmented image arrays for each of the four inputs. These arrays are then stored in a temporal memory structure as described in the next section.

2.3   Temporal Memory Model and Correlation

Creating high-level representations of complex raw data can be improved by introducing a temporal memory structure as a way of reducing noise and increasing system accuracy and reliability. This approach proposes the use of temporal behaviour analysis on the output of the segmentation as a top-level filter before correlation. Specifically, the segments identified by histogram analysis are tracked over a series of video frames in order to check their consistency. This is done by assigning a confidence level to each type of surface, which adjusts depending on whether a similar surface appears repeatedly or not. In this way, the system compensates for noise and image blur on a frame-by-frame basis. Similarly, each grid cell of the segmented images is also assigned a confidence level, which increases if its status as "traversable" or "non-traversable" remains unchanged over time. The final output consists of four new *"traversability"* maps based on the saturation, saturation-based texture, mean chroma and chroma-based texture analysis over time. The final traversability map is then derived by majority voting. Although, more sophisticated techniques could have been implemented, this specific one was preferred as the best compromise between overall robustness and real-time performance. Four different levels of traversability are possible for each pixel as illustrated in *Figure 4b*, where the darker shades of grey indicate non-traversable areas.

3   Results

The presented approach has been evaluated using a video dataset comprising of sequences captured under a wide range of environmental conditions and different terrain types (*Table 1, Figure 5*). In each video, path and obstacle boundaries (ground truth) were manually marked at *1 sec* intervals. The algorithm output was compared to the ground truth and its accuracy was derived as follows:

$$Accuracy\ (\%) = \left(1 - \frac{\sum\limits_{i=0}^{M-1}\sum\limits_{j=0}^{N-1}(|g_{ij} - o_{ij}|)}{M \times N}\right) \times 100 \qquad (2)$$

where g_{ij} is the ground truth array of size $M \times N$ and o_{ij} is the output array of size $M \times N$. In each of the g_{ij} and o_{ij} arrays the traversable pixels are denoted by '1' and the non-traversable pixels by '0'. Error measurement is then performed by calculating the absolute difference of the two arrays. Note that throughout testing no horizon level was used although this would normally increase the system performance and accuracy further. The results for each scenario are listed

Fig. 4. *a)* Chroma-based analysis: Areas of low chrominance are eliminated including the foreground water reflections, *b)* Segmentation result after temporal analysis

Table 1. Environmental and terrain conditions during testing

ID	Conditions	Terrain Type	Vibrations	Samples
1	Cloudy Dry	concrete	Light	81
2	Cloudy Wet	concrete	Light	103
3	Cloudy Muddy	soil, grass, gravel	Medium	10
4	Sunny Wet	concrete	Light	20
5	Complex Shadows	tarmac	Very Intense	100
6	Sunny Dry	poor quality tarmac	Very Intense	18
7	Strong shadows	concrete	Light	56
8	Snow	snow-covered tarmac	Medium	104
	Total			**492**

Table 2. Algorithm accuracy results in changing conditions using varying number of input channels (the numbers in bold-italic font denote the test with the highest accuracy in each row)

ID	Weight	1-channel		2-channel		3-channel		4-channel	
		Accuracy	*Error*	*Accuracy*	*Error*	*Accuracy*	*Error*	*Accuracy*	*Error*
1	0.16	94.87%	3.38%	***97.63%***	1.73%	96.18%	2.20%	97.04%	1.47%
2	0.21	93.68%	4.04%	98.33%	1.09%	98.52%	1.32%	***98.72%***	0.86%
3	0.02	94.35%	2.42%	95.47%	2.96%	97.79%	1.90%	***98.10%***	2.37%
4	0.04	97.12%	4.04%	99.12%	0.74%	***99.42%***	0.24%	99.24%	0.41%
5	0.20	92.47%	8.75%	***96.07%***	5.45%	95.44%	5.50%	95.41%	6.03%
6	0.04	96.46%	3.22%	***98.24%***	1.32%	96.70%	2.81%	96.47%	2.30%
7	0.11	98.95%	1.07%	99.14%	0.73%	***99.20%***	0.66%	99.05%	0.86%
8	0.21	97.01%	4.43%	***98.18%***	3.63%	98.06%	3.04%	98.09%	3.81%
Weighted mean		**95.19%**	**4.57%**	**97.79%**	**2.61%**	**97.44%**	**2.63%**	**97.60%**	**2.70%**

in *Table 2*, where the algorithm accuracy was derived using different number of input channels as follows: *a) 1-channel test*: Using saturation only, *b) 2-channel test*: Using saturation and saturation-based texture, *c) 3-channel test*: Using saturation, saturation-based texture and mean chroma and *d) 4-channel test*: Using saturation, saturation-based texture, mean chroma and chroma-based texture.

The algorithm has generally been robust in predicting the traversability of an area regardless of the image quality, noise and camera vibration. *Figure 5*

Input	Output	Input	Output

Fig. 5. System input and output examples. Areas covered with red lines are nontraversable. The blue lines indicate the path boundaries and the white box indicates the "*safe window*".

provides some characteristic examples of the system output. As we can see from *Table* 2, a performance of between 95.2% - 97.8% against the ground truth is achieved over a range of conditions (cloudy, wet, sunny, shadow, snow) and a range of terrains (concrete, grass, soil, tarmac, snow) with varying levels of vibration (empirically) recorded on the vehicle platform (*Figures 4b, 5*). The error is measured for each test by calculating the standard deviation of the samples. The overall accuracy and error are then derived by calculating the weighted mean. It should also be noted that using more input channels does not always increase the system accuracy and as a matter of fact the system can sometimes perform better with fewer inputs. This is logical since the colour properties of a surface change with weather and lighting conditions. As a matter of fact, if the system had chosen the right number of input channels for each test, the mean accuracy would have been 97.9% ± 2.5% (based on the maximum accuracy per test as highlighted by italic characters in *Table 3*). Given the subjective nature of ground truth labelling such a result is also subject to a ≈2% error, which is highly acceptable within an autonomous driving scenario.

The evaluation was done using the architecture described in *Figure 1*, which performed in real-time (25 frames per second) when implemented in C++ and executed on a 2GHz Intel Core2Duo CPU using up to four input channels. The camera was mounted on a vehicle that was moving at approximately walking pace. While testing, most obstacles were accurately detected as non-traversable areas except in situations where they were indistinguishable from the underlying surface. Regarding changing environmental conditions (*Table 1*), the performance was good, although reflections were sometimes detected as non-traversable areas. *The video dataset, ground truth data and results can be accessed via the following URL: http://tiny.cc/yannis.*

4 Conclusions

In this paper an effective real-time methodology was presented for detecting traversable surfaces by fusing colour and texture information from *HSL*, *YCbCr* and *LAB* colourspaces to perform image segmentation using a temporal memory model. By initially assuming that the area in front of the vehicle is traversable, the algorithm compares the characteristics of the "safe window" to the rest of the image and creates a "traversability" map. Furthermore, the temporal information is used to filter noise and thus improve system robustness. Testing has proved that this approach is well-suited for autonomous navigation in unstructured or semi-structured environments (up to 97.8% ±2.6% accuracy) and can perform in real-time on platforms with limited processing power. Future work will concentrate on developing an algorithm that can be trained to classify the environmental and terrain conditions in order to optimise colour space fusion.

Acknowledgements

This research has been supported by the Engineering and Physical Sciences Research Council (EPSRC, CASE/CNA/07/85) and TRW Conekt.

References

1. Alon, Y., Ferencz, A., Shashua, A.: Off-road path following using region classification and geometric projection constraints. In: IEEE Computer Society Conference on Computer Vision and Pattern Recognition, vol. 1, pp. 689–696 (2006)
2. Amendt, E.M., DePiero, F.W.: Multi-dimensional k-means image segmentation for off-road autonomous navigation. In: 10th IASTED International Conference on Signal and Image Processing (SIP), pp. 623–650 (2008)

3. Batavia, P.H., Singh, S.: Obstacle detection in smooth high curvature terrain. In: IEEE International Conference on Robotics and Automation, vol. 3, pp. 3062–3067 (2002)
4. Bertozzi, M., Broggi, A., Fascioli, A.: Vision-based intelligent vehicles: State of the art and perspectives. Robotics and Autonomous Systems 32(1), 1–16 (2000)
5. Broggi, A., Caraffi, C., Porta, P.P., Zani, P.: The single frame stereo vision system for reliable obstacle detection used during the 2005 darpa grand challenge on terramax. In: IEEE Intelligent Transportation Systems Conference (ITSC), pp. 745–752 (2006)
6. Cucchiara, R., Grana, C., Piccardi, M., Prati, A., Sirotti, S.: Improving shadow suppression in moving object detection with hsv color information. In: IEEE Intelligent Transportation Systems, pp. 334–339 (2001)
7. Desouza, G.N., Kak, A.C.: Vision for mobile robot navigation: a survey. IEEE Transactions on Pattern Analysis and Machine Intelligence 24(2), 237–267 (2002)
8. Goldberg, S.B., Maimone, M.W., Matthies, L.: Stereo vision and rover navigation software for planetary exploration. In: IEEE Aerospace Conference Proceedings, vol. 5, pp. 5-2025–5-2036 (2002)
9. Hsiao, P., Yeh, C.: A portable real-time lane departure warning system based on embedded calculating technique. In: IEEE 63rd Vehicular Technology Conference, vol. 6, pp. 2982–2986 (2006)
10. Kaszubiak, J., Tornow, M., Kuhn, R.W., Michaelis, B., Knoeppel, C.: Real-time vehicle and lane detection with embedded hardware. In: IEEE Intelligent Vehicles Symposium, pp. 619–624 (2005)
11. Agrawal Konolige, K.M., Sola, J.: Large-scale visual odometry for rough terrain. In: International Symposium on Research in Robotics, Hiroshima, Japan (2007)
12. Krïœse, B.J.A., Dev, A., Groen, F.C.A.: Heading direction of a mobile robot from the optical flow. Image and Vision Computing 18(5), 415–424 (2000)
13. Lorigo, L.M., Brooks, R.A., Grimsou, W.E.L.: Visually-guided obstacle avoidance in unstructured environments. In: IEEE/RSJ International Conference on Intelligent Robots and Systems, vol. 1, pp. 373–379 (1997)
14. Nefian, A.V., Bradski, G.R.: Detection of drivable corridors for off-road autonomous navigation. In: IEEE International Conference on Image Processing, pp. 3025–3028 (2006)
15. Shan, Y., Yang, F., Wang, R.: Color space selection for moving shadow elimination. In: Fourth International Conference on Image and Graphics (ICIG), pp. 496–501 (2007)
16. Thorpe, C., Hebert, M.H., Kanade, T., Shafer, S.A.: Vision and navigation for the carnegie-mellon navlab. IEEE Transactions on Pattern Analysis and Machine Intelligence 10(3), 362–373 (1988)
17. Wu, J., Yang, Z., Wu, J., Liu, A.: Virtual line group based video vehicle detection algorithm utilizing both luminance and chrominance. In: 2nd IEEE Conference on Industrial Electronics and Applications (ICIEA), May 2007, pp. 2854–2858 (2007)

Saliency-Based Obstacle Detection and Ground-Plane Estimation for Off-Road Vehicles

Pedro Santana[1], Magno Guedes[2], Luís Correia[1], and José Barata[2]

[1] LabMAg, Computer Science Department, University of Lisbon, Portugal
[2] UNINOVA, New University of Lisbon, Portugal

Abstract. Due to stringing time constraints, saliency models are becoming popular tools for building situated robotic systems requiring, for instance, object recognition and vision-based localisation capabilities. This paper contributes to this endeavour by applying saliency into two new tasks: modulation of stereo-based obstacle detection and ground-plane estimation, both to operate on-board off-road vehicles. To achieve this, a new biologically inspired saliency model, along with a set of adaptations to the task-specific algorithms, are proposed. Experimental results show a reduction in computational cost and an increase in both robustness and accuracy when saliency modulation is used.

1 Introduction

This paper proposes a saliency model adequate to off-road environments. It is based on the work of Itti et al. [1], which is in turn inspired by the pre-attentive human visual system. Biologically inspired saliency models (e.g. [1,2]) are in general more prone to parallel implementations than engineered ones (e.g. [3,4]), which is an important asset for real-time performance. Being inspired by the human visual system, these solutions also tend to be general purpose and consequently useful for more tasks.

Two essential applications for off-road robots are herein considered, namely obstacle detection and ground plane estimation. These applications differ from those typically considered in visual attention literature, such as detecting the most salient region for gaze control [5,6], object recognition [7,8] and landmark detection for visual SLAM [9,10]. The main difference is that previous applications are restricted to indoor/urban, i.e. structured environments. Obstacles in off-road environments are not necessarily the most salient in the image and do not belong to well specified classes of objects.

An essential feature for a robot operating off-road is to determine the ground plane. RANSAC can be used to solve this problem in an efficient way [11]. The explicit handling of the temporal dimension adds some robustness to the method against moving objects [12]. Additional heuristics can be considered in the ground estimation problem, such as removing from consideration 3-D points regarded as obstacles in previous iterations [13] or impose constraints on feasible plane configurations [14]. In this paper a complementary approach is taken. The more salient a pixel is, the less probable it is of being selected by the RANSAC procedure. This novel heuristic, which assumes that saliency is strongly correlated with the presence of obstacles, will be shown to reduce computational cost while increasing robustness.

M. Fritz, B. Schiele, and J.H. Piater (Eds.): ICVS 2009, LNCS 5815, pp. 275–284, 2009.

Obstacle detection can be carried out by simply determining which pixels are above the ground plane. Although this [11] and other ground-plane based approaches [15] work sufficiently well for flat terrains, they fail in rugged ones. There, obstacles are better defined in terms of geometrical relationships between 3-D points, such as in the work of Manduchi et al. [16], which has been extended to cope with real-time constraints and noisy data [13,17]. From these extensions, the space-variant resolution mechanism [17] is the one that can better profit from a saliency modulation and hence herein considered.

This paper is organised as follows. Section 2 proposes the new saliency model, which is then applied to ground plane estimation in Section 3 and obstacle detection in Section 4. Then, experimental results obtained with a stereo vision sensor are described in Section 5, followed by some conclusions and future work in Section 6.

2 Saliency Computation

The following describes the biologically inspired saliency model. It is a specialisation for off-road environments of the one proposed by Itti et al. [1]. Let L be the left image, with width w and height h, provided by the stereo vision sensor. To reduce computational cost, saliency is computed on a region of interest (ROI) of L. The ROI is an horizontal strip between rows u and h, where u corresponds to the upper-most row containing more than 100 pixels with an associated depth within the range of interest r. To further reduce computational cost, all image operators are performed over 8-bit images, whose magnitude is clamped to $[0, 255]$ by thresholding.

A dyadic Gaussian pyramid $I(\sigma)$ with six levels $\sigma \in \{0, \ldots, 5\}$ is created from the intensity channel of ROI. The resolution scale of level σ is $1/2^\sigma$ times the ROI resolution scale. Intensity is obtained by averaging the three colour channels. Then, four on-off centre-surround intensity feature maps $I^{on-off}(c, s)$ are created, to promote bright objects on dark backgrounds, in addition to four off-on centre-surround intensity feature maps $I^{off-on}(c, s)$, to promote dark objects on bright backgrounds. On-off centre-surround is performed by across-scale point-by-point subtraction, between a level c with finer scale and a level s with coarser scale (linearly interpolated to the finer resolution), with $(c, s) \in \Omega = \{(2, 4), (2, 5), (3, 4), (3, 5)\}$. Off-on maps are computed the other way around, i.e. subtracting the coarse level from the finer one. These maps are then combined to produce the intensity conspicuity map, $C_I = \sum_{i \in \{on-off, off-on\}} \left(\frac{1}{2} \bigoplus_{(c,s) \in \Omega} I^i(c, s)\right)$, where the across-scale addition $\bigoplus$ is performed with point-by-point addition of the maps, properly scaled to the resolution of level $\sigma = 3$. Sixteen orientation feature maps, $O(\sigma, \theta)$, are created by convolving levels $\sigma \in \{1, \ldots, 4\}$ with Gabor filters tuned to orientations $\theta \in \{0°, 45°, 90°, 135°\}$. Gabor filters are themselves centre-surround operators and therefore require no across-scale subtraction procedure [2]. As before, all orientation feature maps are combined at the resolution of level $\sigma = 3$ in order to create the orientations conspicuity map, $C_O = \sum_{\theta \in \{0°, 45°, 90°, 135°\}} \left(\frac{1}{4} \bigoplus_{\sigma \in \{1, \ldots, 4\}} O(\sigma, \theta)\right)$.

The saliency map S is obtained by modulating the intensity conspicuity map C_I with the orientations one C_O, $S = \mathcal{M}(\frac{1}{2} \cdot \mathcal{N}(C_I), \frac{1}{2} \cdot \mathcal{N}(C_O))$, where $\mathcal{M}(A, B) = A \cdot sigm(B)$, being $sigm(.)$ the sigmoid operator and $\mathcal{N}(.)$ rescales the provided image's amplitude between $[0, 255]$. Fig. 1(a)-top depicts an example of a saliency map.

(a)   (b)   (c)

Fig. 1. Results of image-pair #6 for $r = 10$ m. (a) saliency map (top) and pixel classification results based on the computed ground-plane (bottom), where red, green and black pixels correspond to obstacles, ground, and points without computed depth, respectively. (b) pixels (red) corresponding to 5000 3-D points randomly sampled for ground-plane estimation without saliency modulation. (c) same as (b) but with saliency modulation.

The proposed saliency model is essentially based on the model proposed by Itti et al. [1] but considering both on-off and off-on feature channels separately, which has been shown to yield better results [2]. Still, two major innovations are present in the proposed model. First, the normalisation operator $\mathcal{N}(.)$ does not try to promote maps according to their number of activity peaks, as typically done. The promotion of some maps over others according to activity peaks showed to provide poor results in the tasks herein considered. This is because spatially frequent objects, which are inhibited in typical saliency applications, may be obstacles for the robot, and thus must also be attended.

A narrow trail may be conspicuous in the intensity channel if it is, for instance, surrounded by dense and tall vegetation. This contradicts the goal of making obstacles salient, rather than the background. Hence, the second major innovation of this work is on the way saliency is computed from the conspicuity maps, i.e. modulating I with O rather than their typical addition, so as to diminish this phenomenon. It focus the saliency on small objects, borders of objects, and on entire objects if considerably textured, which is the most often case off-road. Unfortunately, with this setup, shadows reduce texture and consequently the chances of getting salient. However, as experiments will show, since shadows also originate stereo processing failures, a by-product of saliency is the reduction of false positives caused by inaccurate 3-D reconstruction. A parallel and independent study [18] has also reported on the benefits of using the weighted product of the conspicuity maps instead of their standard summation.

3   Ground Plane Estimation

The proposed solution to modulate the hypothesis-generation step of a conventional RANSAC [19] robust estimation procedure is composed of the following seven steps. **Step 1:** pick randomly a set R of three non-collinear 3-D points within range r, and generate its corresponding ground plane hypothesis, h_R, with some straightforward geometry. Points are considered non-collinear if the area of the triangle defined by them is above threshold t. **Step 2:** the score of the plane hypothesis is the cardinality of the set of its inliers, $score(h_R) = |P_{h_R}|$. An inlier, $j \in P_{h_R}$, is a 3-D point whose distance to plane h_R, $d(j, h_R)$, is smaller than a given threshold d_{plane}. **Step 3:** repeat steps 1 and

2 until n_{hypo} hypotheses, composing a set H, have been generated. **Step 4:** select for refinement, from H, the hypothesis with the highest score, $b = \arg\max_{h \in H} score(h)$. **Step 5:** compute b', which is a refined version of b, by fitting the inliers set of the latter, P_b. This fitting is done with weighted least-squares orthogonal regression, via the well known Singular Valued Decomposition (SVD) technique. The weight w_q of an inlier $q \in P_b$ is given by $w_q = 1 - \frac{d(q,b)}{d_{plane}}$. That is, the farther q is from b, the less it weights in the fitting process. Compute the inliers set of b', $P_{b'}$, and substitute the current best ground plane estimate by the refined one, i.e. make $b = b'$ and $P_b = P_{b'}$. **Step 6:** iterate step 5 until $|P_b|$ becomes constant across iterations or a maximum number of iterations, m_{refit}, is reached. **Step 7:** take b as the ground plane estimate.

To take saliency into account, each 3-D point p selected to build an hypothesis in step 1 must pass a second verification step. This step reduces the chances of selecting p proportionally to the *local saliency* of its projected pixel p'. The underlying empirical assumption (partially confirmed with the experimental results) is that saliency is positively correlated with the presence of obstacles. Preferring non-salient points thus raises the chances of selecting ground pixels (see Fig. 1(c)). Formally, a 3-D point p is rejected in the second verification step if $s_{p'} > \frac{P(x)}{\alpha \cdot n_l}$, where: $n_l \in [0, 1]$ is the number of pixels with saliency below a given threshold l normalised by the total number of pixels; *local saliency* $s_{p'} \in [0, 255]$ is the maximum saliency within a given sub-sampled chess-like squared neighbourhood of p', with size $g \cdot n_l$, being g the empirically defined maximum size; $P(x) \in [0, 255]$ represents samples from an uniform distribution; and α is an empirically defined scaling factor. The goal of using the normalised number of pixels with a saliency value under a given threshold is to allow the system to progressively fall-back to a non-modulated procedure as saliency reduces its discriminative power, i.e. it is too spread in space. This happens for instance in too textured terrains, in which the sampling procedure is too constrained as a result of the saliency map's cluttering.

4   Obstacle Detection

This section describes a way of modulating the space-variant resolution [17] of a well-known off-road obstacle detector [16] with the saliency map.

Formally, two 3-D points $p_a = (x_a, y_a, z_a)$ and $p_b = (x_b, y_b, z_b)$ are considered *compatible* with each other (i.e. pertain to the same obstacle) if $H_{min} < |y_b - y_a| < H_{max}$ and $\frac{|y_b - y_a|}{\|p_b - p_a\|} > \sin\theta$, where, θ is the minimum inclination of a surface to be considered as an obstacle, H_{min} is the minimum height an object must have to be considered an obstacle, and H_{max} is the maximum allowed height between two points to be considered compatible [16]. Assuming that the image is sequentially analysed starting from its bottom to its top and from left to right, then these conditions have the consequence that a point p is compatible to all points encompassed by an upper truncated cone C_U with vertex in p (see Fig. 2(a)). This projected on the image plane corresponds to check the compatibility between p and the points whose projections on the image plane are encompassed by the upper truncated triangle of p', i.e. C_U'.

Rather than checking all pixels during the scanning process [16], the obstacle detector is applied with space-variant resolution [17]. For a given pixel p' (sequentially

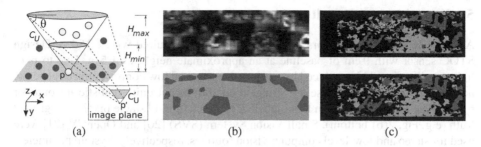

Fig. 2. Obstacle detection process for image-pair #5, with $(n, m, n_{slide}) = (4, 6, 30)$ and ground plane compensation on. (a) compatible points geometrical representation in the camera's reference frame [17]. (b) saliency map (top) and obstacles ground-truth (bottom). (c) obstacle detection without (top) and with (bottom) saliency modulation (same colour code as Fig. 1(a)-bottom).

sampled from $1/n$ of the full resolution, from the image's bottom to its top and from left to right), its C'_U is first scanned for compatible points with $1/m$ of the maximum resolution in a chess-like pattern, where $m > n$. If a compatible point with p' is found, C'_U is rescanned as usual with $1/n$ of the maximum resolution. Then, finished the scanning procedure, the full resolution is recovered as follows. For each obstacle pixel p', all its neighbours within a distance d in the image plane are also labelled obstacles if, their corresponding 3-D points are closer than f from p. The described space-variant resolution [17] operates to great extent blindly. That is, to reduce computational cost n and m are increased and hence many pixels are skipped. The following describes how saliency circumvents this problem by guiding the space-variant resolution.

Differently from the original algorithm which applies the compatibility test along the whole scan, now the compatibility test is applied to pixel p' iff: (1) n_{slide} consecutive pixels in the same row of p' have not been tested so far; or (2) n consecutive pixels, after a pixel whose 3-D reconstruction failed or that has been tested and labelled as obstacle in the same row of p', have not been tested so far; or (3) there is a 10% increment between the *local saliency* of p' and the one of its preceding scanned pixel, provided that both share the same row. Different from the ground plane estimation case, *local saliency* here is computed by taking the maximum saliency from the set of pixels within the same column of p', including itself, and contained in its truncated triangle. This diminishes the effects of poor light conditions, which in some situations make objects' top to appear more salient than their bottom. If only the saliency of p' were used instead, many object's bottom pixels would be inappropriately skipped. Every time a pixel p' is labelled as obstacle, the saliency of all pixels in C'_U, i.e. within its truncated triangle, are increased by an empirically defined scalar i. This mechanism is used to reinforce the presence of an obstacle point by increasing the chances of analysing all pixels associated with it, i.e. which are within the truncated triangle of p'.

The detector's accuracy is directly related to how well the camera's y–axis (see Fig. 2(a)) is aligned with the ground plane's normal vector. Thus, prior to the application of the obstacle detector, all 3-D points are rotated so as to perform this alignment. For this purpose, the ground plane orientation is computed as described in the previous section with $n_{hypo} = 20$ and $m_{refit} = 15$.

5 Experimental Results

A set of 36 stereo image pairs (see Fig. 4) has been acquired with a Videre Design STOC sensor with 9 cm of baseline at an approximate height of 1.5 m. Due to poor light conditions and blur induced by motion, the acquired low contrast images generate noisy 3-D point clouds. These are stringent conditions but quite realistic for outdoor robots. The images have been hand-labelled (obstacle/non-obstacle pixels) for ground truth (e.g. Fig. 2(b)-bottom). Small Vision System (SVS) [20] and OpenCV [21] were used for stereo and low-level computer vision routines, respectively. System parameters have been set to, $r = 10$ m, $t = 100$, $d_{plane} = 0.15$ m, $l = 5$, $\alpha = 4$, $g = 150$, $i = 0.7$, $d = 50$, $f = 0.3$ m, $H_{min} = 0.15$ m, $H_{max} = 0.3$ m, and $\theta = 45°$.

5.1 Ground Plane Estimation Results

A large set M of 10000 ground-plane hypotheses was created with the saliency based approach. This large set results in statistics varying $\approx 1\%$ across experiments. A set U

Table 1. MCC results. (a) ground plane estimation with $\Theta_\mu = \mu_{MCC^M} - \mu_{MCC^U}$ and $\Theta_\sigma = \sigma_{MCC^M} - \sigma_{MCC^U}$. (b) obstacle detection with ground plane compensation, where $\Theta_p = MCC_p^M - MCC_p^U$. (c) obstacle detection without ground plane compensation, where $\Theta = MCC^M - MCC^U$.

#	μ_{MCC^M}	σ_{MCC^M}	μ_{MCC^U}	σ_{MCC^U}	Θ_μ	Θ_σ
#00	0.57	0.36	0.23	0.51	0.34	-0.15
#22	0.68	0.23	0.41	0.37	0.27	-0.14
#23	0.56	0.26	0.30	0.38	0.26	-0.12
#21	0.64	0.22	0.4	0.35	0.25	-0.13
#16	0.75	0.28	0.56	0.41	0.19	-0.14
#33	0.63	0.32	0.48	0.38	0.16	-0.06
#06	0.50	0.24	0.38	0.28	0.12	-0.04
#19	0.79	0.23	0.70	0.34	0.10	-0.11
#31	0.55	0.27	0.47	0.33	0.08	-0.07
#02	0.67	0.18	0.60	0.25	0.07	-0.08
#24	0.23	0.31	0.16	0.29	0.07	0.02
#20	0.68	0.33	0.62	0.38	0.06	-0.05
#07	0.40	0.28	0.34	0.31	0.06	-0.03
#01	0.62	0.16	0.57	0.23	0.05	-0.07
#08	0.39	0.11	0.35	0.12	0.04	-0.02
#27	0.78	0.21	0.73	0.25	0.04	-0.04
#25	0.63	0.28	0.59	0.30	0.03	-0.02
#11	0.54	0.23	0.51	0.26	0.03	-0.03
#34	0.60	0.18	0.59	0.20	0.02	-0.02
#29	0.58	0.29	0.55	0.31	0.02	-0.02
#05	0.39	0.14	0.37	0.16	0.02	-0.01
#35	0.32	0.17	0.31	0.17	0.01	0.00
#26	0.36	0.11	0.35	0.11	0.01	0.00
#10	0.58	0.15	0.57	0.15	0.01	0.00
#15	0.17	0.14	0.16	0.15	0.01	-0.01
#03	0.40	0.19	0.38	0.21	0.01	-0.02
#14	0.21	0.09	0.20	0.09	0.00	0.01
#13	0.00	0.00	0.00	0.00	0.00	0.00
#09	0.02	0.05	0.02	0.05	0.00	0.00
#18	0.00	0.00	0.00	0.00	0.00	0.00
#28	0.20	0.32	0.20	0.31	0.00	0.00
#30	0.27	0.21	0.28	0.20	-0.01	0.01
#12	0.15	0.09	0.16	0.09	-0.01	0.00
#04	0.30	0.15	0.31	0.15	-0.01	0.00
#32	0.50	0.32	0.52	0.30	-0.02	0.02
#17	0.37	0.13	0.40	0.11	-0.03	0.02

(a)

#	MCC_p^M	MCC_p^U	Θ_p
#34	0.38	0.21	0.17
#19	0.69	0.52	0.17
#33	0.11	-0.03	0.14
#29	0.5	0.36	0.14
#7	0.24	0.11	0.13
#0	0.74	0.61	0.12
#2	0.73	0.61	0.12
#27	0.55	0.44	0.11
#31	0.6	0.48	0.11
#22	0.65	0.54	0.11
#1	0.42	0.33	0.09
#6	0.41	0.31	0.09
#26	0.4	0.31	0.09
#5	0.41	0.32	0.09
#21	0.72	0.63	0.08
#12	0.25	0.17	0.08
#20	0.69	0.61	0.08
#4	0.5	0.42	0.07
#25	0.45	0.37	0.07
#23	0.58	0.51	0.07
#16	0.77	0.7	0.07
#28	0.23	0.16	0.07
#30	0.6	0.54	0.06
#3	0.5	0.44	0.06
#35	0.25	0.19	0.06
#32	0.35	0.29	0.06
#17	0.06	0.02	0.04
#11	0.43	0.39	0.03
#8	0.23	0.2	0.03
#10	0.14	0.11	0.03
#9	0.05	0.03	0.02
#24	0.24	0.24	0.01
#14	-0.02	-0.02	0.01
#15	0.29	0.29	0
#13	0	0	0
#18	0	0	0

(b)

#	MCC^M	MCC^U	Θ
#29	0.5	0.33	0.17
#34	0.28	0.11	0.17
#0	0.6	0.45	0.15
#23	0.57	0.44	0.14
#7	0.32	0.19	0.13
#19	0.58	0.45	0.13
#25	0.26	0.13	0.13
#2	0.68	0.55	0.13
#27	0.35	0.23	0.13
#33	-0.02	-0.15	0.13
#16	0.68	0.55	0.12
#30	0.5	0.38	0.12
#21	0.61	0.49	0.12
#31	0.46	0.34	0.11
#28	0.2	0.1	0.1
#22	0.57	0.47	0.09
#20	0.63	0.53	0.09
#3	0.45	0.36	0.09
#26	0.27	0.18	0.09
#1	0.39	0.31	0.08
#5	0.43	0.35	0.08
#12	0.21	0.14	0.07
#35	0.2	0.14	0.06
#32	0.29	0.23	0.06
#6	0.35	0.29	0.06
#4	0.32	0.27	0.06
#11	0.16	0.11	0.05
#15	0.18	0.15	0.03
#10	0.09	0.06	0.03
#24	0.27	0.25	0.02
#14	-0.02	-0.03	0.01
#9	0.03	0.02	0.01
#8	0.24	0.24	0
#13	0	0	0
#18	0	0	0
#17	0.04	0.07	-0.03

(c)

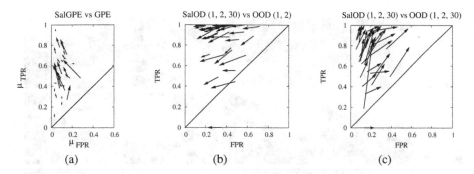

Fig. 3. ROC graphs. (a) ground plane estimation with (SalGPE) vs. without (GPE) saliency modulation. (b) obstacle detection with (SalOD) vs. without (OOD) saliency modulation. (c) same as (b) but skipping n_{slide} pixels for the OOD case. Line $x = y$ displayed for reference.

with the size of M was created without saliency modulation, representing the canonical RANSAC. The set of obstacles detected using each hypothesis in both sets is compared against the ground truth to obtain the True Positive Rate (TPR), False Positive Rate, and the two-class Matthews Correlation Coefficient (MCC). The MCC metric is well known for its ability to handle unbalanced datasets. The closer MCC is to 1, the better the hypothesis matches the ground-truth. Obstacles are those pixels whose orthogonal distance to the plane is above 0.2 cm. Then, the averages (μ) and standard deviations (σ) of the above variables over all hypotheses in both M and U, are computed.

According to the MCC results (see Table 1(a)), two main image sub-sets emerge. One (grey shaded) aggregates images where the RANSAC saliency-based hypothesis generation step significantly wins over the canonical one. The MCC differences are residual (i.e. $< 5\%$) for the remainder images, meaning that saliency is essentially neutral there. Images without obstacles have MCC values of 0. Images benefiting from saliency share a characteristic: a considerable presence of objects. In these situations (e.g. Fig. 2(b)-top) saliency easily segments objects from background. Saliency thus operates better in those situations where it is most required. In the absence of obstacles an uninformed solution should suffice. Fig. 3(a) depicts the ROC graph of the experiment. For each image k, an arrow is drawn to connect its corresponding without-saliency point, $(\mu_{TPR^U}, \mu_{FPR^U})_k$, to its corresponding point with-saliency, $(\mu_{TPR^M}, \mu_{FPR^M})_k$. The closer a point is from the upper-left corner of the graph, the better the corresponding set of sampled hypotheses matches the ground truth. A clear dominance of arrows heading the corner is observed.

5.2 Obstacle Detection Results

Fig. 3(b) shows the results obtained from comparing the Original Obstacle Detector (OOD) with $(n, m) = (1, 2)$ and saliency based one (SalOD) with $(n, m, n_{slide}) = (1, 2, 30)$. With saliency, the detector considerably reduced the False Positive Rate (FPR). The residual reduction of the True Positive Rate (TPR) shows a selective discard of non-obstacle points by using saliency. This signal-to-noise ratio improvement is confirmed by the contrast of the MCC with (MCC_p^M) and without (MCC_p^U) saliency

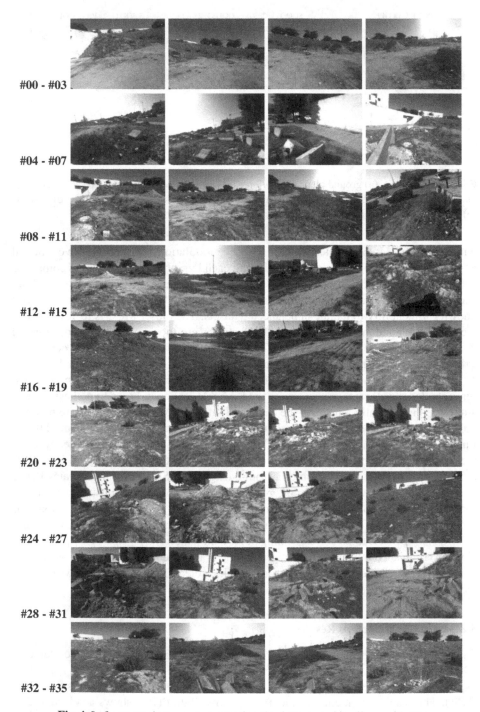

Fig. 4. Left-camera images encompassing the dataset used in all experiments

modulation (see Table 1(b)). Label p means that ground plane compensation is on. Saliency contributes in the same amount when ground plane compensation is off (see Table 1(c)), highlighting its resilience.

To reinforce the evidence that the reduction in FPR is due to the saliency's selective nature instead of the reduced number of pixels being analysed, an additional test was carried out. The OOD was configured to systematically skip n_{slide} pixels, rather than n, when displacing the truncated triangle. The resulting ROC graph (see Fig. 3(c)) shows that although the OOD now produces a smaller FPR, due to blindly skipping more pixels, a considerable reduction in the TPR is also observed. For obstacle detection, smaller TPR means higher risk of collision. Hence, saliency shows itself to be a useful cue for informed false positive removal. With the previous parametrisation, Sa-lOD operates on average at 1 Hz, i.e. $4\times$ faster than the OOD. Further work to cope with real time constraints in its full resolution configuration is necessary. Still, the weaker configuration $(n, m, n_{slide}) = (4, 6, 30)$ suffices to perceive most of the environment's topology (e.g. Fig. 2(c)). It takes on average 50ms, excluding plane fitting and saliency computation cost, which take on average 54ms and 43ms, respectively, on a Centrino Dual Core 2 GHz.

6 Conclusions

A new saliency model, inspired by the human visual system, has been presented and integrated in an obstacle detector, as well as in a ground-plane estimator, both for off-road environments. Saliency allows focusing resources without making hard assumptions on the appearance of obstacles, which is ideal for unstructured environments. To our knowledge this is the first report on the application of a saliency model onto these tasks. The proposed saliency-based modulation of the hypothesis generation step in a RANSAC procedure for ground plane estimation, and of the space-variant resolution for obstacle detection, showed relevant improvements over the original algorithms. These results were only possible with the proposed conspicuity maps' cross-modulation, along with the absence of spatial normalisation. This suggests that the topology of bottom-up saliency models should change with the typology of both environment and task. In this paper the goal was to show that a simple method is already useful for the tasks at hand. In fact, not using 3-D information for saliency computation has been pivotal for the reduction of false positives, as these are mostly caused by noise on the 3-D channel. The addition of texture and colour channels will be considered as future work.

Acknowledgments

We would like to thank the anonymous reviewers for their insightful comments and suggestions. This work was partially supported by IntRoSys, S.A. and by FCT/MCTES grant No. SFRH/BD/27305/2006.

References

1. Itti, L., Koch, C., Niebur, E.: A Model of Saliency-Based Visual Attention for Rapid Scene Analysis. IEEE Trans. on Pattern Analysis and Machine Intelligence, 1254–1259 (1998)

2. Frintrop, S.: VOCUS: a visual attention system for object detection and goal-directed search. PhD thesis, INAI, Vol. 3899, Germany (2006)
3. Kadir, T., Brady, M.: Saliency, scale and image description. Intl. Journal of Computer Vision 45(2), 83–105 (2001)
4. Hou, X., Zhang, L.: Saliency detection: a spectral residual approach. In: Proc. of the IEEE Intl. Conf. on Computer Vision and Pattern Recognition (CVPR), pp. 1–8 (2007)
5. Ude, A., Wyart, V., Lin, L., Cheng, G.: Distributed visual attention on a humanoid robot. In: Proc. of the IEEE Int. Conf. on Humanoid Robots, pp. 381–386 (2005)
6. Ruesch, J., Lopes, M., Bernardino, A., Hornstein, J., Santos-Victor, J., Pfeifer, R.: Multimodal saliency-based bottom-up attention a framework for the humanoid robot iCub. In: Proc. of the IEEE Intl. Conf. on Robotics and Automation (ICRA), pp. 962–967 (2008)
7. Walther, D., Koch, C.: Modeling attention to salient proto-objects. Neural Networks 19, 1395–1407 (2006)
8. Meger, D., Forssen, P.E., Lai, K., Helmer, S., McCann, S., Southey, T., Baumann, M., Little, J.J., Lowe, D.G., Dow, B.: Curious George: An attentive semantic robot. Robotics and Autonomous Systems 56(6), 503–511 (2008)
9. Frintrop, S., Jensfelt, P., Christensen, H.: Simultaneous Robot Localization and Mapping Based on a Visual Attention System. In: Paletta, L., Rome, E. (eds.) WAPCV 2007. LNCS (LNAI), vol. 4840, pp. 417–430. Springer, Heidelberg (2007)
10. Newman, P., Ho, K.: SLAM-Loop Closing with Visually Salient Features. In: Proc. of the IEEE Intl. Conf. on Robotics and Automation (ICRA), pp. 635–642 (2005)
11. Konolige, K., Agrawal, M., Bolles, R., Cowan, C., Fischler, M., Gerkey, B.: Outdoor mapping and navigation using stereo vision. In: Proc. of the 2006 Intl. Symp. on Experimental Robotics (ISER), pp. 179–190 (2006)
12. Mufti, F., Mahony, R., Heinzmann, J.: Saptio-temporal RANSAC for robust estimation of ground plane in video range images for automotive applications. In: Proc. of the IEEE Intl. Conf. on Intelligent Transportation Systems (ITSC), pp. 1142–1148 (2008)
13. Mark, W., Heuvel, J., Groen, F.: Stereo based obstacle detection with uncertainty in rough terrain. In: Proc. of the IEEE Intelligent Vehicles Symposium, pp. 1005–1012 (2007)
14. Chumerin, N., Van Hulle, M.: Ground plane estimation based on dense stereo disparity. In: Proc. of the Intl. Conf. on Neural Networks and Artificial Intelligence, ICNNAI (2008)
15. Broggi, A., Caraffi, C., Porta, P., Zani, P.: The single frame stereo vision system for reliable obstacle detection used during the 2005 DARPA Grand Challenge on TerraMax. In: Proc. of the IEEE Intl. Conf. on Intelligent Transportation Systems (ITSC), pp. 745–752 (2006)
16. Manduchi, R., Castano, A., Talukder, A., Matthies, L.: Obstacle detection and terrain classification for autonomous off-road navigation. Autonomous Robots 18(1), 81–102 (2005)
17. Santana, P., Santos, P., Correia, L., Barata, J.: Cross-country obstacle detection: Space-variant resolution and outliers removal. In: Proc. of the IEEE Intl. Conf. on Intelligent Robots and Systems (IROS 2008), pp. 1836–1841 (2008)
18. Hwang, A.D., Higgins, E.C., Pomplun, M.: A model of top-down attentional control during visual search in complex scenes. Journal of Vision 9(5), 1–18 (2009)
19. Fischler, M., Bolles, R.: Random sample consensus: A paradigm for model fitting with applications to image analysis and automated cartography. Commun. of the ACM 24 (1981)
20. Konolige, K., Beymer, D.: SRI Small Vision System Users Manual. SRI Intl. (May 2007)
21. Bradski, G., Kaehler, A.: Learning OpenCV: Computer vision with the OpenCV library. O'Reilly Media, Inc., Sebastopol (2008)

Performance Evaluation of Stereo Algorithms for Automotive Applications

Pascal Steingrube, Stefan K. Gehrig, and Uwe Franke

Daimler AG Group Research, 71059 Sindelfingen, Germany

Abstract. The accuracy of stereo algorithms is commonly assessed by comparing the results against the Middlebury database. However, no equivalent data for automotive or robotics applications exist and these are difficult to obtain. We introduce a performance evaluation scheme and metrics for stereo algorithms at three different levels. This evaluation can be reproduced with comparably low effort and has very few prerequisites. First, the disparity images are evaluated on a pixel level. The second level evaluates the disparity data roughly column by column, and the third level performs an evaluation on an object level. We compare three real-time capable stereo algorithms with these methods and the results show that a global stereo method, semi-global matching, yields the best performance using our metrics that incorporate both accuracy and robustness.

1 Introduction

Today's stereo algorithms have reached a maturity level that allows the use in real world systems. However, the performance evaluation for such algorithms is still mostly limited to comparisons on the Middlebury database[1] [1]. Most applications have to deal with a lot of different conditions which are not covered by such controlled data sets. For such an outdoor imagery evaluation we need metrics to compare different algorithms (i.e. mainly stereo algorithms in our context) and to compare their impact on different levels of detail. Thus, we introduce a performance evaluation system using the following three levels:

1. low-level: *false stereo correspondences* based on generic stereo data where we use knowledge about object-free volumes to detect violations.
2. mid-level: *freespace* [2] (object-free space in front of the car — the inverse is also called evidence grid/occupancy grid) which is computed directly on the stereo correspondences. The freespace is a basis for many other object detection algorithms and thus suitable for a mid-level evaluation.
3. high-level: *leader vehicle measurement.* We pick one particular application where the leading vehicle is measured in front of the ego-vehicle. This data is needed for all adaptive cruise-control (ACC) variants. Depending on the implemented driver assistance function, different accuracy demands are needed

---

[1] http://vision.middlebury.edu/stereo/

M. Fritz, B. Schiele, and J.H. Piater (Eds.): ICVS 2009, LNCS 5815, pp. 285–294, 2009.

for the distance, relative velocity, lateral position and width of the leader vehicle. We focus on the lateral position and width of the leader vehicle since we have a RADAR system that determines the distance and relative velocity very accurately and serves as ground truth for that part. A comparison between RADAR and vision distance shows mainly the quality of the calibration. For the quality of the relative velocity, a good filtering strategy is the key. The challenge for such applications is a correct object segmentation, and here the choice of stereo algorithm becomes visible.

This three-way analysis system covers the range of applications in which stereo is used in today's automotive industry (e.g. [3]). The ground truth which is needed for evaluating the tasks, is introduced in Section 3. In Section 4 more details on the used metrics to measure the performance are given. Implementation details are presented in Section 5. Mainly we have tested three different stereo algorithms which are discussed in Section 6.

2   Related Work

In recognition tasks (e.g. [4], [5]) ground truth is widely used where Receiver-Operator-Curves (ROC) or classification rates are compared. There, ground-truthing is necessary to provide the recognition algorithms with training data.

The traditional way to determine the performance of a stereo algorithm is to compare its results against the Middlebury database. The evaluation is conducted on 4 image pairs of controlled scenes with known ground truth. Computed depth maps will be compared pixel by pixel and a disparity value for every pixel is required. In our context, we focus on uncontrolled scenes and different weather conditions on a large amount of frames.

Preliminary work has been done by Vaudrey et al. [6] using synthetic driver assistance data where groundtruthing is trivial. But, synthetic data does not reflect the challenges of e.g. bad weather. In [7], an orthogonal method to determine the street plane is used to evaluate stereo. However, the street plane investigation only verifies small parts of the image whereas for real automotive applications there are many other parts of the 3D scene which are important.

In [8], a general framework for performance evaluation of Computer Vision algorithms is presented, with a focus on object detection algorithms. However, all introduced metrics are limited to monocular image sequences and to metrics within the image plane. Both are less relevant to robotics and driver assistance scenarios.

3   Ground Truth Generation

No ground truth data is available for outdoor stereo scenes and it is difficult to obtain. Especially adverse weather conditions pose additional challenges and make groundtruthing almost impossible.

The quality of the ground truth is vital for a good performance evaluation. So, we try to generate ground truth data as well as possible including semi/supervised efforts. The next subsections covers the methods of generating the ground truth for all of the used metrics. We make a trade-off between effort to generate ground truth and quality of ground truth. Ideally, a high-end 3D sensing system with the same resolution as the used cameras would serve the purpose well. A sensor step towards that ideal sensor is the Velodyne sensor used in the Urban Challenge competition[2]. Unfortunately, its vertical angular resolution is still not as good as a camera which is needed for our evaluation purposes.

3.1 Prerequisites for the Performance Evaluation

In order to evaluate stereo algorithms at the three levels the following prerequisites have to be met:

- The cameras have to be calibrated to perform a metric 3D conversion and the rectified images are fed into the algorithms.
- The pose of the stereo camera w.r.t. the street plane has to be known or is estimated from the stereo data (see e.g. [2]).

3.2 False Correspondences

We made some assumptions which lead to an object-free volume in the 3D scene in front of the ego-vehicle which then will be used to detect false stereo correspondences. The ground truth is implicitly given by the assumption that the road is planar and the moving vehicle does not collide with any object in a specific time window. Under normal driving conditions we keep a safe distance of at least 1 second (multiplied by the ego-velocity) from other objects along our driving corridor. So, the object free volume is defined by the road plane, the width and height of the ego-vehicle and a safe distance. We refine it further by taking the yaw rate into account.

If an algorithm computes a 3D point within this object-free volume, a false correspondence has been found. The assumptions are valid for all our collected data sets which gives us a *reliable* ground truth for the low-level metric. If one specifically selects sequences with more space to the next vehicle in front, one may increase the time and hence the object-free space which helps to find more possible false correspondences.

The object-free volume in front of the ego-vehicle is a highly relevant area. All collision avoidance and collision mitigation systems trigger on 3D points close to the ego-vehicle since they indicate an imminent collision. A cluster of 3D points close to the ego-vehicle often leads to the formation of a so-called phantom object which is shown in Figure 4.

3.3 Freespace

The freespace in front of the car is used as a mid level metric. It is directly based on the given stereo correspondences and on a (computed) pitch angle. We use the algorithm proposed by Badino [2]. Starting with a well performing stereo algorithm as initial ground truth we refine the ground truth in a few supervised

---

[2] http://velodyne.com/lidar/products/brochure/HDL-64E%20datasheet.pdf

iteration steps. These refinement steps lead to a best performing algorithm on a sequence basis quickly. In theory, the best-performing stereo algorithm can also be selected on a frame-by-frame basis.

The user employs the sequence-wise accumulated metrics to choose candidates which could outperform the *current* ground truth. These candidates can be determined by choosing stereo setups with differences in the freespace path (see Section 4.2). Then, one sequence is visually compared to the *current* ground truth using the visualization interface. This interface allows the user to see the whole sequence at once (more details in Section 5.3). It takes only seconds to find and inspect relevant frames and to decide if the candidate is a better ground truth or not. The visual inspection of a stereo algorithm running on a 400-frames sequence takes less than 30 seconds to compare to another stereo algorithm.

3.4   Leader Vehicle Measurement

There is a group of measurements which are used to specify a leader vehicle [9], such as distance, width, lateral position, length, height, velocity, etc. Here, we focus on width and lateral position.

The ground truth for the LVM (leader vehicle measurement) is generated by user interaction, frame-wise. To assist the user here, we use a semi-automated tool. It estimates an initial guess for the lateral position and width of the leader vehicle, based on a good stereo algorithm and suitable object detection parameters. Then, the user only has to adjust the measurement data interactively if deviations to the real position in the image are noticeable.

For most of the sequences, the user only has to adjust every 20th frame as the tracking process works well and the initial detection poses the highest challenge.

In contrast to the process of determining freespace ground truth, this is more time consuming (frame-wise instead of sequence-wise). But the LVM metrics are highly distinctive to evaluate the performance of stereo algorithms for automotive applications. In addition, the same framework can be used to validate parameters for other object detection tasks. Groundtruthing a 400-frame sequence takes approximately 5 minutes.

4   Evaluation Metrics

We need metrics to compare different stereo algorithms, including low and mid level metrics to achieve more general results. In addition, we have included an analysis on application level to measure the performance for a real application.

4.1   False Correspondences

Say a stereo algorithm produces a total of N correspondences in an image pair. Each is projected in 3D space and represented as a 3D point. The number of all 3D points which lie inside the object-free volume is counted as a false correspondence $\mathbf{N}_{fc}$ and the metric is the ratio of false 3D points to all 3D points:

$$\mathbf{m}_{fc} = \frac{\mathbf{N}_{fc}}{\mathbf{N}}$$

4.2 Freespace

The freespace is represented by a path through the image from left to right (see Figure 1). For each image column the distance to the first obstacle is stored, assuming a negligible roll angle. These positions yield the freespace path. To compare two sequences we use the following metric m_{fs}:

$$\text{disp}_{\text{measure},i} = \frac{f * B}{\text{dist}_{\text{measure},i}}, \ \text{disp}_{\text{groundtruth},i} = \frac{f * B}{\text{dist}_{\text{groundtruth},i}}$$

$$m_{fs} = \frac{1}{N} \sum_{i=1}^{N} |\text{disp}_{\text{measure},i} - \text{disp}_{\text{groundtruth},i}|$$

with f=focal length, B=baseline, disp=disparity, dist=distance in column i.

Thus we do not directly compare the resulting distances in meters but we first transform them into disparities (in pixels). There are several reasons for this:

– We compare the full freespace path with distances up to 70 meters and errors at larger distances do not lead to erroneous braking or steering interventions. These errors are attenuated.
– Errors (differences) near the ego-vehicle have a higher weight which are the most critical situations (e.g. nearby phantom objects).
– The stereo algorithms measure also in disparities.

Fig. 1. Left: Traffic scene with stereo result (see Section 6). Disparity color encoding: red = near, green = far. Right: Computed freespace is overlaid in green.

4.3 Leader Vehicle Measurement

For a vehicle-following system it is important to know the exact lateral position and the width of the leading vehicle (e.g. in order to guide the driver) .

So, the absolute difference between the value of a chosen setup and the ground truth is a suitable metric to measure the performance of this setup:

$$m_{lp} = |lp_{\text{measure}} - lp_{\text{groundtruth}}|$$
$$m_{w} = |\text{width}_{\text{measure}} - \text{width}_{\text{groundtruth}}|$$

Additionally, we accumulate the number of frames where the LVM algorithm obtained no object because of insufficient stereo data, resulting in a LVM availability.

5   Implementation

5.1   Data Acquisition

For a specific stereo algorithm with an associated parameter set and a recorded image sequence our system dumps a file to disk with the relevant values for the introduced metrics (for each frame). These values are the variables occurring in the metric formulae. Furthermore, we store some additional meta information such as camera parameters for later visualization purposes.

Here, no ground truth is taken into account, thus this basic plain data can be generated in parallel and independently of the rest of the system. Thus, a huge database of image sequences and a variety of different algorithms/parameters setups can be handled easily.

5.2   Database Organization

Once the basic data from a number of setups has been generated for each pair of setup and corresponding ground truth the introduced metrics will be computed and stored in an XML file database. In contrast to the generation of the pre-calculated basic data this step performs very fast and thus it is possible to update the database while using it. If one refines the system by replacing the freespace ground truth with a new (better) setup, the ground truth update for a sequence ($\sim$ 500 frames) and 20 setups takes less than two seconds. To integrate a new setup into the whole database ($\sim$ 22.000 frames) it takes less than 20 seconds. An overview of the system structure is shown in Figure 2.

5.3   Visualization

Based on the XML file database we provide several style-sheets, written in the XML transformation language XSL[3], which transform the huge number of measurements into few compact and easily explorable representations.

We provide different layers of visualization of the metrics generated for each frame and each setup. On the bottom layer we compare results on a frame basis where all frames of a sequence are shown at once. The measurements are plotted on bar charts over frame number. This results in a convenient visualization of the whole sequence. We added an interactive functionality to support the user here with more information for each frame, like disparity map visualization. One example is shown in Figure 3. This representation can be used to inspect a sequence on its own or on a competitive basis with other stereo algorithms (or in comparison to ground truth).

---

[3] http://www.w3.org/TR/xslt

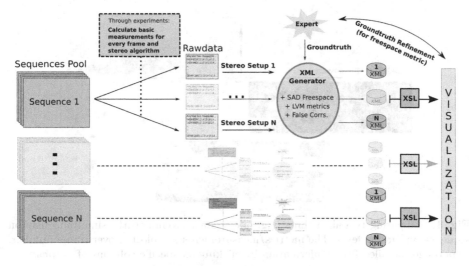

Fig. 2. System Framework

One step further, we integrate the metrics on frame basis to provide a single score for the whole sequence. Here, for a particular setup all sequences' scores are shown at once in the sequences overview. The scores are colored (green to red) according to its absolute value (with empirical specified maximum value). With this color scheme, interesting sequences are easy to identify.

At the highest level, all setups are compared against each other. All sequence scores are integrated for each setup. As before, the scores are colored according to their value. Here, the user can simply plug in different lists of sequences (specified by a single XML file), to evaluate the performance independently for different conditions / situations (rain, snow, clear conditions, etc.).

The resulting representations are mainly SVG (Scalable Vector Graphics) and HTML documents where the interactive functions are implemented via Javascript. They are generated on-the-fly as result of the XSL transformation process which makes it easy when introducing new representations on existing databases. To use the visual inspection system a modern web-browser (support for XSL/XSLT and SVG mandatory) is required.

6   Results and Discussion

Our main interest in building the evaluation system is to compare the three following stereo algorithms (see also Figure 4):

- *Signature-Based Stereo*: A signature based algorithm which searches for unique (corresponding) features of pixels [10].
- *Correlation Stereo*: A patch based correlation stereo algorithm using ZSSD (zero-mean sum of squared differences) [11].
- *Semi-Global Matching (SGM)*: Computes a approximated global optimum via multiple 1D paths in real-time [12].

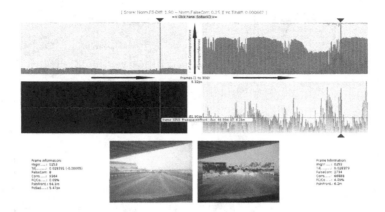

Fig. 3. Comparing two algorithms (e.g. one against ground truth) simultaneously on sequence and frame level. The metrics/measurements are plotted over frame number. Experts get detailed frame information by clicking on specific columns of graphs.

Fig. 4. Stereo results: Signature-Based Stereo (left). Correlation (centre). Semi-Global Matching (right). Disparity color encoding: red = near, green = far. Note the red pixel cluster in the center of correlation - such clusters often generate phantom objects.

We choose these algorithms because of their real-time capability.

The sequences we used are divided into 50% bad weather conditions (rain, snow, night) and 50% normal conditions and contain a total of 22,100 frames recorded at 25 Hz. The mixture is chosen to find failure modes of the algorithms more quickly, so less data is needed. Samples are shown in Figure 5.

The results in Table 1 show that Signature-Based Stereo exhibits shortcomings. Correlation Stereo is far better than Signature-Based Stereo, but the winner at all levels and metrics is SGM. In parentheses the results from the bad weather part of the database are shown. The results have the same order again. Since this data set contains fewer crowded scenes, the LVM availability actually improves compared to the full data set.

Furthermore, the freespace computation and the leader vehicle measurement parameters were tuned on Correlation Stereo and these results underline the overall good and stable performance of SGM. If the applications were tuned w.r.t. SGM, the results of SGM would be even better. Especially the *availability* of the leader vehicle measurements outperforms the correlation approach by far.

Fig. 5. Samples of the used image database. The upper images show example disparity maps and leader vehicle measurements. The red bounding box indicates the leader vehicle width, the white line marks the estimated vehicle center.

Table 1. Results for the stereo algorithms. In parentheses are results from the bad weather part of the database. This data set contains fewer crowded scenes. SGM performs best in all metrics.

Metric	low-level	mid-level	high-level (LVM)		
	False Corr.	*FS Diff.*	$\Delta Lat.Pos.$	$\Delta Width$	*Availability*
Algorithm / Unit	m_{fc} [%]	m_{fs} [px]	m_{lp} [cm]	m_w [cm]	[%]
Signature-Based Stereo	7.45 (10.35)	3.04 (3.06)	19 (22)	26 (35)	80 (88)
Correlation Stereo	1.02 (1.47)	1.26 (1.72)	13 (15)	19 (37)	95 (99)
Semi-Global Matching	0.98 (0.94)	0.68 (0.79)	11 (12)	14 (32)	99 (99)

7   Conclusions and Future Work

We presented a novel approach for evaluation of stereo algorithms for uncontrolled data sets and large amount of frames which can be easily handled by experts. The user can retrace the output of the stereo algorithms up to frame level. Furthermore, the system provides several tools to find relevant and interesting frames which were used to validate the results via eyeballing.

The introduced metrics use different levels of detail to achieve more general statements and to test the performance on real applications. In our evaluations, the ground truth was generated with little effort and was applied on over 22,000 frames. The stable order of the results — SGM better than Correlation Stereo better than Signature-Based Stereo in all metrics — shows the significance of the introduced metrics.

In the future we will focus on more applications and other algorithms. Even algorithms which have no real time performance today could be interesting in a few years.

References

1. Scharstein, D., Szeliski, R.: A taxonomy and evaluation of dense two-frame stereo correspondence algorithms. IJCV 47(1), 7–42 (2002)
2. Badino, H., Franke, U., Mester, R.: Free space computation using stochastic occupancy grids and dynamic programming. In: Workshop on Dynamical Vision, ICCV, Rio de Janeiro (2007)
3. Tech-News: Toyota' lexus ls 460 employs stereo camera (viewed 2009/04/15), http://techon.nikkeibp.co.jp/english/NEWS_EN/20060301/113832/
4. Everingham, M., Zisserman, A., Williams, C.K.I., Van Gool, L., et al.: The 2005 pascal visual object classes challenge. In: Selected Proceedings of the 1st PASCAL Challenges Workshop. LNCS (LNAI). Springer, Heidelberg (2006)
5. Dreuw, P., Steingrube, P., Deselaers, T., Ney, H.: Smoothed disparity maps for continuous american sign language recognition. In: Iberian Conference on Pattern Recognition and Image Analysis, Póvoa de Varzim, Portugal (June 2009)
6. Vaudrey, T., Rabe, C., Klette, T., Milburn, J.: Differences between stereo and motion behaviour on synthetic and real-world stereo sequences. In: IEEE Conf. Proc. IVCNZ 2008 (2008)
7. Liu, Z., Klette, R.: Approximated ground truth for stereo and motion analysis on real-world sequences. In: Wada, T., Huang, F., Lin, S. (eds.) Proceedings PSIVT 2009. LNCS, vol. 5414. Springer, Heidelberg (2009)
8. Mariano, V.Y., Min, J., Park, J.-H., Kasturi, R., Mihalcik, D., Li, H., Doermann, D., Drayer, T.: Performance evaluation of object detection algorithms. In: International Conference on Pattern Recognition, vol. 3, p. 30965 (2002)
9. Barth, A., Franke, U.: Where will the oncoming vehicle be the next second? In: Intelligent Vehicles Symposium, 2008 IEEE (2008)
10. Stein, F.J.: Efficient computation of optical flow. In: Rasmussen, C.E., Bülthoff, H.H., Schölkopf, B., Giese, M.A. (eds.) DAGM 2004. LNCS, vol. 3175, pp. 79–86. Springer, Heidelberg (2004)
11. Franke, U.: Real-time stereo vision for urban traffic scene understanding. In: IEEE Conference on Intelligent Vehicles (2000)
12. Gehrig, S.K., Eberli, F., Meyer, T.: A real-time low-power stereo vision engine using semi-global matching. In: ICVS (2009)

White-Box Evaluation of Computer Vision Algorithms through Explicit Decision-Making

Richard Zanibbi[1], Dorothea Blostein[2], and James R. Cordy[2]

[1] Dept. Computer Science, Rochester Institute of Technology, Rochester, NY 14623-5608
[2] School of Computing, Queen's University, Kingston, Ontario, Canada, K7L 3N6
rlaz@cs.rit.edu, {blostein,cordy}@cs.queensu.ca

Abstract. Traditionally computer vision and pattern recognition algorithms are evaluated by measuring differences between final interpretations and ground truth. These black-box evaluations ignore intermediate results, making it difficult to use intermediate results in diagnosing errors and optimization. We propose "opening the box," representing vision algorithms as sequences of decision points where recognition results are selected from a set of alternatives. For this purpose, we present a domain-specific language for pattern recognition tasks, the Recognition Strategy Language (RSL). At run-time, an RSL interpreter records a complete history of decisions made during recognition, as it applies them to a set of interpretations maintained for the algorithm. Decision histories provide a rich new source of information: recognition errors may be traced back to the specific decisions that caused them, and intermediate interpretations may be recovered and displayed. This additional information also permits new evaluation metrics that include false negatives (correct hypotheses that the algorithm generates and later rejects), such as the percentage of ground truth hypotheses generated (*historical recall*), and the percentage of generated hypotheses that are correct (*historical precision*). We illustrate the approach through an analysis of cell detection in two published table recognition algorithms.

Keywords: Performance Evaluation, Document Recognition, Table Recognition, Scripting Languages, Domain-Specific Languages.

1 Introduction

Current evaluation methods for computer vision and pattern recognition systems are generally *black box*, based solely on observing algorithm inputs and outputs. For example, black-box analysis is standard practice in the document recognition community [1][8][10][11][14][16][17]. Diagnosis of failures is difficult, since black-box observations provide little insight into the causes of poor recognition results. In response to this lack of information, developers who are searching for sources of recognition errors typically write additional code to produce diagnostic output. This is a laborious and error-prone task.

Significant advances can be achieved through *white box* evaluation. We present a technique that explicitly represents decision points where *interpretations* (recognition results) may be altered, and captures decision outcomes at run-time [20][23]. In this

M. Fritz, B. Schiele, and J.H. Piater (Eds.): ICVS 2009, LNCS 5815, pp. 295–304, 2009.

paper we summarize our earlier work, and present new recall and precision-based performance summaries for both complete strategies and individual decisions.

As illustrated in Figure 1, decision points represent the input and output spaces for a decision separately from the function that makes the decision during execution. We represent decision points using the Recognition Strategy Language (RSL), introduced in Section 2. Decision functions themselves may be implemented in any programming language. Section 3 presents new metrics computed using the decision history recorded by RSL programs during execution. An analysis of two published algorithms for table-cell detection [5][7] demonstrates how the technique provides novel insights into algorithm performance, and valuable information for algorithm optimization (Section 4).

2   The Recognition Strategy Language

We represent algorithm decision points as a sequence of operations in the *Recognition Strategy Language* (RSL) [23]. RSL is a scripting language that coordinates the recognition process, maintaining a set of current interpretations while invoking decision functions at run time. In RSL, *what* the algorithm decides is represented separately from *how* the algorithm makes the decisions (see Fig. 1). The six primary decision types are *adaptation* of recognition parameters, *classification* of input regions (e.g. bounding boxes), *segmentation* of input regions, *formation of relations* among regions, *rejection* of parts of an interpretation, and *acceptance/rejection* of complete interpretations.

Each decision point formally defines a decision type, decision function call, and the input and output space of the decision. In Fig. 2, the first decision point takes the set of *Word* regions provided in the input, and then returns one or more sets of *Word* pairs representing horizontal adjacencies (i.e. updating the binary relation *hor_adj*); if

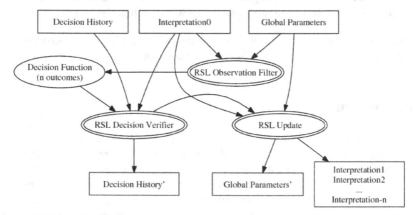

Fig. 1. An RSL decision point. Here a *decision function* produces *n* interpretations for a single input interpretation. Each possible decision outcome contains one or more legal alternatives for the decision type (e.g. valid classes for a classification). The decision-making environment includes a decision history, global parameter set, and RSL book-keeping operations. These operations control the visibility of parameters and interpretations for decision functions, verify outcomes, and update the history, global parameters, and interpretation set.

more than one set of *Word* pairs is returned, RSL produces multiple interpretations (see Fig. 1). This decision is made by the external function *selectHorizAdjRegions*, which is passed the *Word* regions and the parameter *sMaxHorDistance* (the prefix *s* indicates 'static,' i.e. a constant). The second decision point (the *segment* operation) will be applied to *each* of the interpretations output by the previous decision. While not shown here, RSL provides a simple conditional statement to prevent interpretations from being modified at a decision point [23].

To ensure that decision inputs are explicit, RSL hides all interpretation elements and parameters not given in the decision type definition or decision function call. This allows dependencies between region types, relation types, and parameters to be determined by static analysis of RSL source code [23]. For example, at the second decision point (the *segment* decision) *Word* regions are visible, but the *hor_adj* relation must be indicated using the *observing* keyword to be visible to the external decision function (*segmentHorizAdjRegions*). *Classify* decisions have 'neither' (reject) defined by default. For example, *Cells* may be classified as *Header, Entry,* or neither at the third decision point shown in Fig. 2.

Interpretations are represented as attributed graphs, with nodes representing locations for regions of interest, which may have associated types (e.g. bounding box ROIs labeled as *Words* and/or *Cells*), and edges representing region relationships [23]. For example, the built-in RSL *contains* relation encodes region membership, such as the *Cell* regions that belong to a *Column* region.

Decision functions may be implemented in any programming language, provided they are 'wrapped' in order to accept interpretations and parameters from RSL and return text-based decision records. We have prototyped an RSL implementation using the TXL source transformation language [3].

A sequence of decisions produces an *interpretation tree* that RSL records through the history of decision outcomes (see Fig. 1), and by annotating changes directly within interpretations themselves. Every region and relation hypothesis in an interpretation is annotated with a list of the decisions that accepted or rejected it. For example, the annotation "H 1 -2 3" represents acceptance by decision 1, rejection

---

```
model regions
    *REGION Word Cell Header
            Entry Image
end regions

model relations
    *contains adj_right close_to
end relations

recognition parameters
    sMaxHorDistance 5.0    % mms
    aMaxColSep 20.0        % mms
    aMaxHorSep 25.0        % mms
end parameters
```

```
strategy main
    relate { Word } regions with { hor_adj } using
        selectHorizAdjRegions(sMaxHorDistance)

    segment { Word } regions into { Cell }
        using segmentHorizAdjRegions()
        observing { hor_adj } relations

    classify { Cell } regions as { Header, Entry }
        using labelColumnHeaderAndEntries()

    accept interpretations
end strategy
```

Fig. 2. RSL program recognizing table *Cell* regions from *Word* regions. The *model* section defines legal region and relation types. *Recognition parameters* are constants and variables used by the external decision functions. The RSL *strategy function* '*main*' defines the sequence of decision points, here using *relate, segment, classify* and *accept* decision types.

by decision 2, and reinstatement by decision 3 (e.g., for a *Cell* comprised of *Word* regions). This information is used to compute new performance metrics described in Sections 3-4.

For white-box analysis of an *existing* program, decision points to be observed are coded in RSL, which invoke 'wrapped' decision functions called by the RSL program. If analysis is based on published algorithm descriptions, then re-implementation of the decision functions is needed; this is how we carried out the evaluation of table-cell detection algorithms in Section 4, using TXL to program the decision functions. The granularity of decision points can be chosen freely. To model the system as a handful of coarse components, use a small number of decision functions that perform complex computations. To model the system in greater detail, use a large number of simpler decision functions.

3   Decision-Based Performance: Historical Recall and Precision

The accuracy of individual decisions in an RSL program can be determined using the decision history. The RSL source location of decisions that produce false-positive and false-negative hypotheses can also be determined, as discussed in Section 4. Using existing programming practices, it is difficult to obtain this kind of information, because decision points are not explicit in the code, and intermediate decision information is not available in the output.

Recall and precision are commonly used metrics for evaluating detection tasks. *Recall* is the percentage of ground truth hypotheses present in an interpretation, whereas *precision* is the percentage of accepted hypotheses that match ground truth. We may also use historical versions of these measures, which account for rejected hypotheses [22]. Both conventional and historical recall and precision can be evaluated at any point during algorithm execution. The relationship between conventional and historical recall and precision is illustrated in Fig. 3.

Recall is defined by $|TP| / |GT|$, whereas precision is defined as $|TP| / |A|$. *Historical recall* also takes valid rejected hypotheses into account ($|TP \cup FN| / |GT|$), while *historical precision* takes false negatives into account along with the complete set of generated hypotheses ($|TP \cup FN| / |A \cup R|$). If an algorithm never rejects hypotheses ($R = \varnothing$), then the conventional and historical versions of recall and precision are the same. Historical recall is always greater than or equal to recall: historical recall never decreases during execution, whereas recall can decrease as hypotheses are rejected. Precision measures the accuracy of *accepted* hypotheses, while historical precision measures the accuracy of *generated* hypotheses.

Here we discuss only historical recall and precision. Corresponding historical versions of other black-box evaluation metrics can be defined, for example, weighted recall and precision metrics using areas of region overlap [1][10]; Vector Detection Rate, Vector False Alarm Rate, and Vector Recovery Rate used in the GREC arc segmentation contests [19]; and other performance metrics used in document-image analysis competitions [2].

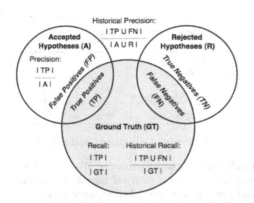

A   The set of accepted hypotheses

R   The set of hypotheses that were accepted and later rejected. At any given time, a hypothesis is accepted or rejected, but not both

GT   A set of ground-truth declarations

TP   The set of true positives, $A \cap GT$

FN   The set of false negatives, $R \cap GT$

Fig. 3. Recall, Precision, Historical Recall, and Historical Precision

4 Illustration: Evaluating Algorithms for Table-Cell Detection

To illustrate the new information provided by white-box analysis, we present an error analysis for cell detection performed by two table-recognition algorithms: Handley [5] and Hu et al. [7], which we refer to as "the Handley algorithm" and "the Hu algorithm" respectively. We chose the Handley [5] and Hu [7] algorithms for our study because they are described in enough detail to permit replication, and exhibit a degree of sophistication.

In this comparison, table-cell detection involves combining *Word* regions to form *Cell* regions, as illustrated in Fig. 4. For our experiments, the input contains *Word* regions, and may also contain *Line* regions if the table is ruled. Our evaluations use test data for which the ground-truth is known; difficulties with defining table ground truth are discussed in [6][12]. Further discussion of table recognition algorithms is presented in [4][9][13][18][21].

The Handley algorithm [5] is a geometry-based approach, making no use of the characters contained in *Word* regions. As illustrated in Fig. 5, the algorithm first hypothesizes that every *Word* region is a *Cell*. *Cell* regions are then merged in a series of steps using weighted projection profiles and cell adjacency relationships.

The Hu algorithm [7] ignores lines, and *Word* regions are classified as alphabetic or non-alphabetic, based on whether more than half the characters in the region are alphabetic. Columns are detected using a hierarchical clustering of the horizontal spans of *Word* regions. Next the table boxhead, stub and rows are located, and then header cells in the boxhead are identified (shown in Fig. 5, Decision 86). Finally cells in the body of the table are identified. We have added a simple step to define text-lines, by projecting *Word* regions onto the Y-axis and defining text-lines at gaps greater than a threshold value. This is necessary because the Hu algorithm is for text files, where text-lines are given.

We re-implemented the Handley and Hu algorithms in RSL and TXL using the published descriptions in [5] and [7] (Handley: 540 lines of RSL, 5000 lines of TXL; Hu: 240 lines of RSL, 3000 lines of TXL, in both cases including comments). For both algorithms, our choice of decision points was informed by the regions and relations that we wished to analyze. The RSL programs may be found elsewhere [20].

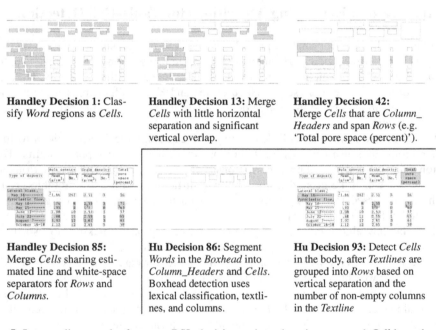

(a) *Word* and *Line* regions (input)   (b) Ground-truth *Cell* regions (ideal output)

Fig. 4. Illustration of the table-cell detection task used in our experiments: *Word* and *Line* regions (a) are analyzed to produce *Cell* regions, which are sets of *Word* regions (b). In our experiments, we manually delimit the *Word* and *Line* regions (a), labeling *Word* regions as alphabetic or other, and we also manually delimit the ground-truth *Cell* regions (b). This table is from page a038 of the University of Washington Database [15]

Handley Decision 1: Classify *Word* regions as *Cells*.

Handley Decision 13: Merge *Cells* with little horizontal separation and significant vertical overlap.

Handley Decision 42: Merge *Cells* that are *Column_ Headers* and span *Rows* (e.g. 'Total pore space (percent)').

Handley Decision 85: Merge *Cells* sharing estimated line and white-space separators for *Rows* and *Columns*.

Hu Decision 86: Segment *Words* in the *Boxhead* into *Column_Headers* and *Cells*. Boxhead detection uses lexical classification, textlines, and columns.

Hu Decision 93: Detect *Cells* in the body, after *Textlines* are grouped into *Rows* based on vertical separation and the number of non-empty columns in the *Textline*

Fig. 5. Intermediate results for some RSL decision points changing accepted *Cell* hypotheses, for the Handley and Hu algorithms given the table in Fig. 5. Gray *Cell* regions are incorrect (false positives), and unshaded *Cell* regions are correct (true positives). Handley Decision 1 accepts 75 cell hypotheses, of which 43 are incorrect. Handley Decision 13 accepts 8 hypotheses (of which 7 are correct) and rejects 16 hypotheses (all of which are incorrect).

4.1 Detailed Error Analysis For a Single Table

Intermediate recognition results can be easily captured when a decision-based algorithm representation is used. A visual display of intermediate states is illustrated in Fig. 5, showing the *Cell* hypotheses at selected decision points in the execution of the Handley and Hu algorithms.

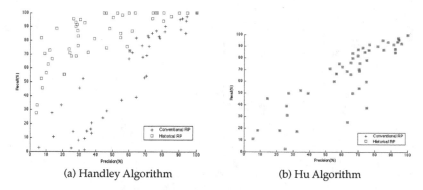

(a) Handley Algorithm   (b) Hu Algorithm

Fig. 6. Precision vs. Recall of *Cell* regions for the Handley (a) and Hu (b) algorithms (test set of 58 tables). Conventional recall and precision is shown by '+', and historical recall and precision by a box. Historical metrics characterize generated *Cell* regions, including those rejected.

From the recorded decision history, we can determine that Decision 42 for the Handley algorithm in Fig. 5 is particularly good: it accepts the only available hypothesis matching ground truth (the upper-right hand header cell), while rejecting two invalid hypotheses. In contrast, Handley Decision 85 (the final interpretation) creates 6 invalid hypotheses, and rejects 12 valid hypotheses. The Hu algorithm uses only two decisions to identify *Cell* regions: Hu Decision 86 identifies header cells, and Hu Decision 93 identifies cells in the table body. The visualizations in Fig. 5 were produced directly from RSL output, which includes decision times that can be matched to specific decision points in the RSL source. This directly locates the part of the source code that caused each recognition error. A decision that 'causes' an error in the output may have been influenced by a poor decision made earlier. Decision histories allow us to also observe which earlier decision points produced the alternatives considered at a decision point.

4.2 Comparing Conventional and Historical Metrics for a Set of Tables

We now compare conventional and historical recall and precision for the Handley and Hu algorithms, for a test set consisting of 58 tables taken from the University of Washington Database [15]. For the final interpretations produced by each algorithm, recall and precision information is shown for individual tables in Fig. 6, and for the test set in Fig. 7. We can see that the Handley algorithm generates far more ground truth cells during execution than are present in the final table interpretations. This is evident from Fig. 6a: the conventional recall for the final interpretations ('+') is generally lower than the historical recall. This is due to over-merging that follows the initial decision to label all *Word* regions as *Cell* regions. The Hu algorithm never discards *Cell* hypotheses, and as a result the historical and conventional recall and precision metrics are identical (Fig. 6b). The conventional metrics for the two algorithms are quite similar; the historical metrics show that the Handley algorithm generates many correct cells that the Hu algorithm does not.

Fig. 8 shows changes in *Cell* recall and precision at each decision manipulating *Cells* in our RSL implementation of the Handley algorithm. In each plot, the center

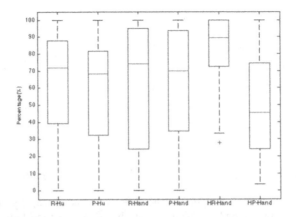

Fig. 7. Distribution of *Cell* detection metrics for Handley and Hu algorithms run on 58 tables. Shown from left to right are Hu recall and precision, Handley recall and precision, and historical recall and precision for the Handley algorithm.

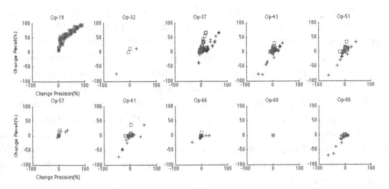

Fig. 8. Changes in precision and recall for *Cell* regions during execution of the Handley Algorithm on 58 tables. '+' show conventional recall vs. precision, and boxes show historical recall vs. precision. Op-19 is an RSL decision labeling all *Word* regions as *Cell* regions. Op-32 is only reached for tables classified as *fully-ruled*; it is executed for two tables in the test set. The following decisions are executed for the remaining 56 tables.

represents no change, with changes in conventional/historical recall shown on the Y-axis, and changes in conventional/historical precision shown on the X-axis. Decision point Op-37 has a positive effect for most tables, as measured by all metrics. In contrast, Op-80 has little effect on historical metrics, and little or negative effect on conventional metrics. Finally, Op-68 was executed for 56 tables, but had no effect.

These new performance summaries visualize patterns in what has been generated and thrown away, for both complete strategies and individual decision points. Along with the ability to identify decision points where specific errors are caused, we believe this information will be useful for machine learning algorithms that tune decision parameters in a recognition strategy, and produce new strategies by combining decision points from multiple strategies (e.g. via genetic algorithms).

5 Conclusion

The Recognition Strategy Language is a scripting language for specifying computer vision algorithms, separating high-level decision points from low-level decision functions expressed in any programming language. This decision-based approach captures intermediate interpretations, permitting white-box evaluation, identifying decisions that cause recognition errors, and analyzing the interaction of decisions. New metrics may be observed, such as *historical recall* and *historical precision*, which measure the set of all hypotheses generated as a decision point is reached. A combination of traditional and historical metrics can then be used to better understand final results and the behavior of individual decisions.

There are some limitations to how RSL may be effectively applied. For heavily numerical/statistical methods, or for decisions that employ significant iteration, it quickly becomes impractical if one records all intermediate values and states; this can be avoided by representing only the inputs and outputs at the outermost level within RSL. Another approach would be to allow the recording of decision outcomes to be modified or disabled using keywords. To improve the speed with which the RSL observation and updating operations are implemented (see Fig. 1), we are also considering producing an interface to 'wrap' the interpretation graphs for direct use by decision functions in various languages. Visible interpretation elements and parameters would be controlled in implementations of the interface for each decision at compile/interpret-time. Finally, we plan to re-implement the RSL compiler to produce Python, which has a number of numerical libraries and interfaces to computer vision libraries (e.g. OpenCV) readily available. This will permit new language features and make RSL useful for a larger group of students and researchers.

RSL is problem-neutral, and a variety of computer vision and pattern recognition algorithms can be represented using RSL. We intend to improve support for feature computations and matrices, develop additional metrics and evaluation methods based on decision histories, and explore constructing hybrid algorithms from existing algorithms implemented in RSL [23], e.g., using genetic algorithms to combine and evolve RSL strategies.

Acknowledgments

This research was supported by the Natural Sciences and Engineering Research Council of Canada, and by Xerox Corporation through University Affairs Committee Grants held by R. Zanibbi and D. Blostein. We also thank Andrew Seniuk for help preparing the test data.

References

[1] Cesarini, F., Marinai, S., Sarti, L., Soga, G.: Trainable Table Location in Document Images. In: Proc. Sixteenth Int'l Conf. Pattern Recognition, vol. 3, pp. 236–240 (2002)
[2] Competitions in Document Image Analysis Organized by ICDAR and GREC (2008), http://www.icdar2007.org/competition.html

[3] Cordy, J.: The TXL Source Transformation Language. Science of Computer Programming 61(3), 190–210 (2006)

[4] Embley, D., Hurst, M., Lopresti, D., Nagy, G.: Table-processing Paradigms: A Research Survey. Int'l J. Document Analysis and Recognition 8, 66–86 (2006)

[5] Handley, J.: Table Analysis for Multi-line Cell Identification. In: Proc. Doc. Rec. and Retrieval VIII (IS&T/SPIE Electronic Imaging), vol. 4307, pp. 34–43 (2001)

[6] Hu, J., Kashi, R., Lopresti, D., Nagy, G., Wilfong, G.: Why Table Ground-truthing is Hard. In: Proc. Sixth Int'l Conf. Document Analysis and Recognition, pp. 129–133 (2001)

[7] Hu, J., Kashi, R., Lopresti, D., Wilfong, G.: Table Structure Recognition and its Evaluation. In: Proc. Document Rec. and Retrieval VIII, SPIE, vol. 4307, pp. 44–55 (2001)

[8] Hu, J., Kashi, R., Lopresti, D., Wilfong, G.: Evaluating the Performance of Table Processing Algorithms. Int'l J. Document Analysis and Recognition 4(3), 140–153 (2002)

[9] Hurst, M.: Towards a Theory of Tables. Int'l J. Document Analysis and Recognition 8, 123–131 (2006)

[10] Kieninger, T., Dengel, A.: Applying the T-RECS Table Recognition System to the Business Letter Domain. In: Proc. Sixth ICDAR, pp. 518–522 (2001)

[11] Liang, J.: Document Structure Analysis and Performance Evaluation. PhD dissertation, Univ. Washington (1999)

[12] Lopresti, D.: Exploiting WWW Resources in Experimental Document Analysis Research. In: Lopresti, D.P., Hu, J., Kashi, R.S. (eds.) DAS 2002. LNCS, vol. 2423, p. 532. Springer, Heidelberg (2002)

[13] Lopresti, D.P., Nagy, G.: A tabular survey of automated table processing. In: Chhabra, A.K., Dori, D. (eds.) GREC 1999. LNCS, vol. 1941, pp. 93–120. Springer, Heidelberg (2000)

[14] Lopresti, D., Wilfong, G.: Evaluating Document Analysis Results via Graph Probing. In: Proc. Sixth Int'l Conf. Document Analysis and Recognition, pp. 116–120 (2001)

[15] Chen, P.S., Haralick, R.: CD-ROM Document Database Standard. In: Proc. Second Int'l Conf. Document Analysis and Recognition, pp. 478–483 (1993)

[16] Phillips, Chhabra, A.: Empirical Performance Evaluation of Graphics Recognition Systems. IEEE Trans. Pattern Analysis and Machine Intelligence 21(9), 849–870 (1999)

[17] Silva, A.E., Jorge, A., Torgo, L.: Design of an End-to-end Method to Extract Information from Tables. Int'l J. Document Analysis and Recognition 8, 144–171 (2006)

[18] Wang, X.: Tabular Abstraction, Editing and Formatting. PhD dissertation, Univ. Waterloo, Canada (1996)

[19] Wenyin, L., Dori, D.: A Protocol for Performance Evaluation of Line Detection Algorithms. Machine Vision and Applications 9(5/6), 240–250 (1997)

[20] Zanibbi, R.: A Language for Specifying and Comparing Table Recognition Strategies. PhD dissertation, School of Computing, Queen's Univ., Canada (2004)

[21] Zanibbi, R., Blostein, D., Cordy, J.R.: A Survey of Table Recognition: Models, Observations, Transformations, and Inferences. IJDAR 7(1), 1–16 (2004)

[22] Zanibbi, R., Blostein, D., Cordy, J.R.: Historical Recall and Precision: Summarizing Generated Hypotheses. In: Proc. Eighth ICDAR, vol. 2, pp. 202–206 (2005)

[23] Zanibbi, R., Blostein, D., Cordy, J.R.: Decision-Based Specification and Comparison of Table Recognition Algorithms. In: Machine Learning in Document Analysis and Recognition, pp. 71–103. Springer, Heidelberg (2008)

Evaluating the Suitability of Feature Detectors for Automatic Image Orientation Systems

Timo Dickscheid and Wolfgang Förstner

Department of Photogrammetry
Institute of Geodesy and Geoinformation
University of Bonn
dickscheid@uni-bonn.de, wf@ipb.uni-bonn.de

Abstract. We investigate the suitability of different local feature detectors for the task of automatic image orientation under different scene texturings. Building on an existing system for image orientation, we vary the applied operators while keeping the strategy fixed, and evaluate the results. An emphasis is put on the effect of combining detectors for calibrating difficult datasets. Besides some of the most popular scale and affine invariant detectors available, we include two recently proposed operators in the setup: A scale invariant junction detector and a scale invariant detector based on the local entropy of image patches. After describing the system, we present a detailed performance analysis of the different operators on a number of image datasets. We both analyze ground-truth-deviations and results of a final bundle adjustment, including observations, 3D object points and camera poses. The paper concludes with hints on the suitability of the different combinations of detectors, and an assessment of the potential of such automatic orientation procedures.

1 Introduction

1.1 Motivation

Automatic image orientation has become mature even in close-range and wide-baseline scenarios with significant perspective distortions between overlapping views. Fully automatic solutions of the relative orientation problem are available for such cases, relying on rotation and scale invariant [1] or even fully affine invariant correspondence detection techniques [2,3,4]. Such systems however do not always perform well: It will turn out that the suitability of detectors varies especially depending on the 3D structure and texturedness of the surfaces.

The applications of automatic image orientation are manifold. Examples are the alignment overlapping subsets of unordered image collections, known as the "stitching problem", which requires to recover the relative positioning of the cameras [5], or the automatic computation of 3D scene models from images, where one needs accurate estimates of the extrinsics for computing dense 3D point clouds.

M. Fritz, B. Schiele, and J.H. Piater (Eds.): ICVS 2009, LNCS 5815, pp. 305–314, 2009.

Fig. 1. Some example images of the datasets used. Top left: ENTRY-P10, top right: HERZ-JESU-P25, bottom left: EMPTY-2, bottom right: GLCUBE-TEXTURE/GLCUBE-COAST.

For evaluating variations of an automatic image orientation system, one may consider two cases: (i) Given a fixed strategy, what is the impact of different operators on the result? (ii) Given a specific operator, how successful are different strategies in solving the problem? In this contribution, we are concerned with (i) and leave the orientation strategy fixed.

We will continue by giving a short overview on the state of the art in local feature detection and automatic image orientation, before describing the system used for this evaluation in section 2, together with the applied keypoint detectors. The experimental setup is detailed in section 3, followed by an analysis of the results in 4. We conclude with a short summary and outlook in section 5.

1.2 Related Work

Fully automated systems for solving the relative orientation problem are available since several years [6,7,8]. The procedure used in our experiments is based on [9], which uses Lowe features [1] for automatic correspondence detection, and related to the approach of [10]. There is a lot of recent work on optimizing such procedures. To only mention a few, in [11] it was shown how to connect pairwise epipolar geometries by first registering the rotations and then globally optimizing the translation vectors in a robust manner, while the authors of [12] use a small Bayesian network for pairwise correspondences in image triples in order to make efficient and statistically sound use of the correspondence information.

Several good feature detectors have been established in the last years. Beyond the classical junction detectors [13,14], based on the second moment matrix computed from the squared gradients, the influential work of Lowe [1] showed that robust automatic correspondence detection is possible under significant illumination and viewpoint changes. Lowe uses a detector searching for local maxima of the Laplacian scale space, yielding scale invariant dark and bright blobs, and computes highly distinctive yet robust "SIFT" descriptors for these local image patches. Subsequent developments brought detectors with invariance under affine distortions for blobs and regions [2,3,4], which is favorable under very strong viewpoint changes. Recently, a robust scale-invariant junction detector has also been proposed [15]. All these detectors can just as well exploit the power of SIFT descriptors for automatic correspondence analysis.

2   A System for Automatic Image Orientation

2.1   Image Orientation Strategy

We follow the scheme published in [9] which will be shortly summarized here. As an input, we assume an unsorted set of N overlapping images with known intrinsics, along with a set of K_n local features each, i.e. $F_{nk} = \{x_{nk}, y_{nk}, \theta_{nk}, \mathbf{d}_{nk}\}$ with $0 < n \leq N$ and $0 < k < K_i$. Here, (x_{nk}, y_{nk}) is the location of the k-th feature in the domain of image n, and θ_{nk} is an additional geometric description of the feature window, possibly its scale σ_{nk} or a matrix A_{nk} containing complete ellipse parameters. The $1 \times M$-vector $\mathbf{d}_{nk}$ is a distinctive description of the feature, in our case a SIFT descriptor [1] with $M = 128$. It is computed over the local neighborhood coded by θ_{nk}.

The procedure starts by comparing descriptors of all possible image pairs (n, m), yielding sets $C_{nm} = \{(p, q) \mid 0 < p < K_n, \ 0 < q < K_m\}$ of initial correspondences. As the intrinsics are assumed to be known, we compute the relative orientation of each image pair using Nister's 5-Point algorithm [16] embedded into a RANSAC scheme [17,18]. This computation step not only allows for robust approximate values for the pairwise epipolar geometries (denoted as EG's in the following), but also acts as a filter on the initial correspondences, usually yielding updated sets C_{nm} with significantly reduced outlier rates.

Based on the filtered sets C_{nm}, we can now directly determine multiview correspondences from the pairs through simple index propagation. The EG's for image pairs are then connected in an iterative manner, prioritized by their quality, which is based on the number of valid coplanarity constraints. Note that some 3-fold correspondences are required to determine the scale between connected EG's. The system only yields one set of connected image orientations: In case that no further EG can be connected, the procedure stops, regardless of another isolated EG cluster.

Subsequently, triplet tests are carried out for further elimination of invalid EG's: For each triple of connected orientations, the product of their rotation matrices has to equal the identity matrix, and the baselines have to be coplanar. After determining 3D object points from the multiview correspondences, the whole block is optimized by a sparse bundle adjustment [19].

2.2   Applied Feature Detectors

Other than proposed in [9], we try different input feature sets F_{nk}. This is motivated by the fact that the Lowe detector (denoted as LOWE in the following) alone is not always the best choice, though most often a good one. Consider the image pair in the bottom left of Fig. 1: The amount of texture is critically low here, and it will turn out that the system is not able to successfully process the whole dataset using only LOWE. We will therefore also present experimental results obtained when using the popular Harris and Hessian affine detectors [2], denoted by HARAF and HESAF, and the Maximally Stable Extremal Regions detector [3, MSER]. Furthermore, we use a scale-invariant junction detector as recently proposed in [15]. Note that the junction features are only a subset of the detector output, determined by restricting to $\alpha = 0$ in [15, eq. (7)]. Lastly we include a new detector based on information theory, which will be described shortly in the following.

*Maximum-entropy-detector (*ENTROPY*).* The maximum entropy detector has been proposed in [20]. It is motivated by the idea of good image coding: We search for local patches of varying size, centered at each pixel position, with locally maximal entropy. Therefore at each position $(\mathbf{x}, \sigma, \tau)$ in the 3D scale space obtained by fixing $\sigma = 3\tau$, we compute

$$H\left(\mathbf{x}, \sigma, \tau\right) = k \sqrt{\frac{\lambda_2(M; \tau, \sigma)}{V_{\mathbf{x}}(\sigma)} \log^2 \left(\frac{V_{\mathbf{x}}(\sigma)}{V_n(\tau)}\right)} \tag{1}$$

Here, $V_{\mathbf{x}}$ denotes the variance of the image intensities within the patch, which can be determined by averaging finite differences of the grayvalues, and V_n is the noise variance at the respective scale level, which can be analytically determined from a given noise estimate of the original image. The result is up to an unknown factor k, which does not affect the maximum search.

3   Experiments

Image Data. We report results for six image datasets, providing a range of different texturings and surface types:

1. The ENTRY-P10- and HERZ-JESU-P25-datasets provided by the authors of [10], at reduced resolutions of 512×768 and 256×384 [pel], respectively (see top row of Fig. 1). The datasets are provided with ground-truth projection matrices. We included HERZ-JESU-P25 especially for having a dataset with full 3D structure, following [21] who pointed out that this is a critical aspect of detector evaluations.
2. Our own EMPTY-1- and EMPTY-2-datasets with a resolution of 512×768 [pel] showing indoor scenes with very low amount of texture (bottom left of Fig. 1). These especially difficult datasets are a challenge for state-of-the-art orientation procedures.
3. Two artificial datasets GLCUBE-TEXTURE and GLCUBE-COAST resulting from a 3D graphics simulation of a cube observed from inside, with natural images as wallpaper textures, rendered at a resolution of 600×800 [pel]. For the texturing we have chosen samples of well-known image datasets from texture analysis and scene category recognition [22,23]. One example pair of each set is shown on the bottom right of Fig. 1.

Investigated feature sets. We computed results (i) for each of the detectors individually, (ii) for all possible pairs complementing LOWE and SFOP, and (iii) for some promising combinations of three or four detectors. The settings of the orientations procedure were otherwise kept constant. The focus on LOWE and SFOP among the pairwise combinations is chosen due to the limited space in the paper, considering that LOWE and SFOP have shown to be most successful.

Indicators. After automatically computing the relative orientation of the images with the system described in section 2.1, we analyzed the following key indicators for each of the combinations and datasets:

1. The percentage P_O of successfully oriented images w. r. t. the overall number of images in a dataset, indicating success in calibrating the whole dataset.
2. The average standard deviation of observations $\hat{\sigma}_{x'}$ as estimated by the bundle adjustment, reflecting the accuracy of observations.
3. The average number $\overline{N}_I$ of 3D object points observed in an image, indicating the stability of the estimated orientation for each particular image.
4. The average number $\overline{N}_O$ of independent observations of the 3D object points in overlapping images, indicating stability of the estimated camera poses.
5. The ratio C between the convex hull of observations and the image plane, as an indicator for good coverage of the image with observations.
6. The average deviation $\overline{D}_{X_0}$ of the estimated projection centers from the ground truth, where available, giving insight into the quality of the estimation.

Note that the differences $\overline{D}_{X_0}$ are computed after a coordinate transformation of the estimated frames into the coordinate system of the ground truth data, using the least squares solution proposed in [24].

As the results vary due to the RANSAC component of the system, we show average values over ten repeated estimates throughout the paper, along with the corresponding standard deviations depicted by black markers.

4   Results

Overall Suitability for Image Orientation. From Fig. 2 we see that not all datasets were successfully calibrated using separate detectors. Only the SFOP detector seems to handle all considered situations. ENTROPY at least solved the problem for all but EMPTY-2. The LOWE and MSER detectors work well with good and medium amount of texture, but yield incomplete results on the difficult EMPTY-2 and EMPTY-1 datasets. Both the HARAF and HESAF detectors yield incomplete results in all cases. Using combinations of two or three detectors however, we were usually able to get complete estimates. Only for EMPTY-2 and EMPTY-1, either LOWE, SFOP or ENTROPY were required for a successful combination.

Using the combination of LOWE and HESAF on GLCUBE-COAST, only 80% of the cameras were calibrated on average, although LOWE alone worked well.

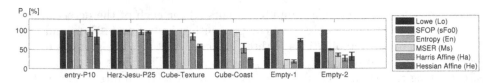

Fig. 2. Percentage P_O of successfully oriented cameras w. r. t. the overall number of cameras per dataset for individual detectors. Throughout the paper, the coloured bars show the mean over 10 repeated estimates, while the black bars denote the standard deviation.

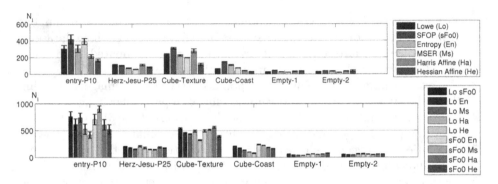

Fig. 3. Average number $\overline{N}_I$ of observed object points per image for individual detectors (top) and pairwise combinations (bottom)

Such negative interaction between two detectors is otherwise rarely observed. We believe that this is due to the fact that both detectors are based on the Laplacian, thus having highly redundant feature sets. One might hence conclude that combinations of very similar detectors should be avoided.

Repeatability and Amount of Observations. The average number $\overline{N}_I$ of object points observed in an image is often highest for SFOP among individual detectors (Fig. 3), while usually some of the other detectors yield comparable scores on particular datasets. On HERZ-JESU-P25 however, LOWE proves best. HESAF has the lowest score in many datasets. In case of pairwise combinations, the $\overline{N}_I$ approximately add as expected. The average number $\overline{N}_O$ of independent observations is significantly better for SFOP junction points on EMPTY-2 and EMPTY-1 (Fig. 4). It is an indicator for the repeatability, and underlines the importance of junction points for processing images of such scenes with poor texture. For combinations of detectors, we get mostly threefold points on average.

Average Accuracy of Observations. The average estimated standard deviation $\widehat{\sigma}_{x'}$ of the observations is worse for ENTROPY and HESAF compared to that of other detectors (Fig. 5). For ENTROPY this may be caused by the lack of a geometric model for the point location, as it is conceptually a window detector. For HESAF we believe that better accuracy could be achieved when using an

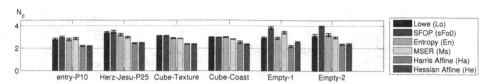

Fig. 4. Average number $\overline{N}_O$ of independent observations of 3D object points

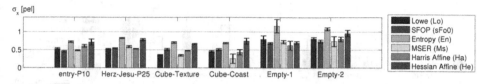

Fig. 5. Average estimated standard deviation $\widehat{\sigma}_{x'}$ of observations for individual detectors

improved subpixel localization method, as the points are conceptually similar to LOWE.

The accuracy of MSER features is noticeably strong on GLCUBE-COAST and GLCUBE-TEXTURE. This is especially interesting because a good performance of MSER on planar surfaces has been reported in other evaluations as well. It is also remarkable that the scores for SFOP are among the best ones on EMPTY-2 and EMPTY-1, although the other detectors did only calibrate part of the images here, usually the subset with less difficult texturings.

For combinations of detectors, the differences vanish due to the averaging.

Image Coverage. We see in Fig. 6 that SFOP and ENTROPY best cover the image with features in case of GLCUBE-COAST, EMPTY-2 and EMPTY-1, which all show rather poor texturedness. On the other datasets they are slightly outperformed by MSER, while LOWE yields very similar results.

Accuracy of Estimated Camera Poses. Comparing the estimated projection centers to the ground truth poses for individual operators (Fig. 7 top), we see that the overall best results are achieved by SFOP and MSER, again with a special suitability of MSER for the planar surfaces. LOWE also yields very good results, but falls back on the smoothly textured GLCUBE-COAST dataset, which also relates to the low number of object points achieved here (Fig. 3). Taking also into account its overall performance on EMPTY-2 and EMPTY-1, it seems that the LOWE detector is more suited for images with high texturedness. ENTROPY performs especially well on the HERZ-JESU-P25 dataset, which is quite surprising as neither the standard deviation $\widehat{\sigma}_{x'}$ nor the number of object points $\overline{N}_I$ was noticeable here. A reasonable explanation for this might be good geometric alignment of the features.

Combining detector pairs significantly improves the results, making them almost all acceptable. However, the pairwise combination of LOWE and HESAF is again conspicuous: While the poor results for HESAF and HARAF (see the

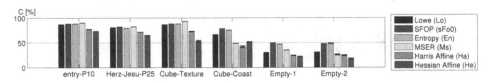

Fig. 6. Average area C [%] of the convex hull of image observations w. r. t. image area

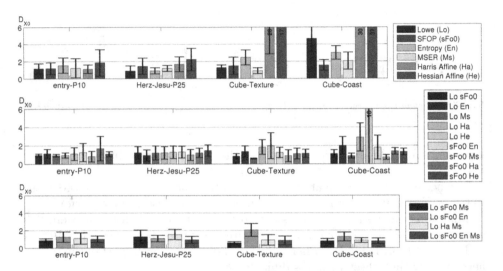

Fig. 7. Average squared distance $\overline{D}_{X_0}$ of reconstructed projection centers w. r. t. ground truth after a transformation into the coordinate system of the ground truth data

top row of Fig. 7) are mostly compensated when combined with other detectors, combining LOWE and HESAF does not seem to be beneficial, especially on GLCUBE-COAST (see second row of Fig. 7 on the right). The triple combinations however are all very stable, but combining LOWE with SFOP and MSER is noticeably the most promising setting.

5   Conclusion

The applied detectors showed quite different performance on the datasets. In particular, the EMPTY-2 and EMPTY-1 datasets with small amount of texture could not be successfully processed by most of the detectors individually, except by the proposed SFOP detector. The latter one showed overall best performance in the sense that it yielded good results on all indicators and datasets.

Under medium or high texturedness of the images, LOWE, MSER, SFOP and ENTROPY are all suitable operators for the orientation problem considered here. The MSER detector showed special strength on planar surfaces, where it delivered very good localization accuracy and repeatability. The HESAF and HARAF detectors however did not reach the same performance as other detectors in our setting. Especially HESAF gave rather weak scores under many indicators; however, from the close relationship to LOWE, we believe that an enhanced subpixel localization and non-maximum suppression might improve the results.

The ENTROPY detector showed worse localization accuracy on the datasets compared to others, but nonetheless yielded acceptable estimation results compared to the ground truth data which may be due to good geometric alignment of the points. This is also indicated by very good coverage of the image area with observations.

Using combinations of features solves most of the problems observed in the individual cases, especially allowing for complete successful orientations, with few exceptions. The overall best results are achieved when combining sFOP with LOWE, possibly complemented by the MSER or ENTROPY detector. Besides computational complexity, negative effects seem to occur only when combining very similar detectors like LOWE and HESAF, which are both based on the Laplacian. This suggests that one should account for the complementarity of feature detectors when combining them; a topic which has been recently addressed in [25].

References

1. Lowe, D.G.: Distinctive Image Features from Scale-Invariant Keypoints. International Journal of Computer Vision 60(2), 91–110 (2004)
2. Mikolajczyk, K., Schmid, C.: Scale and Affine Invariant Interest Point Detectors. International Journal of Computer Vision 60(1), 63–86 (2004)
3. Matas, J., Chum, O., Urban, M., Pajdla, T.: Robust Wide Baseline Stereo from Maximally Stable Extremal Regions. Image and Vision Computing 22, 761–767 (2004)
4. Tuytelaars, T., Van Luc, G.: Matching Widely Separated Views Based on Affine Invariant Regions. International Journal of Computer Vision 59(1), 61–85 (2004)
5. Snavely, N., Seitz, S.M., Szeliski, R.: Photo tourism: Exploring photo collections in 3d. In: SIGGRAPH Conference Proceedings, pp. 835–846. ACM Press, New York (2006)
6. Pollefeys, M., Koch, R., Vergauwen, M., Van Gool, L.: Automated Reconstruction of 3D Scenes from Sequences of Images. ISPRS Journal Of Photogrammetry And Remote Sensing 55(4), 251–267 (2000)
7. Mayer, H.: Robust Least-Squares Adjustment Based Orientation and Auto-Calibration of Wide-Baseline Image Sequences. In: ISPRS Workshop BenCOS 2005, Bejing, China, pp. 11–17 (2005)
8. Roth, D. G.: Automatic Correspondences for Photogrammetric Model Building. In: Proceedings of the XXth ISPRS Congress, Istanbul, Turkey, pp. 713–718 (July 2004)
9. Läbe, T., Förstner, W.: Automatic Relative Orientation of Images. In: Proceedings of the 5th Turkish-German Joint Geodetic Days, Berlin (March 2006)
10. Strecha, C., von Hansen, W., Van Gool, L., Fua, P., Thoennessen, U.: On Benchmarking Camera Calibration and Multi-View Stereo for High Resolution Imagery. In: IEEE Conference on Computer Vision and Pattern Recognition (CVPR 2008), Anchorage, Alaska (2008)

11. Martinec, D., Pajdla, T.: Robust Rotation and Translation Estimation in Multiview Reconstruction. In: IEEE Conference on Computer Vision and Pattern Recognition (CVPR 2007), Minneapolis, USA (2007)
12. Zach, C., Irschara, A., Bischof, H.: What Can Missing Correspondences Tell Us about 3D Structure and Motion? In: IEEE Conference on Computer Vision and Pattern Recognition (CVPR 2008), Anchorage, Alaska (2008)
13. Harris, C., Stephens, M.J.: A Combined Corner and Edge Detector. In: Alvey Vision Conference, pp. 147–152 (1988)
14. Förstner, W., Gülch, E.: A Fast Operator for Detection and Precise Location of Distinct Points, Corners and Centres of Circular Features. In: ISPRS Conference on Fast Processing of Photogrammetric Data, Interlaken, pp. 281–305 (June 1987)
15. Förstner, W., Dickscheid, T., Schindler, F.: Detecting Interpretable and Accurate Scale-Invariant Keypoints. In: 12th IEEE International Conference on Computer Vision (ICCV 2009), Kyoto, Japan (2009)
16. Nister, D.: An Efficient Solution to the Five-Point Relative Pose Problem. In: IEEE Transactions on Pattern Analysis and Machine Intelligence, vol. 26, pp. 756–777. IEEE Computer Society Press, Los Alamitos (2004)
17. Fischler, M.A., Bolles, R.C.: Random Sample Consensus: A Paradigm for Model Fitting with Applications to Image Analysis and Automated Cartography. Communications of the ACM 24(6), 381–395 (1981)
18. Hartley, R., Zisserman, A.: Multiple View Geometry in Computer Vision. Cambridge University Press, Cambridge (2004)
19. Lourakis, M.I.A., Argyros, A.A.: Design and Implementation of a Sparse Bundle Adjustment Software Library Based on the Levenberg-Marquardt Algorithm. Technical report, Heraklion, Crete, Greece (August 2004)
20. Förstner, W.: Local entropy of an image patch. Note (2009)
21. Moreels, P., Perona, P.: Evaluation of Features Detectors and Descriptors Based on 3D Objects. International Journal of Computer Vision 73(3), 263–284 (2007)
22. Lazebnik, S., Schmid, C., Ponce, J.: A Sparse Texture Representation Using Local Affine Regions. IEEE Transactions on Pattern Analysis and Machine Intelligence 27(8), 1265–1278 (2005)
23. Svetlana, L., Cordelia, S., Jean, P.: Beyond Bags of Features: Spatial Pyramid Matching for Recognizing Natural Scene Categories. In: IEEE Conference on Computer Vision and Pattern Recognition (CVPR 2006), Washington, DC, USA, pp. 2169–2178 (2006)
24. Arun, K.S., Huang, T.S., Blostein, S.D.: Least-squares Fitting of Two 3D Point Sets. IEEE Transactions on Pattern Analysis and Machine Intelligence 9(5), 698–700 (1987)
25. Förstner, W., Dickscheid, T., Schindler, F.: On the Completeness of Coding with Image Features. In: 20th British Machine Vision Conference, London, UK (2009)

Interest Point Stability Prediction

H. Thomson Comer and Bruce A. Draper

Computer Science Department
Colorado State University
Fort Collins, CO 80523 USA
thomcom@gmail.com, draper@cs.colostate.edu

Abstract. Selective attention algorithms produce more interest points than are usable by many computer vision applications. This work suggests a method for ordering and selecting a subset of those interest points, simultaneously increasing the repeatability of that subset. The individual repeatability of a combination of 10^6 SIFT, Harris-Laplace, and Hessian-Laplace interest points are predicted using generalized linear models (GLMs). The models are produced by studying the 17 attributes of each interest point. Our goal is not to improve any particular algorithm, but to find attributes that affect affine and similarity invariance regardless of algorithm. The techniques explored in this research enable interest point detectors to improve mean repeatability of their algorithm by 4% using a rank-ordering produced by a GLM or by thresholding interest points using a set of five new thresholds. Selecting the top 1% of GLM-ranked Harris-Laplace interest points results in a repeatability improvement of 6%, to 92.4%.

Keywords: Selective attention, interest points, affine invariance, SIFT.

1 Introduction

Many computer vision systems extract information from large, complex visual scenes. One popular approach is to reduce the data by concentrating on a small set of interest points, sometimes referred to as selective attention windows, local features, image regions, keypoints or extrema. Interest points are distorted less by changes in viewpoint than full images are, and therefore provide repeatable clues to the contents of a scene.

This work looks at properties of interest points extracted by three popular algorithms: Lowe's SIFT interest point detector [8] and the Harris-Affine and Hessian-Affine interest point detectors suggested by Mikolajczyk and Schmid [10,12]. The goal is to predict on a per-interest-point basis which interest points will be invariant to small affine transformations, and which will not. The underlying motivation for this work is that all three algorithms produce large numbers of interest points, often producing more points per image than an application (particularly a real-time application) can handle. As a result, many applications keep and process only a subset of interesting points. Our goal is to provide users with a method for selecting among interest points no matter which interest point

M. Fritz, B. Schiele, and J.H. Piater (Eds.): ICVS 2009, LNCS 5815, pp. 315–324, 2009.

algorithm is used, and for making intelligent trade-offs between increased interest point quantity or increased repeatability. This work may also lead to research into more repeatable algorithms by identifying the attributes that improve individual repeatability the most.

In particular, this work applies the three interest point detection algorithms mentioned above to randomly selected images from the CalTech-101 database [2]. To determine if a point is repeatable, we extract interest points from images before and after the images are subjected to small, randomly selected affine transformations. If the same image position and scale (relative to the transformation) are detected in both images, then the point is said to be repeatable. We measure the repeatability of over one million points in this way. For each point we measure 17 image attributes and fit a generalized linear model (GLM) to predict which points will repeat based on their image attributes. The weights in the resulting model tell us which attributes are most predictive of interest point repeatability.

We also analyze each of the 17 interest point attributes individually, and find that many attributes have a highly non-linear relation to repeatability. In particular, many attributes have a "normal" range which accounts for most samples, and that most of the samples in this range are repeatable. In addition, however, these attributes have "abnormal" ranges in which a smaller number of less reliable interest points fall. As a result, we can predict reliability by selecting a few well-placed thresholds on a few attributes and do almost as well as computing all 17 attributes and using the full GLM. These thresholds are an inexpensive and practical means for computer vision systems to select reliable interest points.

2   Interest Point Detectors

This paper focuses on three pivotal algorithms in selective attention research. The Difference-of-Gaussian (DOG) detection algorithm from Lowe's SIFT system is the most commonly used of all interest point detection algorithms. According to Google Scholar, it has been cited an astonishing 2.4 times *per day* since its publication. More recently, Mikolajczyk and Schmid [10,12] proposed two highly-repeatable algorithms as the basis of their affine-invariant technique. The first of these, the Harris-Laplace, is a multi-scale version of the well-tested Harris corner measure [4], one of the first point detection schemes to gain wide acceptance. The Hessian-Laplace point detector is a multi-scale technique based on second derivatives, and was the best performing derivative-based technique in a comparison of affine-invariant point detectors [14]. It should be noted many other interest point algorithms are also interesting but are outside the scope of this paper, including Matas et al.'s MSER algorithm [9] which performed as well as Hessian-Laplance in previous studies, and Kadir and Brady's Scale-salience algorithm [5,6], which is based on derivatives of entropy (Derivatives of entropy are among the 17 interest point attributes studied in this paper, however).

This paper does not rank interest point algorithms based on a black-box comparison; for such comparisons, see [1,14,11]. Instead, this paper measures attributes of individual interest points (no matter what algorithm they were generated by) and determines whether the repeatability of individual points can be predicted based on these measures.

David Lowe's algorithm approximates Lindeberg's characteristic scale detection [7] with a Difference-of-Gaussians (DOG) pyramid [8]. It selects interest points that are the extrema in the DOG filter response computed over an image pyramid. Lowe's DOG pyramid is able to find extrema in the scale space of an image similar to those found by Lindeberg's LOG. The run time of Lowe's DOG function is significantly improved over LOG by eliminating the convolution with an LOG filter. The DOG approach is the keypoint detection stage of an algorithm called Scale Invariant Feature Transform (SIFT), a popular constellation-of-features based object recognition technique.

Mikolajczyk proposes a new scale invariant interest point generator in his Ph.D. thesis [10]. The Harris-Laplace detector combines scale-sensitive Harris corners with Lindeberg's detection of the characteristic scale. Harris-Laplace uses the Harris corner detector to find maxima in the second moment matrix of first derivatives [4]. Those Harris points that are also extrema in the LOG are then accepted as keypoints. Mikolajczyk and Schmid proposed a similar algorithm using blob detection based on the Hessian second-derivative matrix in place of Harris corner points [13]. In this detector, called Hessian-Laplace, interest points are maximal simultaneously in the determinant and the trace of the Hessian matrix. We examine the features and performance of these two algorithms due to their performance in head-to-head competition with Lowe's algorithm and their recent popularity.

3   Repeatability Prediction

We first detect interest points in a source image and an affine transformed version of the source image, and determine which points appear in both images. We measure the repeatability of 10^6 interest points detected from randomly selected images in the CalTech-101 database [2]. Three algorithms are used for interest point detection: the DOG, Harris-Laplace, and Hessian-Laplace algorithms. While the previous authors suggest various thresholds for these algorithms, no thresholding is performed during interest point detection to increase the informativeness of the corresponding attributes and to verify the previous thresholding results. Interest points for each algorithm are generated on the exact same set of images and transformations. Table 1 shows the relative density, repeatability, and accuracy of interest points extracted by the three algorithms.

Interest points are considered to be repeats if the source and target point fall on the same or neighboring levels of scale space and within each others radii. This differs slightly from Draper and Lionelle [1] who use a set radius of 17 pixels and Mikolajczyk et al. [14,11] who require the distance between the source and

Table 1. Initial results verifying expected repeatability rates for each algorithm. The number of points per image varies considerably with algorithm. DOG, Harris-Laplace, and Hessian-Laplace produce an average of 4,000, 14,269, and 4,896 interest points per image, respectively.

type	number	repeatability	error	IPs/image
SIFT	311,149	88 %	0.31	3989
Harris-Laplace	1,112,983	85 %	0.32	14269
Hessian-Laplace	381,910	85 %	0.28	4896

target interest point be ≤ 1.5. Our repeatability measure is similar to Lowe [8] who allows matches within one-half an octave. Matching interest points up to one-third of an octave follows intuitively from using three levels per octave, allowing matches between neighboring levels only.

The image transformations are randomly selected. One quarter of the transformations are a rotation up to 90 degrees, one quarter undergo uniform scaling from 0.9 to 1.2, one quarter apply a -10% to 10% affine transformation, and one quarter randomly combine all three.

The quantity of Harris-Laplace interest points is the most notable difference between these algorithms. Harris-Laplace produces approximately 3.5 times more interest points than the other algorithms. The repeatability and error rates are similar to those found in [14]. We limit the number of interest points to 10^6 by randomly discarding $806,042$ Harris-Laplace interest points.

3.1   Attributes of Interest Points

In order to predict which points will repeat, seventeen attributes are recorded from each interest point. Each attribute comes from one of five attribute "families" that are based on interest point detection algorithms. Regardless of which algorithm detected a specific interest point, attributes are recorded from every attribute family. The five families of attributes are: position, Harris, Hessian, value, and entropy.

- Position attributes include *xpos*, *ypos*, and *zpos*. *xpos* and *ypos* are the position of the interest point, rescaled according to the image size to be in a range from 0 to 1.0. *zpos* is the position of an interest point in scale space, which for all three algorithms in these experiments we use three levels-per-octave.
- Harris attributes include *harlambda1*, the first eigenvalue of the second moment matrix, *harlambda2*, the second eigenvalue of the second moment matrix, and *hardeterminant*, their product.
- Hessian attributes include *heslambda1*, *heslambda2*, and *hesdeterminant*, where *heslambda1* is the first eigenvalue of the Hessian matrix, *heslambda2* is the second eigenvalue, and *hesdeterminant* is their product.
- Value attributes include *value*, *truevalue*, *dx2*, *dy2*, and *dz2*. The *value* attribute is different depending on which algorithm produced an interest point. For DOG interest points, $value = D(x, y, \sigma)$. For Harris-Laplace interest points, $value = R$, and for Hessian-Laplace interest points $value = \mathrm{DET}(H)$.

Our choice of DET(H) instead of TR(H) follows from the linear modeling of a GLM. Each interest point receives sub-pixel optimization according to Lowe such that *truevalue* = $D(\mathbf{x})$. Computing $D(\mathbf{x})$ provides us with a 3D quadratic, from which we compute $dx2$, $dy2$, and $dz2$. These are the second derivatives of $D(\mathbf{x})$ in the x,y, and z direction. These features describe local curvature around each interest point, regardless of algorithm.

- The interest point detectors used in this study are derivative based, rather than entropy, but we include entropy measures because of their relevance to interest point research (see Kadir and Brady [5,6] and Gilles [3]). In this family we include *entropy*, the entropy $\mathcal{H} = -\sum p(x) log_D p(x)$ of the region defined by each interest point. Also included are *dentropy* and *ddentropy*, the first and second derivatives of the local entropy with respect to scale.

Generalized linear modeling. As a first pass, univariate GLM models were fit to each individual attribute. Models were fit to the raw attribute values, and to three normalizations of the attributes: log-normalization of attributes with variances > 100, mean centering each sample and giving it unit length, and mean centering each sample and dividing by the variance of each attribute. Here we detail only log-normalization, which improves performance in some cases. Univariate models were evaluated by the correlation $r_{E(Y),Y}$ between the 10^6 fitted predictions of the GLM and the measured repeat/no repeat status of each interest point, and AUC, the area-under-curve of an ROC curve produced by points ranked according the their repeatability as predicted by the GLM. These univariate regressions proved not to be very interesting. The models produce $r_{E(Y),Y} \in [0, 0.08]$ and AUC $\in [0.48, 0.55]$, with no attribute producing significantly more interesting results than any other.

The results of the univariate analyses guide a number of multivariate analyses. A full multivariate analysis using all 17 attributes is seen in the first column of Table 2. We produced a variety of models using a subset of the seventeen attributes, the best performing of which is in column two of Table 2.

The coefficients in Table 2 are odds ratios. A priori is the intercept for each model. The three attributes with the greatest effect on repeatability are the second eigenvalue of the second moment matrix, the first eigenvalue of the Hessian matrix, and the local entropy of an interest point. Harris coefficients suggest that edges be minimized by maximizing the second eigenvalue and minimizing the first and their product. Hessian coefficients have a surprisingly inverse relationship to Harris. The first and second eigenvalues should both be optimized, but not simultaneously. Since the first eigenvalue is always dominant, it seems that interest points with a strong Hessian response in any direction are likely to repeat. Most interestingly, none of the detectors used in this research use entropy to select candidate interest points. The local entropy of an interest point is still highly informative, supporting and suggesting further work in entropy based detectors [3,5,6].

Two particular GLM fittings allow us to select a subset of interest points with repeatability better than the original detection algorithms from Table 1. Figure 1 shows the effect on repeatability of selecting the N-"best" interest

Table 2. Odds coefficients produced by a GLM trained to predict the repeatability of an interest point. A coefficient of 1.0 indicates the attribute has no effect on repeatability. Coefficients greater than one increase the probability of repeat as the corresponding attribute increases. Those less than one decrease that probability. All attributes x where $variance(x) > 100$ are normalized with $log(abs(x))$.

Attribute	LOG GLM	Small GLM	LOG(Harris) GLM
AUC	0.60	0.59	0.56
$r_{E(Y),Y}$	0.18	0.13	0.10
A priori	5.990	6.713	8.610
$xpos$	1.000		1.000
$ypos$	1.000		1.000
$zpos$	0.937	0.951	0.952
$log(harlambda1)$	0.933	1.000	0.981
$log(harlambda2)$	1.161	1.096	1.189
$log(hardeterminant)$	0.951		0.945
$log(heslambda1)$	1.187	1.003	
$log(heslambda2)$	1.092	0.970	
$log(hesdeterminant)$	0.876		
$entropy$	1.175		
$dentropy$	0.903	1.000	
$ddentropy$	1.071		
$log(value)$	1.104		
$log(truevalue)$	0.976		
$log(dx2)$	0.979		
$log(dy2)$	1.009		
$log(dz2)$	0.942		

points as predicted by the first two GLMs in Table 2 - the Log GLM and the Small GLM. The GLM produces a set of rank orderings. The interest points with the highest probability are the "best". Log GLM uses 11 log-normalized attributes and 6 un-normalized attributes, producing the best $r_{E(Y),Y}$ and AUC found in our experiments.

Small GLM is the set of attributes that were found to be most consistent across all three algorithms. The small GLM outperforms a multivariate GLM produced from the attributes with the highest $r_{E(Y),Y}$ and AUC in univariate experiments as well as a GLM using the six attributes with the largest coefficients from the *log* GLM experiment. This subset scores nearly as well in AUC and $r_{E(Y),Y}$ as modeling the set of all 17 attributes.

Harris-Laplace prediction. Interest points from each detector were fit to a GLM using only those attributes that are from that detector's attribute family. Of the three detectors, only Harris-Laplace interest points benefit significantly from rank-ordering using a GLM of the log-normalized Harris attributes. Column 3 of Table 2 includes coefficients for a log normalized GLM that can select the top percent of Harris interest points with 92.4% repeatability and the top tenth percentile with 90.6% (Figure 2). These coefficients should plug in to current

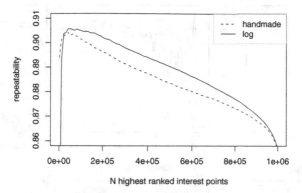

Fig. 1. Repeatability of the N-"best" interest points predicted by a GLM fit to six author selected attributes (small) and to a GLM fit to all 17 attributes (log) including log normalized Harris, Hessian, and value families

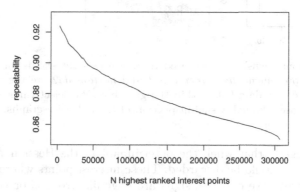

Fig. 2. Performance of a GLM on log normalized Harris attributes predicting the repeatability of only Harris-Laplace interest points

implementations of Harris-Laplace (and we suspect Harris-Affine) with immediate and significant repeatability improvement.

Thresholding. The use of thresholding to improve repeatability and decrease density is supported by Lowe [8] and Mikolajczyk [12]. Lowe recommends discarding interest points where the ratio between Hessian eigenvalues $r > 10$ and when the determinant of the Hessian is negative. Mikolajczyk suggests discarding interest points with Harris corner score $R < 1000$. This research, however, found that no R threshold improves repeatability. We extend on Lowe's thresholds by adding five additional thresholding decisions that improve repeatability performance.

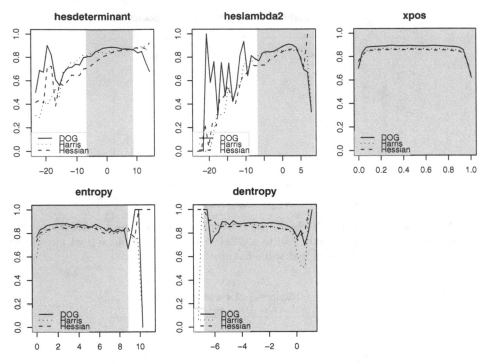

Fig. 3. Conditional density graphs used to create new thresholds for interest point repeatability improvement. *hesdeterminant* and *heslambda2* are the log-normalized attributes. 95% of the data falls within the grey box. We select thresholds where repeatability decreases through visual inspection of these density graphs.

Lowe [8] suggests that when the determinant of the Hessian H is negative the interest point should be discarded. These interest points where the first and second derivatives have opposite signs are edge-like troughs or ridges, instead of peaks. This implies that such interest points will be less repeatable and is well supported by our results. They have 83% repeatability and the points with positive Hessian determinants are 88.3% repeatable. If an application depends on a small number of highly repeatable interest points, discarding Harris-Laplace points according to this threshold is recommended.

We also test the repeatability of interest points for a range of $r = \frac{heslambda1}{heslambda2}$ to verify Lowe's use of $r < 10$. We find that $r < 5$ is most repeatable for DOG, Harris-Laplace, and Hessian-Laplace interest points. We apply the same experiment to the ratio of Harris eigenvalues and find that discarding interest points where that ratio is greater than 20 also improves repeatability slightly.

We estimate the conditional density probabilities that an interest point will repeat based on having a particular attribute scores. The graphs in Figure 3 suggest four new thresholds from this work that each increase repeatability. We include the conditional density graph of *hesdeterminant* to demonstrate the usefulness of this visualization technique.

We combine these results into the following set of seven thresholds which improve repeatability without the computational cost of a GLM:

- $hesdeterminant >= 0$
- $heslambda2 >= 0$
- $heslambda1/heslambda2 <= 5$
- $0.05 < \{xpos, ypos\} < 0.95$
- $harlambda1/harlambda2 <= 20$
- $entropy > 1$
- $dentropy < -1$

Retaining interest points that satisfy these seven inequalities from our set of 10^6 interest points increases mean repeatability from 86% to 90.4% while reducing the total number of interest points to $174, 291$. Thresholding in this fashion provides a fast and easy-to-implement solution to repeatability improvement. These thresholds can be applied only when applicable to the interest point detectors that depend on them or they can be computed for any interest point detector, improving the repeatability of that detector. Training a GLM using this thresholded data offers no improvement, suggesting that the two approaches model equivalent properties of the data.

4 Conclusions

This work models the repeatability of one million interest points with seventeen attributes using generalized linear models. We find three attributes with highest effect on repeatability. Two of these attributes, the first eigenvalue of the Harris and the second eigenvalue of the Hessian, are used by the interest point detectors in this research. Local entropy also has a large effect on repeatability though it is not used by the detectors in this study. Other attributes affect repeatability to a lesser degree.

It is possible to use GLMs to model the relationship between interest point attributes and their repeatability. A GLM using the log-normalized set of all 17 interest point attributes can increase the mean repeatability of a set of interest points by up to 5% while decreasing the density of that set by 50% or more. Another GLM using a set of only 6 author-selected attributes provides comparable performance with less computational complexity. Additionally, using the GLM specialized to Harris-Laplace can provide additional repeatability improvement to researchers who use this detector.

A set of simple thresholds provides a similar performance increase while avoiding the computational expense of fitting the data to a GLM and rank ordering. We support the previous thresholding recommendations of Lowe [8] and provide five additional thresholds that can improve repeatability with nearly identical performance to the GLMs while reducing the number of points by a factor of six. Achieving a set of extremely ($\approx$ 100%) repeatable interest points remains, however, a daunting task.

References

1. Draper, B., Lionelle, A.: Evaluation of selective attention under similarity transforms. In: Proc. of the Int'l Workshop on Attention and Performance in Computer Vision (WAPCV 2003), pp. 31–38 (2004)
2. Fei-Fei, L., Fergus, R., Perona, P.: Learning Generative Visual Models from Few Training Examples: An Incremental Bayesian Approach Tested on 101 Object Categories.. Computer Vision and Image Understanding 106(1), 59–70 (2007)
3. Gilles, S.: Robust Description and Matching of Images. PhD thesis, University of Oxford (1998)
4. Harris, C., Stephens, M.: A combined corner and edge detector. In: Alvey Vision Conference, vol. 15 (1988)
5. Kadir, T., Brady, M.: Saliency, Scale and Image Description. International Journal of Computer Vision 45(2), 83–105 (2001)
6. Kadir, T., Zisserman, A., Brady, M.: An affine invariant salient region detector. European Conference on Computer Vision 1, 228–241 (2004)
7. Lindeberg, T.: Feature Detection with Automatic Scale Selection. International Journal of Computer Vision 30(2), 79–116 (1998)
8. Lowe, D.: Distinctive image features from scale-invariant keypoints. International Journal of Computer Vision 20, 91–110 (2003)
9. Matas, J., Chum, O., Urban, M., Pajdla, T.: Robust wide-baseline stereo from maximally stable extremal regions. Image and Vision Computing 22(10), 761–767 (2004)
10. Mikolajczyk, K.: Interest point detection invariant to affine transformations. PhD thesis, Institut National Polytechnique de Grenoble (2002)
11. Mikolajczyk, K., Leibe, B., Schiele, B.: Local features for object class recognition. In: Proc. ICCV, vol. 2, pp. 1792–1799 (2005)
12. Mikolajczyk, K., Schmid, C.: An Affine Invariant interest Point Detector. In: Heyden, A., Sparr, G., Nielsen, M., Johansen, P. (eds.) ECCV 2002. LNCS, vol. 2350, pp. 128–142. Springer, Heidelberg (2002)
13. Mikolajczyk, K., Schmid, C.: Scale & Affine Invariant Interest Point Detectors. International Journal of Computer Vision 60(1), 63–86 (2004)
14. Mikolajczyk, K., Tuytelaars, T., Schmid, C., Zisserman, A., Matas, J., Schaffalitzky, F., Kadir, T., Gool, L.: A Comparison of Affine Region Detectors. International Journal of Computer Vision 65(1), 43–72 (2005)

Relevance of Interest Points for Eye Position Prediction on Videos

Alain Simac-Lejeune[1,2], Sophie Marat[1], Denis Pellerin[1], Patrick Lambert[2],
Michèle Rombaut[1], and Nathalie Guyader[1]

[1] Gipsa-lab, 961 rue de la Houille Blanche, BP 46, F-38402 Grenoble Cedex, France
[2] Listic (Université de Savoie), BP 80439 74944 Annecy-le-Vieux Cedex, France

Abstract. This papers tests the relevance of interest points to predict
eye movements of subjects when viewing video sequences freely. Moreover the papers compares the eye positions of subjects with interest maps
obtained using two classical interest point detectors: one spatial and one
space-time. We fund that in function of the video sequence, and more
especially in function of the motion inside the sequence, the spatial or
the space-time interest point detector is more or less relevant to predict
eye movements.

Keywords: spatial and space-time interest points, eye position.

1 Introduction

Images contain a very large amount of data, and image analysis often begins
by the selection of some "interest points" which are supposed to carry more
information than the rest of the pixels. The definition of these interest points is
quite subjective, and generally depends on the aim of the analysis.

In the case of still images, many interest point detectors had been proposed.
They are based on the detection of points having a significant local variation of
image intensities in different directions (corners, line endings, isolated points of
maximum - or minimum - local intensity, etc.). The most popular one is probably
the Harris detector [1], with scale adaptive versions ([2],[3]). Different Gaussian
based detectors have also been proposed - LoG (Laplacian of Gaussian), DoG
(Difference of Gaussians), DoH (Determinant of the Hessian). It can be noted
that DoG are used in the definition of the well known SIFT (Scale Invariant
Feature Transform) approach [4][5]. Successful applications of interest points
have been proposed in image indexing [6], stereo matching [7], object recognition
[4], etc.

Only a few interest point detectors had been defined in the case of moving
images. Laptev [8] proposed a space-time interest point detector which is a temporal extension of the Harris detector. He used this detector for the recognition
of human actions (walking, running, drinking, etc.) in movies. In [9], Dollar proposed a space-time detector based on a 2D spatial gaussian filter jointly used
with a quadrature pair of 1D temporal Gabor filters. However, this approach is

M. Fritz, B. Schiele, and J.H. Piater (Eds.): ICVS 2009, LNCS 5815, pp. 325–334, 2009.

limited to the detection of periodic motions, such as a bird flapping its wings. In [10], Scovanner et al. proposed a temporal extension of SIFT descriptor.

Parallel to the research about interest points, other researches have proposed models to predict where people look at when freely viewing static or dynamic images. Given an image or video sequence, these bottom-up saliency models compute saliency maps, which topographically encodes for conspicuity (or "saliency") at every location in the visual input [11]. The saliency is computed in two steps: first, the visual signal is split into different basic saliency maps that emphasize basic visual features as intensity, color, orientation, and second, the basic saliency maps are fuzzed together to create the master saliency map. This map emphasizes which elements of a visual scene are likely to attract the attention of human observers, and by consequence their gaze. The model saliency map is then evaluated using different metrics. These metrics are used to compare the model saliency maps with human eye movements when looking at the corresponding scenes ([12],[13]).

In the same way the visual saliency maps are compared with subject eye movements, in this papers, we test whether the interest points are related to human eye movements. The goal of this papers is to measure the similarity between the interest maps obtained with two successful interest point detectors, one static and one dynamic, and the human eye position density maps. More precisely, we focus on the specificity of these two detectors (spatial/space-time). The papers is organized as follows. Section 2 presents the two interest point detectors which are chosen in this work. The eye movement experiment and the evaluation method are detailed in section 3. A relevance analysis is described in section 4. Conclusions are given in section 5.

2   Selection and Description of Interest Point Detectors

In the case of still images, several works have compared the performances of different interest point detectors. In [14], Schmid et al. introduced two evaluation criteria: the repeatability rate and the information content. The repeatability rate evaluates the detector stability for a scene under different viewing conditions (five different changes were tested: viewpoint changes, scale changes, image blur, JPEG compression and illumination changes). The information content measures the distinctiveness of features. Those two criteria directly measure the quality of the feature for tasks such as image matching, object recognition and 3D reconstruction. Using these two criteria the Harris detector appears to be the best interest point detector. For this reason, this detector will be chosen in the following, either in its spatial and space-time forms.

2.1   Spatial Interest Points: Harris Detector

In an image, Spatial Interest Points (denoted SIP in the following) can be defined as points with significant gradients in more than one direction. In [1],

Harris et al. proposed to find such points using a second moment matrix H defined, for a pixel (x, y) having intensity $I(x, y)$, by:

$$H(x, y) = \begin{pmatrix} \frac{\partial^2 I}{\partial x^2} & \frac{\partial^2 I}{\partial x \partial y} \\ \frac{\partial^2 I}{\partial x \partial y} & \frac{\partial^2 I}{\partial y^2} \end{pmatrix} \qquad (1)$$

In practice, the image I is first smoothed using a Gaussian kernel $g(x, y, \sigma)$ where σ controls the spatial scale at which corners are detected.

To obtain SIP, Harris et al. proposed to use a feature extraction function entitled "*salience function*", defined by:

$$R(x, y) = \det(H(x, y)) - k \times trace(H(x, y))^2 \qquad (2)$$

The parameter k is empirically adjusted between 0.04 and 0.15 (0.04 is chosen in the following). SIP correspond to high values of the salience function extracted using a thresholding step (the salience function being normalized between 0 and 255, typical threshold value is 150).

2.2 Space-Time Interest Points: Laptev Detector

Laptev et al. [15] proposed a spatio-temporal extension of the Harris detector to detect what they call "Space-Time Interest Points", denoted STIP in the following. STIP are points which are both relevant in space and time. These points are specially interesting because they focus information initially contained in thousands of pixels on a few specific points which can be related to spatio-temporal events in an image.

STIP detection is performed by using the Hessian-Laplace matrix H defined, for a pixel (x, y) at time t having intensity $I(x, y, t)$, by:

$$H(x, y, t) = \begin{pmatrix} \frac{\partial^2 I}{\partial x^2} & \frac{\partial^2 I}{\partial x \partial y} & \frac{\partial^2 I}{\partial x \partial t} \\ \frac{\partial^2 I}{\partial x \partial y} & \frac{\partial^2 I}{\partial y^2} & \frac{\partial^2 I}{\partial y \partial t} \\ \frac{\partial^2 I}{\partial x \partial t} & \frac{\partial^2 I}{\partial y \partial t} & \frac{\partial^2 I}{\partial t^2} \end{pmatrix} \qquad (3)$$

As with the Harris detector, a gaussian smoothing is applied both in spatial and temporal domain. Two parameters σ_s and σ_t, one for each domain, control the spatial and temporal scale at which corners are detected. Typical values of σ_s and σ_t are respectively 1.5 and 1.2. In order to highlight STIP, different criteria have been proposed. As in [8], we have chose the spatio-temporal extension of the Harris corner function, entitled "*salience function*", defined by:

$$R(x, y, t) = \det(H(x, y, t)) - k \times trace(H(x, y, t))^3 \qquad (4)$$

where k is a parameter empirically adjusted at 0.04 as for SIP detection. STIP also correspond to high values of the salience function R and are obtained using a thresholding step.

3   Eye Position Experiment and Comparison Metric

Eye positions are usually used to evaluate saliency models. Most of these models are inspired by the biology of the human visual system especially the processing of the retina and the primary visual cortex, ([11],[16],[17]). As the interest point models, these saliency models are based on low level properties of the stimuli. As the aim of this papers is to test whether the interest points are related to human eye movements, an experiment had been carried out in order to get the eye positions of subjects on particular video databases.

3.1   Experiment

We recorded the eye positions of fifteen subjects when they were viewing a video freely. This experiment was inspired by an experiment of Carmi and Itti [18] and is explained in more detail in [17]. Fifty three videos (25 fps, 720x576 pixels per frame) are selected from heterogeneous sources. The 53 videos are cut in small snippets of 1-3 seconds (1.86 ± 0.61), that are strung together to make up 20 clips of 30 seconds. Each clip contains at most one clip snippet from each continuous source. The total amount of snippets over the 20 clips is 305. The eye data are recorded using an Eyelink II eye tracker (SR Research), recording eye positions at 500Hz. As the frame rate is 25Hz, for each frame we compute the median of the 20 values related to this frame in order to get an eye position for each subject and for each frame. To relax the constraint on the exact positions, a 2-dimensional gaussian filtering is applied on each eye position point to obtain the human eye position density map M_h.

3.2   Comparison Metric

The human eye position density map has to be compared to the interest maps provided by the interest point detectors. By looking what is done for saliency model evaluation, we can used several metrics ([12],[13]). In this papers we use the Normalized Scanpath Saliency (NSS) [19],[20] that was especially designed to compare eye positions and the salient locations emphasized by a saliency map M_m, and so it can be easily interpreted. The NSS is defined as follows:

$$NSS(t) = \frac{\overline{M_h(x,y,t) \times M_m(x,y,t)} - \overline{M_m(x,y,t)}}{\sigma_{M_m(x,y,t)}} \qquad (5)$$

where $M_h(x,y,t)$ is the human eye position density map normalized to unit mean and $M_m(x,y,t)$ a saliency map for a frame t. $\overline{M_m(x,y,t)}$ and $\sigma_{M_m(x,y,t)}$ are respectively the average and the standard deviation of the model map $M_m(x,y,t)$.

In this papers the NSS is chosen to compare subjects' eye position and an interest map obtained with the interest-points detector as described below. The NSS is null if there is no link between eye positions and interest regions, negative if eye positions tend to be on non-interest regions and positive if eye positions tend to be on interest regions. To sum up, a interest point model would be a good predictor of human eye fixations if the corresponding NSS value would be positive and high.

4   Relevance Analysis

4.1   Eye Position Density Map and Interest Maps

We chose to transform the sets of points (given by the eye position experiment and the interest point detectors) into maps by applying a 2D spatial gaussian filter on each point. This filtering allows to take the imprecision and the density of measures into account. For each frame of the different snippets presented in the previous section, three maps are worked out :

- Human eye position density map (M_h): which is obtained by applying a 2D Gaussian filtering on each eye position point. In this papers, it corresponds to the reference map.
- SIP interest map (M_{SIP}): this map corresponds to the SIP detector. As for the previous map, it is obtained by applying the same 2D Gaussian filtering on the SIP points.
- STIP interest map (M_{STIP}): this map corresponds to the STIP detector. For this map, we directly use a normalized version of the salience function $R(x, y, t)$ on which a 2D Gaussian filter is applied.

Figure 1 gives an example of these different maps. Human eye position density map $((M_h)$, fig. 1.b) does not look like the two different interest maps $((M_{SIP}),(M_{STIP})$, fig. 1.c/d). There are very few highlighted regions on (M_h) compared to the interest maps. The more the highlighted regions of (M_h) will be also highlighted on the different interest maps, the more the NSS will be high.

In order to determine the relevance of M_{SIP} and M_{STIP} maps according to the human eye position density map M_h, the NSS is calculated for each interest map. In the following, NSS_{SIP} (resp. NSS_{STIP}), denotes the NSS values obtained with M_{SIP} (resp. M_{STIP}).

4.2   Analysis on the Global Database

A temporal analysis of the NSS criteria is realized. Figure 2 shows the evolution of average NSS over time (or frames) of each snippet (see section 3.1).

  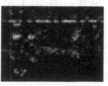 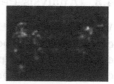

a - Original image b - human eye position c - SIP interest map d - STIP interest map
  ("hand ball")   density map
                                  (M_h) (M_{SIP}) (M_{STIP})

Fig. 1. Example of maps extracted from a snippet

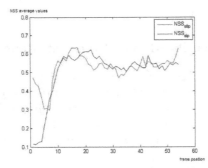

Fig. 2. NSS variations averaged over the 305 snippets over time plotted for the 55 first frames of each snippets. (NSS Average on the global database: NSS_{SIP} 0.50 - NSS_{STIP} 0.54).

First of all, both for SIP and STIP, we can note that the NSS values are positive which means that the interest points are relevant for eye position prediction. The second observation is related to the beginning of the evolution. The two curves present similar aspects after the first ten frames but are quite different at the beginning. That can be explained by the fact that after a shot cut between two snippets, humans' gaze stay at the same position, corresponding to the previous shot, for a short period before going to an interesting region of the new shot. As SIP interest map highlights interest points in a static way, after a shot cut the interest points change immediately and consequently are different from the regions gazed at. Thus the NSS is low. After a small delay, the subjects gazed at regions highlighted on the SIP map, and then the NSS increases. On the contrary, as the STIP interest map is built using a sliding window considering several frames before and after the current frame, during the first frames of a new snippet, STIP saliency map highlights interest points of the previous shot which are still gazed at by subjects.

It is particularly interesting to note that the NSS_{SIP} values are higher than the NSS_{STIP} values for approximately 65% of snippets. However, the $NSS_{STIP}average$ (0.54) is higher than $NSS_{SIP}average$ (0.50). Thus, when NSS_{STIP} is higher than NSS_{SIP}, it is significantly higher.

4.3 Analysis Per Semantical Categories

We want to see if the interest points are more relevant for different semantical categories of snippets. An analysis shows that performances are different according to the snippet content. Among the 305 snippets, we extract a number of classes of similar content. We have chosen to present four examples of interesting behavior: Traffic (18 snippets, 6% of the snippets), Team Sports (44 snippets, 14% of the snippets), Faces and/or Hands (47 snippets, 15% of the snippets) and Demonstration (30 snippets, 10% of the snippets). Figure 3 gives some images of snippets corresponding to these four classes.

Table 1 summarizes the NSS values obtained for these different classes. This table shows the Traffic and Team Sports classes have got average and maximum

| a - Traffic | b - Team sports | c - Faces/hands | d - Demonstration |

Fig. 3. Image examples of the 4 classes

Table 1. Average and maximum NSS values for different classes

		Traffic	Team Sports	Faces/Hands	Demonstration
NSS_{SIP}	Average	0.86	0.17	1.85	0.19
	Maximum	2.10	0.72	4.78	0.78
NSS_{STIP}	Average	1.26	0.77	0.39	0.23
	Maximum	4.24	1.98	3.06	0.95
Number of snippets		18 (6%)	44 (14%)	47 (15%)	30 (10%)

Note that the minimum values of all the interest map is 0.

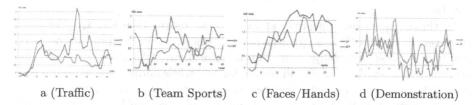

| a (Traffic) | b (Team Sports) | c (Faces/Hands) | d (Demonstration) |

Fig. 4. NSS over time for a snippet of each class

values of NSS greater with STIP than with SIP. Furthermore, for Traffic class, the maximum value is very high. On the contrary, for the Faces/Hands class, SIP gives better average and maximum than STIP. Finally, NSS values for the demonstration class are close to 0, which means that there is a weak link between the eye positions and the interest points. To better understand these results, we give (Fig.4) the NSS evolution for an example of snippet of each class.

Traffic class: This first example comes from the traffic class (fig 3.a), which presents sequences of traffic. Car traffic has special interest: it is characterized by a uniform movement, but with disorderly occasional variations more or less important: file changes, braking, accidents ... These discontinuities are particularly well detected and enhanced by STIP. In addition, these breaks easily attract visual attention. This explains quite well the correct values of the NSS and the improvement brought by temporal component compared to SIP (Figure 4.a).

On this figure, the NSS_{STIP} evolution exhibits a local maximum (value $\simeq 4$) near the thirtieth image. This peak corresponds to the abrupt change in direction of one of the vehicles.

Team sport class (using a ball): The second example concerns the category of team sports (fig3.b) using a ball: basketball, hand ball, rugby. These sports are characterized by rapid movements, rather erratic and with rapid changes. Furthermore, the more a player is close to the ball, or to the action, the more movements are rapid and disorderly. This context is favorable to STIP which tend to detect points with irregular motion.

Figure 4.b shows the evolution of NSS over images for SIP and STIP. Clearly, link with eye positions is better for STIP than for SIP. The local maxima of NSS_{STIP} generally correspond to sudden changes in the action. These changes attract eyes while providing a lot of STIP. So, for this class, the contribution of the temporal component to the interest point detection seems to be relevant. However, this result is not always true for football sequences. This counterexample is probably due to the fact that football images generally gives a wide view, which induces smoother motion.

Face/hand class: The third class is composed of close-up sequences of faces and hands (for instance a music concert - fig 3.c). This class represents the typical situations where the NSS_{SIP} is higher than the NSS_{STIP} (65% of global database).

In these sequences, the areas attracting the most attention are faces [21]. However, motion in these sequences is weak whereas they contain many spatial points of interest, generally located on faces or hands which are areas of visual attention. This explains the good results for SIP while adding the temporal component to interest point detection decreases the performance. Figure 4.c shows the evolution of NSS. NSS_{SIP} has a good level (average level approximately 1.5) and is almost all the time over NSS_{STIP}.

Demonstration/crowd class: The last class contains demonstrations or crowds (fig 3.d). The characteristics of this class is that movements are performed by a multitude of people covering almost all of the image.

Figure 4.d) shows that this class is characterized by a very low NSS relatively constant, around 0.2, as well for SIP as for STIP, even if in some cases STIP seems a little better than SIP.

The result indicates that the eye position do not match with the interest point. The problem is that in these sequences all people move which induces a lot of interest points uniformly distributed within images. But in the same way, visual attention is not captured by a particular area. Thus, the correspondence between eye positions and interest points is rare.

5   Conclusions and Perspectives

The work presented in this papers has shown that interest points provided by specific detectors are globally relevant for eye position prediction. More precisely, we have studied the difference between spatial and space-time interest points, searching in which conditions interest points could be regarded as predictions of eye positions.

In order to analyse the relevance, the reference was built by recording eye position of subject which were compared to interest maps using the NSS metric. Experiment was run on a set of 305 snippets with various contents.

From the obtained results, we can get three main conclusions:

- globally, there is relevant link between eye positions and interest points (SIP and STIP). Hence interest points can be used as a prediction of gaze. The computational cost is very low regarding to other more dedicated methods.
- STIP provide a very good detection of eye positions when the sequence contains specials events, for examples: a car crash, somebody running and suddenly changing the direction of his run,
- On the contrary, when the semantic content is static (for faces and hands for example), the STIP do not work and SIP provide a very good detection of eye positions.

A future extension of this work could be a collaborative use of SIP and STIP according to the video content. If information about the class or type of content is a priori known, the type of detector to use (SIP or STIP) can be easily chosen. If there is no additional information, intrinsic evaluation of STIP could help making this choice for optimum performance.

Acknowledgements

We thank the Rhône-Alpes region for its support with LIMA project.

References

1. Harris, C., Stephens, M.J.: A combined corner and edge detector. In: Alvey Vision Conference (1988)
2. Lindeberg, T.: Feature detection with automatic scale selection. International Journal of Computer Vision, 77–116 (1998)
3. Mikolajczyk, K., Schmid, C.: Scale and affine invariant interest point detectors. International Journal of Computer Vision, 63–86 (2004)
4. Lowe, D.G.: Object recognition from local scale-invariant features. In: International Conference on Computer Vision, pp. 1150–1157 (1999)
5. Lowe, D.G.: Distinctive image features from scale-invariant keypoints. International Journal of Computer Vision, 91–110 (2004)
6. Mikolajczyk, K., Schmid, C.: Indexing based on scale invariant interest points. In: Proc. ICCV, vol. 1, pp. 525–531 (2001)
7. Tuytelaars, T., Van Gool, L.: Wide baseline stereo matching based on local, affinely invariant regions. In: British Machine Vision Conference, pp. 412–425 (2000)
8. Laptev, I.: On space-time interest points. International Journal of Computer Vision 64(2/3), 107–123 (2005)
9. Dollar, P., Rabaud, V., Cottrell, G., Belongie, S.J.: Behavior recognition via sparse spatio-temporal features. In: International Workshop on Performance Evaluation of Tracking and Surveillance, pp. 65–72 (2001)
10. Scovanner, S., Ali, P., Shah, M.: A 3-dimensional sift descriptor and its application to action recognition. ACM Multimedia (2007)

11. Itti, L., Koch, C., Niebur, E.: A model of salincy-based visual attention for rapid scene analysis. IEEE Transaction on Pattern Analysis and Machine Intelligence 20, 1254–1259 (1998)
12. Tatler, B.W., Baddeley, R.J., Gilchrist, I.D.: Visual correlates of fixation selection: effects of scale and time. Vision Research 45, 643–659 (2005)
13. Torralba, A., Oliva, A., Castelhano, M.S., Henderson, J.M.: Contextual guidance of eye movements and attention in real-world scenes: The role of global features on object search. Psychological Review 113(4), 766–786 (2006)
14. Schmid, C., Mohr, R., Bauckhage, C.: Evaluation of interest point detectors. International Journal of Computer Vision 37(2), 151–172 (2000)
15. Laptev, I., Lindeberg, T.: Space-time interest points. In: ICCV 2003, pp. 432–439 (2003)
16. Le Meur, O., Le Callet, P., Barba, D.: Predicting visual fixations on video based on low-level visual features. Vision Research 47, 2483–2498 (2007)
17. Marat, S., Ho Phuoc, T., Granjon, L., Guyader, N., Pellerin, D., Guérin-Dugué, A.: Modelling spatio-temporal saliency to predict gaze direction for short videos. International Journal of Computer Vision 82(3), 231–243 (2009)
18. Carmi, R., Itti, L.: Visual causes versus correlates of attentional selection in dynamic scenes. Vision Research 46, 4333–4345 (2006)
19. Peters, R.J., Iyer, A., Itti, L., Koch, C.: Components of bottom up gaze allocation in natural images. Vision Research 45, 2397–2416 (2005)
20. Peters, R.J., Itti, L.: Applying computational tools to predict gaze direction in interactive visual environments. ACM Trans. On Applied Perception 5(2) (2008)
21. Cerf, M., Harel, J., Einhauser, W., Koch, C.: Predicting gaze using low-level saliency combined with face detection. In: Neural Information Processing System (2007)

A Computer Vision System for Visual Grape Grading in Wine Cellars

Esteban Vazquez-Fernandez[1], Angel Dacal-Nieto[1], Fernando Martin[2], Arno Formella[3], Soledad Torres-Guijarro[1], and Higinio Gonzalez-Jorge[1]

[1] Laboratorio Oficial de Metroloxía de Galicia (LOMG), Parque Tecnolóxico de Galicia, San Cibrao das Viñas, 32901 Ourense, Spain
evazquez@lomg.net
[2] Communications and Signal Theory Department, University of Vigo, Spain
[3] Computer Science Department, University of Vigo, Spain

Abstract. This communication describes a computer vision system for automatic visual inspection and classification of grapes in cooperative wine cellars. The system is intended to work outdoors, so robust algorithms for preprocessing and segmentation are implemented. Specific methods for illumination compensation have been developed. Gabor filtering has been used for segmentation. Several preliminary classification schemes, using artificial neural networks and Random Forest, have also been tested. The obtained results show the benefits of the system as a useful tool for classification and for objective price fixing.

1 Introduction

At present, grape grading systems at cooperative wine cellars combine several criteria. On the one hand, a class categorization is made by an expert according to a visual inspection of the grape container. This inspection focuses on maturation, presence of rotten or damaged grapes, etc. On the other hand, a sample of grape juice is taken to make a later laboratory study, which is mainly an enzymatic and microbial analysis.

The visual inspection is very important since it determines the separation into classes for the preparation of different quality wines. In addition, the price to pay to the cooperative members also depends on this classification, so it must be as objective as possible. The problem is the inherent subjectivity in classification made by human experts. There are too many factors that can influence the final result, like different technicians, fatigue, lighting conditions, inaccurate perception of proportions, etc. Under these conditions, a computer vision system has been developed to make the classification easier and more accurate.

During the last two decades, the use of computer vision systems in the food and agricultural industries has increased. Some recent reviews are available in [1], [2]. These systems offer many advantages for quality assurance and inspection tasks or grading. However, computer vision has never been used for the

M. Fritz, B. Schiele, and J.H. Piater (Eds.): ICVS 2009, LNCS 5815, pp. 335–344, 2009.

inspection of received grapes in wine cellars (or, at least, the authors are un-
aware of this use), probably due to difficulties like outdoor conditions, variable
illumination, etc.

In this paper, we present an incipient computer vision system for grape grading in cooperative wine cellars. The system is intended to work in the hard
conditions of outdoor reception points, so the use of robust image processing
techniques becomes a decisive factor. The achieved results suggest that this development can provide an objective and reliable tool for the correct classification
and separation of different quality grapes. It also ensures a fair price for the cooperative partners.

The paper is organized as follows. Section 2 provides an overview of the image acquisition system. The preprocessing techniques and segmentation methods
applied are presented in Sect. 3 and Sect. 4. Feature selection and classification
are explained in Sect. 5. Finally, results and conclusions are drawn in Sect. 6
and Sect. 7.

2   Image Acquisition System

A schematic view of the reception point, where the system is intended to work, is
shown in Fig. 1a. The region of interest (ROI) for the inspection is a $2\,\text{m} \times 1.3\,\text{m}$
surface of a container full of grapes (see Fig. 1b). The equipment used for the
image capture system is selected according to this real situation, but can be
easily adapted to a different reception point.

The camera used is a JAI BB-500 GE [3] with a 2/3" Bayer Color ICX625AQA
5 Mpixel sensor (2456×2048). An easy calculation can be made to choose a
camera lens according to the field of view (FOV) and the required working
distance [4] given by

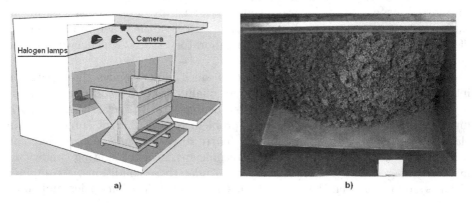

a)   b)

Fig. 1. Image acquisition system: a) Diagram of the grape reception point; b) Obtained
image of the container surface

$$\beta = \frac{Sw}{FOVw} \tag{1}$$

$$f' = \alpha \frac{\beta}{1 - \beta} \tag{2}$$

where Sw is the sensor width in mm, $FOVw$ is the FOV width in mm and α is the distance between the surface to inspect and the lens. For our purposes a Schneider Optics Cinegon 1.4/8mm 2/3" [5] is adequate.

The main problem for the capture system is the illumination due to the outdoor placement and the wide period of operation which frequently goes from day to night. In addition, it is not possible to make an indoor reception point, due to the difficulties in manipulating the containers by a forklift truck. Under these conditions, the best results have been obtained with two high power halogen lamps (1000 W).

3   Preprocessing

Preprocessing commonly comprises a series of image operations to enhance the image before the segmentation process starts. In this application, preprocessing plays a fundamental role due to the difficult capture conditions of the images. The preprocessing stage can be divided in three sections: Camera calibration, continuous white balance and illumination uniformity compensation.

3.1   Camera Calibration

A standard mapping operation is used to correct lens distortions [6]. For this purpose, the following parameters are needed:

$$\text{Intrinsec Matrix} \equiv \begin{bmatrix} f_x & 0 & c_x \\ 0 & f_y & x_y \\ 0 & 0 & 1 \end{bmatrix} \tag{3}$$

$$\text{Distortion Coeficients} \equiv (k_1, k_2, p_1, p_2, k_3) \tag{4}$$

which are used to model the focal, center, radial, and tangential distortions of the optical systems. These parameters are obtained offline by using image sequences of a chessboard pattern, stored and applied as proposed in [7].

3.2   Continuous White Balance

Illumination varies in a wide range during the grading session due to the outdoor placement. Although the illumination from the halogen lamps remains constant, the obtained images suffer a wide color variation due to the frequently and unpredictable changes in external light. In this situation, it is necessary to apply a white balance to every captured image.

Fig. 2. Histogram of the range filtered image

The use of a fixed target for the white balance produces undesirable errors due to the variable positioning of the container, different light incidence between the grapes and the target, etc. To solve this problem, we decided to use the container itself, which is made of stainless steel, as a pattern. An algorithm to automatically detect the region to use as a gray reference has been developed.

To simplify the operations, only the lower left quarter of the image is used, where both grapes and container appear. To locate the steel gray, a texture filtering is applied. It consists on calculating the range value of a pixel $p(x, y)$ in a neighborhood V (empirically fixed to 13×13 pixels) as

$$p(x, y) = \max(V) - \min(V). \tag{5}$$

Looking at the histogram of the filtered image (Figure 2), two clearly different regions can be seen. The first major peak matches the low textured regions (container walls, etc.), while the extended tail matches the highly textured areas (surface of grapes, edges, etc.). A sliding window method [8] based on derivative variations analysis is applied to locate a binarization threshold.

After the binarization process, morphological operations of opening and closing and median filtering are applied to reduce noise. This process allows to label the image in a connected regions map. The selection of the region of interest for the white balance is established by features like area and centroid position. Then, the correction factors sr, sg, and sb, which will multiply the R, G and B planes of the entire image ($m \times n$ size), are obtained in the following way:

$$\bar{r} = \frac{1}{m \times n} \sum_{m,n} R \ , \quad \bar{g} = \frac{1}{m \times n} \sum_{m,n} G \ , \quad \bar{b} = \frac{1}{m \times n} \sum_{m,n} B \tag{6}$$

$$\bar{\imath} = 0.2125\bar{r} + 0.7154\bar{g} + 0.072\bar{b} \tag{7}$$

$$sr = \frac{\bar{\imath}}{\bar{r}} \ , \quad sg = \frac{\bar{\imath}}{\bar{g}} \ , \quad sb = \frac{\bar{\imath}}{\bar{b}} \ . \tag{8}$$

3.3   Illumination Compensation

Another problem in the obtained images is the non uniform illumination. Grapes fill randomly the container, creating different height zones, so light and shadow regions are produced, which need to be compensated. The proposed method is intended to modify the V plane of the HSV color space, while the characteristics of color remain stable. A schematic of the process is shown in Fig. 3.

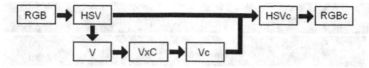

Fig. 3. Schematic view of the illumination compensation process

The most used color space in cameras, screens, etc. is RGB. It also models the way the eye reacts to different wavelength stimulus. However, the high correlation of the three components in RGB linear space makes the three components dependent upon each other and strongly associated with intensity [9]. These relations make it necessary to process the image in a three dimensional color space. To avoid these problems, it is interesting to make a non linear transformation to a HSV color space.

Most of the illumination compensation methods are based on the previous acquisition of the luminance pattern over the scene without the objects of interest [10]. However, we can not take advantage of this method for two reasons: On the one hand, the distribution of illumination depends directly of the objects (grapes) and their placement in the container. On the other hand, the luminance is directly related to the variable incidence of the external illumination all along the day.

To solve this problem, we have designed a method to perform the illumination compensation by using only the information present in the captured image. First, the illumination plane is modeled. An advantage of the grapes surface is their "homogeneity" and their conformation to the shape of the container (in this sense, they could be approached more like a liquid than like a solid). The luminance distribution is approximated by a Gaussian filtering (equations (9) and (10)) of the V plane (HSV space). A smoothing of the sharp texture of the grapes is achieved, while the influence of luminance in a wider area remains unaltered.

$$h_g(x, y) = e^{-(x,y)^2/2\sigma^2} \tag{9}$$

$$h(x, y) = \frac{h_g(x, y)}{\sum_x \sum_y h_g} . \tag{10}$$

To optimize the uniformity of the filtering, its size $n \times n$ should satisfy the following ratio to the standard deviation σ:

$$\frac{n}{2} \approx 3\sigma \Rightarrow \sigma \approx \frac{n}{6} . \tag{11}$$

The illumination compensation matrix, $C(x, y)$, is obtained as:

$$\begin{aligned} C(x, y) &= \frac{k}{L(x,y)} \\ k &= \alpha \bar{L} \\ \alpha &= 1.2 \end{aligned} \tag{12}$$

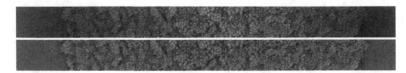

Fig. 4. Comparison detail between images before illumination compensation (above) and after illumination compensation (below)

where $L(x,y)$ is the filtered image. The compensated V plane is obtained by:

$$V_c(x,y) = V(x,y)C(x,y) \ . \tag{13}$$

A detail of the achieved effect on the color image is shown in Fig. 4.

4   Segmentation

The objective of the segmentation process is to separate the surface of the grapes from the rest of the elements in the image. A priori, a colour based segmentation method seems to be adequate for the purpose but, in practice, it turned out not to be robust enough. Variations in grape varieties, maturation or presence of foreign objects in or around the container makes colour an unreliable criteria, so a texture analysis based on Gabor filtering has been used for the segmentation purpose. A 2D Gabor filter can be thought of as a complex plane wave modulated by a 2D Gaussian envelope and can be expressed in the spatial domain as:

$$
\begin{aligned}
G_{\theta,f,\sigma_1,\sigma_2}(x,y) &= \exp\left[\tfrac{-1}{2}\left(\tfrac{x'^2}{\sigma_1^2} + \tfrac{y'^2}{\sigma_2^2}\right)\right]\cos\left(2\pi f x'\right) \\
x' &= x\sin\theta + y\cos\theta \\
y' &= x\cos\theta - y\sin\theta
\end{aligned}
\tag{14}
$$

where f is the spatial frequency of the wave at an angle θ with the x axis and σ_1 and σ_2 are the standard deviations of the 2D Gaussian envelope. In most of the texture filtering applications, and also in this case, the Gaussian envelop is symmetric, so we have $\sigma_1 = \sigma_2 = \sigma$.

The segmentation process is based on the hypothesis that the grapes have the highest variation in texture. The texture operations will be applied to the V plane from the HSV image. The parameters for the Gabor filtering are set to the following values:

- Frequency has been set to a value of $f = 1/16$ pixels. The reason is because the value of the average grape diameter is 8 pixels $(1/2f)$.
- For the standard deviation, a value of $\sigma = \lambda/2 = 1/2\,f$ (measured in pixels) has been selected and tested empirically.
- Two orientations are needed and have been fixed to $\theta_1 = \pi/4$ and $\theta_2 = 3\pi/4$.

The grape texture is uniformly distributed in all orientations, while other highly textured elements, like container edges, are oriented in only one direction. Using two opposite orientations for the filtering and combining them reduces the effects

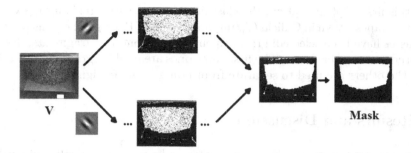

Fig. 5. Mask selection process

of the edges in texture analysis. The best results have been achieved applying first a binarization operation to the magnitude of each filtered image separately and then combining them into one by a logical *AND* operation. The threshold for the binarization is obtained by a histogram analysis in a similar way to that explained in Section 3.2. The mask in the binary image is filled by mathematical morphology operations of opening and closing. Afterwards, the filled areas are labeled in a connected components map and the biggest one is selected for the mask. Figure 5 summarizes the process.

5   Feature Selection and Classification

To test the operation of the system, a preliminary classification scheme has been implemented. It is based on low level features. The method is inspired by the one presented in [11]. Jain and Karu suggested a method for learning texture discrimination masks by using neural networks. This approach is very similar to texture filtering approaches, where the filtering, nonlinearity, smoothing and classification are done all in one. However, this previous work is intended to classify only texture characteristics, so it uses only a 5×5 grey level neighborhood (25 features). In our system a more general classification is desired (e. g. also color is important), so the feature vector is formed by the 5×5 neighborhood values of the corrected planes H, S, V, R, G and B of the image (150 features).

The feature vector feeds the classifier, which is intended to learn higher level features from the input ones. The reason for using this scheme is "Black box" simplicity of implementation: the hard work of obtaining representative features is done by the classifier. Different classification methods have been tested, including Multilayer Perceptron (MLP) and Random Forest classifiers [12] via OpenCV Libraries implementation [6]. For the MLP, several network architectures (number of hidden layers and nodes) have been tested. Divers Random Forest classifiers have been trained with different parameters to obtain several tree populations.

In this first implementation, the classifier is tested with Treixadura, a variety of white grapes grown in Galicia (Spain) and North of Portugal. For this purpose, six classes have been selected: green, ripen, rotten, container fragments, dry leaf and other external elements. The first three ones are used for grape classification, while the others are used to separate from non grading foreign elements.

6   Results and Discussion

Representative regions for the different classes have been manually selected by human experts. This process has provided 140333 samples (5 × 5 pixel neighborhoods), which have been divided in a randomly selected 80 % for training (112266 samples) and 20 % for testing (28067 samples).

In the case of the MLP classifier, several network architectures have been trained to test their performance and to select the most adequate one. The training algorithm is backpropagation. Figure 6 shows the performance of one hidden layer and three hidden layer nets with variable number of nodes. The best results have been achieved by using a three hidden layer network. One can see this approach as a nonlinear generalization of principal components analysis (NLPCA) as proposed by [13], where the first and third hidden layers provide nonlinearity and the second one is the bottleneck. A compromise solution between success rate and computational cost has been achieved by fixing the final architecture to 18, 6 and 18 nodes in the three hidden layers respectively. This results in a 94.1 % and a 93.8 % success rate in the training and test stages. Table 1 shows the confusion matrix for the 18–6–18 three hidden layer MLP.

For the Random Forest classifier, different values of the maximum depth of the trees have been tested. This provides different forest structures and number of trees, since they are pruned at different depths. Figure 7 shows the evolution of the test through the max depth variation, for different number of variables

Table 1. Confusion matrix for the three hidden layer MLP (18, 6 and 18 nodes)

Classified→ Real↓	Green	Ripen	Rotten	Container	External	Dry Leaf
Green	5450	15	16	113	0	0
Ripen	30	4826	202	16	0	149
Rotten	17	309	4079	118	6	6
Container	10	260	67	4300	1	6
External	0	0	1	2	5799	0
Dry Leaf	16	378	8	0	0	1866

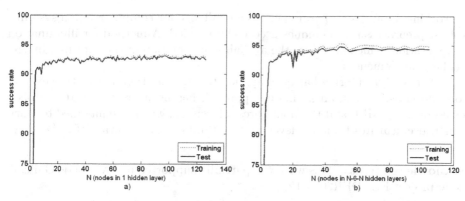

Fig. 6. MLP Network architecture comparison a) MLP one hidden layer net (x–axis represents number of nodes); b) MLP 3 hidden layer net (x–axis represent the first and third hidden layer number of nodes)

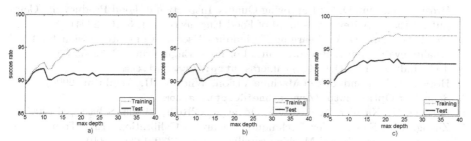

Fig. 7. Random Forest comparison: a) Nvar $= 12$; b) Nvar $= 6$; c) Nvar $= 2$

(Nvar), which are randomly selected at the nodes (and that are used to find the best split). One can see, as the depth level of the trees is increased, an overfitting like effect appears (obtaining much higher rate in the training than in the test).

The obtained results show the feasibility of the system, achieving a success rate over 90 % in all tests. These results lead us to formulate future lines to continue this development:

- Developing specific feature extraction methods to improve the classification.
- Testing the system on different varieties of grapes.
- Extending the classification to other classes (different diseases, abnormal growth, etc.) for obtaining better information for the wine cellar classification, etc.

7   Conclusions

A promising computer vision system for grape grading in cooperative wine cellars has been developed. The system allows grape sorting to produce different quality wines. It also seems to be a useful and objective method to fix an equalitarian price to the cooperative partners.

Working in outdoor environments is a challenge for computer vision systems. Robust preprocessing techniques need to be applied. A method for illumination compensation, which only uses the available information in the captured image, has been implemented.

Texture Gabor filtering has been applied to segmentation. For feature extraction and classification, an all-in-one approach has been presented. It has been tested by using MLP and Random Forest classifiers, which are intended to learn higher level features from low level ones, obtaining a success rate of 94 %.

Acknowledgements. This work was partially supported by "Xunta de Galicia" (code project FEADER2008-12).

References

1. Brosnan, T., Sun, D.W.: Improving Quality Inspection of Food Products by Computer Vision - A Review. Journal of Food Engineering 61, 3–16 (2004)
2. Du, D.W., Sun, D.W.: Learning Techniques Used in Computer Vision for Food Quality evaluation: A Review. Journal of Food Engineering 72, 39–55 (2006)
3. JAI - Industrial CCD/CMOS cameras, http://www.jai.com
4. Hornberg, A.: Handbook of Machine Vision. Wiley VCH, Weinhiem (2006)
5. Schneider Optics, http://www.schneideroptics.com
6. Bradski, G., Kaehler, A.: Learning OpenCV. O'Reilly Media, Sebastopol (2008)
7. Zhang, Z.: A Flexible New Technique for Camera Calibration. IEEE Transactions on Pattern Analysis and Machine Intelligence 22, 1330–1334 (2000)
8. Martin, F.: Analysis Tools for Gray Level Histograms. In: Proc. of SPPRA-2003, pp. 11–16 (June 2003)
9. Cheng, H.D., Jiang, X.H., Sun, Y., Wang, J.: Color image segmentation: advances and prospects. Pattern Recognition 34, 2259–2281 (2001)
10. Russ, J.C.: The Image Processing Handbook, 5th edn. CRC Press, Boca Raton (2007)
11. Jain, A.K., Karu, K.: Learning Texture Discrimination Masks. IEEE Transactions on Pattern Analysis and Machine Intelligence 18, 195–205 (1994)
12. Breiman, L.: Random Forests. Machine Learning 45, 5–32 (2001)
13. Kerschen, G., Golinval, J.C.: Non-linear Generalization of Principal Component Analysis: From a Global to a Local Approach. Journal of Sound and Vibration 254(5), 867–876 (2002)

Inspection of Stamped Sheet Metal Car Parts Using a Multiresolution Image Fusion Technique

Eusebio de la Fuente López and Félix Miguel Trespaderne

E.T.S. Ingenieros Industriales, P° del Cauce 59,
47011 Valladolid, Spain
{eusfue,trespa}@eis.uva.es

Abstract. This paper presents an image processing algorithm for on-line inspection of large sheet metal car parts. The automatic inspection of stamped sheet metal is not an easy task due to the high reflective nature of the material and the nearly imperceptible characteristics of the defects to be detected. In order to deal with the ubiquitous glints, four images of every zone are acquired illuminating from different directions. The image series is fused using a Haar transform into a single image where the spurious features originated by the glints are eliminated without discarding the salient information. Our results clearly suggest that the proposed fusion scheme offers a powerful way to obtain a clean image where these subtle defects can be detected reliably.

1 Introduction

One of the primary objectives for the highly competitive automotive industry is to cut costs guaranteeing the 100 percent of quality parts. However, achieving zero defects in the parts is difficult to accomplish despite years of improvements in the manufacturing processes. In this framework automatic inspection of surface defects has emerged as a necessary task for manufactures who strive to improve product quality and production efficiency.

This paper has been motivated by the need for an automated inspection technique that detects small defects on the sheet metal forming processes. The nearly imperceptible characteristics of the defects and the high reflective nature of the formed metallic surfaces have prevented an early development of an automatic technique.

Sheet metal forming or stamping is a manufacturing process where a sheet is clamped around the edge and formed into a cavity by a punch. The metal is stretched by membrane forces, being conformed to the shape and dimensions to those of the active elements of the pressing device.

Stamping is one of the most common manufacturing processes especially in the automotive sector. Everyday, millions of parts are made by stamping, ranging from small fasteners to large bodywork panels. The extensive application of this manufacturing technique is due to the technical and economic advantages that sheet metal forming presents compared to other manufacturing processes such as casting, forging or machining: presses allow high production rates, lightweight parts with very

M. Fritz, B. Schiele, and J.H. Piater (Eds.): ICVS 2009, LNCS 5815, pp. 345–353, 2009.

complex shapes may be obtained and finally, the manufactured parts do not require any additional mechanical processing.

Despite these remarkable advantages, it is well known that sheet metal forming is an intricate technology. In bodywork manufacturing, the stamping operation is completed using an enormous force in a very short period of time in a process that involves a great number of parameters such as material properties, thickness, geometric shape and dimension, punch velocity, vibration modes, lubrication, surface finish and cleanness of the die. As a result, some unavoidable problems may occur in practice, being one of the most common the fracture of the material due to the thickness diminution when complex parts are stamped into shape.

The apparition of fractures is restricted to some localized zones, where high demands are placed on the material (double curvatures, sharp corners, deep recesses...), however it is visually difficult to detect them because they are not always characterized by an open crack. Often, only a localized reduction of the sheet metal, known as necking, may appear. The localized necking, if the tensile forces continue, is terminated by the final separation or crack.

When necking occurs, an early detection of the defective parts is of crucial importance in bodywork manufacturing. If a defective part slips past the normal quality procedures and arrive at the assembling line, the manufacturer will fall into a very costly lapse. Once the bodywork of the car is completely assembled, it is painted and introduced into a drying oven. There, under the high temperature, the material dilates originating intolerable notorious cracks where the metal fibers were initially broken by necking.

The detection of the defects at this point is extraordinary expensive because the cracks are impossible to repair and there is no other choice but to send the complete assembled and painted bodywork to the scrap yard.

Currently, the only online inspection method for the stamped sheet metal parts is human visual inspection. Human visual inspection is costly, time-consuming, and prone to making errors due to inspectors' lack of experience and fatigue. The task of care-fully inspecting a great number of stamped parts is especially tedious considering the nearly imperceptible characteristics of the necking and the high reflective nature of the metallic surfaces. In a framework where the product quality is mainly a competitive value, it becomes necessary the inclusion of automatic systems in this type of inspection processes.

Several difficulties exist in automatically inspecting stamping defects. The main complication is that the inspection must be performed on complex shaped parts of zinc coated steel. Due to the high reflective nature of this material, a homogeneous illumination of the surface is practically impossible to obtain.

2 Related Work

Image processing technology has enabled to automate many visual inspection tasks in industrial environments especially in the automotive industry. However, online automatic inspection of shaped metallic surfaces has not been accomplished yet. Several solutions have been presented for automatically scanning flat reflective surfaces but have not hitherto been applicable to three-dimensional shaped surfaces. Flat surfaces are inspected in arrangements in which an illumination beam is sent to the surface and their flatness makes it simple to predict where the reflected beam will be and to collect it suitably. In this case, defects and flaws on the material become obvious by the change in the reflection behavior. However, for metallic shaped objects such as stamped parts it is extremely complicated or impossible to predict the path of the reflected beam.

Several methods can be considered for the inspection of car body surfaces but none of them present the accuracy, reliability and speed required in an industrial manufacturing line. Triangulation techniques, such as fringe projection and structured lighting, are difficult to use on metallic surfaces, because they necessitate a diffuse reflectance that is not present on metals. Furthermore these techniques can not provide the accuracy needed to detect the necking defects characterized by a very small variation of the surface curvature. Other systems such as stylus instruments are more sensitive permiting an accurate quantitative characterization of this type of defects but their measuring process are extremely slow to be used in a production line. Other methods based in interferometry such as conoscopic holography have been successfully applied in the inspection of precision components in nanotechnology however they are too fragile to the rough conditions present in the automotive stamping lines.

Due to the lack of feasible methods for on-line inspection of car body parts, this task is mostly done by human operators up to now. Aiming to conquer the above difficulties, this research proposes a computer vision system that employs an image fusion algorithm for detecting the cracks and the necking defects in the stamped parts.

Image fusion algorithms allow integrating a series of images to produce a composite image that will inherit most salient features from the individual images. The series used for fusion can be taken from multimodal imaging sensors or from the same imaging sensor at different times.

In our case, we employ only a CCD camera to acquire four images of the same area but each image is acquired under a different illumination point. The idea is to obtain an image series where the glints appear in different positions in each of the individual images. Combining the information present in all the images of the series we can obtain a clean image where the spurious features proceeding from glints have been eliminated. Then, the resulting combined image could be thought of as an image taken by an advanced yet-not-existing imaging sensor that is immune to glints.

3 Image Fusion

This problem of obtaining a single composite image from an image series is addressed by image fusion. In our case, the goal is to reliably integrate image information from four images to make defect detection more reliable.

Ideally, a fusion algorithm should satisfy the requirements [1]: (i) preserve all relevant information contained in the input images; (ii) minimize any artifacts or inconsistencies in the fused image; (iii) tolerate imperfections avoiding the introduction of noise and irrelevant parts of the image. In our case, the fusion will permit to suppress the irrelevant features of the source images and concentrate only on the salient information. Then the detection of the delicate features corresponding to the defects can be carried out accurately.

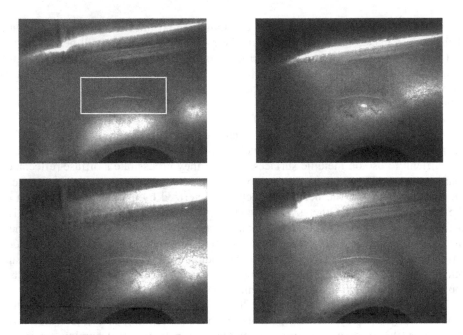

Fig. 1. Four images of the same area are acquired under different illumination. The size of the necking defect (marked on the *top left* image) is about 25 mm x 0.5 mm. Due to the considerable amount of glints, shadows and the microtexture present in the images, the detection of these small defects can not be carried out reliably using only one image.

In the literature [2], the fusion process has been carried out at different levels of information representation: signal; pixel; feature; and symbolic level. In [3], information of interest was extracted from each image separately and then it was combined at a decision level. Unfortunately, because this approach rely upon the initial extraction of features this inevitably results in the reduction of the available information in the image, compared to that contained in the original image's pixels, prior to any fusion process. A more general and powerful approach is to process the two images simultaneously by means of a previous fusion strategy. In this paper we have focused on the so-called pixel level fusion.

Even focussing at the pixel level there are many different fusion techniques: weighted combination, optimization approaches [5][6], biologically-based algorithms and multiresolution (MR) decompositions [7]. MR image fusion techniques decompose the image into several components that embody the information at different resolution scales. We have chosen a multiresolution decomposition scheme because we are interested in separate the structures present in the image at fine and at coarse scale. Furthermore, MR algorithms are computationally efficient.

3.1 Multiresolution Fusion Methods

Multiresolution fusion methods transform each of the input images $I_1, I_2, ..., I_N$ from normal image space into some other domain by applying an MR transform ω.

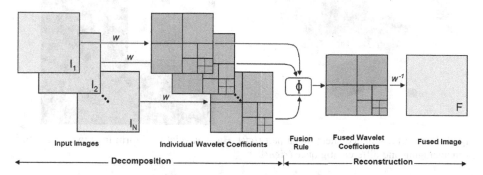

Fig. 2. Pixel based fusion scheme using wavelets

The transformed images are combined using some fusion rule ϕ. Then the fused image F is reconstructed carrying out the inverse transform ω^{-1}:

$$F = \omega^{-1}(\phi(\omega(I_1), \omega(I_2), ..., \omega(I_N))) \qquad (1)$$

Among MR methods, wavelet transforms have been successfully applied in many fusion algorithms. Wavelets can decompose the image information in the localization of both spatial and frequency domains. Another advantage of the wavelet transform is that it can be implemented in a very efficient way extending the one-dimensional operator to compute the two-dimensional image decomposition [9].

3.2 Haar Wavelet Transform

Haar wavelet uses a method for manipulating the matrices called averaging and differencing. The averaging and differencing process is first carried out for every row and then the same process is performed for every column of the image matrix [10].

The Haar wavelet transform framework for image decomposition is shown in Fig. 3. In Fig. 4, an image of a stamped part and its one-level wavelet decomposition are shown.

The Haar wavelet transform can be analyzed in a more abstract mathematical setting using special functions called Haar wavelets [11].

Since the four images of every series are taken at the same time and from the same sensor, no previous registration or rectification is needed to fuse the images.

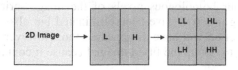

Fig. 3. Haar wavelet transform framework resulting from image decomposition: *(top left)* 2-D lowpass filter (LL); *(top right)* horizontal highpass and vertical lowpass filter (HL); *(lower left)* horizontal lowpass and vertical highpass filter (LH);*(lower right)* 2-D highpass filter (HH)

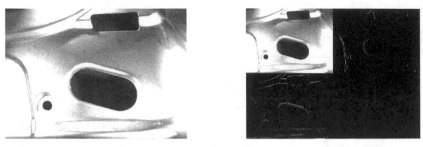

Fig. 4. Image of a stamped sheet metal part *(left)*. Haar wavelet transform framework resulting from averaging and differencing once *(right)*.

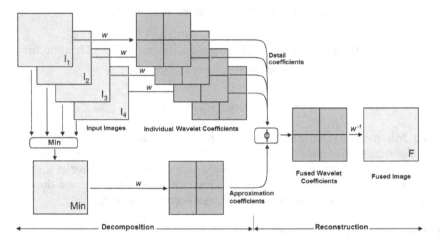

Fig. 5. The fusion is carried out using a one-level Haar transform. The minimum image is previously computed in order to eliminate glints obtaining the low frequency information.

The advantage of combining the images in wavelet space is that different frequency ranges can be processed separately. For example, low frequency information from one image can be combined with higher frequency information from another to increase details in the resulting image.

3.3 Fusion Rule

First, the minimum image will be calculated choosing for every pixel the minimum value among the four homologous pixels of the image series. In this minimum image, most of the glints will have been eliminated but also many interesting features for defect detection will have disappeared too. However, this minimum image provides a first data to obtain the fused image because it contains the low frequency of the scene.

The delicate features corresponding to defects are extracted from the high frequency information present in the four images of the series.

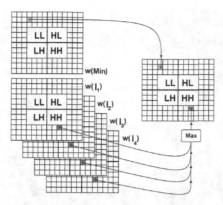

Fig. 6. The approximation coefficients of the fused image *(in LL)* are integrated by the coefficients of the transformed minimum image; the detail coefficients *(in HL, LH and HH)* are established choosing the maximum value at every pixel location in the transformed image series

4 Experimental Results

In figure 7 the result of the fusion of the image series shown in figure 1 is presented. In the fused image, most of the glints, shadows and surface microtexture have been eliminated. The features present in the image correspond faithfully with the details present in the scene. However, even in this image the defect detection is not straight-forward. A number of features that are not defects already remain in the image. It is essential to carefully characterize necking defects in order to distinguish between real defects and features of the surfaces such as moldings marks, creases, corners... which can be present in the surface.

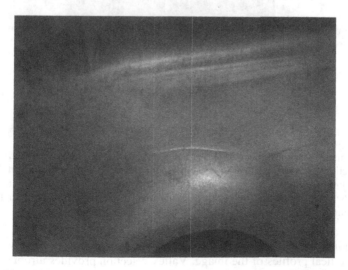

Fig. 7. Fused image obtained from the series of fig.1. The annoying glints have been removed from the image but the salient information of the part surface has been preserved.

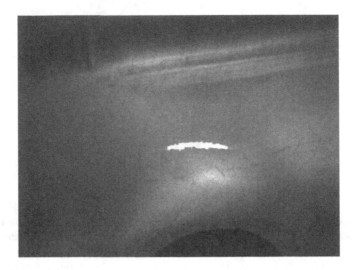

Fig. 8. A valley detection algorithm has been applied in order to detect the defects. A deep sharp valley in the fused image point out the presence of a necking defect in the image.

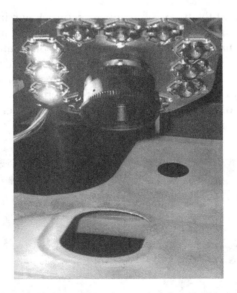

Fig. 9. The image series have been recorded using a robot that displaces the acquisition system to the inspection zones [8]. The illumination is integrated by four independent LED arrays mounted around the camera optics. The lights are triggered separately and controlled by the computer. The intensity of the lights can be programmed independently in order to avoid the complete saturation of the image in some areas with intricate geometry.

The necking defects can be extracted from the intensity image rapidly looking for valleys in vertical profiles of the image. Valley detection provides a robust method to eliminate the remaining spurious features in a very fast manner [4]. In figure 8 the sharp intensity valleys, which correspond to the defect, are highlighted.

5 Conclusions

Automatic inspection of complex shaped surfaces of stamped sheet metal is extremely difficult due to the subtle characteristics of the defects and the high reflective nature of the metallic surfaces. In order to improve the defect detection reliability we acquire series of four image of every inspection zone using complementary lighting conditions. We have presented a multiresolution image fusion algorithm to obtain a meaningful single composite image where the spurious features originated in the image by the glints are eliminated. The fusion has been accomplished using a one-level Haar transform that enables a fast combination of low frequency information from one image with higher frequency information from others. The resulting fused image contain improved quality of information compared to individual source images to infer the presence or absence of necking defects than any of the individual images used in the fusion process.

Acknowledgments. This research was financially supported by the Research Project Program of the Consejería de Educación y Cultura de la Junta de Castilla y León.

References

1. Rockinger, O.: Pixel-level fusion of image sequences using wavelet frames. In: Proceedings of the 16th Leeds Applied Shape Research Workshop. Leeds University Press (1996)
2. Clark, J.J., Yuille, A.L.: Data Fusion for Sensory Information Processing Systems. Kluwer Academic Publishers, Boston (1990)
3. Barrientos, D., de la Fuente, E., Barrientos, F.J., Trespaderne, F.M.: Machine Vision System for Defect Detection in Metal Sheet Forming Processes. In: Proceedings of Int. Conference on Visualization, Imaging and Image Processing, pp. 289–294 (2001)
4. Fuente, E., Trespaderne, F.M., Gayubo, F.: Detection of Small Splits in Car-Body Manufacturing International Conference on Signal Processing. Pattern Recognition and Applications (2003)
5. Puente León, F.: Enhanced imaging by fusion of illumination series Sensors, Sensor Systems, and Sensor Data Processing. In: Loffeld, O. (ed.) Proceedings of SPIE 3100, pp. 297–308 (1997)
6. Puente León, F., Kammel, S.: Inspection of specular and painted surfaces with centralized fusion techniques Measurement. 39, 536–546 (2006)
7. Piella, G.: A general framework for multiresolution image fusion: from pixels to regions. Information Fusion 4(4), 259–280 (2003)
8. Gayubo, F., Gonzalez, J.L., de la Fuente, E., Trespaderne, F.M., Perán, J.R.: On-line machine vision system for detect split defects in sheet-metal forming processes. In: ICPR, vol. 1, pp. 723–726 (2006)
9. Heijmans, H., Goutsias, L.: Nonlinear multiresolution signal decomposition schemes. Part II: Morphological wavelets, IEEE Transactions on Image Processing 9(11), 1897–1913 (2000)
10. Mulcahy, C.: Image Compression Using The Haar Wavelet Transform, Spelman College Science. Mathematics Journal 1(1), 22–31 (1997)
11. Stolnitz, E.J., De Rose, T.D., Salesin, D.H.: Wavelets for computer graphics. Morgan Kaufman Publishers, USA (1996)

Who's Counting? Real-Time Blackjack Monitoring for Card Counting Detection

Krists Zutis and Jesse Hoey

School of Computing, University of Dundee
{kristszutis,jessehoey}@computing.dundee.ac.uk

Abstract. This paper describes a computer vision system to detect card counters and dealer errors in a game of Blackjack from an overhead stereo camera. Card counting is becoming increasingly popular among casual Blackjack players, and casinos are eager to find new systems of dealing with the issue. There are several existing systems on the market; however, these solutions tend to be overly expensive, require specialised hardware (e.g. RFID) and are only cost-effective to the largest casinos. With a user-centered design approach, we built a simple and effective system that detects cards and player bets in real time, and calculates the correlation between player bets and the card count to determine if a player is card counting. The system uses a combination of contour analysis, template matching and the SIFT algorithm to detect and recognise cards. Stereo imaging is used to calculate the height of chip stacks on the table, allowing the system to track the size of player bets. Our system achieves card recognition accuracy of over 99%, and effectively detected card counters and dealer errors when tested with a range of different users, including professional dealers and novice blackjack players.

1 Introduction

Who's Counting? is a computer vision based software prototype designed to track a live game of casino Blackjack, with the primary goal of detecting players that use the technique of card counting in an attempt to gain an edge over the casino. Blackjack (or "21") is the most popular casino table game in the world, in which the aim is to end the round with more points than the dealer, while remaining equal to or under 21 points. The only proven method of gaining an edge over the house is card counting, in which a player tracks which cards have been played, allowing him or her to make optimised betting decisions. Without card counting, the house has a 0.5% higher chance of winning a round. Although card counting without the use of physical aids or equipment is not illegal, the majority of casino establishments do not allow players to count cards. With the rapid advances in portable technology, it has become easier for the average Blackjack player to card count, for instance through the use of an iPhone application that makes counting cards easier, acquired by 500 new users every day [11]. Combined with an increased awareness of card counting due to movies such as "21" , casinos are forced to deal with more card counting attempts.

This paper describes our research into the use of automated systems for detecting card counting. In a user-centered design process, we surveyed and interviewed casino employees, uncovering requirements for such a system. The main

M. Fritz, B. Schiele, and J.H. Piater (Eds.): ICVS 2009, LNCS 5815, pp. 354–363, 2009.

requirements were (1) speed, as blackjack games can be very fast; (2) cost, as casinos are a money-making business; and (3) non invasiveness, as blackjack players and dealers are intolerant of any technological devices on the table or in the chips/cards. Interestingly, these requirements were more important than accuracy, with dealers stating that they would tolerate a small amount of inter-action with the system to ensure 100% accuracy.

We describe a real-time (5fps) system to detect card counting from a single overhead stereo camera. The system uses a combination of contour analysis, template matching and the SIFT algorithm to detect and recognise cards. Stereo imaging is used to calculate the height of chip stacks. The outputs of these two algorithms are combined with a temporal analysis to detect if a person is counting cards based on the pattern of their plays and bets over a period of time. The two key contributions of the work are a user requirements gathering and the demonstration of stereo for chip stack value counting.

2   Background

There has been relatively little work on card counting or card game monitoring from cameras. Recent efforts by casinos have focussed on radio-frequency iden-tification tags (RFID) embedded in cards and chips. However, these solutions are prohibitively expensive, and susceptible to fraud. Due to the blind broadcast nature of RFID, experimentation kits have become widely available (from e.g. ThinkGeek.com), and RFID systems have been plagued with security concerns that players would be able to broadcast a compromised signal, possibly rep-resenting different chip denominations. While encryption within the chips can provide an extra layer of security, this greatly increases the cost of each chip.

Computer vision gives an ideal simple, fast, and inexpensive solution. How-ever, there is little published work in this direction. Clear Deal [4] used a com-bination of line detection, corner detection and template matching to detect the value of the cards as they are dealt throughout the game. The system analysed the quality of the shuffle carried out by the dealer by comparing the deal across hands, and detected card counting by monitoring game decisions and comparing them with basic strategy. However, this system had no way of monitoring the size or variation of bets placed by the player. Card counting strategy shows that 70-90% [6] of the edge developed by a player is applied by changing the size of the bet as the count fluctuates, whereas the remaining 10-30% of the advan-tage goes towards the ability to alter game decisions which, therefore, lead to a higher proficiency. Zaworka [12] tracked a Blackjack game by detecting cards and players' chip stacks as they are bet, in real time. Overall accuracy was 97.5% for detecting playing cards and chip stacks, even with occlusion. However, the system only detected the presence, not the values, of cards and chip stacks. The system used an electronic chip tray, whereas ours uses only computer vision. Template matching and a combination of heuristics was used by Zheng [13] to match cards invariant to rotation, but the technique did not handle face cards well, did not model chips or bet sizes, and did not produce a final usable system. The recognition rate was 99.8% over a range of rotations.

There are a few commercial attempts to market systems for card counting monitoring. Tangam Gaming (tangamgaming.com) produces an automated card recognition system that requires the use of speciality hardware such as RFID. The MindPlay21 system relied on a range of specialized hardware which included 14 cameras, invisible ink, and RFID tags. Cameras were used to scan the cards as they were dealt, as each card had been marked with a unique barcode painted in special ink [10]. The cost of $20,000 per table, the unreliable components and the slow speed of operation led to the company going out of business in 2005.

Generic object recognition has seen much use in the past decade [9]. There are a number of discriminative approaches proposed, perhaps the most common of which is the use of invariant features [8]. In particular, the scale invariant feature transform (SIFT) is used in many areas of image processing, such as 3D modelling, image stitching and object recognition [7]. SIFT extracts distinct keypoints from an image, which can be compared to other sets of keypoints to look for matches. The keypoints extracted by SIFT are invariant to scale, rotation, and location, with partial invariance to view point angle. Template matching is still in use due to its simplicity and efficiency [2].

3   Requirements Gathering

Our primary goal was to develop a working prototype that would meet the requirements of casino operators, croupiers, and players. Thus, a user-centered design approach consisting of informal interviews and discussions, observations of blackjack games, questionnaires, and consultations with local casino employees and managers uncovered design requirements from an end-user perspective.

The questionnaire contained three sections. The first section aimed to find the level of necessity for the proposed system. The second portion gathered non-functional requirements that would determine the performance aspects of the system, and the final part of the questionnaire was used to extract the usability requirements for the system. We received 7 completed questionnaires.

Our requirements analysis uncovered the following needs:

- a necessity for, and an interest in automated card counting detection systems,
- most dealers have suspected a player of card counting,
- error detection features were desired,
- players tend not to play at tables where any technology is visible, particularly if there are cameras at table level.

The requirements analysis also uncovered the following design requirements:

- speed of card detection (2 seconds or less)
- accuracy should be 95% or higher.
- interaction with the system was considered acceptable.
- a graphical user interface (GUI) was preferable to a textual one for croupiers.

4   System Description

Figure 1(a) shows a view of the system, showing the overhead stereo camera (Pt. Grey Research 640x480 Bumblebee2 using IEEE 1394 link), the card dealing table, and the croupier's interface. The computer is an Intel Quad Core 3.2 GHz Processor and 4 Gigabytes of RAM running Linux Ubuntu 8.10. The software is written in C/C++, and uses the OpenCV library [1].

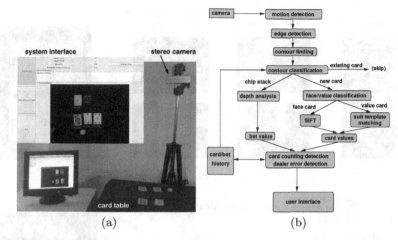

Fig. 1. (a) Who's Counting? system (b) schematic of the software

Figure 1(b) shows a block diagram of the algorithm used. Briefly, the video stream from the overhead camera is fed to a motion detection algorithm that locates stable images (without hands etc) (Section 4.1). Edges and contours are then extracted from the stable images, and are classified into existing cards, new cards, suit blocks, or chip stacks (Section 4.2). Chip stack contours are then further analysed using stereo to calculate the number of chips in the stack (Section 4.3). Suit blocks are saved for future processing, existing cards are recorded, and new cards are classified into face or value cards (Section 4.4). Face cards are then compared to stored models using the SIFT algorithm (Section 4.4). All suit block contours within a value card are counted using template matching to detect the final value of the card (Section 4.4). All card detections also have an associated confidence measure. Finally the card and bet values are passed to the card counting detection system, which stores the current hand, compares the hand to the history, and relays information to the croupier (Section 4.5).

The system uses multiple parameters and thresholds that are specific to a given setup, and are manually specified. The 'area' parameters are dependent on the distance of the camera from the table surface, and the thresholds for contour extraction are dependent upon lighting levels (assumed constant).

4.1 Motion Detection

Motion is detected using image differencing, and triggers a second phase where the system looks for minimal image differences. The first subsequent image with an absolute difference of less than 8000 pixels is valid. This avoids capturing images with dealers or player's hands. Figure 2(a) shows an example.

4.2 Contour Detection and Classification

Canny Edges are found [3], followed by contour-following analysis in OpenCV [1]. Each contour is classified into one of three categories (card, chip stack or suit block) using its area, centroid, and geometry. The classification parameters are

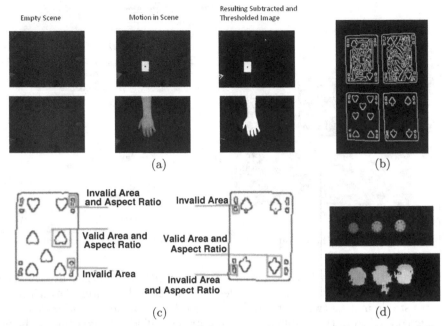

Fig. 2. (a) Example image differencing (b) Binary edge images showing (top row) Face cards with 1407 and 1637 edge pixels and (bottom row) value cards with 630 and 549 edge pixels (c) Binary edge image of a 9 and a 4 of hearts shows valid suit blocks (d) image and disparity map of chip stacks 1, 5 and 10 chips high

dependent on the camera height, here we use 86cm. Any contour with 4 vertices and with an area between 4500 and 12000 pixels is classified as a card. Vertices are found using the OpenCV library for contours. These contours are then further classified as existing or new cards, and as dealer or player cards depending on their centroid. Any contour with an area between 70 and 220 pixels, and with an aspect ratio between 0.5 and 1.5 is classified as a suit block (see Figure 2(c)). The centroid of the suit blocks are used to assign them to cards. Finally, any contour with an area between 1000 and 2000 pixels, with an aspect ratio of the surrounding rectangle between 0.8 and 1.2, and with a Hough transform that matches a circle [5] is classified as a chip stack.

Our system does not compensate for unenclosed contours, thus, a full contour around the circumference of the card and each suit block must be detected in order to successfully recognise a card. We found that, due to the clear difference between the suit blocks and card background, the hysteresis thresholds in the Canny edge detector were easily set to ensure full contours.

4.3   Chip Counting Using Stereo

In a casino, a bet is placed by stacking chips of the same value, and then placing that stack onto the bet area of the table. Our requirements analysis showed that players were not in favour of cameras at table level, so stereo vision from above was used. A BumbleBee2 stereo camera gave accurate and reliable dense stereo estimates, and a depth resolution that was just adequate to detect an individual chip. The average disparity given by the stereo correspondence algorithm at the chip location given by the contour analysis (see Section 4.2) was calculated as the mode of all disparity values within the chip area. This disparity result was then converted to depth and compared to the pre-calibrated chip stack height values to determine the size of the bet. This calibration was learned from a number of runs of the stereo algorithm on chip stacks of known height.

4.4   Card Classification

Cards were classified as face or value cards for further processing using a simple method of counting the number of edge pixels within the card area and comparing to a threshold (1100 was used in our experiments). This method returned consistent results, an example of which can be seen in Figure 2(d). We now describe how the values of face cards and value cards were determined.

Face Cards. We only matched SIFT features on the local areas of each face card: a segmented image size of 100 by 130 was sufficient to find a strong match (100 to 200 keypoints) while maintaining speed. Two keypoints match if the Euclidean distance is less than 0.6. Confidence estimates for face cards were computed by counting how many keypoints the best match had compared to the second best match. A difference of three keypoints was allocated a confidence of 90%, with a further 2% being added for every additional keypoint matched.

Value Cards. The value of a card is determined by counting the number of suit blocks that agree with the highest confidence. A fast normalised cross correlation template matching algorithm is used on each candidate suit block, and all those with a correlation of more than 0.4 are kept. Each suit's template is matched twice, once at the original rotation, and the second time with a 180° vertical rotation. The value of the card is then assigned to be the number of matched suit blocks, N. To determine the suit and confidence of the card, suit block i is matched to suit $k_i \in \{h, d, c, s\}$ with maximum correlation r_i. The card's suit, k^*, is then determined as the one with the highest summed correlation, $k^* = \arg\max_k \sum_{i=1}^{N} \mathbb{I}(k_i, k) r_i$, where $\mathbb{I}(k', k)$ is an indicator function returning 1 if $k' = k$ and 0 otherwise. The card's confidence, c^* is the mean correlation after assigning 0% to all suit blocks with $k_i \neq k^*$: $c^* = \frac{1}{N} \sum_{i=1}^{N} \mathbb{I}(k_i, k) r_i$. It was found this non-linear method yielded more consistent results than a simple maximum of the average of suit correlations.

The area and aspect ratio attributes used to identify candidate contours are invariant to rotation and location, but not the template matching. Automatic rotation of cards to a canonical orientation would help with this problem./

4.5   Card Counting, Dealer Error Detection, and User Interface

To detect card counting, the system looks for correlations between a player's bets and the *card count*, a measure of the likelihood that the next card will have a high value. The *card count* is measured using the "Hi-Lo" method, in which a running count is kept, starting at zero. Each card that is dealt with a value from 2 to 6 adds +1 to the count, 7 to 9 adds 0 to the count, and aces, 10s and face cards all add -1 to the count. If a player increases their bets when this count is high, then card counting is likely. The Hi-Lo card counting strategy was employed because it is the most commonly used method by card counters. However, other methods could also be substituted.

We used a correlation coefficient to calculate the relationship between the sequence of bets b_t and card counts d_t, for $t = 1 \ldots T$ as $r = ((T-1)\sigma_b\sigma_d)^{-1} \sum_{t=1}^{T} (b_t - \bar{b})(d_t - \bar{d})$, where σ_b and σ_d are the sample standard deviations of b and d. A simple threshold on this value is then used to raise an alert to a dealer.

To detect dealer errors, such as paying out a losing hand, our system monitored the payout phase of a round of Blackjack. For any given hand, the game could end in a payout to the player, a loss for the player (removal of the player's chip stack), or a tie (player's chip stack is untouched).

The system required a graphical user interface to show the status of the game and any warning to the dealer. Since the dealer's job is to deal the game of Blackjack, only the basic features are necessary so that the dealer could simply glance at the GUI and ensure that everything was in order. Since testing showed that stereo imaging alone was not reliable enough to calculate the size of the bet placed by the user at all times, an additional input field in the interface allowed the dealer to manually adjust the bet value.

5   Evaluation

Testing was split into three sections, accuracy testing of card recognition and chip stack height, testing of the card counting detector, and user testing to evaluate the system as a whole from the user's perspective.

5.1   Accuracy

To test the accuracy of playing card recognition, each card of two decks was placed onto a green felt lined table ten times. The stereo camera was 86cm above the surface of the table. 8 cards of the same value were then placed onto the table and the results were recorded. This was repeated five times for each set of 8 cards, giving a total of 65 images, with each card being tested ten times. The processing times for a new play was below the required time of 2 seconds.

We first tested the card outline detection and found the system was able to correctly identify cards placed in the scene 100% of the time. We then tested the face/value card differentiation, also finding 100% accuracy. We found 100% accuracy in detecting face cards for both value and suit.

Each value card was tested 40 times, since each card was tested 10 times, and there are 4 suits. The correct value of the card was detected correctly 399 out of 400 times, showing an overall accuracy for card value detection of 99.75%. The results for each suit are Spade: 87%, Club: 98%, Heart: 98%, Diamond: 84%, with an overall accuracy of 92%. However, note that the suit of a card has no impact on the game of Blackjack.

The accuracy of bet value detection was tested using chip stacks of varying heights from 1 to 10 placed directly under the camera. Out of a total 100 chip

Table 1. Results of 30 games showing the correlation r between bets and card counts

card counting	game number														
	1	2	3	4	5	6	7	8	9	10	11	12	13	14	15
no	-0.62	-0.21	0.30	0.27	-0.32	0.36	-0.34	0.33	0.43	0.37	0.28	-0.09	0.32	0.14	0.44
yes	0.68	0.91	0.93	0.89	0.77	0.96	0.71	0.90	0.62	0.82	0.86	0.27	0.65	0.32	0.90

height calculations, with ten for each height, the correct values were detected 97 times. The first two errors occurred when detecting a 1 chip high stack, and resulted in an underestimated stereo depth calculation. The third error came from unsuccessful chip detection from the image processing algorithm with 9 chips in the stack. The results conclude that out of 100 placed bets, 97% of the bet values were successfully calculated. The stereo algorithm worked 97 of the 99 times it was run, giving an overall accuracy level of 98%. The chip detection algorithm had overall accuracy of 99%.

5.2 Card Counting

To test the system's ability to detect card counters, 30 games of Blackjack, each with 20 rounds, were played by the authors, for a total of 600 rounds. In fifteen games, the cards were dealt randomly and the player played according to standard rules (no card counting). In the other fifteen games, the player used the "Hi-Lo" card counting system to vary his bets. The card count correlations (r) for each of the games are shown in Table 1. Thus, we see a threshold on r set between 0.45 and 0.62 would be effective. Games 12 and 14 of the card counting tests gave outlying results. These were caused by a continuous negative card count throughout the test period. In an actual situation such as this, a card counter would continue to bet the minimum amount of chips until the cards shifted to a positive count. However, in these tests, the count did not become positive within the twenty test rounds, and resulted in a low correlation score. Figure 3 shows two screenshots of the system in action, with one showing a card counting detection.

5.3 User Tests

The complete system functionality was tested with users of different backgrounds to evaluate the usability and overall performance. The test group for this study consisted of two professional Blackjack dealers, two average Blackjack players, and four inexperienced players. At the beginning of the test, the background and limitations of the system were described, and example hands were shown to the participants. One participant was then asked to deal a game of Blackjack, while the experimenter played the role of player. Each participant played 15 hands of Blackjack. As well as being observed during the testing, the participants were interviewed after the tests to find the successful and unsuccessful areas of the system. There was general approval of the system. The system successfully detected card counting, and even withstood an attempt to trick the system by placing extremely large bets during the first few hands, then dropping the bet value and proceeding with normal card counting techniques. The system was still able to detect the card counter in fewer than 20 hands after this attempt.

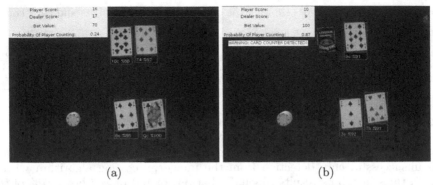

Fig. 3. (a) The interface output after ten rounds of Blackjack, when monitoring a non card counting player. The output shows the state of the current round, as well as the correlation coefficient result of 0.24 - a result which is below the card counter threshold of 0.75. (b) System output when monitoring a card counting player for ten rounds of Blackjack. A correlation coefficient result of 0.87 indicates card counting.

The dealer error detection was also successful, since it not only detected errors which were purposefully included, but also detected genuine, unintended errors. The system detected incorrect dealer payouts, where the dealer wrongly paid out, or collected the chips when the player had won. However, testing also identified certain areas where the system could be improved. The majority of requests were to update the interface to display information more clearly. Dealers would sometimes adjust the card's position on the table, resulting in the card being recognised twice. This was fixed by adding a buffer area around each card, allowing it to have slight changes in location after it has been placed.

6   Conclusion and Future Work

This paper presented a system for detection of card counting and dealer errors in casino blackjack. The system uses a combination of computer vision techniques to track cards and bets, and uses a correlation algorithm to detect card counting. Our requirements analysis and system implementation have demonstrated the need for, as well as the success of detection of card counters. By introducing a pure computer vision solution, the system showed that a cost effective, discrete system can be used to automate casino surveillance.

Several elements could contribute to future developments of similar applications. Contour analysis was well suited to real-time processing needs, and template matching could be used in real time applications, if the region of interest is localised to a small area. The SIFT algorithm functions well for matching objects even when the database of keys taken from images is limited. Therefore, lowering the image resolution and size before extracting keys for the database results in less keys and a much faster recognition time. A significant result from this research was that stereo imaging can be successfully used to detect the height, and therefore the value of chip stacks. In conducting background research, we found that the ability to identify the value of player bets is a highly desired tool from a casino's perspective. This is a particularly promising area to proceed with further research, as it is a feasible method of monitoring chip values without the need for extra hardware, such as RFID tags. Improvements to the system will be more comprehensive detection of unexpected events, support for mutliple players, dealing with occluded cards, automated card and chip threshold calibration, and application to other games such as Roulette or Three Card Poker.

Acknowledgments. The authors thank the users who participated in the surveys and tests, and the staff of the Dundee casino.

References

1. Bradski, G., Kaehler, A.: Learning OpenCV. O'Reilly Media, Sebastopol (2008)
2. Brunelli, R.: Template Matching Techniques in Computer Vision: Theory and Practice. Wiley, Chichester (2009)
3. Canny, J.: A computational approach to edge detection. IEEE Trans. Pattern Analysis and Machine Intelligence 8, 679–714 (1986)
4. Cooper, W., Dawson-Howe, K.: Automatic blackjack monitoring. In: Proc. of Irish Machine Vision Conference, pp. 248–254 (2004)
5. Duda, R.O., Hart, P.E.: Use of the hough transformation to detect lines and curves in pictures. Comm. ACM 15, 11–15 (1972)
6. Fuchs, K.: Knock-out blackjack - the theory. koblackjack.com website, (April 22, 2008), http://www.koblackjack.com/system.html
7. Lowe, D.G.: Distinctive image features from scale-invariant keypoints. International Journal of Computer Vision 60(2), 91–110 (2004)
8. Mikolajczyk, K., Schmid, C.: A performance evaluation of local descriptors. IEEE Transactions on Pattern Analysis and Machine Intelligence 10(27), 1615–1630 (2005)
9. Ponce, J., Hebert, M., Schmid, C., Zisserman, A. (eds.) Toward Category-Level Object Recognition. LNCS, vol. 4170. Springer, Heidelberg (2006)
10. Terdiman, D.: Who's holding the aces now? Blackjack Universe website article, (August 18, 2003), http://blackjackuniverse.com/pages/news/mindplay.html
11. Terdiman, D.: Casinos on lookout for iphone card-counting app. CNET news article, (February 17, 2009), http://news.cnet.com/8301-10797_3-10165861-235.html
12. Zaworka, A., Scherer, S.: Machine vision driven real-time black jack analysis. In: Proc. of 24th workshop of the AAPR (2000)
13. Zheng, C., Green, R.: Playing card recognition using rotational invariant template matching. In: Proc. of Image and Vision Computing New Zealand, December 2007, pp. 276–281 (2007)

Increasing the Robustness of 2D Active Appearance Models for Real-World Applications

Ronny Stricker[1], Christian Martin[1,2], and Horst-Michael Gross[1,*]

[1] Neuroinformatics and Cognitive Robotics Lab,
Ilmenau University of Technology, Germany
{ronny.stricker,christian.martin,horst-michael.gross}@tu-ilmenau.de
http://www.tu-ilmenau.de/neurob
[2] MetraLabs GmbH, Germany

Abstract. This paper presents an approach to increase the robustness of *Active Appearance Models* (AAMs) within the scope of human-robot-interaction. Due to unknown environments with changing illumination conditions and different users, which may perform unpredictable head movements, standard AAMs suffer from a lack of robustness. Therefore, this paper introduces several methods to increase the robustness of AAMs. In detail, we optimize the shape model to certain applications by using genetic algorithms. Furthermore, a modified retinex-filter to reduce the influence of illumination is presented. These approaches are finally combined with an adaptive parameter fitting approach, which can handle bad initializations. We obtain very promising results of experiments evaluating the IMM face database [1].

Keywords: Active Appearance Model, Genetic Algorithm, Retinex-filter, Illumination, Optimization.

1 Introduction

Within the scope of human-robot-interaction, it is often necessary to analyze the identity and the emotional state of the dialog partner. *Active Appearance Models* (AAM) have been established to characterize non-rigid objects, like human heads, and can be used to analyze the user's state based on visual features. Therefore, the parameters of the AAM are adapted, so that the model fits to the current face. Afterwards, the parameters of the AAM can be utilized to determine the expression or gender of the user's face. The main drawback of this approach is that it depends to a large extent on the current operational environment. Especially under real world conditions with uncontrolled observation constraints a mobile robot has to cope with different problems arising from these dependencies. This work suggests improvements of the robustness of the

---

* The research leading to these results has received partial funding from the European Community's Seventh Framework Programme (FP7/2007-2013) under grant agreement no. 216487 (CompanionAble-Project).

M. Fritz, B. Schiele, and J.H. Piater (Eds.): ICVS 2009, LNCS 5815, pp. 364–373, 2009.

adaption step in AAMs to gain a higher independence of the operational environment. This paper is organized as follows: After a brief description of the basics of AAMs, Sect. 3 gives an overview of the related work. Afterwards, we introduce our contribution to increase the robustness of the fitting process. Sect. 5 shows the results which can be achieved with the help of the proposed methods. The paper concludes with a summary and an outlook on ongoing work in Sect. 6.

2   Basics of Active Appearance Models

Active Appearance Models, first introduced in [2], provide a good possibility to model non rigid objects within the scope of image processing and are, therefore, very popular to model human faces or viscera. The AAM itself is a combination of two statistical models. First, the shape model represents the geometry of the object. Secondly, the appearance model allows the modeling of the object texture within the normalized mean shape of the model. The models are built by training images, which are labeled with landmark points on certain positions of the object. These n landmark locations build up the shape $\mathbf{s} = (x_1, y_1, ..., x_n, y_n)^T$ of an AAM instance. Using a Principle Component Analysis (PCA) for all training shapes, the resulting shape model can be represented by a set of shape parameters $\mathbf{p}$ combined with the basis shapes $\mathbf{s_i}$:

$$\mathbf{s}(\mathbf{p}) = \mathbf{s_0} + \sum_{i=1}^{n} p_i \mathbf{s_i}. \tag{1}$$

Afterwards, a triangulation of the mean shape $\mathbf{s_0}$ is used to establish a relation between the labeled points and the surface of the object. With the help of surface triangles, every single point on arbitrary shape $\mathbf{s_i}$ can be warped to a destination shape $\mathbf{s_j}$ using an affine transformation. With respect to [3] we can describe this transformation as $W(\mathbf{x}; \mathbf{p})$, which maps a point $\mathbf{x} = (x, y)^T$ within the model shape to the shape defined by the parameters $\mathbf{p}$. This transformation is used afterwards to build the appearance model, which is very similar to the shape model. The important difference is that each texture sample A_i, defined by the training images, is warped to the mean shape $\mathbf{s_0}$, using the described affine transformation. The texture parameters resulting from the subsequent PCA are denoted as λ. Therefore the texture object is very similar to the *Eigenface* approach:

$$\mathbf{A}(\lambda) = \mathbf{A_0} + \sum_{i=1}^{m} \lambda_i \mathbf{A_i} \quad , \forall \mathbf{x} \in \mathbf{s_0}. \tag{2}$$

The resulting AAM can represent any object instance M covered by the training data using the shape parameter vector $\mathbf{p}$ and the appearance parameter vector λ using (3).

$$M(W(\mathbf{x}, \mathbf{p})) = \mathbf{A_0}(\mathbf{x}) + \sum_{i=1}^{m} \lambda_i \mathbf{A_i}(\mathbf{x}) \quad , \forall \mathbf{x} \in \mathbf{s_0}. \tag{3}$$

The goal of fitting an AAM to an unknown image, as defined by [2], is to minimize the squared difference between the synthesized model and the given image. Using gradient descent to solve this problem leads to a very efficient fitting algorithm. To overcome the problem of simultaneous optimization of shape- and appearance parameters, Baker and Matthews introduced the *Project-Out* gradient descent image alignment algorithm [4]. As the exact formulation of the fitting algorithm lies beyond the scope of this paper, the reader is referred to [3,4] for more detailed information.

3   Related Work

Within the last years, AAMs have become very popular for the purpose of face tracking [5,6] or classification tasks, like facial expression recognition [7,8]. In this context, the problems of illumination independence and robust fitting have been addressed by different approaches. A common method to cope with illumination changes is to model the illumination explicitly as shown in [9]. Besides the construction of the model, this methods add additional parameters to the AAM, which have to be determined during the fitting process and hence increase the complexity. A survey on different approaches dealing with illumination can be found in [10]. The problem of fitting robustness is addressed in [6] by using a hierarchy of models with different complexities. However, this approach involves the toggling between different models which complicates the combination with tracking algorithms. The problem of finding the optimal shape for an AAM, however, has been addressed significantly less in the literature. The only available work concentrates on optimizing the landmarks in terms of their salience as shown in [11]. To our knowledge, this is the only approach which tries to optimize the shape of an existing shape model.

4   Increasing the Robustness

Due to the principle of minimizing the difference between the input image and the synthesized model, the fitting process is very sensitive to differences between the training images and the images used during model fitting [12]. Furthermore, wrong initializations can lead the fitting process to local minima and, therefore, may cause a bad match. This problem increases with the number of model parameters growing as the complexity of the error surface increases as well. Therefore, the AAM shouldn't exceed the needed complexity for the desired application.

4.1   Optimization of the Shape Model

The construction of an AAM is based on training images which are labeled with specified landmark points. As a result, the model quality, defined as its ability to fit to unknown images, depends on the quality of the landmarks and the training images. Unfortunately, the process of adding landmarks to unknown images is quite complex and manual work is indispensable at least to refine the landmark positions. Yet, this process itself is very error-prone as well. Our tests have shown that the variance of the position of hand-labeled landmark points is very

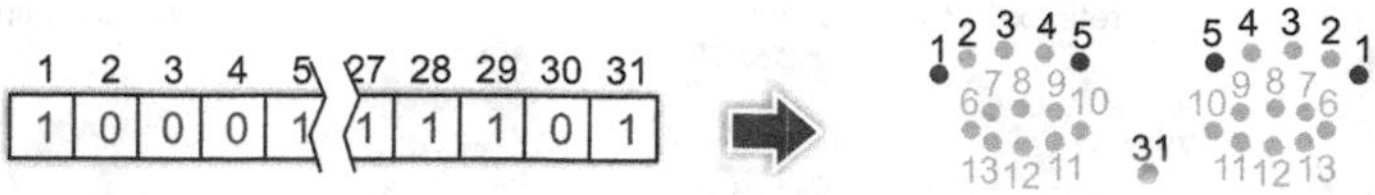

Fig. 1. Exploiting the symmetry constraint, the 58 landmarks of the IMM database shape [1] can be coded using a genome with 31 bits. Only the upper half of the face landmark points are displayed.

high. Furthermore, these errors are not equally distributed, so that landmarks in heavily textured regions can be reproduced very well. One way to find such reliable features using their salience is described in [11]. However, building a model based on the most salient features is not always equal to finding those landmarks optimal for the desired application purpose. Therefore, we present a new method to reduce the number of given landmarks to an explicit set in order to reduce the influence of badly labeled landmarks and to reduce the model complexity. Examples for such a reduced model can be found in [6] and [13], where some kind of *inner-face-model* is used.

Ideally, to reduce a given set of landmarks to an optimal set regarding the desired application involves the analysis of all combinations of different landmarks. Even if the symmetry of the human face it taken into account, the search domain is typically too large to be holistically analyzed. However, it can be expected that the adding and removing of several landmark points from the model have similar effects on different submodels. Therefore, it is a common way to use some kind of evolutionary search, e.g. genetic algorithm, to analyze the search domain in a sparse but purposive way. The different possible shape models are coded as a genome exploiting the symmetry of the human face (Fig. 1). To evaluate a genome, the corresponding AAM is generated and applied to a test dataset afterwards. The dataset should be designed in such a way that the desired application (e.g. emotion recognition) can be represented as good as possible. Therefore, it should contain the respective classification task of interest.

4.2 Adding Robustness to Illumination Changes

Especially within the scope of face recognition, the effects of illumination have been examined very well [10]. The explicit modelling of the illumination can provide satisfying results, but is generally very complex and often not capable of real-time processing. Nevertheless, the model free *retinex filter* first introduced in [14] can achieve promising results within the scope of removing the influence of different kinds of illumination. This filter relates each pixel of the image to its local surroundings:

$$R(\mathbf{x}) = logI(\mathbf{x}) - log|F(\mathbf{x}) * I(\mathbf{x})| \tag{4}$$

where I is the input image and F denotes a function representing the surroundings of the pixel $\mathbf{x}$. Unfortunately, it is necessary to set the size of the surrounding area to an appropriate value to avoid problems of ghost shadows and the loss of detail or insufficient illumination normalization (Fig. 2). This problem has been

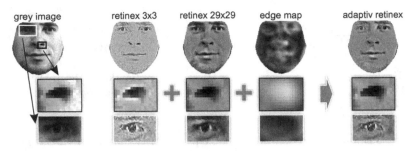

Fig. 2. Comparison of different retinex approaches - the original retinex approach with a surrounding of 3x3 Pixels generates ghost shadows (nostril) and reduces the detail (eye). The retinex filter with a surrounding of 29x29 pixels in turn shows only poor illumination normalization (eye). The adaptive retinex, however, combines the advantages of both filter sizes due to selective combination with the help of the edge map.

addressed with the *multiscale retinex* approach presented in [15], which combines retinex filters with different sizes of the surrounding area. Unfortunately, the described approach only diminishes the problems occurring from wrong parametrisation. Another approach can be found in [16], where the surrounding function is modeled using an anisotropic filter. Unfortunately, the filter is computationally intensive which is not desirable for real time applications. As a combination of the approaches described in [15] and [16], we introduce a kind of *adaptive retinex* filter. We combine the idea of the *multiscale retinex* approach with a dynamic combination function, which depends on the local edge strength. Therefore, we use two retinex filter $R_1(\mathbf{x})$ and $R_2(\mathbf{x})$ with different sizes of the surroundings and add an edge detector $E(\mathbf{x})$, which computes the local edge strength. If the surrounding size of R_2 is smaller than the size of R_1 the combination can be expressed by (5).

$$
\mathcal{S}(\mathbf{x}) = \begin{cases} R_1(\mathbf{x}) & K(\mathbf{x}) < l_l \\ R_2(\mathbf{x}) & K(\mathbf{x}) > l_u \\ \frac{K(\mathbf{x})}{l_u}R_1 + (1 - \frac{K(\mathbf{x})}{l_u})R_2 & l_l \leq K(\mathbf{x}) \leq l_u \end{cases} \tag{5}
$$

Where l_l and l_u denote the lower and upper bounds of the retinex filter with the bigger or smaller surroundings. For edge values between the lower and upper bound, a combination of the two different retinex filter outputs is taken. Due to the dynamic combination of different surrounding sizes, the presented filter is not that addicted to specific illumination conditions. Furthermore, the filter can be computed in a much more efficient manner than the anisotropic one [16].

4.3   Adaptive Parameter Fitting

The *Project-Out* fitting algorithm uses gradient descent and is, therefore, very sensitive to get stuck in local minima. One way to deal with this problem is to apply a hierarchy of models with an increasing number of parameters, as we have already shown in [17]. Nevertheless, it is hard to decide at which point of time the fitting process should switch to a more detailed model. Furthermore, if applied to tracking purpose, the model parameters of a detailed model have to be refused if the fitting process has to switch back to a simple model. This paper introduces an approach for adaptive parameter fitting, which works with only one model of the object (in detail the face).

Due to the applied PCA, used to build the shape model of the face, the shape *Eigenvectors* can be sorted according to their *Eigenvalues*. The *Eigenvalues* in turn represent the variance of the training data in the direction of the associated *Eigenvector*. So, the first *Eigenvectors* have a higher importance to represent the given training data. Standard gradient descent fitting algorithms, like the *Project-Out* algorithm, are based on adapting all model parameters at the same time. However, this approach can force the model parameters, which are associated with *Eigenvectors* with lower importance, to diverge. The reason for this behaviour is that the first, and most important, parameters are not yet stabilized, so that the later parameters are likely to converge into the wrong direction (Fig. 3). We try to address this problem by dividing the model parameters into two different groups. First, the *primary* parameters which are important for the main head movements like pan and tilt, and the *secondary* parameters, responsible to code the shape variance of the inner face. Then, we can suppress changes of the *secondary* shape parameter during the fitting process as long as the *primary* shape parameters have not been stabilized. To detect the strength of the parameter changes, we compute the normalized parameter changes of the n *primary* parameters using the *Eigenvalues EV*:

$$E_p = \sum_{i=1}^{n} \left(\frac{\Delta p_i}{EV(p_i)} \right)^2 .$$

(6)

Afterwards, the parameter changes of the *secondary* parameters can be scaled using a logarithmic coefficient which equals zero if E_p equals the squared sum of all *Eigenvalues* of the *primary* parameters and is equal to 1 if E_p is equal to zero. As shown in Fig. 3 the introduced adaption of the *secondary* parameters can successfully smooth the parameter changes and, thus lead to a more purposive model fitting as we intend to show in Sect. 5.

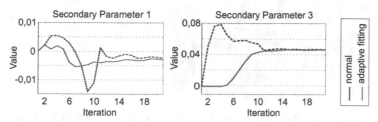

Fig. 3. Simultaneous fitting of all parameters can lead the *secondary* parameter into a wrong direction. Adaptive fitting can improve this behaviour by repressing changes of the *secondary* parameters as long as the *primary* parameters are not stabilized (until iteration 6).

5   Experimental Results

This section presents some experimental results we have achieved by using the described approaches. We decided to use the IMM face database [1] for our studies to produce consistent and meaningful results. The database consists of 6 different images for each of 40 different people. The images contain frontal and side views, as well as sidewise illuminated images and emotion images. To fit the built models to the images, we use the standard *Project-Out* fitting algorithm as described in [3] and start each fitting process with a frontal initialization to give consideration to common face detectors. As the AAMs are prone to initialization errors, we start the fitting process for each model and image for a certain amount of rounds, whereas the initialization is perturbed in every round with increasing variance. Afterwards, the quality of every fitting process is evaluated using a combined measure between the mean and the maximum distance between the ground truth shape, provided by the IMM database, and the fitted shape. This measure is able to distinguish between converged and diverged models using a threshold. Although this threshold appears to be seemingly at random and makes comparisons with other papers more difficult, we found it to be a good and meaningfull measure for quantitative comparisons of the suggested improvements. The fitting rates given below always refer to the declared images of every person within the IMM database (frontal images refer to the images 1 and 2; sidewise view images refer to the images 3 and 4; illumination image refers to image 5).

Optimization of the Shape. This section presents the optimization of the shape, given by the IMM database, with respect to fitting accuracy. Therefore, we evaluate each computed genome with respect to its fitting accuracy, computed as the mean and maximum distance between the ground truth and the resulting shape. Thereby, the generated shapes show a significant improvement over the complete shape with respect to the distance values. Having a closer look at the

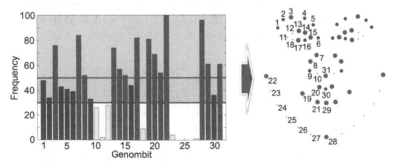

Fig. 4. The different landmarks of the 100 best genomes are color coded according to their frequency of employment. The lower surrounding of the face can be represented sufficiently by labels 22 and 28, whereas labels 23 to 27 can be ignored. For the sake of clarity only half of the labelpoints are annotated.

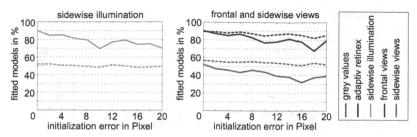

Fig. 5. Using the *adaptive retinex* filter significantly improves the fitting performance for sidewise illuminated images. Unfortunately filter tends to be more sensitive to bad initialization.

used landmark points of the 100 best shapes, it can be seen that especially the surrounding of the face is not necessary for accurate model fitting (Fig. 4). This is an interesting finding in contrast to commonly used AAM labeling instructions. The landmarks in the inner face region are least affected by the shape reduction. This points seem to be necessary for reliable model fitting given different poses and emotions.

Robustness to Illumination Changes. To show the benefit of the proposed *adaptive retinex* filter we build the AAMs based on the images with frontal illumination. The models are applied afterwards to the images with sidewise illumination (Fig. 5). Although the fitting can be significantly improved for images with sidewise illumination, the image preprocessing seems to be more sensitive to bad initialization. The *adaptive retinex* filter also removes slight illumination changes occurring from the three-dimensional structure of the head – for example the illumination on the cheek. This seems to complicate the fitting process, especially for rotated heads. Nevertheless, this disadvantage seems to be uncritical in most cases due to the great benefit achieved for sidewise illumination.

Adaptive Fitting. The effect of applying adaptive fitting to the *Project-Out* algorithm on frontal and sidewise views is illustrated in Fig. 6. While the fitting

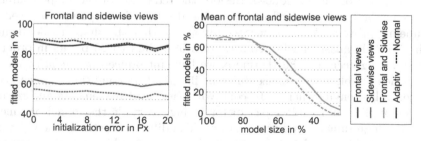

Fig. 6. *Adaptive fitting* improves the fitting performance for images with bad initialization. Therefore sidewise views and models with wrong scaling initialization can be improved. Left: Shape perturbed in *x* and *y* direction. Right: Shape with perturbed scaling.

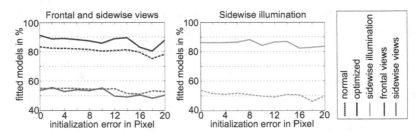

Fig. 7. The combined approach achieves better fitting performance. Especially the performace for sidewise view can be significantly improved from 50 % to 85 %.

performance remains almost the same for frontal views, it can be improved for sidewise views. This result indicates that the adaptive fitting successfully enables the algorithm to rotate the model, before the adaption of the *secondary* parameters is carried out. The same improvement can be observed for a model initialization with perturbed size parameters. Again the model is able to scale the main shape before the *secondary* parameters were fitted and, therefore, is able to produce significantly better results.

Full Optimization. After having discussed the effects of each of the introduced methods, now the results for the combined approach are presented in Fig. 7. Although the different methods degrade under certain circumstances, the combined approach produces better results for all kinds of images of the IMM database. Although the fitting performance is only slightly increased for neutrally illuminated images, it can be significantly improved for sidewise illumination conditions. Therefore, the fitting performance can be increased by approximately 10 percent for frontal views, and by 35 percent for sidewise illuminated images.

6   Conclusion and Future Work

In this paper, we have presented different methods to increase the robustness of AAMs. First of all, an approach to adapt the complexity of the shape model to certain applications is introduced. Besides the reduction of the shape complexity, this method may be used to find reduced sets of label points to speed up the labeling process. We have successfully shown that the shape model defined by the IMM database can be reduced from 58 points to 25 points in order to increase fitting accuracy. Furthermore, we have introduced an *adaptive retinex* filter, which is able to normalize different illumination conditions, which occur in uncontrolled environments. To cope with fast head movements and rotated faces, we applied an adaptive parameter fitting, to guide the model parameter within the high dimensional error surface. The different methods show promising results for different AAM specific problems. The combination of all methods leads to a robust and real-time capable approach which has been tested in our lab on the mobile robot SCITOS and performs significantly better than standard approaches. Continuing our work, we will cope with the problem of shape optimization within the scope of emotion classification.

References

1. Stegmann, M.B., Ersbøll, B.K., Larsen, R.R.: FAME – A Flexible Appearance Modelling Environment. In: IEEE Trans. on Medical Imaging, pp. 1319–1331 (2003)
2. Cootes, T.F., Edwards, G., Taylor, C.J.: Active Appearance Models. In: Proc. of the European Conf. on Computer Vision (1998)
3. Baker, S., Matthews, I.: Lucas-Kanade 20 Years On: A Unifying Framework. Int. Journal of Computer Vision, 221–255 (2004)
4. Baker, S., Matthews, I.: Equivalence and efficiency of image alignment algorithms. In: Proc. of IEEE Conf. on Computer Vision and Pattern Recognition, pp. 1090–1097 (2001)
5. Baker, S., Matthews, I., Xiao, J., Gross, R., Kanade, T.: Real-time non-rigid driver head tracking for driver mental state estimation. Robotics Institute, Carnegie Mellon University (2004)
6. Kobayashi, A., Satake, J., Hirayama, T., Kawashima, H., Matsuyama, T.: Person-Independent Face Tracking Based on Dynamic AAM Selection. In: 8th IEEE Int. Conf. on Automatic Face and Gesture Recognition (2008)
7. Ratliff, M.S., Patterson, E.: Emotion Recognition using Facial Expressions with Active Appearance Models. In: Proc. of HRI (2008)
8. Saatci, Y., Town, C.: Cascaded Classification of Gender and Facial Expression using Active Appearance Models. In: Proc. of the 7th Int. Conf. on Automatic Face and Gesture Recognition, pp. 394–400 (2006)
9. Kahraman, F., Gokmen, M., Darkner, S., Larsen, R.: An Active Illumination and Appearance (AIA) Model for Face Alignment. In: IEEE Conf. on Computer Vision and Pattern Recognition, pp. 1–7 (2007)
10. Zou, X., Kittler, J., Messer, K.: Illumination Invariant Face Recognition: A Survey. In: IEEE Int. Conf. on Biometrics: Theory, Applications, and Systems, pp. 1–8 (2007)
11. Nguyen, M.H., la Torre Frade, F.D.: Facial Feature Detection with Optimal Pixel Reduction SVMs. In: 8th IEEE Int. Conf. on Automatic Face and Gesture Recognition (2008)
12. De la Torre, F., Collet, A., Quero, M., Cohn, J., Kanade, T.: Filtered Component Analysis to Increase Robustness to Local Minima in Appearance Models. In: IEEE Computer Society Conf. on Computer Vision and Pattern Recognition, pp. 1–8 (2007)
13. Kim, D., Kim, J., Cho, S., Jang, Y., Chung, S.-T., Kim, B.G.: Progressive AAM Based Robust Face Alignment. In: Proc. of world academy of science, engineering and technology, pp. 483–487 (2007)
14. Jobson, D., Rahman, Z., Woodell, G.: Properties and performance of a center/surround retinex. In: IEEE Transactions on Image Processing, pp. 451–462 (1997)
15. Jobson, D., Rahman, Z., Woodell, G.: A multiscale retinex for bridging the gap between color images and the human observation of scenes. In: IEEE Transactions on Image Processing, pp. 965–976 (1997)
16. Wang, H., Li, S., Wang, Y.: Face recognition under varying lighting conditions using self quotient image. In: Proc. of the IEEE Int. Conf. on Automatic Face and Gesture Recognition, pp. 819–824 (2004)
17. Martin, Ch., Gross, H.-M.: A Real-time Facial Expression Recognition System based on Active Appearance Models using Gray Images and Edge Images. In: Proc. of the 8th IEEE Int. Conf. on Face and Gesture Recognition, paper no. 299 (2008)

Learning Query-Dependent Distance Metrics for Interactive Image Retrieval

Junwei Han, Stephen J. McKenna, and Ruixuan Wang

School of Computing, University of Dundee, Dundee DD1 4HN, UK
{jeffhan,stephen,ruixuanwang}@computing.dundee.ac.uk

Abstract. An approach to target-based image retrieval is described based on on-line rank-based learning. User feedback obtained via interaction with 2D image layouts provides qualitative constraints that are used to adapt distance metrics for retrieval. The user can change the query during a search session in order to speed up the retrieval process. An empirical comparison of online learning methods including ranking-SVM is reported using both simulated and real users.

1 Introduction

Critical components in any content-based image retrieval (CBIR) system are the methods used to compute the dissimilarity of images and to obtain feedback from users during search. Most early CBIR systems relied on pre-defined distance functions (e.g., Euclidean distance in feature space) for image dissimilarity measurement. Although these so-called computer-centric systems are relatively easy to implement, some inherent drawbacks limit their performance. Image understanding is highly subjective; each user will have different personal intentions and preferences when searching for images. These can vary from session to session even if identical queries are posed. Therefore, pre-defined distance metrics based on fixed combinations of features are inadequate.

Relevance feedback (RF) was proposed to help address this limitation [11]. It attempts to adapt to a user's preferences by performing on-line learning of a query-dependent distance function based on user feedback. Most RF techniques operate under the assumptions that users are looking for a category of images and start with a query example from that category. After each iteration of retrieval, the user provides feedback on the relevance of the retrieved images. Machine learning methods such as support vector machines [14] or manifold learning [4] are then used to refine the distance function based on the feedback. The refined distance function is then applied to obtain new retrieval results.

In general, traditional RF techniques learn from user feedback that consists of labelling returned images as relevant or irrelevant, or perhaps assigning quantitative relevance scores to them. The first type of feedback ignores information on the degree of relevance. The second type of feedback can be difficult and time-consuming for users to provide. For example, a user might puzzle unnecessarily over whether a relevance score should be 0.80 or 0.85. A more appropriate

M. Fritz, B. Schiele, and J.H. Piater (Eds.): ICVS 2009, LNCS 5815, pp. 374–383, 2009.
© Springer-Verlag Berlin Heidelberg 2009

form of feedback is based on relative comparisons or ranks, e.g. "the query image is more similar to image A than it is to image B". The study of how to learn from relative comparisons is attracting increasing attention. Joachims [7] proposed a ranking-SVM method which converted the learning task to a standard SVM classification task. It was applied to learning from 'clickthrough' data for Web search engines. Schultz and Joachims [12] extended this approach to learn distance metrics. Freund *et al.* [2] presented the RankBoost algorithm.

Rank-based distance learning has been used to solve vision problems. Frome [3] proposed a method to learn local image-to-image distance functions for classification by combining relative comparison information and image shape features. Hu *et al.* [5] explored a multiple-instance ranking approach based on ranking-SVM to order images within each category for retrieval. Lee *et al.* [8] employed a rank-based distance metric to retrieve images of tattoos. However, these three approaches [3,5,8] were evaluated under the scenario of *offline* learning.

This paper proposes a target-based interactive image retrieval approach that incorporates on-line rank-based learning. It makes the following contributions. (i) A novel user feedback mechanism is proposed. Instead of asking users to label training data as relevant or irrelevant, the users are able to offer relative, qualitative information to the system. (ii) Rank-based online learning is used to refine the distance metric based on constraints generated from user feedback. (iii) The user can change the query example during a session in order to speed up retrieval. (iv) An empirical comparison of methods including ranking-SVM is reported. This includes evaluations based on simulated users and a preliminary evaluation with real users.

2 Problem Formulation

The scenario considered here is that of search for a specific target image in an image set I. Search is terminated when the target is found or the user decides to give up the search. This contrasts with many CBIR systems in which it is assumed that users are searching for images that belong to some category of images. Target-based retrieval is very useful in applications such as logo, trademark, historical photograph, and painting search [1].

A search session consists of a series of iterations. At the tth iteration, the user is presented with a 2D visualisation of a set of retrieved images, a subset of I. These appear as a 2D layout, L_{t-1}, and are arranged based on their content. The user selects a query image, q_t, from this layout. The selected query may or may not be the same image as the previous query, q_{t-1}. The user can also move the images in the layout to express judgements about relative similarity to the query. The user's similarity judgements will depend on the target and the context. This results in a set of inequality constraints, P_t. A learning algorithm then uses the selected query and the constraints to obtain a new distance metric, D_t. This metric is then used to retrieve the closest matches from the image set and a visualization algorithm produces a new 2D layout from these matches for the user. This sequence can be summarised as follows.

$${L_{t-1}} \xrightarrow{\text{user}} {q_t, P_t} \tag{1}$$

$${I, q_t, P_t} \xrightarrow{\text{learner}} {D_t} \tag{2}$$

$${I, q_t, D_t} \xrightarrow{\text{matcher and visualizer}} {L_t} \tag{3}$$

Let $\mathbf{q}$ and $\mathbf{x}$ denote feature vectors of a query image and an image in the database, respectively. A parameterized (Mahalanobis) distance metric can be used: $D(\mathbf{q}, \mathbf{x}; \mathbf{W}) = \sqrt{(\mathbf{q} - \mathbf{x})^T \mathbf{W} (\mathbf{q} - \mathbf{x})}$, where the symmetric matrix $\mathbf{W}$ should be positive semi-definite (i.e., $\mathbf{W} \succeq 0$) to ensure that D is a valid metric. If $\mathbf{W}$ is a diagonal matrix, the distance metric becomes a weighted Euclidean distance, which is adopted here:

$$D(\mathbf{q}, \mathbf{x}; \mathbf{w}) = \sqrt{\sum_i W_{mm}(q_m - x_m)^2} = \sqrt{\langle \mathbf{w} \cdot ((\mathbf{q} - \mathbf{x}) * (\mathbf{q} - \mathbf{x})) \rangle} \tag{4}$$

where q_m and x_m denote the mth elements of $\mathbf{q}$ and $\mathbf{x}$. The mth diagonal element, W_{mm}, of $\mathbf{W}$ reflects the importance of the mth feature. "$\langle \cdot \rangle$" denotes the inner product and "$*$" the element-wise product of two vectors. $\mathbf{w}$ is the vector consisting of diagonal elements of $\mathbf{W}$. Note that $\mathbf{w} \succeq 0$.

An initial layout L_{-1} can be generated using a representative (or randomly selected) subset of I. Alternatively, if the user has a query example q_0 already to hand, the first two steps, (1) and (2), are omitted in the first iteration and $\mathbf{w}_0$ is taken to be a vector of ones so that D_0 is a Euclidean distance metric.

Key to the proposed target-based retrieval approach is to learn the parameter $\mathbf{w}_t$ based on the user-provided constraints, P_t. This learning component of the system will be described in Section 4. First, the user interaction and the visualization component are introduced.

3   User Interaction Based on 2D Visualization

In a CBIR system, the user interface must present retrieval images to users and enable interaction for the purpose of providing feedback. A well-designed interface will make this interaction easy and quick for users, and enhance the efficiency of the system. Firstly, retrieval results are visualised as 2D layouts. Secondly, users can move images on the layout to convey their preferences. The relative locations of the images are then taken to provide ranking information from which the system can learn.

Most traditional CBIR systems show retrieval results as lists sorted in order of decreasing similarity to the query. Moghaddam et al. [9] argued that visualizing images in a 2D space can be superior, allowing mutual similarities to be reflected. Rodden [10] performed user studies which demonstrated that 2D layouts could enable users to find a target image or group of images more quickly.

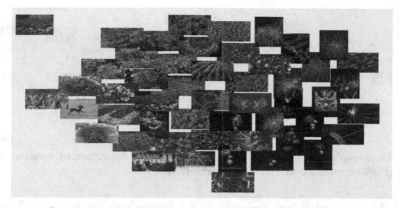

Fig. 1. An example layout showing a query (top left) and 50 closest matches

The visualisation method of Wang *et al.* [15] was modified here in order to generate 2D layouts, L_t. The main idea of this method is to combine an unsupervised dimensionality reduction algorithm with a term that rewards layouts that have high entropy. It enables layouts to be generated that represent a trade-off between (i) preserving the relative distances between images and (ii) avoiding image overlaps and unoccupied layout regions. The distance between two images was measured using D_t. Whereas Wang *et al.* [15] used an ISOMAP term, a multi-dimensional scaling (MDS) term was used instead in this paper because of the relatively small number of images in each layout. In common with [15], Renyi quadratic entropy was used. Fig. 1 shows an example layout. The query is at the top-left of the interface. The 50 most similar images to this query are arranged automatically based on color correlogram features [6]. Visually similar images are grouped together which is helpful for users when making judgements and providing feedback on their preferences.

Traditional RF techniques assume that users are searching for a category of images and require users to label results as relevant or irrelevant thus indicating whether or not they are in the same category as the query. Such feedback is essentially a set of class labels. Cox *et al.* [1] argued that this burdens the user by forcing them to decide upon a useful categorization of images even if unfamiliar with the database. It is appropriate to category-based search rather than target-based search. In this paper, users are allowed to drag images in the 2D visualization space and the relative locations of images and query image convey their preferences. Fig. 2 shows an example in which only five retrieved images are used, for clarity of presentation. Fig. 2(a) shows the automatically generated layout. Fig. 2(b) shows the layout after the user has chosen to move the images to reflect their perceived relative similarity to the query (image q). This user-defined layout yields an ordering of the images in terms of similarity to the query, in this case $1 \succ 2 \succ 3 \succ 4$, where $\succ$ denotes a ranking relationship. This ordering implies a set of inequalities on the distance measure being used by the user. If the user arranges N images relative to the query then there are $\frac{N(N-1)}{2}$ such inequalities. However, if we assume that the user's measure is a metric then

Fig. 2. An example of user interaction in which images are arranged relative to the query. (a) Before interaction. (b) After interaction.

most of these are redundant and only $N - 1$ inequalities are needed. These are used to provide constraints for the learning algorithm to learn a new metric D_t. In the example shown in Fig. 2(b) the constraints would be $P_t = \{D_t(q_t, 1; \mathbf{w}) < D_t(q_t, 2; \mathbf{w}), D_t(q_t, 2; \mathbf{w}) < D_t(q_t, 3; \mathbf{w}), D_t(q_t, 3; \mathbf{w}) < D_t(q_t, 4; \mathbf{w})\}$.

Moghaddam *et al.* [9] also used 2D visualization to collect feedback but their method differs in two main respects. Since their purpose was to group images for browsing, all relationships between images were used. Instead, this paper is concerned with target-based retrieval so only relationships between images and query are used. Secondly, [9] used absolute locations of images for learning. Instead, a more qualitative feedback is adopted here for reasons discussed earlier.

4   Rank-Based Distance Metric Learning

The objective of the learner is to infer the parameter $\mathbf{w}$ of the distance metric $D(.,.;\mathbf{w})$. Ideally, this metric should satisfy the constraints P. (For clarity, the subscript t is omitted in this section). A maximal-margin formulation with slack variables is adopted here to perform this learning task. The task is formulated as the following optimization problem which has the same form as in [3] and [12].

$$\min_{\mathbf{w},\xi_{(q,i,j)}} \tfrac{1}{2} \| \mathbf{w} \|^2 + C\sum_{(q,i,j)} \xi_{(q,i,j)}$$

$$
\begin{aligned}
&s.t. \\
&\forall(D(q,i;\mathbf{w}) > D(q,j;\mathbf{w})) \in P: \ D^2(q,i;\mathbf{w}) - D^2(q,j;\mathbf{w}) \geq 1 - \xi_{(q,i,j)} \\
&\forall(q,i,j): \ \xi_{(q,i,j)} \geq 0 \\
&\mathbf{w} \succeq 0
\end{aligned}
\tag{5}
$$

Here, $\| \mathbf{w} \|^2$ is a regularization term and indicates structural loss, $\xi_{(q,i,j)}$ are slack variables, and C is a trade-off parameter. Substituting (4) into the first set of constraints in (5) leads to

$$\langle \mathbf{w} \cdot (\mathbf{d}_{q,i} - \mathbf{d}_{q,j}) \rangle \geq 1 - \xi_{(q,i,j)} \tag{6}$$

where $\mathbf{d}_{q,i} = (\mathbf{q} - \mathbf{x}_i) * (\mathbf{q} - \mathbf{x}_i)$, and $\mathbf{x}_i$ is the feature vector for the ith image.

The constraint $\mathbf{w} \succeq 0$ is needed to ensure that the learned distance is a valid metric. Incorporating this constraint is non-trivial. Without this constraint, the setting of the optimization would be the same as that of ranking-SVM and standard quadratic programming solvers such as SVM-Light could be used [7]. The purpose of ranking-SVM is to learn a ranking function which is expected to correctly sort data. In ranking-SVM, elements of $\mathbf{w}$ can have negative values and the ranking values can be negative. Although image retrieval can be formulated as a ranking problem using such an approach [5], it is not suitable for query-by-example. If ranking-SVM is used to perform query-by-example, the output for the query itself will be zero as desired. However, outputs for other images can be negative since elements of $\mathbf{w}$ can be negative. It leads to an undesirable situation in which other images can be deemed to be more similar to the query than the query itself. In Section 5, this point will be demonstrated empirically.

Frome [3] proposed a custom dual solver for the optimization problem which is adopted here. This approach can guarantee that $\mathbf{w}$ is non-negative. Moreover, its fast optimization speed and good performance make it suitable for online learning. It iteratively updates dual variables until convergence:

$$\mathbf{w}^{(t)} = \max \{ \sum_{(q,i,j)} \alpha_{(q,i,j)}^{(t)} (\mathbf{d}_{q,i} - \mathbf{d}_{q,j}), 0 \} \tag{7}$$

$$\alpha_{(q,i,j)}^{(t+1)} = \min \{ \max \{ \frac{1 - \langle \mathbf{w}^{(t)} \cdot (\mathbf{d}_{q,i} - \mathbf{d}_{q,j}) \rangle}{\| \mathbf{d}_{q,i} - \mathbf{d}_{q,j} \|^2} + \alpha_{(q,i,j)}^{(t)}, 0 \}, C \} \tag{8}$$

where $0 \leq \alpha_{(q,i,j)} \leq C$ are the dual variables and are initialized to zero. The reader is referred to [3] for implementation details.

5 Experiments

A set of $10,009$ images from the Corel dataset was used for experiments. These images have semantic category labels and there are 79 categories such as tiger, model, and castle. Each category contains at least 100 images. Category labels are not used in what follows. Three types of low-level feature were used: a 36-dimensional color histogram, an 18-dimensional texture feature based on a wavelet transformation [13], and a 144-dimensional color correlogram. In all experiments, the trade-off parameter C was set to 20. The computational speed mainly depends on the learning algorithm and the visualization algorithm. A Matlab implementation normally takes a few seconds to perform both learning and visualization on a 2.4GHz, 3.5GB PC which is adequate for on-line processing.

It is common to evaluate CBIR systems using simulated users since interactions from real users are expensive to collect. This is usually done using pre-defined, fixed category labels. Retrieved results are automatically marked as relevant if they share a category label with the query. Rank-based learning has been evaluated similarly [3,8,5]. The underlying assumption is that images within the same pre-defined category are always more similar to each other than images from other categories. In contrast, the purpose of the system in this paper is to find a target image without the use of pre-defined categories. Therefore, a different evaluation method is proposed.

Two experiments were performed. In the first experiment, the user was simulated. The second experiment involved online evaluation with four real users.

5.1   Evaluation Using a Simulated User

Experiments using a simulated user were performed as follows. A fixed distance metric, $D_{user}(\mathbf{q}, \mathbf{x}; \mathbf{w}_{user})$ based on the image features was used by the simulated user. Each simulated search session was initiated by randomly selecting two images from the database, one as query and one as target. In the first iteration, the system retrieved images based on a pre-specified metric $D_0(\mathbf{q}, \mathbf{x}; \mathbf{w}_0)$ that differed from D_{user}. At each iteration, the simulated user used D_{user} to select the closest retrieved image to the target and rank ordered the retrieved images in terms of distance to the query. In this way, $N - 1$ inequality constraints were generated and used by the learning algorithm to update the distance metric to better approximate D_{user}. Search terminated when the target was retrieved or when a maximum number of iterations was reached. Once an image had been retrieved it was excluded from being retrieved in subsequent iterations.

More specifically, 36-dimensional color histograms and 18-dimensional texture features were concatenated to give 54-dimensional feature vectors to represent the images. A total of 100 search sessions was simulated with up to 50 iterations per session. The distance metric was initialised to only use the texture features. In other words, the weights in Eqn. (4) were set to equal, non-zero values for each of the 18 texture features, and to zero for each of the 36 colour features. In contrast, the simulated user used a distance metric in which colour features had equal, non-zero values and texture features had weights of 0.

The number of images retrieved at each iteration is a free parameter, N. Larger values of N result in more feedback information at each iteration and greater choice of query for the subsequent iteration. However, large N also results in increased time and effort from the user at any given iteration. Fig. 3 shows results obtained by using different values of $N \in \{5, 10, 20, 30, 40, 50\}$. Performance was measured as the fraction of trials in which the target was retrieved within a given number of iterations. The proposed method retrieved nearly all targets within a few iterations provided that N was large enough.

The method was compared to several alternatives. Ranking-SVM was used to learn $\mathbf{w}$ from the inequality constraints. Code from SVM Light [7] was used. Another method involved randomly selecting N images without any simulated user interaction. Another method used the initial metric (i.e. texture only) for matching. Finally, the methods were compared to retrieval using the ideal metric, D_{user} (i.e. colour only). Fig. 4 shows comparative results for various values of N. The results demonstrate that the proposed approach is better than ranking-SVM especially when the value of N is small. For example, for $N = 10$, the proposed method achieved the retrieval rate of 59% and ranking-SVM achieved the retrieval rate of 7% at the tenth iteration. For $N = 20$, the performance of the proposed method and ranking-SVM was 96% and 50% respectively at

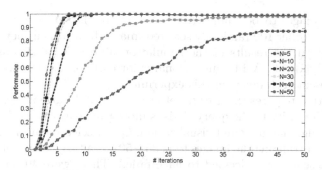

Fig. 3. Performance comparisons with different N

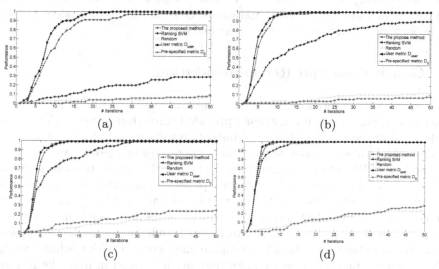

Fig. 4. Performance comparisons using different methods. (a) $N = 10$, (b) $N = 20$, (c) $N = 30$, and (d) $N = 40$.

the tenth iteration. Retrieval rates obtained by the proposed method quickly approached those obtained using the ideal metric as N increased. When $N = 40$, the proposed method differed from the ideal metric by about 5% only between the second round and fifth iterations. This indicates that the method was able to capture preferences.

5.2   Interactive Online Experiment with Users

Future work will be needed to fully evaluate the proposed approach with users. Here we report only a preliminary user experiment. Four subjects (2 male and 2 female) tested the system. Each subject performed ten search sessions. Target images were selected by users and came from 36 different categories. Before each session, the system displayed a layout of 100 images selected randomly from the image database. The user selected whichever of these images was most similar to the target as the initial query image unless the user did not consider any of these 100 images to be similar to the target. In the latter case, the system offered them another 100 randomly selected images from which they were forced to choose. Given the results of the simulation above, $N = 20$ was chosen as a reasonable trade-off. A 144-dimensional color correlogram feature vector was used to represent each image in this experiment.

Each iteration requires the user to select a query and move images to provide feedback on similarity to the query. This is more time-consuming than the CPU time for learning, matching and visualization. Query selection normally took less than $10s$ while arranging the images took $25 - 50s$. If a target was not found after 10 iterations, search was deemed to have failed. There were 40 search sessions in total and, of these, 5 failed, 3 found the target without any interaction other than initial query selection, 20 were successful within 5 iterations, and 12 others were successful using more than 5 iterations. Overall, successful sessions required an average of 5 iterations to retrieve the target.

6   Conclusions and Recommendations

An approach to adaptive target-based image retrieval was proposed. Maximal-margin learning based on constraints provided through user feedback was used to learn distance metrics. The experimental results suggest that the approach has potential for application to real-world interactive image-retrieval.

The idea of RF is to bring users into the loop and so evaluations with the real users are essential. However, few previous papers report interactive online tests. The interactive online test lead to two useful observations. Firstly, some retrieved images were considered irrelevant to the query by users. As such, users were not interested in them and did not like or found it difficult to provide judgements about them. Future work should investigate improved feedback mechanisms that allow users to efficiently select images they are interested in from the retrieval layouts and only provide feedback on those images. A second observation is that selecting appropriate query images to start a search session plays an important role in yielding success. Most failed searches were due to the initial query being very dissimilar to the target image. This problem would be reduced by selection of the initial query using an image browsing system that can present a global view of the whole database [16].

Acknowledgments. The authors thank A. Ward for valuable discussions. This research was supported by the UK Technology Strategy Board grant "FABRIC: Fashion and Apparel Browsing for Inspirational Content" in collaboration with Liberty Fabrics Ltd., System Simulation Ltd. and Calico Jack Ltd. The Technology Strategy Board is a business-led executive non-departmental public body, established by the government. Its mission is to promote and support research into, and development and exploitation of, technology and innovation for the benefit of UK business, in order to increase economic growth and improve the quality of life. It is sponsored by the Department for Innovation, Universities and Skills (DIUS). Please visit www.innovateuk.org for further information.

References

1. Cox, I.J., Miller, M.L., Minka, T.P., Papathomas, T.V., Yianilos, P.N.: The Bayesian image retrieval system, Pichunter: Theory, implementation, and psychophysical experiments. IEEE Trans. on Image Processing 9(1), 20–37 (2000)
2. Freund, A., Iyer, R., Schapire, R.E., Lozano-Perez, T.: An efficient boosting algorithm for combining preferences. J. Machine Learning Research 4, 939–969 (2003)
3. Frome, A.: Learning Distance Functions for Examplar-based Object Recognition. PhD thesis, UC Berkeley (2007)
4. He, X., Ma, W.-Y., Zhang, H.-J.: Learning an image manifold for retrieval. In: Proceedings of the 12th Annual ACM international conference on Multimedia, New York, pp. 17–23 (2004)
5. Hu, Y., Li, M., Yu, N.: Multiple-instance ranking: Learning to rank images for image retrieval. In: IEEE Conference on Computer Vision and Pattern Recognition, Anchorage, USA (2008)
6. Huang, J., Ravi Kumar, S., Mitra, M., Zhu, W., Zabih, R.: Spatial color indexing and applications. Int. J. of Computer Vision 35, 245–268 (1999)
7. Joachims, T.: Optimizing search engines using clickthrough data. In: The Eighth ACM SIGKDD International Conference on Knowledge Discovery and Data Mining, Alberta, Canada, pp. 133–142 (2002)
8. Lee, J.-E., Jin, R., Jain, A.K.: Rank-based distance metric learning: An application to image retrieval. In: Computer Vision and Pattern Recognition (CVPR), Anchorage, USA (2008)
9. Moghaddam, B., Tian, Q., Lesh, N., Shen, C., Huang, T.S.: Visualization and user-modeling for browsing personal photo libraries. International Journal of Computer Vision 56, 109–130 (2004)
10. Rodden, K.: Evaluating Similarity-Based Visualisations as Interfaces for Image Browsing. PhD thesis, University of Cambridge (2001)
11. Rui, Y., Huang, T.S., Ortega, M., Mehrotra, S.: Relevance feedback: A power tool in interactive content-based image retrieval. IEEE Trans. on Circuits and Systems for Video Technology 8, 644–655 (1998)
12. Schultz, M., Joachims, T.: Learning a distance metric from relative comparisons. In: Neural Information Processing Systems (NIPS), Berlin (2003)
13. Smith, J.R., Chang, S.-F.: Automated binary texture feature sets for image retrieval. In: IEEE International Conference on Acoustics, Speech, and Signal Processing, Atlanta, USA, pp. 2239–2242 (1996)
14. Tong, S., Chang, E.: Support vector machine active learning for image retrieval. In: ACM Conference on Multimedia, Ottawa, Canada, pp. 107–118 (2001)
15. Wang, R., McKenna, S.J., Han, J.: High-entropy layouts for content-based browsing and retrieval. In: ACM International Conference on Image and Video Retrieval, Santorini, Greece (2009)
16. Ward, A.A., McKenna, S.J., Buruma, A., Taylor, P., Han, J.: Merging technology and users: applying image browsing to the fashion industry for design inspiration. In: Content-based Multimedia Indexing, London, pp. 288–295 (2008)

Consistent Interpretation of Image Sequences to Improve Object Models on the Fly*

Johann Prankl[1], Martin Antenreiter[2], Peter Auer[2], and Markus Vincze[1]

[1] Automation and Control Institute
Vienna University of Technology, Austria
{prankl,vincze}@acin.tuwien.ac.at
[2] Chair of Information Technology (CiT)
University of Leoben, Austria
{mantenreit,auer}@unileoben.ac.at

Abstract. We present a system, which is able to track multiple objects under partial and total occlusion. The reasoning system builds up a graph based spatio-temporal representation of object hypotheses and thus is able to explain the scene even if objects are totally occluded. Furthermore it adapts the object models and learns new appearances at assumed object locations. We represent objects in a star-shaped geometrical model of interest points using a codebook. The novelty of our system is to combine a spatio-temporal reasoning system and an interest point based object detector for on-line improving of object models in terms of adding new, and deleting unreliable interest points. We propose this system for a consistent representation of objects in an image sequence and for learning changes of appearances on the fly.

1 Introduction

Typical vision systems integrate low-level visual cues in a hierarchical fashion, and extract relevant output from this bottom-up processing. More recent approaches try to establish feed back loops and combine different vision methods at different levels, but these methods also reach their limitations if dynamical scenes get crowded up and objects get partly or even totally occluded.

Our system is inspired by findings of Gredebäck [1] and Spelke [2], who have shown that even infants at the age of 4 month build a spatio-temporal representation of objects and accurately predict the reappearance after full occlusion. To incorporate such an ability, our system fuses bottom-up visual processing with top-down reasoning and inference to keep track of occluded objects and to learn appearances of objects that continuously change due to rotation or lighting. The system reasons about occlusion and hiding events and maintains a hypotheses graph that is updated according to the visual input. In case of a plausible hypothesis a learning event is triggered and the vision component updates the interest

---

* The work described in this article has been funded by European projects under the contract no. 6029427, no. 215821 and no. 216886, as well as by the Austrian Science Foundation under the grant #S9101 and #S9104 ("Cognitive Vision").

M. Fritz, B. Schiele, and J.H. Piater (Eds.): ICVS 2009, LNCS 5815, pp. 384–393, 2009.

point based object model. If the object is moving, interest points adjacent to the assumed object boundary are tested for consistent motion. Furthermore an interest point statistic is maintained that allows deleting interest points with a low information content. Hence we are able to keep a smart and manageable object model, which is necessary for high recognition performance.

We tested our system with a scenario where a human moves different objects, which interact several times, i.e., get occluded and reappear again. The goal is that the system tracks the objects even under full occlusion while enhancing the object model with never seen interest points and removing unreliable interest points.

The paper is structured as follows: After an overview of related work in the next section, the overall system is presented in Sec. 2. Then object recognition (Sec. 4), spatio-temporal reasoning (Sec. 5), and improving object models while tracking (Sec. 6), are explained in detail. Finally, experiments and results are given in Sec. 7.

1.1 Related Work

There exist some occlusion reasoning systems for tracking or segmenting objects, mostly for traffic scenes or persons. Elgammal and Davis [3] use a probabilistic framework for segmenting people under occlusion. Their system operates on a pixel level, whereas our system does the occlusion reasoning on a more abstract object level.

Huang and Essa [4] present an approach for tracking a varying number of objects through temporally and spatially significant occlusions. The method is built on the idea of object permanence. The system can track objects in presence of long periods of full occlusions. They assume that a simple colour model is sufficient to describe each object in a video sequence, therefore they do not have to update their object models.

The approaches in [5] and [6] use image regions for occlusion reasoning. A region may consist of one or more objects, the relative depth between objects is not considered. If occlusion happens, the system merges the affected regions into a new region. On the other hand a region is split, if the system is able to discriminate objects within this region. Thus these approaches handle occlusion not at the object level.

Bennett et al. [7] enhances tracking results of moving objects by reasoning about spatio-temporal constraints. The reasoning engine resolves error, ambiguity and occlusion to produce a most likely hypothesis, which is consistent with global spatio-temporal continuity constraints. However, the whole system does only bottom-up processing.

A way to incorporate knowledge into vision systems is to use a knowledge-based approach, e.g. [8] for an aerial image understanding system, and [9] for traffic monitoring applications. Matsuyama and Hwang [8] identified two types of knowledge in an image understanding system, that is, knowledge about objects and about analysis tools, and built a modular framework which integrates top-down and bottom-up reasoning. The system extracts various scene descriptions, and an evaluation functions selects the most complex scene description from the database. The evaluation function is simple and trusts the low-level vision output more than the reasoning output. While reasoning in [9] is based on image regions using trajectories and velocity information, our reasoning is based on more abstract object behaviour to achieve a consistent scene interpretation even if objects are totally occluded.

2 System Overview

Our system consists of three main parts (Fig. 1, right): the object detector, the reasoning component, and the knowledge-base used by the reasoning component. The reasoning component maintains a graph of hypotheses (Fig. 1, left). Each hypothesis describes the content of a particular frame of the video, and it is linked to plausible hypotheses for the previous as well as for the next frame. A hypothesis is an assumption about the states of all relevant objects. It is calculated from the vision inputs for the current frame, from one of the hypotheses for the previous frame, and from the rules in the knowledge-base. Our current knowledge-base includes the rules about the appearance of interacting physical objects. Examples for such rules are given in Sec. 5. Communication between the object detector and the reasoning component is not just bottom up, but also includes top-down instructions from the reasoning component to the object detector, such as a request to detect a specific object at a certain location, or the command to update the object model with interest points at a specified position. The following list describes the main steps:

1. Top-down processing: Feed information from the hypotheses about the previous frame to the vision components.
2. Bottom-up processing: Create new *pre-hypotheses* from the output of the vision components. These pre-hypotheses give possible object positions and the confidence of the vision components for these positions.
3. Reasoning: Apply the *construction rules* of the knowledge base to the pre-hypotheses. The construction rules construct all plausible hypotheses.

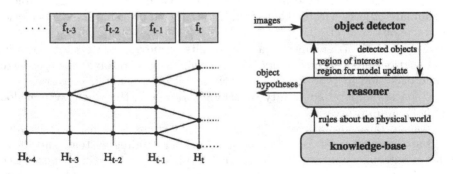

Fig. 1. System overview, including the hypotheses graph (left), the structure of the system and the communication between components (right)

4. Hypotheses selection: Prune the hypotheses graph from unlikely hypotheses.
5. Object model update: Provide the boundary of the visible object area to update the object model if the actual hypothesis is reliable.

The next sections describe the involved components and the main steps in detail, starting with the object detector.

3   Object Representation

In Sec. 2 we described our system which is designed to process image sequences. The first step is to learn the initial object models. To this end the user has to mark the object boundaries in the first frame. In case of an existing initial object model this interaction can be omitted.

As object representation, we use a part based model proposed by Agarwal et al. [10] and improved by Leibe et al. [11] for the task of object class recognition. The idea is to build up a vocabulary (in the following termed a *codebook*) of interest points and to compose the geometric structure out of this vocabulary.

The initial set of codebook entries is generated from the first image. As proposed by Lowe [12] the Difference-of-Gaussian (DoG) operator and SIFT are used for detection and description of interest points. These interest points are clustered and each codebook entry represents a cluster of interest points with a similar SIFT descriptor. The codebook is then used to build up a structural model of the object. Therefore detected interest points on the object are matched with the codebook and the relative locations of interest points with respect to the centre of the object are assigned to codebook entries.

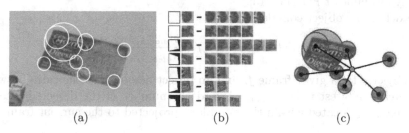

(a)   (b)   (c)

Fig. 2. Fig. 2(a) shows detected interest points and Fig. 2(b) the codebook representation, cluster means and occurrences (interest points). In Fig. 2(c) the star-shaped object representation is sketched.

Summarised, each codebook entry represents a part of the object and stores the possible locations where this part can be found relative to the object centre. The result is a star-shaped structural model of the object, that is shown in Fig. 2.

4   Object Detection

Likewise as described in Sec. 3 for generating the codebook, interest points are detected using the DoG-operator and the SIFT-descriptor for object recognition.

The detected interest points are matched with the codebook and activated codebook entries vote for an object centre.

Consistent votes are accumulated in the Hough accumulator array. We use a four dimensional space where occurrences of activated codebook entries vote for an object location $\mathbf{x}_v = (x_v, y_v)$, a scale s_v and an object model m:

$$s_v = \frac{s_i}{s_{occ}}, \tag{1}$$

$$\mathbf{x}_v = \mathbf{R}\mathbf{x}_{occ}s_v + \mathbf{x}_i. \tag{2}$$

In (1) s_i is the scale of the detected interest point in the current image and s_{occ} denotes the scale of the occurrence in the learning image respectively. In (2) $\mathbf{x}_i$ is the location of the detected interest point in the current image, $\mathbf{x}_{occ}$ denotes the location of the object centre with respect to an occurrence of the model and $\mathbf{R}$ stands for the matrix that describes the rotation from model to image orientation of the interest point.

Once all matched interest points have voted, the Hough accumulator array is used to find the most promising object hypotheses. The probabilistic votes in each Hough bin i are summed up and – starting with the best hypothesis, i.e. the heaviest bin – the object location is refined. This is done in a mean shift like procedure, for which the neighbouring bins are examined for contributing votes. This handles the typical boundary effect of Hough voting schemas.

The result of the mean shift refinement is a cluster of interest points, that consistently vote for an object location. This cluster is used to compute an affine homography H_{aff}, for which we use a Least Median of Squares implementation, publicly available at FORTH [13].

We define the object confidence

$$detected(o|m, f_t) = \frac{n_{matched}}{n_{detected}} \tag{3}$$

of an object o for a given frame f_t and an object model m as the ratio between the matched interest points $n_{matched}$ and the number of the detected interest points $n_{detected}$ located within the boundary projected to the current frame.

5   Reasoning

The main idea is to split a hypothesis into two or more plausible hypotheses, if the correct hypothesis cannot be inferred. What can be inferred mainly depends on what can be observed. In our setting we use one static camera. Thus the distance of objects from the camera cannot be observed. If two boundaries intersect, it cannot be decided ad hoc which object is in front of the other object. Thus the current hypothesis is split in two and each possibility is represented by one of the hypothesis. Examples for hypotheses construction rules:

1. If the boundaries of two objects intersect, then split the hypothesis into two. One hypothesis states that the first object is in front, the other hypothesis states that the second object is in front.

2. If an object is partially occluded by one object (occluder), then we generate two hypotheses. One hypothesis states that the object does not move and reappears at the old position. The other hypothesis states that the occluded object can reappear along the trajectory of the occluder.
3. If the object detector returns two or more possible object positions with similar confidence for an object, then generate one hypothesis for each plausible object position.

5.1 Evaluation Criterion of a Hypothesis Path

After running the object detectors and constructing the hypotheses graph, an evaluation criterion is used to calculate the most likely hypothesis path which explains the video sequence. The evaluation function $Q(\mathcal{H}|\mathcal{F})$ evaluates a hypothesis path $\mathcal{H} = \langle h_1, \ldots, h_m \rangle$ from the root hypothesis at frame 1 to a hypothesis for the current frame where $\mathcal{F} = \langle f_1, \ldots f_m \rangle$ is the corresponding sequence of frames. It is a quality measure of a hypothesis path compared to other paths. We sum the quality measures q for each hypothesis on the path to calculate the overall evaluation measure Q,

$$Q(\mathcal{H}|\mathcal{F}) = \frac{1}{m} \sum_{i=1}^{m} q(h_i|f_i). \tag{4}$$

The quality measure for a hypothesis of frame f_t is then the sum of all normalised plausibility values,

$$q(h_i|f_t) = \frac{1}{\#\{o : o \in h_i\}} \sum_{o \in h_i} \frac{p(o|h_i, f_t)}{\max_{h \in H_t} p(o|h, f_t)} \tag{5}$$

where $H_t = \{h : h \text{ is a hypothesis for frame } f_t\}$ is the set of all hypotheses for frame f_t. The plausibility value $p(o|h_i, f_t)$ is a mapping of the detector stage and the current state of the hypothesis h_i.

The inconsistency function ι combines the confidence value $detected(o|h_i, f_t)$ of the detector component with the relative occluded area $occludedarea(o|h_i)$, and should detect inconsistency between these values.

$$\iota(o|h_i, f_t) = \left| -\frac{\sqrt{2}}{2} + \frac{\sqrt{2}}{2} detected(o|h_i, f_t) + \frac{\sqrt{2}}{2} occludedarea(o|h_i) \right| \tag{6}$$

The function $occludedarea$ returns the normalised area of the occluded object area, depending on the state of the given hypothesis, ranging from 0 to 1. We assume, that if the detector confidence is small then the occluded object area should be large. The inconsistency ι is small if the low-level vision confidence is small and the occluded object area is large, or vice-versa.

The plausibility function p maps the inconsistency value to a value between one and zero. For objects which are not totally occluded we define

$$p(o|h_i, f_t) := -\frac{2}{\sqrt{2}} \iota(o|h_i, f_t) + 1. \tag{7}$$

A different definition of plausibility is needed if an object is totally occluded. It would be misleading if a plausibility value of 1 were assigned to totally occluded objects, since a visible object will not typically receive a plausibility value of 1 due to noise, illumination changes, etc. Then a hypothesis with a total occluded object would have higher plausibility than a hypothesis where the same object is partially visible. Therefore we bound the plausibility of a total occluded object by its maximal plausibility when it is visible:

$$p(o|h_i, f_t) = \max_{\substack{h \in H_t \\ o \text{ is visible}|h}} p(o|h, f_t) \tag{8}$$

If there does not exists a hypothesis $h \in H_t$ such that object o is visible, then set $p(o|h_i, f_t) = 1.0$. This is the case where all hypotheses assume, that the object o is totally occluded.

6   Improving the Object Model on the Fly

The reasoning engine described in Sec. 5 keeps track of correct object locations even under full occlusion. Furthermore it triggers learning new object interest points in situations where it is plausible that the object is correctly detected.

If learning is triggered we distinguish between two cases. The first case is that the object is staying, then we insert interest points, that are not matched and located within the object boundary, to the object model. The second case is a moving object. Then interest points adjacent to the visible surface are compared to the actual affine motion of the object. If they have a similar motion they are also added to the object model. In this way we are able to handle rotating objects and we can add interest points of object parts that are never seen before to the model. In our experiments we use a threshold for motion similarity, which is half of the object motion.

During recognition we further compute interest point statistics, which are used to remove unreliable interest points. We compute a interest point related detection rate r which counts how often a descriptor detects the associated object. We set the detection threshold to 50%, i.e., interest points only survive if they are detected at least in each second frame. This method keeps the size of the codebook manageable.

7   Results

We processed four video sequence to test our system. In our first video sequence we arranged the objects within three layers. A person moved the objects between the layers and the objects get partially or totally occluded. The system has to interpret the sequence correctly, such that it can update the object models accordingly. This is important, because wrong model updates can accumulate to a wrong model, which can lead to false detection results. On the other

(a)   (b)

Fig. 3. Two possible interpretation of an observed scene are shown. Fig. 3(a) shows the best interpretation of the frame 290, which is the correct one. The confidence value of this hypothesis path is 0.9669, compared to the other interpretation in Fig. 3(b), which is only 0.8913. The system explained the occlusion event correctly.

hand – without updating the object models – the system will not be able to detect the objects reliably. Small objects are usually not reliably detected during motion and rotation. In our first test sequence the object with id 'I-2' is an example of such a small object. Fig. 3 shows an occlusion event and two possible interpretation from the observed detection results. In Fig. 3(a) the system concludes, that the object with id 'I-1' is occluded by the two objects 'I-4' and 'I-5'. It therefore can update the model for 'I-1' accordingly. The system draws the visible boundary for the object 'I-1'. In Fig. 3(b) the system tries to explain the scene with an other object ordering. This leads to a different and wrong object model for object 'I-1'. The new learnt model for object 'I-1' gives good detection result, because the system learnt additional keypoints from the surrounding objects, but the overall hypothesis cannot explain the scene properly. The contradiction is, that all detectors give good detection results even under occlusions. The evaluation function can detect such a contradiction, the corresponding hypothesis of Fig. 3(a) has a confidence value of 0.9669, which is higher than the confidence value 0.8913 of the hypothesis from Fig. 3(b). In Fig. 4 we show a more complex arrangement of objects from the first sequence. Every object has an id label and a boundary. The system draws the estimated visible boundary, therefore the images show the estimated relative depth between objects. The id label, within the boundary, is bracketed if the reasoning does not use the detection result. Question marks indicate that the reasoning has assumed a detection failure. A dashed box around the last known object position is drawn, if the reasoning has not enough evidence for an exact object position. In frame 420 (Fig. 4(a)) the object with id 'I-1' is placed between the objects 'I-4' and 'I-5'. The relative depth is correctly estimated. The next frame (Fig. 4(b)) shows nearly total occlusion of object 'I-1', 'I-4', and 'I-5'. In Fig. 4(c) detection results are used for objects 'I-2' and 'I-3', but not for object 'I-4' which is totally occluded by the hand and object 'I-2'. In the frames 570 and 595 (Fig. 4(d) and 4(e)) there is less occlusion and the reasoning uses the detection results (bottom-up processing). In the last frame the object 'I-3' is rotated and placed

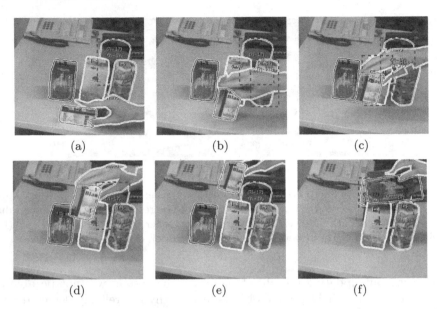

(a)   (b)   (c)

(d)   (e)   (f)

Fig. 4. The first box sequence showing the various occlusion events (Frames: 420, 495, 545, 570, 595, and 845). The relative depth between the objects is correct in every frame.

Table 1. Comparison of using a static model versus a dynamic model

	static model		online learned model	
Video sequence	detection rate	depth ordering	detection rate	depth ordering
box1	95.90%	88.86%	97.81%	85.05%
box2	74.31%	66.43%	98.71%	97.84%
box3	81.43%	74.80%	99.07%	91.24%
cap	32.86%	21.40%	99.95%	93.21%

on top of the object 'I-4'. The object 'I-1' and 'I-2' are totally occluded by the other objects in the scene. In Table 1 we show a comparison of a system which learns the object model from the first image (static model). The static model is used with the reasoning component to explain the scene. The first column is the detection rate for all visible objects. The second column indicates how well the reasoning can infer the correct depth ordering. As can be seen from Table 1, our online model improves the detection results, compared to the static model. Additionally, the reasoning component can prevent the system to learn a wrong model even under occlusion events.

8   Conclusion and Further Work

We use a reasoning system to build a spatio-temporal representation of object hypotheses. Depending on this hypotheses objects are assigned to different depth layers and the visibility of the object surface is computed. Plausible object locations are used to update the object models, which leads to improved object models. These adaptive models can detect objects more reliably than simple detectors trained offline. An interest point statistic is computed while tracking, which is used to delete unreliable interest points from the object models and therefore keeps the object models manageable.

References

1. Gredebäck, G.: Infants Knowledge of Occluded Objects: Evidence of Early Spatiotemporal Representation. Number Dissertation, Acta Universitatis Upsaliensis; Faculty of Social Sciences (2004) ISBN 91-554-5898-X
2. Spelke, E.S., von Hofsten, C.: Predictive reaching for occluded objects by 6-month-old infants. Journal of Cognition and Development 2(3), 261–281 (2001)
3. Elgammal, A.M., Davis, L.S.: Probabilistic framework for segmenting people under occlusion. In: ICCV, pp. 145–152 (2001)
4. Huang, Y., Essa, I.: Tracking multiple objects through occlusion. In: IEEE Conference on Computer Vision and Pattern Recognition (CVPR 2005), San Diego, CA, USA, June 2005, vol. 2, pp. 1051–1058 (2005)
5. Brémond, F., Thonnat, M.: Tracking multiple non-rigid objects in video sequences. IEEE Transaction on Circuits and Systems for Video Technology Journal 8(5) (september 1998)
6. McKenna, S., Jabri, S., Duric, Z., Rosenfeld, A., Wechsler, H.: Tracking groups of people. Computer Vision and Image Understanding 80(1), 42–56 (2000)
7. Bennett, B., Magee, D.R., Cohn, A.G., Hogg, D.C.: Using spatio-temporal continuity constraints to enhance visual tracking of moving objects. In: ECAI-2004, pp. 922–926 (2004)
8. Matsuyama, T., Hwang, V.S.: SIGMA: A Knowledge-Based Aerial Image Understanding System. Perseus Publishing (1990)
9. Cucchiara, R., Piccardi, M., Mello, P.: Image analysis and rule-based reasoning for a traffic monitoring system. IEEE Transactions on Intelligent Transportation Systems 1(2), 119–130 (2000)
10. Agarwal, S., Awan, A., Roth, D.: Learning to detect objects in images via a sparse, part-based representation. IEEE Transactions on Pattern Analysis and Machine Intelligence 26(11), 1475–1490 (2004)
11. Leibe, B., Leonardis, A., Schiele, B.: Robust object detection with interleaved categorization and segmentation. Int. J. Comput. Vision 77(1-3), 259–289 (2008)
12. Lowe, D.G.: Distinctive image features from scale-invariant keypoints. International Journal of Computer Vision 60(2), 91–110 (2004)
13. Lourakis, M.: homest: A c/c++ library for robust, non-linear homography estimation (July 2006), http://www.ics.forth.gr/~lourakis/homest/ (Accessed on 20 July 2006)

Nonideal Iris Recognition Using Level Set Approach and Coalitional Game Theory

Kaushik Roy and Prabir Bhattacharya

Concordia Institute for Information Systems Engineering
Concordia University, Montreal, Quebec, Canada
{kaush_ro,prabir}@ciise.concordia.ca

Abstract. This paper presents an efficient algorithm for iris recognition using the level set approach and the coalitional game theory. To segment the inner boundary from a nonideal iris image, we apply a level set based curve evolution approach using the edge stopping function, and to detect the outer boundary, we employ the curve evolution approach using the regularized Mumford-Shah segmentation model with an energy minimization approach. An iterative algorithm, called the Contribution-Selection Algorithm (CSA), in the context of coalitional game theory is used to select the optimal features subset without compromising the accuracy. The verification performance of the proposed scheme is validated using the UBIRIS Version 2, the ICE 2005, and the WVU datasets.

Keywords: Iris recognition, level set based curve evolution, coalitional game theory, contribution selection algorithm, Mumford-Shah segmentation model.

1   Introduction

Iris recognition has been receiving extensive attention over the last decade, with increasing demands in automated person identification [1]. Most state-of-the-art literatures on iris biometrics focused on preprocessing of on-axis iris image of an eye, which is achieved through a stop and stare interface in which a user must align his/her optical axis with the camera's optical axis [2]. However, new dimensions have been identified in iris biometric research, including processing and recognition of 'nonideal irises', and 'iris on the move and at a distance' [2,3]. It is not practical to assume that a user always aligns his/her optical axis with the camera's optical axis due to the increasing security issues. Therefore, it is important to deploy the methodologies to account for the nonideal irises in order to design a nonideal iris recognition scheme. For iris segmentation, most of the researchers assume that iris is circular or elliptical. However, in the cases of nonideal iris images, which are affected by gaze direction, motion blur, pupil dilation, nonlinear deformations, eyelids and eyelashes occlusions, reflections, etc, iris may appear as noncircular or nonelliptical [4,5]. Because the inner boundary may be partially occluded by the reflections, and the outer boundary may be partially occluded by the eyelids, it is important to fit the flexible contour that can stand for such disturbances. Another constraint is that inner and outer boundary models must form a closed curve [2]. Therefore, we can deploy the geometrics active contours to represent the inner and outer boundaries accurately. In [2], inner and outer boundaries are detected in terms

M. Fritz, B. Schiele, and J.H. Piater (Eds.): ICVS 2009, LNCS 5815, pp. 394–402, 2009.
© Springer-Verlag Berlin Heidelberg 2009

of active contours based on the discrete Fourier series expansions of the contour data. Authors proposed two approaches in [3] where the first approach compensated for the off-angle gaze direction, and the second approach used an angular deformation calibration model. In [4,5], curve evolution approaches were applied based on active contours to segment the nonideal iris images. The parametric active contours based iris segmentation scheme may terminate at certain local minima such as the specular reflections, the thick radial fibers in iris or the crypts in ciliary region. The iris segmentation schemes based on active contours with the edge stopping function proposed in [4,5] may fail to detect the outer boundary accurately since iris is separated from the sclera by relatively a smooth boundary. Addressing the above problems, we propose two-stage iris segmentation algorithm, in which we first apply the level set based curve evolution approach using the edge stopping function to detect the inner boundary. In the second stage, we evolve the curve based on the level set method towards the outer boundary using the energy minimization algorithm in order to detect the boundary between iris and sclera [6,7,8]. Prior to apply the curve evolution approach using the active contours, we deploy Direct Least Square (DLS) elliptical fitting to approximate the pupil and the iris boundaries. The iris biometrics template with a large number of features increases the computational complexities. Hence, the optimal features set selection from a feature sequence with a relative high dimension has become an important factor in the field of iris recognition. The conventional feature selection techniques (e.g., principal components analysis, independent components analysis, singular valued decomposition, etc.) require sufficient number of samples per subjects to select the most representative features sequence. However, it is not realistic to accumulate a large number of samples due to some security issues. Therefore, we apply a feature a selection scheme called the 'Contribution-Selection Algorithm (CSA)', a notion from game theory to select the subset of informative features without losing the recognition accuracy.

2 Level Set Based Iris/Pupil Localization

The segmentation of the nonideal iris image is a difficult task because of the noncircular shape of the pupil and the iris [3]. First, we segment the iris and pupil boundaries from the eye image and then unwrap the localized iris region into a rectangular block of fixed dimension. We divide the iris localization process into two steps: (a) Inner boundary detection and (b) Outer boundary detection.

2.1 Inner Boundary Detection

First, we use DLS based elliptical fitting to approximate the pupil boundary. However, the accuracy of the ellipse fitting process degrades in the presence of the outliers such as eyelashes. Therefore, we apply a morphological operation, namely the opening to an input image to suppress the interference from the eyelashes. DLS based elliptical fitting returns five parameters $(p_1, p_2, r_1, r_2, \varphi_1)$:the horizontal and vertical coordinates of the pupil center (p_1, p_2), the length of the major and minor axes (r_1, r_2), and the orientation of the ellipse φ_1.In order to find the optimal estimate of the inner (pupil) boundary, we apply the geometric active contours based on the edge stopping function in a narrow band over the estimated inner boundary by considering that the pupillary region is the darkest part of the eye and is separated by relatively strong gradient from the iris [6,7]. A brief discussion of the level set based curve evolution approach is given as follows: Let Ω be the image domain, and I be the two dimensional image. Let us consider the evolving curve C in Ω, as the boundary of an open subset ω of Ω. The main idea is to embed this evolving curve as the zero level set of a higher dimensional function ϕ. We can define the following function:

$$\phi(x, y, t = 0) = \pm d \tag{1}$$

where d denotes the distance form (x, y) to C at time $t = 0$. The plus (minus) sign is selected if the point (x, y) is outside (inside) of the curve C. Therefore, in the curve evolution approach for pupil segmentation, we need to solve the *partial differential equation* (PDE) of the following form [8]:

$$\frac{\delta\phi}{\delta t} = g(I)(S_1|\nabla_\phi| + S_2|\nabla_\phi|), \phi(x, y, 0) = \phi_0(x, y) \tag{2}$$

where S_1 is a constant advection term that forces the curve to expand or contract uniformly based on the its sign, S_2 depends on the curve geometry and is used to smooth out the high curvature region, the set $\{(x, y), \phi(x, y) = 0\}$ defines the initial contour, and $g(I)$, an edge stopping function, which is used to halt the evolution of the curve at the inner boundary, can be defined as:

$$g(I) = \frac{1}{1 + |\nabla G_\sigma(x, y) * I(x, y)|^\rho}, \rho \geq 1 \tag{3}$$

where $G_\sigma(x, y) * I(x, y)$ is the convolution of I with the Gaussian $G_\sigma(x, y) = \sigma^{-\frac{1}{2}} e^{-\frac{|x^2 + y^2|}{4\sigma}}$. Now to discretize ϕ, we apply the finite differences scheme proposed in [7]. To evolve the curve, we perform the discretization and linearization of (2) [7,8]:

$$\phi_{i,j}^{n+1} = \phi_{i,j}^n - \Delta t[\hat{g}(I)(\hat{S}_1|\nabla_\phi| + \hat{S}_2|\nabla_\phi|)] \tag{4}$$

where Δt is the time step, (x_i, y_j) are the grid points for $1 \leq i, j \leq M$, and $\phi_{i,j}^n = \phi(x_i, y_j, n\delta t)$ approximates $\phi(x, y, t)$ with $n \geq 0, \phi^0 = \phi_0$. In [7], an upwind scheme is used to estimate $S_1|\nabla_\phi|$ of (4):

$$S_1|\nabla_\phi| = [max(\Delta_-^x \phi_{i,j}^n, 0)^2 + min(\Delta_+^x \phi_{i,j}^n, 0)^2 + max(\Delta_-^y \phi_{i,j}^n, 0)^2 + min(\Delta_+^y \phi_{i,j}^n, 0)^2]^{\frac{1}{2}} \tag{5}$$

and the term $S_2|\nabla_\phi|$ depends on curvature $K(K = div(\frac{\nabla_\phi}{|\nabla_\phi|}))$ and can be estimated as:

$$S_2|\nabla_\phi| = -\epsilon K[(\frac{\phi_{i+1,j}^n - \phi_{i-1,j}^n}{2})^2 + (\frac{\phi_{i,j+1}^n - \phi_{i,j-1}^n}{2})^2] \tag{6}$$

where ϵ is a constant. Now, the active contour ϕ_0 is initialized to the approximated pupil boundary, and the optimum estimate of the inner boundary is measured by evolving the initial contour in a narrow band of ± 10 pixels. Fig. 1(b) shows segmentation of pupil based on the algorithm mentioned above.

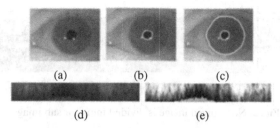

(a)   (b)   (c)

(d)   (e)

Fig. 1. (a) Original image from WVU dataset (b) Pupil detection (c) Iris detection (d) Normalized image (e) Enhanced image

2.2   Outer Boundary Detection

To approximate the outer boundary, we apply the DLS based elliptical fitting again, and obtain five parameters $(I_1, I_2, R_1, R_2, \varphi_2)$: the horizontal and vertical coordinates of the iris center (I_1, I_2), the length of the major and minor axes (R_1, R_2), and the orientation of the ellipse φ_2. This method, thus, provides the rough estimation of iris boundary. To find the exact outer boundary, we apply the level set approach based on the energy minimization algorithm by assuming that the iris has relatively smooth boundary [9,10].In order to evolve the curve towards the outer boundary, we use Mumford-Shah segmentation model with the regularization terms [10]. Therefore, the main objective is to minimize the length of the curve and the area of the region inside the curve. We introduce the following energy function E:

$$E(C, c_1, c_2) = \mu \int_\Omega \delta(\phi(x,y))|\nabla_\phi(x,y)|dxdy + v \int_\Omega H(\phi(x,y))dxdy +$$

$$\lambda_1 \int_\Omega |I(x,y) - c_1|^2 H(\phi(x,y))dxdy + \lambda_2 \int_\Omega |I(x,y) - c_2|^2 (1 - H(\phi(x,y)))dxdy \quad (7)$$

where $\mu \geq 0$, $v \geq 0$, $\lambda_1 > 0$, $\lambda_2 > 0$ are the positive constants, C is the evolving curve, c_1, c_2 are the averages of I inside and outside of C respectively, ϕ denotes the zero level set of the signed distance function representing C as in (1), H is the Heaviside function, and δ is the Dirac measure. In (7), the first and the second terms on the right hand side denote the area and length at $\phi = 0$, respectively. Therefore, the main goal is to estimate the values of C, c_1, c_2 such that $E(C, c_1, c_2)$ is minimized. We parameterize the descent direction by $t \geq 0$, and deduce the Euler-Lagrange PDE from (7) which leads the following active contour model:

$$\phi'_t = \delta(\phi) [\mu \, div \frac{\nabla_\phi}{|\nabla_\phi|} - v - \lambda_1(I - c_1)^2 + \lambda_2(I - c_2)^2] \quad (8)$$

Now, we regularize the Heaviside function H, and the Dirac measure δ as in [8]:

$$H_\epsilon(\phi(x,y)) = \frac{1}{2} + \frac{1}{\pi} \arctan(\frac{\phi(x,y)}{\epsilon}) \quad (9)$$

and thus,

$$\delta(\phi(x,y)) = \frac{1}{\pi} \cdot \frac{\epsilon}{\epsilon^2 + (\phi(x,y))^2} \quad (10)$$

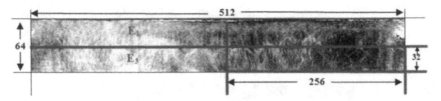

Fig. 2. Normalized image is divided into four sub images

From (9) and (10), we can observe that the evolution scheme has the tendency to measure the global minimizer with the applied regularizations. By discretizing and linearizing (7), we obtain:

$$\frac{\phi_{i,j}^{n+1} - \phi_{i,j}^n}{\Delta t} = \delta_\epsilon\,(\phi_{i,j}^n)[\mu K - v - \lambda_1(I_{i,j} - c_1(\phi^n))^2 + \lambda_2(I_{i,j} - c_2(\phi^n))^2] \qquad (11)$$

Now, we use the rough estimation of the iris boundary as the initial contour ϕ, and the curve is evolved in the narrow band of ±15 pixels to detect the exact outer boundary. Fig. 1 (c) shows the iris segmentation results.

Besides reflections, eyelid occlusion, and camera noise, the iris image data may be corrupted by the occlusion of the eyelashes [14,15]. We apply 1D Gabor filters and variance of intensity to isolate the eyelashes [16]. We unwrap the iris region to a normalized rectangular block with a fixed dimension of size 64×512 [2]. Since the normalized iris image has relatively low contrast and may have non-uniform intensity values due to the position of the light sources, a local intensity based histogram equalization technique is applied to enhance the contrast of the normalized iris image within a small image block of size 20×20. Fig. 1 (d, e) shows the unwrapped image and the effect of contrast enhancement.

In this paper, Daubechies wavelet transform (DBWT) is used to extract the distinctive features set form normalized and enhanced iris image block of size 64×512 pixels. We first divide the normalized image block into four sub images of size 32×256 and then apply Daubechies four coefficient wavelet transform to each sub image as shown in Fig. 2. The values of HH_4 of each sub-block are considered as the components of the distinctive features vector, and the region HH_4 contains the information of 2×16=32 data for each image sub-block. The iris information on HH_1, HH_2, and HH_3 are also obtained by calculating the mean value of each such region and assigning to one dimension. This procedure is applied for each image sub-block. Therefore, the normalized image is represented by a distinctive features set of (2×16+3)×4=140 components.

3 Feature Selection Using Coalitional Game Theory

We apply a feature a selection scheme in the context of coalitional games, a notion from game theory [17]. An iterative algorithm for feature selection, called the Contribution-Selection Algorithm (CSA), is used to optimize the performance of the classifier on unseen data. The CSA algorithm combines both the filter and wrapper approaches. However, unlike filter methods, features are ranked on each step by using the classifier as a black box. The ranking is based on the Shapley value [17], a well known concept from game theory, to estimate the importance of each feature for the task at hand by taking into account the interactions between features. In coalitional game theory, a set of players is associated with a payoff, a real function that denotes the benefit achieved by different sub-coalitions in a game. Formally, we can define the coalitional game theory by the pair (N, u), where $N = \{1, 2, \cdots, n\}$ is the set of all players and $u(S)$, for every $S \subseteq N$, denotes a real number associating a value with the coalition S. Game theory represents the contribution of each player to the game by constructing a value function, which assigns a real-value to each player and the values correspond to the contribution of the players in achieving a high payoff. The contribution value calculation is based on the Shapley value [17]. We briefly discuss about the Shapley value in the following paragraph:

Let us consider the marginal importance of a player i to a coalition C, with $i \notin C$ be:

$$\Delta_i = u(S \cup \{i\}) - u(S) \tag{12}$$

Then, we can define the Shapely value by the payoff as follows:

$$\Phi_i(u) = \frac{1}{n!} \sum_{\pi \in \Pi} \Delta_i(S_i(\pi)) \tag{13}$$

where Π denotes the set of permutation over N and $S_i(\pi)$ is the set of players appearing before the i th player in permutation π. Actually, the Shapley value of a player is a weighted mean of its marginal value, averaged over all possible subsets of players. If we transform the concept of game theory into the arena of iris features subset selection, in which the contribution of each feature is estimated to generate a classifier, the players N are mapped to the features of a dataset and the payoff is denoted by a real valued function $u(S)$, which measures the performance of a classifier generated using the set of features S. In this paper, we use accuracy as the payoff function.The CSA is iterative in nature, and in this work, we adopt a forward selection approach. Each feature is ranked according to its contribution based on Shapely value, and the features with the highest contribution values are selected with the forward selection approach. The algorithm continues to calculate the contribution values of the remaining features given those already selected, and selecting new features, until the contribution values of all candidate features exceed a contribution threshold with forward selection. The algorithm is a generalization of filter method. However, the main idea of the algorithm is that the contribution value for each feature is estimated according to its assistance in improving the classifier's performance, which is generated using a specific induction algorithm, and in conjunction with other features. In our feature selection algorithm, we use the Shapley value heuristically to estimate the contribution value of a feature. The decision tree is used for feature selection, and the linear SVM [16,17] is deployed to perform for actual prediction on the selected features.

In this paper, we use Hausdorff Distance (HD) for iris templates matching. The HD is used to measure the dissimilarity between two sets of feature points. If $A = \{a_1, a_2, a_3, .., a_m\}$ and $B = \{b_1, b, b_3, .., b_n\}$ are two sets of iris features, the HD between A and B are given by:

$$H(A, B) = (h(A, B), h(B, A)) \qquad (14)$$

where $h = maxmin \, |a - b|$ and $|\cdot|$ is the norm of the vector.

4 Results and Analysis

We conduct the experimentation on three iris datasets namely, the ICE (Iris Challenge Evaluation) dataset, [11], the WVU (West Virginia University) dataset [12], and the UBIRIS version 2 dataset [13]. The ICE database consists of left and right iris images for experimentation. We consider only the left iris images in our experiments. There are 1528 left iris images corresponding to the 120 subjects in our experiments. We evaluated the performance of the proposed iris recognition scheme on the WVU dataset. The WVU iris dataset has a total of 1852 iris images from 380 different persons. The performance is also evaluated using UBIRIS version 2 (Session 1 and Session 2) dataset which contains 2410 iris images from 241 different persons. In order to perform an extensive experimentation and to validate our proposed scheme, we generate a non-homogeneous dataset by combining three datasets which contains 741 classes and 5790 images. We select a common set of curve evolution parameters based on level set approach to segment the nonideal iris images accurately. To detect the inner boundary with the edge stopping function, the selected parameters values are $\Delta t = 0.05$ and $\epsilon = 0.015$. The selected parameters values to find the outer boundary using energy minimization algorithm are $\mu = 0.00001, \upsilon = 0.02, \lambda_1 = \lambda_2 = 1, \Delta t = 0.1$ and $\epsilon = 1$. Fig 3 shows the segmentation results on three datasets. Leave-One-Out Cross-Validation (LOOCV) is used to obtain the validation accuracy for the linear SVM to select the optimal features using coalitional game theory. Fig. 4 shows the accuracy of the feature subsets with a different number of selected features over all the datasets, and this figure also demonstrates that CSA achieves a reasonable accuracy when the number of features is around 120 in the cases of all the datasets when the permutations size and number are 5 and 2000 respectively. Therefore, we use an iris template of 120 elements for matching using HD. In order to provide a comparative analysis, we apply the proposed level set approach (LS), integro-differential operator (IDO) method [1] and the Canny edge detection and Hough transform (CHT) based approach [16] for segmentation on all the datasets. ROC curves in Fig. 5 show that the matching performance is improved when the level set approach is used for segmentation on all the datasets. The Genuine

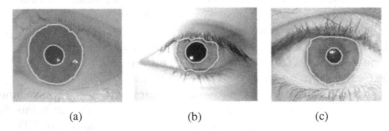

(a)   (b)   (c)

Fig. 3. Segmentation results on datasets (a) WVU (b) ICE (c) UBIRIS

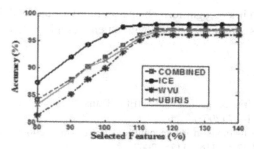

Fig. 4. Game theory based feature selection using forward selection scheme

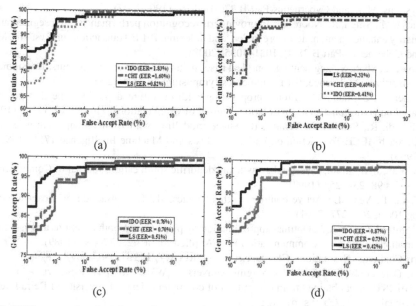

Fig. 5. ROC curve showing the performance on (a) WVU (b) ICE (c) UBIRIS (d) Combined datasets

Acceptance Rate (GAR) at a fixed False Accept Rate (FAR) of 0.001% is (a) 96.21% in WVU, (b) 98.13% in ICE, and (c) 97.10% in UBIRIS datasets. However, the overall GAR on the combined dataset at the fixed FAR of 0.001% is 97.27%.

5 Conclusions

The accurate segmentation of the iris plays an important role in iris recognition. In this paper, we present an nonideal iris segmentation scheme using the level set based curve evolution approach with the edge stopping function and energy minimization method. The distinctive features are extracted using the Daubechies wavelets, and a feature selection scheme in the context of coalitional game theory is used to find the subset of informative texture features that can improve the analysis of iris data. We validate the proposed iris recognition scheme on the ICE, the WVU, the UBIRIS, and the nonhomogeneous combined datasets with an encouraging performance.

References

1. Daugman, J.: How iris recognition works. IEEE Transaction on Circuits, Systems and Video Technology 14(1), 1–17 (2003)
2. Daugman, J.: New methods in iris recognition. IEEE Transactions on Systems, Man, and Cybernetics-Part B 37(5), 1167–1175 (2007)
3. Schuckers, S.A.C., Schmid, N.A., Abhyankar, A., Dorairaj, V., Boyce, C.K., Hornak, L.A.: On techniques for angle compensation in nonideal iris recognition. IEEE Transactions on Systems, Man, and Cybernetics-Part B 37(5), 1176–1190 (2007)
4. Vatsa, M., Singh, R., Noore, A.: Improving iris recognition performance using segmentation, quality enhancement, match score fusion, and indexing. IEEE Transactions on Systems, Man, and Cybernetics-Part B 38(4), 1021–1035 (2008)
5. Ross, A., Shah, S.: Segmenting non-ideal irises using geodesic active contours. In: Biometric Consortium Conference, IEEE Biometrics symposium, pp. 1–6 (2006)
6. Osher, S., Sethian, J.A.: Fronts propagating with curvature dependent speed: algorithms based on Hamilton-Jacobi formulation. Journal of Computational Physics 79, 12–49 (1988)
7. Malladi, R., Sethian, J., Vemuri, B.: Shape modelling with front propagation: a level set approach. IEEE Transaction on Pattern Analysis and Machine Intelligence 17(2), 158–174 (1995)
8. Sethian, J.A., Strain, J.: Crystal growth and dendritic solidi cation. Journal of Computational Physics 98, 231–253 (1992)
9. Chan, T., Vese, L.: Active contours without edges. IEEE Transaction on Image Processing 10(2), 266–277 (2001)
10. Mumford, D., Shah, J.: Optimal approximation by piecewise smooth functions and associated variational problems. Communication Pure Applied Math. 42, 577–685 (1989)
11. Iris Challenge Evaluation (ICE) dataset found, http://iris.nist.gov/ICE/
12. Iris Dataset obtained from West Virginia University (WVU), http://www.wvu.edu/
13. UBIRIS dataset obtained from department of computer science, University of Beira Interior, Portugal., http://iris.di.ubi.pt/
14. Roy, K., Bhattacharya, P.: Iris recognition based on zigzag collarette region and asymmetrical support vector machines. In: Kamel, M.S., Campilho, A. (eds.) ICIAR 2007. LNCS, vol. 4633, pp. 854–865. Springer, Heidelberg (2007)
15. Roy, K., Bhattacharya, P.: Optimal features subset selection using genetic algorithms for iris recognition. In: Campilho, A., Kamel, M.S. (eds.) ICIAR 2008. LNCS, vol. 5112, pp. 894–904. Springer, Heidelberg (2008)
16. Roy, K., Bhattacharya, P.: Adaptive Asymmetrical SVM and Genetic Algorithms Based Iris Recognition. In: International Conference on Pattern Recognition ICPR 2008, pp. 1–4 (2008)
17. Cohen, S., Dror, D., Ruppin, E.: Feature selection via coalitional game theory. In: Neural Computation, vol. 19, pp. 1939–1961. MIT press, Cambridge (2007)

Incremental Video Event Learning

Marcos Zúñiga[1,*], François Brémond[2], and Monique Thonnat[2]

[1] Electronics Department - UTFSM, Av. España 1680, Valparaíso, Chile
marcos.zuniga@usm.cl
http://profesores.elo.utfsm.cl/~mzuniga
[2] INRIA - Projet PULSAR, 2004 rte. des Lucioles, B.P. 93, 06902 Sophia Antipolis
Cedex, France
Francois.Bremond@sophia.inria.fr, Monique.Thonnat@sophia.inria.fr
http://www-sop.inria.fr/pulsar

Abstract. We propose a new approach for video event learning. The only hypothesis is the availability of tracked object attributes. The approach incrementally aggregates the attributes and reliability information of tracked objects to learn a hierarchy of state and event concepts. Simultaneously, the approach recognises the states and events of the tracked objects. This approach proposes an automatic bridge between the low-level image data and higher level conceptual information. The approach has been evaluated for more than two hours of an elderly care application. The results show the capability of the approach to learn and recognise meaningful events occurring in the scene. Also, the results show the potential of the approach for giving a description of the activities of a person (e.g. approaching to a table, crouching), and to detect abnormal events based on the frequency of occurrence.

1   Introduction

Video event analysis has become one of the biggest focus of interest in the video understanding community [3]. The interest of researchers has been mainly focused on the recognition of predefined events [8] and off-line learning of the events [9]. To date, very little attention has been given to incremental event learning in video [5], which should be the natural step further real-time applications for handling unexpected events.

We propose **MILES** (**M**ethod for **I**ncremental **L**earning of **E**vents and **S**tates), a new event learning approach, which aggregates on-line the **attributes** and **reliability information** of tracked objects (e.g. people) to **learn** a hierarchy of concepts corresponding to **events**. Reliability measures are used to focus the learning process on the most valuable information. Simultaneously, MILES **recognises** new occurrences of events previously learned. The only hypothesis of MILES is the availability of tracked object attributes, which are the needed

---

* This research has been supported in part by the Science and Technology Research Council of Chile (CONICYT) in the framework of INRIA (Sophia Antipolis) and CONICYT cooperation agreement.

M. Fritz, B. Schiele, and J.H. Piater (Eds.): ICVS 2009, LNCS 5815, pp. 403–414, 2009.

input for the approach. This work centres its interest in learning events in general, and is validated for specific events for home-care (e.g. approaching to a table, crouching).

MILES is an incremental approach, as no extensive reprocessing is needed upon the arrival of new information. The incremental aspect is important as the available training examples can be insufficient for describing all the possible scenarios in a video scene. Also, incremental approaches are suitable for on-line learning, as the processing cost is very low.

This approach proposes an automatic bridge between the low-level image data and higher level conceptual information. The learnt events can serve as building blocks for higher level behavioural analysis. The main novelties of the approach are the capability of learning events in general, the utilisation of a explicit quality measure for the built event hierarchy, and the consideration of measures to focus learning in reliable data.

This paper is organised as follows. After the state-of-the-art, Section 3 describes the proposed event learning approach and illustrates the learning procedure. Then, Section 4 presents the results obtained for an elderly care application.

2   State-of-the-Art

Most of video event learning approaches are supervised using general techniques as Hidden Markov Models (HMM) and Dynamic Bayesian Network (DBN) [2], requesting annotated videos representative of the events to be learned. Few approaches can learn events in an unsupervised way using clustering techniques. For example, in [9] the authors propose a method for unusual event detection, which first clusters a set of seven blob features using a Gaussian Mixture Model, and then represents behaviours as an HMM, using the cluster set as the states of the HMM. In [6], the authors propose an approach for learning events using spatial relationships between objects (e.g. the proximity between a person and kitchen dishes) in an unsupervised way, but performed off-line. Also, in [7], they learn in an unsupervised way composite events using the APRIORI clustering algorithm. This technique requires the manual definition of the simple events to build the composite ones. However, these unsupervised clustering techniques request to (re)process off-line (not real-time) the whole cluster distribution.

Some other techniques can learn on-line the event model by taking advantage of specific event distributions. For example, in [5], the authors propose a method for incremental trajectory clustering by mapping the trajectories into the ground plane decomposed in a zone partition. A new trajectory cluster is created as soon as the trajectory extremity does not belong to any of the zone corresponding to a trajectory cluster. Their approach performs learning only on spatial information, it cannot take into account time information, and do not handle noisy data.

Therefore, a new approach for incremental event learning is needed to handle unexpected situations.

3   MILES: A New Approach for Incremental Event Learning and Recognition

MILES is based on *incremental concept formation models* [1]. Conceptual clustering consists in describing classes by first generating their conceptual descriptions and then classifying the entities according to these descriptions. *Incremental concept formation models* is a conceptual clustering approach which incrementally creates a new concept without extensive reprocessing of the previously encountered instances. The knowledge is represented by a hierarchy of concepts partially ordered by generality. A *category utility* function is used to evaluate the quality of the obtained concept hierarchies [4].

MILES is an extension of incremental concept formation models for learning video events. The approach uses as input a set of attributes from the tracked objects in the scene. Hence, the only hypothesis of MILES is the availability of tracked object attributes (e.g. position, posture, class, speed). MILES constructs a **hierarchy of state and event concepts h**, based on the **state and event instances** extracted from the tracked object attributes.

A **state concept** is the modelisation of a spatio-temporal property valid at a given instant or stable on a time interval. A **state concept** $S^{(c)}$, in a hierarchy **h**, is modelled as a **set of attribute models** $\{n_i\}$, with $i \in \{1, .., T\}$, where n_i is modelled as a random variable N_i which follows a Gaussian distribution $N_i \sim \mathcal{N}(\mu_{n_i}; \sigma_{n_i})$. T is the number of attributes of interest. The state concept $S^{(c)}$ is also described by its **number of occurrences** $N(S^{(c)})$, its **probability of occurrence** $\mathcal{P}(S^{(c)}) = N(S^{(c)})/N(S^{(p)})$ ($S^{(p)}$ is the root state concept of **h**), and the **number of event occurrences** $N_E(S^{(c)})$ (number of times that state $S^{(c)}$ passed to another state, generating an event).

A **state instance** is an instantiation of a state concept, associated to a tracked object **o**. The state instance $S^{(o)}$ is represented as the set attribute-value-measure triplets $\mathbf{T_o} = \{(v_i; V_i; R_i)\}$, with $i \in \{1, \ldots, T\}$, where R_i is the reliability measure associated to the obtained value V_i for the attribute v_i. The measure $R_i \in [0, 1]$ is 1 if associated data is totally reliable, and 0 if totally unreliable.

An **event concept** $E^{(c)}$ is defined as the change from a starting state concept $S_a^{(c)}$ to the arriving state concept $S_b^{(c)}$ in a hierarchy **h**. An **event concept** $E^{(c)}$ is described by its **number of occurrences** $N(E^{(c)})$, and its **probability of occurrence** $\mathcal{P}(E^{(c)}) = N(E^{(c)})/N_E(S_a^{(c)})$ (with $S_a^{(c)}$ its starting state concept).

The state concepts are hierarchically organised by generality, with the children of each state representing specifications of their parent. A unidirectional link between two state concepts corresponds to an event concept. An example of a hierarchy of states and events is presented in Figure 1. In the example, the state S_1 is a more general state concept than states $S_{1.1}$ and $S_{1.2}$, and so on. Each pair of state concepts $(S_{1.1} ; S_{1.2})$ and $(S_{3.2} ; S_{3.3})$, is linked by two events concepts, representing the occurrence of events in both directions.

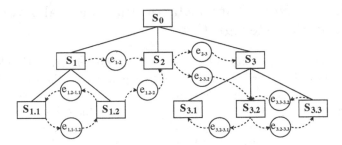

Fig. 1. Example of a hierarchical event structure resulting from the proposed event learning approach. Rectangles represent states, while circles represent events.

3.1   MILES Learning Process

The input of MILES corresponds to a list of tracked object attributes. MILES needs that the objects are tracked in order to detect the occurrence of *events*. There is no constraint on the number of attributes, as MILES has been conceived for learning state and event concepts in general. For each attribute, MILES needs a normalisation value to be defined prior to its computation. This value corresponds to the concept of *acuity*.

The **acuity** [1] is a system parameter that specifies the minimal value for numerical attributes standard deviation σ in a state concept. In psychophysics, the *acuity* corresponds to the notion of a *just noticeable difference*, the lower limit on the human perception ability. This concept is used for the same purpose in MILES, but the main difference with its utilisation in previous work [1] is that the *acuity* was used as a single parameter, while in MILES each numerical attribute n_i has associated an acuity value A_{n_i}. This improvement allows to represent different normalisation scales and units associated to different attributes (e.g. kilo, meter, centimetre) and to represent the interest of users for different applications (more or less coarse precision). The acuity parameter needs to be set-up manually to enable the user to regulate the granularity of the learned states.

Initially, before the first execution of MILES, the hierarchy **h** is initialised as an empty tree. If MILES has been previously executed, the incremental nature of MILES learning process allows that the resulting hierarchy **h** can be utilised as the initial hierarchy of a new execution.

At each video frame, MILES utilises the list of all tracked objects **O** for updating the hierarchy **h**. For each object **o** in **O**, MILES first gets the set of triplets **T_o**, which serves as input for the state concept updating process of **h**. This updating process is described in Section 3.2. The updating process returns a list **L_o** of the current state concepts recognised for the object **o** at each level of **h**.

Then, the event concepts $E^{(c)}$ of the hierarchy **h** are updated comparing the new state concept list L_o with the list of state concepts recognised for the object **o** at the previous frame.

Finally, MILES gives as output for each video frame, the updated hierarchy **h** and the list of the currently recognised state and event concepts for each object **o** in **O**.

3.2   States Updating Algorithm

The state concept updating algorithm is described below by pseudo-code.

```
list_of_states updateStates (hierarchy h, list_of_triplets To) {
      list_of_states L;
      C = getRootOfHierarchy( h );
      if emptyTree( h ) {
         insertRoot( h, To );
      } else if isTerminalState( C ) {
         if cutoffTestPassed ( C, To )
            createNewTerminals( h, To );
         incorporateState( C, To );
      } else {
         incorporateState( C, To );
         P = highestScoreState( h );
         Q = newStateConcept( h, To );
         R = secondScoreState( h );
         y = mergeCategoryUtilityScore( P, R );
         z = splitCategoryUtilityScore( P});
         if score( P ) is bestScore
            updateStates( getSubTree( h, P ), To );
         else if score( Q ) is bestScore
            insertChild (Q, h);
         else if y is bestScore {
            M = mergeStates( P, R, h );
            updateStates(getSubTree( h, M), To );
         } else if z is bestScore {
            splitStates( P, h );
            updateStates( getSubTree( h, C), To );
         }
      }
      insertCurrentState( C, L );
      return L;
}
```

The algorithm starts by accessing the analysed state **C** from the current hierarchy **h** (with function *getRootOfHierarchy*, which returns the root state of **h**). The initialisation of the hierarchy is performed by creating a state with the triplets **T₀**, for the first processed object.

Then, for the case that **C** corresponds to a terminal state (the state has no children), a *cutoff* test is performed (function *cutoffTestPassed*).

The **cutoff** is a criteria utilised for stopping the creation (i.e. specialisation) of children states. It can be defined as:

$$\text{cutoff} = \begin{cases} \text{true} & \text{if} & \{ & \mu_{n_i} - V_{n_i} \leq A_{n_i} \\ & & | & \forall\ i \in \{1, .., T\} & \} , \\ \text{false} & \text{else} \end{cases} \tag{1}$$

where V_{n_i} is the value of the i-th triplet of $\mathbf{T_o}$. This equation means that the learning process will stop at the concept state $S_k^{(c)}$ if no meaningful difference exists between each attribute value of $\mathbf{T_o}$ and the mean value μ_{n_i} of the attribute n_i for the state concept $S_k^{(c)}$ (based on the attribute *acuity* A_{n_i}).

If the *cutoff* test is passed, the function *createNewTerminals* generates two children for $\mathbf{C}$, one initialised with $\mathbf{T_o}$ and the other as a copy of $\mathbf{C}$. Then, passing or not passing the *cutoff* test, $\mathbf{T_o}$ is incorporated to the state $\mathbf{C}$ (function *incorporateState* described in Section 3.3). In this terminal state case, the updating process then stops.

If $\mathbf{C}$ has children, first $\mathbf{T_o}$ is immediately incorporated to $\mathbf{C}$. Next, different new hierarchy configurations have to be evaluated among all the children of $\mathbf{C}$. In order to determine in which state concept the triplets list $\mathbf{T_o}$ is next incorporated (i.e. the state concept is recognised), a quality measure for state concepts called **category utility** is utilised, which measures how well the instances are represented by a given category (i.e. state concept).

The category utility CU for a class partition of K state concepts (corresponding to a possible configuration of the children for the currently analysed state $\mathbf{C}$) is defined as:

$$CU = \frac{\displaystyle\sum_{k=1}^{K} \frac{\mathcal{P}(S_k^{(c)}) \displaystyle\sum_{i=1}^{T} \left(\frac{A_{n_i}}{\sigma_{n_i}^{(k)}} - \frac{A_{n_i}}{\sigma_{n_i}^{(p)}} \right)}{2 \cdot T \cdot \sqrt{\pi}}}{K}, \tag{2}$$

where $\sigma_{n_i}^{(k)}$ (respectively for $\sigma_{n_i}^{(p)}$) is the standard deviation for the attribute n_i of $\mathbf{T_o}$, with $i \in \{1, 2, .., T\}$, in the state concept $S_k^{(c)}$ (respectively for the root state $S_p^{(c)}$).

It is worthy to note that the category utility CU serves as the major criteria to decide how to balance the states given the learning data. CU is an efficient criteria because it compares the relative frequency of the candidate states together with the relative Gaussian distribution of their attributes, weighted by their significant precision (predefined acuity).

Then, the different alternatives for the incorporation of $\mathbf{T_o}$ are:

(a) The incorporation of $\mathbf{T_o}$ to a existing state $\mathbf{P}$ gives the best CU score. In this case, the function *updateStates* is recursively called, considering $\mathbf{P}$ as root.

(b) The generation of a new state concept $\mathbf{Q}$ from instance $\mathbf{T_o}$ gives the best CU score $\mathbf{x}$. In this case, the function *insertChild* inserts the new state $\mathbf{Q}$ as child of $\mathbf{C}$, and the updating process stops.

(c) Consider the state $\mathbf{M}$ as the resulting state from merging the best state $\mathbf{P}$ and the second best state $\mathbf{R}$. Also, consider $\mathbf{y}$ as the CU score of replacing states $\mathbf{P}$ and $\mathbf{R}$ with $\mathbf{M}$. If the best CU score is $\mathbf{y}$, the hierarchy is modified by the **merge operator** (function *mergeStates*). Then, *updateStates* is recursively

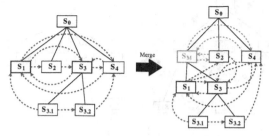

Fig. 2. Result of a merging operation. Blue boxes represent the states to be merged. The green box represents the resulting merged state. Red dashed lines represent the existing events, while the green dashed lines are the new events from the merging process.

called, using the subtree from state **M** as the tree to be analysed. The **merge operator** consists in merging two state concepts S_p and S_q into one state S_M, while S_p and S_q become the children of S_M, and the parent of S_p and S_q becomes the parent of S_M, as depicted in Figure 2. The merge operator also generates new events for state S_M which generalise the transitions incoming and leaving states S_p and S_q. (d) Consider **z** as the CU score of replacing state **P** with its children. If the best CU score is **z**, the hierarchy is modified by the **split operator** (function *splitStates*). Then, *updateStates* is called, using the subtree from the current state **C** again. The **split operator** consists in replacing a state S with its children, as depicted in Figure 3. This process implies to suppress the state concept S together with all the events in which the state is involved. Then, the children of the state S must be included as children of the parent state of S.

At the end of function *updateStates*, each current state **C** for the different levels of the hierarchy is stored in the list **L** of current state concepts for object **o**, by the function *insertCurrentState*.

3.3   Incorporation of New Object Attribute Values

The incorporation process consists in updating a state concept with the triplets $\mathbf{T_o}$ for an object **o**. The proposed updating functions are incremental in order to improve the processing time performance of the approach. The incremental updating function for the mean value μ_n of an attribute n is presented in Equation (3).

$$\mu_n(t) = \frac{V_n \cdot R_n + \mu_n(t-1) \cdot Sum_n(t-1)}{Sum_n(t)}, \tag{3}$$

with

$$Sum_n(t) = R_n + Sum_n(t-1), \tag{4}$$

where V_n is the attribute value and R_n is the reliability. Sum_n is the accumulation of reliability values R_n.

The incremental updating function for the standard deviation σ_n for attribute n is presented in Equation (5).

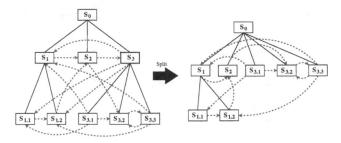

Fig. 3. Split operator in MILES approach. The blue box represents the state to be split. Red dashed lines represent events.

$$\sigma_n(t) = \sqrt{\frac{Sum_n(t-1)}{Sum_n(t)} \cdot \left(\sigma_n(t-1)^2 + \frac{R_n \cdot \Delta_n}{Sum_n(t)}\right)}.$$
$$with$$
$$\Delta_n = (V_n - \mu_n(t-1))^2$$

(5)

For a new state concept, the initial values taken for Equations (3), (4), and (5) with $t = 0$ correspond to $\mu_n(0) = V_n$, $Sum_n(0) = R_n$, and $\sigma_n(0) = A_n$, where A_n is the *acuity* for the attribute n.

In case that, after updating the standard deviation Equation (5), the value of $\sigma_n(i)$ is lower than the *acuity* A_n, $\sigma_n(i)$ is reassigned to A_n. This way, the acuity value establishes a lower bound for the standard deviation of an attribute.

4   Evaluation of the Approach

The capability of MILES for automatically learning and recognising real world situations has been evaluated, using two videos for elderly care at home. The video scene corresponds to an apartment with a table, a sofa, and a kitchen, as shown in Figure 4. The videos correspond to an elderly man (Figure 4a) and an elderly woman (Figure 4b), both performing tasks of everyday life as cooking, resting, and having lunch. The lengths of the sequences are 40000 frames (approximately 67 minutes) and 28000 frames (approximately 46 minutes).

The input information is obtained from a tracking method which computes reliability measures to object attributes, which is not included due to space constraints.

The attributes of interest for the evaluation are 3D position (x, y), an attribute for standing or crouching posture, and interaction attributes $SymD_{table}$, $SymD_{sofa}$, and $SymD_{kitchen}$ between the person and three objects present in the scene (table, sofa, and kitchen table). For simplicity, The interaction attributes are represented with three flags: $FAR : distance \geq 100[cm]$, $NEAR : 50[cm] < distance < 100[cm]$, and $VERY\_NEAR : distance \leq 50[cm]$. The contextual objects in the video scene (sofa, table, and kitchen) have been modelled in 3D.

(a)   (b)

Fig. 4. Video sequences for elderly care at home application. Figures (a) and (b) respectively show the observed elderly man and woman.

All the attributes are automatically computed by a tracking method, which is able to compute the reliability measures of the attributes. These reliability measures account the quality and coherence of the acquired data.

The learning process applied over the 68000 frames have resulted in a hierarchy of 670 state concepts and 28884 event concepts. From the 670 states, 338 state concepts correspond to terminal states (50.4%). From the 28884 events, 1554 event concepts correspond to events occurring between terminal states (5.4%). This number of state and event concepts can be reduced considering a state stability parameter, defining the minimal duration for considering a state as stable. Two learned events are described below.

This evaluation consists in comparing the recognised events with the ground-truth of a sequence. Different 750 frames from the elderly woman video are used for comparison, corresponding to a duration of 1.33 minutes. The recognition process has obtained as result the events summarised in Figure 5.

The evaluation has obtained 5 true positives (TP) and 2 false positives (FP) on event recognition. This results in a precision (TP/(TP+FP)) of 71%. MILES has been able to recognise all the events from the ground-truth, but also has

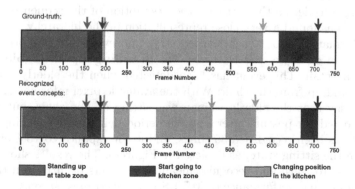

Fig. 5. Sequence of recognised events and ground-truth for the elderly woman video. The coloured arrows represent the events, while coloured zones represent the duration of a state before the occurrence of an event.

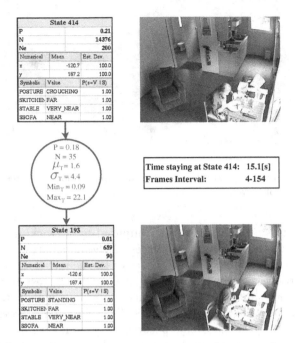

State 414		
P		0.21
N		14376
Ne		200
Numerical	Mean	Est. Dev.
x	-120.7	100.0
y	187.2	100.0
Symbolic	Value	P(s=V I S)
POSTURE	CROUCHING	1.00
SKITCHEN	FAR	1.00
STABLE	VERY_NEAR	1.00
SSOFA	NEAR	1.00

$$P = 0.18$$
$$N = 35$$
$$\mu_T = 1.6$$
$$\sigma_T = 4.4$$
$$\text{Min}_T = 0.09$$
$$\text{Max}_T = 22.1$$

Time staying at State 414:	15.1[s]
Frames Interval:	4-154

State 193		
P		0.01
N		659
Ne		90
Numerical	Mean	Est. Dev.
x	-120.6	100.0
y	187.4	100.0
Symbolic	Value	P(s=V I S)
POSTURE	STANDING	1.00
SKITCHEN	FAR	1.00
STABLE	VERY_NEAR	1.00
SSOFA	NEAR	1.00

Fig. 6. Event *standing from the table zone*. On the left, the learned event is in red and the learned states are in black. The right-top image corresponds to a video frame before the event, while the right-bottom image corresponds to the frame which has caused the occurrence of the event. The black square contains the information about the starting state at the moment of occurrence of the event.

recognised two inexistent events, and has made a mean error on the starting state duration of 4 seconds. These errors are mostly due to bad segmentation near the kitchen zone, which had strong illumination changes, and to the similarity between the colours of the elderly woman legs and the floor. The results are encouraging considering the fact that the description of the sequence generated by a human has found a very close representation in the hierarchy.

Rich information about each learned state and event can be obtained with MILES. As an example, the learned event **Standing up at Table Zone** is explained in detail. This event has been detected when the elderly woman has begun to stand up from the chair. With the available pixel information it is not possible to say that the elderly woman was sitting on the chair, but just that she has changed her posture after a stable period being in a crouching posture. This event has been recognised 35 times, and it corresponds to 18% of possible events from the sitting state, as depicted in Figure 6. The results show that the system is able to learn and recognise meaningful events occurring in the scene. The computer time performance of MILES is $1300[frames/second]$ for a video with one tracked object and six attributes, showing the real-time capability of the learning approach. However, the learned events are frequent and stable, but are not always meaningful for the user. Despite the calculation of the category utility, which formally measures the information density, an automatic process for measuring the usefulness of the learned events for the user is still needed.

5   Conclusions

A new event learning approach has been proposed, able to incrementally learn general events occurring in a video scene. The incremental nature of the event learning process is well suited for real world applications as it considers the incorporation of new arriving information with a minimal processing time cost. Incremental learning of events can be useful for abnormal event recognition and for serving as input for higher level event analysis. MILES allows to learn a model of the states and events occurring in the scene, when no a priori model is available. It has been conceived for learning state and event concepts in a general way. Depending on the availability of tracked object features, the possible combinations are large. MILES has shown its capability for recognising events, processing noisy image-level data with a minimal configuration effort. The proposed method computes the probability of transition between two states, similarly as HMM. The contribution MILES is to learn the global structure of the states and the events and to structure them in a hierarchy.

However, more evaluation is still needed for other type of scenes, for other attribute sets, and for different number and type of tracked objects. The anomaly detection capability of the approach on a large application must be also be evaluated. Future work will be also focused in the incorporation of attributes related to interactions between tracked objects (e.g. meeting someone). The automatic association between the learned events and semantical concepts and user defined events will be also studied.

References

1. Gennari, J., Langley, P., Fisher, D.: Models of incremental concept formation. In: Carbonell, J. (ed.) Machine Learning: Paradigms and Methods, pp. 11–61. MIT Press, Cambridge (1990)
2. Ghahramani, Z.: Learning dynamic bayesian networks. In: Giles, C.L., Gori, M. (eds.) IIASS-EMFCSC-School 1997. LNCS (LNAI), vol. 1387, pp. 168–197. Springer, Heidelberg (1998)
3. Hu, W., Tan, T., Wang, L., Maybank, S.: A survey on visual surveillance of object motion and behaviors. IEEE Transactions on Systems, Man, and Cybernetics - Part C: Applications and Reviews 34(3), 334–352 (2004)
4. McKusick, K., Thompson, K.: Cobweb/3: A portable implementation. Technical report, Technical Report Number FIA-90-6-18-2, NASA Ames Research Center, Moffett Field, CA (September 1990)
5. Piciarelli, C., Foresti, G., Snidaro, L.: Trajectory clustering and its applications for video surveillance. In: Proceedings of the IEEE International Conference on Advanced Video and Signal-Based Surveillance (AVSS 2005), pp. 40–45. IEEE Computer Society Press, Los Alamitos (2005)

6. Sridhar, M., Cohn, A., Hogg, D.: Learning functional object-categories from a relational spatio-temporal representation. In: Proceedings of the 18th European Conference on Artificial Intelligence (ECAI 2008), Patras, Greece, July 21-25, pp. 606–610 (2008)
7. Toshev, A., Brémond, F., Thonnat, M.: Unsupervised learning of scenario models in the context of video surveillance. In: Proceedings of the IEEE International Conference on Computer Vision Systems (ICVS 2006), January 2006, p. 10 (2006)
8. Vu, T., Brémond, F., Thonnat, M.: Automatic video interpretation: a novel algorithm for temporal scenario recognition. In: Proceedings of the 18th International Joint Conference on Artificial Intelligence (IJCAI03), Acapulco, Mexico (August 2003)
9. Xiang, T., Gong, S.: Video behavior profiling for anomaly detection. IEEE Transactions on Pattern Analysis and Machine Intelligence 30(5), 893–908 (2008)

A System for Probabilistic Joint
3D Head Tracking and Pose Estimation
in Low-Resolution, Multi-view Environments

Michael Voit[1] and Rainer Stiefelhagen[1,2]

[1] Interactive Analysis and Diagnosis, Fraunhofer IITB, Karlsruhe, Germany
[2] Institute for Anthropomatics, Universität Karlsruhe (TH), Karlsruhe, Germany

Abstract. We present a new system for 3D head tracking and pose estimation in low-resolution, multi-view environments. Our approach consists of a joint particle filter scheme, that combines head shape evaluation with histograms of oriented gradients and pose estimation by means of artificial neural networks. The joint evaluation resolves previous problems of automatic alignment and multi-sensor fusion and gains an automatic system that is flexible against modifications in the available number of cameras. We evaluate on the CLEAR07 dataset for multi-view head pose estimation and achieve mean pose errors of 7.2° and 9.3° for pan and tilt respectively, which improves accuracy compared to our previous work by 14.9% and 25.8%.

1 Introduction

The automatic visual analysis of human social interaction and individual behavior strongly relies on the recognition of peoples' gaze and its derived visual focus of attention. No less than that, the observation of natural cooperation between people can only be ensured if their environment provides unconstrained work places and does not limit the scope of human actions to restraining sensors. Primary challenges hence originate from compromised sensor setups, as for example camera captures with bad lighting, low resolution or, as in the case of tracking gaze, the problem of rear and profile views of the people under study. Especially the problem of non-frontal observations can however be tackled with camera setups, that allow views from different angles. The low-resolution of far distant face captures however, and the still necessary selection between rear and possibly frontal appearances, still put limitations on every perception. A common approach to approximate gaze and the person's overall attention is therefore to use head orientation. Yet, most challenges also apply here besides the large variety of head appearances, that different poses and hair styles provide.

Official evaluations of multi-view head pose estimation, and with such, a common dataset to compare international systems, was conducted with the CLEAR evaluation workshop in 2006 and 2007. With them, several different approaches to integrate multi-sensor information and enhancements of single-view pose classifiers to fit this new scenario were presented and still provide current state of the art achievements.

M. Fritz, B. Schiele, and J.H. Piater (Eds.): ICVS 2009, LNCS 5815, pp. 415–424, 2009.

Fig. 1. Example scene from the CLEAR 2007 dataset for head pose estimation. The dataset provides four camera views from the room's upper corners. From this distance, facial details appear blurred and depending on the used camera view, the captured head region happens to be as small as 20 × 30 pixels and less.

Canton et al. [8] introduced color descriptors on 3D ellipsoidal shapes to derive likely pose distributions. Although the use of skin color is often used as a very strong feature in visual human-computer interaction tasks, the unrestricted environment challenges its robustness by introducing rear views of people with less or very short hair, whose hair color might even match the previously learned skin color cluster. Furthermore, our own experiments showed, that depending on lighting and background noise, the skin color segmentation is likely to happen on background objects that surround the detected head region, which strongly disbalances the color model of the person under study.

In [7], Ba et al. used a monocular pose classifier, consisting of texture and color analysis, and fused the individual single-view estimates upon the percentage of detected skin color in the respective view's head bounding box. Altough the underlying classification scheme achieves a high accuracy on monocular samples, its disadvantages are the strong dependence on a robust skin color segmentation in every view and the yet missing automatic 3D multi-view alignment.

Another work was presented by Lanz et al. in [12], in which a set of key views of the target is used to compute corresponding color histograms of the head and to generate new poses in between by interpolating from these pre-acquired key models. The training however has to happen on the same video sequence, as individual models have to be created that match the current color distribution of the corresponding person. Furthermore, the groundtruth pose angles during initialization are derived online, by applying frontal face template matching with symmetry analysis to find the best view and hence the observed rotation. With such, the model only allows to estimate in the scope of the initial setup and strongly depends on a robust color description with enough key views to interpolate over the complete set of possible pose angles.

Very good results on the CLEAR07 dataset were achieved by Yan et al., who presented in [10,11] a manifold learning algorithm, based on each individual's set of simplexes with propagated pose labels through the approximated submanifold. The submanifolds of all subjects in the training set are synchronized and new samples are classified by their median of the nearest neighbors in the manifolds' reduced feature space. A sample hereby consists of the concatenated intensities of cropped head image boxes over all camera views and, as above, does not yet include the automatic head alignment but relies on predefined head bounding boxes. Furthermore, the applied fusion on feature level, restricts the system to cope with modified camera setups where new views are added or existing cameras removed.

Considering above limitations and challenges, we now present a new fully-automatic 3D head tracking and pose estimation approach for low-resolution, multi-view environments. In a combined particle filter framework, we rate head appearances with local shape descriptors and estimate pose angles with artificial neural networks. Monocular observation likelihoods are computed for state projections into the respective camera views. The individual probability distributions are then merged by their joint product, which allows the overall system to be flexible for increasing or decreasing the number of available cameras without further retraining. Section 2 thereby describes our framework and both evaluations against pose and shape. Our results are presented in Section 3 where we discuss our testing on the CLEAR07 dataset for head pose estimation and put our experiments in contrast to our previous work. The conclusion in Section 4 then summarizes this paper and gives a short overview of yet unaddressed problems and future plans.

2 Head Tracking and Pose Estimation

We assume that the head's shape can be represented by the quadruple $s = (x, y, z, r_z)$, describing a 3D ellipsoid at position $(x, y, z) \in \mathbb{R}^3$ with radiuses of fixed proportions $r_x = r_y = k \cdot r_z$, and $k, r_z \in \mathbb{R}$. The ellipse's pose is represented by $\theta = (\theta_{pan}, \theta_{tilt})$, to describe rotations in horizontal (pan) and vertical (tilt) direction. In-plane rotation does not influence the overall viewing frustum, which is why we neglect it in this work. Hence, be $X_t \in \{s, \theta\}$ the head's state space at time t, then tracking the head's configuration can be defined as to follow the state evolution $X_t | X_{1:t-1}$, from gathered observations $Z_{1:t}$ up to now. A common Bayesian approach is to recursively calculate the state space density $p(X_t | Z_{1:t}, X_{1:t-1})$, for letting its expectation value $\mathbb{E}[X_t | Z_{1:t}, X_{1:t-1}]$ be the state hypothesis. If we assume, that state evolution is a first order Markovian process, i.e. letting the head's configuration X_t only depend on its predecessor and present measurement, such density is defined by:

$$p(X_t | Z_{1:t}) = \frac{p(Z_t | X_t) p(X_t | Z_{1:t-1})}{p(Z_t | Z_{1:t-1})} \tag{1}$$

with $p(X_t|Z_{1:t-1})$ as the Chapman-Kolmogorov prediction

$$p(X_t|Z_{1:t-1}) = \int p(X_t|X_{t-1})p(X_{t-1}|Z_{1:t-1})dX_{t-1} \qquad (2)$$

2.1   Sequential Monte Carlo Sampling

To cope with the non-linear and non-Gaussian nature of the problem, we approximate equation 1, by applying sequential Monte Carlo sampling by means of a particle filter (PF) with sampling importance resampling (SIR) [9].

Following the law of large numbers, particle filters approximate a possibly multimodal target function with a set of support points $\{X_t^i, i = 1, \ldots, N_s\}$ and associated weights $\{\omega_t^i, i = 1, \ldots, N_s\}$. The sum of Dirac functions over this set of weighted samples then results in a discrete representation of the underlying signal, in our case the state space's probability distribution function (PDF):

$$p(X_t|Z_{1:t}) \approx \sum_{i=1}^{N_s} \omega_t^i \cdot \delta(X_t - X_t^i) \qquad (3)$$

With this, a configuration hypothesis is easily obtained from the weighted mean of the support set:

$$\mathbb{E}[X_t|Z_{1:t}] = \sum_{i=1}^{N_s} \omega_t^i \cdot X_t^i \qquad (4)$$

To propagate state evolution, the set of particles is updated as soon as a new measurement is available. New samples are drawn according to a predefined proposal distribution $X_t \sim q(X_t|X_{t-1}, Z_{1:t})$, which suggests samples in interesting regions of the state space. A corresponding weight update is then successively calculated with:

$$\omega_t^i \propto \omega_{t-1}^i \frac{p(Z_t|X_t^i)p(X_t^i|X_{t-1}^i)}{q(X_t^i|X_{t-1}^i, Z_t)} \qquad (5)$$

The SIR filter scheme is applied to cope with these updates but provides two advantages: i) it sets the proposal function $q(\cdot)$ to the often applied and implicitly available prior PDF $p(X_t|X_{t-1}^i)$ and ii) instead of simply drawing new samples and propagating their old weights over time, it resamples and replaces the set of support points with every update step. This sets the particle priors to a uniform distribution with $\omega_{t-1}^i = N_s^{-1}$ and allows us to simplify equation 5 to a less complex reweighing scheme, which only depends on the observation likelihoods:

$$\omega_t^i \propto p(Z_t|X_t^i) \qquad (6)$$

Resampling is usually done by drawing new samples from the current set of support points with probabilities according to their corresponding weights. These weights are then updated with respect to the given observation, as the particles' respective state hypotheses are propagated along a known process motion model, including explicitly added noise, that is to cope with observation variances. The applied motion model filters state evolution for that diffused particles do not persist to local maxima of observation likelihoods and less particles become necessary for a matching approximation of the underlying signal. This is especially useful for complex motion patterns in high dimensional state spaces. However, since we only track the head's 3D position and rotation along two axes, we neglect state motion and only add Gaussian noise on top of the state vector.

2.2   Evaluating Pose Observations

To make use of the multi-view environment, our goal is to merge individual estimates from every camera in a combined framework, instead of applying a best view selection beforehand that introduces a further error source. This can easily be achieved with training the classifier to estimate pose angles with respect to the particular camera's line of sight. However, applying the same classifier on different views, introduces rear captures of the tracked head, as well as large distances to the observing camera, depending on the trajectory of the person under study. The trained system needs to cope with possibly low-resolution head captures and noise induced from different hair styles. It therefore has to show strong generalization capabilities and should allow to measure its confidence along with its given hypothesis. In [6], we showed that classifying artificial neural networks (ANN) sufficed all these conditions. We trained two feed-forward networks with three layers, to respectively estimate a PDF over a set of possible pose angles. One network was applied for pan, another for tilt angle classification. The class width was chosen to span over $10°$, hence leading to 36 output neurons for an estimate over $-180° - +180°$ horizontally, and 18 output neurons for $-90° - +90°$ in vertical direction. By using a Gaussian PDF as target output during training, we implied uncertainty concerning neighbor angle classes. In our experiments this has shown to enhance robustness when applying the same network on different camera views: unimodal estimates, that peaked over wrong angles, could still provide enough support, if the actual class lied in the near neighborhood. A joint PDF over all obtained network outputs hence still managed to average its peak near the correct target angle.

We therefore applied this classifier in our current framework as follows: With Z_t^c the observation of camera c, be $Z_t^c(s_t^i)$ the cropped image patch, which is obtained from projecting the 3D bounding box around state estimate X_t^i's ellipsoid into camera view c. This 2D region is preprocessed, for that it is resampled to a fixed size of 32×32 pixels in order to provide invariance to different head sizes and observation distances. After resampling, the head region is grayscaled and equalized in intensity to deliver a better contrast. The result is concatenated with its 3×3 Sobel magnitude response, to provide a vectorized feature vector $\Upsilon(Z_t^c(s_t^i))$, consisting of the head intensity and edge appearances. The ANN then estimates the posterior PDF over the set of relative angles θ_{pan}^c or θ_{tilt}^c, for horizontal or vertical rotations. Since we consider both angles to be conditionally independent, we can build a joint posterior with:

$$p^{pose}(\theta^{i,c}|\Upsilon(Z_t^c(s_t^i))) = p^{ann}(\theta_{pan}^{i,c}|\Upsilon(Z_t^c(s_t^i)))p^{ann}(\theta_{tilt}^{i,c}|\Upsilon(Z_t^c(s_t^i))) \qquad (7)$$

If we assume a uniform distribution of training samples per pose class, then following Bayes' rule gains an observation evaluation, proportional to the ANNs' estimated posterior:

$$p^{pose}(Z_t^c|X_t^i) = p^{pose}(Z_t^c|s_t^i, \theta_t^c) \propto p^{pose}(\theta^{i,c}|\Upsilon(Z_t^c(s_t^i))) \qquad (8)$$

2.3   Evaluating Head Alignment with Local Shape Descriptors

The nature of the trained ANNs is to output pose likelihoods for any given image patch along with strong generalization capabilities. This makes the estimates only as reliable as the implicit head alignment, that is to crop 2D image head regions consistent with used training samples. To gain a measurement for the fitness of an aligned head region and with such, confidence in the ANN's estimates, we use local shape descriptors by means of histograms of oriented gradients (HOG) as a second evaluation of a state hypothesis.

HOGs were presented by Dalal and Triggs in [1] and describe an appearance-based approach to represent an object's shape by merging local histograms of its binned edge orientations into a joint feature vector. The histograms are computed for non-overlapping subwindows of fixed size, to cover the object's image patch in total. The concatenation of histograms of neighboring subwindows then gives the final description. In the original work, a support vector machine then discriminatively detects learned objects.

We adopt the descriptor and directly rate possible head appearances against a given head model by means of the l^2 norm. An initial mean HOG representation of heads is computed over a set of training samples. This model is then gradually adapted online with sparse head detector hits from a custom-trained Haar-like feature cascade using OpenCV's implementation [2,3]. A general preprocessing thereby happens similar to 2.2: a given image patch $Z_t^c(s_t^i)$ is resampled to a fixed width and height, grayscaled and equalized for a better contrast. Its HOG descriptor is then computed on its 3×3 Sobel filter response. We obtained satisfactory results, by scaling image patches to 24×24 pixels, using 8 bins for discretizing orientations into $45°$-wide segments and concatenating the final descriptor over 3×3 neighboring histograms.

With defining $\Gamma(Z_t^c(s_t^i))$ to be the respective HOG descriptor of the image patch corresponding to hypothesis s_i, and $\widehat{\Gamma}$ a mean shape model that we computed upon training samples, a corresponding observation likelihood equates to the similarity of the two vectors:

$$p^{shape}(Z_t^c|X_t^i) = p^{shape}(Z_t^c|s_t^i) = p^{shape}(\Gamma(Z_t^c(s_t^i))|\widehat{\Gamma}) \propto \lambda exp - \lambda|\Gamma(Z_t^c(s_t^i)) - \widehat{\Gamma}| \qquad (9)$$

The parameter λ defines how strong the fitness converges against zero and was empirically set to 0.25.

Fig. 2. Histograms of oriented gradients for an exemplary head image patch. The head region was grayscaled and resampled to fit a width and height of 24×24 pixels (left). A division into 8×8 pixel sized subregions (middle) then defines the areas for which individual histograms over the edge orientations are computed (right). Each line in the right image, resembles an orientation bin in that local histogram. The brighter the line, the stronger that edge orientation is supported.

2.4 Joining Multi-sensor Observation Likelihoods

Using two or more cameras implies a set of multi-view sensor stream observations denoted by $Z_t = \{Z_t^c, c = 1, \ldots, N_C\}$, with pose and shape observations $Z_t^c = \{\Upsilon(\cdot), \Gamma(\cdot)\}$. Both evaluations estimate likelihoods invariant to the used camera view. To cope with multiple streams, a common acceptance in Bayesian tracking is therefore to build the product density over the set of all single-view likelihoods [12]. Considering that observations for pose and shape evaluations are conditionally independent in every camera view, we can therefore build a final joint observation PDF with:

$$p(Z_t|X_t^i) = \prod_{c=1}^{N_C} p^{pose}(Z_t^c|X_t^i)p^{shape}(Z_t^c|X_t^i) \tag{10}$$

3 Experimental Validation

To allow a comparison with current state of the art systems, we evaluated our approach on the CLEAR07 dataset for head pose estimation [5].

Provided are four camera views from a room's upper corners with 640×480 pixels at 15 frames per second. The dataset contains 15 different persons, whose head poses were captured with a magnetic pose sensor [4] and who showed rotations over the whole range of angle classes. We stayed consistent with training our system on the same video subset, that was officially used during the workshop. To directly distinguish between head detection and pose estimation tasks, manually annotated head bounding boxes for every 5th frame in all camera views are included in the dataset, which automatically lets us assess implied head tracking and alignment. Evaluations only take place on these dedicated selected frames.

With each evaluation video, we initialized our system to randomly spread particles in a spherical radius of 20 cm off the true head position in 3D. We considered this to be a valid assumption for state-of-the-art body tracker and as it showed, our particles converged very fast onto the real head nearby. Aside from initialization, the remaining videos were processed fully automatic. With this, the implicit tracking only showed a mean absolute difference of only 2 cm compared to the annotated head centroids. As can be seen in Table 1, for the individual camera views, this resulted in a mean difference of 3.6 pixels for the

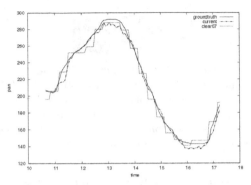

Fig. 3. Pan rotation over 7 seconds for the sequence depicted in Figure 1. Shown is the groundtruth head rotation, estimates we gained with our previous system from CLEAR07 [6] and results from this work. As can be seen, the previous system only estimated the pan angle on every 5th frame, because only then annotated head bounding boxes were available within the dataset. Our current implementation includes automatic tracking and alignment, hence we achieve estimates on every frame.

Table 1. Mean and standard deviation of the distance of our hypotheses to the annotated ground truth

	μ	σ
3D head box centroid [cm]	2.0	0.7
2D head box centroid [px]	3.6	2.0
2D head box width [px]	4.0	3.0
2D head box height [px]	3.9	2.8

projected 2D head box centers. Their width and height fit with a mean error of 4.0 and 3.9 pixels respectively.

Considering head poses, we observed mean errors of 7.2° and 9.3° for pan and tilt estimation. In CLEAR07, we presented a system that simply used the included head box annotations directly, instead of providing a custom tracking and alignment scheme [6]. Table 2 shows both systems' results in contrast. The overall decrease in error by 14.9% and 25.8% thereby emphasizes the advantages of a joint position and orientation state filtering. With such, we experienced that observation likelihoods were sometimes maximized by decreasing ellipse sizes, so that projected 2D image patches concentrated on face regions instead of the whole head with its hair and further background noise.

Furthermore, the joint tracking of both rotation angles in one state, mostly helps to resolve ambiguities that e.g. arise with poses that show downwards tilting. Here, views from above mostly depict hair in every view, which strongly resembles rear or even profile shots where parts of the face are occluded from long hairstyles. Smoothing the joint pose trajectory over time hereby restricts unlikely and sudden rotations in either direction and removes ambiguities that come along with them.

Table 2. Results on head pose estimation, compared to our previous system

	$\mu_{pan}[°]$	$\mu_{tilt}[°]$
voit07 [6]	8.46	12.54
voit09	7.2	9.3
$\varDelta$	14.9%	25.8%

4 Conclusion

In this paper, we presented a new approach for tracking the head's position and rotation in a 3D environment with multiple low-resolution cameras. We implemented a particle filter framework, that uses artificial neural networks for pose estimation and head shape evaluations by means of histograms of oriented gradients in a joint sampling importance resampling scheme.

We evaluated our implementation on the CLEAR07 multi-view subset for head pose estimation and obtained 7.2° and 9.3° mean errors regarding pan and tilt estimation. In contrast to our previous system we presented for CLEAR07 [6], which respectively showed errors of 8.46° and 12.54°, this approach jointly models the head's position, size and orientation in single state hypotheses. Besides the hereby gained full-automatic head tracking and alignment, both in 3D as well as 2D camera views, this tight integration increased the overall accuracy by 14.9% and 25.8% in horizontal and vertical direction. A comparison to further state of the art results on the same dataset can thereby be found in [5].

Still unaddressed problems in this work include the normalization of camera view distortions and coping with in-plane rotations for a more robust recognition. Since head appearances not only vary with respect to pose and person, but also to the distance of the observing camera, observations from above result in differences due to their high viewing angle the nearer a person gets. Yet other enhancements can be found in using different shape models for individual pose classes, hence obtaining a coarse estimate of head orientations implicitly from the alignment observation, and successively applying neural networks for pose refinement only.

Acknowledgments

This work was supported by the FhG Internal Programs under Grant No. 692 026.

References

1. Dalal, N., Triggs, B.: Histograms of Oriented Gradients for Human Detection. In: Proceedings of IEEE International Conference Computer Vision and Pattern Recognition, San Diego, USA, pp. 886–893 (2005)
2. Viola, P., Jones, M.: Robust Real-time Object Detection. International Journal of Computer Vision (2001)
3. OpenCV Library: http://sourceforge.net/projects/opencvlibrary

 4. Ascension Technology Corporation., http://www.ascension-tech.com/
 5. Stiefelhagen, R., Bernardin, K., Bowers, R., Rose, R.T., Michel, M., Garofolo, J.S.:
    The CLEAR 2007 evaluation. In: Stiefelhagen, R., Bowers, R., Fiscus, J.G. (eds.)
    RT 2007 and CLEAR 2007. LNCS, vol. 4625, pp. 3–34. Springer, Heidelberg (2008)
 6. Voit, M., Nickel, K., Stiefelhagen, R.: Head pose estimation in single- and multi-
    view environments - results on the CLEAR 2007 benchmarks. In: Stiefelhagen, R.,
    Bowers, R., Fiscus, J.G. (eds.) RT 2007 and CLEAR 2007. LNCS, vol. 4625, pp.
    307–316. Springer, Heidelberg (2008)
 7. Ba, S.O., Odobez, J.-M.: A Probabilistic Head Pose Tracking Evaluation in Single
    and Multiple Camera Setups. In: Stiefelhagen, R., Bowers, R., Fiscus, J.G. (eds.)
    RT 2007 and CLEAR 2007. LNCS, vol. 4625, pp. 276–286. Springer, Heidelberg
    (2008)
 8. Canton-Ferrer, C., Casas, J.R., Pardàs, M.: Head orientation estimation using par-
    ticle filtering in multiview scenarios. In: Stiefelhagen, R., Bowers, R., Fiscus, J.G.
    (eds.) RT 2007 and CLEAR 2007. LNCS, vol. 4625, pp. 317–327. Springer, Heidel-
    berg (2008)
 9. Arulampalam, S., Maskell, S., Gordon, N., Clapp, T.: A Tutorial on Particle Fil-
    ters for Online Nonlinear/Non-Gaussian Bayesian Tracking. IEEE Transactions on
    Signal Processing 50, 174–188 (2002)
10. Yan, S., Zhang, Z., Fu, Y., Hu, Y., Tu, J., Huang, T.: Learning a person-
    independent representation for precise 3D pose estimation. In: Stiefelhagen, R.,
    Bowers, R., Fiscus, J.G. (eds.) RT 2007 and CLEAR 2007. LNCS, vol. 4625, pp.
    297–306. Springer, Heidelberg (2008)
11. Yan, S., Wang, H., Fu, Y., Yan, J., Tang, X., Huang, T.: Synchronized Submanifold
    Embedding for Person-Independent Pose Estimation and Beyond. IEEE Transac-
    tions on Image Processing (TIP) 18(1), 202–210 (2009)
12. Lanz, O., Brunelli, R.: Joint Bayesian Tracking of Head Location and Pose from
    Low-Resolution Video. In: Stiefelhagen, R., Bowers, R., Fiscus, J.G. (eds.) RT 2007
    and CLEAR 2007. LNCS, vol. 4625, pp. 287–296. Springer, Heidelberg (2008)

Robust Tracking by Means of Template Adaptation with Drift Correction

Chen Zhang[1], Julian Eggert[2], and Nils Einecke[2]

[1] Darmstadt University of Technology, Institute of Automatic Control, Control
Theory and Robotics Lab, Darmstadt D-64283, Germany
[2] Honda Research Institute Europe GmbH, Offenbach D-63073, Germany

Abstract. Algorithms for correlation-based visual tracking rely to a
great extent on a robust measurement of an object's location, gained by
comparing a template with the visual input. Robustness against object
appearance transformations requires template adaptation - a technique
that is subject to drift problems due to error integration. Most solutions
to this "drift-problem" fall back on a dominant template that remains
unmodified, preventing a true adaptation to arbitrary large transformations. In this paper, we present a novel template adaptation approach
that instead of recurring to a master template, makes use of object segmentation as a complementary object support to circumvent the drift
problem. In addition, we introduce a selective update strategy that prevents erroneous adaptation in case of occlusion or segmentation failure. We show that using our template adaptation approach, we are able
to successfully track a target in sequences containing large appearance
transformations, where standard template adaptation techniques fail.

1 Introduction

Visually tracking arbitrary moving objects in a dynamic real-world environment
is a difficult task. Tracking systems face many challenges like cluttered background, fluctuating environment conditions, occlusions, large object movements
due to limited processing frame rate and not at least object appearance transformation. A robust tracking system must be able to cope with all these difficulties,
in order to succeed in real-world applications

Modern Bayesian tracking systems (as e.g. described in [1], [2]) track arbitrary moving objects in a way that they estimate the object's parameters by
first predicting the state and consecutively confirming the predicted state by incorporating a measurement of the state. In our case, the measurement of a target
object is gained by comparing a template (as an appearance model) of the target object with the input image containing the sought object, using template
matching techniques (see e.g. [3]). The quality of the measurement essentially
depends on how up-to-date the template is. In order to make template matching
robust in a sequence of images with changing object appearance, the template
needs to be continuously updated towards the current appearance.

M. Fritz, B. Schiele, and J.H. Piater (Eds.): ICVS 2009, LNCS 5815, pp. 425–434, 2009.

Under the assumption of small object appearance changes, different approaches were proposed to update the template towards the current appearance. These approaches apply parametric transformations depending on the type of assumed appearance change ([4]), e.g. using a linear appearance transformation (e.g. in [5], [6]) or an active appearance model (e.g. in [7]). Apart from the fact that these methods are gradient-descent based and therefore not suited for large transformations, they are not designed to cope with arbitrary appearance transformations.

However, in order to cope with large appearance transformation of arbitrary type, the most generic way is rather simple. The template is updated using the current input image at the position where the object is currently found. Unfortunately, due to small errors in the position estimation, the great drawback of this naive approach is the risk of a loss of the target by a systematic drift introduced by the template update process. Previous authors have addressed this problem (see e.g. [4], [8]), but the solutions are based on falling back on a master reference template in regular intervals, which is not suitable for large, irreversible transformations.

To tackle the template drift problem, we propose in this paper a novel method for template adaptation by cutting out a new template with drift correction. The drift problem is solved in the way that the drift is first detected by analyzing the segmented object mask and then the drift is immediately corrected after each cut-out of the new template. A further update strategy prevents an erroneous adaptation, e.g. in case of occlusion or segmentation failure. In this paper, we first present our tracking framework with its three constituting components: I) multiple-cue based measurement by template matching, II) Bayesian based dynamic state estimation and III) template adaptation with drift correction. Then we demonstrate the performance of our tracking system by means of an experimental evaluation using different template adaptation methods.

2   The General Tracking Framework

2.1   Framework Overview

We want to track an arbitrary object in 2D images by estimating its state vector $\mathbf{X}_k = (\mathbf{x}_k, \mathbf{v}_k, \mathbf{a}_k)$ - comprising position, velocity and acceleration - at time step k, given all its past and current measurements $\mathbf{Z}_k, \mathbf{Z}_{k-1}, ..., \mathbf{Z}_1$.

The general tracking framework can be separated into three main components: I) The multiple-cue based measurement part for calculating the likelihood, II) the dynamic state estimation part for obtaining $\mathbf{X}_k$, and III) the template adaptation part for keeping the template up-to-date in favor of a robust likelihood calculation.

Part I: This part starts with a color image as input. Indicated as step 1 in Fig. 1, the image is then preprocessed into an array $\mathbf{Z}_{i,k}$ of N 2D planes corresponding each to an activity field that indicates the degree of response to a given cue. In step 2, a tracking template array $\mathbf{T}_{i,k}$ and an object mask $\mathbf{W}_k$ are used to find positions in the 2D planes that indicate a high probability for the presence of the tracked pattern. This template array consists of the same number of 2D planes as the preprocessed input after step 1, so that all the different cues

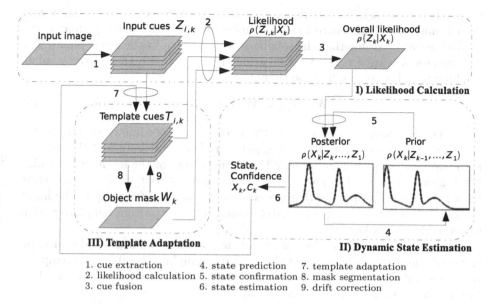

Fig. 1. Overview of tracking framework: the entire tracking system consists of nine processing steps within three main components: I) Calculation of measurement likelihood. II) Dynamic state estimation. III) Template adaptation. Details about the steps are described in sections 2.1-2.4.

are taken into consideration. The result is the likelihoods $\rho(\mathbf{Z}_{i,k}|\mathbf{X}_k)$ which are fused in step 3 to an overall likelihood $\rho(\mathbf{Z}_k|\mathbf{X}_k)$ as a single 2D plane.

Part II: The overall likelihood is used for a dynamic estimation of the tracking state $\mathbf{X}_k$ in a Bayesian manner in steps 4, 5 and 6 of Fig. 1.

Part III: Depending on the confidence of the state vector (which mainly depends on the quality of the likelihood and therefore, of the current template), a decision is made in step 7 whether to adapt the template. In the case that a new template is extracted, a segmentation of the target object from the new template provides an up-to-date object mask (step 8) which is used to prevent the drift during the template adaptation (step 9).

Steps 1-9 are iterated, so that the state estimation and if necessary also the template and object mask adapt to changing input. The system has to be initialized with a starting state vector $\mathbf{X}_0$, a template $\mathbf{T}_{i,0}$ and an object mask $\mathbf{W}_0$ for the target object. This is assumed to occur from outside of the system, either by human interaction or by some higher-level processing centers that communicate down a hypothesis on which parts of the scene should be tracked.

2.2 Likelihood Calculation

In the evaluations, we used RGB color channels and structure tensors (see e.g. [9]) as cues. This leads to $N = 6$ cue planes which are correlated with a template pattern consisting of N corresponding planes which specifies the particular properties of the selected 2D region that is being tracked. We perform a windowed, normalized cross correlation of the cue planes with the template pattern.

We basically assume that the sought object/pattern in the input planes $\mathbf{Z}_{i,k}$ of time step k can be found by comparing the planes with their corresponding tracking template planes $\mathbf{T}_{i,k}$, so that

$$\mathbf{W}_k \odot \mathbf{T}_{i,k} \approx \mathbf{W}_k \odot \mathbf{Z}_{i,k}^{\mathbf{x}} \qquad . \tag{1}$$

Here, $\mathbf{W}_k$ is a window operating in the two spatial coordinates that indicates the approximate limits of the tracked pattern. The contribution of the window is to suppress background clutter. $\mathbf{Z}_{i,k}^{\mathbf{x}}$ are cue planes of the input image which are centered around the spatial position $\mathbf{x}$ which is part of the overall state vector $\mathbf{X}_k$. Eq. (1) expresses that we expect the pattern of activity of the input around position $\mathbf{x}$ to be approximately matching the tracking template within the considered window $\mathbf{W}_k$.

We additionally assume that the input may contain a shifted and scaled (in terms of cue intensity) version of the tracking template, to make the template comparison and the tracking procedure contrast and brightness invariant. This means, that instead of Eq. (1), we consider

$$\mathbf{W}_k \odot \mathbf{T}_{i,k} \approx \lambda_i \mathbf{W}_k \odot \mathbf{Z}_{i,k}^{\mathbf{x}} - \kappa_i \mathbf{W}_k + \eta_i \mathbf{1} \qquad . \tag{2}$$

Here, λ_i is a contrast scaling parameter and κ_i a brightness bias. The factor η_i is additive Gaussian noise with variance σ_i^2. It is important that all the input image patches $\mathbf{Z}_{i,k}^{\mathbf{x}}$ centered around different positions $\mathbf{x}$ get scaled to the corresponding reference template $\mathbf{T}_{i,k}$, and not the other way round.

The likelihood that the input $\mathbf{Z}_{i,k}^{\mathbf{x}}$ centered around position $\mathbf{x}$ matches the tracking template $\mathbf{T}_{i,k}$ within a window $\mathbf{W}_k$ can then be expressed as

$$\rho(\mathbf{Z}_{i,k}|\mathbf{X}_k) \sim e^{-\frac{1}{2\sigma_i^2}\left\|\lambda_i \mathbf{W}_k \odot \mathbf{Z}_{i,k}^{\mathbf{x}} - \kappa_i \mathbf{W}_k - \mathbf{W}_k \odot \mathbf{T}_{i,k}\right\|^2} \qquad . \tag{3}$$

Eq. (3) constitutes an observation model that expresses the similarity between the real measurements $\mathbf{Z}_{i,k}$ and the measurements expected from knowing the state $\mathbf{X}_k$.

We now proceed to make Eq. (3) independent of λ_i and κ_i. For this purpose, we maximize the likelihood Eq. (3) with respect to the scaling and shift parameters, λ_i and κ_i. This amounts to minimizing the exponent, so that we want to find

$$\{\lambda_i^*(\mathbf{x}), \kappa_i^*(\mathbf{x})\} := \operatorname{argmin}_{\lambda_i, \kappa_i} \left\|\mathbf{W}_k \odot \left(\lambda_i \mathbf{Z}_{i,k}^{\mathbf{x}} - \kappa_i \mathbf{1} - \mathbf{T}_{i,k}\right)\right\|^2 \qquad . \tag{4}$$

This leads to:

$$\lambda_i^*(\mathbf{x}) = \frac{\varrho_{\mathbf{Z}_{i,k}^{\mathbf{x}}, \mathbf{T}_{i,k}} \cdot \sigma_{\mathbf{T}_{i,k}}}{\sigma_{\mathbf{Z}_{i,k}^{\mathbf{x}}}} \qquad \text{and} \tag{5}$$

$$\kappa_i^*(\mathbf{x}) = \lambda_i^*(\mathbf{x})\, \mu_{\mathbf{Z}_{i,k}^{\mathbf{x}}} - \mu_{\mathbf{T}_{i,k}} \qquad \text{with} \tag{6}$$

$$\mu_{\mathbf{A}} = \langle \mathbf{A} \rangle := \frac{\mathbf{1}^T \mathbf{A} \odot \mathbf{W}_k^{\textcircled{2}} \mathbf{1}}{\mathbf{1}^T \mathbf{W}_k^{\textcircled{2}} \mathbf{1}} \quad , \tag{7}$$

$$\sigma_{\mathbf{A}}^2 = \langle \mathbf{A}^{\textcircled{2}} \rangle - \langle \mathbf{A} \rangle^2 \text{ , and} \tag{8}$$

$$\varrho_{\mathbf{A},\mathbf{B}} = \frac{1}{\sigma_{\mathbf{A}} \cdot \sigma_{\mathbf{B}}} \langle (\mathbf{A} - \mu_{\mathbf{A}} \mathbf{1}) \odot (\mathbf{B} - \mu_{\mathbf{B}} \mathbf{1}) \rangle \text{ ,} \tag{9}$$

where $\mathbf{A}$ and $\mathbf{B}$ have to be replaced by $\mathbf{Z}_{i,k}^{\mathsf{x}}$ and $\mathbf{T}_{i,k}$, respectively. Here, the operators $\odot$ and $\textcircled{2}$ indicate element-wise multiplication and element-wise squaring, respectively.

Inserting Eqs. (5) and (6) into Eq. (3), so that $\lambda_i = \lambda_i^*(\mathbf{x})$ and $\kappa_i = \kappa_i^*(\mathbf{x})$, leads to the final likelihood formulation:

$$p(\mathbf{Z}_{i,k}|\mathbf{X}_k) \sim e^{-\frac{1}{2}\left(\frac{\sigma_{\mathbf{T}_{i,k}}}{\sigma_i}\right)^2}\left(1 - \varrho_{\mathbf{Z}_{i,k}^{\mathsf{x}},\mathbf{T}_{i,k}}\right) . \tag{10}$$

For all cues, Eq. (10) is calculated, which basically amounts to the computation of the normalized, locally windowed correlation $\varrho_{\mathbf{Z}_{i,k}^{\mathsf{x}},\mathbf{T}_{i,k}}$ of a cue with its template. This is done for each pair of cue/template planes separately, and the overall likelihood $p(\mathbf{Z}_k|\mathbf{X}_k)$ is then additively composed of all the planes computed according to Eq. (10)

$$p(\mathbf{Z}_k|\mathbf{X}_k) \sim \bigoplus_{i=1}^{N} p(\mathbf{Z}_{i,k}|\mathbf{X}_k) . \tag{11}$$

From Eq. (11) it is expected that, for cues which temporarily characterize the tracked object to some extent, there will be a pronounced peak at the position of the tracked object.

2.3   Dynamic State Estimation

The fundamental problem that a tracking system has to solve is that of recursive, dynamic target state estimation. This means that it has to estimate continuously the state $\mathbf{X}_k$ of the dynamic system

$$\mathbf{X}_k = f_{k-1}(\mathbf{X}_{k-1}) + v_{k-1} \tag{12}$$

$$\mathbf{Z}_k = h_k(\mathbf{X}_k) + w_k \tag{13}$$

using a series of measurements $\mathbf{Z}_k, \mathbf{Z}_{k-1}, ..., \mathbf{Z}_1$ gained from an observable that can be put in relation to the state $\mathbf{X}_k$. Here, $f_{k-1}(.)$ and $h_k(.)$ are models for state transition and object observation, respectively, and v_{k-1} and w_k are additive noise.

Bayesian tracking equations (see e.g. [1], [2], [10]) express this formally in two stages of the filtering process, usually termed *prediction* and *update* stages

$$p(\mathbf{X}_k|\mathbf{Z}_{k-1}, ..., \mathbf{Z}_1) = \int p(\mathbf{X}_k|\mathbf{X}_{k-1}) p(\mathbf{X}_{k-1}|\mathbf{Z}_{k-1}, ..., \mathbf{Z}_1) d\mathbf{X}_{k-1} \tag{14}$$

$$p(\mathbf{X}_k|\mathbf{Z}_k, ..., \mathbf{Z}_1) \propto p(\mathbf{Z}_k|\mathbf{X}_k) p(\mathbf{X}_k|\mathbf{Z}_{k-1}, ..., \mathbf{Z}_1) \tag{15}$$

with

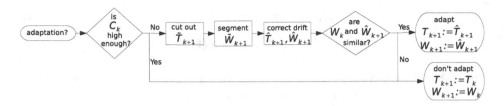

Fig. 2. Template adaptation strategy: a template adaption is only done for small calculated confidences C_k. For each template adaptation an object segmentation mask is calculated, which is used to correct the drift of target object in the template. A plausibility check between the newly segmented mask and the currently used mask is applied to prevent a possible wrong segmentation, which can happen e.g. due to occlusion or if the segmentation algorithm fails.

- $p(\mathbf{Z}_k|\mathbf{X}_k)$ as the measurement likelihood expressing the comparison between measurement and expected measurement (given by Eqs. (10), (11) for our correlation-based tracker),
- $p(\mathbf{X}_k|\mathbf{Z}_k, ..., \mathbf{Z}_1)$ as the posterior of the state given all past and current measurements, and
- $p(\mathbf{X}_k|\mathbf{Z}_{k-1}, ..., \mathbf{Z}_1)$ as the prior which is gained from the posterior of the last step using a state transition model $p(\mathbf{X}_k|\mathbf{X}_{k-1})$.

For coping with the six dimensional state space and multimodal distributions of the posterior, we use a *particle filter* approach in our framework for the estimation problem, with a linear prediction model for $p(\mathbf{X}_k|\mathbf{X}_{k-1})$. The particle filter produces estimates for $\mathbf{X}_k$ from the posterior $p(\mathbf{X}_k|\mathbf{Z}_k, ..., \mathbf{Z}_1)$.

2.4   Template Adaptation

In real-world applications objects may undergo arbitrary types of appearance transformations. To ensure a robust likelihood calculation $p(\mathbf{Z}_k|\mathbf{X}_k)$, the template $\mathbf{T}_{i,k}$ and corresponding object mask $\mathbf{W}_k$ need to be adapted to the current object appearance.

The most generic way to do template adaptation for coping with all types of appearance transformations consists in cutting out the patch at the determined object position $\mathbf{x}_k$ which is part of $\mathbf{X}_k$ and set it as the new template $\mathbf{T}_{i,k+1}$. However, apart from the fact that the object mask $\mathbf{W}_{k+1}$ must be recalculated after every template adaptation, the weakness of this method is that the target may drift from the template in course of time, because of the integration of small inaccuracies in the object measurement. In order to fix this problem, in our framework the drift problem is solved in a correction step after each cut-out.

As Fig. 2 illustrates, the first step of our template adaptation strategy is to check if it is necessary to adapt the template. For high confidences of state vector $\mathbf{X}_k$ there is no need to adapt template, since likelihood calculation works robustly. A possible confidence is for instance the value of the highest posterior peak. In the case if the confidence is starting to get worse, the new template

$\tilde{\mathbf{T}}_{i,k+1}$ on position $\mathbf{x}_k$ is cut out. A segmentation algorithm is applied to the newly cut-out template patch in order to generate a new object mask $\tilde{\mathbf{W}}_{k+1}$. Different segmentation algorithms are suitable for calculating the object mask, here we have chosen a Level-Set based segmentation algorithm as described in [11]. From the mask, the center of gravity of the object mask $\mathbf{x}_{\tilde{\mathbf{W}}_{k+1}}$ is calculated. The distance

$$\mathbf{d}_k = \mathbf{x}_{\tilde{\mathbf{W}}_{k+1}} - \mathbf{x}_k \tag{16}$$

is considered as the template drift which is therefore used to recenter the template and the mask in order to get the corrected template $\hat{\mathbf{T}}_{i,k+1}$ and mask $\hat{\mathbf{W}}_{k+1}$.

As a second criterion for excluding detrimental template adaptations, e.g. after an object loss, occlusion or failure of the segmentation algorithm, the newly gained mask $\hat{\mathbf{W}}_{k+1}$ undergoes a plausibility check, in the way that it must be similar to the current mask $\mathbf{W}_k$. A possible similarity measure is the correlation coefficient between $\hat{\mathbf{W}}_{k+1}$ and $\mathbf{W}_k$. Only in case of high similarity, the new template and mask are updated, otherwise the current template and mask are kept for the next frame, according to:

$$\mathbf{T}_{i,k+1} = \hat{\mathbf{T}}_{i,k+1} \text{ and } \mathbf{W}_{k+1} = \hat{\mathbf{W}}_{k+1} \text{ , if both adaptation criteria fulfilled} \tag{17}$$

$$\mathbf{T}_{i,k+1} = \mathbf{T}_{i,k} \text{ and } \mathbf{W}_{k+1} = \mathbf{W}_k \text{ , otherwise} \tag{18}$$

On applying these two criteria during template adaptation, a persistently low confidence value C_k of state $\mathbf{X}_k$ is a strong indication for target object loss, e.g. because of occlusion. In this case, the second criterion prevents to update the template $\hat{\mathbf{T}}_{i,k+1}$ in such cases.

3   Evaluation

This section demonstrates the evaluation results of our tracking system with the template adaptation mechanism as described in section 2.4.

In a sequence of 250 frames (illustrated in Fig. 3) a hand is tracked. As listed in the table of Fig. 3, this sequence contains four phases of different motions (each with translation and/or other types of appearance transformations, like 2D/3D rotation or change of hand shape). The appearance transformation that the template update system has to adapt to is easiest in phase I and gets increasingly harder for phases II-IV.

In the evaluation three methods for template adaptation are compared. In *method 1* **no** template and mask adaptation is applied. The template $\mathbf{T}_{i,0}$ and the object mask $\mathbf{W}_0$ from the first frame are used throughout the rest of the sequence. *Method 2* adapts template and its object mask as described in section 2.4 but **without** drift correction. That means, if the plausibility check is fufilled, the cut-out template $\tilde{\mathbf{T}}_{i,k+1}$ and its object mask $\tilde{\mathbf{W}}_{k+1}$ are used to update template and mask instead of using $\hat{\mathbf{T}}_{i,k+1}$ and $\hat{\mathbf{W}}_{k+1}$. *Method 3* applies the full template adaptation strategy described in section 2.4 according to Eqs. (17) and (18) which corresponds to method 2 but **with** drift correction.

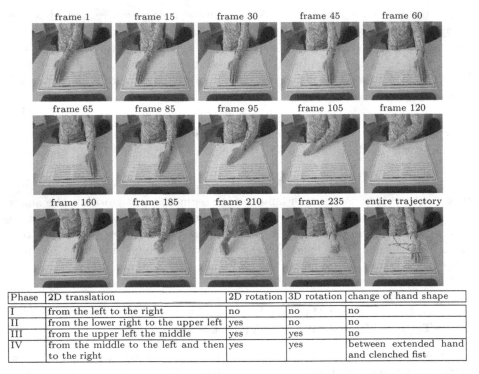

Phase	2D translation	2D rotation	3D rotation	change of hand shape
I	from the left to the right	no	no	no
II	from the lower right to the upper left	yes	no	no
III	from the upper left the middle	yes	yes	no
IV	from the middle to the left and then to the right	yes	yes	between extended hand and clenched fist

Fig. 3. This figure illustrates selected frames of an evaluation sequence composed of 250 frames. The images are taken with a frame rate of 10Hz and have a size of 256×256 pixels. The sequence can be approximatively separated into four phases with individual motion types which are described in the table.

The evaluation results are shown in Fig. 4. They reveal that the tracking system fails to track the target object in cases using method 1 and method 2. Using method 1 the object is already lost at around frame 50 when the object starts to perform 2D rotation, because the correlation based measurement method as presented in section 2.2 can only cope with 2D translation, scaling intensity and baseline shift. Using method 2 the object is lost in phase II. In this case, the object smoothly drifts away from the template. After a while the template hardly contains any object parts so that the tracker sticks on the background. This drift process is illustrated in Fig. 5. Only by using method 3 the object is successfully tracked throughout all 250 images of the sequence. In no single frame the target object is lost or misplaced. Template adaptation is mainly triggered in phases III and IV when object appearance transformation is strongest.

In further evaluations (not shown) this framework was tested during occlusion conditions. In the cases of occlusion, the mask plausibility check failed, which prevented a template adaptation, although the measurement confidence was below threshold.

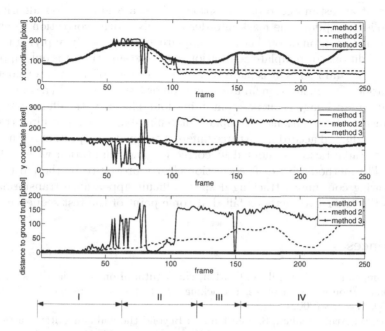

Fig. 4. Comparison of the three methods from section 3. Method 1 looses the target when the tracked object starts to perform 2D rotation. Method 2 looses the object in phase II, after the object more and more drifted out of the template and the tracker therefore confuses the background with the object. Only method 3 can successfully track the object throughout the entire sequence. For a more detailed description refer to section 3.

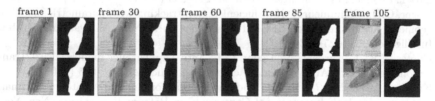

Fig. 5. This figures shows the template and its corresponding object mask during the tracking process in cases without and with drift correction. In the case of no drift correction (first row) one can see that the target object is lost from the template step by step, leading to a tracker failure. In the case with drift correction (second row) the template drift is corrected after every adaptation step using a newly calculated object mask, keeping the object steadily in the middle of template.

4   Conclusion

In this paper we presented a novel template adaptation approach for robust template-matching-based object tracking which allows large appearance transformations of arbitrary types. The approach consists of cutting out a new template at an estimated object position, where a segmentation algorithm is then applied to update the mask in order to apply a drift correction to prevent integration of position errors between template and object. By applying two criteria as conditions for template adaptation, we make sure that it is only applied if it is necessary and its result is plausible. A large change of mask is considered as an indication of segmentation failure, occlusion or loss of target. In a comparative setting using an image sequence containing four phases with different types of appearance transformations, a template-matching-based particle filter tracking system is evaluated according to three different template adaptation methods: no adaptation, adaptation without drift correction and adaptation with drift correction. The method with drift correction clearly proved to be the most robust one, allowing continuous tracking despite difficult appearance transformations whereas the other two methods failed at some point of the test sequence.

References

1. Arulampalam, S., Maskell, S., Gordon, N.: A tutorial on particle filters for online nonlinear/non-gaussian bayesian tracking. IEEE Transactions on Signal Processing 50, 174–188 (2002)
2. Ristic, B., Arulampalam, S., Gordon, N.: Beyond the Kalman Filter: Particle Filters for Tracking Applications. Artech House, London (2004)
3. Gonzalez, R.C., Woods, R.E.: Digital Image Processing. Prentice Hall International, Upper Saddle River (2007)
4. Matthews, I., Ishikawa, T., Baker, S.: The template update problem. IEEE Trans. Pattern Anal. Mach. Intell. 26, 810–815 (2004)
5. Baker, S., Matthews, I.: Lucas-kanade 20 years on: A unifying framework. International Journal of Computer Vision 56, 221–255 (2004)
6. Hager, G.D., Belhumeur, P.N.: Efficient region tracking with parametric models of geometry and illumination. IEEE Transactions on Pattern Analysis and Machine Intelligence 20, 1025–1039 (1998)
7. Cootes, T.F., Edwards, G.J., Taylor, C.J.: Active appearance models. IEEE Transactions on Pattern Analysis and Machine Intelligence 23, 681–685 (2001)
8. Kaneko, T., Hori, O.: Template update criterion for template matching of image sequences. In: 16th International Conference on Pattern Recognition, New York, pp. 1–5. IEEE Press, Los Alamitos (2002)
9. Bigun, J., Granlund, G.H.: Optimal orientation detection of linear symmetry. In: First International Conference on Computer Vision, Washington, DC,pp. 433–438. IEEE Computer Society Press, Los Alamitos (1987)
10. Isard, M., Blake, A.: Condensation - conditional density propagation for visual tracking. International Journal of Computer Vision 29, 5–28 (1998)
11. Weiler, D., Eggert, J.P.: Multi-dimensional histogram-based image segmentation. In: Ishikawa, M., Doya, K., Miyamoto, H., Yamakawa, T. (eds.) ICONIP 2007, Part I. LNCS, vol. 4984, pp. 963–972. Springer, Heidelberg (2008)

A Multiple Hypothesis Approach
for a Ball Tracking System

Oliver Birbach[1] and Udo Frese[2]

[1] Deutsches Forschungszentrum für Künstliche Intelligenz GmbH,
Safe and Secure Cognitive Systems, Enrique-Schmidt-Str. 5, 28359 Bremen, Germany
Oliver.Birbach@dfki.de
[2] Fachbereich 3 - Mathematik und Informatik, Universität Bremen,
Postfach 330 440, 28334 Bremen, Germany
ufrese@informatik.uni-bremen.de

Abstract. This paper presents a computer vision system for tracking
and predicting flying balls in 3-D from a stereo-camera. It pursues a
"textbook-style" approach with a robust circle detector and probabilistic models for ball motion and circle detection handled by state-of-the-
art estimation algorithms. In particular we use a Multiple-Hypotheses
Tracker (MHT) with an Unscented Kalman Filter (UKF) for each track,
handling multiple flying balls, missing and false detections and track
initiation and termination.

The system also performs auto-calibration estimating physical parameters (ball radius, gravity relative to camera, air drag) simply from
observing some flying balls. This reduces the setup time in a new environment.

1 Introduction

Robotics is not only about relieving mankind from laborious and dangerous
tasks. It is also about playfully exploring the world of dynamic motion and perception from the perspective of a machine. The latter view led to the RoboCup
2050 vision of a human-robot soccer match as proposed by Kitano and Assada [1].
Our interest lies in the vision part, namely visually perceiving a soccer match
from the players perspective. In previous work [2] we have investigated how to
predict a flying ball from images of a *moving* camera. This paper presents a
system for *robust* tracking and prediction of *multiple* balls from a static camera.

We provide three contributions with the overall system: First, a novel circle
detector avoids hard decisions and thresholds for the sake of robustness. Second, a multi-hypothesis tracking (MHT) system based on the implementation
by Cox [3] robustly handles several flying balls and false or missing measurements. And third, an auto-calibration mechanism learns physical parameters
(ball radius, gravity vector in camera coordinates, air drag) simply by observing
flying balls.

Ball tracking is important in TV sport scene augmentation. The vision systems in [4,5,6] exploit the TV perspective, with the field as a static uniform

M. Fritz, B. Schiele, and J.H. Piater (Eds.): ICVS 2009, LNCS 5815, pp. 435–444, 2009.
© Springer-Verlag Berlin Heidelberg 2009

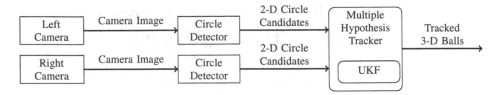

Fig. 1. System Overview: In the left and right image circle candidates are detected. These are fused by an MHT establishing the stereo correspondence, assignment to tracks and track initiation and termination. The two detectors run in parallel.

background. In contrast, in the long run our system shall work from the player's perspective with a moving camera. Hence we propose a novel circle detector to find the ball in front of moving and cluttered background. The system by Gedikli et al. [6] uses MHT as we do, but for player tracking, complementary to our task.

In RoboCup tracking is often 2-D with a coloured ball and manually tuned heuristics as for instance in the CMVision [7] software. Experience in the competitions shows, that usually hours are needed to tune the vision system to new environments. We experienced the same with a trade-fair demonstration of a ball catching robot [8]. This motivated our ball detection algorithm that does not need tuning parameters. Voigtländer et al. [9] propose a tracking system that fits a 3-D parabola to stereo triangulated ball positions. This ignores the uncertainty structure of stereo triangulation, where depth is most uncertain. We model the metrical uncertainty of circle detection in an UKF [10] to improve accuracy and the uncertainty, whether the circle is actually a ball, in an MHT to improve robustness.

Indeed, we see our contribution in presenting a "textbook-style" algorithm without heuristics that still works in real-time.

2   System Architecture

The architecture for our proposed ball tracking system is a two-staged bottom-up process (Fig. 1). In the first stage, circle candidates are extracted from a pair of cameras exhaustively searching through all centers and radii (Sec. 3). In the second stage, the circle candidates of both images are fused to ball tracks using the MHT algorithm (Sec. 5). We use the implementation by Cox [3]. This algorithm defines a systematic method for setting up association-hypotheses between multiple-targets and measurements considering false-alarm and missing measurements and evaluating them probabilistically. For our system, a target corresponds to a single ball trajectory whereas a measurement is a circle candidate from the detector. Hypothetical associations between tracks and measurements are evaluated by an UKF, which provides the probabilistic model for a single track (Sec. 4). The most likely association hypothesis and its tracked ball trajectories are returned by the MHT.

After the system description, the method for learning the parameters of the physical model is given in Sec. 6. Last, experimental results are presented.

3   Circle Detection

This section describes the circle detection algorithm that is used to find the flying ball(s) in the image. It assumes that the ball has a circular outline in the image with a radial intensity gradient. The algorithm ignores the circle's interior, which could in future be used for recognising false detections.

3.1   An Improved Definition for a Circle Response

Our approach is related to the well known circle Hough-transform [11,12] as both define a circle response $CR(x_c, y_c, r)$ as a function of the circle center (x_c, y_c) and radius r and search for local maxima of $CR(x_c, y_c, r)$. The circle Hough-transform basically goes through all edge pixels of the image and moves perpendicular to the edge for a distance of $r \in [-r_{\max} \ldots r_{\max}]$. For all resulting pixels $(x(r), y(r))$ the circle response $CR(x(r), y(r), |r|)$ is incremented.

So, $CR(x_c, y_c, r)$ is the number of edge pixels closer than $r_{\max}$, where this perpendicular line goes through (x_c, y_c) within half a pixel. This definition involves two hard decisions designed to facilitate efficiency. The first is the classification of edge pixels with a threshold that is sensitive to illumination and image blur. The second is the half-a-pixel criterion for the perpendicular line, which is sensitive to noise. Such early decisions impair robustness.

We now present a circle response definition that is illumination invariant and continuous with no thresholds. It represents *the average fraction of image contrast along the circle that can be explained as a radial intensity gradient.* This notion can be formalized mathematically, but we omit the derivation here for lack of space. The idea is as follows: A local image patch around a point can be decomposed into a sum of components, similar to Fourier decomposition. One component is the image structure we expect, namely a linear intensity gradient in radial direction. The sum of the squared norm of all components, is the local image variance. So, if we take the squared norm of the linear intensity component and divide it by the local image variance, we get an illumination invariant measure that indicates which fraction of the local image contrast is a radial gradient.

Practically, the result is a contrast-normalized Sobel filter C, where the vector length indicates *gradient purity* rather than *gradient intensity*. The circle response $R(\alpha)(x, y)$ in a point (x, y) is then the squared scalar product of the radial direction ($\begin{smallmatrix} \cos\alpha \\ \sin\alpha \end{smallmatrix}$) with C.

$$R(\alpha) = \left(\begin{pmatrix} \cos\alpha \\ \sin\alpha \end{pmatrix} \cdot C \right)^2, \quad C = \frac{\sqrt{2}\left(\begin{pmatrix} -1 & 0 & +1 \\ -2 & 0 & +2 \\ -1 & 0 & +1 \end{pmatrix} * I, \; \begin{pmatrix} -1 & -2 & -1 \\ 0 & 0 & 0 \\ +1 & +2 & +1 \end{pmatrix} * I \right)^T}{\sqrt{16 \begin{pmatrix} 1 & 2 & 1 \\ 2 & 4 & 2 \\ 1 & 2 & 1 \end{pmatrix} * I^2 - \left(\begin{pmatrix} 1 & 2 & 1 \\ 2 & 4 & 2 \\ 1 & 2 & 1 \end{pmatrix} * I \right)^2}} \tag{1}$$

It can be seen, that in (1) the nominator is the ordinary Sobel filter. The denominator is the image variance computed as the weighted mean of I^2 minus the squared weighted mean of I. This follows from the well known variance formula $\mathrm{Var}(X) = \mathrm{E}(X^2) - (\mathrm{E}(X))^2$. The factors $\sqrt{2}$ and 16 make $R(\alpha) \in [0 \ldots 1]$.

The circle response is now the average fraction of radial gradient on the circle.

$$CR(x_c, y_c, r) = \frac{1}{2\pi} \int_{\alpha=0}^{2\pi} \left(\begin{pmatrix} \cos\alpha \\ \sin\alpha \end{pmatrix} \cdot C \begin{pmatrix} x_c + r\cos\alpha \\ y_c + r\sin\alpha \end{pmatrix} \right)^2 d\alpha \qquad (2)$$

Normalizing the contrast on each pixel individually is important. Otherwise one large gradient dominates the response making it higher than for a small gradient on the whole circle. False circles tangential to intense edges would result.

Finally, the N_{cand} largest local maxima are circle candidates for the MHT.

3.2 Real-Time Implementation

We have taken considerable effort to implement (2) in real-time[1]. C in (1) is only computed once per pixel and well suited for Single Instruction Multiple Data (SIMD) optimization (Intel SSE here). We exploit that the convolutions in (1) are all combinations of blurring by $\frac{1}{4}(1,2,1)$ and differentiation by $(-1,0,1)$ in x and y respectively. This shows again the relation to the Sobel filter. The result is well represented with 7 bits plus sign reducing memory throughput.

The key challenge is computing the integrand of (2) for every pixel on every circle considered ($\pi r_{\text{max}}^2 wh = 15 \cdot 10^9$ times in our case). Furthermore, the pattern of memory access on C is regular regarding x_c, y_c but not for r and α. Hence, we iterate on r, α, y_c, x_c from outer to inner loop, so we can SIMD-parallelize in x_c. However, this sequence of loops would require C to be loaded many times (πr_{max}^2) from memory. To avoid the bottleneck, we process blocks of 16×16 pixel in x_c, y_c and nest the loops as y_c block, x_c block, r, α, y_c in block, x_c in block. Furthermore, the vector $\begin{pmatrix} \cos\alpha \\ \sin\alpha \end{pmatrix}$ and the relative memory address of $\begin{pmatrix} r\cos\alpha \\ r\sin\alpha \end{pmatrix}$ is precomputed in a table with one entry for every pixel along each circle.

Even though the integrand of (2) is computed in 0.42ns, the whole computation still needs 6.6s (Intel Xeon, 2.5GHz). Our solution is a multi-scale approach where we define a detection radius r_{det} (3 pixel) and successively halve the image. Starting from the lowest resolution we search for circles of radius $r_{\text{det}} \ldots 2r_{\text{det}} - 1$ and successively refine the circles found before. So every circle is detected at that resolution where its radius is in the above interval. This multi-scale approach just needs 13.1ms in which the image is scaled down up to one fourth of the original size.

For comparison, the openCV implementation of circle Hough-transform needs 85ms. However, we believe that with comparable implementation effort, Hough-transform would be faster than our detector. The main advantage is, that our detector uses no thresholds making detection more robust from our experience.

4 Single Track Probabilistic Model

This section describes the Kalman Filter used to track the ball as a single target from circle measurements of the camera images. It presents the probabilistic model both for the motion of the ball and for the cameras observing the ball.

---

[1] The implementation is available upon request.

When tracking a ball, we are interested in its position over time. We also need the velocity to predict the ball's upcoming position. Therefore, the estimated state vector $x_b = [x\ v]$ consists of the ball's 3D-position x and 3D-velocity v.

The change of the ball's state during flight, required by the filter's prediction step, is modeled by classical mechanics including gravitation g and air drag α.

$$\dot{x} = v, \quad \dot{v} = g - \alpha \cdot |v| \cdot v + \mathcal{N}(0, \sigma_v^2), \quad \alpha = \tfrac{1}{8}\pi c_d \rho d^2 m^{-1} \tag{3}$$

The factor α determines the air drag, with c_d drag coefficient, ρ density of air, d ball diameter, and m ball mass. The uncertainty in this process is modeled as Gaussian noise with zero mean and the covariances σ_v perturbing the velocity.

The measurement equations used in the update step model the position and radius of the circle detected in a single camera image. We use a pin-hole camera model plus radial distortion [2] that provides a function h which maps a point from a 3D-scene into the image plane. To project a ball into an image, we calculate two orthogonal vectors with length $d/2$ orthogonal to the ball's line-of-sight. We then add x and project these four points using h into the image plane. The results $(p_{x,i}, p_{y,i})$ are recombined to center and radius:

$$\begin{pmatrix} x_c \\ y_c \end{pmatrix} = \tfrac{1}{4}\sum_{i=1}^{4} \begin{pmatrix} p_{x,i} \\ p_{y,i} \end{pmatrix}, \quad r = \sqrt{\tfrac{1}{4}\sum_{i=1}^{4}(p_{x,i} - x_c)^2 + (p_{y,i} - y_c)^2} \tag{4}$$

This method implicitly triangulates at the ball diameter to obtain depth.

Generally, tracking systems of this kind use the Kalman filter which represents the state distribution as a Gaussian random variable and requires linear dynamic and measurement models. For our models linearization is required. One could use the Jacobians which is known as the Extended Kalman Filter (EKF). Better results are achieved by the Unscented Kalman Filter (UKF) [10] which utilizes the so-called unscented transform to linearize the model at a given state. It represents the state's mean and covariance by a set of so-called sigma points, which are computed such that their sample mean and covariance corresponds to the state's mean and covariance. With these, the whole Gaussian is transformed by propagating each sigma-point through the nonlinear function. The propagated sigma-points are then combined to mean and covariance of the transformed state. This method reduces linearization errors that perturb tracking. Therefore, we use the UKF to estimate the state of a single track over time.

5 Multiple Hypotheses Tracking

In the previous section, we considered how to track a single ball (the target) from a series of measurements originating from that ball. In practice, associating a series of measurements with its corresponding track, when there are multiple measurement candidates and multiple targets, is difficult for a number of reasons. First, measurements might be missing, i.e. occluded or not detected. Second, all false measurement candidates (e.g. a person's head) need to be correctly classified as false-alarm measurements and therefore not associated with any track. Finally, tracks start and finish at an unknown points in time.

5.1   The Approach of Cox and Reid

One solution to such a data association problem was proposed by Reid [13] and later enhanced to our case by Cox and Hingorani [3] and is known as the multiple hypothesis tracking algorithm (MHT). This algorithm systematically maintains a set of association hypotheses involving multiple targets and multiple, possibly false-alarm, measurements. Formally, a hypothesis is an assignment of each measurement candidate to a track or to "false-alarm". On arrival of new measurement candidates, each hypothesis from the previous time-step is expanded to a set of new hypotheses by considering all possible associations of measurement candidates to tracks in the current time-step. Each measurement may be at most associated with one track and vice versa. Furthermore, the initiation or termination of tracks are considered while generating hypotheses.

The algorithm computes the probability for each hypothesis. This probability is effectively the product of individual probabilities for "everything that happened". For most events (track initiated, track terminated, measurement missed, false-alarm) it is simply a preconfigured constant. For the event of a measurement being associated with a track, the single track model gives the probability. This probability expresses, how well the measurements assigned to the track fit metrically to the model. If they fit well, the most likely hypothesis is that they form a track, otherwise it is more likely that they are false-alarms. This behaviour is the essence of the functionality provided by the MHT.

Formally, for the hypothesis m at time k the probability is [3]

$$P(\omega_m^k|Z^k) = \frac{1}{c}P(\omega_{l(m)}^{k-1}|Z^{k-1})\lambda_N^v\lambda_F^\phi\prod_{i=1}^{m_k}\mathcal{N}_{t_i}(z_i(k))^{\tau_i}$$

$$\prod_t(P_D^t)^{\delta_t}(1-P_d^t)^{1-\delta_t}(P_\chi^t)^{\chi_t}(1-P_\chi^t)^{1-\chi_t} \tag{5}$$

where c is a normalizing factor, $P(\omega_{l(m)}^{k-1}|Z^{k-1})$ is the probability of the parent hypothesis and known from the previous time-step, λ_N is the density of new targets, λ_F is the density of false-alarm measurements, v is the number of new targets and ϕ the number of false alarms in this hypothesis. $\mathcal{N}(z_i(k))^{\tau_i}$ is the likelihood of the measurement z_i at time k given the target t_i provided by the single track model, P_D^t is the probability of detecting and P_χ^t is the probability of ending track t. τ_t, δ_t, χ_t are 1 if $z_i(k)$ is associated with a known track, if track t detected at time $k-1$ is also detected at time k or if track t known at time $k-1$ is terminated at time k, respectively. Otherwise they are 0.

Although, we can evaluate the probability of every hypothesis, the exponential complexity of the ever-growing tree of hypotheses makes an efficient implementation infeasible. Therefore, several strategies for removing unlikely hypotheses proposed by Cox and Hingorani [3] are used. Ratio pruning removes all hypotheses whose ratio to the best hypothesis is below a certain threshold. This is efficiently done by generating only the k best hypotheses following Murty. Last, N-scan-back pruning removes hypotheses based on the assumption, that ambiguities can be resolved within N time-steps.

5.2   Track Initiation

Within the MHT algorithm, a track is automatically created for every observed measurement. Obviously, one measurement defines the ball's position via the inverse of (4) by triangulating over the ball diameter. However, it does not define velocity. So we set the initial velocity covariance to a large prior representing an upper bound on typical velocities. When later a nearby measurement is associated with the track, the velocity is implicitly computed by the UKF. Still, such a prior is important, because it bounds the area where measurements could be associated with this track thereby limiting the number of hypotheses.

Furthermore, we correctly initialize the covariance of the ball's position using the Jacobian of the inverse of (4). This prevents false associations compared to the widely used initialization with a constant covariance.

5.3   Circle Candidate Correspondence

When using stereo vision, correspondences between features found in both camera images must be established. With MHT there are two possibilities. First, one could match candidates from both images prior to the tracking and integrate the result as 3D-measurements into the MHT. Second, one could integrate the set of circle candidates of each camera image successively. Then, MHT implicitly handles the correspondences when associating candidates to the same track, leading to more hypotheses though. We implemented this, because it could process tracks observed from just one camera, where the other one would not find a match.

Future work is to compare with a particle filter replacing both UKF and MHT. The challenge is the following: Due to the low dynamic noise, a particle filter effectively selects from the particles initialized from the first few measurements the particle fitting best with all measurements. This requires many particles since, in particular the velocity uncertainty decreases by a large factor.

6   Physical Parameter Learning

The model (3) and (4) require the gravity vector g (relative to the camera), the air drag α, the ball diameter d and the stereo-camera calibration. The latter is calibrated only once, but g, which depends on the camera's orientation, and α, d, which depend on the used balls, change with every new environment.

For easy setup, the parameters are estimated from flying balls during a calibration phase. There the UKF runs with (g, α, d) in the state. The first challenge is that with the additional states, many more false tracks fit to the model, leading to wrong estimates. It would be most rigorous to run another MHT or robust estimator to fuse (g, α, d) estimates of different tracks. We currently proceeds simpler. First, we provide some rough prior information ($|g| = 9.81 \pm 0.05\frac{m}{s^2}$, $d = 0.21 \pm 0.1$m, $\alpha = 0.015 \pm 0.1$m^{-1}) and second, only estimates from tracks which lasted at least 15 frames are accepted. Technically, the prior on $|g|$ can only be integrated after the uncertainty in g is low enough to linearize $|g|$.

Fig. 2. Camera view of the tracking scenario and overlaid detection results (red circles) and predicted ball trajectories (coloured circles). A filled circle denotes an association to a track. For a video of the tracking results visit http://www.informatik.uni-bremen.de/agebv/en/MHBallTracking.

Tracks in roughly opposite direction are needed to distinguish g and α. This is because air drag and the component of g in the direction of flight have similar effect. Hence, when a track is accepted, the final (g, α, d) estimate with covariance becomes the prior for new tracks. So information is collected over several tracks.

7   Experiments

The system described above has been implemented and evaluated. The experimental setup consists of a calibrated camera pair (1024×768 pixel, 30Hz) with a 20cm baseline. Both images are processed in parallel by Two Quad-Core Xeon 2.5 GHz processing units and then fused by the MHT (see Fig. 1). The preconfigured constants for the MHT algorithm were $P_D = 0.3$, $\lambda_\chi = 40$, $\lambda_N = 4 \cdot 10^{-9}$ and $\lambda_F = 3.65 \cdot 10^{-6}$. P_D was chosen lower than the actual detection probability, to allow tracks to continue for a few frames without the integration of measurements. This compensates for correlation between detection in successive frames which is not modeled by the MHT. The pruning strategies were initialized with 0.01 for ratio, 5 for k best hypothesis and 10 for N-scan-back pruning.

In the experiment, four people were throwing up to three volleyballs to each other outdoors. Fig. 2 shows two camera images, with overlaid detection and prediction. Not only the trajectory of the ball flight is visible, but also trajectories created by false-alarm measurements. This is inevitable, since every measurement might be a possible new track. To evaluate the performance of the system, the detection and tracking results were manually analyzed by annotating ball detections and tracks (Fig. 3). In the sequence of 417 stereo frames 2257 balls were visible forming 32 trajectories. The detector postulated 13637 candidates, from which 1567 were balls, leading to 69.4% detection rate. The large number of false alarms was intended, because the detector is used to return the $17 - 20$ circle candidates with highest response. This avoids making early decisions in the detector, where the MHT has much more information. When forming the best hypothesis, the MHT rejected to associate 100 correctly detected measurements. On the other hand, it wrongly associated 76 false-alarm measurements.

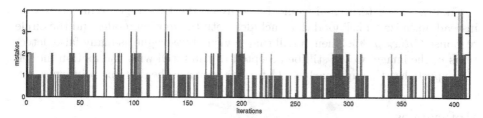

Fig. 3. Stacked bar chart denoting the number of errors the system made at each time-step. The red bar indicates missed balls, the blue bars show correctly detected balls not associated with any track and the green bars visualize the number of false-alarm measurements that were associated with a track.

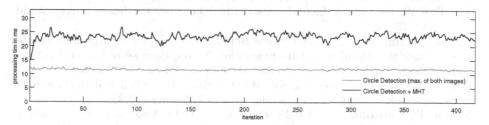

Fig. 4. Processing time of the circle detector (left/right parallel) and the overall system

A large part of these occurs when the circle detector mistakes a shadow on the ball for the ball returning a circle that is slightly of center and too small. This suggests to avoid the two-stage feed-forward approach and instead look back in the original circle responses during tracking. Then the true circle could be accepted by the tracker, even though it has a slightly worse response than the false circle because it fits better to the motion model [14].

The computation time is shown in Fig.4. One could also be interested in evaluating the metrical prediction. This is left to future work since here the focus is on the MHT.

8 Conclusion and Outlook

We have presented a system for tracking and predicting multiple flying balls from a static stereo camera, consisting of a novel circle detector and the MHT algorithm applied to the physical model of a flying ball. The system is very "textbook-style" containing almost no heuristics and no tuning parameter in the circle detection. Still it works very robustly in real-time.

In the long term, we want to move the system onto a helmet worn by a human player and track the ball from the player's perspective [14]. This requires integrating an inertial sensor for egomotion perception into the single track model. It also poses a subtle challenge for the MHT tracker, because different tracks are not independent any more, but linked by the unknown pose of the camera.

Finally, a long term goal would be to avoid the two-stage architecture and instead optimize a likelihood that includes both the motion model and the circle response $CR(x_c, y_c, r)$. Then, a ball that is visually as vague as many false detections in the image, would still be accepted if it fits well with the motion model. We expect that this approach could further increase the systems robustness.

References

1. Kitano, H., Asada, M., Kuniyoshi, Y., Noda, I., Osawa, E.: Robocup: The robot world cup initiative. In: Proc. of IJCAI-1995 Workshop on Entertainment and AI/Alife (1995)
2. Birbach, O., Kurlbaum, J., Laue, T., Frese, U.: Tracking of Ball Trajectories with a Free Moving Camera-Inertial Sensor. In: RoboCup 2008: Robot Soccer World Cup XII (2008)
3. Cox, I.J., Hingorani, S.L.: An Efficient Implementation of Reid's Multiple Hypothesis Tracking Algorithm and Its Evaluation for the Purpose of Visual Tracking. IEEE Trans. on Pattern Analysis and Machine Intelligence 18(2) (1996)
4. Ren, J., Orwell, J., Jones, G., Xu, M.: Real-time 3D football ball tracking from multiple cameras. In: British Machine Vision Conference (2004)
5. Yan, F., Christmas, W., Kittler, J.: Layered Data Association Using Graph-Theoretic Formulation with Application to Tennis Ball Tracking in Monocular Sequences. IEEE Trans. on Pattern Anal. and Machine Intel. 30(10) (2008)
6. Gedikli, S., Bandouch, J., von Hoyningen-Huene, N., Kirchlechner, B., Beetz, M.: An adaptive vision system for tracking soccer players from variable camera settings. In: Proc. of the 5th Intern. Conference on Computer Vision Systems, ICVS (2007)
7. Bruce, J., Balch, T., Veloso, M.: Fast and inexpensive color image segmentation for interactive robots. In: Proc. of the Intern. Conference on Intelligent Robots and Systems (2000)
8. Frese, U., Bäuml, B., Haidacher, S., Schreiber, G., Schaefer, I., Hähnle, M., Hirzinger, G.: Off-the-Shelf Vision for a Robotic Ball Catcher. In: Proc. of the Intern. Conference on Intelligent Robots and Systems, pp. 1623–1629 (2001)
9. Voigtländer, A., Lange, S., Lauer, M., Riedmiller, M.: Real-time 3D ball recognition using perspective and catadioptric cameras. In: Proc. of the 3rd European Conference on Mobile Robots (2007)
10. Julier, S.J., Uhlmann, J.K.: A New Extension of the Kalman Filter to Nonlinear Systems. In: The Proc. of AeroSense: The 11th Intern. Symposium on Aerospace/Defense Sensing, Simulation and Controls, Multi Sensor Fusion, Tracking and Resource Management II (1997)
11. Hough, P.V.C.: Machine analysis of bubble chamber pictures. In: Proc. of the Intern. Conference on High Energy Accelerators and Instrumentation (1959)
12. Yuen, H., Princen, J., Dlingworth, J., Kittler, J.W.: A comparative study of hough transform methods for circle finding. In: Proc. of the Alvey Vision Conf. (1989)
13. Reid, D.B.: An Algorithm for Tracking Multiple Targets. IEEE Trans. On Automatic Control 24(6), 843–854 (1979)
14. Frese, U., Laue, T. (A) vision for 2050: The road towards image understanding for a human-robot soccer match. In: Proc. of the 5th Intern. Conference on Informatics in Control, Automation and Robotics (2008)

Fast Vision-Based Object Recognition Using Combined Integral Map

Tam Phuong Cao, Guang Deng, and Darrell Elton

Department of Electronic Engineering, La Trobe University, Vic 3086, Australia
t.cao@latrobe.edu.au, D.Deng@latrobe.edu.au, D.Elton@latrobe.edu.au

Abstract. Integral images or integral map (IMap) is one of the major techniques that has been used to improve the speed of computer vision systems. It has been used to compute Haar features and histograms of oriented gradient features. Some modifications have been proposed to the original IMap algorithm, but most proposed systems use IMap as it was first introduced. The IMap may be further improved by reducing its computational cost in multi-dementional feature domain. In this paper, a combined integral map (CIMap) technique is proposed to efficiently build and use multiple IMaps using a single concatenated map. Implementations show that using CIMap can significantly improve system speed while maintaining the accuracy.[1]

1 Introduction

Computer vision mimics the real-time vision-based object recognition capability of human beings. However, due to large amount of computation and bandwidth required to process the image, real-time or high frame rate performance is still a significant challenge. With the improvement in computer technology, many techniques and frameworks have been proposed to improve the efficiency of vision processing algorithms. Among them is a technique proposed by Viola and Jones [1], called integral image or integral map (IMap), which can be used to efficiently compute Haar features. The IMap was one of the major factors contributing to the high speed performance of the face detection system proposed in [1]. This IMap technique has been used in many other applications. For example, Fasola [2] has used the IMap in a vision-based robot detection task. With the IMap the system can achieve a real-time frame rate with some restrictions such as restriction (assumption) on background color.

Pan [3] proposes a method that uses the IMap applied to a different feature space, the Histogram of Oriented Gradients (HoG) proposed by Dalal [4]. This method is used to detect printed characters in natural scene images. There are several IMaps used, each corresponding to a different gradient angle bin. Similarly, Zhu [5] has shown that using IMaps for HoG features signiffcantly improves the speed of the pedestrian detection system originally developed to use the HoG

---

[1] This work has been supported by AutoCRC Australia.

M. Fritz, B. Schiele, and J.H. Piater (Eds.): ICVS 2009, LNCS 5815, pp. 445–454, 2009.
© Springer-Verlag Berlin Heidelberg 2009

feature set. In these applications, IMaps were used as a simple extension or application of the original IMap technique proposed in Viola and Jones [1]. In these cases, using IMaps significantly improved the speed of the application system when compared to the conventional method of finding the histograms. However, building different IMaps is still costly in terms of computing time. The process of building up the IMap at every pixel's location has to be repeated several times for each angle bin, resulting in a high computational cost.

Messom [6] has shown that the performance of the IMap can be further improved by using a modern graphic processing unit (GPU). There are multiple processing cores in each GPU. A face detection algorithm using a GPU and the IMap showed a significant speed improvement. However, 'the IMap technique was not altered. The improved performance was the result of using additional computing power provided by the GPU.

Lienhart [7] proposed a rotated version of the integral map called rotated sum area table (RSAT). This concept is essentially is integral image rotated by 45°, where entry at a location can be computed from its previously computed neighbours. The RSAT is also a single pass algorithm, in that it only needs to be computed once per image. Lienhart [8] shows that RSAT can be used to efficiently compute the extended Haar features which are standard Haar features rotated by 45°.

Porikli [9] proposes an extension of the conventional IMap to the 2-D domain to compute 2-D histogram efficiently. This method is more efficient than building separate IMaps in that the location of the pixels of interest only need to be computed once. However, this method still requires sequential processing of each bin, where the histogram record is incremented appropriately depending on the bin value. This method has been used in many applications, such as human detection and tracking [10,11]. Like the IMap and previously proposed variants, the size of each entry to the map has to be large enough to hold the possible sum of the entire image. For example, the bottom right hand corners of the IMaps have to be at least a 27-bit value for a 640×480 pixel grayscale image. This results in a large amount of memory accesses, decreasing the speed of the algorithm.

In this paper, a variant of the IMap called the combined integral map (CIMap) is proposed, which integrates more than one IMap into each CIMap. This CIMap is more efficient than building IMaps separately for two main reasons:

1. The CIMap reduces the total amount of memory storage required for IMaps, hence reducing time required to transfer data into and out of memory
2. The CIMap increments and accesses multiple histogram bins per visit to a pixel location, and hence is more computationally efficient

This CIMap is also fast and efficient to implement on a hardware platforms such as field programmable gate array (FPGA). This paper is organised as follows. Section 2 briefly describes the IMap [1]. Section 3 describes how to build up a CIMap and provides details of the over flow control technique used. Section 4 shows an example using CIMap, which demonstrated to be faster than using different IMaps separately. Finally, conclusions are presented in Section 5.

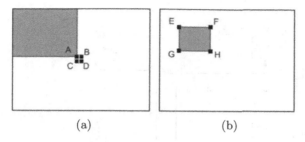

(a)   (b)

Fig. 1. IMap build up and use

2   Overview of Integral Map

Integral Map (IMap) was introduced by Viola and Jones [1] for fast calculation of Haar features. The IMap has the same size (number of rows and columns) as the image. In an IMap, each entry is the sum of all pixel values to the left and above the current pixel's position in the original image. For example, in Fig.1.(a), the entry to the IMap at point D is the sum of all pixels to the left and above (as marked by shaded areas) in the original image. To build the IMap more efficiently, neighbouring entries are used. For example, the IMap entry at point D in the IMap $M(D)$, as shown in Fig.1.(a), is calculated as:

$$M(D) = M(B) + M(C) - M(A) + P(D) \tag{1}$$

where A,B,C are D's direct neighbours in the IMap, $M(A),M(B),M(C)$ are IMap values at A,B,C in the IMap, and $P(D)$ is the pixel value at D in the original image. When it is required to find the sum of all pixels bounded by E,F,G and H as shown in Fig.1.b, then the sum S will be calculated by:

$$S = M(H) - M(G) - M(F) + M(E) \tag{2}$$

where $M(E),M(F),M(G)$ and $M(H)$ are coresponding values of E,F,G and H in the IMap.

For the Haar feature set, only one IMap is required for the whole image and the process of building the IMap only happen once. Therefore, the IMap is extremely efficient to implement on PC as well as on hardware platform such as FPGA.

3   Combined Integral Map (CIMap)

3.1   Building Up

IMap was adapted to efficently calculate HoG feature [4] in which one IMap was built for each angular bin. Nine angular bins used, hence nine different IMaps needed to be built. In the proposed CIMap technique, multiple IMaps, one for each bin, are built and stored as a single equivalent concatenated map. A CIMap can be built and used in a similar way to the IMap shown in Fig.1.(a).

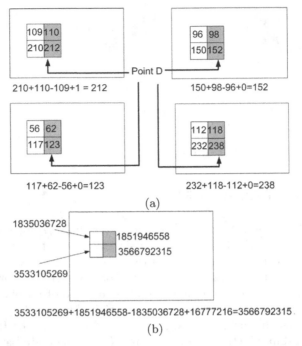

(a)

3533105269+1851946558-1835036728+16777216=3566792315

(b)

Fig. 2. Building up IMap and CIMap. (a).4 different IMaps are built represented by 4 separate 8-bit binary additions. (b) CIMap is built using 1 32-bit binary addition according to (3) with $R(A) = 1835036728$, $R(B) = 1851946558$, $R(C) = 3533105269$ and $V(D) = 2^{24} + 0 + 0 = 16777216$.

For example , when an CIMap is used for a 4-Bin HoG unnormalized feature space, the CIMap value at position D, denoted as $R(D)$ is calculated as:

$$R(D) = R(B) + R(C) - R(A) + V(D) \tag{3}$$

with

$$V(D) = P_1(D)2^{x+y+z} + P_2(D)2^{y+z} + P_3(D)2^z + P_4(D) \tag{4}$$

where $R(A)$, $R(B)$, $R(C)$ are CIMap entry at point A, B, C respectively; x, y, and z are number of bits required to store an entry in the IMap. P_i is defined as:

$$P_i(d) = \begin{cases} 1 & \text{if the gradient angle of } D \in \text{Bin } i, \\ 0 & \text{otherwise.} \end{cases} \tag{5}$$

where $i = 1, 2, 3, 4$ is the bin number. In this way 4 different IMaps are built at the same time. When the total number of pixels belong to bin 1, 2, 3 or 4 within the area S, as shown in Fig.1(b), is required, S can be computed using CIMap by:

$$S = R(H) - R(G) - R(F) + R(E) \tag{6}$$

Where $R(E)$, $R(F)$, $R(G)$, $R(H)$ are CIMap entries at points E, F, G, H respectively. From the definition of an CIMap (according to (3) and (4)), S is given by:

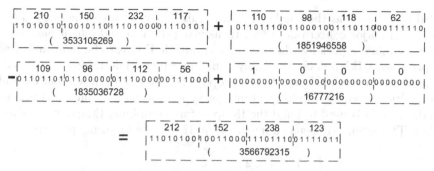

Fig. 3. Details equivalent of combined addition in CIMap. These number are binary number of CIMap entry shown on Fig.2(b).

$$S = b_1 2^x + b_2 2^y + b_3 2^z + b_4 2^t \tag{7}$$

where b_i is number of pixel belong to Bin i ($i = 1, 2, 3, 4$) within the area bounded by E, F, G and H. Using integer division, it is straightforward to find b_i using bit shifts, adds and subtracts without loosing precision. For example $b_1 = \frac{S}{2^x}$ and $b_2 = \frac{S - b_1 2^x}{2^y}$ and so on.

The comparison between the CIMap and the conventional IMap is illustrated in Fig.2. Suppose we have to find four entries for four IMaps (one for each bin) at location D of the original image. Using the conventional method of calculating the IMap, four separated adds are required for the pixel D as shown in Fig.2(a), one for each angular bin's IMap. However, according to Viola and Jones [1], three out of four additions (according to e.q.(1) are adding zero to the current IMap entry (as a pixel at location D is quantised to only one of the four angular bins). Using the CIMap method, only one addition is required for all four IMap as shown in Fig.2(b) following (3), (4) and (5) with $R(A) = 1835036728$, $R(B) = 1851946558$, $R(C) = 3533105269$ and $V(D) = 224 + 0 + 0 = 16777216$ (assuming current pixel gradient's angle falls in to bin 1). The details binary content of the addition is shown in Fig.3. It should be noted that the each 8-bit section, marked by a decimal number of top of the equivalent bits, has equivalent value to one of the four entries shown in Fig.2(a). In this case, the allocated size of the CIMap is assumed to be of adequate size.

3.2 Controling Overflow

It is necessary to allocate enough space for each IMap in the CIMap to prevent overflow. Overflow occurs when the value of an IMap entry exceeds the maximum value that can be stored in one IMap entry. Considering an image of size 480×752, the maximum value of an IMap entry for a bin could be as large as 360960 at the bottom right corner of the image following e.q.(1). To accomodate this large number, each entry of the original IMap (of a particular Bin) needs to be 19 bits wide (as $2^{19} > 360960$). Following the original method of implementing the IMap on a PC, each IMap for an angular bin is made of 480×752 integer numbers, i.e., one 32-bit integer for each entry of the IMap. The number of IMap needed is the same as the number of bin required. Even though memory capacity is not a major concern on a PC, transfering data in and out of memory is time consuming, especially when there are multiple IMaps to be built and used. The proposed CIMap does not simply concatenate multiple IMaps as originally proposed into a single CIMap. In the proposed CIMap, a data set that extends the definition of standard unsigned integer type (normally 32 bit long) is used. This data set H is used to build the IMap before combining IMaps into a single CIMap. The extended unsigned integer type H has the following properties:

$$
H: \begin{cases}
1.\ a, b < 2^n \\
2.\ a = a + 2^n \\
3.\ a - b = a + 2^n - b \text{ if } a < b \\
4.\ a - b = a - b \text{ if } a > b \\
5.\ a + b = a - 2^n + b \text{ if } a + b > 2^n \\
6.\ a + b = a + b \text{ if } a + b < 2^n
\end{cases} \tag{8}
$$

where n is the number of bits to represent a, b. For example, suppose we need to calculate the subtraction $6 - 9$, in the signed integer domain the result is $6 - 9 = 3$. In the 8-bit (n = 8) unsigned integer H domain (from property 3 of (8)) $6 - 9 = 6 + 256 - 9 = 253$. The result 253 in 8-bit binary format is 11111101 which is the same as -3 in singed 8-bit two's complement [12] format. At a later stage, the result -3 is added to another number, say 250, the calculation in signed integer domain will be: $-3 + 250 = 247$. The calculation in 8-bit unsigned integer domain H will be $253 + 250 = 503 = 503 - 256 = 247$ (as from property 5 of (8)).

The process of building and extracting information from an IMap using the normal signed integer and integer data-types belonging to the data type H are the same. An example of building up and extracting information from an IMap is shown in Fig.4, in which a grey pixel indicates an entry of 0, a white pixel indicates a 1 entry to an IMap of an angular bin (as a pixel can only either fall into a particular angular bin (entry 1) or not fall into that bin (entry 0)). The number on each position is the IMap entry at that location, which is calculated as (1). As shown in Fig.4(a), point A has direct neighbours with entry values of 258 (above and to the left), 260 (above) and 262 (to the left), and the current pixel is 1 (white)and according to e.q.(1), the value at current position of point A is: $262 + 260 - 258 + 1 = 265$. Similarly, for an IMap calculated using the unsigned integers in H, shown in Fig.4(b), the equivalent calculation is: $6 + 4 - 2 + 1 = 9$. As shown in Fig.4(a), the number of white pixels within the marked area S_1 is calculated using (2) as:

$$S_1 = 289 - 259 - 257 + 253 = 26$$

Using the IMap built with integers in H, shown in Fig.4(b), the total number of white pixels within the marked area S_2, property 5 of (8), is:

$$S_2 = 33 - 3 - 1 + 253 = 282 = 282 - 256 = 26$$

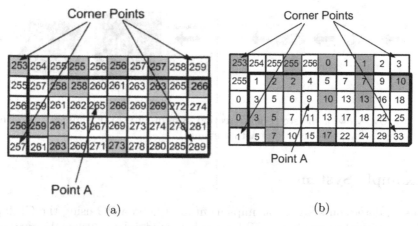

Fig. 4. Example of normal IMap calculation and overflow controled CIMap calculation. (a). IMap calculated by normal 32-bit integer. (b). IMap calculated by 8-bit unsigned integer.

Thus we have $S_2 = S_1$. This result agrees with manually counting the number of white pixels within the marked area.

The most appropriate value for n in (8) depends on the size of the target object being detected. The calculations of integers in the H domain depends on the detection window being much smaller than the original image. As a result, the size of each entry to each individual IMap (in the CIMap) needs only to be large enough to hold the maximum value of m×n, where m and n are number of rows and collumns in the detection window. The product $m \times n$ is much smaller than the maximum possible value of summations in the entire image as employed by the original IMap [1]. If we further know the maximum size of a feature, then we could even reduce number of bits n. Using the integer type H, overflow will occur in the IMap (in the CIMap) but it is guranteed not to occured more than once in any detection window because n is selected to be large enough. For example, if the detection window size is 30×30 pixels, then each entry in the IMap can be represented by a 10-bit number, instead of 32 bits as in the original techique of computing an IMap. As a result, a CIMap made up of 480×752 64-bit extended integer can hold upto 6 IMaps, while 6 IMaps built in the original technique requires 6×32×480×752 bits of memory. Hence, the memory efficiency (total amount of memory required for IMaps) and the computational efficiency (number of computation required to construct IMaps) increases significantly. There is a small amount of computation overhead required to perform overfow control calculations in the H domain. In addition, less memory usage can make a big difference when the CIMap buffer can fit into CPU's L2 cache whose bandwidth is very large.

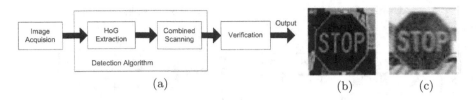

(a)   (b)   (c)

Fig. 5. (a). Overview of the stop sign detection system. (b),(c). Examples of positive sample images. (image noise is from actual images)

4   Example System

A stop sign detection system was implemented in C on a PC using the CIMap. For fairness of the test result, the CIMap implemented did not utilize the overflow control technique. This means the implemented system has maximum computational efficiency of the CIMap but moderate memory efficiency (compactness) since more bits are needed for each IMaps in a CIMap. The detection algorithms uses a variant of the HoG [4] feature set where only the gradient angle is used. The gradient magnitude in this example is irgnored for faster computation in fixed point domain. The effect of irgnoring the gradient magnitude is tolerated during the trainging processing. An overall system block overview is given in Fig.5.(a). The performance of this system is compared against a similar system use separate IMaps for different angular bins.

4.1   Training Data

A database of positive and negative sample images has been used to train the classifiers employing AdaBoost and cascaded classifier techniques as in [1]. The positive sample set is made up of 210 extracted images containing stop signs which may be affected by size variations, rotation, skew, motion blur or added white noise. The stop signs in these positive sample images are of the size 36 ± 2 pixels across. The extracted targets are of size of 36×36 pixels. Some example of positive samples are shown in Fig.5(b). The negative sample set (images without any stop sign) contains 195 negative images mostly at the resolution of 480×752 pixels. These negative images capture scenes of roads, buildings people, and road signs (other than stop sign).

Negative input vectors are collected by a detection window of size 36×36 pixel at different locations in the negative images. There are upward of over three hundred thousand possible negative samples in a negative images and we sample about 11 million of them to create the negative sample data set. Data for training and testing were collected with a camera system that consists of an automotive grade CMOS sensor, the Micron MT9V022IA7ATC, and a C-mount lense with $43.8°$ field of view. The sensor has a native resolution of 480×752 pixels at 60 fps. The camera system was mounted on the windscreen near the

Table 1. Performance comparision between system using IMaps separately and using CIMap. The computing system used for testing is an entry level laptop equipped with a 1.8GHz processor and 1 GB of RAM.

Factor	IMaps separately	CIMap
Detection	98.84%	98.84%
FPPW	7.99×10^{-7}	7.99×10^{-7}
Frame Rate (Average)	$\approx$4 fps	$\approx$7 fps

rear view miror of the car. Video sequences were recorded on a 1.8 GHz dual core laptop using software provided by Micron corp.

A large test data set consists of about 9700 hand-annotated images extracted from the 29 recorded video sequences. None of the video sequence was part of the training data set. These images are used to test the performance of classiffiers using CIMap and separate CIMaps. In the video sequences used for the test set, there are 24 positive video sequences in which some frames contain a valid stop sign, and 5 negative sequences with no stop sign in any of the frames in the sequence. There are between 99 to 966 image frames in each video sequence.

4.2 Experimental Results

The system was trained using a modified version of the HoG [4] feature set and the cascade of classifier approach [1]. AdaBoost was used to select the best feature in every round (stage) of training. After training 30 HoG features was selected and a cascade of classifier is formed. Based on the training result, C-based systems were implemented using the original IMap and the proposed CIMap. These two systems were tested against the test data set, and compared to each other in terms of speed and accuracy (detection rate and FPPW). The comparision of results is shown in Table.1, in which the frame rate comparision based on unoptimize C-code and post-processing step (spatial and temporal correlation between detected candidates) was used.

The false positive rate is greatly affected by the inconsistencies in the stop sign's size when the video sequences are manually annotated. If considering the overall outcome per video sequence, the system detects 28 out of 29 video sequence, and failed to detect only one sequence due to incorrect settings caused by human error when performing recording. The detection and FPPW rates of the system using CIMap is the same as the system that uses IMaps separately, However, the system using CIMap run at more than twice as fast.

5   Conclusions and Future Work

In this paper, a CIMap technique has been proposed. The CIMap efficiently builds multiple IMaps at once which improve the data efficiency of using multiple IMaps in multi-dimensional feature spaces such as HoG. This technique reduce number of memory accesses and computation required when building up different IMaps. The CIMap technique has been employed in a stop sign detection system and shown more than three times speed improvement. The CIMap technique can be extended to efficiently implement on hardware platforms. More analysis is planned to further study the improvement of the CIMap technique. Similar to the 2-D integral histogram [9], this CIMap works most efficiently on unnormalized features. Additional modifications may be required to apply the CIMap on normalised features.

References

1. Viola, P., Jones, M.: Rapid object detection using a boosted cascaded of simple features. In: 2001 IEEE Computer Society Conference on Computer Vision and Pattern Recognition (CVPR 2001), vol. 1, pp. 511–518 (2001)
2. Fasola, J., Veloso, M.: Real-time object detection using segmented and grayscale images. In: Proc. 2006 IEEE International Conference on Robotics and Automation, Orlando, FL, pp. 4088–4093 (2006)
3. Pan, Y.F., Hou, X., Liu, C.L.: A robust system to detect and localize texts in natural scene images. In: IAPR International Workshop on Document Analysis Systems, pp. 35–42. IEEE Computer Society, Los Alamitos (2008)
4. Dalal, N., Triggs, B.: Histograms of oriented gradients for human detection. In: 2005 IEEE Computer Scociety conference on Computer Vision and Pattern Recognition, vol. 1, pp. 886–893 (2005)
5. Zhu, Q., Avidan, S., Yeh, M.C., Cheng, K.T.: Fast human detection using a cascade of histogram of oriented gradients. In: Proc. IEEE computer society conference on computer vision and pattern recognition, New York, USA, pp. 683–688 (June 2006)
6. Messom, C., Barczak, A.: Stream processing of integral images for real-time object detection. In: PDCAT 2008: Proceedings of the, Ninth International Conference on Parallel and Distributed Computing, Applications and Technologies, Wasington, DC, USA, pp. 405–412. IEEE Computer Society, Los Alamitos (2008)
7. Lienhart, R., Kuranov, A., Pisarevsky, V.: Empirical analysis of detection cascades of boosted classifiers for rapid object detection. Technical report, Microprocessor Research Lab, Intel Labs (December 2002)
8. Lienhart, R., Maydt, J.: An extended set of haar-like features for rapid object detection. In: 2002 International Conference on Image Processing, vol. 1, pp. 900–903 (2002)
9. Porikli, F.: Integral histogram: A fast way to extract histograms in cartesian spaces. In: CVPR 2005: Proceedings of the 2005 IEEE Computer Society Conference on Computer Vision and Pattern Recognition (CVPR 2005), Washington, DC, USA, vol.1, pp. 829–836. IEEE Computer Society, Los Alamitos (2005)
10. Nejhum, S.S., Ho, J., Ming-Hsuan, Y.: Visual tracking with histograms and articulating blocks. In: Proc. 2008 IEEE International Conference on Computer Vision and Pattern Recognition, Anchorage, AK, pp. 1–8 (2008)
11. Chen, Y.T., Chen., C.S.: Fast human detection using a novel boosted cascading structure with meta stages. IEEE Transactions on Image Processing 17, 1452–1464 (2008)
12. Brown, S., Vranesic, Z.: Fundamentals of Digital Logic with VHDL Design. Mc Graw Hill, New York (2005)

Author Index

Aldavert, David   204
Antenreiter, Martin   384
Auer, Peter   384

Barata, José   275
Barnich, Olivier   104
Başeski, Emre   235
Behley, Jens   164
Bergström, Niklas   245
Beveridge, J. Ross   21
Bhattacharya, Prabir   394
Birbach, Oliver   435
Blostein, Dorothea   295
Bohg, Jeannette   245
Bolme, David S.   21
Breckon, Toby P.   265
Brémond, François   403
Butakoff, Constantine   33

Cao, Tam Phuong   445
Chessa, Manuela   184
Comer, H. Thomson   315
Condell, Joan V.   84
Cordy, James R.   295
Correia, Luís   275
Crumpler, Steve   265
Czyz, Jacek   144

Dacal-Nieto, Angel   335
Debeir, Olivier   144
de Jong, Sjoerd   94
de la Fuente López, Eusebio   345
Demirdjian, David   1
Deng, Guang   445
Detry, Renaud   235
Dickscheid, Timo   305
Dittes, Benjamin   255
Draper, Bruce A.   21, 315

Eberli, Felix   134
Eggert, Julian   124, 425
Einecke, Nils   425
Ekenel, Hazım Kemal   43
Elton, Darrell   445
Engel, Karin   114

Fels, Sidney   215
Fink, G.A.   73
Formella, Arno   335
Förstner, Wolfgang   305
Frangi, Alejandro F.   33
Franke, Uwe   285
Frese, Udo   435
Frintrop, Simone   63
Fritsch, Jannik   255

Gehrig, Stefan K.   134, 285
Gepperth, Alexander   255
Goerick, Christian   255
Gonzalez-Jorge, Higinio   335
Gross, Horst-Michael   364
Guedes, Magno   275
Guyader, Nathalie   325

Han, Junwei   374
Heracles, Martin   255
Hiromoto, Masayuki   53
Hoey, Jesse   354
Hosotani, Daisuke   154
Houben, Quentin   144

Kastner, Robert   255
Katramados, Ioannis   265
Klein, Dominik Alexander   63
Kogler, Jürgen   174
Kootstra, Gert   94
Kraft, Dirk   235
Kragic, Danica   245
Krüger, Norbert   235
Kubinger, Wilfried   174

Lambert, Patrick   325
Leens, Jérôme   104
López de Mántaras, Ramon   204

Marat, Sophie   325
Marchegiani, Maria Letizia   11
Martin, Christian   364
Martin, Fernando   335
May, Stefan   194
McKenna, Stephen J.   374
Meyer, Thomas   134

Michalke, Thomas   255
Miguel Trespaderne, Félix   345
Miller, Gregor   215
Miyamoto, Ryusuke   53

Nam, Seungjin   225
Nüchter, Andreas   194

Oh, Juhyun   225
Oldridge, Steve   215

Pavani, Sri-Kaushik   33
Pellerin, Denis   325
Piater, Justus   235
Piérard, Sébastien   104
Pirri, Fiora   11
Pizzoli, Matia   11
Plötz, T.   73
Prankl, Johann   384
Prasad, Girijesh   84
Pratheepan, Yogarajah   84
Pugeault, Nicolas   235

Qiu, Deyuan   194

Ramisa, Arnau   204
Rebhan, Sven   124
Richter, Andreas   124
Rombaut, Michèle   325
Roy, Kaushik   394

Sabatini, Silvio P.   184
Sakaue, Katsuhiko   154
Santana, Pedro   275
Schauerte, B.   73

Schomaker, Lambert R.B.   94
Schulz, Dirk   63
Simac-Lejeune, Alain   325
Sohn, Kwanghoon   225
Solari, Fabio   184
Steingrube, Pascal   285
Steinhage, Volker   164
Stiefelhagen, Rainer   43, 415
Stricker, Ronny   364
Sukno, Federico M.   33
Sulzbachner, Christoph   174
Szasz-Toth, Lorant   43

Thonnat, Monique   403
Tocino Diaz, Juan Carlos   144
Toennies, Klaus   114
Toledo, Ricardo   204
Torres-Guijarro, Soledad   335

Van Droogenbroeck, Marc   104
Varri, Chenna   1
Vazquez-Fernandez, Esteban   335
Vincze, Markus   384
Voit, Michael   415

Wagner, Jean-Marc   104
Wang, Ruixuan   374
Warzee, Nadine   144

Yoda, Ikushi   154

Zanibbi, Richard   295
Zhang, Chen   425
Zúñiga, Marcos   403
Zutis, Krists   354